Art Today

FRANK STELLA. *Sinjerli Variation IV*. 1968.
Fluorescent acrylic on canvas, diameter 10′.
Collection Mr. and Mrs. Burton Tremaine,
Meriden, Conn.

Art Today

An Introduction to the Visual Arts

FIFTH EDITION

Ray Faulkner
Stanford University

Edwin Ziegfeld
Teachers College, Columbia University

HOLT, RINEHART AND WINSTON, INC.

New York   Chicago   San Francisco   Atlanta   Dallas
Montreal   Toronto   London   Sydney

Library of Congress Catalog Card Number: 69–19919

SBN 03–072245–4

0123 75 98765432

*A Helvetica Press production : Printed in black-and-white
gravure by the Presses Centrales Lausanne, Switzerland;
color offset by the Imprimeries Réunies, Lausanne;
bound by Mayer & Soutter S.A., Renens, Switzerland.*

First printing, 1969

Designer : Marlene Rothkin Vine

Preface

Art Today is about that vital phase in our human environment which we term the visual arts. They touch us at every point and affect all our activities, and they range from humble, handmade, or machine-produced utensils to the masterworks of painting, sculpture, and architecture. Those visual arts that surround us have the most immediate, continuous effect, but those that are experienced only occasionally in visits to museums, in travel, or through photographs are also cultural influences. The primary purposes of this book are to increase the understanding and enjoyment of all the visual arts, to create awareness of the extent to which they influence the quality of living, and to suggest ways by which the visual arts can be made to improve the condition of man.

In this century there has been a lively, constructive rebellion in the visual arts, similar to the revolutions that have taken place recurrently throughout the history of art. Exploration and experimentation have greatly extended our horizons and sensibilities. New goals and values, together with new materials and technologies and different ways of using older ones, have led to art forms uniquely expressive of this age. This radical change has been paralleled by an avid interest in historic achievements in the visual arts from all parts of the world, an interest that has deepened and broadened our knowledge of and respect for both past and present world cultures.

This century also has brought an astonishing increase of interest in the most diverse phases of creative endeavor. Art works are being purchased by individuals in unprecedented numbers; attendance at public and private galleries and museums has set new records; and millions of Americans are amateur painters, sculptors, and weavers. Cultural activities are supported by government, by private foundations, by individuals, and by business, the latter a uniquely twentieth-century sponsor. Many corporations have leading architects design their buildings and industrial designers shape their products. They may have extensive collections of paintings to enhance their offices and murals and sculpture in reception areas, and their advertising may reflect a knowledge of the power of art.

Architects, urban planners, and industrial designers are increasingly aware of the relationship of the visual arts to the patterns and qualities of contemporary living. To provide shelter for man's varied activities, they build structures for home life and community functions, for religious expression, for research and manufacture and the many facets of commerce. Because it is usually desirable or necessary to live in groups and to be able to move from one place to another, communities are developed and the means of transportation provided. But the structures that are built can be more than shells that protect their contents and give basic physical comfort; they can aid in man's search for identity and give dignity to his life. Most of the millions of products that are manufactured for sale are designed basically for efficiency, but they serve best when they go beyond utility.

Human needs are by no means limited to the practical. Since his earliest days man has continuously sought ways to express and communicate his inner thoughts and feelings through painting and sculpture, ceramics and textiles, and a variety of other creations. There are vases and bowls that came out of someone's urge to make an object deeply satisfying in shape and color, inviting to the sense of touch, and strong in the feeling of the clay or glass from which it was made. There are paintings and edifices that eloquently communicate religious aspirations, sculpture and community plans that tangibly manifest the ideals of people living together. The number of individuals creatively engaged, from the amateur weaver to the environmental planner and the most avant-garde painter, has increased enormously, and their products face us on all sides, inviting critical appraisal.

Because art is engendered by human needs, both practical and esthetic, and is intended to satisfy them, these needs deserve primary consideration. But when an artist begins to search for a solution to them, he is faced with two important decisions: What materials are most appropriate, and how can they be used to full advantage? How can the form, space, color, and texture be composed to produce a work of art that fulfills all of its purposes? Hence, the emphases of the first three parts of this book are as follows:

Part I. ART AND HUMAN NEEDS
The art problems that arise in the home, community, religion, industry, and commerce are discussed in Chapters 1 through 5.

Part II. MATERIALS AND PROCESSES
The potentialities and limitations of such varied materials as wood, metal, plastics, clay, and glass and the processes by which they can be transformed into useful and pleasing objects are considered in Chapters 6 through 10.

Part III. THE VISUAL ELEMENTS AND THEIR ORGANIZATION
The expressive qualities of form, space, line, texture, light, and color, the possibilities for their organization, and the principles of design by which their quality may be understood and assessed are emphasized in Chapters 11 through 14.

Each of these three general concerns is vitally interrelated to the others, and they are brought into unison in the most satisfying works of art. Although architecture, painting, and sculpture are discussed in the first three parts of the book, the great significance of these fields of art justifies more intensive consideration in the concluding chapters:

Part IV. PAINTING, SCULPTURE, AND ARCHITECTURE
The general and specific problems faced by painters, sculptors, and architects in transforming raw materials into works of art are examined in Chapters 15 through 17.

Art is a complex subject and can be approached in many ways. We can read and talk about it, see and appreciate it, or produce it. Each of these activities contributes to the depth and breadth of our understanding. True art appreciation is more than knowing the names and dates of important artists and their works. It involves attitudes, emotions, and personal preferences as well as knowledge. It is our hope that this book will be a catalytic agent in helping the reader to react to the visual richness that surrounds him and that it will also stimulate him to make the human environment a better one in which to live.

Many individuals and institutions have helped in the preparation of this new edition of *Art Today*. Among them, we wish to thank Professors Ralph G. Beelke of Purdue University, Irving Block of San Fernando Valley State College, and R. W. McMillan of Grinnell College for the critiques they prepared of the fourth edition of *Art Today*. Their ideas and recommendations, formulated in response to the old editions, have been immensely helpful to us in our attempts to make the fifth edition genuinely relevant for its time. We also have a debt of gratitude that we wish to acknowledge to Professors Gibson Byrd of the University of Wisconsin, Roger Easton of Ball State University, and Warren Faus of San José State College, who had the great patience to examine and comment on the entire manuscript for the new edition. Edward F. Fry, Associate Curator of the Solomon R. Guggenheim Museum, has been good enough to review the manuscript for the chapters on painting and sculpture and to give us the benefit of his extraordinary knowledge of modern art. Professor David Gebhard of the University of California at Santa Barbara read the manuscript for the chapter on architecture and did much to help us understand the most recent developments in building design and construction. Professor Lincoln F. Johnson, Jr., of Goucher College, made not only a critical but a genuinely substantive contribution to the section on the film. We received yet further help on the photography chapter from Hugh Edwards, Curator of Photography at the Art Institute of Chicago, and from Professor Charles Swedlund at the State University of New York College in Buffalo. We are grateful to Professor Glenn C. Nelson of the University of Minnesota at Duluth and to Mr. and Mrs. Dominick Labino for their advice on Chapter 7, "Ceramics and Glass."

At Holt, Rinehart and Winston we are pleased to acknowledge the help of the staff who prepare the art books. Our editor, Dan Wheeler, contributed invaluable ideas and criticisms and was the guiding force in the book's production. His editorial colleague Herbert J. Addison shared special knowledge with us in his comments on the manuscript for Chapter 17. Karen Dubno spent many months getting our manuscript ready for publication, and Rita Gilbert managed the huge task of securing the illustrations and the permission to reproduce them. It is Marlene Rothkin Vine who designed and laid out what we believe to be a stunning and appropriate format for the fifth edition of *Art Today*.

We wish especially to express our appreciation to the museums, the private collectors, the art galleries, the commercial and industrial organizations, as well as the photographers who have provided us with illustrations and granted us permission to use them in this edition of our book.

Anna Lacovara typed the manuscript for Chapters 13 through 17 and deserves full thanks for the skill she brought to this edition of the book. As in the past, Sarah Key Faulkner went far beyond the call of duty in making major contributions to every phase of this publication. To these and many others we extend our thanks.

Stanford, California
New York, New York
January 1969

RF
EZ

Contents

part I Art and
Human Needs

overleaf: 1. Downtown Chicago is where the skyscraper was developed in the late nineteenth century to take care of the rapidly increasing population. Now it is a vibrant cityscape of styles and of solutions to the problem of the human need for space in which to live and work.

2. In order to take full advantage of the sun and views, architect Richard T. Foster designed a house in Connecticut (1968) that rotates 360 degrees around a central fixed stair core on a ball-bearing assembly such as that used for revolving radar antennae. The speed of the rotation can be controlled to take from 48 minutes to 4 hours for a complete turn. The eight-room house is glass-walled, and cedar shingles sheathe the roof and supporting structure and allow the unusual shape to be the dominant feature.

1 The Arts of the Home

Shelter that physically and psychologically inspirits man is a vital factor in his total welfare because so much time is spent in the home. Never before have homes been so diversified as they are today. Caves and tents, mobile homes and houseboats, college dormitories and retirement communities, multiple-unit apartment complexes and single-family houses, mansions and deplorable slums all serve as dwellings. Some are decades or even centuries old, others are new. Contemporary technological developments and a resurgence of architectural creativity have resulted in a greatly extended range of materials and a multiplicity of architectural forms. Large sums of money are expended annually on construction. In the United States from one to two billion dollars, depending on economic conditions, are spent each year on residential buildings. This is nearly one-half of the country's total construction outlay, and yet there is still an acute housing shortage in many areas, and a great many persons live in substandard buildings. There is abundant evidence that inadequate living quarters result in varied expressions of wasteful unrest and cause man to fail in the realization of his full potential.

Our homes are significant far beyond their dollar cost because they directly affect family living patterns. A few fortunate families live in homes that were specifically designed for them, while others do as much as they can to make the

If efficiently planned and appropriately furnished, a small apartment can be a satisfying environment. David Parmelee, designer.

right : 3. One end of the living-dining area is organized for daytime living, nighttime sleeping, and storage. The predominantly rectangular furniture fits compactly into the limited space, enlivened by the unexpected shape of the coffee table and by strong, contrasting colors.

below : 4. The efficient plan gives direct access to the clothes closets and bath, the kitchen, and the living-dining space.

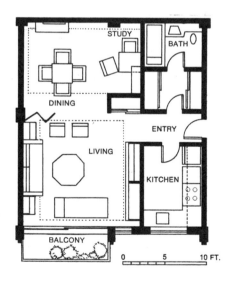

space available to them an expression of their individuality. Creating beneficial space for living is so complex a task that it has challenged experts in such diverse fields as architecture, city planning, sociology, and economics; but some indication of the basic factors involved can be gained through study of several homes.

A Small Apartment

For many persons a small apartment is the first home that can really be called one's own. As such it has special problems and a special meaning. The first step is finding an apartment that has adequate and well-arranged space to promote convenient and gratifying home life. Equally important, the space should allow the occupant to express his individuality in furnishing it.

Figures 3 through 6 illustrate how a young American designer solved this problem. The apartment has approximately 460 square feet of floor space, which is adequate for one person but is not costly to rent or to maintain. The entry gives convenient access to all parts of the dwelling. At the left is a compact kitchen with a large window over the sink; at the right, two large closets and a bath form a dressing area. Beyond these is a room of about 13 feet wide and 23 feet long, with a window wall at one end that opens onto a small balcony. At the right of the entrance a projecting closet suggests a logical division of the area.

By the use of handsome, mass-produced, multiple-purpose furniture and lively colors and accessories, this space has been transformed into a home environment of character and individuality. For practical purposes and visual pleasantness, the long room has been divided into a major area for conversation, casual reading, listening to music, watching television, entertaining friends, and, at night, sleeping; and into a secondary area at the other end for dining and study. The two areas are

demarcated by a folding screen that extends toward the closet and by two large rugs. The living zone is furnished with two couches that double as beds, two lightly scaled chairs, and an ample coffee table. The large size of this table is mitigated by its transparent glass top and shelf and by its octagonal shape, which allows easy passage around it. One couch is framed by storage units joined at the top by a built-in lighting unit. This group is dominant because of its importance in the occupant's pattern of living, because of the large size of the off-white couch set against a dark-green wall, and because of the vigorous painting.

At the other end of the room the secondary furniture group is subdivided into a dining area and a study area. Each centers around one of two identical rosewood tables with chromed steel legs, supplemented by matching chromed steel chairs with upholstered cushions and by a hanging shelf. The tables and chairs can be used separately, as shown, or placed together to seat six.

The selection and organization of space and furniture in this apartment demonstrate some basic principles in home planning and furnishing. First, the amount and kind of space that was needed and economically feasible were considered. Second, the space was subdivided into areas of appropriate size, shape, and location for different activities. Third, circulation paths were planned to minimize both steps and interference with furnishings and activities.

Efficiency, however, was not the only consideration, for homes are most satisfying when they stimulate the eyes, the hands, and the spirit. Many factors combine to make this apartment a heartening environment. Each object unhesitatingly reveals its purpose and its materials and is a component of the unifying theme of predominantly simple shapes and broadly treated surfaces. Monotony is avoided by introducing many differences and contrasts. In size, the furnishings have a full range from room-size rugs to small accessories. In character, they vary from mass-produced objects to original paintings.

left : 5. The elegantly precise dining furniture is enhanced by the beauty of rosewood and metal, a textured rug, a painting judiciously placed on a white wall, and the boldly striped wall pattern at the left.

right : 6. A table and a hanging shelf that match those in Fig. 5 comprise a compact study area. A dark green wall makes the space seem secure and inviting, while the mirror on the wall visually enlarges it at the right.

Materials, textures, and colors introduce both unity and diversity. Very smooth, transparent glass in the windows and in the coffee table enable one to see what is beyond, but the mirrored wall in the study reflects what is opposite it. Gleaming metal, repeated throughout the living-dining space in the legs of tables and chairs, contrasts sharply with the textured upholstery and the intricately grained wood. Plaster walls and ceilings differ markedly in surface character from the shaggy rugs.

All of this adds up to a bold and brilliant composition, suited to the tenant, fulfilling his needs, and expressing his personality. No matter what the form of art—a modest home, a place of public quietude and worship, an automobile, or a community mural—personal and group needs and interests deserve serious consideration. The designing of pots and pans, of chairs and apartments is a comparatively minor art problem, but these objects are seen and used every day and can be constant sources of satisfaction and delight or of irritation and the deadening of the spirit. At the other end of the art continuum are the paintings, sculpture, and edifices that develop out of untrammeled imagination, great skill, and a full comprehension of man's higher endowments and that offer the opportunity for profound spiritual experiences. There are enormous differences between chairs and cathedrals, yet both can be justly included in the scope of art.

The Homes of Three Architects

When an architect designs his own home, he can express his convictions without compromise. Although he must solve the basic problems common to all domestic architecture, which are discussed in detail on pages 18 to 28, his design can be highly individual. This is a situation quite different from that faced by the designers of most apartments and mass-produced houses, which must appeal to a large number of varied tenants or owners. The three homes now to be discussed were planned and built under the close supervision of three influential architects and represent some of the major trends in contemporary architecture. All three are "modern," but the first is an example of *Organic Architecture*, the second exemplifies the *International Style*, and the third belongs to a general category that has been called *Domestic Vernacular*.

Frank Lloyd Wright's Home near Spring Green, Wisconsin

Taliesin North (Pl. 1 and Figs. 7, 8), designed by Frank Lloyd Wright, is a noble complex of buildings set just below and encircling a hilltop in rolling, wooded farmland. Taliesin, a Welsh term meaning "shining brow," is an apt name for a structure placed near the top of a sunlit hill. It is referred to as "North" or sometimes as "East" to distinguish it from Taliesin West in Arizona (Fig. 626). Begun in the 1920s as a home for Wright's mother, it was expanded into a spacious dwelling for his family, a private studio, a school of architecture, and a farm. Only a portion of the Wrights' living quarter, built in 1925, is discussed here.

The architect's purpose was to evolve an organic edifice that was an outgrowth of its natural environment. With deep reverence for nature, Wright chose his materials and shaped his home so that it is rooted to its site. Local stone, laid by country masons in patterns reminiscent of the quarry in which it was found, extends into garden courts and paths, forms the lower walls, and thrusts upward in the massive block to the left. The other walls are lighter, wood-framed screens against the weather, and they are surfaced with plaster that is colored and textured with sand from the river below. Exterior wood walls were treated with transparent preser-

Plate 1. In Frank Lloyd Wright's own home, Taliesin North (1925—), in Spring Green, Wisconsin, interlocking planes of roughhewn masonry and smoother plaster, wood, glass, and shingles gradually merge into the pastoral countryside. Without any sharp division between man-made forms and materials and those of nature, the structure is responsive to the site and is, in Wright's words, "a natural house." Frank Lloyd Wright, architect. (See also Figs. 7, 8.)

above : Plate 2a. A glass box (1949) is the main living pavilion of Philip Johnson's home in New Canaan, Connecticut. The interior is shielded from the weather but seems part of the landscape. The colors are subdued and in harmony with the greens of trees and grass, and the dark brick floor and leather upholstery are polished to a soft luster. The sense of lucid space is paramount. Philip Johnson, architect. (See also Figs. 9, 10.)

right : Plate 2b. The guest house, set across the lawn from the glass house, retains the same simplicity but is closed and private. Windowless except for three circular windows high on one side, the guest house has a draped and domed interior, is sparsely furnished, and is aglow with a soft radiance created by hidden lights. Philip Johnson, architect.

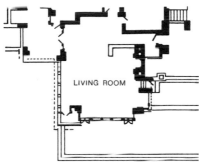

Taliesin North (1925–), Spring Green, Wisconsin. Frank Lloyd Wright, architect.

7. Each surface that encloses the living room is clearly defined by its material, shape, and direction, but all are interwoven into a complex flow of space.

8. The plan of the living room shows how Wright destroyed traditional boxlike confinement.

vatives to make them a slightly violet gray, or a deep, warm orange, and the shingled woods were allowed to weather to a natural gray.

This is a northern house where spring brings a profusion of gay wild flowers, summer a luxuriant variety of greens, autumn a burst of reds and yellows, and winter the dazzling whiteness of snow and icicles. The house welcomes these seasonal changes.

The exterior, however, is but a prelude to the interior, where Wright demonstrated what he meant when he spoke of interior space as being the essence of architecture. The floors, walls, fireplaces, and ceilings are of the same stone, wood, and plaster that comprise the exterior. Although they give a secure sense of shelter, the space seems open and unconfined, never boxlike. As in all great architecture, the dominant esthetic enjoyment comes from the manner in which the enclosing surfaces are an inevitable development from the plan. The interior is perceptively modulated, not rigidly partitioned. Walls of varied heights and materials activate the space by inviting exploration in all directions, and on two sides they open wide onto terraces. The ceilings are a complex interplay of low, flat areas related to broad shelves a little above head height that give a sense of human scale. Above the shelves the sloping ceiling soars upward following the lines of the roof. Wide and thin strips of wood accentuate the different planes. The house was oriented and windows were placed so that sun comes into every room sometime during the day and to allow views of the fields, hills, and sky. Taliesin North literally and spiritually grows upward and outward from its solid foundation into the outdoor space of which it is an integral part.

Although this house has well-planned circulation and areas for living, it transcends such practical matters in fulfillment of Wright's philosophy of Organic Architecture. In Taliesin North the visible forms are so completely integrated with the specific purpose of the building, the materials from which it is constructed, and the environment of which it is a part that the structure develops a life pattern of its own.

Philip Johnson's Home in New Canaan, Connecticut

The home that architect Philip Johnson designed for himself (Pl. 2 and Figs. 9, 10) is different from Taliesin North in almost every respect except its integrity.

The Philip Johnson glass house (1949), New Canaan, Connecticut. Philip Johnson, architect.

right : 9. Clarity of structure, beauty of proportions, and meticulously refined details give the exterior a poised serenity.

below : 10. The plan shows extreme simplicity of design coupled with sensitivity to space and form. A comparison with the plan of Taliesin North reveals how differently one can handle rectangular shapes.

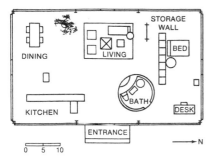

Johnson's house is as precise as a mathematical formula, as logically conceived as a philosophic discourse, a lyrical statement of geometric space and materials. Built in 1949, the house and its furnishings have withstood the test of time remarkably well. The house influenced many other structures, but none to date has equalled its purity and refinement.

Johnson's structure is no typical house planned for a family; it is a bachelor's audacious experiment in living with nature in a transparent prism poised a few inches above the ground. In the approximately 1800 square feet of glass-enclosed space, zones for different activities are barely suggested by three fixed space dividers. The food-preparation space is separated from the dining and living areas by nothing more than a walnut cabinet 3½ feet high. Between the area for sleeping and that for living is a walnut storage wall 6 feet high. The only interior element that goes from floor to ceiling is a brick cylinder 10 feet in diameter that secludes the bathroom and opens into a fireplace. The "living room" is furnished with five pieces of impeccably beautiful furniture resting lightly on a white wool rug that, in turn, seems to float at anchor on the polished brick floor. Its boundaries are intimated by an unframed painting suspended from an iron stand, by a large sculpture, and by a plant. The plan is indeed as open as are the walls of the house.

This house is one of several precisely positioned units on a large, tree-bounded estate. The others include a guest house as securely enclosed with brick as the house is opened with glass; an underground museum that is all but hidden under a low mound of earth; and a naturalistic lake with a summer pavilion. Man-made landscaping consists primarily of a beautifully tended lawn and screens of trees and shrubs placed at strategic points.

In its twentieth-century machined precision, the house contrasts as strikingly with its simple, natural setting as the beautifully sculptured, formal Parthenon (Fig. 592) contrasts with its rocky eminence. In neither did the architects try to harmonize the structure with its surroundings. The transparent walls, however, let one see not only into Johnson's house but through it to the landscape beyond; and in places they mirror the trees and the sky. Thus, the house and its setting are intimately related in a way that is distinctly different from Taliesin North.

The Johnson house represents the International Style, a movement in architecture that emerged in the 1920s and is still a vital force. Study of it and other examples of this style, such as the New Bauhaus (Fig. 152) and the Tugendhat house (Fig. 411) shows that they emphasize volumes and space rather than solid mass, openness and flexibility rather than tight enclosure. These qualities are also fundamental in Organic Architecture, but the International Style differs from it in a marked emphasis on regularity, precision, and visual simplicity. Regularity comes from repetition and standardization of predominantly rectangular forms. Precision comes from machine technology. Simplicity is achieved through the elimination of everything that is unnecessary. Interest comes from the total composition of space and enclosing planes, which are sparingly accented with rich materials and works of art. (See Pl. 2 and Fig. 11.)

As its name implies, the International Style developed out of widespread twentieth-century technology and ideals rather than out of local traditions or geographic environments. It is a "world architecture" that aims to coordinate basic, generalized human needs and the techniques of standardized industrial production. Philip Johnson made no attempt to create the informality and "naturalism" inherent in the design and furnishings of the Wright house. Nor was he concerned with such factors as economical heating and cooling. But he achieved what he wanted—a formal, precise, highly disciplined design of great clarity.

Hugh Stubbins' Home in Cambridge, Massachusetts

Whereas Frank Lloyd Wright's Taliesin North grew organically from its pastoral, geographical environment, and Philip Johnson's glass-and-metal house is a bold proclamation of twentieth-century technology, Hugh Stubbins' home (Figs. 12–15)

11. For a benign climate at Cap Bénat, France, Philip Johnson designed Boissonas House II (1964) as a series of five separate pavilions. Three of them cluster around an outdoor living terrace that has an undulating roof of poured concrete and tapered columns.

was developed from the needs of its owners in a manner that is compatible with American Colonial houses and with the later "traditional" dwellings that surround it. Stubbins' house, planned for his wife and himself, is an ingenious integration of old and new ideas and materials. In the New England tradition are the simple rectangular mass of the house, the double-pitched shingled roof, and the exterior walls of wood. The interior space that reaches to the ceiling, the loftlike bedrooms, and the frankly exposed structure are reminiscent of New England barns. Strictly contemporary are the living room wall of fixed and sliding glass and the varied windows that are placed where needed rather than in a stereotyped formal arrangement. The roof shingles are asphalt, and the exterior is covered with resawn redwood—materials that were not used in New England until recently. Also new are the dramatic interior spatial composition and the integration of the enclosed space with the swimming-pool terrace at the east and the shaded terrace on the west.

The Stubbins house (1966), Cambridge, Massachusetts. Hugh Stubbins, FAIA, architect.

left : 12. The front of the house uses glass in an informal geometric composition. It is different from the house in the background, but the similarity of shapes and materials and the juxtapositions of light and dark result in a harmonious relationship.

below : 13. The plan has the same rectangular simplicity as the exterior.

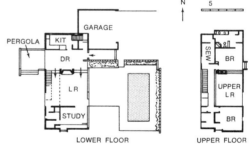

LOWER FLOOR　　　　UPPER FLOOR

14. The living room intensifies the interplay of forms by sharp contrasts of color. The clear-cut furniture is an effective foil for the complexity of the rug pattern.

15. On the south wall of the Hugh Stubbins house, the triangular shape of the roof is dramatized by the upward thrust of the window bay.

Protected by the garage and garden wall, the entrance door leads into a vestibule that can be left open into the dining area or separated from it by a folding room divider. With the exception of the kitchen and bath, all of the first floor is a continuous flow of space, partially subdivided by the fireplace and a spur wall, into zones for living, dining, and study. The bedrooms, accessible from an open, balcony-like corridor, can be secluded from the living area or joined with it by movable shutters.

The group-living area is an intriguing, multidimensional composition that combines great freedom of spatial movement with a reassuring sense of substantial architectural enclosure. Built of dark-red brick, the 26-foot chimney accentuates the loftiness of the room. The low-ceilinged entrance-dining area and the study are inviting havens. Contrasting materials emphasize the size and shape of the space. Walls and ceiling of rough plaster painted white accentuate the darker elements and make the room light and airy. Dark, reddish-brown tiles, similar in color to the bricks of the fireplace, are used on the floor of the entrance-dining area. Traditional, random-width oak boards are a quiet background for the large Oriental rug intricately patterned in dark reds, blues, and white. A chair, an ottoman, and sofas upholstered in white, and a natural wood chair and tables, are arranged in an open yet sociable conversation group.

The exterior is as straightforward as New England rural architecture, but it is notable for its satisfying proportions and refined details. The main block of the house is a 26-by-56-foot rectangle, with a garage projecting from the northeast corner, a dining pergola to the west, and a brick-walled and -paved terrace to the east that more than doubles the space for group living. Closer study of the exterior reveals enough unexpected elements to awaken and hold interest. When viewed from the brick-paved street, the total exterior design is a tightly knit composition of rectangular forms underlined by an ever-changing juxtaposition of light, shade, and shadow. The brick garden walls are varied in height and offset along the street side. The recessed garage doors produce shadows that act as a frame. At each end of the upper floor, the bedrooms extend beyond the lower walls to increase interior space and add visual interest. On the south side the projecting bay has a tier of windows reaching from the lower-floor study to the roof and contrasting effectively with the plain walls to the right and the very small window to the left.

Mass-Produced Homes

Architects have long been aware of the need for less-expensive ways of building and have recognized the potentialities inherent in prefabrication. The assembling of architectural structures from standardized, factory-built components can reduce costs, shorten construction time, and assure a specified degree of quality. Prefabricated houses, however, often have a monotonous uniformity because the results cannot be tailored to individual needs and preferences. Many of them suffer from a mediocre approach to design, and some of them are poorly engineered. In spite of this, manufactured houses have steadily increased in number, and many architects have attempted to devise systems using standardized parts to produce individualized results.

Modular Prefabrication

In the 1950s, architects Carl Koch and Associates, who had designed numerous one-of-a-kind buildings, started creative research into methods of producing components that could be assembled into houses appropriate for many middle-income families. Their system, called Techbuilt houses, is one example of the possibilities in mass production. Unlike custom-built houses that are designed for individual families and specific sites, Techbuilt houses (Figs. 16–19) were designed to appeal

right : 16. Typical two-story dwellings are often awkwardly raised on foundations, but Techbuilt houses are lowered into the ground and are pleasingly related to their sites.

below : 17. Composed and simple in basic shape, Techbuilt houses have a quality of coherence and an informal appeal. Alfred Della Paolera, architect.

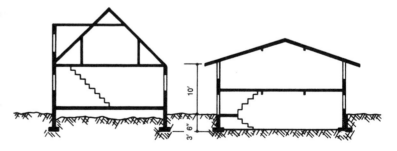

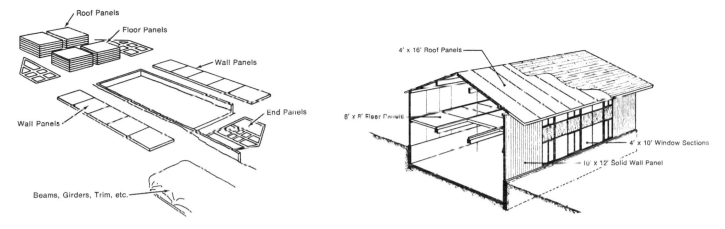

Roof Panels

Floor Panels

Wall Panels

End Panels

Wall Panels

Beams, Girders, Trim, etc.

4' x 16' Roof Panels

8' x 8' Floor Panels

4' x 10' Window Sections

10' x 12' Solid Wall Panel

to many potential customers, to be appropriate for many climates and sites. In searching for a solution, the architects considered many facts and factors relating to costs, structural systems, and appearance. Although it seems almost impossible to reconcile all of the requirements, the architects succeeded in combining economy and individuality with an ingenious system of prefabrication.

■ All of the space that will be required eventually is enclosed in the initial building of the house because merely enclosing space is comparatively inexpensive. The space needed at first is completely finished. Then, when more space is needed and funds are available, some or all of the remainder is finished.

■ Two-story houses,* which are often high and look boxy, can be made to fit comfortably into their setting. In essence, what Koch did was to build a basement and an attic without the intervening floors (Fig. 16). Houses in cold climates need foundations three or more feet below ground level, and it costs very little more to excavate all of this area and use the foundation to enclose the lower part of the ground floor. Rooms below grade are warmer in winter and cooler in summer, and modern technology can easily dispel the cold dampness of old-fashioned basements. Attics are mostly wasted space, but if the walls are raised 5 or 6 feet higher and adequate windows installed, the space becomes comfortably livable. The net result is that the side walls need be only 10 feet above the ground, which is little higher than that of single-story dwellings.

■ Construction systems in which the exterior walls plus widely spaced posts and beams hold the house up give remarkably flexible interiors that can be altered to suit changing family needs or different families. The inside space can be partitioned with lightweight, easily changed walls, storage units, folding doors, or screens. This is possible because only four posts break the space in an area that measures 24 by 36 feet.

■ Entrances and stairways, furnaces and fireplaces, plumbing and kitchen equipment are expensive to move, and for this reason, as well as for convenience in living, the central portion of a house is their logical location. This leaves both ends, or almost two-thirds of the enclosed space, completely flexible.

■ The major components of a house—walls, roof, floors—can be made in a factory and shipped to the site on one truck (Fig. 18). In two days four men can put these in place, and from then on all of the other work can be completed regardless of weather.

■ Licenses to fabricate the panels are granted to manufacturers in many parts of the country, while such items as doors and heating equipment are economically purchased in wholesale quantities. By such means costs are reduced.

The construction of Techbuilt houses is ingenious and efficient. Carl Koch and Associates, architects.

left: 18. The basic components of the structure can be delivered to the site on a single truck.

right: 19. Roof, floors, and interior and exterior walls can be surfaced with whatever materials the owner may think appropriate. Window and door panels can be placed where they serve best.

---

* Although some Techbuilt houses have only one story, those with two stories make the most significant contributions.

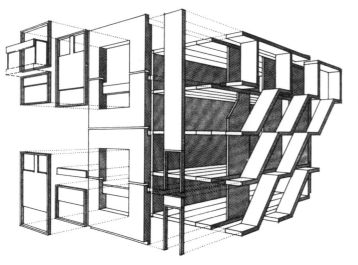

Houses of various sizes can be speedily constructed from a system of modular components, either singly between existing buildings or in a row. Stull Associates, Inc., architects.

above left : 20. Diagram of the system of basic components.

above right : 21. Model of a typical house.

left : 22. Other plans for Fig. 21.

This concept of prefabrication differs greatly from the typical manufactured houses that come in a comparatively few, difficult-to-change models. Perhaps most significant is the choice of at least sixteen different room arrangements. The 4-foot-wide panels, which are solid and opaque or can have doors and varied window arrangements, are selected and placed to suit the owner's preferences in relation to his special needs and the site on which the house is to be built. Finally, the owner has complete freedom in choosing the materials and colors for interior and exterior walls and the roof. Thus, Techbuilt houses are not a completed, unalterable package but a series of components that can be assembled on the site as the owner wishes.

The possibilities of modular prefabrication are also being considered for urban renewal programs. One such proposal (Figs. 20–22) consists of a series of precast, prestressed concrete wall, floor, and roof panels that can be assembled at the site into modular boxes with door and window units cast into the walls. A variable number of the components could be used to produce a variety of plans, exterior designs, and sizes to fit specific lots. The architects conceived the program as a way of filling in the many empty lots scattered over the city of Boston to provide quick housing for families that would be displaced by massive urban renewal projects.

Total Prefabrication

Another approach to prefabricated shelter is evident in those dwelling units that are completely assembled before leaving the factory, much as automobiles are. These include truly mobile vacation homes that can travel easily from one location to another (Fig. 23), and those that are hauled to a trailer park and semipermanently installed. Some are designed to be deposited by helicopter in remote areas where highways are nonexistent (Figs. 24, 25). In addition to these detached units are those planned as components to be joined together. Habitat 67 (Figs. 620, 621) was one of the first notable attempts to construct a massive urban complex from large factory-made elements hoisted into place. Another such structure of assembled units by the same architect is shown in Figure 26. These concepts of total prefabrication are being explored as one solution to the overwhelming need for more, and less costly, shelter.

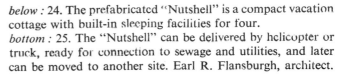

below : 24. The prefabricated "Nutshell" is a compact vacation cottage with built-in sleeping facilities for four.
bottom : 25. The "Nutshell" can be delivered by helicopter or truck, ready for connection to sewage and utilities, and later can be moved to another site. Earl R. Flansburgh, architect.

above : 23. Completely equipped, prefabricated mobile homes are available in many sizes and price brackets. Some are trailers, which are planned for semipermanent sites. Others, such as this Cortez coach, are intended for those who want freedom to travel. Ford and Earl Design Associates.

left : 26. "Habitat Puerto Rico" is an experimental proposal by architect Moshe Safdie to test the validity of total prefabrication for low to middle income urban housing. Precast hexagonal interchangeable concrete modules would be placed in staggered pyramidal clusters down a hill site with a network of roads giving direct access to each level from the rear. (See also Figs. 621, 622.)

Criteria for Determining Architectural Effectiveness

The consideration of house planning in terms of the interrelated problems of *use*, *geography*, *community*, *materials*, *individuality*, and *beauty* will suggest useful criteria for determining the effectiveness of domestic architecture for both efficiency and delight.

Use

Houses are built for people to live in. Obviously, then, the physical, psychological, and spiritual needs of a family should indicate the forms and materials of a home. How architects, builders, and prospective homeowners wish that the solution were as simple as the statement of the problem!

Comfortable Shelter   A prime requisite of homes is protection from excessive cold and heat, wind and dust, rain and snow, insects, and intruders. A sealed box, however, is not the answer because we also enjoy natural light, pleasing outlooks, and adequate ventilation. Walls, roofs, and floors give the needed physical protection and also assure psychological enclosure and privacy. Today, walls can be comparatively thin yet strong and weatherproof and can be made of opaque, translucent, or transparent materials. Windows and doors bring contact with what is beyond the enclosure of the structure. They can be large or small and located where they function best in varied geographical settings.

Areas for Living   Many people have to live in one-room huts or apartments, but almost everyone appreciates segregated areas planned for entering and circulating through the house, relaxing and entertaining, cooking and eating, sleeping and bathing, and outdoor activities. Storing possessions is also a real problem. Organizing these areas is one of the most important aspects of home design.

The planning of space may be approached either as enclosure or as extension. *Closed plans* divide the space into sharply separated rooms. When heating was difficult and low building costs permitted many rooms for specific purposes, closed plans functioned well. They still retain the notable advantages of giving privacy and minimizing the disturbance of conflicting activities. *Open plans*, which have fewer floor-to-ceiling partitions, minimize the separateness of areas used for relaxation and entertainment, eating and cooking. Broad openings, partitions and storage dividers of less than ceiling height, and folding or sliding doors are some of the devices that relate one part of the house to the others. Because open plans give a greater sense of spaciousness and permit more flexible use of actual space, they gained favor as houses became smaller and heating was improved.

The homes discussed so far in this chapter exemplify open planning because it is a concept that has met the needs of twentieth-century living. The Japanese house on page 29, however, shows that this way of organizing space has been enjoyed by people for centuries and in other parts of the world.

Relaxation and entertainment suggest large spaces and furnishings adaptable to varied situations. Living and dining spaces that permit many different furniture arrangements can be changed to suit the family, the occasion, or the season. Large doors that open onto terraces or decks unite these spaces with the outdoors and enlarge the living areas. A family room nearby also extends group-entertainment space, but one at some distance allows two groups to operate independently.

The preparation of food does not have to be walled off from the rest of family life, but it does suggest a specially ventilated area near space for eating. In many houses, the kitchen is secluded from halls and dining space by walls, but it opens into the family room over a counter (Fig. 28). This not only facilitates serving informal meals in the family room but gives those in the kitchen a pleasant outlook and opportunity to supervise children's play.

Dining areas can be varied. They can be at one end of the living room, in one leg of an L-shaped living-dining space, in the family room, in a totally separate room, or even on a different floor. Convenience is increased if outdoor dining space is located near the kitchen.

Bedrooms need privacy, good ventilation, and quiet. In one-story houses they are usually grouped together in the quietest part of the house, sometimes in a segregated wing, but children's and adults' bedrooms can be separated to give each age group privacy. In the typical two-story house all bedrooms are on the upper floor away from other activities; but placing bedrooms on more than one floor also has advantages, especially when children are older and need a degree of independence. Bedrooms that are large enough to double as studies or retreats are particularly useful.

The space enclosed by a Techbuilt house can be organized to meet the family's needs and can easily be altered as the family pattern changes.

top left : 27. When a family is small, only part of the 1920-square-foot house needs to be completed. The unfinished room on the lower floor can be used for storage or play; the living-dining room is a lofty two-story space.

top right : 28. For a family with young children, ample space for group activities is provided on the lower floor and for privacy and quiet on the upper floor.

below left : 29. When the children have grown up, the house may be converted into a two-family dwelling.

below right : 30. The 2304 square feet of a larger plan are arranged to minimize the conflicts between the activities of older children and adults. The children's bedrooms on the lower floor are close to the family room. The upper floor is planned for the generally quieter work of adults.

upper floor

upper floor

lower floor

lower floor

upper floor

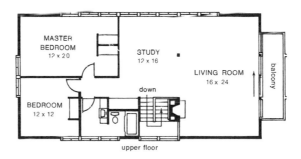

upper floor

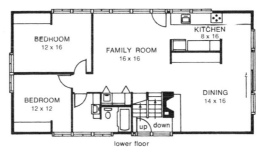

lower floor

lower floor

19

Bathrooms should be placed to suit each family's needs. It is desirable to have at least one centrally located on each level, in addition to any accessible only through the bedroom it serves.

Laundry equipment located near either the kitchen or bathroom consolidates plumbing and is also well placed for convenience.

Storage is a major concern today when there are so many things to be put away in limited space. Convenience indicates that objects be stored near where they are to be used and that each object be easily available. Homes need adequate cabinets in the kitchen and large closets in bedrooms. Other rooms should have ample space for movable storage units, supplemented by a special storage room or storage space in the garage or carport for putting accumulations out of the way.

The enjoyment of outdoor activities—gardening, entertaining, and just relaxing—is a function of the way a house is related to its setting and the manner in which the landscaping is planned. An intimate relationship to the ground and banks of windows and doors is an excellent start. Garages, terraces, and balconies can extend the home out into the landscape (Figs. 31, 33) in one or more directions. Lawns, shrubs, and trees as well as flowers and fences—whatever the owner wishes—can complete the composition.

Circulation   Short, pleasant routes from one part of the house to another are desirable, but excess space in hallways is an extravagance in construction cost, upkeep, and the occupants' energies. This important aspect of home planning is ingeniously handled in the plans on page 19. The compact but adequate, well-lighted entries, midway between the two levels, lead directly to small halls on both floors. From these one can get to any room without walking through another room. Little space is devoted to circulation alone, but greater convenience is hard to imagine. Efficient, economical circulation results when the plan is compact, functionally related areas are adjacent to each other, and furniture is out of the way of traffic.

Furnishings and Equipment   Furniture and household equipment transform the architectural shell into a livable home. Beauty and individuality in furnishings are discussed elsewhere in this chapter, but the possibilities for the arrangement of furniture and equipment in a house are important considerations in terms of use. Rooms should be large enough to accommodate needed pieces of furniture with space to spare. Dead-end rooms, with doors in the corners and windows grouped together, leave uninterrupted and usually alternative wall spaces to accommodate large furniture groups. Thermostatically controlled heating and cooling units automatically keep the rooms at comfortable temperatures. Artificial lighting should be planned for maximum flexibility, efficiency, and pleasantness. Kitchen and laundry equipment incorporating the latest advances in these fields are often great work- and time-savers.

In summary, the purpose of a house, in terms of use, is to provide an environment for convenient, gratifying home life. Thus, the first criterion for domestic architecture is: The building (with its furnishings and equipment) should meet the human needs for which it was designed.

Geography

In the past, geographical factors strongly affected home design. The American Indians of the Pacific Northwest made sturdy houses of wood; those of the Southwest built theirs of adobe brick. The nomadic Plains Indians depended on lightweight, easily transportable tepees made of poles and buffalo skins. Each group

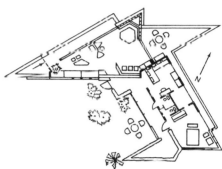

left : 31. Climate and site were important factors in Peter Jefferson's design for a cottage in the Bahamas (c. 1965). The house was shaped to deflect the full force of hurricanes but to take advantage of the trade winds. The main living areas project into the expansive view.

below : 32. Plan for Fig. 31.

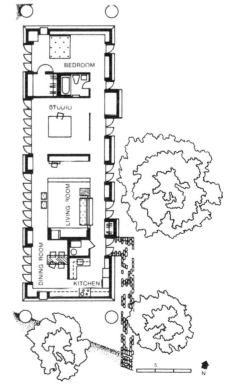

left : 33. Architect Remmert W. Huygens, of Huygens and Tappé, Inc., designed his own home in Wayland, Mass., to be as solid and satisfying as the old New England homes in the same area. (See also Fig. 398.)

below : 34. The plan for Fig. 33 has a studio that could be converted into two bedrooms and a large closet that could become another bath.

used native materials to shape distinctive dwellings that were a direct outgrowth of the group's mode of living in relation to the climate, the building materials, and the character of the landscape.

Today architectural concepts spread rapidly over the world. Building materials, new and old, can be transported far from their point of origin, and much work that was done on the site is now done more efficiently in factories. New heating and cooling equipment, together with improved insulating materials, makes the interiors of houses relatively independent of the weather outside. These factors markedly lessen the differences among houses in varied geographical settings. Thus, contemporary architecture has less regional character than does most historic work; but this does not mean that the same house is equally good everywhere.

So far geography has been discussed in regional terms, but specific sites are just as important. The shape and size of the lot, whether the land is flat or rolling, the presence of trees, a lake, or a good view, which point of the compass the major rooms should face are all of great concern in the design of a home.

The two houses in Figures 31 through 34 were built for specific sites in quite different locations. The vacation cottage in the Bahamas is poised on a bluff overlooking the ocean. The main living areas project into the expansive view through window walls shaded by wide overhangs, and a protected veranda faces the sunset. The Huygens house is in Massachusetts, a section of the country subjected to heavy winter snows. The tentlike roof and thick concrete walls protect the large window areas and have a feeling of solidity and shelter appropriate to the climate.

Orientation   Relating a house to the sun, wind, and views is important in home design. Generally, in the Northern Hemisphere it is desirable to have the major rooms face south and east and to concentrate windows on these sides. The gains are numerous. The winter sun, lower in the sky, sends a warm, good feeling deep into the house, but an overhanging roof keeps the high summer sun from the windows. Cold winter winds are kept at bay. Outdoor living areas can be integrated with their interior counterparts. Entrance and stairway, storage areas and bathrooms can be placed toward the north and west. Special situations may suggest a change in this ideal orientation, however. The Huygens house faces southwest to take advantage of the view over a river valley and the hills beyond, but being only one room deep, the house also receives morning sun on the eastern exposure (see Fig. 398).

From this discussion emerges the second criterion for domestic architecture: The house should be suited to its setting and climate.

Community

A home is usually a part of a community, seldom an isolated dwelling. This brings additional problems and potentialities. Building ordinances usually regulate some factors to ensure safe construction, adequate window area, the covering of only a certain percentage of the land, and location of the house on the lot in a desirable position in relation to the rest of the community. A few communities go farther by prescribing minimum size and cost, and occasionally even the exterior design of a home. In most situations, however, each man has the freedom to make his home look the way he wants it to. Usually he wants his home to be pleasantly related to the general character of the community, but herein lies a difficulty. The community may be a jumble of pseudo-Colonial confronting pseudo-Tudor, or of imitation French Provincial arguing with Hollywood Spanish. It may be simply block after block of nondescript houses, or it may proclaim that creative thinking stopped a century or so ago. This, of course, is a challenge that each architect meets in his own way.

Architect Remmert Huygens was required by deed restrictions to design his own house "to relate to its historic neighbor," a large white, eighteenth-century frame house and a red barn. He achieved this by using traditional forms but interpreting them in a contemporary and very personal manner (Fig. 33). The simple rectangular shape of the house and the double-pitched roof go back to early Colonial days, as do the cedar shingles that cover the roof and the massive chimney. But the gable end is filled in with a huge glass window that floods the kitchen and dining room with light. The thick walls are of concrete—a twentieth-century material when used for homes—that has been given a somewhat rustic, battered finish. The windows are actually a series of doors that open the house to the landscape and are deeply set between thick piers to protect them from the weather. Thus, although the house expresses the architect's concepts in the rhythm of voids and solids, and is thoroughly modern in its relationship to the outdoors, it has the enduring, uncomplicated forms and quality of many older homes in New England.

As we continue our study, it should become increasingly evident that every art object was created in a period of time, in a place, and in a social order. Significant

35. Lofty, projecting brick walls control the sun and create a lively, three-dimensional interplay of light, shade, and shadow on the Richard Henrich house (c. 1965) in Barrington, Illinois. Edward D. Dart, architect.

art expresses all of these without hesitancy or flamboyance, as demonstrated by the homes that have been discussed. From this comes our third criterion for domestic architecture: The home should express the time and place in which it was created.

Materials

The usefulness and beauty of a home are directly related to the selection and handling of the materials from which it is built.

Wood is one of the most commonly used and versatile materials for domestic structures. Beams that run the length of the house and support the roof or second floor attest to the strength of wood. Roof and wall panels, made of plywood sheathing or grooved plywood siding bonded to insulated wood frames, are remarkably strong for their weight and thickness. Wood siding can be used on the exterior and sometimes on the interior as well. Steel, which is much stronger and more expensive than wood, is often used for the posts that support the beams and sometimes for the shell of the house. Brick is a logical material for fireplaces and can also be used for walls and floors, making these as durable as they are handsome. Brick was also used for the dramatic piers that frame the windows of the house designed by Edward Dart (Fig. 35) because their precise shape leads naturally to an elegant simplicity. Roughhewn masonry would have necessitated a different type of construction and resulted in a completely different character. Throughout the houses in this chapter each material has been employed with sympathetic understanding of its nature. None has been assigned a task for which it was unsuited, nor have its special qualities been hidden.

The fourth criterion of domestic architecture, then, is: The materials should be appropriately chosen and handled.

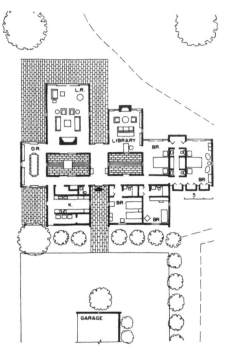

above : 36. The plan of the house in Pl. 3 shows six pavilions clustered around two open courts that separate the various phases of home life. Hugh Newell Jacobsen, A.I.A., architect.

right : 37. Vertical siding of untreated cypress that will weather to a gray tone in the salt air sheathes the handsomely detailed exterior of the Jacobsen house and accentuates the unusual roof line that rises over the center of each wing.

Individuality

In an age marked by standardization and conformity, individuality runs the risk of being stifled, but the urge to be one's self comes out strongly in home planning and furnishing. A satisfying home goes beyond mere physical shelter to become intimately related to its occupants. This includes such factors as family size, financial and social status, way of living, and tastes and preferences. Although family size and income are the most obvious determinants, others deserve equal consideration. For example, families that often entertain large groups or enjoy such active relaxation as dancing may need larger homes than do those that enjoy smaller groups and quieter activities.

The house illustrated in Plate 3 and in Figures 36 and 37 is a one-story structure set in a broad meadow by the sea. As the plan and Plate 3b show, the house has been designed to give privacy and quiet to different activities by a system of pavilions placed around two inner courts. On the landward side of the house, tall, thin windows allow broken glimpses of the surroundings, but seaward the rooms open out through broad window walls with sliding doors. The interior treatment juxtaposes plain flat surfaces with abrupt changes of height, a feeling of warm enclosure with sweeping views. The colors used have a quietly glowing quality that shows to advantage a collection of large modern paintings. In the living room, the furniture has been grouped away from the wall and special lighting installed to further enhance the paintings.

Every person in a home has a right to some space that expresses his personality. It may be through use of favorite colors, shapes, or textures, through pictures on the wall, or through plants in the garden. It may be through interests or hobbies, which merit as much space and equipment as the pocketbook permits. The photographer wants his darkroom and the weaver his loom. Other persons are gratified by planning and cooking meals, arranging flowers, reading, or enjoying music.

In almost all of the rooms illustrated in this chapter, paintings, sculpture, and accessories make their unique contributions. Since prehistoric times man has found emotional and spiritual satisfaction in painted or carved expressions of significant human experiences. So universal is this human need that it is difficult to find a home devoid of this opportunity to escape from daily routine. Painting and sculpture can be intense focal points that express the owner's individuality as well as that of their creators (Pl. 3a). Today many painters, printmakers, and sculptors are creating moderately priced work with homes, rather than museums, in mind.

The fifth criterion of domestic architecture is: The home should state its owners' preferences and interests.

above : Plate 3a. In a pavilion house (1967) in Bristol, Rhode Island, white living room walls, an off-white area rug on a dark slate floor, and black and white furniture are sparked by intense colors in a sofa and accessories and create a restrained but positive setting for a collection of modern paintings. One wall has sliding glass doors that join the living room to the surrounding terrace. Hugh Newell Jacobsen, A.I.A., architect. (See also Figs. 36, 37.)

left : Plate 3b. The thoughtful, meticulous detailing evident throughout the pavilion house can be seen in this view looking down into the inner courts, which are lighted at night by outside sources, opening up and illuminating the interior.

Plate 4. The three-story window wall of the Fred I. Smith house (1967) in Darien, Connecticut, stands clear of the inner structure. White-painted wood and brick and large areas of glass are a sparkling contrast to the green landscape and blue sky. Richard Meier, architect. (See also Figs. 38, 39, 497.)

Beauty

In designing a home, beauty is seldom the architect's *primary* preoccupation in the *beginning* stages, although he is always aware of the ultimate need for it. The first, consciously intellectual steps in designing a house are usually concerned with such technicalities as how the family wants to live and the most economical ways of meeting these needs. Countless sketches are made and the most promising are refined for greater beauty and for efficiency. But even though an architect does not concentrate on beauty at first, his long experience in finding esthetically energizing forms leads him, perhaps intuitively, to favor some possibilities above others. The true artist, whether builder or carver, never denies that he is a whole man—his feelings for the usable, the rational, and the emotional are all deeply involved in his creations.

The house designed by architect Richard Meier (Pl. 4 and Figs. 38, 39, 497) has an innate coherence that grew directly from the plan and that is expressed in the framework, both visual and structural. All the rooms are harmoniously rectangular, but they differ in size and proportion. Some are privately withdrawn, others open freely into adjacent areas. Locating them on three levels allowed the architect to open the living spaces up to the balcony study and down to the large dining room. The bedrooms and kitchen are enclosed and secure within the bearing-wall framework on one side of the house. On the other side a regularly spaced, columnar steel structure provides support and allows the freestanding window wall to express on the exterior the openness of the living areas. The height of the almost all-glass façade is emphasized by placing the fireplace chimney as a separate vertical element. Its rectangularity is thrown into relief by the precise curves on the staircases and the tubular steel columns.

The beauty of the Meier house is based on clean, crisp, unstereotyped design, asymmetrical in detail but assured and balanced. The house is painted white inside and out, and much of the furniture has the same crisp rectangularity relieved by curves as do the building forms, all leading to an unusual degree of unity.

Each of the houses in this chapter has its own personal and individual beauty. The glowing colors of the Jacobsen pavilion house emphasize the coherence of the

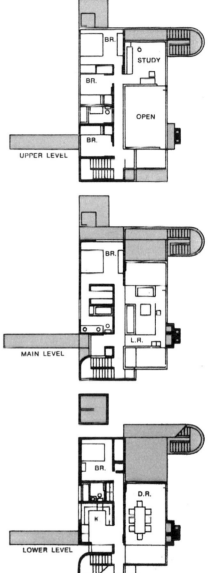

above: 38. The severity of the three-level rectangular plan of the Smith residence, designed by Richard Meier, is eased by unexpected set-backs in the house wall and by the rounded forms on the interior and exterior stairs.

left: 39. The diagonal view that Richard Meier created from the third level down through the house reveals the consistency of the geometric design, extending even to the furnishings. Beyond is the broken shoreline on which the house stands.

structural design and the balanced placement of the furniture. In the Huygens residence, the three-dimensionality of the enclosing walls gives a forceful rhythm to the exterior and balances the visual weight of the large roof. The house designed by Edward Dart, although somewhat similar in concept to the one by Meier, is quite different in execution and impact. The brick piers break up the façade, shield the interior, and create a play of light and shadow that is forceful and dramatic. The cottage in the Bahamas is an intriguing composition of diagonals that de-emphasize the house and carry sightlines out into the view. Each of the houses is the result of interaction between the site, the needs and desires of the owners, and the personal vision of the architect, and attests to the scope of beauty in domestic architecture today.

Beauty defies exact definition, explanation, and prescription, but there are some elementary factors that contribute to the comeliness of the houses discussed in this chapter and in Plates 1 through 4. In each the design of the whole and of every part is harmonious with and expressive of its use and materials. All of the parts belong together, but they are not monotonously repetitious. Satisfying balance, rhythmic relationships, and appropriate dominance and subordination mark each composition. Perhaps most important, the houses seem to have an inner vitality that gives them a wonderful relevance and rightness.

Thus, the sixth criterion of domestic architecture is: The home should be beautiful.

The homes examined so far in this chapter are called modern because they satisfy today's needs directly, take advantage of technological progress, and exemplify current concepts of beauty. They put to good use what has been learned in the past, but they do not imitate earlier work. Following a basic principle in architecture, they were designed *from the inside out*: the exterior developed from the interior, which in turn grew out of contemporary living patterns. This approach leads to architecture that is a self-renewing, continually changing manifestation of man's psychological and physical necessities rather than to a fixed style.

Three Historic Homes

To broaden our horizons, we now look at three homes from varied cultures. Each exemplifies fitness to its purpose, expression of its cultural and geographic environment, and adroit use of materials. Each is beautiful in its own terms.

A Japanese Home

Having evolved over several centuries, the traditional Japanese house (Figs. 40, 41) is serenely calm and has a remarkable feeling of sheltered openness. It is basically simple and clear, yet intricately complex in details and space relationships. It is designed on a standardized module: woven mats measuring about 3 by 6 feet not only cover the floor but determine the building's proportions. This basic regularity allows the designers to introduce variety and surprise without loss of composure. Sliding panels flexibly subdivide interior space and relate it to the garden. The natural colors of wood, plaster, and woven reeds further tie the house to its natural setting and produce a singleness of effect amid variety. The size and shape of each unit is so in scale with the occupants that a truly great harmony is achieved. It is no wonder that many contemporary architects have found inspiration and guidance in Japanese buildings.

A traditional Japanese house built by native craftsmen in the garden of the Museum of Modern Art, New York

right : 40. An impeccable sense of order unites diverse, asymmetrically disposed elements.

below : 41. The continuing lines of the exposed structure, the broad openings, and the refined details produce a feeling of spaciousness transcending the actual dimensions.

Mary Arden's Home

The home of Mary Arden, Shakespeare's mother, typifies smaller dwellings of sixteenth-century England (Figs. 42, 43). In contrast to the refined lightness and flexibility of Japanese homes, it is almost boisterously vigorous, heavy, and solid; but it, too, consistently reveals its structure and materials, inside and out. Heavy wood timbers form the structural and ornamental framework. Plaster-covered masonry fills the spaces between the timbers and provides a strong contrast of color and texture. Everything works together to make the house a secure haven against the environment,

Mary Arden's home (16th century), Wilmcote, near Stratford, England.

right : 42. A straightforward, functional use of materials contributes to its appeal. The dark timbers not only support the structure but make a strong visual pattern.

below : 43. Heavy and dark, but warm and safe, the interior and its furnishings are totally consistent with the exterior.

but the large-scale beams, a room-heating fireplace, heavy furniture, and small windows make the rooms seem even smaller than they are. The exterior, too, promises protection against weather and marauders.

Judged by contemporary standards, it is cramped, dark, poorly ventilated, and difficult to heat, yet it functioned efficiently when judged by sixteenth-century standards of living. Its relationship to contemporary American houses is similar to that between Elizabethan stagecoaches and our latest automobiles. Even today, though, it has a consistently heartwarming, roughhewn integrity that gives it an undeniable beauty and that tells much about the period in England when medieval traditions were giving way to Renaissance ideals.

A Dwelling from Colonial Williamsburg

From 1699 to 1779, Williamsburg was the governmental, economic, religious, and social center of the colony of Virginia. It declined during the Revolutionary War and remained a quiet college town and country seat until restoration was begun in the 1930s. It now stands as a museum of an eighteenth-century American capital.

The Brush-Everard house (Figs. 44, 45) now looks much as it did in 1750. It is far more refined, and less vigorous, than Mary Arden's cottage, and it is more formal than the Japanese house or Hugh Stubbins' home. The exterior is unpretentious yet dignified. The simple, economical shape establishes a strong horizontal feeling, which is reinforced by the cornice marking the juncture of wall and roof as well as by the horizontal lines of the siding and shingles. Vertical doors, windows, and dormers are a lively contrast. The small-paned, shuttered windows reflect the high cost of large panes of glass and the need for protection against cold. Their pleasing shape and orderly placement show deep concern for proportion and regularity. The simple doorway gains prominence through its central position, dark color, and brick platform. Color contributes to the total effect: the walls are golden-yellow, shutters and dormers are white, the window bars and the trim around the roof are biscuit, and the door is a dark, intense green.

The handsomely designed and richly furnished living room more than fulfills the promise of gracious living suggested by the exterior. The architectural background is as decisively rectangular and clearly defined as the exterior. The centered fireplace, a logical focus of interest, projects into the room. Its importance is underlined by sensitively shaped moldings, the whiteness of the firebrick, and its soft green color, which differentiates it from the oak floor and the white plaster walls and ceiling. However, its color extends onto the wall at the left and carries around the room in the cornice where walls and ceiling meet. The furnishings bring diversity of many sorts. Draperies and upholstery are bright cherry red, a color echoed in the Oriental rug. Mahogany chairs and tables are gracefully and comfortably curved. Color, shape, and intricate pattern are introduced in the rug, tea set, and other decorative objects. Views into other worlds are offered by the paintings. The Brush-Everard house is consistent yet diversified, as was the spirit of the age. It stands today as a unified expression of eighteenth-century living in Virginia.

The integrity of the contemporary and historic homes discussed in this chapter comes when art grows directly and naturally from its whole environment. The Colonial builder constructed according to what is now called the Colonial style because he was building a house for Colonial family life. The art from different historic periods may seem to have little in common, but each style is invariably a direct, sincere expression of the life of its time and place. We, too, are creating an art of our own.

Furnishing the Home

The problem is to *furnish* rather than to *decorate* space for living. This is not a complicated procedure, but there are ways of approaching the task that will help to assure a pleasing and workable result. An analysis of the problem can be made by considering the following questions:

What activities will take place in each area? A consideration of the uses to which each space will be put is a fundamental first step in furnishing. Will the room be used for relaxation, reading, talking, listening to music, study, eating, or sleeping? Each activity makes its special demands. The more comprehensive and detailed this analysis, the better the chances of getting good results.

What furnishings and equipment does each activity require? Casual reading, for example, necessitates only a seat and a light, but a convenient place to keep reading materials helps. Serious and prolonged reading or study indicates a really comfortable chair, very good light, freedom from distractions, and perhaps a desk. Conversation, games, eating, sleeping, dressing, and hobbies have their own special requirements. The designer of the one-room apartment on pages 4 and 5 used double-duty and component furniture to satisfy these needs in a remarkably small space.

The Brush-Everard house (c. 1750), Williamsburg, Virginia.

left : 44. The exterior shows the sureness of design, subtlety of proportion, and simple yet dignified quality of eighteenth-century American architecture.

right : 45. A handsome fireplace, comfortable furniture, and appropriate paintings and accessories recall a stable, assured era.

What basic character should each room and the whole house have? If life were merely a matter of eating, sleeping, and working, there would be no need for art. But we have an enduring need for qualities beyond the strictly practical. This is the time for self-analysis, for realism but also for dreams. Frank Lloyd Wright's and Philip Johnson's homes, for example, are indicative of their characters, and their enthusiasms, as well as their design philosophies.

What furnishings are most appropriate? The answer to the question of basic character provides the key to appropriateness. Does the character desired suggest formal symmetry with a balanced repetition of furniture forms, as in Philip Johnson's home, or does it indicate a more informal, asymmetrical balancing of unlike shapes, as in Taliesin North? If the living quarters are reasonably permanent, each object can be selected with a particular space in mind. If not, furnishings that will fit other situations may be most appropriate, as on pages 4 and 5. Should the forms be predominantly rough or smooth, sturdy or delicate, plain or ornamented? Then there is the question of whether the colors should be rich or pale, high-keyed or muted, contrasting or harmonious. These factors of design and color are discussed fully in Chapters 11 through 13.

How can furnishings be arranged for comfort, convenience, and attractiveness? The importance that is attached to each phase of a person's life affects both purchases and arrangements. If reading is a major interest, good conditions for reading are a necessity. Music, gardening, or cooking is most enjoyable when the surroundings encourage the hobby. The joy of space or the exhilaration of color may seem more important than any specific activity. Again, it is a matter of putting human needs first, and then selecting and arranging furnishings so that they relate to one another and give each object its just emphasis. This is a matter of balance and rhythm, dominance and subordination—principles of design that in themselves are constant, but application of which will vary with the individual and his time. These principles are covered in greater depth in Chapter 14.

Planning the Landscape

Each of the houses in the preceding sections has its own distinctive landscape development. The Foster house (Fig. 2) floats independently above its pastoral site and visually extends itself into the panoramic view. Taliesin North, in contrast, is as deeply rooted in its site as are the trees around it in order to minimize the differences between man-made structure and natural ground forms and vegetation. The landscaping around Philip Johnson's home—as simple, open, and restrained as the glass-walled structure—consists of a spacious lawn, a lake, and a greenbelt of native trees and shrubs. Hugh Stubbins' average size, unexceptional city lot is enclosed with walls that together with the paved terraces make the limited space eminently usable. The restricted site on which the Japanese house was built was developed along the principles of carefully studied naturalism. A small lawn and two fully branched trees comprise the entrance area of the Brush-Everard house, while picket fences define the modest side and rear gardens. The garden of Mary Arden's house is a picturesque profusion of flowering plants, trees, and vines in harmony with the informality of the architecture and stone wall.

The Egyptians, Greeks, Romans, and Spaniards extended their houses into the gardens as true outdoor living rooms enclosed by the house, high walls, and arcades. Pools and fountains, sculpture and plants provided visual delight. Medieval Europeans protected their beds of roses and herbs and their arbored walks with the strong walls of castle and monastery. The artists of the Italian Renaissance opened their

The Grosenick house (c. 1966), Medina, Washington. Anton Mueller, architect. Robert W. Chittock, landscape architect.

above : 46. The house merges almost imperceptively with the garden by means of decks at various levels, raised planting beds, extended roofs, and steps and paths that lead to the lawn.

right : 47. The placement of the house at the back of the property allows the group-living areas, both indoors and out, to take advantage of the southern exposure.

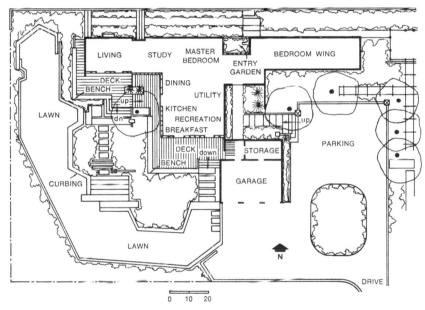

gardens to nature with broad walks and shady groves, but related them to their houses with richly embellished walls, balustrades, fountains, and pavilions. The English, who "jumped the fence and discovered that all nature was a garden," developed the naturalistic landscape based on the theory that a straight line does not look natural. The inspiring history of gardens is the story of man's delight in nature and of his achievements in adapting nature to his needs.

Because most people today want their landscaping to provide usable areas for outdoor living, the principles of house design apply directly. In the Carl P. Grosenicks' home (Figs. 46, 47) a strongly unified composition of architecture and landscape joins the indoors with the outdoors so adroitly that it is difficult to tell where one stops and the other begins. A section of an old estate, the gently rolling site was blessed with many fully grown trees and shrubs. The architect and landscape architect collaborated from the beginning in locating and designing the house and landscape elements to preserve as much of the site's idyllic character as possible. Grading was reduced to a minimum. Only a few trees and shrubs were removed, others were pruned to admit more sun and to reveal their structure, trunks, branches, and foliage masses. The land and the T-shaped house were effectively zoned: a garage and a parking area in the southeast corner are conveniently near storage areas, the guest entrance, and doors into the group-living area. An ample living terrace overlooks the major landscape development on the south and west; and the bedrooms are secluded on the north side.

The plan and photographs show how the series of decks, landscaped areas, and paths that encircle the house invite outdoor living. The raised wood deck, benches, and steps; the exposed aggregate walls and paving; and the lawn, shrubs, and trees form a lively, three-dimensional interplay of light, shade, and shadow.

In designing a landscape, as in planning a room, an analysis of needs is the first step, followed by a decision about the general character wanted. If the list of needs emphasizes comfortable outdoor living, attention should be given to *enclosure* for privacy and protection from wind; *overhead protection* from sun, wind, rain, and snow; and *comfortable and weather-resistant furniture.* In the Grosenicks' home, the deck area outside the dining room has a protective roof. Benches along the edges of the decks are weatherproof, provide seating, and eliminate the need for much more furniture. What furniture there is, is lightweight and movable. The variety of exposures of the outdoor areas would take care of many climate conditions. Other interests, such as gardening, might lead to a different program. Whatever the goals, the landscape deserves as much thought as the house and its furnishings.

Single-family dwellings asserting their independence on their own piece of private property have long been held as the ideal of many people in the United States. Such houses can have the advantages of individuality and privacy when they fit the preferences and pocketbooks of their owners and when the lots are sufficiently large to encourage outdoor activities. More often than not, however, there is nothing to be seen in uncounted real estate developments but an endless repetition of identical structures crowded together on lots that are too small for them. This kind of suburban sprawl precludes the potential advantages of either country or city living. No matter how well planned, single-unit projects have numerous drawbacks. These include comparatively high original and continuing costs, the necessity for private automobile transportation, the time spent in commuting to work or running household errands, and the lack of real community feeling. Even more serious in the long run is the extravagant squandering of land. Alternatives such as clustered or semidetached houses, attached town houses, and high-rise apartment complexes offer many advantages and will be discussed in Chapter 2.

The topic of art in the home is so large that no one could hope to exhaust the material on it. This chapter can do little more than act as an introduction.

The following sections of the book will present further discussions of color, design, and materials that can be applied to the home. Part I, with its emphasis on human needs, serves as a foundation for the more intensive study of materials, form and color, and design covered in Parts II and III.

48. "City Shape/21," a visionary project by architect Stanley Tigerman, would enlarge the central core of cities by building out over adjacent water areas on a system of gigantic pontoons. The shape of the inverted, hollow pentahedrons, forty-six stories high, opens each unit to the sun.

2 The Arts
of the Community

Communities, ranging in size and character from small isolated settlements to vast metropolitan agglomerations, are comprised of individuals with some common concerns and some kind of communal organization. The remote, fast-disappearing rural communities were necessarily more or less self-sufficient. In striking contrast are New York City, Los Angeles, Tokyo, and London, which have millions of persons living and working in one complex. Most of the population depend on trains, buses, subways, or private automobiles to get from home to work. They rely heavily on public utilities and the services of many persons to maintain their way of living. A single breakdown, such as a power failure, is a critical factor. Already overcrowded, the metropolitan areas are still growing and now contain more than 60 percent of our total population.

Between these extremes are communities of many sizes and types. They may be independent towns or satellite complexes related to a large city; or they can be sections within a town or neighborhoods within a larger community held together by similar ideals or interests. Communities may also be specialized in nature, such as retirement centers, trailer parks, or vacation areas. Also, they can be much larger than a metropolis, extending hundreds of miles and even crossing state boundaries, as does the Tennessee Valley Authority. They may in fact be world wide, as is the United Nations. All of these diverse communities generate art problems similar to those of the home, but they are much broader in scope and larger in scale and have deeper implications. Through city or regional plans, recreation facilities, public buildings, painting and sculpture, each community has magnificent opportunities to take care of its practical needs and to express its ideals.

The Community of Williamsburg

In the eighteenth century, Williamsburg covered approximately a square mile of land and had a resident population of around three thousand persons. When the assemblies and courts were in session, as many as four thousand more persons came to stay in the taverns and inns. Some came on government business, others to see the newest fashions from London or to be entertained by fairs and horse races, lotteries, cockfights, and other diversions. Merchants and planters came to transact business. Colonel Spotswood boasted that his supper guests at the Governor's Palace numbered four hundred.

Out of the busy life of eighteenth-century Virginia developed the community of Williamsburg. Common goals banded the citizens together, and their arts expressed their activities, philosophies, and ideals. The builders of Williamsburg were English colonists imbued with the contemporaneous attitudes of their mother country. Because their way of life and the geographical conditions rather closely resembled those in England, they adapted the architecture they had known in their native country to the conditions and materials of America. The entire community was designed in the style of the period, a style that the inhabitants of Williamsburg had helped develop and that expressed their pattern of life.

The Plan of Williamsburg

Williamsburg, the first planned community in the United States, was designed with impressive dignity and good sense (Fig. 49). Duke of Gloucester Street, the main avenue, is a noble thoroughfare 99 feet wide and almost a mile long. At the east end it is terminated by the Capitol, which, as the major public building, was given the most important position. At the west end Duke of Gloucester Street forks into main roads to Richmond and Jamestown, and at this strategic intersection stands the College of William and Mary. Between these public buildings the major thoroughfare is lined with other community buildings, shops, and important residences. Parallel to Duke of Gloucester Street are several narrower residential streets. Between the college and the Capitol is Palace Green, a broad lawn extending two blocks to the Governor's Palace and providing a dignified approach to the residence of the colony's most important political personage. In the eighteenth century there were farms in the countryside beyond the Governor's Palace that provided food for the community.

The plan of Williamsburg is simple, and its rectangular pattern resembles the gridiron pattern of most American cities. There are, however, important differences that give Williamsburg a pleasant, distinctive character: the widths of streets vary according to their importance; the blocks vary in size and shape; and the chief buildings have impressive locations. Thus, the streets in this Colonial capital were not merely traffic arteries but played their part in giving the city a simple grandeur that typifies eighteenth-century living. For its purpose and its time, the plan was both beautiful and useful.

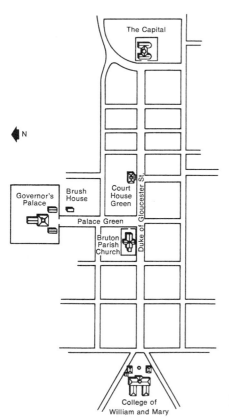

49. The plan of Williamsburg, Virginia, is a modified gridiron with blocks of varied sizes and shapes and appropriately dominant locations for important buildings.

The Governor's Palace

The Governor's Palace (Fig. 50) is orderly, dignified, and impressive. It indicates at once that it was more than an ordinary home, that it was the official center of hospitality for eighteenth-century Virginia.

Many factors contribute to this impression. First, the location of the Governor's Palace at the end of Palace Green gives it a distinguished setting. Second, its size makes it imposing, for it is the largest home in Williamsburg. Third, it is handsomely framed by the two flanking buildings and by the curved forecourt wall leading up to the richly ornamented gate. Finally, the main building is masterfully designed. Symmetrical and precisely ordered, it is saved from monotony and stiffness by the rightness of its proportions and the grace of its detail. The building is a simple rectangle that gains stability and repose through its horizontality. The roof is a truncated pyramid that serves as a transition between the lower portion and the cupola. The verticality of the windows, the chimney, and the cupola tempers the dominant horizontality. Subtle progressions give vitality to the window shapes and to their placement: they diminish in height from the first floor to the third floor, and the distance between them increases from the center to the ends. Both of these devices direct attention toward the central doorway. Restrained, judiciously placed ornament enriches the total composition.

The design of the building suggests comparison with the musical concept of theme and variations practiced by many eighteenth-century European composers. The composer would begin with a simple melody of his own or with a well-known song or hymn and then would rework the original tune in many and varied ways. The architects of Williamsburg handled architectural forms in a similar way. For example, the truncated pyramid is repeated and varied in the roof of the main building, the dormers and chimneys, and the roofs of the two smaller structures. Echoing and diversifying a basic form bestows importance on it and helps to unify the design.

Just as conversation in the drawing rooms of Williamsburg was characterized by gracefully turned phrases, delicately poised innuendoes, and correctly balanced sentences, so too was the architecture marked by gracious proportions, delicately molded ornaments, carved brackets and balustrades, and airy cupolas. Throughout Williamsburg the graceful design and the adroit use of ornament are so effective

The Governor's Palace and Garden at Williamsburg have a gracious regularity typical of much eighteenth-century design.

left : 50. The symmetrical exterior of the Palace is enlivened by the measured spacing of windows, the delicate detail of cornices and cupola, and the curved wall of the forecourt. Red brick, white trim, and gray slate roof contrast pleasantly with the colors of sky and foliage.

right : 51. The formal garden behind the Palace is in harmony with the architecture, echoing and emphasizing the geometric shapes of the building.

that today, as we look at the whole community, we are transported across the intervening centuries to that age in which reason and functionalism underlay imaginative yet ordered beauty.

The Governor's Garden

The Governor's Garden (Fig. 51) carries the precision, formality, and elegance of the Palace into the landscape. It, too, is basically rectangular, but the diagonal hedges echo the roof lines, and the rounded shrubs recall the cupola. The Garden, like the Palace, expresses the love of orderly and elaborate surroundings of people who wore powdered wigs and lacy jabots.

In the eighteenth century the effect of the garden, standing in such startling contrast to the wide forests a few miles away, must have been breathtaking. One can imagine how the Indian chief felt when he walked its formal paths, how the wilderness-worn traveler felt when he first saw the mathematical precision of the clipped shrubs. The garden belonged not only to the Governor and his family, but to Williamsburg, to the colony of Virginia, to Colonial America. It served home needs, it impressed local visitors, it refreshed travelers, and it reminded the colonists of their mother country. It was truly a community garden.

The community of Williamsburg needed other public buildings, including the Capitol, the Courthouse, and Bruton Parish Church (Fig. 95). Each was planned with the same fundamental ideas that molded the Governor's Palace: simple, rectangular forms of red brick as a foil for the refined white ornamentation; cupolas and spires; formally placed openings; windows with small panes of glass; and restrained ornamentation.

Contemporary Communities

Since the time Williamsburg was built, the changes in the United States and in most parts of the world have been phenomenal. In the eighteenth century American civilization was concentrated along the Atlantic Seaboard. Farming was the major occupation, and cities were few and small. The nineteenth and twentieth centuries brought tremendous expansion of both the geographical boundaries and the population. Industry and research expanded and became increasingly specialized and interdependent. The telegraph, the telephone, radio, and television, and the widespread availability of printed material accelerated communication among institutions and individuals. Rapid transit systems, automobiles, buses, trucks, airplanes, and elevators brought undreamed-of mobility. They also resulted in exasperating traffic congestion (Fig. 52).

Until fairly recently man proceeded as though the world's supply of land was unlimited and as if population was not a matter of concern. These false assumptions led to an extravagant use of land and natural resources. Man now realizes that there are only about 135 million square miles of land on this earth. So far only 10 percent of the most desirable area is intensively cultivated. With astute planning and advanced technology another 10 to 20 percent could be made useful and habitable according to contemporary estimates. Population is another matter. In 1920 the number of persons living in the United States was 105 million, but by the 1960s that figure had doubled and more than one-half lived in cities that occupied only 1 percent of the land. Estimates for the year 2000 indicate that there will be about 330 million people in the United States and that 80 percent will be living in cities. In 1895 only four automobiles were registered in the United States. Now it is esti-

52. Ninth Avenue, New York City.

mated that cars occupy from 60 to 70 percent of the land in Los Angeles. The result of this growth is that cities have mushroomed upward and outward but often without comprehensive, enlightened planning, and overcrowded slums and overburdened transportation systems have made city life a grim experience for many.

Quite recently planners have taken a long, realistic look at what has happened and have taken some of the steps necessary to improve the situation. Most of these steps can be classified in three categories: *new communities*, which have been built in sparsely settled areas; *urban renewal* projects, which have made encouraging progress in revitalizing and humanizing central districts of cities; and *regional planning*, such as the vast area in the Tennessee Valley Authority and the more modest perimeters of Washington, D. C., which attempts to utilize the resources and to channel the growth of large areas of land.

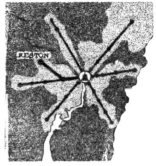

A New Town: Reston, Virginia

In 1898 an Englishman, Ebenezer Howard, pioneered the "garden city" movement. Distressed by the conditions in which he found English factory workers living and rearing children, he advocated smaller communities planned from the beginning for a limited number of well-placed industries and for a limited number of dwellings. Growth was not to proceed unchecked, since that always led to the congestion common to ill-planned cities. Each garden city was planned to grow to a healthy size, and then, if necessary, a new one separated from the original by farm or woodlands would be started.

Early in the 1960s it was predicted that the population of the metropolitan area around Washington, D.C., would increase from around two million to five million persons by the year 2000. The National Capital Planning Commission proposed "The Year 2000 Plan" to take care of this tremendous increase. The plan envisioned a series of satellite towns spaced out along the radial corridors leading into the city. Instead of a constantly proliferating spawn of formless bedroom suburbs, the new towns would be at least partially self-contained communities with a variety of housing types, diversified commercial and industrial enterprises, schools and parks, and cultural, medical, and recreational facilities. Hopefully, a large proportion of the inhabitants of a new town would also work there.

Reston (Fig. 53), a privately financed venture that was planned under the leadership of Robert E. Simon, Jr., to be developed over a period of some twenty years, is one component of The Year 2000 Plan. It is a bold adventure in designing an environment that eventually will enhance the lives of 75,000 people. Located on a 10-square-mile tract of gently rolling land, it is 17 miles from Washington and around 100 miles from Williamsburg, with which it invites comparison. Two watercourses, a lake, hills and valleys, and many groves of trees give it a distinctive character that will be altered as little as possible. Every portion of the land was carefully studied so that roads and buildings would fit into the topography with a minimum of grading and tree cutting. The over-all plan, which can be flexibly adapted as the need arises, allots 1500 acres for recreational and open space, such as a natural amphitheater near the proposed college campus, golf courses, parks, playgrounds, and facilities for horseback riding, swimming, and boating. More than 500 acres along the highway that bisects the property will be used for light industry and governmental agencies to provide employment near housing. A town center is planned for the area around the intersection of the highway and the railroad.

The remainder of the land will be organized into seven "villages," each identified with a special geographical feature. Each village will offer diversified housing—about 70 percent town houses, 15 percent apartments, and 15 percent detached

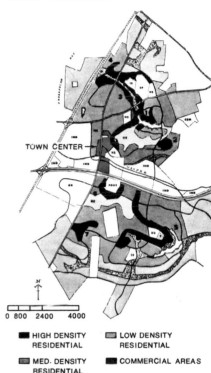

TOWN CENTER

0   800   2400   4000

■ HIGH DENSITY RESIDENTIAL   □ LOW DENSITY RESIDENTIAL

▨ MED. DENSITY RESIDENTIAL   ■ COMMERCIAL AREAS

53. Reston, Virginia, follows the contours of the rolling topography to emphasize its distinctive qualities. The town center, near the intersection of the major highway and railroad, is the hub of seven villages (indicated by numerals). Land for light industry is convenient to but segregated from residential areas. High-density housing is interspersed with areas for lower densities and open space. The plan indicates the location of the cemetery (CEM), golf courses (GC), governmental reserve (GR), health complex (HC), high school (HS), industrial areas (IND), intermediate schools (IS), parks (P), sports park (SP), and post-graduate high school (PGHS). Whittlesey, Conklin, and Rossant, planners.

houses. All of the housing units will be within safe walking distance of commercial and community village centers, schools and churches, and open space. To avoid the wasteful, monotonous urban sprawl that is all too common in typical suburbs, the high-density housing (about 60 persons per acre) is concentrated in sinews adjacent to lower density complexes of town houses (14 persons per acre), and surrounded by greenbelt areas. A density of 3.4 persons per acre is planned for clusters of detached houses. Automobile circulation is provided by loop roads around the periphery of each area and is well separated from pedestrian walkways. Rapid transit offers those who work in Washington the possibility of reaching their jobs quickly and safely without further congesting the highways.

Lake Anne Village (Figs. 54–57, 196) was the first of the seven Reston villages to be developed, and it is marked by exceptionally high standards of design. To give variety, several architectural firms were commissioned for different phases of this unit. The major segment is the village center designed by Whittlesey, Conklin, and Rossant to bring together in a seemingly new but actually long-proven way the varied activities of people. The dominant feature is a tall apartment tower whose corner windows and balconies emphasize the predominantly diagonal views of the community center, the lake, and the woodlands. It contrasts effectively with the

right : 54. The Lake Anne Village Center (1965) combines commercial enterprises with community facilities and varied residential accommodations. Whittlesey, Conklin, and Rossant, planners and architects.

below : 55. Town houses and a tall apartment building face the lake and open onto lawns and trees at the rear.

below right : 56. A second cluster of houses, located around a wooded flood plane that has been preserved as a natural feature, is rigorously rectangular. Open terraces, exposed structural members, and light, shade, and shadow emphasize three-dimensionality. Charles M. Goodman, architect.

much lower, horseshoe-shaped complex that has shops, community facilities, a restaurant, apartments, and studios. Town houses, set in irregular groups to give them a residential character, were planned to combine privacy with views of the public space and the lake. The waterfront areas are restricted to pedestrian use; all automotive traffic and parking is placed behind the buildings. Although all of the architecture of this area is compatible, the apartment building, the town houses, and the community center are clearly differentiated from one another. Outdoor sculpture, tables and seats, distinctive store fronts and signs, and paving patterns add up to a spirited, urbane congregating space that is in scale with people and with its setting. It is reminiscent of Venice, where towers and lower buildings, great paved areas, sky, water, and people are in harmony.

Charles M. Goodman's town houses (Fig. 56) consist of three clusters of homes organized around access courts that are in part the roofs of parking spaces below. The site is a natural flood plain, and the landscaping accentuates this with streams and pools that carry the water downhill. Strongly accented horizontal and vertical members establish a regular three-dimensional grid that integrates the units in each building group. The space within the grid is inventively varied with eleven plans.

No aspect of design was neglected in Lake Anne Village. Topography and vegetation were changed as little as possible, and structures were designed and placed to emphasize the character of the site. Chermayeff and Geismar Associates designed distinctive road and street signs and all other graphic markers to make them legible but not obtrusive. Seymour Evans Associates treated the artificial illumination of public areas as a succession of eventful experiences. Trees along roads are flood-lighted to emphasize their character at night, while overhead lighting in pathways and parking lots illumines the paved areas without glare. At night the village center is transformed by festive patterns of light.

Because of a change in management in the late 1960s, no one can accurately predict how the now-vacant land of Reston will eventually be developed. However, a basic point in the design philosophy was that planning done in the 1960s should be flexibly adaptable during the next twenty years in response to inevitable changes, new developments and trends. It remains true that what has been done to date is a landmark in planned communities. Another planned community is illustrated in Figures 75 and 76.

57. Other town houses on the waterfront of Lake Anne in Reston, Virginia, are informally varied and located in an effort to achieve individualized domesticity. Cloethiel Woodard Smith and Associates, architects.

Urban Renewal

Despite the deplorable conditions in many large cities, few would deny that the unique advantages of urban living make them worth saving. As cities grow, large areas in the central districts tend to deteriorate, often to a degree that is tragic. Replacing or remodeling outdated structures, improving transportation, and providing more usable open space can revitalize the core of a city. Usually this involves buying or leasing the property in several or many city blocks, removing or renovating the structures, and creating a new, more humane organization of land and buildings. Ideally, urban renewal projects increase population density but not city congestion, for they encourage people to live in well-planned housing units near their places of work, education, recreation, and worship. To date, most of these projects have been primarily or completely residential and, until recently, were designed for a restricted income group—either low, middle, or high. Many have been monotonous, barren, almost brutal blocks of masonry monumentally arranged in space for which there was no implicit use. Such developments repelled rather than attracted people. Fortunately, the approach has changed, as can be seen in examples from San Francisco and Boston in this chapter, from Philadelphia in Chapter 5 (Figs. 201–204),

above : 58. The site on which the Golden Gateway Center stands was formerly a wasteland of vacant debris-filled lots and substandard buildings.

left : 59. The Golden Gateway Center, begun in 1960 and more than half completed by 1969, is located between San Francisco Bay and the city's financial center. Varied types of housing are combined with parks, stores, and an office building at the right. Architects Wurster, Bernardi, and Emmons in association with De Mars and Reay, with consultation by Belluschi and Schwartz, and landscape architects Sasaki, Walker and Associates, Inc.

and in Plate 5, which shows a view of part of the design proposed for the United States Pavilion at Expo 70 in Osaka, Japan. The imaginative forms and explosive colors of this playground are for inspiration, a welcome change of pace in an urban environment.

Golden Gateway Center, San Francisco   The San Francisco Redevelopment Agency invited nine groups of architects, builders, and financiers to submit proposals for redeveloping a dilapidated downtown area comprising 19.7 acres adjacent to the city's financial core yet with magnificent views of the bay. The design of the winning team (Pl. 6 and Figs. 59–61) is remarkable in many respects:

■ The general layout, as revealed in the model (Fig. 59) and the plan (Fig. 77), acknowledges the rectangular street grid that dominates San Francisco to provide a readily understandable pattern of circulation and to mesh the new project with its surroundings. It is not, however, a restrictive grid but is developed as an asymmetric yet orderly organization of land and buildings.

Plate 5. Part of a proposal for the United States Pavilion at Expo 70, to be held in Japan, is "The Garden of the Moon," a playground for children and rest area for weary sightseers. Artificial turf scattered with enticing "play shapes" integrates sculpture with functional open space. Isamu Noguchi, designer; Shoji Sadao, Peter Floyd, and John McHale, associate architects.

Plate 6. The Golden Gateway Center in San Francisco (1960–1968) is a complex of housing, offices, and shops that combines the advantages of a small community with the invigorating character of the city. Congestion has been ameliorated by raising circulation plazas two levels above the street and by spacing the large structures in such a way that light and air can penetrate the whole composition. Lower buildings and landscaped areas produce a sense of human scale. The 25-story Alcoa Building, braced with aluminium-sheathed structural steel, brings office space close to housing and stands on a two-block-long parking garage. A variety of shops and restaurants are in the substructure under the town and apartment houses, and the area around the center is undergoing rebuilding and renovation as an additional result of this large-scale redevelopment. Skidmore, Owings, and Merrill, architects for the Alcoa Building; architects for the Golden Gateway Center Development, Wurster, Bernardi, and Emmons in association with De Mars and Reay, with consultation by Belluschi and Schwartz, and landscape artists Sasaki, Walker, Lackey, and Associates. (See also Figs. 58, 59, 77.)

■ Pedestrian and vehicular traffic are completely separated by concentrating traffic-free areas two stories above convenient garages and neighborhood shops.
■ The 16.3 acre residential area is diversified (Fig. 60). Seven structures, human in scale and character despite their twenty-two stories, are widely spaced for good views, sun, and air. They contain 2174 apartments, which range from "efficiency" to four-bedroom units. Most have outdoor balconies. Further variety is offered by 106 two-story town houses, each with its private outdoor area.
■ All types of neighborhood shops necessary to any residential area are centrally located on the ground level, and it is only a short distance to the city's central shopping area.
■ Only 20 percent of the residential area is covered by buildings. This leaves ample space for park and recreation areas ranging from formal courts (Fig. 61) to a block-size wooded park, producing a sense of continuous, diversified spaciousness.
■ An area of 3.4 acres nearest the city's financial center is the site of a 25-story office building distinguished by its boldly exposed vertical and diagonal structural members (Pl. 6). Beneath it is a 1500-car public parking area.
■ Sculpture, fountains, and murals enrich the architecture and open spaces.

Now that the project is nearing completion, the hope of the redevelopment agency that this project would "provide San Francisco with distinguished architecture" and the wish of the architectural advisory panel that the design would "make the greatest contribution to an environment for the totality of human experience—physically, culturally and spiritually" have been realized.

Waterfront Renewal in Boston A small segment of the extensive "Boston Downtown Waterfront—Faneuil Hall Urban Renewal Program" is illustrated in Figures 62 and 63 (see also Figs. 77, 78). It was decided that in this project, which is in a section of the city rich in historic tradition and with many important old buildings, the traditional character should be preserved as much as possible. The first step was transforming an old, empty macaroni factory, known as the Prince Building, into a very desirable, residential structure with thirty-two apartments. When emphasized by contrasting materials and colors, the basic framework of verticals and horizontals

left : 60. The rush and splash of water from a fountain by François Stahly dominates a block-size park of the Golden Gateway Center. Tall apartment buildings rise above a two-story arcade that gives access to shops. The low town houses, with sloping roofs at either side of the tower, bring human scale to the urban landscape.

right : 61. The courts between the buildings are large in size and enlivened with pergolas, paving patterns, changes in level, and trees and shrubs. The apartment houses in the background are compatible with each other, but each has its own identity in design and color.

The rehabilitation of outmoded structures in desirable, central locations is an important way to revitalize cities, as exemplified by one phase of the Boston waterfront renewal program. J. Timothy Anderson & Associates Inc., architects.

right : 62. The Prince Building was remodeled in 1967 into an attractive apartment house.

right : 63. Proposed town houses are notable for their diversified, strongly three-dimensional designs.

became a visually pleasant architectural composition that is thoroughly contemporary yet harmonious with Boston traditions. The next step in the program will be the remodeling of the dock warehouses into up-to-date apartments and the construction of row town houses from strong, individual designs scaled to human proportions.

A Regional Plan: The Tennessee Valley

The Kentucky Dam and Powerhouse (Figs. 64, 65), gigantic and monumental as they are, only hint at the size of one of the largest, most comprehensively planned developments in the United States. The Tennessee River, whose valley lies in the seven states of Tennessee, Kentucky, Virginia, North Carolina, Georgia, Alabama, and Mississippi, was an uncontrolled river that carried away tons of precious topsoil and caused disastrous floods. In 1933 the Tennessee Valley Authority went into operation with one hydroelectric dam and two others in the process of being built. By

The TVA Kentucky Dam and Powerhouse (c. 1935) express the monumental grandeur of attempts to utilize natural resources by controlling a formerly wayward river.

above : 64. An aerial view shows a portion of the 184-mile-long reservoir and the dam.

right : 65. The shape of the powerhouse is as strong as the force of the river.

1937, over 400,000 kilowatts of much needed power were produced. By the middle of the 1960s there were thirty-one major power dams and ten steam plants generating 12 million kilowatts of electricity, which were distributed over 80,000 square miles. More than two-thirds of the 900-mile river is now a series of lakes that greatly reduce soil erosion and floods, create navigable waterways for inexpensive transportation, and provide 10,000 miles of shoreline that have become one of the country's great inland recreational centers. These developments have also attracted private industries that have provided jobs for many individuals and significantly raised the region's economy.

Important as this is, the TVA would not find its place in a book concerning art today were it not for the fact that some of the concepts it pioneered are now more vitally important than ever before. City and regional planners, architects, landscape architects, designers, painters, and sculptors cooperated with governmental officials, private industry, *and the residents of the region* to change an environment that produced an overabundance of poverty and misery into one that enabled people to achieve a much higher standard of living in more equable surroundings. The TVA also showed that such complex projects, which often encompass more than one governmental jurisdiction, need the kind of unified execution that can only come with a new kind of cooperative confederation. Air pollution, mass transportation, and the relieving of congestion in the inner city by providing more living and working accommodations beyond the fringes of present-day urban and suburban areas are all problems that cannot be solved by a single city. They are inextricably tied to a whole area that may cover 50 or 100 square miles. The TVA has shown that environmental planning on a large scale can be accomplished.

Environmental Planning

Communities are living organisms created to make group living satisfying and efficient. In the last few decades we have become acutely aware that environmental planning is far more than laying out identical, rectangular city blocks, regardless of topography or land use. The chief concern of today's planners is with the lives of men. The Golden Gateway Center (Pl. 6) shows one solution to the problem of creating human as well as functional urban areas.

The basic problem in environmental planning is the organization of land, streets, and buildings for group living. It is an art and science large in scale and complex in nature. As with other art forms, environmental planning not only expresses the culture that produces it, but continuously affects the thoughts and feelings of people. Dwelling in slums is degrading to man's spirit (see Fig. 66) and tends to foster undesirable patterns of behavior. Smog and other types of air pollution are fast negating many of the advances of medical science that would prolong life, as well as ruining the natural resources in and around the urban areas. Traffic congestion is choking the centers of cities (see Fig. 52), the proliferation of highways is scarring the land beyond redemption, the airplane produces still higher decibels of noise, and airports devour more and more acreage. Well-planned communities could prevent or greatly mitigate such evils, and they can do much more. Like great paintings, sculpture, and architecture, they should invigorate the spirit of man.

When communities were small and changed slowly, they developed in an orderly, organic, creative way. This is equally true of New England villages, English rural communities, and Italian hill towns. But simplicity vanished when city growth became almost malignant with the industrialization of society and the startling population increase during the past two hundred years. The demoralizing drabness of many

66. The squalor and dilapidation of slum areas, such as this one in New York City, are detrimental to the physical and moral health of the people who must live in them.

cities is equally serious, and this applies not only to older, dilapidated areas, but also to many redeveloped and new sections in which an overemphasis on so-called efficiency and economy have led to an inhuman monotony and sterility (see Fig. 80). Fortunately, experts in environmental planning and community groups are facing this situation with a broader, more realistic and insightful comprehension of the broad spectrum of human needs. They recognize the desirability of mixing ages and races, of providing outdoor living and shopping areas, restaurants, and recreation facilities in residential sections, so that the amenities of life are readily accessible and divergent groups can intermingle.

Centralized Planning

One of the basic questions in city planning, and one on which experts and laymen, today and in the past, have expressed varying points of view is, how many persons living and working on how much land should be served by one major city center?

Centric is the name given to those plans (Fig. 67) in which all developments are grouped around a single major center regardless of the community's size. When a new community is begun, no one can predict accurately its future size—unless, as in Reston, limits on its growth are set.

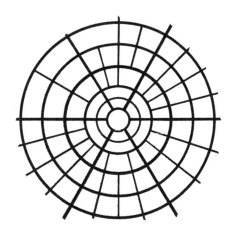

67. Centric city plans tend to focus on one major center. Street patterns can be of any type. This example combines radial and ring streets.

Most American communities are centric. At one end of the scale are the small centric communities—New England villages, Williamsburg, and numerous small towns throughout the country. The plan of Reston combines centralized and decentralized characteristics; when completed, it will have a dominant community center supplemented by seven village centers. Centric plans function well when communities remain small, either by chance or by intent, so that distances from the center to the edges are short. At the other end of the scale are the vast metropolises centered around their commercial and industrial districts. Even though the population in a metropolis is densely concentrated, distances from home to work become long for most people, and traffic tends to strangulate the city's inner core. Sunlight, pure air, and open green spaces are at a minimum, air pollution at a maximum.

In bygone days when moats and walls gave effective military protection, when transportation and communication between communities were poorly developed, and when cities by today's standards were small, concentration around one center offered conspicuous advantages. It still has its good points. In both New York City and Paris, for example, one finds in the few square miles of the central district an almost fantastic concentration of varied business and cultural opportunities packed tightly together—and served by an almost hopelessly tangled and congested transportation system.

Le Corbusier's Voisin Scheme Some planners, believing that great concentrations of population at some city centers are inevitable or even desirable, envision an intensification of present patterns—even taller high-rise structures to bring more people to the center—but with tremendously improved transportation and with more open space. This sounds like a paradox, but the Swiss-French architect, planner, and painter Le Corbusier has shown how the apparent contradictions can be reconciled. In his "Voisin" scheme of 1925 (Figs. 68, 69), he made a bold proposal to open up a large area near the center of Paris with efficient transportation and tall buildings. Six hundred acres of a jumbled, unhealthy, inefficient section would be transformed into a sparkling and orderly commercial city. Some adjacent areas would be rebuilt with multifamily residential units.

Circulation would be handled by an efficient supersubway system and by broad, widely spaced streets. The subway, with stations under each skyscraper and with a

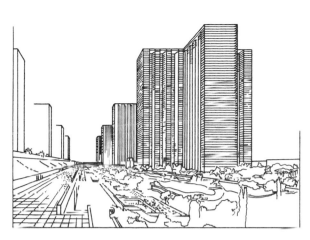

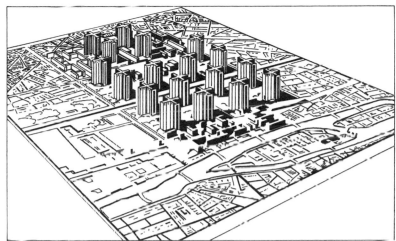

central station far greater in size and efficiency than any yet built, would carry passengers quickly, safely, and economically. Roads would be planned on a large-scale gridiron pattern, their widths varying from 150 to 400 feet and spaced 1200 feet apart. (The present streets in this section are from 20 to 35 feet wide, and the distances between them range from 60 to 150 feet.) A new east-west thoroughfare would reduce traffic on the once daringly wide but now congested Champs Elysées, shown in Figure 71. Quite as important as the provision for streets and subways is the fact that ample residential areas conveniently adjacent to the commercial zone would greatly reduce the need for home-to-work transportation.

Sixteen enormous skyscrapers would rise 600 feet from the centers of the super-blocks carved by the roads. Each of these glass-walled, cruciform towers would accommodate from 20,000 to 40,000 employees. Along the tree-lined roadways between the towers, low buildings for shops and restaurants would provide human scale and diversion. Although the population density in this section was far too great in 1925 with the existing plan, the Voisin scheme would increase it fourfold. In the existing plan, buildings cover from 79 to 80 percent of the land. In the new scheme, buildings would cover only 5 percent of the land, and the remaining 95 percent would be given over to boulevards, parking areas, and parks. Thus, it would be a 600-acre garden city, providing a healthy, pleasant working environment for a great many persons. Visually it would be an impressive, but somewhat overwhelming, twentieth-century organization of voids and solids, architecture and landscape.

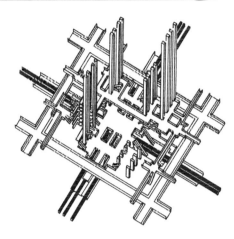

An imaginative concept of how a section of Paris could be replanned contrasts markedly with an existing section of the city.

top left: 68. Le Corbusier's bold Voisin plan (1925) would relieve congestion by concentrating work space in widely spaced building of grand scale set in parks and by providing wide traffic thorough-fares.

top right: 69. A model of the Voisin plan shows a traffic thoroughfare, which would replace the Champs Elysées, and the relation of the building complex to its surroundings.

above: 70. The Regional Plan Association of New York has proposed principles similar to Le Corbusier's in its study on future planning for midtown Manhattan (1968).

left: 71. Twelve streets radiate from the Place de l'Étoile, in the center of which stands the Arc de Triomphe. Buildings are crowded and traffic congested, but it is human in scale and rich in diversity and historical association.

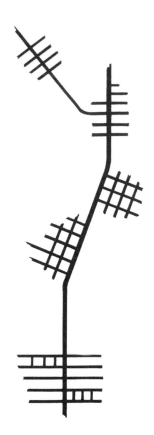

Le Corbusier did not expect that the Voisin scheme would be carried out in its entirety, nor did he regard it as the final solution. His primary aim was to raise the level of discussions of city planning from what he termed "silly little reforms" to reasonable, twentieth-century standards and principles. Among those principles to which he would give great attention are decongestion of city centers even though population is increased, concentration of the population in tall, widely spaced buildings, a great increase in parks and other open spaces, and more efficient transportation. Some of these principles underly the planning of San Francisco's Golden Gateway Center, New York's much earlier Rockefeller Center (Fig. 584), and Brazil's new capital, Brasilia (Pl. 64, p. 510, and Fig. 646). The Voisin scheme has been selected for discussion from the many and varied proposals formulated by Le Corbusier because it carries centralization to a logical, inspired extreme. A recent instance of his concept is that suggested by the Regional Plan Association of New York. A graphic representation of the principles it advocates is shown in Figure 70. Very high "access trees" are placed over subsurface transportation stations and allow direct vertical passage to offices in the towers; lower office buildings cluster nearby; and multi-level movement systems separate the pedestrian and various types of transportation.

Decentralized Planning

Decentralized planning (Fig. 72) is advocated by those who believe that increased concentration is neither efficient, because of the already serious congestion of transportation systems, nor desirable, because too many people are crowded into too little space. They propose complete, identifiable, self-sustaining communities that would not be allowed to grow beyond an optimum size, often defined by walk-to-work limits. Decentralized planning can be achieved through totally new self-sustaining communities not closely related to other centers or by "satellite towns," such as Reston, which are near large cities and may be only partially self-sustaining.

above : 72. Decentralized city plans reduce concentration by having a number of centers. They, too, can have varied street layouts.

below : 73. Small businesses and housing developments crowd the old road extending out from the city. A freeway nearby speeds traffic but divides the land into segments.

Ribbon and Linear Planning

As early as 1882 the Spanish writer Soria y Mata suggested that cities might expand along transportation routes so that Cadiz, for example, might be at one end of a continuous development and Leningrad at the other. In many parts of our country this type of growth has been proceeding haphazardly where communities once separated by natural greenbelts are stretching out until they merge. This is happening on the East Coast from Boston to Washington, D.C. Unfortunately, in most instances, lack of regional planning has merely lined the highways with unrelated stores (Fig. 73), drive-in restaurants, filling stations, and automobile sales lots, behind which gridiron street plans have been ruthlessly imposed upon the land. These elongations have almost nothing in common with the concepts under discussion.

Ribbon plans have several advantages: expansion can proceed almost indefinitely by establishing new units, each of which remains an identity limited in size; open space for farms and gardens and for light and air is adjacent to more densely settled sections; and much of the traffic within each unit can be pedestrian.

A generalized ribbon plan developed by planner Ludwig Hilberseimer is illustrated in Figure 74. The plan has four continuing bands of land zoned for different uses. The backbone is a broad traffic artery for automobiles and trains that runs through a continuous greenbelt from one community to the others. Industry lines the leeward side of the traffic artery so that smoke and fumes will not blow into the other areas. On the windward side is a ribbon of parklike land for commercial and community activities. Beyond this are the residences, facing dead-end streets, and the schools, surrounded by ample space yet convenient to the homes. Each community is limited in size and is permanently separated from others by farms, fields, and forests. A rectilinear plan is illustrated here, but the communities can have any shape and character indicated by specific local conditions.

Cumbernauld, Scotland   In 1910 Edgar Chambless proposed that the buildings along traffic arteries be integrated with the transportation system. One of his ideas was a continuous narrow concrete structure of indefinite length with public transportation at the lowest level, shops, offices, and apartments above, and a sheltered pedestrian street on the roof. Major economics in construction and utility costs, and preservation of the natural landscape by compact, multiple-purpose structures would result.

Le Corbusier drew sketches in 1929 for a 14-mile-long, 14-story structure that would follow the contours of a site in Rio de Janeiro. It would be a genuine linear city, incorporating all vehicular traffic in the building. Recently a 3-mile sample has been built in Tokyo.

The new Scottish town of Cumbernauld (Figs. 75, 76) incorporates some of the ideas of these visionary planners. Designed to be self-sustaining, the town is centered

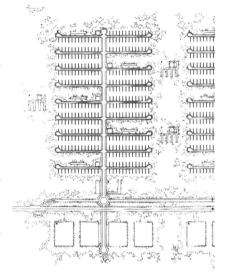

74. In this idealized ribbon plan (1945), a railroad and arterial highway separate industrial areas from residential areas.

Cumbernauld, Scotland (c. 1955–), 15 miles from Glasgow, is one of many British "New Towns" planned to relieve congestion in large cities. The project will be completed around 1970. L. Hugh Wilson, chief architect and planning officer; Peter Youngman, landscape architect.

right : 75. An aerial view of Cumbernauld shows the organization of zones for the town center (in the upper right, straddling the highway), several kinds of housing, and ample open space. A portion of another neighborhood appears in the lower left, and in the upper left are some industrial areas.

below : 76. The model of the town center reveals the complex relationships of the integrated structure.

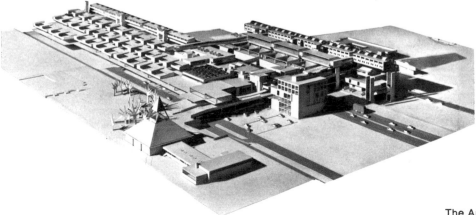

on a hilltop but extends into the valley below. The major unit is a compact, urban complex a mile long that is built, on multiple levels, over the spinal highway linking the town with Glasgow, 15 miles away. Stores and offices, cultural, recreational, and educational facilities, roads, parking areas, and penthouses are integrated in this one structure. Pedestrian and vehicular traffic are completely separated. The protected internal circulation is particularly appropriate to the Scottish climate. Low apartment houses and town houses for 50,000 occupants, all within walking distance, are linked by pedestrian pathways to the town center. Around the base of the hill and separated by greenbelts are neighborhoods with their own community and commercial facilities that will house up to 30,000 additional persons in somewhat more widely spaced residential units. Industrial areas in which many of the citizens can find employment are located near the town's boundaries. A major concern of the planners was to create an environment that would encourage people to enjoy both spontaneous and planned interaction, and they have accomplished this by providing large parks and small play areas, ball fields and an indoor sports center, theaters, a dance hall, and covered gathering spaces.

Few communities are exclusively centralized, decentralized, or built along a linear belt, and this includes the many wholly new towns that are now being planned or built. Each of the three types of planning has its particular advantages, and function often indicates that the best of each be combined. Reston and Cumbernauld are representative of a large number of new communities. Although the two differ from each other in many respects, they have much in common. Both are within commuting distance of major cities, but they are more or less self-sufficient entities separated from nearby settlements by greenbelts. The ultimate size of each will be limited to preserve a feeling of communality and identity. Housing accommodations are diversified, and some opportunities for local employment are provided. They demonstrate that private living, community activities, recreation, and work can be brought conveniently together so that traffic congestion is reduced. Above all, they show that the complexity and size of the problem of providing a habitable and rewarding environment can be met only by enlightened, collaborative planning.

City planning

The basic problems of city planning can be considered under two major aspects—zoning and circulation.

Zoning

There are four general types of land use: residential, community, commercial, and industrial. Communities usually have zones for these varied land uses so that unnecessary conflicts are minimized, but in many instances a too insistent, rigid separation of areas for different activities has split cities and the lives of their citizens into overly discrete segments. This weakens the sense of a community entity and minimizes the benefits of a lively interplay of man's diverse activities. The planning of Reston (Fig. 53) and of the Golden Gateway Center (Fig. 77) demonstrates how perceptive zoning can locate areas for specific purposes without segregating them from one another too drastically.

Residential Areas   The most desirable, healthful land, land that is free from unnecessary noise, smoke, smog, and congestion, is generally reserved for residential areas. Dividing this land into neighborhoods with homes for several hundred families, with

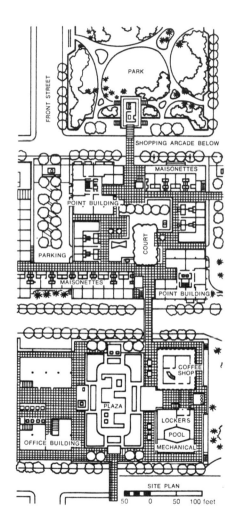

above : 77. The Golden Gateway Center is sensibly zoned. Areas for different purposes are separated from each other in this gridiron plan but not by a great distance. At the top of a portion of the plan is a large park. The middle block has two high apartment buildings and rows of two-story houses above a shopping arcade. The third block has a large office building facing an open plaza, a coffee shop, and a swimming pool.

schools and recreational areas near their centers, and with appropriately located churches creates a good environment for family living. Having convenient local shopping centers and access to transportation makes them efficient. This suggests superblocks, as in Reston, that are penetrated by roads for local traffic only. The size of these blocks is important. Ideally, they should be large enough to support an elementary school, but not so large that the sense of neighborhood is lost. From 600 to 1000 families make a good neighborhood. Much more acreage will be required if these superblocks are planned for single-family houses than if they are designed for apartments.

Community Areas   Residential areas vie with community areas for choice sites. In addition to the small community areas that should be part of each residential neighborhood, cities require sites for city halls, libraries, schools, auditoriums, and parks as well as other recreational areas to serve several or all of the neighborhoods. In contemporary and historic cities the major public edifices are often grouped in civic centers near the heart of the community. Institutional and recreational areas are most convenient when distributed throughout the city. Wherever they are located, community areas ought to express sensitively the spirit of their cities and be a source of pride to their citizens.

Commercial Areas   There are three general types of commercial areas: neighborhood, regional, and central "downtown" districts.

■ *Neighborhood centers* serve the day-to-day needs of nearby families. These are at their best when unified groups of stores and community facilities are located within walking distance of residences, as in Reston, or when small shopping centers have convenient, pleasant parking areas.

■ *Regional centers* are a new development that has resulted from traffic density in city centers, the trend toward suburban living, and the use of family automobiles as the chief means of transportation. They are small-scale versions of downtown commercial sections and are located on large parcels of land, with attractive pedestrian malls and parking areas. Grouped around at least one big department store and a supermarket there are in the typical regional center a variety of specialty shops, restaurants, service stores, banks, and offices. When well planned, such centers make shopping a delightful experience instead of a tiresome chore. (See Pl. 17, p. 151, and Figs. 197–200).

■ *Downtown commercial centers* have the advantage of conveniently concentrated, diversified shopping and business areas, but they can become seriously congested with unseparated vehicular and pedestrian traffic. An enlightened way of revitalizing a central area in Philadelphia to eliminate this problem is illustrated in Plate 18 (p. 152) and Figure 201 through 204.

Industrial Areas   Two categories, called "heavy" and "light," distinguish industrial areas. Heavy industries include the large factories usually associated with noise, smoke, and railroad yards. Until their undesirable aspects can be eliminated, they remain necessary nuisances that ought to be convenient to but segregated from residential, community, and commercial zones. A minimum essential is to locate them so that they are separated by a buffer zone from other sections of the community and so that the community can be protected from the inevitable smoke and fumes carried by prevailing winds. Light industries, in contrast, are relatively clean and quiet plants for such enterprises as processing photographic film or assembling electronic equipment. When well designed and on sufficient land, they can be conveniently close to residences with no deleterious results.

Although the four types of areas differ in function and deserve some separation from each other, in many instances this separation has been carried to an inefficient, monotonous extreme. It has become almost normal for many persons to live at some distance from their work in spite of the time-consuming inconvenience and the burden on transportation systems. Hilberseimer's plan (Fig. 74) and Reston demonstrate that areas for disparate activities can be set apart from one another without great distances between them.

Circulation

When one realizes that about 80 million automobiles are driven more than 1 billion miles every twenty-four hours on our network of well over 3.7 million miles of road, the critical seriousness of the circulation problem becomes apparent. And the problem is as complex as it is big.

Even in horse-and-buggy days there were roads that differed in size and purpose, as did those in Williamsburg. Between towns there were main roads from which branched minor ones. But traffic was light, quiet, slow, and comparatively safe. Intersections were not hazardous. All of this had changed by the time Reston was built. In the Reston plan, city-to-city highways were routed around the town centers, a few major streets within the town carried most of the traffic, and thought was given to pedestrians as well as to vehicles. Most cities, however, were laid out when traffic was light, and they are therefore totally unsuited to the present-day traffic load.

Street patterns can be put into four categories: gridiron, radial, ring, and organic.

Gridiron Plans   A typical solution is gridiron plans, and they have a long but interrupted history. Extensively used by the Egyptians, Greeks, and Romans, they were so uncritically revived in the nineteenth century that little thought was given to alternatives. Their distinguishing characteristic is two sets of parallel streets at right angles to each other. Gridiron plans can be efficient and can even have monumental grandeur (Fig. 69), but in many situations other solutions are preferable. Their major asset is clear-cut, easy-to-understand orderliness. Too often they have been nothing more than a rigid application of a cut-and-dried formula that wastefully chops land into many small, monotonous blocks separated by a plethora of undifferentiated streets. When ruthlessly imposed on such hilly topography as that in Duluth or San Francisco, the result would be laughable were it not costly and dangerous. The gridiron concept can be modified by interspersing superblocks, as in Figure 68, or by separating levels for vehicular and foot traffic, as in Figure 77.

Radial Patterns   Streets radiating from one or more centers, as illustrated in Paris (Fig. 71), characterize radial patterns. Usually, the radial streets are important thoroughfares and are combined with a gridiron pattern. Such plans tend to make traffic direct, to give impressive settings for monuments and buildings, and to provide interest and variety; but unless adroitly planned they dangerously congest traffic at the point where the radial streets converge.

Ring Plans   In cities where successive edges of a growing city are marked by circular boulevards, much like the growth rings of a tree, ring plans are to be found. In some European cities these boulevards have replaced old walls, moats, or canals. In such American cities as Detroit they were originally laid out as streets. The distinctive characteristic is a series of streets in concentric rings.

Organic Patterns   Street plans that follow no set rules or predetermined patterns are considered organic. Streets are placed where human need and topography indicate. Curved and straight, wide and narrow, dead-end and arterial streets are combined for efficiency and beauty, as in Reston. The differences between a stereotyped and a functional approach are illustrated in the proposed plan for remodeling a section of New York City (Fig. 78). The new design greatly reduces street area, clearly distinguishes thoroughfares from local traffic streets, and adapts block size and shape to the use of the land. This reduces cost and traffic hazards, leaves more land for productive use, and provides the basic pattern for good living.

The planning and replanning of our urban complexes is often frustrating, but it can be a rewarding union of art and science that is never finished. As patterns of living change, planning necessarily develops in new directions, and experts need the assistance of well-informed citizens to make and keep cities desirable environments in which to live and work.

One of the most critical aspects of planning, which for some decades was submerged by narrow interpretations of order, economy, and efficiency, is man's innate longing for social interaction and for surroundings that excite and invigorate him. Experiments with rats living in a visually enriched environment have shown that they developed more in brain weight and message capacity, in problem solving, and in learning than did those in groups kept in standard or impoverished environments. Related experiments with people indicate that challenging conditions increase human development. Although some degree of comprehensible order is essential in communities, such qualities as surprise, delight, ambiguity, even contradiction are revitalizing. We need the expansiveness of long vistas and the enclosure of small spaces; the flavor and warmth of eventful display windows, street furniture, and nighttime illumination; the contrast of growing plants and man-made structures; the stimulation of paintings, sculpture, and fountains; and, when feasible, the juxtaposition of the old and the new. Above all, people should be encouraged to feel that they are the reality of the city's existence. The planners of the new towns and the redeveloped areas discussed in this chapter were fully aware of these factors.

Parks and Parkways

As communities become more urbanized, the need for open spaces planned for varied types of recreation and enjoyment arises. These outdoor areas can range from

78. Existing (*left*) and proposed (*right*) plans for a section of New York City. The proposed plan reduces street area, increases open space, and provides thoroughfares for traffic and dead-end streets for residential sections.

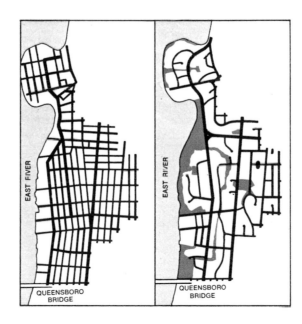

Riis Plaza (1966), New York City. M. Paul Friedberg and Associates, landscape architects; Pomerance and Breines, architects.

below : 79. The amphitheater shows the complex but coherent juxtaposition of forms and materials pervading the entire design. An interplay of raised and lowered levels and of open, partially enclosed, and enclosed spaces activates every part of this area.

bottom : 80. The site of Riis Plaza was formerly a flat expanse of lawn, hard to cultivate and difficult to maintain.

right : 81. The plan is basically a simple series of rectangular areas organized along a major and a minor axis, but each area is developed in a distinctively different way in accord with its function.

intensively planned plazas in residential areas to extensive parks that benefit all. We are, however, the most mobile society in history and frequently want to travel from one community to another by automobile. Freeways designed for pleasure as well as rapid transportation meet this need. Three different kinds of outdoor facilities are illustrated in Figures 79 through 83. The first is an intensively developed city plaza, and the second is a much larger, informal park in New York City; the third is a parkway on the west bank of the Hudson River near New York City.

Riis Plaza (Figs. 79, 81) is a two-acre mid-city development that offers the residents of Jacob Riis Houses, a New York City Housing Authority project, richly diversified recreational facilities. What was an off-bounds plot of scrub grass and malnourished trees has become a succession of areas designed to satisfy the leisure and recreational interests of all age groups. Terminating the central axis at the left is a children's playground that is very different from the typical ones with drab asphalt paving and dull, standardized equipment. Everything invites uninhibited play. Youngsters can wade or splash in pools, scramble over fountains, sculpture, and giant concrete blocks, climb up or hang down from suspended ladders, and find seclusion in niches and alcoves. Next to the playground is the large plaza and sitting area that combines open spaciousness with sheltered retreats. Beyond it is an amphitheater for group entertainment or casual relaxation. From the lowered stage area rise ingeniously planned wide steps that provide seating, surrounded by a pergola that shelters and defines this unit. At the far right is a secluded, walled garden for the elderly. The space along the secondary axis toward the left has been transformed into a pedestrian mall. Throughout the plaza, textured paving that can take hard use with minimum maintenance also provides visual delight. Although all existing trees were saved and hardy shrubs were added, geometric forms related to architecture predominate. Used intensively by all age groups, Riis Plaza demonstrates that inspired physical planning can bring the individuals of a community together.

Larger parks generally show a markedly different character. Central Park (Fig. 82), an oasis 2½ miles long and ½ mile wide, opens up a densely populated section of Manhattan. Usually parks as large as this are informally naturalistic. They often include natural features of interest—lakes, hills, rocks, or groves of trees— and these features, not buildings and straight-line design, are dominant. Insofar as it is feasible, the rugged, natural topography is preserved. Lawns and meadows are diversified in shape and size and are bounded by masses of trees and shrubs similar to those seen in the countryside. They are refreshing contrasts to a man-dominated environment. As it stands at present, Central Park is the result of more than one hundred years of planning, but there have been few deviations from the original concept. Thirty-two miles of winding footpaths encourage people to walk from one center of interest to another. Adroitly located in this rural setting are sculpture and fountains, a bird sanctuary and a zoo, playgrounds and athletic areas, a lake for boating and an amphitheater with an artificial ice-skating rink, and a long

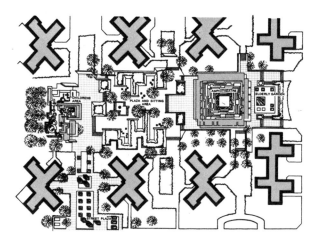

above: 82. Central Park, New York City, was begun in 1858 from plans prepared by Frederick Law Olmsted and Calvert Vaux. It is an outdoor haven of 840 acres in a city of more than 81,000 persons per square mile.

below: 83. The Palisades Interstate Parkway, on the west side of the Hudson River, provides a pleasant and fast route for motorists in New Jersey and lower New York State.

formal mall terminating in a concert area. These attractions encourage people from all walks of life to intermingle while enjoying the park's benefits.

Parkways are a new development fostered by widespread automotive transportation. Although freeways and parkways have numerous historic antecedents, contemporary examples are so much larger and more complex that they can be regarded as distinctively twentieth-century achievements. Freeways are simply superhighways with no interference from cross traffic. Parkways (Fig. 83) are any kind of road system that is designed as an elongated park with greenbelts along each side and sometimes between opposing lanes of traffic to help protect adjacent areas from noise and exhaust fumes as well as to give travelers refreshing surroundings. Both freeways and parkways must be planned for maximum safety at designated speed limits and should efficiently use the vast amounts of land they take up. Each fully developed traffic interchange, for example, requires from 50 to 150 or more acres.

At their best, freeways and parkways not only provide efficient transportation facilities but also are innovative compositions that can elicit new esthetic experiences. The precisely engineered curves of the highways and clover-leaf intersections can have the continuously developing character of growing organisms. When well handled, they bring men, machines, and nature together in an exhilarating, contemporary fashion.

The parks and parkways discussed illustrate three fundamentally different approaches to design. Riis Plaza illustrates the man-made, highly ordered, complex urbanity that draws people into groups and fosters social communication while at the same time it relieves the pressures of crowded private living spaces. Central Park, on the other hand, brings the country into the city with its natural informality. In the midst of the crowded heart of the city, it provides open space and green vistas, places to wander and facilities that draw people together. Although tremendously expensive in terms of the land it occupies, it is almost priceless in its humanity. The parkway is controlled but not rigid, free-flowing but not wayward or haphazard, and it unites the firm circulation paths of the city with the landscape through which it flows. The basic concept from which it grew and the forms that it uses express natural forces without imitating natural forms.

Community Architecture

The buildings that a community erects for its governmental agencies, schools and libraries, and public housing offer unlimited opportunity for tangible expression of the citizens' needs, interests, and tastes. When communities are planned and built within a comparatively short time span, as in Williamsburg and Reston, the architecture is usually coherent, rather than monotonously repetitious. Population centers having a long history, such as Rome or Paris, have had to respond to many changes. These are reflected in the highly diversified architecture that makes them stimulating experiences. In spite of the short history of the United States, this is also true of many of its older cities. However, the inevitable changes that society undergoes create a need for new approaches to architectural planning. Conflicts between the new and the old, the established and the innovative, are as old as the history of man, or of the universe for that matter. Architects who design contemporary civic edifices are always faced with the problem of being sympathetic toward old traditions but expressing the present and keeping the future in mind.

United Nations Headquarters

Designing an architectural environment for the world organization of many nations was one of the most complex tasks ever assigned to a group of architects. They were faced not only with the problems of use and construction, but with the unique challenge of making the buildings a monumental symbol of a world community (Figs. 84, 85).

The United Nations Headquarters in New York City (1950) shelters an extremely complex world organization in three differentiated buildings. Wallace K. Harrison, Director of Planning.

left: 84. The tall Secretariat is a rectangular slab of glass and marble. The low General Assembly Hall has curved walls and a roof through which the dome of the auditorium asserts itself. The Conference Building is a horizontal structure linking the other two buildings together.

below: 85. The auditorium has walls leaning inward and curving to the end of the hall. Two abstract murals by Fernand Léger enliven the space.

86. Scarborough College (1966) is a new satellite branch of the University of Toronto, Canada. The twisted axial relationships that open the building to the scenic ravine are a refreshing relief from the conventional, often rigid, rectangular designs, and they help give each of the three major units its own identity. John Andrews, Page and Steel, architects.

The Secretariat has been described as a "vast marble frame for the world's two largest windows." It is a 39-story slab only 72 feet wide and 287 feet long. The narrow north and south walls are unbroken planes of marble. On the east and west, two glass curtain walls 544 feet high and 287 feet wide have been made from 5400 panes of blue-green glass that at times look like gigantic reflecting mirrors. Dramatically simple and elegantly proportioned, the shaft of glass and marble is impressive.

The General Assembly, in which sweeping curves predominate, is radically different in form. Resembling the shape of a tarpaulin supported by four posts, the roof swings down to a low point near the center, from which a low dome over the circular central auditorium rises. Only the rectangular end walls relate this structure to its rigorously geometric neighbors. The auditorium interior (Fig. 85) is a bold, sculptural space in which verticals, horizontals, diagonals, and curves are united. It is the world's first meeting room to be surrounded by press, radio, and television booths and to use all available architectural and mechanical devices for control of air, light, and sound. These utilitarian complexities take their place quietly in an architectural composition that imbues its occupants with a sense of the dignity of man.

The Conference Building is a five-story structure stretching 400 feet along the East River. In terms of use, it provides numerous rooms for official conferences and lounges for employees. Visually, it becomes a base for the towering Secretariat and a transitional link between it and the General Assembly. Along the side facing the river, a busy traffic thoroughfare runs inconspicuously under the building and the plaza beyond it.

At the time these buildings were built, they were both praised and condemned. Some critics admired their pure, sensitively proportioned dignity. Others regarded them as inhumanly abstract and cold. In the years since, their orderly beauty and vigorous yet peaceful quality have become familiar and accepted. Along with Philip Johnson's house (Pl. 2a, p. 8, and Figs. 9, 10), they exemplify basic concepts of the International Style in architecture, an approach that has influenced architecture in almost all the great cities of the world.

Scarborough College

Aligned along the top of a ridge overlooking a wooded ravine, Scarborough College (Fig. 86) is effectively housed in one continuous structure. The advantages of this linear approach to planning are many. Had each instructional unit been located in a separate structure, the land would have been spotted with many buildings too small to make much impact, and costs would have been increased. In a rigorous climate, the skylighted, multiple-level interior "streets" that give access to all facilities are far more protected and therefore more pleasant than typical open courts and walkways exposed to the weather. The central portion is a large, indoor plaza in which the all-commuter student body can study or find relaxation. The humanities are concentrated in the wing at the right. The sciences are located in the left wing, the sloping wall of which encloses numerous laboratories that get natural illumination through skylights. When necessary, the structure can be extended at both ends or from the pivotal center section. The design of the classrooms, many of which seat only twenty students, grew out of the educational program, which calls for nearly half of the teaching to be by lectures telecast from the college's own production studios.

The ruggedly picturesque terrain suggested open-ended asymmetry and the bold sculptural forms that are eminently suited to concrete construction. Walls canted inward and outward, stepped-down roofs and terraces, and occasional units that project beyond the face of the structure result in a complex configuration that clearly articulates the interior volumes. The whole development is a notable example of the growing concern of some contemporary architects with the interaction between interior spaces and exterior forms, which inevitably leads to greater complexity and animation of exterior design.

Boston's City Hall

A major phase of Boston's extensive urban renewal project is the Government Center in the heart of the city, where there were no buildings worth saving with the exception of some notable historic landmarks. The new center, to which numerous architects have contributed their talents, is a coordinated complex of city and state agencies as well as private office and commercial buildings, a motel, and a large parking garage. Three young architects won the competition for the design of the City Hall (Figs. 87, 88).

Impressively monumental, the structure of precast and poured-on-the-site concrete rises boldly above a large plaza. The courageous design grew directly out of

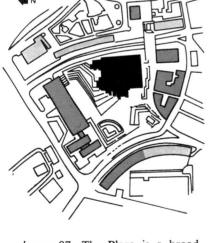

above: 87. The Plaza is a broad, stepped plane that flows through the central court of the City Hall to the buildings beyond.

right: 88. The Boston City Hall (1968) is an imposing public edifice that comands its site, but the openness of its lower structure makes it welcoming and receptive. Kallman, McKinnell, and Knowles, architects.

60

Plate 7. The library of the University of Mexico, completed in 1953, is boldly enhanced
with mosaic murals that memorialize the history of the Mexican people. Their strongly
architectural character is in keeping with the huge block of the structure. Juan O'Gorman,
architect and mosaicist.

Plate 8. Marc Chagall. *The Triumph of Music*. 1966. Mural, oil on canvas, 30 × 36′. Metropolitan Opera House, Lincoln Center for the Performing Arts, New York. Rhythmically related, emerging as separate notes or clustered in harmonic chords, as sudden bursts of brilliance or complex interweavings of line and color, the forms and figures in Chagall's mural are a chromatic, visual interpretation of the music that fills the Opera House.

the building's functions, but it goes far beyond material concerns. The efficiency of any work of architecture, but especially of a public edifice visited by many people for varied purposes, is based on a logical allocation of space and readily comprehensible paths of circulation. Through large openings, citizens can quickly reach offices on the lowest floor for such matters as paying bills, obtaining licenses, and lodging complaints. Broad steps lead to an open central court, around which council chambers, a municipal library, and the mayor's offices are located. Offices seldom visited by the public are concentrated on the three top floors.

The exterior design is a complex, yet ordered, correlation of diverse components. The lower two-thirds of the mass is an audaciously scaled, vigorously three-dimensional juxtaposition of solids and voids. In some places, tall piers rise to the upper floors, but, for emphasis, important units of the interior space project beyond the plane of the wall. The overhanging top floors, with their horizontal bands of regularly aligned windows, become the equivalent of a classical cornice. Coherence of the whole structure is strengthened by the all-pervading rectangularity of the concrete forms. Vitality comes from the multiplicity of unconventional relationships. Unlike the ubiquitous "package" exteriors, whose monotonous two-dimensional surfaces tell one nothing about the space they enclose, the structure of City Hall gives immediate clues as to where the different activities take place. Equally important is the visual stimulation that it offers to all who see it. As with the United Nations Headquarters, the design of the Boston City Hall has elicited both approval and condemnation. It does not follow the traditions formulated in the eighteenth and nineteenth centuries, but speaks definitely of today and quite possibly of the future.

Community Murals

Prehistoric man painted community murals and carved statues that were meaningful factors in his pattern of living. Some evidence indicates that he may have produced these expressive works of art before he gave much attention to the making of utilitarian objects. Since those times many peoples in all parts of the world have enriched their buildings with paintings, murals, mosaics, and sculpture that recorded significant events or vivid group ideals and accomplishments.

In the twentieth century a renewed interest in community murals has been spearheaded by a group of Mexican artists that includes Diego Rivera, José Clemente Orozco, David Alfaro Siqueiros, and Juan O'Gorman. They saw that their people needed to know more about themselves, their history, and their potentialities. In a series of heroic programs, they covered the walls of many public buildings with deeply moving murals. The Mexicans' love of richly decorated surfaces, strong forms, and vibrant colors is a tradition that predates the Spanish conquest (see Pl. 10). Thus, when the new University of Mexico was planned, it was natural that "artists" should make their contributions not as decorative afterthoughts but as part of the total concept of architecture. O'Gorman not only designed the Library (Pl. 7) but did the mosaic murals as well. The south wall is a "symbolic and pictorial memorialization" of the Spanish Colonial period. Intricately woven together are the arms of Charles V, a Christian church built over an ancient pyramid, and astronomical symbols. Varicolored stones, many of which came from the building site, create a vibrantly glowing surface strongly related to the lava beds on which the university stands. The stone-mosaic technique and the figures and symbols are deeply rooted in Mexican art history, but the result is not imitative. It is, rather, a new development of an old tradition that makes the mural truly belong to the Mexican people of today.

The Triumph of Music (Pl. 8) is one of two large mural paintings recently created by Marc Chagall for the lobby of the new Metropolitan Opera House. It can be enjoyed at the sensuous level for its visually stimulating, brilliant red tonality, for the complex interweaving of swirling, curvilinear figures and abstract forms accented by a few angular shapes, and for the painterly handling of oil paint on canvas. More detailed study reveals groups of singers, musicians, and ballerinas that seem to float in space. There are sly references to American, French, and Russian folk music, jazz, and operas; and glimpses of the New York City skyline, St. Patrick's Cathedral, and Rockefeller Center. Chagall was eminently suited to the commission because of his rare ability to weld such diverse emotions as profound joy or sorrow, youthful playfulness, and tender humor into noble, dreamlike compositions. Born in a small Russian village, Chagall was deeply impressed with the importance that his peasant family and friends gave to music and imaginative folklore, but most of his adult life was spent in France, where he absorbed more sophisticated influences. He anticipated the Surrealists' irrational imagery, then mastered the Cubists' disciplines, and later participated in the Expressionists' search for forms that communicate inner sensations and personal emotions. The essentials of all of these experiences are amalgamated in his later work.

Community Sculpture

With the unveiling of "Chicago's Picasso" (Fig. 89), so called because the sculptor did not give it a specific title, a vociferous controversy arose. People asked, "What is it? A long-eared dog, a dodo bird, a woman, a Barbary ape, a cruel joke, a Trojan dove, or a Communist plot?" One alderman introduced a resolution that it be replaced with a naturalistic statue of the Chicago Cubs' first baseman, but this was quickly voted down. Another official said, "If it is a bird or an animal, they ought to put it in the zoo. If it is art, they ought to put it in the Art Institute." But there were also many positive responses. Mayor Richard Daley called it "an expression of the vitality of the city." The Chairman of the National Council of the Arts declared, "Chicago has taken a giant step forward esthetically." The Director of the Art Institute explained, "Those who haven't experienced this type of art may not like it. But that's all right. Not so many years from now, it will be accepted by the man on the street as Van Gogh and others are today." This process of assimilation has already started. A policeman is quoted as having said, "I like it fine—whatever it is," and a cab driver, "The longer you look at it, the more you see."

The sculpture is fundamentally an arresting, abstract composition of lines and planes interweaving in space that is, in itself, valid. It does, however, have subject matter, because the forms are a stylized presentation of a woman's face, shoulders, and hair. Although the model that Picasso generously gave to Chicago was done in 1965, its characteristics can be traced back almost sixty years to the days when Picasso and Georges Braque, influenced by "primitive" African and Iberian sculpture, began to develop the Cubist style. Seeking significant essentials rather than copying external actuality, they worked with abbreviated planes, lines, and angular fragments organized in space so that they established their own reality and meaning. "Chicago's Picasso" embodies the high idealism and intellectual exaltation, the intentional ambiguity and equivocacy that are basic to Cubism (see pp. 432, 437). Each person who sees this sculpture can arrive at his own interpretation.

The composition is a basically simple organization of three pairs of steel plates and a number of slender steel rods. Two planes are joined to form the supporting base: one is a rectangle that slopes up from the front to the back; the other is vertical, with curved ends that rise up to meet the hair. Eyes and nostrils are schematically depicted on a frontal plane that slopes back from the slender nose and curves out where it meets the upper part of the hair. This plane rests on a vertical member whose comparatively complex outline suggests the mouth and chin in double profile above rounded shoulders. The hair is treated as two large, billowing shapes that spread out like wings. A cage of steel rods fans out from the face to meet the hair. The unexpected juxtaposition of these powerful shapes calls attention to their individual distinctiveness and evokes the special enigmatic magic for which Picasso is well known. Space within and around the sculpture becomes charged with vitality. For those who can walk around and see it in many kinds of weather, each view offers a new experience.

Even with contemporary technology, the construction from a 41¼-inch model of a 50-foot-high sculpture that has 6500 square feet of steel weighing 162 tons was a monumental undertaking. The engineers, who had designed and built many huge bridges, had never faced a task like this. With a specially designed, electric-eye cutting tool, they shaped the steel members to follow the curves of the original work exactly. It was fully assembled at the factory to test its strength and resistance to

89. "Chicago's Picasso" (1967) is a 50-foot-high steel sculpture that stands in the large plaza of the new Chicago Civic Center.

90. Aristides Demetrios' 16-foot-high sculptural fountain (1964) is a central feature in the large plaza planned for varied student activities at Stanford University.

wind, then taken apart, trucked to its final site, and finally welded together. Although the concept was evolved by the artist in a studio on the French Riviera, the final result could have been achieved only with the sympathetic cooperation of highly skilled technical experts.

Picasso, in discussing the joy he derives from his work in sculpture, has stated:

. . . I am caught up in shaping my vision of the world. . . . I cut through appearances to the marrow, and rebuild the essentials from there. I cannot invent a detail that has not been carefully planned, and my wish is that the public, through thinking and meditation, may retrace my intentions. . . . in sculpture there is combat with raw materials. When I triumph over such odds, I feel the joy of an athlete. . . .*

It is, perhaps, Picasso's ability to project these concerns and emotions that involves the viewers, willingly or not, in his art.

"Chicago's Picasso" stands in a plaza before the new Civic Center in Chicago, where it gives scale to the 31-story building and acts as a focal point in the great expanse of space. In another part of the plaza a large square pool, dotted with jet fountains, provides the refreshing, cooling sight and sound of splashing water. Because of their three-dimensional quality, sculpture and fountains are natural choices to enhance open spaces in cities. Sometimes they are used separately, as they were here, but many times they are combined into one effective composition (Pl. 18, p. 152).

A fountain of activated forms and spraying water is the dynamic focal element of a landscaped mall on the Stanford University campus (Fig. 90). It is related not only to the vistas, buildings, and planting around it, but also to the coming

---

* *Look*, November 28, 1967, p. 88.

and going of the students who walk through the plaza. Benches and low walls around it provide seating in sun or shade for those who wish to relax, read, or talk to friends. Copper is the basic structural material of the fountain, covered with molten bronze that coruscates the surface. Rising from a substantial circular base, a series of intertwining elements become progressively lighter and more pointed as they swirl upward. They are carefully shaped to maximize the interplay of eighty jets of water that heighten the exuberant movement. Although the abstract forms do not depict any specific natural objects or happenings, they remind most viewers of leaping forms, of waves breaking high on a rocky coastline, of the upward striving of growing things. The result is an experience of spontaneity, extension, and excitement.

The arts of the community belong to and affect large numbers of persons, and consequently they differ in some respects from the arts of the home that are of major concern only to those who live in them. Community planning immediately and constantly influences daily living patterns. Public buildings are seen by the many persons who pass them, and they affect those who work, live, learn, or seek relaxation or cultural experiences in them. Because they symbolize the spirit of the community, they inevitably transcend purely utilitarian requirements. Mural paintings, mosaics, sculpture, and fountains continue their traditional roles as tangible embodiments of group ideals and aspirations.

3 The Arts in Religion

Although radically different in appearance, the two Finnish churches illustrated in Figures 92, 93, and 94 have much in common. Each has a bell tower and a place in which to worship. They are in similar geographical surroundings, their builders are of the same nationality, and the religious creed is basically the same.

The difference in their appearance lies chiefly in the fact that they were built more than five hundred years apart, and this half millennium has brought drastic changes in ways of thinking, living, and building. The older of the two, the church at Sipoo, is simple in basic shape and ruggedly solid, and attests to an uncomplicated, rigorous faith. Its massive walls and steep roofs staunchly resist the elements. Hand-chiseled stone and rough shingles, varied in texture, create the rugged picturesqueness that sometimes comes with handcraftsmanship. Soft light comes from small windows and flickering tallow candles. The single bell will sound only when the bell ringer slowly sets the heavy mass of bronze into ponderous motion.

The twentieth-century church at Imatra is lithe, resilient, and complex. Exterior and interior walls are of reinforced concrete and brick painted white, and the roof is sheathed with copper. Natural wood pews and red tile floors contrast with the smooth white walls. Many diverse shapes, dynamically held together, indicate the church's manifold functions as an educational and social center as well as a place for worship. The building program specified that the interior be planned so that it could be subdivided into two or three separated spaces by movable walls or become one large space for special celebrations. A slender bell tower with mechanically operated chimes rises audaciously above the large, low building that hugs the ground. Precisely smooth surfaces envelop intricately elegant forms that are enlivened by an unexpected, but functional, placement of doors and windows. Ample light comes from these windows and from electrical fixtures. The trees around the building create a lively interplay of light and shadow.

Five hundred years ago the Finnish people were predominantly farmers and lumbermen who worked long hours six days a week. Sundays were spent at church,

opposite: 91. Robert Indiana. *God Is a Lily of the Valley*. 1962. Oil on canvas, 5 × 4'. Collection Eleanor Ward, New York. Indiana's painting belongs to one phase of Pop Art. Taken from a Negro spiritual, the text "God is a Lily of the Valley, He is a Tiger, He is a Star, He is a Ruby, He is a King" is presented in five circles of boldly contrasting colors.

right: 92. A fifteenth-century church in Sipoo, Finland, was built of massive stone masonry forms expressive of a rural, handcraft society.

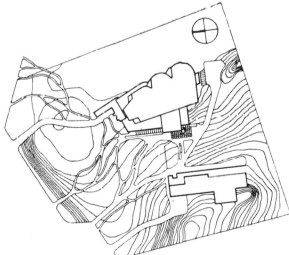

left: 93. Built in 1956, the Vuoksenniska Church in Imatra, Finland, acknowledges the machine age without becoming rigidly mechanistic. Alvar Aalto, architect.

above: 94. By planning the space in the Vuoksenniska Church with organic freedom instead of conventional ideas, Aalto solved many practical demands in a fresh manner.

The Arts in Religion 69

the religious as well as community center. Families rose early and put on their Sunday clothes. Most of them walked to church, but some rowed across the lakes, and the older persons were taken to church in stout wagons. They gathered at the church, and the men talked of such things as the weather, their crops, and farm animals. The women exchanged news of their families and hints about cooking and weaving. When the bell rang out, the group moved toward the church doors and was greeted by the minister, who also glanced down the paths to see how far away the latecomers were. But there was no great haste; Sunday was the day for meditation and relaxation.

Today Finland is a fast-moving, complex nation. Although many people still work and live close to the land, the country has numerous industries and an active commerce served by an efficient transportation system. The Imatra church is near a highway, and the parishioners come by automobile, not only to seek spiritual guidance but to participate in cultural and social events throughout the week. Other comparisons could easily be made. But although geography and climate, nationality and creed normally are powerful factors affecting artistic expression, in the two churches under discussion they are constants. Time is the element that is sharply different. A comparatively simple, slow-paced country has become a swift, busy, and energetic one. The two Finnish churches manifest man's religious thoughts, beliefs, and activities in the tempo of their periods.

Two Eighteenth-Century American Churches

Although the passage of time accounts for some of the most conspicuous differences in the forms through which men objectify their ideals, other significant determinants are rooted in traditions, climate, geography, and availability of materials.

The Bruton Parish Church (Fig. 95) belongs in general character, in basic form and details, and in materials to eighteenth-century Williamsburg, a community discussed in the preceding chapters. Because most of the buildings were completed within a relatively short period when one style prevailed, the church has much in common with the homes and public buildings nearby. The symmetrical masses of red brick enhanced with classical details stamp it as the product of the same English Georgian architectural tradition that produced the Governor's Palace. It differs from the other buildings in its dominant bell tower, its tall and narrow windows, and its cruciform plan, which give it *one kind* of religious expressiveness.

The Mission St. Francis of Assisi (Fig. 96), built in Ranchos de Taos, New Mexico, is also an American Colonial church, but it grew out of Spanish traditions and a geographical environment quite unlike that of Virginia. In converting the Pueblo Indians to Catholicism, the Spanish missionaries needed to build churches. Although not trained as architects, the zealous priests were familiar with religious structures, especially the fortress-churches of Mexico. In New Mexico labor of any sort was scarce, and there were no artisans who could work stone or wood skillfully. The semiarid land was thinly vegetated, the light had unfiltered brilliance, and the scale of the landscape was tremendous. Mud was plentiful and stone could be had, but timber was scarce.

Out of these conditions grew the churches of New Mexico. Their massive, thick, almost unbroken walls look defensive, for there was need for protection against marauding enemies and against extremes of heat, cold, and light. Literally raised from the earth, the Mission church was made of adobe bricks (sun-dried mud) and wood. It illustrates how materials and construction techniques affect

Two eighteenth-century American churches decisively reflect their different cultural and geographic environments.

left: 95. The Bruton Parish Church (1710–1715) at Williamsburg, Virginia, harmonized with the other buildings, the climate, and the citizens of the colonial community.

below: 96. The Mission St. Francis of Assisi (1772–1816) at Ranchos de Taos, New Mexico, is typical of the Spanish-American culture of the southwestern United States.

architecture. Walls could be no higher than was safe with unreinforced adobe brick, and the building could be no wider than the length of timbers available to support the roof. The length was determined by the size of the congregation. But even with such strict limitations, there was freedom to create a structure with spiritual significance.

The result was a new kind of architecture, organically developed from rigorous conditions but fulfilling all of its functions as admirably as did the Bruton Parish Church. It has its own beauty of simple masses, strong and decisive, yet enlivened by a sensuous, handmade quality.

Contemporary Religious Buildings

Today's freedom of religious expression and the prodigious technological advances allow the creation of architecture with a new independence of spirit. Four centers of devotion demonstrate that sympathetic understanding of the religious, cultural, and geographical environments and of divine and secular functions leads to distinctive developments. Three of them make evident the potentialities of concrete, a material favored today for large structures, and one shows how an old shop in a densely settled section of Paris was transformed into a "chapel of ease."

Temple and School, North Shore Congregation Israel, Glencoe, Illinois

Built of concrete, the slender, soaring forms of the Temple of the North Shore Congregation Israel (Figs. 97–99) are illustrative of the thin, light, self-supporting shell structures that new techniques make possible. For many years, architect Yamasaki has been interested in the structure of living organisms. The commission

The Temple and School for the North Shore Congregation Israel (1964) at Glencoe, Illinois, are structures that symbolically express the plant forms that inspired them. Minoru Yamasaki and Associates, architects.

for the Temple of the North Shore Congregation Israel was a great opportunity for him to create an edifice that is congruent with the wooded site on the shores of Lake Michigan and that evokes the reverence given to natural beauty in the Jewish religion.

Skylights, rows of low windows at floor level, and glass around the arches flood the interior in daytime with natural, diffused light that accentuates the airy shell structure. At night, artificial illumination in the skylights, controlled by dimmers, produces a similar effect. For special celebrations, the seating capacity can be more than doubled by using the broad, raised platforms at both sides of the regular seating area and also by opening the folding wall under the balcony to join the main hall with a large memorial vestibule.

The North Shore Congregation Israel Temple and its related buildings are a complex architectural project handled with imaginative freedom and individuality. A serene place for worship, the sanctuary soars far above the lower buildings, which were planned for secular activities. The total design, with its unfolding, rhythmically integrated forms, forcefully signifies the purpose of the whole and of each part. Its fluent movement, openness, and flexibility are characteristic of a dynamic architectural trend that has emerged during the last half of the twentieth century.

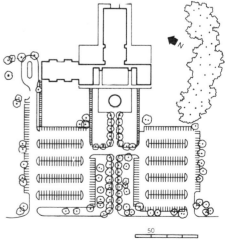

opposite : 97. The side walls of the Temple are composed of seven tall arches that fan outward at the top. The windows and doors of the lower memorial hall on the left are slenderized versions of the sanctuary's ogival windows.

above : 98. Looking toward the rear of the interior, the delicacy of the thin concrete shells that support and enclose the building is apparent.

right : 99. The site plan indicates the placement of the temple at the rear of the property with a forecourt flanked by smaller buildings for offices and a school building at the far left. Ample areas on either side of a tree-lined approach provide parking space.

St. Francis de Sales, Muskegon, Michigan

At a recent International Congress of Religions, Architecture, and the Visual Arts, architects and theologians representing many faiths discussed the functions and forms of contemporary religious architecture. Some speakers stated that new churches and temples would serve best if they were small, hospitable structures that would quietly take their place in the neighborhood. Others thought that they should be noble, enduring structures expressively symbolizing the eminence of God. The parish church of St. Francis de Sales (Figs. 100, 101) in Michigan and the Glencoe temple follow the latter philosophy. Marcel Breuer, one of the architects of St. Francis de Sales, said, "How much this building affects those who see and enter it, how much it signifies its reverent purpose, will depend on the courage its designers manifest in facing the age-old task: to defeat gravity and to lift the material to great heights over great spans—to render the enclosed space a part of infinite space. There the structure stands—defined by the eternal laws of geometry, gravity, and space."*

The arresting exterior mass of the center of worship is composed of unbroken, double-curvature side walls that, canted inward at the front and outward at the rear, gradually revolve as they rise from bases parallel to the long axis of the building. In contrast, the end walls are both inward-sloping planes, but the front wall widens while the back wall narrows toward the top to accommodate the side walls. Their

---

* *Architectural Record*, November, 1967, p. 130.

The parish church of St. Francis de Sales (1967) in Muskegon, Michigan, is an audacious, monumental concrete structure. Marcel Breuer and Herbert Beckhardt, architects.

opposite : 100. Rising above the low walls of the entrance court and vestibule, the front of the church is a huge trapezoidal plane standing boldly against the sky. The side wall is a hyperbolic paraboloid that twists out to meet it.

right : 101. The 75-foot-high nave is lighted by skylights and a special artificial-lighting slot between the ribs of the ceiling. The Chapel of the Blessed Sacrament, in an elevated niche, is dramatically illuminated by two spotlights and a stained-glass skylight.

warm, light-gray surfaces are boldly textured by the wood forms in which the concrete was cast.

Each of the major surfaces that shape the interior volume is an active element clearly differentiated from the others. The side walls—curved, smooth, and white— are a splendid foil for the darker end wall, in which the structural members are an intriguing visual event. The strong ascending forms continue in the horizontal ceiling to the other end of the church. The red brick floor slopes down 5 feet from back to front to aid visibility and then steps up into the podium. The plain white altar and the canopy overhead echo the trapezoidal shapes that are evident in the walls. Dark wood screens, diagonally placed at the ends of the sanctuary, form a background for the choir at the left and seclude offices and storage rooms at the right. The Chapel of the Blessed Sacrament is raised high above the brick podium so that all can see and become involved with the celebrant as he elevates the Host in benediction. Artificial illumination can be controlled to focus attention on either the altar or the chapel.

Approaching and entering the church provides the congregation with a sequence of varied spatial experiences. The massive building can be seen from some distance, but it is approached through a large, paved court that is open to the sky but protected from high wind by walls. The low-ceilinged narthex is not only an ample vestibule but contains the baptistry, confessionals, and seating for those who are waiting. Finally, the nave has a voluminous spaciousness that forms an exhilarating contrast with the comparatively low narthex. By providing emotional and esthetic encounters in these ways, religious architecture can be one factor in lifting man's spirit into a mystical communion with the divine.

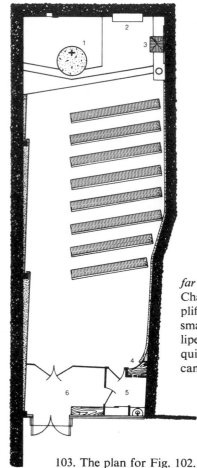

far left : 102. The Saint Anne Chapel (c. 1965) in Paris exemplifies the renewed interest in small "chapels of ease." Phillipe Vuarnesson and Jean Fourquin, architects. Olivier Descamps, sculptor.

103. The plan for Fig. 102.

Saint Anne Chapel, Paris

Situated in one of the poorest, most crowded areas of Paris' Montmartre district, the Saint Anne Chapel (Figs. 102, 103) differs markedly from the religious edifices previously discussed. It is a very small, unpretentious but heartwarming place of worship, planned to give renewed validity to prayer and meditation in the daily lives of those who live nearby. Formerly an ironworker's shop, it is in the center of a city block and can be approached only through a long, narrow court. Notable bronze entrance doors (Fig. 237), hung at the end of the court, are the first indication that this is a holy place. The interior space has an irregular, rectangular plan, painted masonry walls, and a staunch timber framework that supports the slanting roof. To create an informal atmosphere and to make the space seem larger, all of the elements are asymmetrically disposed. The rustic stone altar stands at the left on a diagonal stone podium raised three steps above the floor. Placed off center to the right on the rear wall is a gleaming brass retable that combines the tabernacle with a sculptural panel depicting the Christ Child, the Blessed Mother, and Saint Anne. Eight wood benches for the worshipers are diagonally placed against the right wall. No trace of meaningless elaborations disturbs the elemental simplicity of this quiet space because the chapel was designed as a haven in which the faithful could concentrate on spiritual concerns. Although it manifests contemporary trends, its stalwart, handcrafted forms are reminiscent of old, unpretentious, rural places of veneration.

The First Presbyterian Church, Stamford, Connecticut

When the members of the First Presbyterian Church in Stamford, Connecticut, outgrew their old Romanesque-revival structure, they felt that their new building should have lasting spiritual significance. Architect Wallace K. Harrison (who was also in charge of designing the United Nations Headquarters and Rockefeller Center, reproduced in Figs. 84, 85, 584) began thinking about the great European cathedrals. Why not bring together, thought Harrison, the luminous magic of stained glass and the technological attainments of our period?

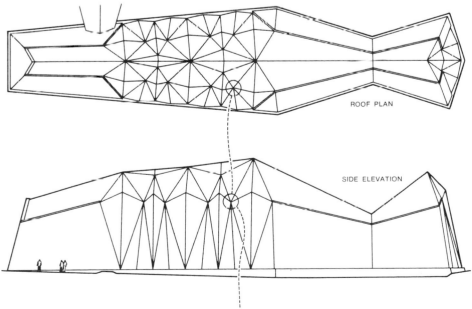

ROOF PLAN

SIDE ELEVATION

above: 104. Tilted, trapezoidal planes of concrete and stained glass support each other in an intricate interplay of stress and counterstress in the First Presbyterian Church at Stamford, Connecticut.

left: 105. The roof and side elevation of the church show the complex structural design that allows the interior to be free of supports.

The church (Pl. 9 and Figs. 104, 105) is large enough to seat eight hundred worshipers in "an enormous envelope of stained glass" as high as a six-story building and 135 feet long, completely uncluttered by structural supports. The frame of concrete reinforced with steel, only 8 inches thick and without buttresses or columns, was perfected by structural engineer Felix Samuerly. Gabriel Noire, the great stained-glass maker of the city of Chartres, produced the 20,000 pieces of amber, amethyst, emerald, ruby, and sapphire-colored glass that are embedded in the concrete frame. This is an intricate structure without a single right angle. In plan and in profile it resembles a fish, an ancient symbol for Christ. Although related to Gothic cathedrals, it is a valid, twentieth-century statement of man's need for churches that give a "sense of the presence of the Almighty."

It would be imprudent to say that any of the four buildings just discussed is superior in every way to the others, but each of us is justified in having his own preferences. Architectural history abounds with magnificent churches and temples. It is clear that no single architectural style or form can satisfy a human need so universal and multiform as religious expression. In Chapter 17, examples from many places can open our eyes further to the exhilarating diversity of religious architecture. Different as these buildings are in specific respects, they were all built as sacred centers. In each, the creativity of the designers and builders brought religious beliefs and temporal and geographical environments into unison with contemporaneous building technology and ideals of beauty.

Religious Sculpture

When sculptors carve a human head on which the ears are as high as a man, and when builders construct a tomb as high as a 48-story skyscraper, size alone makes the results imposing. If, however, such monuments are to have enduring significance, their forms must be as powerful as their hugeness demands. The men who created the Sphinx and the Great Pyramid of Khufu at Giza in Egypt (Fig. 106) understood well the magnitude of this challenge and produced monuments that

Religious sculptures from Africa (Figs. 106, 107), separated in time by 4500 years, are distinguished by a depth of feeling and conviction characteristic of profound religious art.

106. The Sphinx and the Great Pyramid of Khufu (c. 2600 B.C.) at Giza, Egypt, have long stood as symbols of religious permanence in which individuality was less important than generalized idealism.

78

Plate 9. For the First Presbyterian Church (1957) in Stamford, Connecticut, the architect created a lofty interior illumined by walls of stained glass to give a sense of spiritual exaltation. Wallace K. Harrison, architect. (See also Figs. 104, 105.)

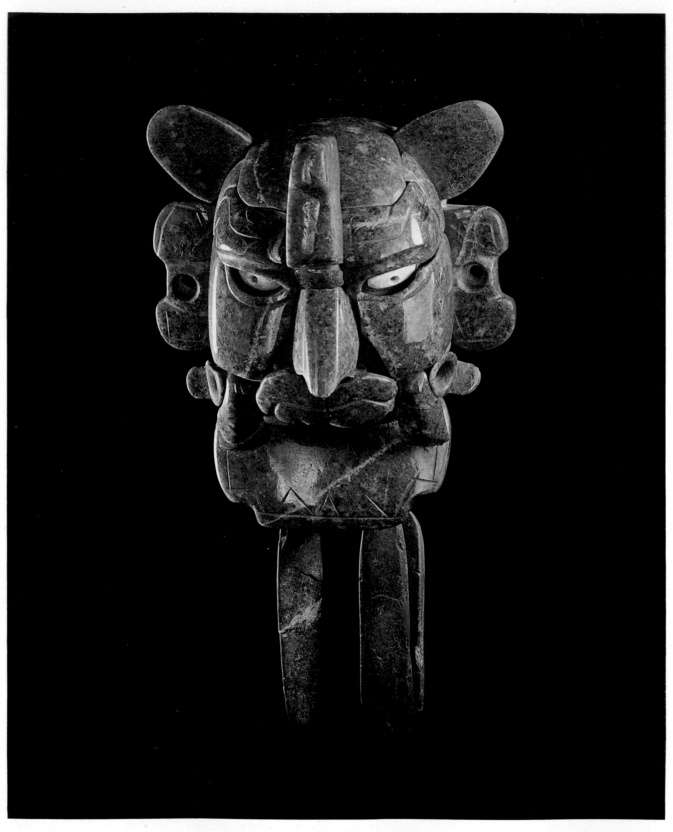

Plate 10. Zapotec bat mask. Mexico, c. 3d–8th centuries. Mixed media, height c. 7″. Museo Nacionạl de Anthropologia, Mexico City. This mask of the bat god of darkness and death, who was prominent in the mortuary rites of the Zapotec culture centering at Monte Albán, Oaxaca, Mexico, has jadeite features, shell eyes, and slate pendants fashioned into a fearsome object of worship.

have become symbols of permanence. Completed about 2600 years before the birth of Christ, the Great Pyramid of Khufu and the Sphinx are magnificent expressions of one of the most slowly changing religious, social, and political systems the world has ever known.

The pyramids were built as tombs, and the Great Pyramid was built to protect the mortal remains of the Pharaoh Khufu. The largest of the Egyptian pyramids, the Great Pyramid covers about 13 acres, measures 755 feet on each side, and was originally 480 feet high. Colossal blocks of limestone, some weighing 30 tons, were quarried with metal tools on the far side of the Nile, ferried over on rafts, and then laboriously hauled up ramps to their final position. It is estimated that this stupendous achievement took ten years of labor on the part of 100,000 men. Except for three small chambers deep in the interior and the narrow passages leading to them, the pyramid is a solid mass of masonry calculated to contain 2.5 million cubic yards of stone. Such prodigal use of labor and material attests to the great importance that the Egyptians attached to the afterlife. Believing it essential to protect the mummies of their rulers, they spared nothing to attain that goal. The pure pyramidal form, which evolved from stepped pyramids and earlier mortuary structures with flat roofs and sloping side walls, is one of the most durable of architectural shapes. Originally the sides were smoothly surfaced with stone, and then its strict, unadorned geometry was in compelling contrast to the forms of nature around it. Even now, although some of its precise simplicity has been lost, its unequivocal order and intense restraint command attention.

The Sphinx is probably an idealized portrait of the Pharaoh Khafre, who was Khufu's son. It joins a human head to the body of a lion in order to symbolize the godlike wisdom and strength of the princely priest who ruled both the religion and the politics of his country. Carved partly from living rock and partly from stone hauled to the site, it is immediately awe inspiring because of its colossal size (140 feet in length and 65 feet in height). Its lasting significance, however, comes far less from its bulk than from the grandeur of its massive forms. The head has a timeless majesty, a grave eloquence that tells us how deeply its creators were motivated by intense belief. Reproducing in exact detail the physical appearance of the Pharaoh was not their aim. Their mission was to communicate the spirit personified by Egypt's ruler, and the material chosen for the message was stone. This naturally led to generalizing and perfecting the features, to imbuing them with dignity, and to giving them an architectonic quality in keeping with the mass of stone from which they were carved. Both in size and in character the Sphinx, like the Great Pyramid, is magnificently at home in its vast desert setting, where it stands as one of the world's most monumental religious sculptures.

At first glance the African ancestor figure in Figure 107 seems to have little in common with the Sphinx. The nineteenth-century ancestor figure is only 22¾ inches high and was made from perishable wood. It emerged from a dissimilar religio-social pattern and geographical environment. Its intended setting is a small, dim hut on a mountain plateau covered with coarse grasses and scattered trees. Whereas the Sphinx asserts bold confidence, the ancestor figure is withdrawn and reclusive.

Further study, however, discloses significant similarities. Both were created in response to religious beliefs profoundly concerned with the continuity of life. The forms in both are compact and tightly knit. There is no twisting, turning, or suggestion of imminent movement. They do not invite strict comparison with natural forms because their creators felt no urge toward literal imitation: the size and the shape of each part were determined by the importance each part held for the idea that was to be expressed. In short, both the ancestor figure and the Sphinx are universalized abstractions of human figures.

The ancestor figure came from an agricultural community in which a cult of the dead is bound up with the continuity of family life. Death is regarded as a transformation of life into another kind of "being," which continues in *this* world. The souls of the departed wander uneasily until they find an appropriate abode. Then, in their statuettes, they settle down as "living" members of the family, often occupying a place of honor in the home. In return for little sacrifices, they can be asked for advice and may permit the use of their power.

With this background we can look at the form and materials of the statue. The sculptor's basic intent was to embody in his work the feeling of his group's religion and to make visible its conception of the world and the qualities of its social order. Because he was not making a literal portrait, he could adapt forms from older statues or from any aspect of nature, yet he was held within the bounds of tribal taste. The carver selected a piece of green wood and worked, through successive stages, from large masses down to intricate details. The head, which held the all-important soul and mind, was emphasized through size and elaboration. Torso and limbs were simplified because they were considered to be of secondary consequence. The shape of the log from which the statue was released by carving is clearly shown in the outline of the whole sculpture and is echoed in the neck, torso, arms, and legs. The strict parallelism of vertical and horizontal forms knits them together. All of this leads to a quiet but strangely vital gravity. Many modern sculptors and painters have been attracted by the powerful design of African sculpture, but the real power comes less from the formal design than from vivid communication of spiritual ideas and emotions. The spirit gave birth to the forms so completely that the work achieves a life of its own. How different this is from art in which there is little or nothing beyond a decorative arrangement of form, space, and color.

In most pre-Columbian cultures in Mexico the gods were all-powerful beings to be feared and placated. Although the same intensity of expression and abstraction of forms can be seen in the African sculptures, the total effect is quite different. A small bat-god mask from Monte Albán (Pl. 10), near Oaxaca, represents a supernatural figure made remote and intimidating by staring eyes of jet inlay set in rigid, disjunctive segments of jadeite. Even more formidable is the statue of *Coatlicue* (Fig. 108), the Aztec goddess of the earth, of death, and of man, who played the combined role of creator and destroyer. This was not a simple concept to portray in stone, for it demanded that hope and fear be brought together in a sculptural unity much as they were reconciled in the Aztec way of life. Until about 1325 the Aztecs were migratory hunters. Then they settled on the site of Mexico City and in two centuries had not only conquered all of Mexico but had developed an astonishing civilization. Their religious sacrifices of thousands of captives, even of children, may seem inhumanly brutal; but in their faith new life came out of destruction, and slaughter, therefore, was necessary.

The statue of *Coatlicue* was carved from a massive block of andesite, a granite-like stone whose gray color and mottled texture suit it well to the subject matter. Standing a little more than 8 feet high, it is surmounted by a fearsome tusked mask.

From a necklace formed of hands and hearts a skull hangs as a pendant, and twisted snakes form the skirt. All of this might have been a conglomeration of unrelated details. That such is not the case results from the skillful use of several compositional devices: strict bilateral symmetry, rhythmic relationship of each part to the whole, and emphasis on the important units through size and depth of carving. The figure is further unified by the simple, rectangular outlines that recall the first shape of the block of stone. When it was serving its religion, this "Lady of the Skirt of Serpents" must have had great emotional impact. Even today, its savage intensity and powerful forms cannot be taken lightly.

Two examples of religious sculpture from Europe give further evidence of the degree to which specific theologies affect the portrayal of human figures.

109. Praxiteles. *Hermes and the Infant Dionysus.* c. 340 B.C. Marble, height 7′ 1″. Archeological Museum, Olympia. The humanistic philosophy and religion of Greece in the fourth century B.C. is exemplified by this sculpture. Emphasis on physical beauty through softly rounded, well-proportioned forms is lifted above the materialistic by a serene idealism.

Hermes and the Infant Dionysus (Fig. 109), a statue probably carved by Praxiteles around 340 B.C., more than 2200 years later than was the Sphinx, is a warm, humanized interpretation of divinity. In contrast to the great size of the Sphinx and the small size of the ancestor figure, *Hermes* is slightly larger than life size. Unlike the Egyptians, the Africans, and the Aztecs, the Greeks wanted to understand what they believed. To understand their gods, they conceived them in the image of men and women but somewhat larger and more beautiful. They believed that their gods, although invisible, had great concern with their daily lives and that they visited them frequently. And like peoples in many parts of the world, the Greeks felt that their deities could be approached through images that gave substance to their ideas of the gods. The interest in man as the measure of all things and the devotion to formal order led to such works as this.

Hermes was herald and messenger of the gods, and in this statue he holds on his arm the infant Dionysus, who introduced man to the grape and its wine. His pose is relaxed and graceful, his expression serene and detached. There is no great fire of inner spirit, no regal austerity, no lowly supplication or intense fear. There is, instead, a transcendent idealization of physical beauty. In the total effect the fine-grained, creamy-white polished marble plays an important part, and it has been carved with the greatest skill. Imagine, if you can, this statue done in coarse limestone, mottled granite, or coarsely grained wood! Its material was carefully selected and sensitively handled to communicate an idea. In addition to its beauty and the insight this statue gives into Greek ideals of the fourth century B.C., the *Hermes*

110. West portal, detail. Chartres Cathedral. c. 1145–1170. Height, 20′ 6″. Representing the kings, queens, and prophets of the Bible, the compressed, columnar statues are strikingly different from the outgoing, full-bodied figures in Fig. 109.

is of interest because it is the only existing statue believed to have been created by any of the great Greek sculptors.

In contrast to the sensuous physical beauty of *Hermes* and the brutal, coiled force of *Coatlicue* is the spiritual idealism of the sculpture on the west portal of Chartres Cathedral (Fig. 110). The Chartres figures differ in almost every way from *Hermes*. They and the columns to which they are attached are over 20 feet high, but *Hermes* is only about 7 feet in height. The figures are unrealistically tall and slender, and their bodies tightly compressed. They are an integral part of a large, complex architectural composition, while *Hermes* is freestanding; and they are carved from opaque, gray limestone rather than from creamy marble. These are the most obvious differences, but there are many others. In *Hermes* emphasis has been placed on the whole body; with its placid, generalized features, the head gets no more than its just share of attention. The heads of the Chartres sculptures seem conspicuously large and more boldly carved than the rest of the figures and somewhat individualized in features and expression. The treatment of the bodies is just the reverse. In the Chartres sculptures the draperies fall in abstract folds that no more than hint at what they cover; in *Hermes* there is an unabashed exposure of a supple, muscular figure and of cloth that is heavily modeled in realistic, three-dimensional curves. This is but one evidence of fundamentally different ideas and, accordingly, different organizations—an easy, graceful, curvilinear treatment of forms in space as opposed to a strict, formal rigidity. These variances are, of course, the result of two religions that had relatively little in common.

Religious Painting

The *Lamentation* (Fig. 111) painted by Giotto in the Arena Chapel at Padua is one of Christianity's most powerful paintings. Seldom has there been such mastery of expressive form and color, such a direct and vital portrayal of passionate grief. After more than six centuries, this fresco retains its immediate and its sustained impact, because Giotto was one of those rare persons capable of a deep understanding of humanity and able to express this understanding with technical mastery. The figures and the composition as a whole are roughhewn and angular, heavy in their downward movement. All of the important action takes place in the lower half of the panel, and the body of Christ lies near the bottom. Mourners grouped in two asymmetrical, rectangular units frame His body and express through their bodies as well as their faces the irreparable loss. No extraneous details distract from the tragedy, for Giotto knew full well the power of simplicity. Although the composition is masterful, it properly plays a secondary role to the purpose of the painting—a convincing presentation of a Biblical story.

The *Sistine Madonna* (Fig. 112) was painted by Raphael in the early years of the sixteenth century, approximately two hundred years after Giotto's *Lamentation*.

Two paintings done in Italy approximately two centuries apart illustrate the manner in which art of the same religion and same country changes.

opposite : 111. Giotto. *Lamentation.* 1305–1306. Fresco, 7′ 7″ × 7′ 9″. Arena Chapel, Padua. The direct, forceful expression of intense grief is realized through means not unlike those in the sculptures in Fig. 110.

right : 112. Raphael. *Sistine Madonna.* c. 1515. Oil on canvas, 8′ 8″ × 6′ 5 ¼″. State Museums, Dresden. The opulence of form and sensuous physical beauty of this painting are similar to the characteristics of the sculpture in Fig. 109.

In contrast to the earnest, spare severity of Giotto's work, the *Sistine Madonna* combines a tender and lyrical treatment of the faces with a monumental, symphonic composition of curves. Basically triangular, the design begins its upward sweep in the figure at the left, swirls around Christ and the head of the Madonna for a momentary pause, and then returns through the figure at the right to the two cherubs at the base. Because both Giotto's and Raphael's paintings were created under the influence of the Roman Catholic religion and since both artists are Italian, they have an underlying similarity. Yet there are many differences. In the earlier painting, the forms are direct and forceful, show an angular, architectural sense of weight and solidity, and are tightly knit into compact groups. In the *Sistine Madonna* the forms are much softer and have a gentle, flowing quality, quite unlike anything in the earlier painting, and the composition is more open and expanding. Its appeal is to the tender and sentimental aspects of human nature. These differences, to be sure, arise in part from the differences in the personalities of the two painters, but they also reflect the great changes in social and religious thought that took place from the fourteenth to the sixteenth centuries in Italy.

Modern painters present fundamental religious concepts in fresh but timeless forms.

left : 113. Georges Rouault. *Christ Mocked by Soldiers.* 1932. Oil on canvas, 36 ¼ × 28 ½". The Museum of Modern Art, New York. The brilliant colors of stained glass are combined with intense expressionism.

opposite above : 114. Rico Lebrun. *Crucifixion.* 1949–1951. Oil on Upson board, 16 × 26'. Collection Syracuse University. This painting elicits compassion by its deeply felt sincerity, wrath by its shocking contrasts.

opposite below : 115. South wall window. Church of Maria Königin, Cologne, Germany. c. 1954. A continuous curtain of stained glass from floor to ceiling forms the wall of a contemporary church in Germany. Dominikus Bohm and Heinz Beinefeld, designers.

To close the discussion of religious painting, let us consider two modern examples, Georges Rouault's *Christ Mocked by Soldiers* (Fig. 113) and Rico Lebrun's *Crucifixion* (Fig. 114). Rouault is one of the few modern painters who has been able to represent the great ideas of the Christian faith in twentieth-century forms. His paintings were built up slowly, often over a period of years, by means of patches of rich, glowing colors overlaying one another and then reinforced with black outlines. Inevitably they remind one of stained-glass windows. The compositions are strong, simple, and sincere. Thus Rouault's paintings have an immediate appeal of color and design, but they go far beyond that in their deep penetration of subject matter. Infinite compassion and resignation are conveyed by the curved figure of Christ, a startling contrast to the coarse mockery of the soldiers leering over His shoulders.

Anger at man's inhumanity to man, today and in the past, compelled Rico Lebrun to lay bare the horror of the Crucifixion. Lebrun explained, "The awesomeness and cruelty should be in the forms themselves. The poetry should be in the pity. . . . There is no end to horror and pain." Slashing diagonals, strident color contrasts, and tortured forms build up to violent movement and a sense of destruction. With the exception of Christ, all of the figures are dehumanized to portray the evil that is within them. Christ is emaciated, and His face is hidden so that he symbolizes all people who are lonely and rejected. Thus Lebrun denounces the past and the present in a single image of shattering intensity. Neither of these two paintings is for entertainment or decoration. They both show deep concern with fundamentals and with the problem of communicating them vividly to us.

Stained-Glass Windows and Bronze Doors

In northern countries where the natural light is not intense, stained-glass windows were a distinctive feature of medieval churches. Recently, a heartening revival of this art has resulted in numerous, thoroughly contemporary creations. A vibrant

wall of stained glass (Fig. 115) animates an otherwise unexceptional new church in Cologne. The simple interior of the church with walls of brick painted white, red brick floors, and naturally finished wood benches is a quiet setting for the shimmering intricacy of the glass panels. In harmony with the wooded park in which the church stands, the glass is predominantly of silvery tones of gray and neutral green, but even within this limited color range it was possible to achieve much variety. The over-all pattern is based on a series of slender, gently curving motifs that suggest

a thicket of trees intertwining as they rise from the floor to the ceiling. The "trees" are composed of countless small pieces of curved, trapezoidal, triangular, and rectangular glass. Structural steel posts divide the wall into seven panels, each of which is punctuated by two medallions of liturgical significance. Fragments of brightly colored glass gleaned from the ruins of old, bombed-out churches were used in the medallions and contrast effectively with the new, more neutral pieces. These focal points are generally circular in shape, and their radiating movement extends into the design that surrounds them. The over-all effect is a joyous testimonial to the glory of God.

Another art form whose association with religious expression constitutes a tradition in itself is the bronze doors hung at the principal portals of great churches. Elements that open up space and close it in, doors have long been invested with symbolic meaning for some of the major moments in human experience. They suggest both life and death, the beginning and the end, freedom and confinement, and the immemorial rites of passage to and from places of grave and solemn meaning. In the Renaissance, the bronze reliefs prepared by Lorenzo Ghiberti for the doors of the Baptistry in Florence were so beautiful they have since been called *The Gates of Paradise*, a commentary ascribed to none other than Michelangelo. For the nineteenth-century French sculptor Auguste Rodin, monumental bronze portals were an occasion to create *The Gates of Hell*, vast metaphors for human destiny.

Cathedrals seem never to be completed, and the Basilica of St. Peter's in Rome (Figs. 601, 602) entered the twentieth century with only a single set of bronze doors—those taken from the original Early Christian basilica demolished to make place for the present St. Peter's—for the portals of the five porches leading to the basilica's interior. In 1949 Giacomo Manzù, one of Italy's most distinguished modern sculptors, won the competition for one pair of the four sets of door panels the Vatican decided to have made for St. Peter's. The subject of the project assigned to Manzù was specified as "Glorification of the Saints and Martyrs of the Church."

Although steeped in the heritage of Western art, especially that related to life in the Mediterranean countries, Manzù is a man born of poor parents in the provincial town of Bergamo and an artist largely self-taught. For Manzù the commission was an honor, for it placed him in the artistic company of Bramante, Michelangelo, Raphael, and Bernini, all of whom worked at St. Peter's, but the theme of legendary, historical saints came to seem irrelevant to him. After a period of inactivity Manzù found in Pope John XXIII, also from a poor family of Bergamo, the inspiration and courage to develop a strong and appropriate theme directly out of his own profound but individualistic sense of human value. Simplification—both of content and form—became the artist's goal. Thus, in the completed doors the traditional attributes of sainthood and such accessories as palms, lights, rays, and halos are gone. Timelessness and universality have been achieved through perfection of form only, not through classic decorative devices. Manzù is religious in an unorthodox way and a humanist at heart, and like many Europeans of his generation, he was much affected by the outrages against humanity perpetrated during World War II. To him the real witnesses to faith are the anonymous, ordinary people of everyday life, and it is their suffering and martyrdom that Manzù wanted to celebrate in his doors for St. Peter's. The bronze panels have come to be called the *Doors of Death* (Fig. 116).

In the upper left panel is a scene entitled "Death of Mary"; in the upper right panel, the "Death of Christ." Just below them, in the position of door handles, are the Eucharistic symbols of vine leaves and sheaves of wheat, the emblems of peace and salvation among scenes of suffering and destruction. In the top row of the lower two groups of reliefs, from left to right, are: "Death of Abel," the first murder

left: 116. Giacomo Manzù. *Doors of Death,* Basilica of St. Peter's, Rome. 1964. Bronze (alloy of tin, zinc, lead, nickel, iron, and copper), 25′ 3 ¹/₂″ × 12′ ³/₄″.

below: 117. Giacomo Manzù. *Pope John XXIII Receiving Cardinal Rugambwa,* detail from the reverse side of Fig. 117.

victim; "Death of Joseph," the pilgrim dying from the exertions of long and painful travel; "Death of Stephen," the Christian church's first martyr, stoned to death by a hostile mob; and "Death of Gregory VII," a religious leader in exile abused by a military figure.

It is in the lowest row of four reliefs that Manzù placed the heart of his program, for here are the scenes of deaths endured by common man. They are, on the extreme left, "Death by Violence," a torture victim watched over by a compassionate woman; the second from the right, "Death in the Air," the uncoordinated bundle of a man entangled high above ground in the limp ropes of a failed parachute; and at the extreme right, "Death on the Earth," a woman dying nameless and unaided on a chair in the presence of a helpless child. Among these scenes, second from the left, is a portrait of Pope John XXIII kneeling in the simple expression of deep private prayer. It was made by Manzù after Pope John died as a tribute to a good and much-loved spiritual leader. In this panel are the words *Pacem in Terris*, the title of John XXIII's great encyclical on the rights of human beings to freedom and dignity and on peace among nations. It is the only inscription on the face of the door, except for "3 VI 63," the date the Pope died, recorded in the Stephen panel.

The reverse side of the doors is blank sheet bronze adorned only by a narrow frieze running across both door panels about two-thirds down from the top. It depicts prelates at the Ecumenical Council (Vatican II) and contains a second portrait of John XXIII, receiving Cardinal Rugambwa from Africa (Fig. 117).

Characteristics of Religious Art

What are the characteristics of religious art? What binds together the humble wooden idols of Africa, the sensuous marble gods of the Greeks, the paintings of Giotto and Lebrun, and the stained-glass windows of the Stamford church? Two sacred architectural monuments, widely separated in time and place, give one answer.

The prehistoric, Cyclopean construction at Stonehenge in England (Fig. 118) and the modern, unfinished cathedral in the new city of Brasilia (Fig. 119) attest to man's ability to objectify his religious beliefs. Stonehenge was probably built as a setting for the religious observances of sun worshipers. Two huge concentric circles, the largest almost 98 feet in diameter, and two horseshoe-shaped rows of tall stone monoliths surround a 16-foot-long altar and are oriented to the summer and winter solstices. It took the labor of many men and unbelievable ingenuity to transport these huge stone blocks from their source 134 miles away, to raise them into their upright positions, and then to cap them with gigantic horizontal members. The culture and religion that created Stonehenge disappeared long ago, but what remains is a testament to man's indomitable vision.

Almost 350 centuries later and halfway across the world, other men had an equally compelling vision—that of the ideal city, newly created in a plain 3000 feet above sea level in the huge, unpopulated center of Brazil. Because the land space available was enormous, the buildings in Brasilia can be set apart from each other, viewed from all sides, and sculptured against the great arch of the sky (see Pl. 64, p. 510). One of the new capital's most important structures is the unfinished, crown-shaped cathedral, called Our Lady of the Apparition after the patron saint of Brazil. Great ribs of warm-toned, reinforced concrete, standing on narrow tips, spring from a circular base, come together and support each other, and then flare outward against the ever-changing cloud patterns passing overhead. Eventually, large and in-curving stained-glass windows will fill in the inverted V-shaped spaces to create an enclosed but spacious place of worship, alive with the light coming through the varicolored glass. As Stonehenge was a supreme effort of man pitted against the almost unmovable, the cathedral at Brasilia states modern man's supremacy over the forces of gravity, and in so doing glorifies the spiritual forces sustaining such an effort.

opposite : 118. Stonehenge, Wiltshire, England, built in successive stages from about 1800 to 1400 B.C., stands as a silent, moving memorial to the power of religious beliefs.

right : 119. The cathedral (1960—) at Brasilia, Brazil, even in its unfinished state, exemplifies man's ability to visualize and fulfill a great dream. Oscar Niemeyer, architect.

4 The Arts of Industry

There are such marked differences between the purposes and forms of religious art and of those arts created to make everyday living more efficient and gratifying that going from one to the other requires a major shift of attitude. As stated in the Preface, anything that man makes creatively and skillfully deserves consideration in a book on art. Textiles and teapots, telephones and furniture are a few of the products made by hand or machine that belong to the arts of industry.

Today's world is a vast network of cities and towns, farms and mines interlaced with a web of split-second communication and swift transportation. In the United States, Australian wool, Japanese ceramics, Italian glass, and Scandinavian steel are found side by side with domestic products, which, in turn, are sent to many other countries. But before discussing present-day mass production of useful objects, let us observe a craft culture.

Handcraft Cultures

Communities that depend primarily on what they make with their own hands are increasingly rare, but a few still exist. In Guatemala there are villages in which craftsmen working with primitive looms, potter's wheels, and other simple equip-

opposite : 120. Robert Grosvenor. *Still No Title*. 1966. Fiber glass, steel, and plywood, length 27″. Park Place Gallery of Art Research, New York. A union of art and industry is achieved in Grosvenor's Minimal sculpture, made in a factory to his specifications.

ment supply most of the textiles, utensils, and objects needed by the community. They are used by the families who make them or are sold or exchanged in the nearby markets. Until very recently little was produced that was not used within the area.

The sturdy cotton textile in Figure 121 is from a remote Guatemalan village and is typical of the work done in this area. It is a carrying cloth, used for carrying bananas, beans, and babies. Humble though it is in purpose, the cloth is enriched with abstract human and animal figures. These figures are a continuation of a tradition developed in this village over the centuries. All of the other weavers in the locality follow similar patterns. To be sure, each weaver infuses his work with subtle, often hardly noticeable individual variations, much as the singer of folk tunes makes the songs his own. But, as with folk songs, these are patterns that not only have withstood the test of time but have been improved over long periods. Weaknesses have been eliminated and strengths emphasized until the results are "right." Although no two textiles are identical, they conform so closely to one another that they are almost standardized. They are comparatively minor variations on a traditional theme. When a thoroughly satisfactory design has been achieved, there is, at least in simple cultures, little impetus to change. Of course, if there were no change at all, the vitality of the design would soon ebb into monotonous, stereotyped repetition. At the other extreme, change without real need leads to senseless fads and fashions.

The fact that the Guatemalan textile is enriched beyond simple utilitarian requirements is important. Throughout the world man has expressed his need for this kind

In handcraft societies, articles made by the local craftsmen usually represent slowly evolving traditional types, as shown at left and in Fig. 122.

121. A handwoven Guatemalan cloth (1936) of traditional design is enlivened by the irregularity of weaving and the varied treatment of the figures.

122. A silver teapot made by Paul Revere in eighteenth-century Boston exemplifies the refined craftsmanship and subtlety of design possible in more advanced craft societies. The Metropolitan Museum of Art, New York (bequest of A. T. Clearwater, 1933).

of enhancement of life. Even when merely keeping alive demands almost all of a people's energy, craftsmen have found time and enthusiasm to make their everyday objects good to see and to touch. Sometimes this enhancement comes directly from the material: the sensuous beauty of silk or wool, the color and texture of clays and glazes, or the grain and color of wood. At other times it grows directly out of the process, as in the patterns produced in weaving. But there are other types of enrichment: the figures in the Guatemalan textile were put there consciously and purposefully for esthetic stimulation and satisfaction.

One other aspect of the Guatemalan textile deserves attention—the charm of irregularity, the appeal of the "human touch," which is characteristic of many craft products. The figures are not always aligned, and some are larger than others. The yarns are of uneven thickness, and the weave varies in tightness throughout the textile. In short, the textile does not have machinelike regularity.

But much craftwork is precise and disciplined. In the eighteenth century in the United States, to cite but one example, craftsmanship reached a high level of technical and artistic perfection, as can be seen in Paul Revere's silver teapot (Fig. 122) and the handsome chest of drawers by John Pimm (Pl. 11). These, too, came from a long tradition, but one in which meticulous refinement was of great importance.

The Industrial Revolution

By the time of the Industrial Revolution, which got well under way in the nineteenth century, the high level of craftsmanship was changed in many parts of the world. The advent of power machinery and the consequent technological changes threw thousands of craftsmen out of work and, understandably, met with strong opposition from them. One of their arguments, well founded in the early stages of industrialization, was that the machine destroyed individuality and beauty. Certainly, traditions as old as man were almost swept away.

Plate 11. A masterpiece of craftsmanship, this high-chest-of-drawers, made of maple and pine c. 1740–1750 in Boston, has elaborately carved finials and shell and garland motifs, complemented by painted scenes, called japanned decoration, that imitate Oriental lacquerwork. John Pimm, cabinetmaker; probably painted by Thomas Johnson. Henry Francis du Pont, Winterthur Museum, Delaware.

Plate 12. In the "red-blue chair" (1917) designed by Gerrit Rietveld of Holland cubic forms and rectangular planes are lightly poised and the structure is exposed and simply joined. A complete break with traditional forms, it is a forthright statement of a chair and an experimental rather than a final solution. Stedelijk Museum, Amsterdam.

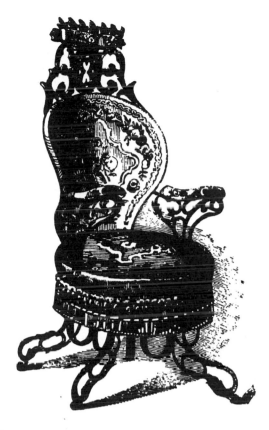

Extremes in nineteenth-century American design mark two chairs.

left : 123. Like most furniture designed and handcrafted by Shaker groups, this armed rocking chair (1830–1850) is remarkable for its honesty and satisfying proportions.

right : 124. A floridly curved and ornamented chair with centripetal springs was designed later and patented for machine production.

The industrialists' first consideration was to make objects cheaply, and this was achieved by producing them in large quantities with minimum labor. A hundred spoons could be made by machine as quickly as a craftsman could make one, and they could be sold for a fraction of their former price. But cheapness was the only virtue of the early stages. Through long years of work with their materials and in their traditions, craftsmen had become competent designers, but by fighting instead of accepting the machine, they left it without a master. Design degenerated, and ornament, as profuse as it was senseless, took its place. Ornamentation had been used thoughtfully in the handcrafts, because it took time and skill. But the machine could cover any object with curlicues in a few seconds, and because it was so fast and easy, ornament became an obsession (Fig. 124) and was indiscriminately applied to everything. It became the symbol of "art"; and, even worse, it was often used to disguise cheap materials and poor workmanship. Contemporary trends toward severe simplicity are in part the last vestiges of a reaction against nineteenth-century abuse of enrichment.

Gradually, however, conditions changed. Manufacturers found that quality, as well as quantity and cheapness, was important. In achieving quality they needed help, which they obtained from a few artists, craftsmen, and designers who saw that the realities of mass production called for new theories of design. The chair by Gerrit Rietveld (Pl. 12), for instance, is a pioneering example of some of the forms that resulted from a reexamination of furniture design.

Industrial Design

Industrial design, the design of objects for machine production, is an integration of art, engineering, and merchandising. Although its foundations go back to prehistoric man's first attempts to better his life by shaping tools and equipment, industrial design as we know it was born in the 1920s. At first it was often hesitant and superficial. "Art" was "applied" to machine-made objects in a superficial "styling" of external appearances by persons who had "good taste" or "flair." Often it amounted to little more than suggesting different colors for bath towels or tablecloths, simplifying the appearance of typewriters by covering the working parts, or giving furniture more pleasing proportions. By mid-century, though, it had become a major factor in the industrial economy. Only a few decades ago, no more than a handful of objects benefited from the skills of professional designers. Today there is little on the market that has not been influenced, directly or indirectly, by them. Industrial design has become a field as complex as architecture or community planning, and, like them, it is a serious business that works from the inside out, from basic human needs to products that satisfy those needs. Experts in many fields pool their skills in the design of everything from tableware to the shapes of automobiles.

Although there is no single procedure that is followed by all industrial designers, one approach to the problem is the four-stage program described by Raymond Loewy (in Raymond Loewy, *Never Leave Well Enough Alone.* New York: Simon and Schuster, 1955).

The first step is *fact finding*, a process that has two phases. One is the gathering of full information on the product to be designed or redesigned and of comparative information on the major competitors. Although the client can readily supply the designer with some of the pertinent data, such as sales booklets and sales records, additional independent investigation is in order. The designer's representatives go into the field for firsthand information from dealers and salesmen, and they also take several similar products into their shop for thorough comparative testing. Not only are the products studied, but the whole promotional procedure is scrutinized—wrappers, packing boxes, sales literature, and even the company's stationery and trademark. The second fact-finding phase is getting all the pertinent information on the manufacturer's mechanical facilities for production and on his key personnel. For this, a task force from the designer's office visits the client's factory to see what equipment is available, and, equally important, to become well acquainted with the experience, skills, and attitudes of the personnel.

The second step, *designing*, begins with many preliminary sketches and models. This is a period of creative exploration during which literally hundreds of drawings may be made. The sky is the limit, but appearance is by no means the only consideration. If the fact-finding program discloses, among many other points, that the current product is bulky and heavy, alternative materials and manufacturing techniques are checked with the company's engineering department. Then the many sketches are judged, and the three or four that hold the greatest promise are selected. Models of these are made and are attractively displayed for a meeting with company officials. Discussions may last only a few hours, or they may go on for several days. As a result of this conference, the designs are revised. Again models are made, but this time they are finished to look exactly as though they were ready to be used. These are studied in detail from all points of view, even to the taking of photographs to see how well the product will show up in television or newspaper ads. Again there is a conference between designer and client and more design revisions then follow (Fig. 125).

The third step is *the making and testing of working models*. From accurate mechanical drawings, the company produces by hand a few working models (Fig. 126). These models are checked on such factors as ease of operation, maintenance, and cleaning under normal use. They are also tested for durability under abnormally rough use. If they stand up well, final drawings lead to the necessary changes in the manufacturer's plant and program. When the first units are manufactured, the designer checks everything again but is now able to pay special attention to such details as finish, color, trademark, and packaging. Then full-scale production begins, and the final products are soon in the distributor's hands.

Promotion is the fourth step, but planning for this stage begins early in the program. Celebration parties may be organized in hotel ballrooms or a convention hall. After refreshments, speeches, and perhaps some entertainment, the new product is unveiled to buyers from representative stores. Then the arts of advertising call it to the attention of the buying public, and it succeeds or fails in terms of how millions of potential purchasers react to it.

Designing a combination can opener and knife sharpener involves many steps.

right : 125. Several design possibilities are explored in sketches, renderings, model studies, and a final working model.

below : 126. The final design shows the result of careful study in the placement of the knife sharpener and the control handle, and the over-all integration and balance of the appliance.

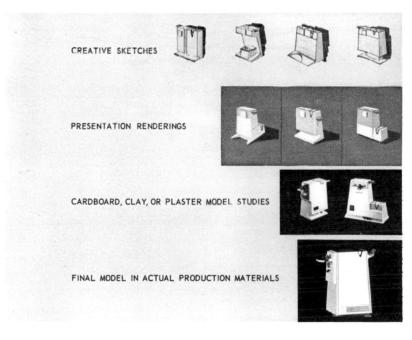

CREATIVE SKETCHES

PRESENTATION RENDERINGS

CARDBOARD, CLAY, OR PLASTER MODEL STUDIES

FINAL MODEL IN ACTUAL PRODUCTION MATERIALS

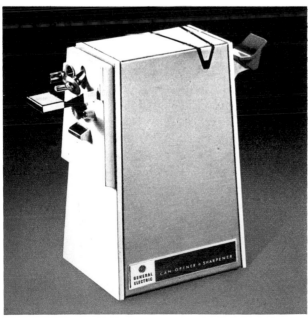

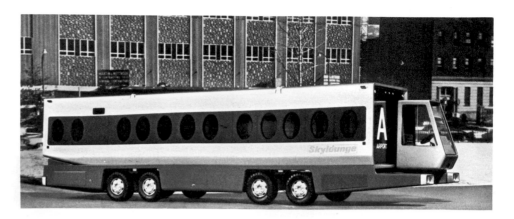

The skylounge, manufactured by the Budd Company, is a new idea for speeding transportation from the center of the city to the airport. The system should save passengers 50 minutes of commuting time. Peter Muller-Munk Associates, Inc., design consultants.

above : 127. Capable of carrying forty-four passengers, the skylounge will be driven from midtown to the pickup locations. The body, made of lightweight aluminum, rests on a specially designed flatbed truck.

left : 128. A helicopter will lift the body from the final pickup station to the airport.

Although industrial design projects usually involve intensive fact finding, and many preliminary possibilities may be developed, the length of time the process takes varies greatly. If the problem is simply to update something that is basically satisfactory, it may be solved in a relatively short time. The design of a new kind of bus (Figs. 127, 128), however, may take several years, and it requires many years to create a new airplane or space vehicle (Fig. 156).

Four Musical Instruments

What should a musical instrument look like? Admittedly this is of far less importance than the sound it produces, but still it is a factor. There is not much leeway, however, in the design of most instruments and not much impetus toward change. Thus, violins made by Stradivarius, the great Italian violin maker of the seventeenth and eighteenth centuries, look very much like those produced today. This is less true of the piano and its ancestors. Although the varying lengths of the strings are usually reflected in the body of a grand piano, the case and its supports can be treated in many ways. The four examples illustrated in Figures 129, 130, 131, and 132 show how the predominant trends in three centuries of furniture design affected their form.

From eighteenth-century Rome comes the harpsichord supported by Tritons, a vivid expression of the Baroque spirit that swept over Europe in the seventeenth and early eighteenth centuries. Far removed from anything we would—or could—do now, it embodies the Baroque urge for vivid excitement, heavily modeled and contorted forms, and dynamic movement. Sculptor and cabinetmaker put their talents together to create a sumptuously rich experience—too rich, perhaps, for those today who ask for nothing more than simplicity, but a magnificent statement of its place and period, an environment not suited to timid souls. We, too, in the twentieth century seek dynamic movement in many of our art forms, but seldom if ever as full-bodied and ingeniously complex as this harpsichord.

The second example, designed in 1836, belongs to the Neoclassic style that developed out of a renewed interest in the forms and ornament of ancient civilizations, especially that of Rome. Thin strips of inlaid wood emphasize the basic form of the case and the precisely curved, vase-shaped legs. The handsomely grained wood is the only other ornament. In comparison with the Baroque harpsichord, this piano is simple and restrained.

Four musical instruments (Figs. 129–132) show markedly different design character.

above : 129. An eighteenth-century Italian harpsichord is a triumphant example of Baroque exuberance. The Metropolitan Museum of Art, New York (The Brosby Brown Collection of Musical Instruments, 1889).

right : 130. An early nineteenth-century design is remarkable for its restrained elegance and grace.

The Arts of Industry   103

right : 131. A robust Victorian grand piano (1857) is ornamented with rich, vigorous carving.

below : 132. The twentieth-century concert grand has a monumental grandeur worthy of great piano music.

The third instrument was constructed in the middle of the nineteenth century and exemplifies Victorian design at its best. The swirling grain of the wood is adroitly used, and the vigorous carving is sensitively and sensibly integrated with the shapes and purposes of the parts and the whole. The piano has the same confident Romanticism as the music of the period.

The concert grand piano shown in Figure 132 has a remarkable history. Designed in the early years of the twentieth century, this model, with only slight modifications, has been in continuous production since that time. Anticipating later twentieth-century trends, it is about as simple as possible, restrained to the point of austerity. Nothing distracts from the basic form. Even the grain of the wood is concealed under coats of lustrous black paint. This instrument majestically expresses a quest for essentials, for forms that gain beauty from intense, singleminded clarity and precision.

The harpsichord-piano sequence shows how tastes changed during three centuries. The pendulum swung from the emotionally charged Baroque harpsichord to the restrained Neoclassic piano. Then it reversed to the vigorous Victorian example and came back to the calm simplicity of the modern concert grand. Even within a single period of history, such as the last four decades, a range of design can be observed.

Contemporary Chairs

The primary purpose of a chair is to offer one the opportunity to relax the muscles in a bodily position somewhere between the vertical and the horizontal. Merely satisfying this physiological necessity is comparatively simple, but the total problem is not so easy. There are many kinds and degrees of relaxation, and, consequently, chairs have many configurations. They can be fabricated from diverse materials and put together in a seemingly inexhaustible variety of ways, and each material and process determines to some degree what the final form will be. There are also changes in taste from one decade to the next as well as the all-important factor of individual differences in designers and consumers. Each of the chairs in Figures 133 through 140 has its own distinctive, expressive character. Each promises one kind of physical comfort and in turn calls up a fairly specific chain of reactions, although these may vary greatly from one person to another. Beyond this, each chair arouses emotional and esthetic feelings, related to what it will do for one's physical needs, but by no means limited to that alone.

The "Barcelona" chair (Fig. 133), so named because it came to worldwide attention at the Barcelona International Exhibition, was designed by Miës van der Rohe in 1929. It still stands without peer among the thousands of modern machine-made chairs. Its polished stainless steel frame has one simple and one reverse-curved member, and the removable leather cushions are supported on straps

133. The "Barcelona" chair (1929), designed in Germany by Miës van der Rohe, has a timeless beauty.

left : 134. Yrjö Kukkapuro's Finnish lounge chair (1965) is low, broad, and bulky.

opposite : 135. Warren Platner's chair (1966) has an airy, structural framework of parallel wires that creates an intriguing, changing pattern of light and dark as one walks around it.

of saddle leather. Not only are the shape and materials exquisitely beautiful, but the workmanship is, of necessity, perfect. It exemplifies its designer's philosophy of "less is more," a belief that demands a hard, intense search for essences and should not be confused with the all-too-prevalent notion that modern simplicity comes through mere elimination. The latter more often than not leads only to esthetic impoverishment. The character of the Barcelona chair is not easy to describe. Although formal, it is not stiff or rigid. It is elegant but not ostentatious. For the past forty years it has been used in the public reception areas of hotels and office buildings, and in the living rooms of homes in Europe and the Americas with equal felicity. Because it is an exceptionally coherent design in which each part is coordinated with its purpose, it has continued to be manufactured while many derivations have come and gone. It is indeed a classic.

Although thoroughly contemporary in materials and production methods, the second chair (Fig. 134), designed by Yrjö Kukkapuro, is reminiscent of old-fashioned, informal ease. Constructed of separate, machine-made elements that are also used to make sofas of different lengths, it is shipped in parts and assembled at its destination. The structural frame is of steel tubes that fit into sockets; the seat rests on rubber suspension bands that are hooked onto the frame. Wood panels support and stabilize the loose arm and back cushions. Leather or fabric upholstery, held in place by zippers, is easily removable for cleaning. The design of these seating pieces represents a current trend toward furniture that is massive and sheltering and that adapts to the body of the sitter.

The apparent simplicity of the third chair (Fig. 135) gives little hint of the complex technology on which it is based. The company that produced it had had considerable experience in making meshed-wire and plastic-shell furniture, but this design raised new problems of precision. Architect-designer Warren Platner chose steel wire as his basic material and shaped it so that the supports become the framework in one continuous flow. The wires are first individually shaped by hand to very precise measurements, then laid over a form and welded to the tie wires that hold them in place. A plastic shell is molded to fit inside the contours of the frame,

padded with latex cushions, and covered with fabric that may be removed for cleaning. Although much of the work is done by machines, the design necessitates a considerable amount of hand labor. The result is a buoyant, curvilinear composition in which handcraft and machine production are each used for the contributions they can make. Although Platner has designed other chairs and tables on this same principle, each one requires individual shaping. This is quite different from the concept underlying the Kukkapuro chair, which is assembled from components that can be used in a variety of pieces.

For some years a reaction against the many coldly mechanistic shapes that surround us has led designers to seek fresh inspiration in the possibilities of new materials and techniques. In the fourth chair (Fig. 136), which is more a lounge than a chair, Olivier Mourgue followed this direction. He took advantage of the

136. Sinuous forms shaped to fit the entire body make French designer Olivier Mourgue's lounge chair (1965) an inviting piece of furniture.

tensile strength of tubular steel, the pliancy of rubber webbing and foam rubber, and the stretch properties of some of the new fabrics. From these he developed a line of furniture that is sculptural and uniquely personal.

The first four chairs were specifically designed for contemporary machine production, although some handworkmanship is involved, and they clearly state this fact in their form and materials. In contrast, the chairs in Figures 137 through 140 are allied to handcraft traditions. The first two evolved from ancient Far Eastern and Danish methods. The handcrafted plastic chair is a bold, direct use of a new material, and the Mexican hand-foot seat is a humorous expression of an age-old interest in carving wood.

The cane chair (Fig. 137) is one of the many designs handmade by native craftsmen in the Far East. As is the case with the familiar Windsor chair, its designers are unknown. Its design evolved naturally through the experience of several generations of craftsmen working with materials they knew well. The result is a truly remarkable achievement. A framework of lightweight bamboo is ingeniously structured for strength and then wrapped with split cane. Seat, back, and sides are of woven cane. Not only is this chair shaped to fit the sitter's body, but it responds resiliently to different positions. Although its structure is evident, it is not emphatic because the seat, back, and sides are literally woven and bound together. The character of the cane chair is humble and unpretentious, its design unselfconscious and unaffected.

A Danish chair (Fig. 138) designed by Hans Wegner and made by Johannes Hansen, a cabinetmaker, demonstrates the collaboration that exists between designers and craftsmen in some European countries. This continuing traditional relationship accounts for the persistence of a handcrafted character apparent in certain European products, even though much of the work is now done by machines under the close supervision of craftsmen. As in the Barcelona chair, the parts are distinctly and systematically enunciated and are coherently related to each other and to the whole. The two chairs, however, are quite unlike each other in several important ways. In the former, the structural members that support the seat and back are continuous, curved steel bars of uniform width and thickness. In Wegner's chair, the upright legs and the horizontal seat, arms, and back are clearly differentiated from one another. Each part is shaped in accordance with its function. The legs are slender at the base, thicken to the point at which they are joined to the seat, and then diminish as they go up to support the arms and backrest. The seat, back, and arms are gently curved to fit the human body. Wegner chose wood as the basic material because it has long been favored for Scandinavian furniture, is pleasing to see and to touch, and naturally suggests the forms he had in mind. The result is a chair that integrates the old and the new in a design that satisfies modern taste for things minimal, elegant, and functional.

Aagard Anderson's chair (Fig. 139) was not intended to be a model for a salable, mass-produced line of furniture, but it is a creative exploration of the intrinsic character of a new man-made material, urethane foam. While it is being processed, urethane foam is a viscous substance that can be made to take almost any desired form. It can, for example, be worked and finished so that it somewhat unconvincingly imitates wood, as some furniture manufacturers are already doing. Anderson, however, was concerned with its distinctive fluidity, which seems always to be in the process of completing itself. Although the seat, back, and arms are comparatively simple and smooth, the globular masses supporting them are an agglomeration of intricately varied convolutions. Such projects may or may not have any immediate, practical application, but they offer original ideas in experimental forms and open new vistas of design possibilities.

left : 137. A cane chair, largely handmade in the Far East, has had widespread appeal for many years because it combines comfort, lightness, and low price with a pleasing and durable design.

right : 138. Hans Wegner's pull-up chair (1949) developed out of traditional Danish handcraft techniques and forms. Johannes Hansen, cabinetmaker.

below : 139. Aagard Anderson's experimental chair (1964) from Denmark exploits one of the potentials of poured urethane, a plastic foam. The Museum of Modern Art, New York (gift of the designer).

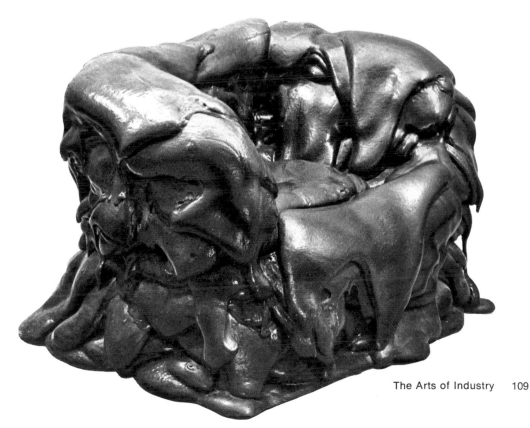

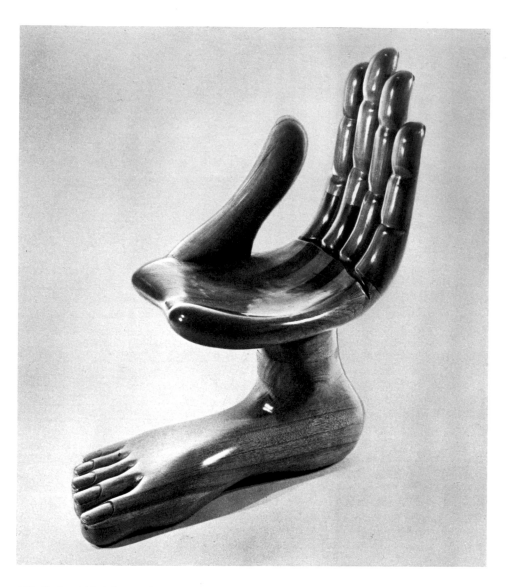

140. Pedro Friedeberg's foot-hand chair (1966), hand carved in Mexico from wood, is a surprising departure from conventional seating shapes.

The wood seat shown in Figure 140 represents a reaction to repetitive mechanization, fast-paced but uneventful living, and contemporary Scandinavian furniture design. Born in Italy while Mussolini was in power, the designer, Pedro Friedeberg, immigrated to Mexico to get away from regimentation. Unlike the other chairs in this series, his has a stalwart, crude vigor that is more closely related to massive pre-Columbian Mexican pyramids and carving than to most products of contemporary technology. It reaffirms the esthetic values of heavy, solid wood carved by hand, which has been neglected in today's preoccupation with lightweight efficiency. Although it offers some degree of comfort, it is primarily an unexpected, witty, sculptural form that can provide a focal point among other, less exotic furnishings.

The diversity of these eight chairs demonstrates that modern design need not be stereotyped. Their materials include steel and leather, rubber and plastic foam, and wood and cane. They express lean elegance, casual comfort, and sculptural grace, fluidity, and monumentality. They offer the individual consumer great freedom for expressing his own taste and design ideas.

Characteristics of Contemporary Industrial Design

Certain identifiable qualities distinguish the industrial arts of the third quarter of the twentieth century.

Diversity The most obvious characteristic of contemporary design is the diversity of approach. Never before have so many materials and ways of processing them been at man's command, and this challenges designers. Never before have there been such widespread buying power and such freedom of choice. The eight chairs discussed earlier were selected from hundreds now on the market.

Simplicity In spite of the many differences, there is a general trend toward restraint in external design (Fig. 141). As with our bodies, this simplicity often conceals a great complexity of inner working parts. Smooth surfaces, color in large areas, and minimal ornament, if any, emphasize basic forms. Unity and harmony overshadow variety and contrast, perhaps as an expression of our quest for comprehending a perplexing epoch. Figure 142 shows an electric desktop computer that works in the way large computers do but in a space of only 7½ by 19 by 24 inches. A clean, uncluttered cover protects the complicated working mechanism that sorts, computes, makes logical decisions, and then prints out the information on a roll of paper. The keys are clearly visible, shaped for comfort and convenience, and disposed in a pattern that is first of all efficient but also pleasingly balanced. It is an excellent example of the good design that is often evident in purely utilitarian objects when the designer has been able to express both mechanical and human functions.

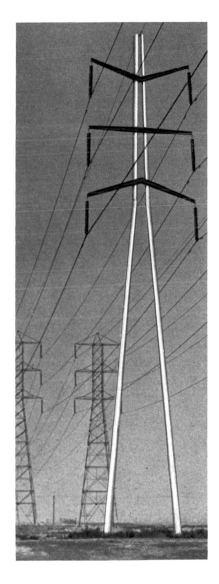

right : 141. Tapered steel tubing provides needed strength and allows great simplicity in the design of Southern California Edison's new 220 KV Double-Circuit Transmission Tower, which replaces the model in the background. Henry Dreyfuss & Associates, N. Diffrient, design consultant.

Geometry is a natural design element in machinery, but usually the human element is also taken into consideration, as in Figs. 142 and 143.

below : 142. The Programma 101 Desk-Top Computer (1967) is based on geometrical forms that have been modified to eliminate sharp edges that would intimidate the user.

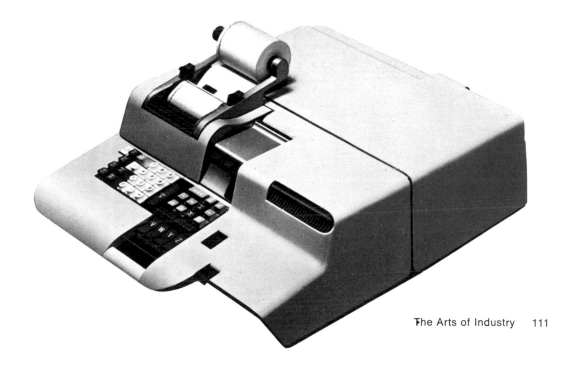

below : 143. In a steel-wheel road roller (1967), the circular rollers are joined together by slant-sided geometrical forms. Their slightly rounded angles humanize the contours.

Standardized modular furniture and equipment bring economy and unity.

opposite above : 144. A variety of components can be combined in a wall-to-wall storage and display installation using a minimum of floor space. Henry Robert Kann, architectural designer.

opposite below : 145. Borge Mogensen's sofas, chairs, and tables fit compactly together to save space. Although the pieces are not identical, they relate harmoniously to one another.

Implied motion   Activity often underlies surface quietness. We live in a dynamic age. While we do not often seek such vehement movement as that in the Baroque harpsichord, neither do we derive pleasure from objects that look inert. Each of the chairs previously discussed has its own rhythmic pattern, and the new transmission tower in Figure 141 has a quiet but compelling upward thrust, in contrast to the galvanic activity of the older model in the same illustration.

Approaches to Contemporary Industrial Design

Of the many approaches to form, three are dominant.

Geometrical Approach   The furniture and storage units in Figures 144 and 145 are based on geometrical modules, or units of measurement. Working on this system, a manufacturer can make many pieces of furniture from a relatively small number of parts. Because the storage units are dimensionally coordinated, purchasers can arrange and rearrange them in many orderly, space-saving combinations. Strictly geometrical shapes also occur in most dinnerware (Fig. 146) and in machines, such as the road roller in Figure 143, where precision is an indispensable requirement.

146. Designer Hans Theo Baumann took advantage of the geometrical precision of the cylinder in his THOMAS ABC tableware that stacks easily, safely, and economically. Bold contrasts of color and freely formed handles accentuate the simplicity of the shapes.

Sculptural Approach   The second approach to form leads to free-form sculptural shapes, such as those in the chairs designed by Mourgue, Platner, Anderson, and Friedeberg. These humanized shapes, reminiscent of our own bodies, can be almost infinitely varied, and their naturalness arouses sympathetic responses.

Modified Geometrical Approach   A great body of industrial design, however, falls into a third category in which angular forms are modified to permit an easy transition from one unit to another—a transition that brings a smoothly flowing quality. The effect is far less sharp than that which would have come from unaltered rectangles and much more natural. At the same time, it brings the feeling that underneath the sculptural contours lies the structural certainty of the right angle. This both strengthens the forms when seen by themselves and relates them to the rectangularity that characterizes most architecture and equipment today. The desktop computer in Figure 142 is composed of harmonious, smoothly interlocking forms that look comfortable and easy to use, desirable traits in objects that are meant to be handled.

In the competitive field of business, many products are designed to create new needs rather than merely to satisfy those needs of which the public is aware. This can lead to progressive innovations, and it can also put on the market numerous contraptions and gadgets that do little if anything to improve daily living. The desire to sell more and more frequently results in built-in or enforced obsolescence. In many fields, such as the automotive, new models are put out each year. Other fields, of which clothing and home furnishings are examples, may introduce two or more new lines in a twelve-month period. To keep sales high, only one of a number of possible improvements may be incorporated at any one time, thereby making a large number of products seem old-fashioned every year whether they are or are not functionally obsolescent. It is true, of course, that many new models perform better than their predecessors, and new designs are also needed to keep pace with fundamental changes in taste and the development of new materials (Pl. 13).

Even a casual survey of today's machine-made products will reveal that there are exceptions to every possible generalization. There is, for example, comparatively little variety in the appearance of kitchen stoves and refrigerators produced by competing companies, but the slight differences, referred to as "marginal differentiation," are accentuated in advertising. Although some textiles and wallpapers are unornamented, there are also many with rich patterns. And a few products are intentionally designed to have long, useful lives.

above : Plate 13a. New inventions bring forth new forms in industrial design. The Smith-Corona Mail Call TM is a cordless, miniature, transistorized tape recorder for producing "talking letters" by means of a cartridge half the size of a pack of cigarettes and which can be mailed in an ordinary envelope. The edges have been slightly rounded to make the units comfortable to hold, but the essentially geometric forms are sturdy and uncontrived.

right : Plate 13b. New materials are also influential in the design of products. The canoe in the foreground, 10′ long, weighs less than 50 pounds and is unsinkable because it is made of plastic that can be molded into lightweight, watertight forms. Howard Benjamin, designer. The sailboat, of fiber glass and polyurethane foam, 13′6″ × 44″, is sleek and buoyant and requires minimum maintenance. John Redfield and staff, designers. The shapes of both products are similar to older models made of different materials, but the forms have been inventively developed in response to the possibilities of the materials. California Design 10, Pasadena Museum of Art.

Plate 14. The handcrafted and manufactured articles reproduced here were chosen for exhibit at the California Design 10 show at the Pasadena Museum of Art in 1968. *Mini* is a vat-dyed painted linen and appliqué wall hanging (12 × 12′) by Ragnhild Langlet. The laminated walnut-rib chair was made by designer-craftsman Espenet. A do-it-yourself sculpture called *Sculptron 106* is the creation of Charles F. Ulrich, a limited production designer-craftsman. Buckminster Fuller designed the geodesic dymaxion light fixture (diameter 20″), which is made by Xavier Lanier as a do-it-yourself kit. John Caldwell's nested rosewood end tables are manufactured by Brown Saltman Company.

The Handcrafts Today

Seemingly doomed to extinction by the machine, the handcrafts have turned out to be hardy perennials with roots so deep in human nature that they give every indication of persistence. By the middle of the nineteenth century the protests against the ugliness of machine products, the disastrous unemployment of craftsmen, and the cities made ugly by factories and uncontrolled expansion led to the Arts and Crafts Movement. William Morris, its English founder, was an idealistic social reformer who envisioned an integrated society, well housed, working under good conditions, and producing beautiful handmade objects for everyday use. Viewed as a whole, the movement was unsuccessful because machine production had too many advantages to be abandoned. But it focused attention on good design, sympathetic use of materials, and the gratification that comes from handmade articles.

Today the handcrafts flourish at professional and amateur levels. From the hands of skilled craftsmen come many handsome objects (Figs. 147–149). Not aimed toward the common denominator of public taste, these one-of-a-kind works can be experimental and can be conceived and developed without compromise (Pl. 14). In an age threatened by stereotypes and conformity, these singular expressions are highly valued. Of great importance, too, is the influence of handcrafts on industrial design, as illustrated by the color reproduction in Plate 14. All the crafts provide an inexpensive way to explore new ideas that may later be adapted to machine production.

We should not overlook the personal satisfaction that amateurs get from making something entirely with their own hands. Handcraftsmanship, ranging from simple sewing to complex cabinetmaking, is a rewarding avocation. In public schools and colleges the crafts are recognized as creative disciplines, and many homes have workshops or hobby rooms. Books on the subject run into the thousands. Although this is not exactly what William Morris had in mind, he would undoubtedly have been pleased with the amateur craftsman's accomplishments, which are boons to mental health and to the individual economy.

Now that the machine has been domesticated and the handcrafts have again proven their usefulness, it is clear that they can exist side by side harmoniously.

left : 147. Oscar Bucher's handcrafted stoneware branch jar (1964) has a vigorous shape, emphasized by the two spouts and the roughly tooled texture.

center : 148. Dominick Labino's free-blown vase (1966) of green glass with trapped bubbles preserves the character of the molten material from which it was made. Collection the artist. (See also Pl. 24.)

right : 149. Kay Sekimachi's three-dimensional wall hanging (1966), handwoven of clear nylon monafilament, is an innovative handling of a new material.

150. In making a pin (1965), Resia Schor took advantage of the malleability of gold to produce a sculptural design, then backed it with sterling silver for strength.

Each makes its contribution, and although each contribution differs in certain important respects, the products are often markedly similar in appearance. This raises issues about honesty, sincerity, and imitation. It could be argued that industrial designers ought to avoid conscientiously anything resembling handcraft designs and that craftsmen should consciously, perhaps self-consciously, refuse to be affected by machine products. Such arguments have some validity, for in accentuating differences one gets variety and intensity. On the other side, if carried to extremes, these attitudes are hardly realistic. Few would criticize a skilled craftsman for reproducing with split-hair precision a dozen or a hundred or a thousand glass goblets to be used as sets. Why, then, look askance at machine-woven textiles that have pleasing variations simply because irregularity has been associated with handweaving? Here, again, it is necessary to get back to human needs, physical and spiritual, as the first concern. Both hand and power looms are available, and they perform as they are directed to. Neither has a "soul" of its own that dictates what it should do. This issue, however, is one on which there is considerable difference of opinion.

The Problem of Selection

Inevitably a considerable amount of money is spent on the industrial arts. For the consumer, the most pressing challenge is to select wisely from the bewildering variety that changes from day to day. Fads and fashions follow one another as rapidly as promoters can make them. Sometimes they emphasize newness, sometimes they stress a return to the past. Neither is a sound criterion for judgment. It has been remarked that we are "galloping consumers," and our period has been described as a "Kleenex culture" in which just about everything is disposable. Such things as paper napkins are intended to be used only once, but others, such as silverware, may be expected to last more than one generation.

Distinguishing between useful objects that have lasting interest and those of fleeting appeal requires serious thought and continued study, but it yields high dividends. Before making any purchase, it is wise to decide exactly *why* the object is wanted and *when*, *where*, and *how* it will be used. Questions to be asked and answered include the following: How well does it perform its utilitarian functions? How suitable are the materials, and how well have they been processed? How satisfying are the form, color, and texture? The answers to these questions, especially the last one, are subjective, because concepts of beauty vary greatly from person to person and from period to period. Evaluating the experience of others and oneself helps build a sound basis for judgment. In the long run, however, it is the total response of the individual consumer that is critically important.

Industrial Architecture

A phenomenon as significant as the Industrial Revolution should bring about a new kind of architecture, and it did. At first this new architecture consisted of nothing more than undistinguished factories and warehouses. Pathetically futile attempts were made to "beautify" these structures by appliquéing historic ornament —classical columns, a frosting of Gothic, Romanesque, or Renaissance embellishment—that had nothing in common with the structure or its uses. The "art" could have been stripped from the "engineering" with a chisel.

Then, to step up production, engineers began to design sensible, straightforward buildings that were adequately illuminated and ventilated but seldom beautiful. Countless experiments took advantage of new possibilities in architectural construction. Metal posts and beams together with new kinds of concrete and metal arches made possible spacious interiors with few interrupting supports or walls. Large areas of glass became feasible. The engineer, with his interest in function and materials, taught architects a much-needed lesson.

Some architects were ready to learn, and among them Walter Gropius was a leader. He designed a structure known as the Bauhaus (Fig. 152) to house a revolutionary program of teaching the arts. In this school, with its many studios and

Two contemporaneous workshops function well in their environment.

right : 151. A home factory in Cuernavaca, Mexico, shows the potter working outside his home with a primitive footpower potter's wheel.

below : 152. The epoch-making Bauhaus (1926) in Dessau, Germany, was designed to house a school that brought art and industry together again as they were in the past.

Distinctive, powerful forms expressive of their purpose have evolved in industrial architecture and, incidentally, have provided some painters with new subject matter (Fig. 154).

153. The Bull Run Steam Plant, built for the TVA in the 1960s, is a vigorous expression of power.

workshops, architects, craftsmen, and designers worked side by side with painters and sculptors to educate artists for a machine age. A primary aim was the re-integration of all of the arts, with emphasis on bridging the gap between art and industry. Artistic sensitivity was aroused and developed by projects based on the study of structural principles and the qualities of materials. Experiments led to the revelation of numberless potentialities. The effect, especially on industrial design and architecture, was enormous and continues to be a vital influence today.

The building itself was a landmark in modern architecture. The workshop, referred to as the "Glass Box," had walls almost entirely of glass to give abundant light and a great sense of spaciousness. When finished, it attracted worldwide attention, not because it was the first glass-walled building (London's Crystal Palace, for example, antedated it by almost seventy-five years), but because more than any of its predecessors it achieved a thoroughly satisfying sense of architectural design in glass and steel. The bold yet sensitive character of this early example of the International Style profoundly affected the course of modern architecture.

The designers of the TVA Bull Run Steam Plant (Fig. 153) were given a program quite different from that of the Bauhaus. Massive, comparatively inflexible equipment was to be kept in working order by a few skilled technicians and workmen. Although not innovative, as was the Bauhaus, the building has its own beauty, if beauty is regarded as a coherent interrelationship of functions, forms, and materials. Marked by decisive simplicity and vigor, the exterior is an abstract expression, not a literal description, of the power generated inside. The severity of the huge blocks of the buildings is punctuated by offset forms. In striking contrast are the rising, elongated coal conveyers, sheathed with ridged metal and boldly supported by steel-girder frameworks. The 800-foot-high chimney, one of the tallest in the world, indicates the tremendous size of this plant complex. The clean-cut patterns of lights and darks and the play of dynamic, thrusting forms with and against blocky masses produce a compelling composition.

There have also been notable advances in making the interiors of factories better places in which to work. The shapes of rooms and of machines and their surfaces have become more stimulating and satisfying. Bright colors replace drabness. In some oil refineries and manufacturing plants, red, blue, yellow, orange, and green create almost a festive atmosphere. Not only do these colors affect the employees' sense of well-being, but they help them do their jobs more effectively. Red, for example, warns of potential danger, and light hues improve visibility. Used according to a code, colors give immediate clues as to what each piece of equipment does.

Research is a big industry today. As centers for the development of new ideas, materials, processes, and products that will improve our environment and our economy, "think" factories call for a new kind of architecture. Typically they contain a complex of laboratories, computer rooms, private offices, and conference

154. Charles Sheeler. *Incantation.* 1946. Oil on canvas, 24 × 20″. The Brooklyn Museum, New York (Ella C. and John B. Woodward Memorial Funds). Sheeler's painting is a compelling statement of the purposeful and orderly complexity of industrial architecture.

155. The National Center for Atmospheric Research (1967) near Boulder, Colorado, is a workshop designed to facilitate scientific advances. I. M. Pei, architect.

spaces needed by scientists in their conduct of coordinated basic and applied research. The National Center for Atmospheric Research (Fig. 155), erected on a rugged site where the Great Plains rise up into the Rocky Mountains, has research facilities for four to five hundred meteorologists, astronomers, chemists, and air-pollution experts involved in solving one of mankind's most urgent problems.

When architect I. M. Pei started to design the center, he was challenged to create strong, elemental forms that would be in scale with the rugged majesty of the site. Offices and laboratories are efficiently grouped in tall, blocklike towers around a plaza and lower building for common-use activities. Corridors in these buildings are much more than hallways, for they have many alcoves and niches where scientists can pause for unscheduled exchanges of ideas. Vertical ribbons of windows accentuate the height of the towers; larger windows in conference rooms at the top of each tower are shielded by projecting hoods from the dazzling sun and violent winds of the mile-high setting. The boldly rectangular masses stand out resolutely against the mountainous background, but the dark reddish-brown aggregate used in the rough-finished concrete walls harmonizes with the mountains from which it came.

Architect Pei's authoritative design acknowledges the surroundings while embodying the excitement of contemporary science. This architecture is quite unlike that of the International Style of the Bauhaus, which at its extreme is based on the premise that the same or similar forms are equally appropriate on any site. Yet both approaches grew out of a similar concern for the fundamentals of basic shape and a respect for materials and structure. Both examples present new and eloquent images of their periods.

Today architects, craftsmen, designers, engineers, and scientists are avidly experimenting with new and old concepts of design, materials, and processes. Being at the utilitarian end of the scale, industry primarily seeks efficiency. Design and construction are shaped toward economical output, but ideas of efficiency and economy differ markedly from those held a century or even twenty years ago. Instead of concentrating wholly on machinelike capability, designers and manufacturers think of the total human economy that brings both profit and satisfaction to all. Industrial designers and manufacturers are influenced by and dependent upon the buying public. It is now up to the consumers, as well as the designers, to make certain that artistry and humanistic ideals keep pace with scientific advances.

Inevitably, there is some interaction and reciprocal influence between the arts designed primarily for use and those created for esthetic stimulation, because both are concerned with the manipulation of form.

above : 156. An experimental "lifting body" vehicle, the M2-F2 (1965) is one of many research models for manned spacecrafts that can penetrate the atmosphere and make a horizontal landing on the earth. Theoretical studies, begun in the early 1950s, soon centered on the half-cone shape as most efficient for adequate lifting power. The cone was blunted to reduce heating on reentering the atmosphere; fins and other control devices were added to give stability and maneuverability.

below: 157. Peter Voulkos. *Firestone.* 1965. Cast bronze and aluminum, 48 × 80″. Los Angeles County Museum of Art. When the American artist Peter Voulkos produced this sculpture, he concentrated all of his energy on searching for forms that would awaken our esthetic sensibilities. Utility was of no concern, but he was clearly aware of the contemporary technology that pervades our environment.

5 The Arts of Commerce

Commerce, the lifeline of industry, gives producers a means of familiarizing prospective consumers with their goods and services. It is a fast-changing, competitive field of selling to which artists make notable contributions and which has had, in turn, a definite impact on some contemporary painting (Pl. 15, p. 133), printmaking, and sculpture.

The central task of the arts of commerce is to focus interest on a product, service, or idea so that observers or listeners are favorably impressed and the buying urge is aroused. This is achieved through capturing the consumer's attention and then holding it long enough to make a forceful, lasting impression. Major divisions of the field include trademarks, packaging, and display; posters, advertisements, and television commercials; and commercial architecture. When all of these are coherently developed by one organization, they add up to an image of corporate identity.

Corporate Identity and Trademarks

In the field of marketing there is great rivalry among the many manufacturing firms in their struggle to attract the consumer's money. Many products, such as light bulbs or toothpaste, look so much alike that there is need for some differentiation

1894

1927

to help consumers tell quickly and unerringly just which one they are buying. Other commodities may be distinctive in themselves, but the identity of the manufacturer can help to indicate quality. And in these days of diversification, when one corporation may market a widely disparate array of goods or services, consumer acceptance can be transferred from one product to another by means of established images. The creation of a visible image is achieved through graphics, a trade term relating to the art of expressing ideas by means of lines, forms, colors, letters, and numerals. Images usually center around the company's trademark—the name, initials, and symbol that identify products and express corporate identity.

Trademarks are important devices because they can be used in countless ways. Their history has been traced back to potters' marks used over three thousand years ago to protect buyers from inferior merchandise. Today there is renewed interest in their effectiveness, and their creation is an exacting design assignment. Effective trademarks share the following characteristics:

■ They are a distinctive, easily remembered identification of *one* company. This tends to raise questions about such well-known abstract shapes as crosses, stars, and triangles unless they are inventively differentiated or unless they incorporate the name or initials of the producer, as has been done in the ALCOA trademark (Fig. 159). Historical examples of visual forms that have long been successful as associative images, albeit noncommercial, are the cross of the Christian religion, the Solomon's Seal of Judaism, and the blocky Red Cross of the international rescue agency.

■ They maintain their viability over long periods of time, but they can be slightly modified to meet new needs. Detailed, pictorial representations of products or of people in contemporary clothing are not suitable because the rapidity of evolving taste quickly dates them.

1929 VARIATION

1943

1955

The Herman Miller trademark is varied in its use and appearance.

below : 160. The symbol, an abstract white *M* that could also be an *H*, is used to identify one of the Herman Miller buildings from a distance.

bottom left : 161. The symbol alone, in dark gray, is used on the spine of the company's catalog. It is repeated on the cover in a distinctive, white-against-gray abstract pattern.

bottom right : 162. On letterheads and envelopes, the dark gray symbol is above the name and address.

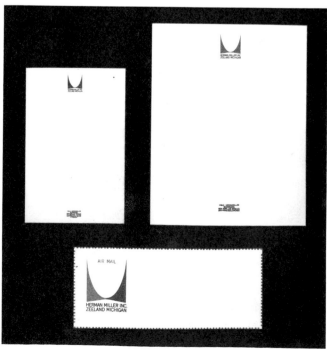

■ They are adaptable to many different applications (Figs. 160–163). In addition to letterheads and packaging, they are used on products, catalogs, small and large advertisements, the exteriors and interiors of offices and showrooms, and delivery vehicles. Although typically printed, they may be woven, embossed, transcribed into neon lighting, or transmitted as moving images on television. Colored trademarks are usually more easily remembered than are those in black and white, but the color used in the primary design should be selected so as to make an effective image when the design is reproduced in black, gray, and white, as in the IBM trademark (Pl. 16, p. 134).

■ They signify the diversity that characterizes the output of most large companies.

Some experts believe that using a symbol together with the name or initials of the manufacturer is redundant, but until thoroughly established through repeated use, abstract shapes alone seldom convey a specific message to many people. It is an endless challenge to designers to create lettering that is inherently related to the products, such as the letter *S* in the trademark shown in Figure 167, reminiscent of the curves assumed by the hoses that bring air to the scuba diver. Although trademarks are the keynote of corporate identification, other means include distinctive colors, repeated use of characteristic shapes, and the design of products that among themselves have a strong family resemblance.

Containers, Packaging, and Display

Early in this century grocery stores were a confusion of barrels, bins, and bags exposing peas, beans, brown sugar, and coffee to all who came in. Counters and shelves were lined with boxes and tubs, most of them wide open, holding soda crackers, dried prunes, and pickled herring. When a customer asked for a pound of soda crackers, the grocer reached into the cracker box, measured out a pound,

163. Furniture cartons must above all protect their contents, so the cautionary words and symbols are unmistakably clear. The trademark has been varied (white against a bold black rectangle, with the company's full name and address above) to provide a balanced arrangement on each side.

and stuffed them into a brown paper bag, all of which required that he handle the crackers several times. Customers knew little about the quality of the crackers because they did not know the brand, and their trust in the grocer's scales was all they had to go on to ensure quantity. Such simple means, of course, have their own colorful appeal and are occasionally revived in respect for the taste of nostalgia.

Today a great many products are sold in containers or packages, because, for the consumer, well-designed packages are readily identifiable, they increase the delight of a purchase, they often add some visual attractiveness to shelves and cupboards at home, and they offer the pleasure of opening a new package. Packaging reaches a high point in such products as perfume and jewelry, which are often bought as gifts (Fig. 178). In a more material vein, packages protect the product and can assure purchasers of the standard quality and quantity of their contents; also, they simplify the handling, storing, and use of the many things brought into the home or to a place of business. Merchants also appreciate the fact that packages are convenient to handle and store, take much less time to manage on the part of the sales force, and can improve a store's appearance. Manufacturers have learned that in stores, in newspaper and magazine advertisements, and on television, a distinguished package is a potent selling factor. Pop artists such as Andy Warhol (Pl. 15) have become aware of the profound but largely unobserved influence of commercial designs on our environment and have used them as subject matter in their paintings, prints, and sculpture.

The design of containers and packages becomes more challenging every year, as products increase in number and variety and as stores increase in size. The trend toward self-service stores has placed advertising and much of the selling burden that was formerly carried by the store's employees squarely on the shoulders of package designers. The shopper is often on his own in a perplexing environment crowded with merchandise and hurried customers. More frequently than not, there is no salesman nearby to give assistance. This has led some commercial artists to think seriously about how their packages can contribute to a more relaxed atmosphere and, at the same time, focus attention on the product being sold. Designers first study the product: what it is, what it does, and how it is used. They search for ways of expressing its special characteristics, and they keep in mind the fact that the package will be more effective if it bears a family resemblance to the other products the manufacturer puts on the market. This can be achieved by conspicuous use of the company's trademark, and by distinctive shapes, colors, and graphics. Because a package is seldom displayed alone, a major consideration is the visual impact that many of them stacked together will have. One device employed to achieve this goal is to use lines and forms that will be aligned horizontally, vertically, or even diagonally in an arresting, coherent composition (Figs. 166, 167).

164. A transparent acetate window tantalizes the prospective buyer by displaying the shining chromium automobile horn. The tiretread marks around the sides are composed of a closely set repetition of the words "Rallye Sports Horn," an ingenious use of evocative graphics. Edward C. Kozlowski Design.

top : 165. For one line of foods the name BIRDS EYE is superimposed on an appropriate symbol. The naturalistic representation of the contents is unequivocal; the weight and other pertinent information are clearly shown.

right : 166. Wizard air freshener containers use full-color photographs to quickly indicate their specialized scents or where they are to be used. When aligned on shelves, they make an effectively unified but varied display. Design by Miles R. Grove, Inc.

above : 167. SCUBAPRO's comprehensive design program includes containers and packages that feature the company name, a distinctive letter *S*, and the semiabstract depiction of a diver's head and headgear. Whether used singly or in different combinations, the packages are an effective identification. Porter and Goodman Design Associates.

1924 1925 1926

1928 1929 1930

Changes in taste are quickly reflected in packaging.
168. Six different compositions were used in a six-year period.

The package should be strong enough to protect its contents, but no heavier than necessary. Shapes that are easy to handle, to pack for shipping, to display on shelves, and to store in closets are desirable. In one sense, packages are posters that arouse the buying urge. But unlike posters, packages are three-dimensional and, therefore, are expected to carry their message when viewed from any angle or side (Fig. 168). The manufacturer's sales force may suggest how they could be best displayed, but the store's manager and clerks make the final decisions. Thus, it is up to the designer to make the package effective under varying circumstances.

There are many ways in which packaging can convey specific messages. One effective approach is a partially or entirely transparent container (Figs. 164, 178). Glass jars and glass bottles are still widely used, and plastic containers are becoming increasingly popular. Another selling device is a pictorial representation of the contents, as illustrated in Figure 165 and in countless canned fruits and vegetables, that tells immediately and more forcefully than words what to expect inside. But many commodities, such as air fresheners, are neither distinctive nor inviting in themselves. In such instances, the buyer is often tempted with an alluring representation or suggestion of the end result, as in Figure 166.

169. The 1960 design made an effective pattern when stacked on store shelves and was identifiable from the top or any side by the distinctive *K*. Saul Bass, designer.

Many products, such as disposable tissues, are not suitable to enticing pictorial representation, and for these a distinctive abstract design is often the best solution. The history of one company's packages, of which many billions have been sold, can be seen in Figures 168 through 170. The packages displayed in 1924 and 1925, legible but dull and with the name of the product visible on only one side, were superseded in 1926 by an incoherent design in which the pertinent information was scattered in a loose arrangement of unrelated shapes. Visually, the 1928 attempt is strong and straightforward, but it did not convey its message from the side most commonly seen. This was partially remedied in 1929. In 1938 an outstanding package was put on the market. A bold organization of dark blue and white rectangles that acknowledged the shape of the box made an immediately recognizable and esthetically satisfying pattern. The identifying name was clearly visible on the top and four sides. However, in 1960 it was replaced by an excellent but less distinctive design that was said to be "consumer tested and proved . . . modern, decorative . . . greater acceptance in all rooms of the house . . . especially appealing to women."

In 1966, it was decided to broaden the scope of appeal by a variety of designs. The rectangular composition of the 1938 box was retained in most of these, but it was softened with an overlay of curvilinear motifs derived from natural forms. The new containers are quite different in character from those of their rivals. They have a family resemblance, achieved through the consistent use of the trade name, both in its graphic form and in its placement, and through the basic similarity of the swirling patterns disposed on the geometrically divided backgrounds. Although the new packages do not stand out as boldly as did the 1938 design, they differ noticeably from other tissue boxes, and at the same time the unemphatic treatment allows them to fit into most home backgrounds in an unobtrusive manner.

170. The two most recent designs (1966) come in different colors, identifying the color of the tissue, and in patterns that vary with the size of the box. The name is prominent on all sides in order to identify the package in any stacking position. Raymond Loewy-William Snaith, Inc., designers.

The Arts of Commerce   131

171. Some of the rapt eloquence of India's traditional music is captured in a dramatic presentation of Ravi Shankar's head.

Record albums and the covers and dust jackets of books and magazines are specialized types of "packages." Although they, too, are point-of-sale advertisements, their contents differ in kind from such quickly consumed commodities as soups, crackers, and cosmetics. Magazines are usually kept around for only short periods of time, but records and books often retain their value and interest for many years. Whether of long-term or of temporary value, these types of packaging offer designers great range for graphic expression. Until a few decades ago, records came in sedate, somber-colored albums or jackets that were inconspicuously identified only by the names of the composers, the compositions, and the performers. Today, nearly all are distinctively differentiated from one another by a wide array of expressive colors and representational or abstract design. Often, as in Figure 171, the performer is featured, but this is only one of the directions that may be taken.

The "abstract" quality of much music makes nonrepresentational design especially suitable. In Figure 172, the idea of *Provocative Percussion* is conveyed by an emphatically active and unexpected visual composition. Ten large squares placed at different angles, organized into four major groups and linked by nine smaller squares, produce a lively, staccato, syncopated effect. *Persuasive Percussion* (Fig. 173) suggests a quieter approach. A broad band of small circles, densely and regularly aligned, establishes a secure background rhythm. Above this, a few freely spaced circles float spontaneously and playfully.

The simplest geometric shapes, if sensitively selected and organized, constitute an inexhaustible source of expressive designs.

left : 172. Squares positioned at varied angles convey a sense of excitement and activity.

right : 173. Regularly aligned circles produce a quiet, stable effect despite the few that freely float.

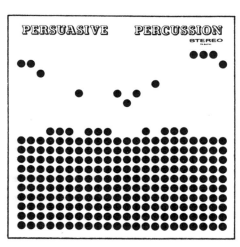

132

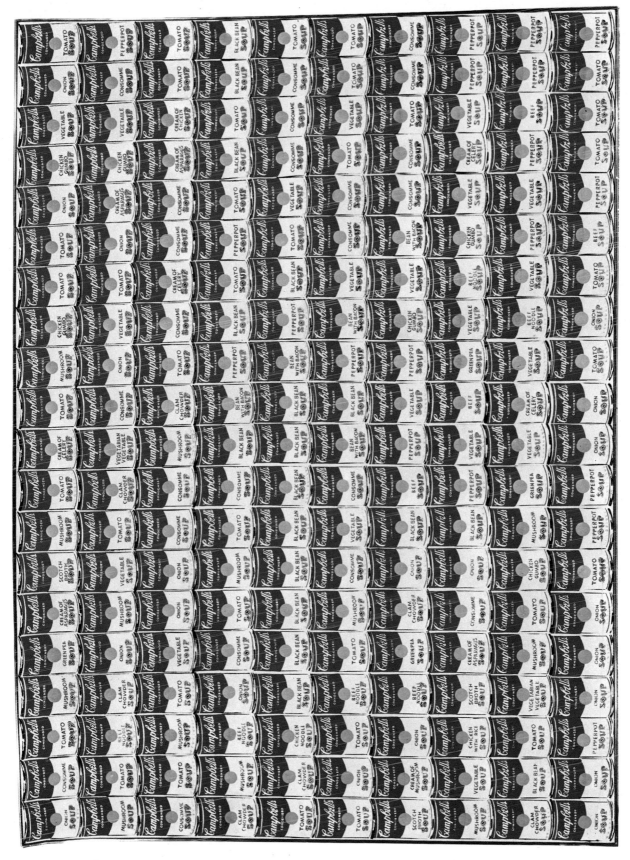

Plate 15. Andy Warhol. *200 Campbell's Soup Cans.* 1962. Casein on canvas, 6′ × 8′ 4 ¹/₈″. Collection John Powers, Aspen, Colorado. The design of containers and packages is a phase of commercial art that has interested some Pop artists as subject matter for paintings and sculpture. Warhol has used the theme of the visual repetitiveness of the commercial environment, in this case tiers of cans on the shelves of a supermarket; by placing this theme in a different context—that of art—he makes us consciously aware of our casual surroundings and of their possible impact.

Plate 16. The trademark of the International Business Machines Corporation is sufficiently well known that it alone identifies its packages and products. The simplicity of design allows it to be used in an over-all pattern that is varied solely by color changes. Although the company identification appears only on the face of the packages, the consistent use of blue side panels is a visual clue when the packages are stacked one on top of another.

Contemporary book and magazine covers are as diversified as their contents. Figure 174 graphically states the substance of the book by means of an intriguing example of optical illusion, and the pertinent information is printed on both the cover and the spine. Typical magazine covers emphasize what the journal contains. The cover for *Print* (Fig. 175) calls attention to a feature article on an exhibit at the Bettman Archive, a notable repository of old prints and photographs. Occasionally, however, a design that makes one wonder why it was used attracts attention, and this kind of design is most often found on specialized journals. The cover of *Architectural and Engineering News* (Fig. 176), repeated at alternating angles and in diminishing size so that each one fits within the other, creates an illusion of rapidly receding space, a perspective such as might be seen by looking straight up through the center of a high-voltage tower. The effect is strengthened by the use of violently contrasting colors—pure red and green—that are seasonally appropriate to the December issue.

Although the design of containers and packages, and of families of packages, acts as a point-of-sale enticement, producers know that more than attractive packaging is needed in order to sell their wares. That is why they turn to the field of advertising.

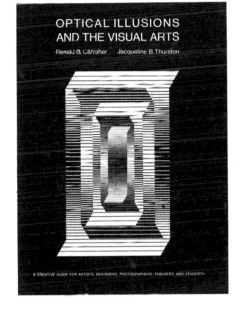

right : 174. A composition of forms that seem to move in and out of space is an eye-catching incentive to examine a book more closely.

below left : 175. The cover of *Print*, a graphic design magazine, bears a reproduction of *Panopticon I*, created by Peter Max as one of a series of posters advertising an exhibit of modern graphic design that is reviewed in the issue. Using several old prints as a motif, Max repeated them for a kaleidoscopic effect. Art director Andrew Kner.

below right : 176. The cover design of *Architectural and Engineering News* is appropriately geometrical and precise. Tony Palladino, designer.

Advertising

Nobody knows who made the first advertisement. Perhaps it was a potter thousands of years ago who identified his pots with a distinguishing trademark. We do know, though, that the Romans used advertisements and that in the sixteenth century posters and handbills appeared in England. Surprisingly, it was the clergy who in comparatively modern times made the first use of advertising notices to inform people of their services.

Today advertising is a national phenomenon of tremendous magnitude, and although it usually is a persuasive accelerator of business, advertising is costly. One full-page black-and-white advertisement in a magazine can cost upward of $50,000, and recently one company spent over $66,000,000 in a single year to tell consumers about its products. Advertising as we know it became firmly established about fifty years after the United States was first settled, but it did not get into full swing until the Industrial Revolution brought mass production on a large scale, railroads carried products great distances, and periodicals with nationwide circulations were read by millions of people.

It has been said that the best advertisements tell you *what, why, where, when,* and *how much.* In general this is true, but there are outstanding exceptions, examples of which are illustrated in Figures 177 and 178. The design of a new typeface was used by the advertising firm Sudler and Hennessey, Inc., to illustrate their services and the felicity with which the typeface might be used. The design of the advertisement itself suggests the answers to the first two questions; the next two are answered in the small block of information worked into the format at the left. An example of *pioneering* advertisements, it announces a new product and reminds potential customers of the company's services, but it discreetly leaves the last question open.

Used virtually without change since 1939, except for the gradual elimination of all captions, the advertisement for Chanel No. 5 has come to be a classic. While it tells *what* with unforgettable clarity, the other four pieces of information are left to the viewer to discover. Rarely do advertisements survive for so many years. This is a *reminder* advertisement and falls into the *prestige* category. It is starkly simple yet distinctive, and, therefore, stands out from the typically cluttered pages

177. A new typeface is appropriately introduced (c. 1962) by displaying its grace and commenting on its own versatility. Herb Lubalin, designer.

136

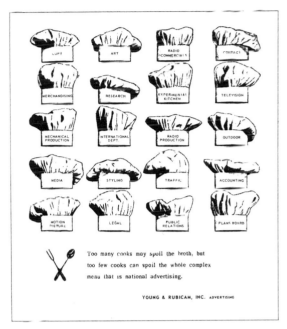

left : 178. Some advertisements remind us that a well-known product is still available (1968).

below : 179. An advertising agency's own bid for attention (c. 1950) depicts some of the many areas that are involved in this field.

of magazines and newspapers. Its effectiveness comes from long-continued, regular repetition. But it would not have been repeated this long had it not been effective in the first place.

Effective advertising is the result of a long process in which many experts participate in preliminary research, planning, and evaluation. The numerous areas that are involved in national advertising are shown in Figure 179, an ad produced by an advertising agency to illustrate the scope of its services.

Marketing and Psychological Research

Marketing research seeks facts about potential consumers and about the appropriateness of the possible advertising media— newspapers, magazines, radio, television. Some of the questions to be answered are:

- Who uses the product and why?
- How does the product come to the attention of the *consumer,* and how does it get into his hands?
- What factors, positive and negative, determine his choice?

Psychological research is concerned with the general and specific human reactions to varied kinds of display and copy. It has given advertising experts such findings as these:

Size increases attention by approximately the square root of the space used (for example, if the attention value of a full page is 100 percent, that of a half-page is about 71 percent and of a quarter-page about 50 percent). The Chanel advertisement, shown in Figure 178, is usually on a full page in such magazines as *The New Yorker.* This allows its highly restrained technique to be fully effective.

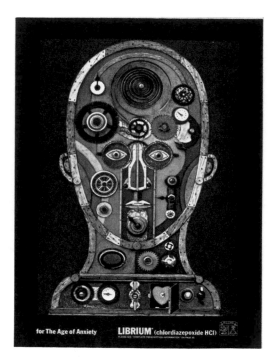

180. A fanciful, mechanized transcription suggesting the intricacies of the human head is a provocative image for publicizing a tranquilizer (c. 1964).

Position is important. The first and last pages of periodicals get most attention. Right-hand pages are preferable to left-hand pages. If less than one page is used, the outer column captures more attention than the inner column, and the top more than the bottom.

Movement, suggested by illustrations and layout, invades the readers' consciousness quickly and deeply. The harmonious, unified, but varied and striking rhythms of the Sudler and Hennessey advertisement (Fig. 177) would be effective at almost any size that was legible and in most positions.

Color catches the eye, but it should center the readers' thoughts and feelings on the product, service, or idea for which the advertisement was created. This is a fundamental point, for the advertisement will fail if its color merely attracts attention to itself.

Contrast, *unexpectedness*, and *uniqueness* are almost always effective for a time at least, although they may not hold up under repetition. The presence of springs, wheels, buttons, and gauges on the shape of a human head and shoulders is certainly unexpected, as Figure 180 reveals. As an expression of what a head can feel like in the "Age of Anxiety," this unusual image is, with a minimum of words, quite telling in its pictorial suggestiveness of the condition that the medicine Librium is for.

Planning the Advertisement

After the preliminary study of marketing and psychological factors, the next step in creating advertising is planning an advertisement or an entire promotional campaign. A theme or an idea, in both text and illustration, is developed from the research results and out of the advertising experts' imagination and ingenuity. Anything that is extraneous or irrelevant or that diverts interest from the basic idea weakens an advertisement just as it would weaken a painting, a statue, or an architectural structure. It is somewhat easier, however, to weed out the unnecessary elements in advertising than it is in other art media because the aim is single and simple: to sell. To succeed it must capture attention, arouse and hold interest, make a lasting impression, and lead to the action deemed desirable by the man who pays the bill. The final step is *checking the effectiveness of the advertising* in selling products, services, or goodwill.

Posters

A form of advertising predating the newspaper, the poster has the unique function of catching the attention of people who are themselves in motion. To do this it must be both clear and distinctive in order to effect and persuade one even at some distance. Four notable posters from England, Switzerland, and the United States (Figs. 181–184) present their messages in markedly different ways. If the poster proclaiming "Come on the Telephone" were located, in its full size and colors, along your path, it would affect you in many ways. Its brief, urgent message would remind you of that important means of communication, the telephone. You would think of what the telephone can do because the designer, E. McKnight Kauffer, centered attention on the handiness of the telephone and the magical ease with which it carries voices over great distances. This poster might make you decide to install another extension in your home or to put in a call at the nearest pay phone, but its primary purpose is to bring to mind again what a wondrous invention the telephone is. Advertising of this type is often appropriately called *reminder* advertising.

Vigorous, clear, and simple, this poster can be visually grasped and understood at a glance. It can also be seen repeatedly without losing its impact because it is both strong and subtle. An emphatic element, the telephone, is thrust into the left side of the poster as though it were being handed to the viewer. This movement is carried downward at the right with the words "Come on the Telephone." There are many ways of looking at any worthwhile design, and thus this poster could also be analyzed in the following way: An emphatic vertical is held above a sturdy horizontal, and these are brought together in a triangular composition by the diagonals of the wrist and of the words "Come on the." It is difficult to imagine a more simple basic design. What Kauffer did with it is another matter. Although immediately recognizable, the illustration is suggestive rather than representative. The hand and wrist are almost contained within a form as rigidly angular as the blocks of letters—but notice the subtle shading that gives the hand life and motion, and the thumb that escapes through the boundaries to point toward the first word of the sentence. Motion is further suggested by the accurately specific outline of the tele-

Effectiveness in posters can be achieved in many ways, as shown in Figs. 181–184.

181. E. McKnight Kauffer employed a simple, dynamic design (c. 1934) to project a forceful idea.

phone that overlays and pulls forward the expressive but generalized black shape behind it. This progression from the specific to the general is carried one step further in the vague, cloudlike shapes behind the hand and phone. They evoke associations of things far away, yet allow each observer to make his own interpretation. From the specific and commanding sentence to the intentionally amorphous shapes, this poster is addressed to the viewer. It is at once specific and unconfining, as is the service it advertises.

The second poster transports one to Pontresina, a sunny valley in the Swiss Alps filled with spring flowers (Fig. 182). At first glance the poster looks completely naturalistic. So hirsute is the hat, so glistening the edelweiss, and so hard and shiny the sunglasses and pick that through his eyes alone the viewer can sense in his fingertips the contrasting textures. Gay flowers and warmth where the climbers are resting and, just beyond, snow and rocks that almost touch the sky suggest an exhilarating paradox near the top of the world. With material such as this, it is no wonder that Herbert Matter, the designer, took nature as his inspiration, but he was not slavishly literal. He selected, organized, emphasized, and subordinated his images so that the underlying idea makes a vivid, lasting impression.

The art of the poster enjoyed a revival of interest during the 1960s, encouraging participation by many more artists. Frank Stella, well known for his hard-edge, geometric paintings, designed the poster for the Lincoln Center Festival (Fig. 183). Concentric semicircles of gay color roll down from the top of the poster to the word "Festival," drawing attention to the message spaced across the bottom. The movement of the interrupted arcs of color has a dancing, syncopated rhythm appropriate to the theme. The five semicircular compositions suggest the several performing arts featured at the festival, and, linked together, they signify the interrelationships possible among arts included in a single festival.

The rock-pop music of the 1960s has engendered new styles in posters, as in Figure 184. Although it is reminiscent of Art Nouveau design of the turn of the

right : 182. Herbert Matter's poster (c. 1951) catches attention with its brilliant naturalism and enforces its message with well-selected, inventively organized subject matter.

opposite left : 183. Frank Stella's pure geometric forms (1967), festive in color for the most part, create a buoyant but decisive design that draws attention to the pertinent information. (See also Pl. 45, p. 379, and p. ii.)

opposite right : 184. Wes Wilson incorporated the necessary information within an entwined, densely packed composition (1967) that compels notice but requires scrutiny to decipher.

century, its particular amalgamation of verbal message and pictorial content is a unique approach. Instead of clinging to the time-honored, valid, but somewhat tired convention of decisive clarity, Wes Wilson, the designer, explores the involvement that near-illegibility arouses. Two reverse curves fit around each other. The first curve conveys in barely discernible graphics and in eccentric phrasing the information that the Byrds, Moby Grape, and Andrew Staples may be seen at Winterland on Friday, March 31, and Saturday, April 1, for $3, and on Sunday, April 2, at 7 P.M., for $2, at Fillmore Auditorium. The other curve contains a fanciful black-and-white representation of some birds. The poster gives all the information about the performance, but in a form that involves the viewer only if he is really interested. It is taken for granted that anyone who bothers to unriddle the message already knows where the Fillmore and Winterland are in San Francisco. The swirling, elusive design in red, blue, black, and white gives, as far as possible on a flat plane, some of the psychedelic sensation of the light-and-color displays that often accompany rock concerts.

Each of the posters just discussed grew from an idea in which there was a distinctive aspect of the service advertised. Each artist created a design that vividly expressed what he wanted to communicate, and each design is quite different. The first is simple, strong, and semiabstract; the second is realistic and intricately detailed; the third is completely abstract, but striking and lively; while the fourth unifies a complexity of semiabstract, semirealistic shapes. The poster is an art form that offers a limitless range of expression to the imaginative designer.

Television Titles and Commercials

The newest form of advertising, television program titles and commercials introduce actual movement in time, a captivating device of considerable consequence. Program titles attempt to arouse the viewer's interests, to give them information,

141

and to hold their attention until the program starts. Giving the designers much more scope than do motionless advertisements, they are uniquely suited to the medium. They are often fast-paced, disjunctive sequences that gradually build up into a recognizable image, and then they may or may not rapidly disintegrate and perhaps build up again in a somewhat different pattern. Because they are never static, they encourage people to stay around to see what is going to happen. At the same time, the changing designs *can* have a stimulating esthetic effect.

Two illustrations show some of the possibilities. Figure 185 is built on sequential patterns of four letters, *P*, *O*, *S*, and *T*. The designs gradually become more dense until they fill the screen. Then the letters grow larger and are more scattered until, finally the name of the program appears. Bernard Lodge, the designer of *Doctor Who* (Fig. 186), used electronically created patterns that coalesce into an identifiable image. Sequences of this type are particularly appropriate in that the patterns themselves are produced by light.

With the advent of color, the range possible for design has broadened considerably. Television has been credited as being one source of the trend toward more

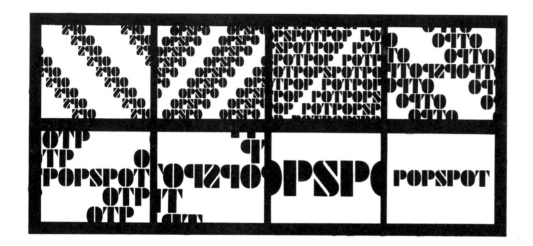

above : 185. A title sequence for a television program is composed of the letters of the program's name in varying sizes and patterns that rapidly appear and disappear on the screen. John Stamp, designer and director.

right : 186. A sequence of light patterns that could only be created electronically suggests the mystery and eeriness of the television program. Bernard Lodge, designer.

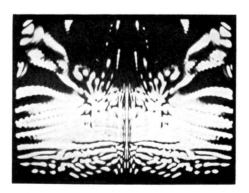

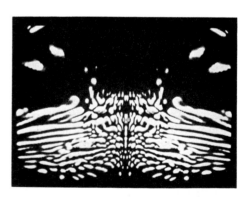

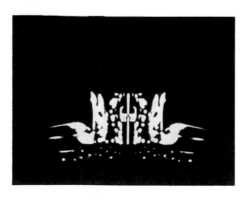

187. The Millinery Shop In eighteenth-century Williamsburg, Virginia, is set back and raised four steps above the ample brick sidewalk. A modest sign and two oval plaques depicting women's hats provide sufficient identification.

colorful clothing and interior design. Program titles and commercials in particular have used bright hues to add sparkle to their messages. Often changing or pulsating colored light intensifies the action, and the almost psychedelic effects of stroboscopic lighting are used with force and imagination.

Commercial Architecture

In the twentieth century, commercial architecture has undergone a revolution. The first stages were little more than face-lifting and "brightening up" old stores and offices. Ornament was scraped off; fresher colors were used; illumination was improved. Sometimes old equipment was rearranged or perhaps replaced by what seemed more up-to-date. But, with few exceptions, these changes were rightly called "modernization"; they did not really meet new needs. Later, the many problems connected with store and office design were freshly studied in the light of contemporary human needs and habits. As with the home and the city, new solutions emerged.

Eighteenth-Century Williamsburg

The Millinery Shop (Fig. 187) in Colonial Williamsburg is a handsome building, smaller in size and more humble in purpose than the Governor's Palace (Fig. 50), but imbued with the same spirit and built from the same materials. It is set back from the ample brick sidewalk and raised four steps above it in a reserved manner. A modest sign and two oval pictures emphasizing women's hats tell the stranger what this building is. But almost everybody in eighteenth-century Williamsburg knew what it was, and it had little competition. It is a friendly, tranquil, nonassertive structure that fulfilled its function in its own time and place.

In many respects, the Millinary Shop differs markedly from the commercial enterprises of the nineteenth and early twentieth century, with their brash, hard-sell attempts to stand out blatantly from their environment. More recently, however, merchandisers have begun to sponsor structures that are compatible with their surroundings, even though each one is distinctively individualized.

Frank Lloyd Wright's design for the V. C. Morris store (1949) in San Francisco is a distinct departure from the trend toward making store exteriors into gigantic display windows.

left: 188. The massively solid, brick exterior expresses stability and dignity and lures one inside with the promise of richness and surprise.

right: 189. The interior is voluminously spacious yet has the intimacy appropriate for the display of small, costly objects.

A Shop without Windows and a Bank with Glass Walls

When built, the V. C. Morris store and the Manufacturers Hanover Trust Company's building (Figs. 188–191) were pioneer statements of what commercial architecture could be in the mid-twentieth century, and they still stand as enduring landmarks. In designing the Morris store, Frank Lloyd Wright soared far above the rules that tie lesser men down. And in the Manufacturers Hanover Trust Company building, architects Skidmore, Owings, and Merrill went so far beyond stereotypes that the bank has been called a "crystal lantern." At that time, stores without display windows were rare, and banks with glass walls were virtually unprecedented. Both were surprising, a quality especially valuable in commercial art, but neither of these buildings depends only on unexpectedness.

Situated on a very short and narrow street in San Francisco, the Morris store presents a great wall of golden-yellow bricks. Although not large in size, it is monumental in feeling. Elegant and substantial, it has no need to shout its wares. No sign tells what it is, for with an exterior as distinguished as this, no applied advertising is needed. But the brick-and-glass archway arouses interest and invites exploration. The exterior announces a theme of circles in squares as simply and boldly as the opening measure of Beethoven's Fifth Symphony states its first great theme. Inside, this theme is magnificently developed. Within the confines of a cube, a spiral ramp carves the space with a powerful singleness of purpose. Without diverting too much attention from the main floor, it leads up to the circular balcony—and, visually, up to the ceiling. This ceiling of luminescent plastic bubbles, suspended from above so that it floats between the walls, is a disciplined flight of fancy that inspirits the whole interior with gaiety. The rectangularity characterizing the floor and many of the cabinets throws into prominence the use of numerous variations of circular forms: cylinders, discs, holes, domes, and spheres.

As one moves through the store, led on but not coerced by the organization of the interior, the integration of beauty and usefulness becomes evident. One notices the predominant gold, gray, and white color scheme against which dark walnut cases and tables act as foils for the glass, silver, china, and linens. The ramp allows the visitor to participate physically in the circular movement. There are tables and chairs for comfortable sitting while one experiments with table settings either before or after looking at the objects on display. Although the store seems uncluttered, it offers an astonishing amount of display and storage space. Because the displays cannot all be seen at once, the visitor is not overwhelmed, as in a typical store, by seemingly endless rows of cases and shelves. Instead, he sees a little at a time, often in quite small spaces, which gives a feeling of homelike intimacy and minimizes shopping fatigue. All of this, said the architect, "transforms the visitor into a dignified customer."

The Manufacturers Hanover Trust visually opens a corner on New York City's crowded Fifth Avenue. It is a five-story structure screened from the weather by sheets of glass held in slender, polished, aluminum frames. These walls do not support the building but are suspended from the roof, which in turn is supported by the widely spaced, slender piers visible in the photograph of the interior. A bank building with walls of transparent glass functions well. The interior is pleasant for customers and employees. Bank deposits are insured, burglar alarms have been perfected, and robbery in full view of the public would be foolhardy. Perhaps most important, banks today sell services more than they sell old-fashioned security, and the Manufacturers Hanover Trust advertises its services by letting passersby see them in action.

The Manufacturers Hanover Trust Company building (1954) in New York City, remarkable for its assured, forthright design, is as open and inviting as the Morris store is closed and intriguing. Skidmore, Owings, and Merrill, architects.

above : 190. The exterior walls of glass and metal are reduced to their simplest structural terms but are beautifully proportioned.

below : 191. The interior continues the feeling of uncluttered space announced by the exterior. Surfacing materials are bathed by light from luminous ceilings.

Even though almost all of the interior is visible from the sidewalk, there is no letdown when one steps inside. The promise of light and spaciousness is handsomely fulfilled. The first two floors of this bank are for customers, a fact that might have been surmised from the exterior. Inside and outside, the exterior walls are unbroken for two stories; the second floor is a mezzanine that stops about 8 feet from the exterior walls and whose edges are guarded only by low but firmly fastened planting boxes. An escalator makes the ascent quite effortless. Almost everything inside has the beauty of highly polished precision. Pale yellow, corrugated plastic ceilings diffuse a soft and even radiance throughout the area. Some walls are smooth plaster painted in light, spacious colors, while others are of rich brown teakwood, gray marble, or black granite. Creamy figured marble from Italy, black-brown ebony from Makassar, and lustrous stainless steel are combined in the writing tables and the long counters.

Harry Bertoia's 70-foot gold-colored sculptured screen is the one dramatic exception to the clean-cut geometry elsewhere. Innumerable sheets of metal are suspended from a slender framework, much as the glass walls are suspended from the building's structural framework. But no two units of the screen are identical. Some are merely textured, others are imaginatively bent, cut, and modeled. Although predominantly rectangular, the individual units vary slightly in size, shape, and angle. Whereas the building is regular and precise, the screen is intricate and irregular. In the words of Lewis Mumford, ". . . it humanizes these quarters . . . mainly because it suggests something frail, incomplete, yet unexpected and defiant of the rational statement, and thus lovable, a note that is not audible in most of the representative architectural expressions of our time."

Different as these two buildings are in many respects, they have a surprising number of similar characteristics. Most important, from the commercial point of view, is the fact that both structures are distinctively self-identifying, and they both fulfill their initial promise from the first big ideas animating their initial conception down to the smallest details of design applied to the purposes of function and delight. From the artists' point of view, both structures offer esthetic experiences alive with a creative vigor that communicates directly to those customers and employees with the sensibility to respond to the excitement of moving through space, form, color, texture, and light.

A Flexible Showroom

The Rosenthal Studio-Haus in Düsseldorf (Figs. 192–195) which is tightly packed in between other shops, has a narrow front of about 46 feet on a busy thoroughfare. The clearly designed, legible sign immediately identifies the store, but the distinctive character of the form, space, and materials, and the restrained display would be sufficient identification, for they communicate the fact that the merchandise is not ordinary.

A remarkable feature of the store is its flexibility. All of the standardized, lightweight equipment can be easily rearranged in many different ways. Suspended from ceiling tracks laid out on a module roughly 28 inches square, Plexiglas and wood panels, as well as doors and walls of showcases, can be placed almost anywhere. The entire store can be a recessed display window (Fig. 194) or a deep display area arranged close to the street (Figs. 192, 195). In the second arrangement, three square showcases stand in front of a long, rectangular case, with the rest of the store visible through transparent walls and doors. The passerby who is intrigued by recesses, nooks, or crannies is drawn first into the show-window area and then into the store proper. The only stationary elements in the sales area are the side and back

The Rosenthal Studio-Haus (c. 1966) in Düsseldorf, Germany, is adaptable, distinctive and cleanly detailed.

top : 192. The sign incorporates the Rosenthal trademark with the crown that identifies their fine porcelain goods. The clear Plexiglas cases display some products and reveal another showcase behind, as well as the interior of the store.

left : 193. The interior is uncluttered by counters or dividing walls. Articles on open shelves and tables are accessible to the customers.

below left : 194. Another easily arranged variation of the floor plan has the showcases stepped back from the street.

below right : 195. A circulation path around the entire sales area is a third possibility.

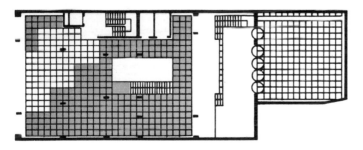

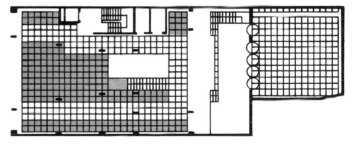

walls, a pool, and a Plexiglas stairway that takes customers to the second-floor sales room. Lighting is equally flexible. In the ceiling there are 668 reflector units, each of which is controlled by its own switch, and these are supplemented by luminous boxes that radiate light upward or downward in shelves and cases. To concentrate attention on the diversified merchandise, the architectural background was kept simple. Basalt lava tiles, neutral in color, are the basic flooring material, but rugs can be placed where wanted. Aluminum, Plexiglas, and naturally finished wood comprise the cabinets and shelving. Curtains can be drawn to produce soft backgrounds or subdivided areas. The Rosenthal Studio-Haus has an atmosphere of polished restraint appropriate to the quality of its wares, while at the same time it is architecturally open, airy, and versatile, giving the store a unique quality.

Shopping and Commercial Centers

In the eighteenth century, when there were no automobiles and most shoppers traveled short distances on foot, the main street of Williamsburg was an efficient commercial area. Although all of the shops had the same architectural character, each one stood freely on its own plot of ground and was identified by a nonassertive sign (Fig. 187). But conditions have changed. In many communities, the distance from homes to shopping areas is very much greater than it was for the eighteenth-century residents of Williamsburg. Family cars and inefficient public-transportation systems bringing hordes of shoppers into already overcrowded cities have led to exasperating traffic congestion. Today we are trying to cope with this problem in three major ways: by planning neighborhood centers near homes, by building shopping centers in outlying districts, and by revitalizing downtown areas.

Lake Anne Village Center   A refreshing example of the small neighborhood center is the Lake Anne Village Center at Reston, Virginia (Fig. 196), which was discussed in Chapter 2. Located within walking distance of most of the homes in this community, the center consists of a pedestrian plaza surrounded on three sides by stores for day-to-day shopping, integrated with offices and apartments. The fourth side is open to a refreshing view of Lake Anne. A sculptural group, sturdy enough for people to sit on and for children to play around, provides a focal point in the expanse of open space. It is a natural gathering place that brings people together in a casual, friendly way while they shop for routine needs.

196. Washington Plaza in the Lake Anne Village Center (1965) at Reston, Virginia, brings together in a pleasant, open setting the convenient shops and services needed by residents of the area. Whittlesey, Conklin, and Rossant, architects.

The NorthPark Shopping Center (1966), Dallas, Texas, is based on the premise that accessibility, convenience, order, and pleasure attract customers more powerfully than chaotic competition. Harrell and Hamilton, and Kevin Roche of Eero Saarinen Associates, architects. Lawrence Halprin and Associates, landscape architects.

top : 197. The strong Texas sunlight creates juxtapositions of light and shadow on the bold, geometric exterior forms.

above : 198. The air-conditioned interior malls and plazas on which the shops face were designed as an environment in which people could enjoy physical comfort and visual stimulation.

right : 199. A band of semicircular projecting bays dramatically contrasts with the basic rectangularity of the structure.

NorthPark Shopping Center   Located in a 94-acre superblock 5 miles from downtown Dallas, NorthPark Shopping Center (Pl. 17 and Figs. 197–200) is a regional complex serving the city and the surrounding suburbs and was planned to make shopping a leisurely, rewarding event. The major unit is a three-story, L-shaped structure that houses three large department stores and about a hundred smaller shops. To unify this diversification, the architects decided to treat the exterior as a monumentally simple composition of decisive, rectangular masses that are activated by many projecting, receding, and overhanging elements. White brick, cast stone, and concrete are the materials chosen for the exterior, and their use is repeated inside, in the courts and malls providing entrance to the stores. Display windows are all framed with bronze-colored, anodized aluminum, but the shops are clearly differentiated from one another by brick pillars or columns and by individualized signs and displays. As can be seen in the plan (Fig. 200), interior circulation is handled by two long, air-conditioned malls that are punctuated by a series of plazas.

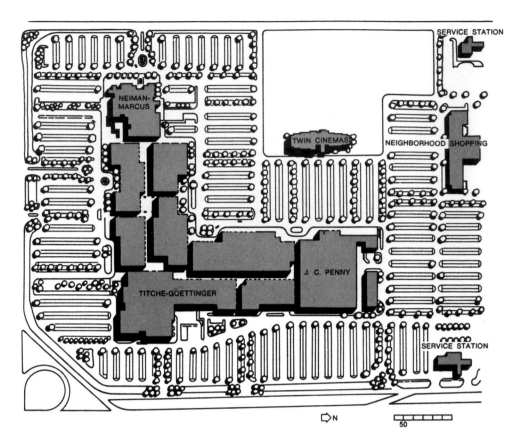

200. A schematic plan shows the many entrances from the parking lots and the relation of the malls and plazas to the shops.

This sequence of expanding and contracting spaces is strengthened by changes in floor levels and ceiling heights to provide a stimulating spatial experience. Large skylights flood the public areas with natural light during the day and artificial illumination at night. Benches, fountains and pools, trees and masses of flowers humanize the expanses of masonry and glass (Pl. 17).

Parking lots with spaces for 6000 cars surround the major unit, but the depressing, confusing atmosphere of most parking areas has been mitigated by planting trees and shrubs that subdivide the space into more than twenty smaller units. These have been arranged so that no car is more than 350 feet from one of the nine entrances into the mall. Twin cinemas, two service stations, and neighborhood shopping facilities are located in separate buildings. Sufficient land has been reserved for office and medical buildings, apartments, and recreational facilities to be built in the future. The development of this center required extensive cooperation among the owners, architects, consultants, and tenants to achieve a unified, vital environment that would be esthetically satisfying as well as commercially successful.

Independence Mall and Market Street East   Two segments of the plans for the redevelopment of Philadelphia proposed under the leadership of Edmund N. Bacon, the executive director of the Philadelphia City Planning Commission, are Independence Mall and Market Street East. For many years, civic leaders in Philadelphia have been concerned with the acute need for revitalizing the city's core and have studied the many problems pertaining to such a mammoth project. Nearly four million persons live within a thirty-minute drive of this section. Regional rail, bus, and subway lines and expressways focus on the area, but they are poorly coordinated. Streets are congested, many buildings are obsolete, and commercial activities have declined.

above : Plate 17a. In the North-Park Shopping Center (1966) in Dallas, Texas, stores open in a friendly way through large sliding glass doors onto the circulation mall. Stepped-down reflecting pools, pyramidal fountains and planting boxes, and round tubs for seasonal displays of flowers add interest and color to the predominantly beige, gray, and white interior street. Eero Saarinen Associates, architects; Lawrence Halprin Associates, landscape architects. (See also Figs. 197–200.)

left : Plate 17b. the Neiman-Marcus store exhibition hall in the NorthPark Shopping Center has winglike canopies of white stretch fabric, designed by architect Charles Forberg, that reduce the scale of a large, cavernous space intended for special art and merchandise exhibits. Eleanor Le Maire Associates, interior designers.

Plate 18. The Fifteenth Street subway garden in Philadelphia is an example of the possibilities inherent in the revitalization of cities. The common materials of concrete and metal have been given forms that delight as well as fulfill their primary functions of utility. Graceful stairs arch down from the upper plaza to the subway level mall, and both areas are brightened and given a human context by the use of fountains, sculpture, and plants. Utescher, sculptor. (See also Figs. 201–204.)

The varied solutions for revitalizing different areas generally aim to reinforce major activity centers in their present locations. Many of these are still proposals for the future, but some are underway (Pl. 18). Around Independence Hall (Figs. 201, 202) numerous buildings in a formerly blighted neighborhood have been torn down and replaced by a large green mall that opens up this section of the city and focuses attention on the historic buildings at one end. In the areas bordering on the mall, new buildings are going up that will reinforce the dignity and significance of this prestigious area.

The Independence Mall area of Philadelphia has undergone intensive renewal.

left : 201. Before the improvement was begun, a jumble of rundown buildings and unsightly parking lots did little to enhance Independence Hall or to attract people to this section.

below : 202. After the work was completed (1966), a three-block-long mall opened up a section of the city, providing a suitable setting for this historically and architecturally important building. Two large, usable masonry structures on either side have been preserved, and new ones are rising along the periphery of the mall.

153

The most concentrated and comprehensive of the redevelopment projects is that proposed for the main downtown commercial area centering on East Market Street. This major section of the core city, stretching from Independence Mall on the east to the City Hall on the west, contains four large department stores, many small shops, and innumerable small businesses, interspersed with office buildings, open parking lots, and parking garages. The latest in a series of constantly evolving plans for this complicated enterprise are shown in Figures 203 and 204.

The Market Street East Plan (Fig. 204) is based on the need for integrating the primary means of transportation with the retail, commercial, and parking facilities of the area, while at the same time providing a more human environment. The complex, ingenious scheme would transform Market Street East into a pleasant shopping

203. A map of the central section of Philadelphia shows Independence Mall running north and south along 6th Street, linked to a series of other open areas; City Hall set on a large landscaped plaza on Broad Street; and between the two, the four-block spine of Market Street East, with ramps leading off to the ring of highways that surround the area.

BROAD

13th

12th

11th

10th

9th

8th

7th

6th

WALNUT CHESTNUT MARKET ARCH RACE

N.

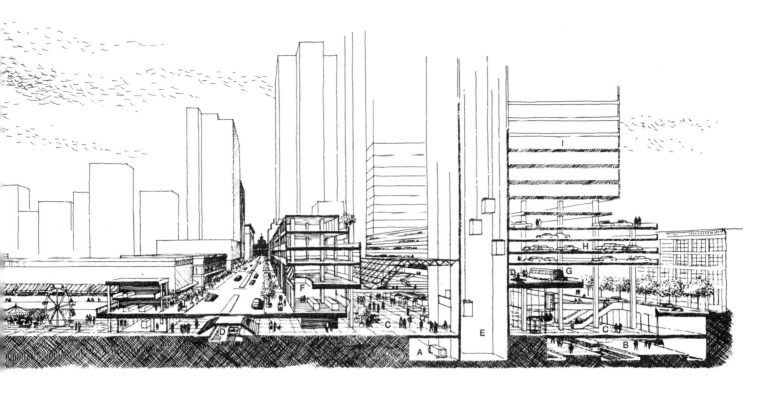

artery by diverting buses, trucks, and parked cars into a multiple-level, multiple-purpose spine running through the section to City Hall at the west end. At the lowest level of the spine are two tunnels for trucks (A) and newly combined loop railroad tracks (B) that will bring commuters into the area. Above this is a large glass-roofed, air-conditioned, landscaped pedestrian mall (C) one level below the street but easily accessible to it. The mall is open to the subway (D) that runs under Market Street, and it widens into plazas in the middle of each block. The plazas are the hub of circulation, with escalators taking people up to the street and banks of elevators (E) for people and goods rising from the lowest levels to the office buildings above. Shops line the mall at main and balcony levels; kiosks, street furniture, and planting will humanize the great structure. At one side of the mall, along Market Street, low-rise structures (F) are planned for shops and offices. On the other side of the mall a continuous structure provides a linear commuter bus terminal (G) two levels above the street, surmounted by four levels of parking (H). A series of high-rise structures (I) are spaced along the spine to admit light to the mall and plazas and to relate to the vertical circulation cores. Cross traffic is carried on bridges, and landscaped pedestrian paths lead to other areas.

Around this new spinal structure, many of the buildings already there would remain, such as the large department stores. Those buildings that have definitely outlived their usefulness would be replaced with open spaces or spot redevelopment, but the planners recommend proceeding with caution, for in this part of Philadelphia, but especially to the south of Market Street (beyond the structures shown at the left of the drawing), there are many buildings on narrow, crowded streets that are old but not blighted beyond redemption. The planners wisely decided that the character of this area should be conserved because it has its own special delights and gives a sense of continuity with the past.

Urban renewal is dismayingly slow and extremely costly. Although Philadelphia is noted for the vigor and foresight of its planners, who have established excellent public relations with the community, not everyone agrees with their proposals. To date, the necessary funds for the entire project have not yet been appropriated,

204. The projected plan for Market Street East (1966) indicates one possibility for integrating but separating transportation, parking, shops, and office buildings.

and the Federal Government has not given its final approval. The plan, however, can be developed in segments as conditions permit. No one can predict exactly when and how the specific projects will be realized. But regardless of the final outcome, the concept represents one enlightened approach to the revitalization of city centers.

The arts of commerce deserve consideration because they are the most ubiquitous of all the arts, with the possible exception of the arts of industry, to which they are linked. Every year more than five billion magazines are distributed in the United States, and in some of them more than half the pages carry advertising. Television programs without commercials are rarities. Not only in stores but in our homes, packages are constantly at hand, protecting food, detergents, and many other everyday articles. The arts of commerce are primarily selling devices. They do not deepen our understanding of eternal truths nor do they give us profound esthetic experiences, but they are inescapable influences in our daily lives. Instead of passively receiving the impact of this plethora of advertising, we can profit from a critical analysis of the quality of the messages and the ingenious, sometimes insidious, means by which they are conveyed. By being aware and appreciative of good commercial design, whether in packaging or in architecture, the general public can assure itself a more pleasant environment.

Industries sometimes advertise through the use of their products as art forms.

left : 205. The Rohm and Haas Company commissioned Gyorgy Kepes to design some innovative chandeliers (1967) from the acrylic plastics they produce to illuminate and enrich the lobby of their new building (on the left in Fig. 202) in Philadelphia. Welton Becket and Associates, architects.

right : 206. Bernard Rosenthal. *Sculpture Wall.* 1966. Aluminum, 35' ×13'6". Gateway Buildings, Los Angeles. Rosenthal's aluminum sculptured walls enhance the Gateway Buildings of Century City in California and were built by the Aluminum Company of America.

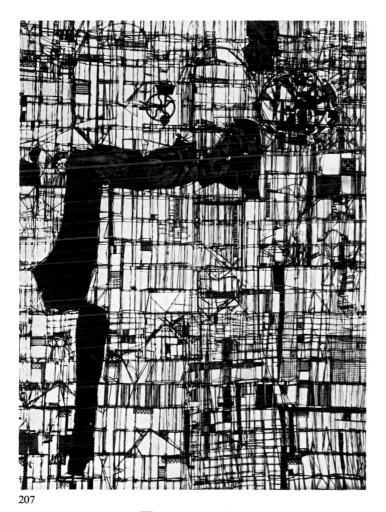

207

208

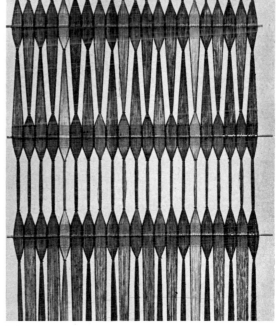

209

210

part **II** Materials
and Processes

overleaf:

207. Max Neufeld. *Metal Tapestry*, detail. 1967. Welded metal, 8′6″ × 11′.
California Design 10, Pasadena Art Museum. Neufeld's work is an
intricately varied network of thin wires accentuated
by crumpled and pierced sheets of metal.

208. John Kapel. Cupboard doors, detail. 1964. Wood, 24 × 42 × 12″.
Collection the designer. The doors are faced
with pieces of wood whose rough-sawed texture and angled shapes
create a lively pattern of light and shadow.

209. H. Crane Day. *Festival in Siena*, detail. 1967. Acetate and rayon, 42″ × 16′.
California Design 10, Pasadena Art Museum.
The rhythmic pattern of the woven banner is achieved
by knotting the warp in alternate positions.

210. Tom McMillin. Stoneware panel. 1967. Ceramic, 2′6″ × 8′6″.
California Design 10, Pasadena Art Museum.
The panel is composed of heavy,
rugged motifs that are well-suited to clay.

211. A Venini glass vase and bowl, made in Italy, is boldly stroked with color.

Introduction

The primary concern of artists is to satisfy human needs. These needs are fulfilled when ideas that exist in the artist's mind are given tangible expression in materials. Thus, a major art problem is that of selecting appropriate materials and handling them with respect. Each material has its own range of characteristics, its special possibilities and limitations, its inherent beauty, as the illustrations in this section demonstrate. Exploring the nature of materials and discovering ways in which they can be fabricated is a constant challenge. The achievements of the past and of the present deserve study, because each age makes its own contributions.

There is no single, rigid system by which an artist decides what materials and what processes he will use. The materials most suitable for a chair, for instance, depend primarily on the specific purposes of the chair and where it would be placed. An outdoor chair is most serviceable when it withstands weather and hard usage and most satisfying when it is in harmony with an outdoor setting. Weather-resistant woods, such as cypress or redwood, or such durable metals as aluminum, copper, or weatherproofed steel come to mind. In contrast, a chair in a living room leads a comparatively protected existence and is usually expected to have a greater degree of grace and refinement. Mahogany and walnut are possibilities for the frame, and the upholstery might be of linen, silk, wool, leather, or a synthetic fabric. Each material has its own kind of comfort and durability and its unique expressive qualities. Silk seems luxurious, and wool is noted for its durability, but much depends on how each material is worked. Without denying the intrinsic nature of the fibers, coarsely spun silk can be woven into thick, roughly textured cloth, and wool can be gossamer-thin and lustrous. From all this we can generalize the following major factors to be considered when selecting materials:

- The *use* to which the object will be put
- The *expressive qualities* that are desired
- The *nature* of the material
- The *processes* with which the material is worked

There are two additional determining factors. First is the *time and place* in which the object was created. Every aspect of the wall and furniture in Figure 213, a room in Sutton Scarsdale, connotes eighteenth-century England. Max Neufeld's welded metal composition (Fig. 207), designed to stand a few inches from the wall, clearly belongs to the second half of the twentieth century, but in this period of internationalism its place of origin (California) is not readily apparent.

The second factor is the *artist's creative individuality*. George Nelson's office furniture (Fig. 215), expresses his philosophy of design for mass production, while the detail of Lawrence Hunter's table (Fig. 222) evinces his concern with sensuous, handcrafted wood. The transformation of materials for purposes of utility and enjoyment is a constantly rewarding impetus to designers and artists and a source of delight to appreciative laymen.

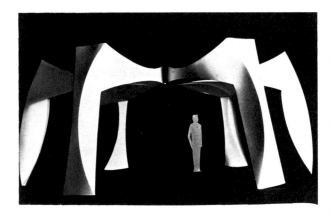

above : 212. This is one of many investigations of the possibilities of large, prefabricated building units. Components could be stamped out of sheets of plastic or other materials, shipped to the building site, folded to shape, and filled with rigid foams for stability. Samuel Lebowitz, designer.

right : 213. The versatility of wood when fashioned by skilled artisans is demonstrated in a room from Sutton Scarsdale, a home built in Derbyshire, England, in 1724. The strong architectural character of the columns contrasts with the more delicate forms of the chair and small table, as do the diverse kinds of carving and molding on the walls with the intricate patterns of inlay in the clock cases. Philadelphia Museum of Art.

214. Bruce Beasley.
Untitled sculpture. 1967.
Cast Lucite, 30 × 24". Hansen
Gallery, San Francisco.
This is one of Beasley's
many experiments in a search
for sculptural forms that
exploit the ability of Lucite
to reflect, distort,
and refract light into
dramatic, changing patterns.

6 Wood, Metal, and Plastics

Wood and metal are two of nature's most abundant and useful resources. To these, man has added a third—plastics. New uses are constantly being discovered for these astonishingly versatile materials, and their beauty is ever more apparent and varied.

George Nelson's office furniture (Fig. 215), designed to minimize clutter and yet give ready access to everything that is needed, combines all of these materials. Brightly polished aluminum was chosen for the slender but strong furniture legs and frames. The desk and the typing table have work surfaces of laminated plastic with soft vinyl edges. A deep file bin of oiled walnut or ash extends across the back of the desk, and shallow wood drawers line up along the front. A tambour top of the same woods can be rolled forward to cover the file and the top of the desk. The light-weight, easily moved chair has an aluminum base, a one-piece seat and back of molded plastic, and cushions covered with a colorful, trouble-free synthetic fabric. A high, convenient storage unit provides the user with additional work surface as well as files and bookshelves.

Each material was chosen because of its distinctive qualities and used where it would be most functional. However, other choices would also have been feasible.

The furniture could have been made entirely of wood or of metal, in which case the design and effect would have been different. A plastic, too, might have been the major material, but as yet no man-made material has sufficient strength to permit very slender supports for heavy furniture. In short, wood, metal, and plastics have enough common characteristics so that designers can choose from among them for many objects. They are by no means identical, however, and discerning designers select the material most appropriate for each purpose.

Wood

Wood is still preeminent in the manufacture of furniture because it is widely available, moderately durable, inexpensive, and easy to work. So are metal and plastics, and either could be used as far as utility is concerned; but wood has a warmth and an organic beauty that have appealed to man throughout history and are especially welcome in a mechanized civilization.

Characteristics and Kinds of Wood

The *grain* of wood reveals its growth history and usually has a deeply satisfying color and pattern. If a board is painted well, it is not easy to distinguish it from some plastics or enameled metals. Therefore, if a designer wishes to take advantage of the most distinctive qualities of wood, he will keep the grain visible. This was done in the tambour desk top in Figure 215, the carved fireplace wall in Figure 213, the chair in Figure 227, and the table in Figure 222.

Wood grain differs with various kinds of wood. Birch, maple, mahogany, walnut, ebony, teak, pine, redwood, fir, and many others have their own distinctive patterns.

215. Action office furniture (1966) was designed by George Nelson after an investigation of office activities that assessed not only the efficiency of work patterns, but the effect of the worker's moods on those patterns.

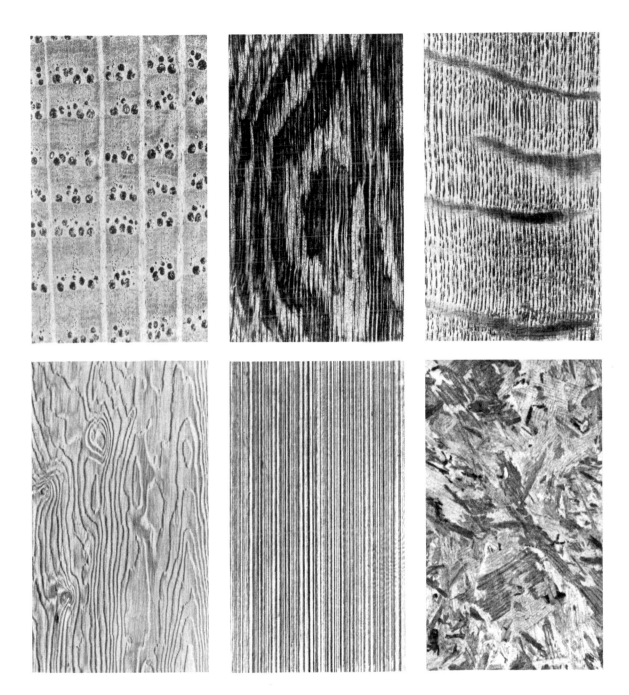

top left : 216. Oak sawed across the grain.
top center : 217. Plain-sawed oak.
top right : 218. Quarter-sawed oak.

above left : 219. Etched plywood.
above center : 220. Striated plywood.
above right : 221. Particle board of cedar.

Further, grain is notably affected by the way in which the wood is processed—whether it is sawed across the grain (Fig. 216), plain-sawed (Fig. 217), or quarter-sawed (Fig. 218). It can be smoothly sanded, etched to make the grain three-dimensional (Fig. 219), textured with parallel ribs (Fig. 220), shaved into chips that are then bonded together with resins (Fig. 221), or transformed into paper.

The *color* of wood also varies according to the kind of wood and the method of treatment. A few woods are naturally almost white or black, some are grayish or greenish, but most are in yellow, orange, and red tones. Oak tends to be yellowish; rosewood, cherry, and mahogany are red; walnut and teak are brown. With bleaches and stains, however, the natural color of wood can be changed, sometimes attractively.

Although grain and color are the most readily noticed qualities of wood, many other factors are important in selecting a suitable wood for a specific purpose:

- relative hardness, weight, and strength
- freedom from shrinkage, swelling, warping, and splitting
- ability to hold nails and screws
- ease of working with hand and power tools
- number and size of knots
- resistance to decay
- cost

Let us compare two woods.

White oak is hard and heavy, shrinks and swells considerably, but has only average warpage. White oak is hard to work with hand tools but easy with power machinery. It holds nails and screws well, but has only average resistance to splitting. In bending strength and in stiffness it ranks high, but it is only average in supporting weights from above. It is tough, resists decay, and has interesting grain but few knots. Its cost is moderately high.

Northern white pine is light and soft, average in shrinking and swelling, but has little warpage. It is easy to work with hand tools and is average in nail-holding power. Although stiff, it is not exceptionally strong or tough. The grain is of little interest, but it has many small knots. Finally, it is not expensive.

To the craftsman, designer, and builder, this information indicates that the comparatively hard and strong, interestingly grained white oak deserves consideration for such uses as flooring, the interior trim of buildings, and furniture, as well as for implements and heavy timbers. Northern white pine—softer, weaker, less expensive, without special beauty of color or grain, but easily worked with hand tools—is, in the better grades, useful for those structural parts of buildings in which great strength is not needed and for cabinetwork that will be protected by paint. The poorer grades can be made into boxes and crates.

Finding the best wood for a job is a challenge. Here are some of the qualities of four other woods:

Mahogany was so highly prized and widely used for furniture in the eighteenth century that the period has been called the "Age of Mahogany." Although the several varieties of true mahogany differ from one another, all are moderately hard and very strong; yet they are amenable to the most delicate carving and can be polished to a high luster. The color ranges from pale red to dark brownish red, and beautifully figured patterns of grain often occur.

Redwood is light and soft. However, it is also strong, resists attacks of decay and insects, shrinks little, and is easy to work. The colors resemble those of mahogany. No one would suggest using it for delicately carved, highly polished furniture, but it is valued for outdoor furniture, interior and exterior walls, and garden fences.

Teak, used extensively in the Orient and recently in Europe and the United States, is admirably suited to furniture. It ranges in color from straw yellow to tobacco brown and has striped or mottled grain patterns. Heavy and durable, it can be elaborately carved or fashioned into sculptural forms, and it responds beautifully to natural oil finishes. The cost is moderately high.

Walnut has been a favored furniture wood since early in man's history. Strong and hard yet comparatively light in weight, walnut, like mahogany, lends itself to

222. A detail of a walnut table (1965) handcrafted by Lawrence Hunter reveals not only the character of the wood but the hands and tools of the craftsman shaping and joining the parts in organic relationships.

carving and lustrous finishes (Fig. 222); also, it comes with an amazingly varied pattern of grain. With the introduction of mahogany around 1730, walnut temporarily lost favor, but it made a strong comeback in Victorian "black walnut" and is esteemed today in its normal brown tones.

Without proper treatment, most wood deteriorates rather quickly, and its surface is often too soft and absorbent to resist wear and stains. Hence some kind of finish is usually needed. *Oils* and *waxes*, the oldest preservatives, produce a beautiful, soft surface if many coats are properly applied. *Varnish* and *clear lacquer* give a hard surface that is easily cleaned. *Opaque paints*, in any color and degree of luster wished, dry to a durable, protective surface. New methods include soaking wood in or impregnating it under pressure with highly effective preservatives to provide a saturate finish that is integral with the material.

Shaping Wood

Wood usually grows in pole-shaped trunks and branches that can be

- refined into columns, furniture legs, and lamp bases
- squared into rectangular beams
- cut into planks or thin slabs for siding, tabletops, and the like
- sawed into blocks suitable for turning on the lathe into bowls, plates, and convoluted shapes
- bent under heat and pressure
- ornamented with carving and inlaid patterns
- sliced into very thin sheets suitable for veneers or plywood
- ground or split into small pieces and made into wallboards, paper, and synthetic fibers

The vocabulary of shapes that can be produced with such hand and machine tools as saws, knives, chisels, lathes, and planes is almost limitless (Fig. 213).

Wood was certainly one of the earliest, most widely used sculptural materials. Even today a sculptor may delight in shaping a section of a tree trunk, subtracting and adding a piece here and there, and slowly evolving a work that expresses his

Hans Hokanson. *The Cannon*. 1965. Wood, height 6'. Collection of the artist. Two photographs show how Hokanson transformed raw materials into sculpture.

left : 223. The basic form is that of the huge tree trunk from which the sculpture was cut and roughed out with a chain saw.

right : 224. The finished sculpture has various wheel shapes, cut from crosswise blocks of tree trunks and joined to the form by dowls. Gouged and chiseled surfaces create a rippling, rhythmic pattern.

affinity for the material in terms of his own esthetic sensibilities and creativity (Figs. 223, 224).

Few objects show greater fitness to purpose and more respectful use of materials than the Windsor chair (Fig. 225). Its design is based on two of the most appropriate forms of wood—the slab and the pole—supplemented by two pieces of bent wood. Projecting boldly beyond its supports, the writing arm demonstrates that wood is remarkably strong for its weight. So does the seat, which will support up to 300 pounds, even though it is less than 2 inches thick and is supported only near the corners. Four slender legs carry this weight to the floor. Notice especially the very slight spindles in the back, held in place by the two pieces of bent wood. Although extremely lightweight and airy, this structure will withstand the considerable pressure of a sitter who leans against it. Not only is the wood *strong in compression* (it holds its shape under pressure, as demonstrated by the legs), but it is also *strong in tension* (it resists breakage when bent or pulled, as in the back of the chair). The basic design of the Windsor chair seems so well thought out that contemporary designers continue to explore its potentialities (Fig. 226).

Veneer, Plywood, and Laminated Wood   Layer constructions of thin sheets of wood, thicker boards, or paper greatly extend wood's repertory. *Veneers* are sheets of wood as thin as $1/_{28}$ inch, produced by slicing, sawing, or rotary-cutting large logs. They can be glued to thicker lumber to make "veneered wood," to other veneers as in plywood and laminated wood, or to paper for wall coverings. *Plywood* is a sandwich composed of an odd number of veneers glued together with the grain of adjacent sheets at right angles to each other. *Laminated wood* is a type of plywood in which the grain of successive layers goes in the same direction. It bends easily with the grain and is very strong in one direction, which makes it especially suitable for the legs of furniture.

The advantages of these layer constructions are many. All are readily available in much larger pieces than is solid wood and can be surfaced with carefully matched, handsome woods that would be prohibitively expensive if they were solid. Typically, they are strong and resist shrinking and warping. Plywood and laminated wood can be molded or bent into curved forms.

Figure 227 shows one of the most remarkable chairs our age has created. Man has long known that he could *bend* wood for skis, snowshoes, and Windsor chairs, but designer Charles Eames, experimenting in his own apartment, found that he could *mold* plywood into new shapes through heat. When his apartment oven exploded, he continued his work in a bakery and later in a well-equipped laboratory. The organic shapes of the *plywood* seat and back echo those of the human body and are surprisingly comfortable for uncushioned seating. *Laminated wood* is an ideal material for the legs. Each part of the chair expresses its special function as clearly as do the parts of the Windsor chair, and yet the chair is convincingly unified. Above all, it has an unusually spontaneous but assured sculptural quality.

Designed for machine production, these chairs are based on three significant technological developments. First, the wood is rapidly, precisely, and permanently molded under heat and pressure. Second, the parts of the chair are joined by shock welding, a technique in which synthetic resin sheets are placed between the parts and sufficient heat is transmitted electronically to produce a bond stronger than the wood. Third, the wood is impregnated with resin, which makes it water-resistant and hardens the surface against scratches and dents. Not many examples of contemporary or historic work show as complete mastery and integration of the problems of human needs, materials, processes, and design as do Eames's chairs.

This is a brief introduction to the wondrous potentialities of wood. There are also the magnificently strong or delightfully intricate carvings in historic architecture and furnishings, as in the musical instruments in Figures 129 through 131 and the room from Sutton Scarsdale (Fig. 213). We hear much about the new "wonder materials," but to date none of them is more versatile, useful, and beautiful than wood. It can be made into innumerable shapes with hand or power tools. It is strong in relation to its weight and bulk, and it is easy to repair. Many new processes are making it resistant to rot and decay, fire and insects, as well as to shrinking, swelling, and warping. Its feel of warmth and intimacy make it uniquely endearing to man.

The basic concepts underlying the design of the Windsor chair are so strong and fundamentally right that they have inspired innumerable variations.

left : 225. An eighteenth-century American writing chair is comfortable, sturdy, and handsome. Museum of Fine Arts, Boston.

center: 226. Hans Wegner's oak spindle-back chair is a contemporary Danish interpretation.

right : 227. Charles Eames used wood inventively in this sculptural chair developed in 1946 and still in production with virtually no changes. Seat and back are of molded plywood; supports are of bent laminated wood.

right : 228. The Verrazano-Narrows Bridge, completed in 1964 and still the longest suspension bridge in the world in 1969, links two sections of New York City. Ammann and Whitney, consulting engineers; John B. Peterkin, Aymar Embury II, and Edward D. Stone, consulting architects.

below : 229. Pendant from Colombia, South America. Before A.D. 1600. Gold, height 7″. Museum of Primitive Art, New York. This object in the form of a ceremonial knife illustrates the ductility of gold, which may be hammered into thin sheets and cut and molded with simple tools.

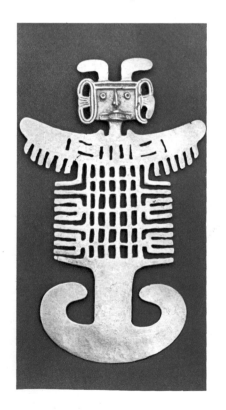

Metal

The Verrazano-Narrows Bridge (Fig. 228) was built to help solve some of New York City's transportation problems by providing a direct link between Staten Island and Brooklyn over the main approach to New York Harbor. Architects and engineers collaborated to create a majestic composition out of 143,000 miles of wire and 120,000 tons of structural steel. Gigantic cables, each $35\,^7/_8$ inches in diameter and composed of 26,108 wires, hang in curves as beautiful as they are efficient over the two 690-foot-high towers. These cables suspend two levels of traffic thoroughfares, each six lanes wide, for 6690 feet between the two anchorages. The bridge dramatically demonstrates one of the most distinctive qualities of metal, *great tensile strength*.

In an age concerned with technology, it is natural for art and engineering to reflect one another, and Richard Lippold's *Variation within a Sphere* (Pl. 19) has more than a little in common with the Verrazano-Narrows Bridge. Both were

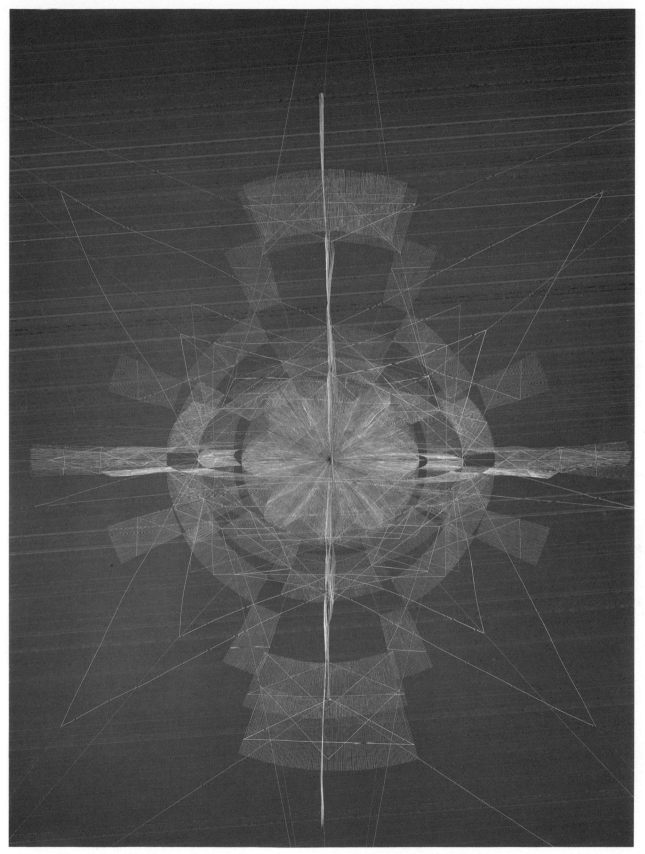

Plate 19. Richard Lippold. *Variation within a Sphere, No. 10 : The Sun.* 1963–1956. Gold-filled wire, 21' 11³/₄" × 10' 11⁷/₈" × 5' 57/₈". The Metropolitan Museum of Art, New York (Fletcher Fund, 1956). A shimmering luminosity seems to spread outward from the radiant center of Lippold's sculpture and animates the space in which it is suspended.

Plate 20. Barbara Hepworth. *Sphere with Inner Form.* 1963. Bronze, height 38″. Courtesy Marlborough-Gerson Gallery, New York. A sculpture of cast bronze illustrates the rich tonality that may develop in this age-old material. By the appropriate treatment, the artist has achieved a glowing verdigris patina on the inner form, accentuated by the mellow brown surface of the protective enclosure.

meticulously planned and constructed, and both employ metal wire as a major material because of its resistance to longitudinal stress. But whereas the bridge is primarily utilitarian, the sculpture was created solely for esthetic delight. Lippold spent two years in making sketches and models of paper and many months in cutting and welding thousands of parts by hand. Approximately 2 miles of wire twice the thickness of human hair and composed of 96 percent pure gold with a bronze core were used in the final work. This inherently beautiful material can be bent but has sufficient strength to retain the shape that it is given. The symmetrical composition is based on geometric circles, triangles, and starlike shapes positioned at many angles. An emphatic focal point is firmly established at the center by intersecting discs with pronounced, radiating lines. This is strengthened by the dominant vertical and horizontal units that form a cross. Surrounding the center are more open shapes that seem to float freely in space. The construction is held in tension by stainless-steel wires diagonally attached to the ceiling, walls, and floor, but the central core is suspended by an almost invisible wire from the ceiling so that air currents turn it in an endless succession of patterns that change gradually as one watches.

When first exhibited, the sculpture was thought by some critics to be a stunt rather than a work of art. Others felt it was expressive of a golden sunburst with its corona separate from the core. To many observers it evokes the shimmering luminosity of celestial bodies in the nocturnal sky. Whatever the judgment of the observer, it is obvious that the artist used the quality of the material and the processes by which it can be worked to give form to his concept.

Another artist in another time and place, a native of the Tohina culture in Colombia, South America, fashioned gold (Fig. 229) with the same respect for and attunement to the possibilities of the material and produced a work quite different from the Lippold sculpture but equally valid in its realization.

Metals and Their Qualities

Aluminum, one of the most abundant metals, was not discovered until 1727 and was not commonly used until the twentieth century. In its natural state it is bluish white in color, and it oxidizes to a soft gray. It can, however, be highly polished or softly brushed, and anodizing gives it a wide range of bright or dull colors that are integral with the primary metal. Except when used near salt water, it does not deteriorate. One of its most distinctive qualities is its light weight. Adding even very small amounts of other metals greatly increases its hardness and strength. Because it is light, durable, and easily worked, it is used in cooking utensils, furniture, transportation vehicles, architecture, and sculpture (Fig. 206).

Bronze, an alloy of copper and tin (silicon, aluminum, and manganese may be used instead of tin), is harder than brass but less easily worked. When exposed to air and moisture, it becomes a rich brownish black or develops a strikingly beautiful green patina, or mellow surface film. When treated with various chemicals, a wide range of colors is produced. Bronze has long been used for sculpture (Pl. 20), for long-lasting vessels (Fig. 236), and for ornamental doors (Figs. 116, 117, and 237).

Iron and *steel* are the great structural metals of our age. Iron is almost as abundant as aluminum, and man has used it for many centuries. Steel is produced by combining iron and carbon, heating the compound to a high temperature, and then cooling it suddenly. Both iron and steel have great strength and can be worked easily by hand or machine (Figs. 235, 238). Their great limitation is deterioration caused by rust. This, however, has been overcome by such new developments as nonrusting stainless steel and by "CorTen" (see Fig. 89), which when exposed to air quickly develops a rich brown surface coating that prevents deterioration.

230. Brent Kington. *A-Way-We-Go.* 1966. Silver, length 31″. Collection the artist. This frolicsome version of an automobile has complex forms embellished with many jewel-like ornaments.

Silver was known and prized from early times, because it is sometimes found in a pure state and because it is the whitest of metals. Next to gold it is the most ductile and malleable metal. A single gram can be drawn into a wire over a mile long, or it can be beaten into leaves only 0.00025 millimeter thick. In its pure state it is too soft for most uses, but small additions of copper increase its toughness and hardness. Frequently it is employed as plating over less costly metals. Soft buffing creates an inimitable satiny luster, or it can be polished to dazzling brilliance. Its color and its ability to reflect light suit it ideally to the delicate detail of the automobile sculpture in Figure 230 and to silverware (Fig. 234).

In spite of their many differences, metals have important common characteristics:

- All are inorganic and therefore do not rot or decay, although many rust or corrode.
- They are long lasting, in part because, even when thin, they do not break so readily as glass, ceramics, or wood.
- They are heavy, dense, and homogeneous (whereas wood is comparatively light, porous, and fibrous).
- They are seldom found in a pure, usable state and therefore must be refined, the materials with which metalsmiths work bearing almost no resemblance to the ores from which they were extracted.
- They tend to look hard and cool, and when highly polished they have a glittering brilliance.

The distinctive qualities of metals greatly expand our range of visual and tactile enjoyment. Few sights are more heartwarming than brass or copper glowing with light reflected from a fireplace, or more exciting than the metallic sleekness of aircraft, or more treasured than the richly luminous highlights in jewelry.

Shaping Metal

The methods of fabricating metals are many:

- In its solid state, metal can be sawed, drilled, cut with dies or blow torches, turned on a lathe, or engraved.
- When thin, it can be hammered, bent, twisted, and embossed.

■ With heat and pressure, it can be hammered, pressed, or rolled into thin sheets, drawn into slender wires, fused together as in soldering, welding, or plating, or melted and cast into forms.

Three typical processes are described below.

Making metal hollow ware by hand is illustrated in Figure 231. With the silversmith's tools, a pitcher is gradually raised from a flat disc into a three-dimensional, hollow receptacle. No nonmetallic material would respond in this way to the repeated blows of a mallet; the word *malleable* was derived from the mallets used in hammering metal. When a final form is reached, the delicate, precisely engraved pattern is "chased" into the metal. Joining the separately made handle, spout, and base completes the piece. The handsome contemporary pitcher in Figure 232 shows the subtle texture of hammer marks and was made by similar means. So was the teapot made in the eighteenth century by Paul Revere (Fig. 122). Iron, too, can be hammered and bent, especially when hot, into shapes ranging from horseshoes to fireplace equipment and wrought-iron furniture.

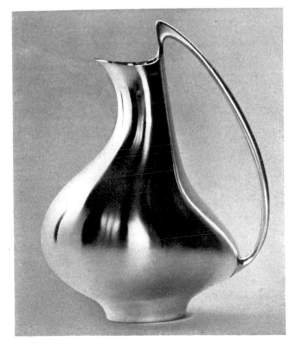

Handworking a flat piece of metal into hollow ware is an ancient process that is still used today.

above : 231. A pitcher is literally "raised" from a disc of silver with hammers and chasing tools.

left : 232. The body of Henning Koppel's voluptuous sterling silver pitcher (1952) has an asymetric contour when seen from the side. The slender, elegant handle is an effective contrast.

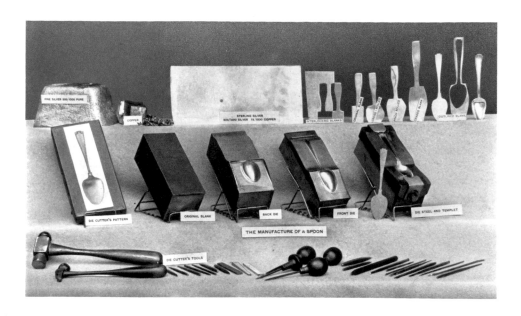

Transforming silver and copper into sterling silver forks and spoons is accomplished by hammering or pressing.

above : 233. In making spoons, flat sheets of silver are cut to approximate shape and then formed in a mold.

below : 234. Part of the distinctiveness of the design of these forks and spoons is in the logical concentration of ornament near the ends of the handles and at the junctions of bowls and handles.

Shaping metal under pressure in molds is somewhat similar to hammering but is a much faster process for mass production. In Figure 233 the steps in the manufacture of spoons can be seen. Dies for the front and back are carefully made; and a sheet of silver, rolled to the proper thickness, is cut in the shape of the spoon. Then an indefinite number of spoons can be stamped mechanically in a heavy press. Silverware can also be made by hand, a much more expensive process than making them by machine, but having the possibility of such individualized beauty as that shown in Figure 234.

Casting molten metal in a mold is a third way of shaping metal. In this process, molten metals are poured into molds. The resulting products can be as unpretentious as the cast-iron firelighter in Figure 235. Adapted from an old Cape Cod invention, the pot holds kerosene or coal oil. The easily held, self-cooling coil handle is attached to an absorbing firestone that, when lighted, takes the place of kindling. But cast metal objects can also be richly ornamented, as study of the Chinese bronze vessel (Fig. 236) will prove. The bronzes of the Shang Dynasty have never been surpassed in craftsmanship, creative handling of complex symbols, and powerful but controlled intensity of feeling. A lighthearted, playful, contemporary interpretation of an automobile (Fig. 230) shows another of the many potentialities of casting in metal.

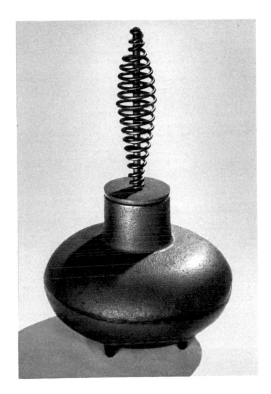

Metal objects can be highly enriched or severely plain.

left : 235. A contemporary cast-iron firelighter, designed by George Nelson, is simple, sturdy, and useful.

below : 236. Shang ceremonial vessel. Chinese, c. 1500–1028 B.C. Bronze. The Metropolitan Museum of Art, New York (Rogers Fund, 1943). This bronze vessel represents a combination of great technical skill, creative power, and discipline.

175

The ways in which metals are handled reveal their qualities.

left : 237. Olivier Descamps. Ornamental doors. c. 1966. Bronze. St. Anne Chapel, Paris. Descamps' cast bronze doors have an enduring character in their weightiness and age-old technique, but the design is of today. (See also Figs. 102, 103.)

right : 238. A detail of the United States Pavilion at Expo 67, Montreal, shows the unique bolted clusters of mass-produced, lightweight steel bars organized as a series of triangles in hexagonal frames—the most efficient, economical structural system man has yet devised. R. Buckminster Fuller, architect. (See also Pl. 61, p. 507, and Figs. 634, 637.)

It is almost as difficult to imagine a world without metal as to imagine it without color. From airplanes to safety pins, from suspension bridges to wrist watches, metal products serve us constantly. Steel construction has given architecture a new character, and metals have made possible systems of heating, lighting, and plumbing. But in addition to utilitarian concerns, the beauty of metal is a continuing source of esthetic satisfaction.

Plastics

Plastics are one of man's greatest triumphs in creating new substances to meet his needs. Chemists have transmuted such materials as cotton, wood pulp, soybeans, milk, natural resins, salt, silica, coal tar, and formaldehyde into crystal-clear substances that resemble glass but are tough, into durable, brilliantly colored strips that can be woven into chair seats and backs, into dishes that do not break easily, and into surfaces that resist scratches and stains. Wood and especially metal are considerably altered when transformed into useful objects or works of art, but plastics bear not the slightest relation (except chemically) to the raw materials from which they were developed.

The history of plastics goes back to 1868, when celluloid was made (from a highly improbable fusion of cotton, nitric acid, and camphor) as a substitute for the ivory used in billiard balls. Progress, though, was relatively slow until the 1920s. Since then, each year brings many new developments in substances tailormade to meet the fantastically diversified and specialized demands of contemporary society. The annual production of plastics rose from 4 million tons in 1958 to more than 14 million tons in 1968, and it is predicted that the next decade will bring increases at least as great.

Characteristics and Uses of Plastics

Plastics are grouped into families on the basis of their chemical composition, but within each family there is considerable variety. Five of the twenty or so families will serve to introduce the greatly diversified qualities and uses of plastics.

Acrylic plastics are noted for their exceptional clarity and for their transmission of light when transparent (Figs. 214, 239), but they also come in a considerable range of translucent and opaque colors. Strong, stiff, and rigid, they withstand weather and sharp blows. Their uses include skylights, windows, airplane cockpit canopies, furniture, lampshades, tableware, costume jewelry, and sculpture.

Melamines are among the hardest of plastics. They retain a lustrous finish and are unaffected by detergents, cleaning fluids, and oils. Their range of textures and lightfast colors is great. These qualities suit them to laminated surfaces on desks and tables (Fig. 215) and to colorful dinnerware.

Nylons withstand extreme temperatures, and their high tensile strength makes them resistant to bending or hard blows. They are not harmed by most ordinary

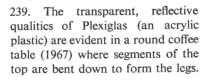

239. The transparent, reflective qualities of Plexiglas (an acrylic plastic) are evident in a round coffee table (1967) where segments of the top are bent down to form the legs.

chemicals and can be made weather-resistant. Their color range is almost unlimited. Although a textile fiber, nylon is also easily processed into handles and bristles for brushes, appliances, electrical and automotive parts, tumblers and lamp shades.

Urethane polymers can be produced as resilient or rigid foams and as coatings and adhesives, or they can be injection-molded, cast, or machined into almost any shape the designer may wish. The foams can be given densities matching those of wood, and they can be worked, finished, and repaired much like wood. Their low cost leads some manufacturers to predict that within ten years more plastics than wood will be used for furniture. Figure 139 shows the possibilities that one designer saw in this unique material, while Figure 243 illustrates some of the illimitable shapes to which the quick-setting foams are suited.

Vinyls, which can be flexible, rigid, or a foam, are used for upholstery, draperies, floor and wall coverings, phonograph records, and lamp shades. They, too, are strong and tough, and they resist normal abrasion but not direct heat. Vinyls can be clear or in a wide range of translucent or opaque colors. Articles made from them can be printed or embossed.

Shaping Plastics

The processes by which plastics are formed are the same as many of those used for metal and glass, plus some additional ones. They can be

- molded in forms under pressure or blown into molds
- cast by methods similar to those used for metal and glass
- rolled or pressed into sheets
- extruded through dies to form continuous sheets, filaments, rods, tubes, or pipes
- blown full of air or gas to make lightweight upholstery and structural and insulation materials
- sprayed onto other materials
- used to impregnate other substances to combine the virtues of both

240. Street furniture (1967) of fiber glass (fibrous-glass-reinforced plastic) exhibits the large scale, sculptural possibilities of the material. The covered bus-stop bench was designed by Douglas Deeds; the round planter with seats, by Elsie Crawford, and the street lights, translucent acrylic ellipsoids, by Wayne Compton and Associates.

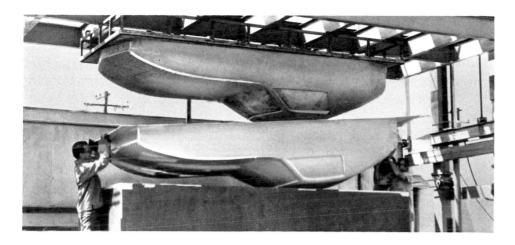

The speed with which plastics can be formed offers exciting prospects.

above : 241. An auto body of ABS (acrylonitrile-butadiene-styrene) can be molded from a single sheet, 25 by 10′, in less than three minutes.

right : 242. Experimental cars formed of Cycloac ABS (1967) have been successfully road-tested and crash-tested.

Plastics can be quickly and economically molded or cast into hulls for boats, bodies of automobiles (Fig. 241), independent units for architectural structures (Fig. 212), whole rooms or parts of rooms, furniture and tableware, packaging and diverse industrial components. Foam plastics can have twice the resilience of foam rubber and also can have their own protective skin that makes other surface coverings unnecessary. Also, plastics can be handworked into sculptural creations, as illustrated in the Bruce Beasley piece (Fig. 214) and in Plate 58 (p. 472).

No other group of materials can be used in so many ways; no others are so truly *plastic*. The ease with which they can be handled, together with the abundance of the raw materials from which they are made, are great virtues, but they have many other assets *when appropriately selected and used*. Many of them are surprisingly durable, yet lightweight and pleasant to handle. Some are remarkably resistant to mars and scratches. Because the color is usually integral with the plastic, it does not wear off, and when properly selected and used the color does not fade. Only recently, however, have the special characteristics of specific plastics been intensively studied and the best uses for each plastic become known to designers, manufacturers, and some consumers.

Designing in plastics is challenging because there are no historical precedents, as there are for wood, metal, ceramics, glass, and textiles. Furthermore, the raw materials have little intrinsic character and can be made to do almost anything.

As is typical under such conditions, designers first directed their energies toward making these new materials look like old familiar ones that consumers were accustomed to purchasing. It is still common to find tabletops and flooring materials that unconvincingly imitate wood, cloth, marble, tiles, and bricks. Gradually, however, the inherent qualities of plastics are being accepted and sympathetically revealed to make a new and positive contribution to our living.

Woods, metals, and plastics are a group of fantastically varied substances that can be processed in a multitude of ways to produce an endless number of objects for use and for esthetic pleasure. In enjoying and appraising them, one might concentrate on how well—or how poorly—the materials have been selected and shaped in terms of their purposes. Furniture, for example, can be made from wood, metal, or plastics, but it is hard to think of any one design equally suitabie for all three materials.

Many people derive greater satisfaction from those man-made creations that are forthright statements of their materials than from those that imitate other substances. This raises a basic question to which all creators and consumers do not give the same answer, as even a quick survey of the many facsimilies and imitations will reveal: Should materials be used only in ways that remain true to their basic nature, or is it permissible to use them in ways that simulate other materials? In other words, are plastics more gratifying when they reveal their inherent and unique qualities than when they copy forms and designs that seem to belong to wood, ceramics, or glass?

Answers to these questions take one in the direction of philosophy and personal values, to a consideration of the valuation of sincerity and frankness, the desire for honesty in art, and the contentment with imitation and pretense. One's attitudes toward these concerns govern many reactions to art objects in all fields.

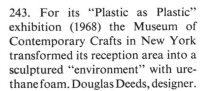

243. For its "Plastic as Plastic" exhibition (1968) the Museum of Contemporary Crafts in New York transformed its reception area into a sculptured "environment" with urethane foam. Douglas Deeds, designer.

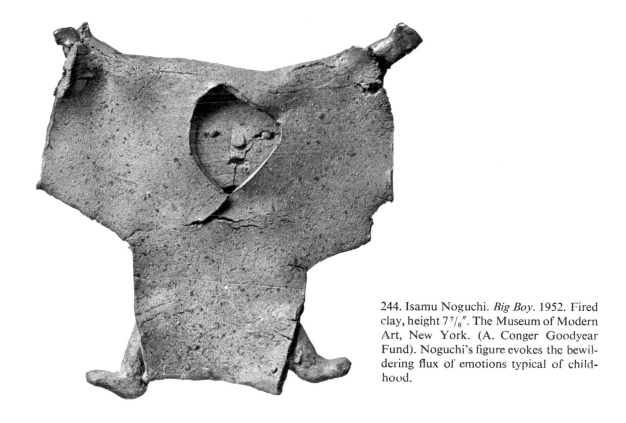

244. Isamu Noguchi. *Big Boy*. 1952. Fired clay, height 7⁷/₈". The Museum of Modern Art, New York. (A. Conger Goodyear Fund). Noguchi's figure evokes the bewildering flux of emotions typical of childhood.

7 Ceramics and Glass

It is logical to consider ceramics and glass together because they have marked similarities. Both are made from decomposed rocks, and, being inorganic, they do not rot or decay like wood, nor do they rust or corrode like metal. They are shaped while still in a plastic or liquid state, and both are subjected to high temperatures. Generally, ceramics and glass have less tensile strength than wood, metal, and plastics, for they may break if bent and shatter if dropped on a hard surface. All glazed ceramics are closely related to glass because of their glazes, which are in fact glass; and porcelain, although rightfully classified with ceramics, has almost as many "glass" characteristics as those associated with clay. Both glass and ceramics can be shaped by hand or machine. Although the hand processes have changed very little basically, historic techniques have been given new vitality, and their range has been extended with new ways of shaping materials. Industrialization has greatly increased speed and economy. For example, a year's output of a medieval potter could be hardened at one firing in some of our large kilns. In one minute a machine can make a thousand glass bulbs for electric lights, while only a few decades ago it would have taken two men an entire day.

There are, however, important differences between glass and ceramics. Glass is usually thought of as being transparent (even though it can be opaque), and ceramics are usually opaque (although porcelains can be translucent). Glass is made

245. An archaic jug from Cyprus (7th or 6th cent. B.C., height 10″) is decorated with motifs that seem surprisingly modern in their abstraction and unconstrained disposition.

from sharply pointed grains of sand that become plastic or fluid only when fused at great heat; ceramics are made from clays that become plastic or fluid when mixed with water. Glass is shaped while very hot, but ceramics do not undergo heat until they have been shaped. Glass can be remelted and reshaped, but fired clays can never again be made plastic or fluid. Finally, the tensile strength of glass far exceeds that of ceramics, for glass can be drawn or rolled into large, thin sheets for windows or spun into thin filaments for textiles and insulation.

Ceramics

"Objects made of fired clay" is a short definition of *ceramics*, a category that includes tableware, vases, sculpture, tiles, bricks, and drain tiles. No one knows when or where the art of fashioning vessels from clay and hardening them by heat arose; nor do we know how the first ceramics were made. Inevitably, however, early man must have noticed that some fires hardened the ground under them; and, then as now, the soft clay along riverbanks invited shaping, perhaps halfway over a round boulder. Someone might have learned that lining a wicker basket with clay made it more nearly waterproof and then have discovered that when this clay-lined basket was left in a fire, the wicker burned away to leave a hardened clay pot. Somewhere it was discovered that different clays, turning different colors in firing, could be used for colorful enrichment, and that some common materials, such as ashes, would produce glassy coatings. Glazes were used in Egypt before 3200 B.C. on tiles, jewelry, and small pieces of sculpture, but they were not widely used on pottery until centuries later.

Many of the basic materials and processes in ceramics were discovered hundreds of years ago, and the artistry of ancient potters (Fig. 245) was notable. This art soon reached the stage where significant steps ahead became few and far between. The twentieth century has to its credit the discovery of new clays and glazes, faster and more accurate methods of firing, and mass-production techniques. It has applied power to turn old machines, found new sources of heat, and greatly developed the

246. Marguerite Wildenhain's contemporary, hand-thrown stoneware bowl is appropriately enriched with scratched (sgraffito) patterns in white and brown.

chemistry of ceramics to meet such new demands as that for insulators for high-voltage electricity and crucibles for chemists. Today, almost everyone can own ceramic objects, whereas in 1750 only the wealthy could afford a set of ceramic dinnerware.

Recently, artists have taken a fresh look at the age-old materials of glass and ceramics in terms of contemporary needs and possibilities. They have rebelled against confining rules and practices with unfettered experimentation in their quest for new freedom. In many instances this is expressed in such boldly unexpected, assertive statements as Peter Voulkos' plate and Daniel Rhodes' *Guardian Figures*, illustrated in Figures 268, 272, and 273. Seeking vigor rather than smooth perfection, they have created works that are deliberately rough and dynamically asymmetrical. Ornamentation, if any, is not servile to the shapes on which it is put, as in Roy Lichtenstein's cup and saucer (Fig. 247) and Hui Ka Kwong's vases (Pl. 21b). But the basic components are still *clays* and *glazes*.

Clay

Minute particles of decomposed granite-type rocks form clays suitable for ceramics. They are found all over the world and vary as much as woods and metals, but their common characteristic is a flat, flakelike structure that causes them to slide together and adhere to one another whether they are wet or dry. Clays vary in their plasticity —the ability to hold a shape while being formed—which varies in accordance with the size of the clay particles. In general, the finer clays are the more plastic. They also differ in the temperatures at which they will melt and in the colors they develop when fired. Some turn red, others tan or brown. Some remain gray, and a few become white.

Because a single clay as found in its natural state is seldom completely satisfactory for ceramics, two or more clays are generally mixed together, often with the addition of such materials as feldspar or flint, to give the desired properties. In order to be workable, especially by hand, some degree of plasticity is desirable. For all ceramics it is requisite that the clay keep its shape during drying and firing and that the particles fuse together in the kiln.

Ceramic wares can be categorized in terms of the clays used and the temperatures at which they are fired. Both of these factors affect the use, shape, glaze, thickness, durability, and enrichment of the piece.

Earthenware includes brick and floor tiles, flower pots and terra-cotta sculpture, and some vases, bowls, and dishes. Made from coarse surface shales and clays, earthenware is fired at low temperatures (1740–2130° F). The coarser earthenware, such as flower pots and "pottery" bowls or plates, is comparatively rough and porous, red to brown in color, and thick (Fig. 247). More refined earthenware is produced by adding other clays and flints. Fired at higher temperatures, this "fine earthenware" is stronger and smoother than the coarse wares, facts that suggest thinner pieces with more delicate, more formal shapes and a measure of enrichment (Figs. 264, 266).

Stoneware, frequently used for ornamental vases and bowls, some of the better "pottery" dinnerware, and sculpture, is made from finer clays and fired at higher temperatures (2130–2300° F) than earthenware. When fired, stoneware generally becomes tan or gray, and the clay particles are partially to completely fused. They have smoother surfaces and greater strength than earthenware and are usually impervious to water and other liquids. The range of shape, glaze, and ornamentation is great (Figs. 246, 248, 255).

Porcelain is used for high-grade dishes and ornamental wares. Usually made from mixed clays containing goodly amounts of kaolin (very pure, fine, white clay) and feldspar (a mineral component of most crystalline rocks), porcelain is fired at high temperatures (2300–2786° F). The result is a completely vitrified (changed into a glassy) substance that is a waterproof, strong, and white or bluish-white material. It is often translucent. Precise, refined, formal shapes and enrichment, such as the dinnerware in Figure 249, are suggested by this costly, usually thin type of ceramic.

Although stoneware and porcelain are standard categories, they tend to merge with each other rather than maintain separate distinctions. There are, for example, clay bodies that fall between stoneware and porcelain, and one very common hybrid, china, deserves mention.

China, from which much commercial dinnerware is made, is white in color, durable, and not expensive. The term was originally used for European ceramics that imitated Chinese porcelains. China is fired at medium temperatures (2200–2280° F) and is semivitreous. Ranging from medium to high in thinness, translucency, and strength, it suggests somewhat formal shapes and enrichment.

Practical and attractive dinnerware can be made by casting and jiggering.

opposite : 247. Going beyond conventional tenets, painter Roy Lichtenstein's designs for dinnerware (1966) deliberately contradict the commonplace shapes to which they are applied. The shadow of the cup's handle painted on the saucer is delightfully whimsical. Leo Castelli Gallery, New York.

below : 248. This sturdy stoneware in strong, informal shapes has a smooth, white mat glaze on the inner bowls and a dark textured glaze on brims and outsides.

bottom : 249. Thin and refined porcelain shapes are covered with a smooth, white glaze that is appropriate to the material and form. Sylvia Leuchorius, designer.

250. A fired, unglazed planter (12 × 24″) with a crisply curled brim was made with the slab method by William Daley.

Shaping Clay by Hand Clay, moistened to a putty-like plasticity, can be shaped by several methods. The results vary from the simple, pure forms of the Natzler pieces (Pl. 21a) to the more intricate shapes of Hui Ka Kwong (Pl. 21b) and Daniel Rhodes (Figs. 272, 273).

The *coil method* goes back to the earliest days of pottery making, is quite easy to do, and still holds many possibilities for forms that differ from those natural to the other methods. Starting with a flat disc of clay for the bottom, the potter then rolls out ropelike strands of clay. He builds these up into layers of coils, pinching and smoothing them together, until the desired size and shape are attained. The process can result in either a symmetrical or an asymmetrical form. When the coiled pot is nearly dry, the potter may smooth and polish it with a pebble or spoon, or he may let the successive layers of coils remain as structural ornament.

The *slab method* involves rolling clay out like biscuit dough, cutting it into pieces, and fastening them together (Fig. 250). Rectangular, rounded, or irregular forms are all possible and are sometimes joined to thrown forms. Clay slabs can also be pressed into a hollow mold or onto a convex mold.

Throwing is the term for shaping clay on a potter's wheel (Figs. 251–254). Dating back to at least 4000 B.C., the potter's wheel is a heavy, flat disc that is rotated by

Throwing pottery on a potter's wheel is an age-old art still widely practiced.

251–254. Four stages in forming a vase. *below left :* 251. Placing the ball of clay on the wheel. *below right :* 252. Centering the clay. *bottom left :* 253. Raising the clay into a cylinder. *bottom right :* 254. Shaping the vase.

left : Plate 21a. Four simply formed vases by Gertrud and Otto Natzler (c. 1965) are distinguished by mellow, earth-colored glazes that are modulated by the light that strikes them.

below : Plate 21b. Four unconventionally shaped vases by Hui Ka Kwong (1968) have equally imaginative glazed decoration, which, by definitely accentuating or defying the forms on which it is placed, heightens the individual effect of each. The swirling pattern of the fabric is an unexpectedly effective background.

187

Plate 22. N. Pellipario and Master Giorgio of Gubbio. Plate with Presentation of the Virgin in the Temple. 1532. Luster-painted majolica. Museo Civico, Bologna. Majolica pottery originated in Spain and so greatly influenced Italian ceramists of the fifteenth and sixteenth centuries that much Italian Renaissance pottery is called majolica ware. After a first firing with tin-bearing glazes, the pieces were often painted with colorful luster glazes and refired at a lower temperature. An inscription on the back of the plate shown indicates that Master Giorgio completed the work of Pellipario by a third firing of metallic lusters. A Biblical scene covers the entire surface. The plate is obviously decorative rather than utilitarian.

left: 255. The beautiful proportions of the basic form and
the shaping of the lid and
handles in Arthur Baggs'
stoneware cookie jar make
additional ornamentation unnecessary. Syracuse Museum
of Fine Arts.

right: 256. Paul Soldner's
vase (14 × 9″) is unglazed
but decorated with white
opaque slip and copper oxide.
After firing at low temperature, it was partly smoked, a
process that smudged and
speckled the surface.

hand, foot, or motor. Few art processes are more exciting to watch than a skilled
potter raising a shapeless lump of clay into a symmetrical, thin-walled bowl or vase.
A ball of clay is "thrown," or placed onto the middle of the wheel, which is then
rotated. When the potter has a squat, symmetrical, truncated cone of clay, he begins
to open it by pressing both thumbs into the center while his fingers keep it from
spreading too much. Then he forms a cylinder by pressing on the inside with one
hand and on the outside with the other. From this point on, the potter shapes his
pot by varying the pressure on the inside and outside. An almost unlimited variety
of round, symmetrical shapes is possible. The potter's skill, imagination, and taste,
and the available clays are the important controlling factors. The cookie jar in
Figure 255 is a consummate example of wheel-thrown pottery. The full, flowing
contours and the unobtrusive concentric rings show clearly that a plastic material
was shaped on a rotating wheel.

Although wheel-thrown pottery is typically symmetrical, some contemporary
potters have experimented with less rigid forms. Creating spontaneously, Paul Soldner has modified a wheel-thrown form by altering the perfectly circular shape and
adding clay to produce a distorted and very personal version of a vase (Fig. 256).

Shaping Clay by Machine For mass production, ceramic objects are first designed in clay, plaster, or on paper; then models are made; and finally thousands of
replicas can be turned out quickly in molds or with a jigger and jolley.

Casting in molds is a typical way of making hollow ware—vases, coffee pots, and
pitchers. The process is based on two facts: plaster of Paris absorbs water readily,
and clay particles can be suspended in water. A one-piece mold for a simple shape
in which the top is the largest dimension can be made by simply turning the model
to be cast upside down and pouring plaster of Paris over it to form a thick wall.
If the model is more complicated and has undercuts or extrusions, a mold of two
or more coordinated, interlocking segments is needed. Then, when the plaster has
hardened sufficiently for it to retain its shape, the original model is removed and
the mold is dried.

Figures 257 and 258 show the casting of a pot in a three-piece mold. *Slip*, a mixture of clay and water, is poured into the top of the mold. Being very "thirsty," the mold absorbs the water from the slip that comes in contact with it. Thus a layer of clay, which varies in thickness with the length of time the slip is left in the mold, builds up inside the mold. When this layer is thick enough, the excess slip is poured out. Then the piece is allowed to dry; and because clay shrinks in drying, it eventually pulls away from the plaster of Paris. The cast pot is removed from the mold, steam marks or other imperfections are smoothed out, and any handles or knobs not cast with the main pieces are fastened on. After thorough drying the mold can be used again.

Shaping with a jigger and jolley is the process by which most machine-made cups, bowls, saucers, and plates are formed. Basically it is much like throwing on a potter's wheel, but a mold and a template are substituted for the potter's hands (Fig. 259). Jiggered pieces are finished and dried in the same manner as those that are cast.

While being shaped, clay is typically either plastic or fluid and is amazingly responsive to the ceramist's imagination and skills. When fired, it is comparatively hard and brittle. If one thinks of this material in relation to a potter's wheel, rounded, symmetrical, and fairly compact forms come to mind, and these are predominant in historical and contemporary pieces. Sharp edges, angles, and slender extended parts typically are excluded. But there are many other methods that lead to a great diversity of possible forms. The qualities of the material are of great importance, but they are only one factor in determining the final outcome. In many cultures, especially the Oriental, angular forms have been used felicitously. We readily accept the angularity of bricks and tiles, and we may find delight in such contemporary work as that of Noguchi (Fig. 244) and Rhodes (Figs. 272, 273). Cups and pitchers can have slender, extended handles; bowls and vases can have thin, flaring rims. Potters bring into unison the forms a material and a process suggest or imply, their skill and daring to exploit any of the potentialities, the spirit of the age in which they work, and the human needs, specific and general, for which the object is made.

Drying and Firing   Clay objects must be dried carefully and slowly to prevent warping or cracking. In drying, they may shrink as much as 10 percent, and they may shrink another 10 percent in firing. Before firing, they are called *greenware*, and at this stage they break easily and soften or even disintegrate in water.

Firing at sufficiently high temperatures completely changes the character of clay. This change is called *maturing*. As mentioned, various clays are fired at different heats. At temperatures suitable for earthenware, porcelain will harden but not vitrify; and at the high heats needed to mature porcelains, earthenware clays lose their shape. Successful firing demands careful control. Temperatures must not go too high or stay too low.

Most ceramic objects are fired twice. *Biscuit firing* hardens the ware, and this is the only firing that such unglazed pieces as flower pots get. *Glaze firing* produces a glossy or lustrous coating. A few objects are hardened and glazed in one firing, and some glaze effects or types of ornament require several firings.

Glazes

Most ceramics are covered with glazes, glasslike coatings joined at high temperature to clay objects. Their major utilitarian function is to give pottery a hard, durable, easily cleaned, and usually waterproof surface. Glazes differ in the way they join the clay body. A broken piece of earthenware shows that the glassy coating and earthy body are distinctively different, but in porcelains the glaze and body are so

Mass-produced ceramics are usually made in molds or with jiggers and jolleys.

below left : 257. In casting, liquid clay is poured into a plaster mold that absorbs the water and leaves a layer of clay on the inside of the mold.

below right : 258. After the clay has partially hardened, the object is removed.

bottom : 259. In the jigger-and-jolley method, the mold on the jigger shapes the inside of the bowl or plate while the template on the jolley arm shapes the outside.

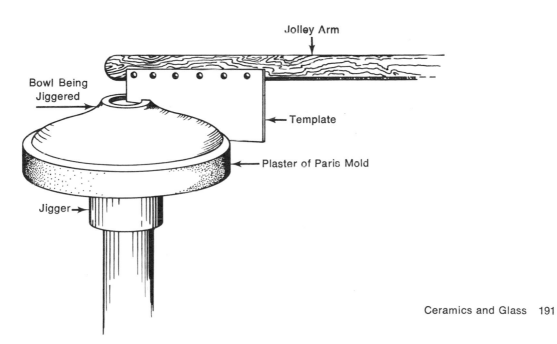

similar chemically that they fuse together. If glaze and body do not shrink at the same rate while cooling, the glaze may *craze*, or crack into many fine or coarse lines. On such frequently used pieces as dinnerware this is usually not desirable. Sometimes, however, "crackling" is deliberately planned as an attractive enrichment. In the Sung Dynasty bowl (Fig. 260) the long crackle lines stained a dark color emphasize through contrast the shape of the bowl while adding their own intricate tracery.

The colors of glazes range from soft, earthy colors to those of gemlike brilliance. Their surfaces can be very smooth or have uncounted kinds of other textures. They can be thin and transparent, translucent, or thick and opaque. These qualities are determined by the ingredients used in the glazes and by the methods of firing and cooling the pieces. Endlessly fascinating to potters, glazes range from such simple types as the salt glaze on Arthur Baggs' earthenware cookie jar (Fig. 255) to those illustrated in Figures 260 through 263, which are technically and visually complex. This challenging wealth of possibilities makes glazes a primary type of enrichment. At their best, glazes rise above utility to intensify the esthetic character and the purpose of the piece. If the potter wishes the basic form to be dominant, then comparatively smooth, subdued glazes are a sensible choice (Figs. 249, 263). Should he want glazes that are eventful in themselves, he might use the kinds that produce such visual textures as the crackle on the Chinese bowl (Fig. 260) or the rugged encrustation of Beatrice Wood's bowl (Fig. 261). Maija Grotell used several glazes to create a decisive pattern in color and texture (Fig. 262), while in the Natzler pieces in Plate 21a the glazes have a depth and richness that impart a glowing intensity to the forms.

Shape and glaze give these ceramics great beauty of different kinds.

opposite above: 260. Sung begging bowl. China, c. A.D. 960–1280. Gray porcelanous clay. The Metropolitan Museum of Art (Rogers Fund, 1917). The heavy gray glaze on this simply shaped bowl has crackle patterns produced by sudden chilling in a pigmented liquid.

opposite below: 261. Vigorous textures of clay and glaze accentuated by contrasting colors vitalize Beatrice Wood's contemporary bowl (c. 1960). M. H. de Young Memorial Museum, San Francisco.

right above: 262. Maija Grotell's vase (c. 1960) is enriched with a pattern that retains the qualities of glazes fusing and melting in a kiln.

right below: 263. Triple-spouted vase. China, 18th cent. Stoneware. Stanford University Museum. This gourd-shaped vase retains the plasticity of the clay from which it was made. The body is covered with softly textured green glaze.

Plates on which ornamentation is harmonious with their shapes and the varied types of clay are demonstrated by Figs. 264–268.

left : 264. This Spode plate is of high-grade earthenware, cast in a mold, with a raised design that is precise and formal in character.

right : 265. On a coarser earthenware body this freely drawn, vigorous design seems at home. Hjorth, designer.

Enrichment of Ceramics

Although many ceramics are beautiful through shape and glaze alone, man has often responded to the need for some additional ornamentation. As in the other arts, ceramic enrichment is most satisfying when it in itself is tellingly related to the object's useful and expressive functions, to its material, and to the basic shape.

A study of five plates will introduce some of the potentialities of ornament. Plates with a lip (or rim) and a well (concave inner part) suggest that these two important divisions be acknowledged. Figure 264 shows a plate made of highly refined earthenware. The lip is covered with an over-all pattern of raised diamond shapes that at first appear completely angular but actually have curved sides. The lines make these shapes seem to be going out from the center and returning to it; the result is a lively circular movement. An indistinct wreath of conventionalized leaves slightly emphasizes the sloping sides of the well, the center of which is plain. Quite different is the vigorous, hand-painted design on the coarser earthenware plate (Fig. 265), on which abstract forms suggest varied natural shapes and rhythms. A circular "bull's-eye" emphasizes the plate's center, and from this focus five plant-like patterns radiate. Two circular bands not only check this outward movement but indicate the division between lip and well. A freely drawn serpentine band accented with concentric motifs completes the design.

Less symmetrical than the plates just discussed are the next two. On the Wedgwood plate (Fig. 266) a wreath of semirealistic grapevines with a hint of three-dimensionality is combined with an informally fluted and scalloped rim that is actually three-dimensional. The whole design is remarkable for its consistent informality. In this example, ornamentation is concentrated on the lip, but it wanders down the sides of the well and spreads a little onto the flat bottom of the plate. Typical of informal art, this design does not confine itself within rigid boundaries. In so doing, it tends to merge, rather than to differentiate, the parts of the plate. Figure 267 illustrates the Oriental's ability to adapt and modify natural forms without either making them superficially imitative or losing their organic qualities. The

intricately elaborated lip becomes a rich but subordinate enclosure for the floral design in the well. Each part maintains its identity and yet truly belongs with the others. The plate subtly and creatively goes beyond many tedious little rules of design to become a beautifully integrated whole. Its expressive communication does not grow stale with repeated study.

Strikingly different in intent and execution is the plate created by Peter Voulkos (Fig. 268). Massive, its contour split and broken, its surface dented, lumpy, and leathery, it is not meant to be used as a "plate" in the conventional way but is a muscular, impetuous expression of the weight and plasticity of clay. The asymmetrical distortion and disintegration, emphasized by dark, richly toned glazes, lead to an uneasy contradiction of forces in search of resolution.

above left : 266. Fine-grade earthenware with a printed pattern.

above right : 267. Plate. China, 18th cent. Porcelain. Stanford University Art Gallery (Mortimer C. Leventritt Collection). The hand-painted embellishment was done with enamel-like glazes.

below : 268. Peter Voulkos' plate (1963, width 16 ½"), with its earthy glazes, conveys a feeling of the potter's hands and tools.

Painted or Printed Ornamentation   Painting or printing is one of the two basic categories of ceramic ornamentation. The typically smooth, uninterrupted surface of pots and plates invites drawing and painting almost as much as do walls and canvases. Very early, men discovered that clays and minerals could be mixed with liquids and painted on clay. The prehistoric urn in Figure 245 has black and brown designs painted on its reddish body; the eighteenth-century Chinese plate in Figure 267 was painted with enamel-like glazes of glowing colors; and the luster-painted majolica platter in Plate 22 (p. 188) depicts the Presentation of the Virgin.

A great variety of "paints," tools, techniques, and effects is possible. Diverse pigments can be used, and they can be mixed with liquids to many consistencies. Clays can be combined with water to the consistency of rich cream and applied thickly, as in much Pennsylvania German ware, or they can be as thin as milk. These latter can be applied with fingers, sticks, brushes, eye droppers, or syringes; and the designs can be boldly vigorous or precise and intricate. Glazes, stains, and enamels can also make the patterns. All of these methods are used in handmade ceramics, but similar effects on mass-produced wares are achieved by printing (Fig. 266). In one of the many ways in which this is done, copper rollers are engraved with the designs, heat-softened color is rubbed into the engraved lines and then printed on special tissue paper to produce *decalcomanias*, from which the design can then be transferred to the surface of the ceramic ware. This printed paper is placed on the piece with its color side down; it is vigorously rubbed to make the color adhere to the object; and then the paper is washed off.

So far, only the pigments, tools, and effects have been mentioned. But pigments can be applied to clay objects as soon as they are dry enough to hold their shape, after they are biscuit-fired, or after they are glazed. After application of the pigment, the piece can be glazed or reglazed. Painted or printed decoration covered by a glaze (usually colorless and transparent) is called *underglaze* decoration. If no glaze covers the design, it is called *overglaze* decoration. Protected by a glassy coating, underglaze decorations are more durable; but overglaze pigments have a greater color range, and all gilding is done after the final glaze firing.

below : 269. The convoluted and bulbous forms on Jerry Rothman's footed bowl with handles (1966) are accented with painted glazes.

Hui Ka Kwong's new ceramics (Pl. 21b) are inventive in both shape and decoration. Although many of his decorative motifs have been used before, he has made them seem startlingly fresh. All of his pieces were thrown on a potter's wheel, but not all are symmetrical. The piece at the left has a firm, circular base and thick stem with black and orange bands accenting their roundness. The dome form that they support has somewhat irregular diamond shapes and culminates in a red cap with white stripes that follow its contours. The squat vase next to it has an over-all pattern in black and white. The design is not rigidly geometric and rectangular, and the optical illusions, aided by circular bands around the neck of the vase and radiating lines on the top, draw attention to the roundness of the form itself. On the tallest piece jagged patterns accentuate the three divisions, whereas the almost biomorphic designs on the softly flaring yellow vase at the right flow freely from top to bottom. In sum, the ornamentation on each piece is compatible with but not a slave to the form it enhances.

Modeled or Carved Ornamentation   Clay in its plastic state invites handling because it responds so readily to every pressure. While hand-thrown pottery is still soft it can be given concentric raised or lowered rings and thumbprint borders. It can be textured with about everything from modeling tools and pocket combs to burlap and screen cloth, or it can be impressed with designs carved in wood or plaster. Also, it can be modeled into the sculptural forms of the Luca della Robbia plaque in Figure 270.

When *cheese hard* or *leather hard* (firm enough to be handled safely but not so dry that it powders or chips when cut away), other kinds of enrichment are possible. Three-dimensional enrichment can be *incised*, or cut into the clay (Fig. 264); *excised*, or the background cut away to leave the design in relief (Fig. 271); or *pierced*, cut through the body of the piece. *Sgraffito*, a process with a very long history, is produced by coating the whole piece with a slip of clay different from that of the body; the design is then scratched through the outer layer to expose the body underneath (Fig. 246).

Clay is a natural material for carved or modeled ornamentation.

left : 270. Luca della Robbia. *Prudence.* Italy, 15th cent. Enameled terra-cotta, diameter 5′4 ¹/₂″. The Metropolitan Museum of Art, New York (Purchase, 1921, Joseph Pulitzer Bequest). The sensitively modeled forms of this ceramic plaque are emphasized by richly colored glazes.

right : 271. Dirk Hubers' contemporary jar (1959, 15 × 14″) is deeply carved with a vigorous abstract pattern. The naturally dark brown stoneware body is lightened with a spotted, cream-colored mat glaze in the deep relief.

197

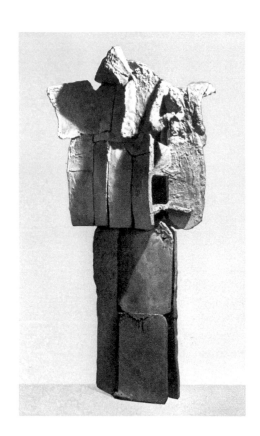

Ceramic Sculpture

The extraordinary manipulative qualities of clay have also made it a favorite material of sculptors from prehistoric times to the present. A sampling of some contemporary ceramic sculpture indicates the possibilities. In Figure 244, Isamu Noguchi created by the simplest means possible a haunting evocation of a small boy struggling into a shirt too large for him. Daniel Rhodes' recent experiments in combining fiber glass with clay have permitted intricately complex personal expressions in forms that previously were not feasible. In firing these pieces, the glass fibers and the clay fuse together to become a homogeneous material with greater tensile strength and resilience than clay alone would have. In Figure 272, one of Rhodes' *Guardian Figures*, large, vertical slablike and sculptural forms surmount a tall, hollow base and convey the impression of a strong and vigilant sentinel. In Figure 273, the interlacing configurations are more dynamic and confident, suggesting some kind of determined combat.

Because it is far too large to have been fired in one piece, *Memorial Wall II* (Fig. 274), by Harold Paris, is built up of irregular tiles assembled into the finished sculpture. In some places forms on one tile overlap the adjoining one, effectively concealing the break; in other places the lines of separation are allowed to be part of the total design. Its great size and three-dimensional occupation of space reinforce the power of its statement.

Glass

The oldest man-made synthetic, glass is used today in countless ways in almost every part of the world. Throughout its history, it has affected human concerns but never so significantly as in the twentieth century. This is because of its fabulously expanded repertory. One glass company checks an average of thirty new formulas each day; in more than a century it has tested over 100,000 formulas. Glass now can be lighter than cork or almost as heavy as iron, as soft as cotton or nearly as hard as gems. Some glasses transmit heat or electricity readily, while others do not. There are types of glass that survive sudden temperature changes; others are sufficiently strong and flexible to serve as diving boards. There are windshields that resist shattering, and a telescopic mirror, cast in one flawless piece, that weighs 20 tons and is 200 inches in diameter. Special types of glasses have been developed that measure atomic radiation; others temporarily darken when exposed to ultraviolet radiation to reduce sun glare. But in spite of these tremendous advances, almost 90 percent of today's glass has much the same soda-lime-silica composition as did very ancient examples.

Like ceramics, glass has a long history that has not yet been completely disclosed. Also, we do not know just when or where man first made glass, but we do know that nature has been producing such glassy substances as obsidian for eons. The making and shaping of glass developed slowly, and some processes resembled those used in ceramics. Thus some of the first vessels were probably made much like coil pottery, by winding rods of hot, softened glass around a core of sand or

left : 275. This tiny multicolored vase of translucent glass was made in Egypt more than 3000 years ago.

above : 276. Tapio Wirkkala's clear, cut-glass bowl (c. 1959, height c. 8″, diameter 13″), designed for the Iittala Glass Works, Finland, transforms light into complex patterns.

by dipping the molded sand into a vat of molten glass (Fig. 275). By 1200 B.C. the Egyptians knew how to press glass, but the blowpipe was not invented until shortly before the birth of Christ and has changed remarkably little from its first form. Comparable in importance to the invention of the potter's wheel, the blowpipe caused an early "industrial revolution." With the new, efficient tool, glass descended a little from the category of a rare luxury, but not until the Industrial Revolution of modern times did it become a product for common use.

Glass, according to one definition, is "a rigid, brittle but amorphous inorganic substance, usually transparent, composed chiefly of silicates." The strangest and most distinctive physical characteristic of glass is that it is a "supercooled liquid" which at ordinary temperatures becomes so viscous it is rigid. Technically speaking, glass is not a solid, for there is no abrupt physical change when it ceases to be a substance that will flow and becomes one that will not. This would be of little concern were it not that glass actually looks like a liquid, which is an important factor in designing.

Despite the diversified characteristics of special glasses, ordinary glass is comparatively brittle and fragile, and it will not withstand sudden temperature changes. But it does not rust, corrode, or rot when in contact with water or most acids; it exceeds any plastic to date in its combined transparency and hardness; and it reflects and breaks up light as few other common materials can (Fig. 276). Although one usually thinks of glass as thin, transparent, and colorless, man struggled for thousands of years before unlocking the secrets that made this kind of glass possible. Glass can be translucent or opaque, filled with bubbles or other textures.

It can be thick or thin, colorless, delicately tinted, or richly hued. It can be blown, cast, molded, pressed, "drawn," rolled into sheets, or spun into threads; and it can be enhanced by cutting, engraving, etching, sandblasting, and enameling. No wonder it remains one of the most spectacularly useful and beautiful of materials. As though this were not enough, glass is made from common materials and is inexpensive to manufacture.

The Materials of Glass

Even though thousands of glass formulas include almost every chemical element known, glass is basically composed of silicates such as sand and alkalies such as sodium or potassium fused at very high temperatures. To these basic substances, many others may be added to give special qualities, but the great majority of glasses fall into one of three major categories, as determined by their basic materials. In addition to *silica*, *soda* and *lime* are the principal ingredients of ordinary household and window glass. *Potash* and *lime* are used in a finer grade of glass. *Lead*, from 25 to 50 percent by weight, is used in "crystal," which has exceptional clarity, brilliance, and luster.

Colors come from various minerals: gold and copper oxides give reds; copper or cobalt oxides give blues; and cadmium and uranium produce yellows and oranges. Other effects, such as translucency, opacity, or bubbles, result from chemicals or the way in which the glass is treated.

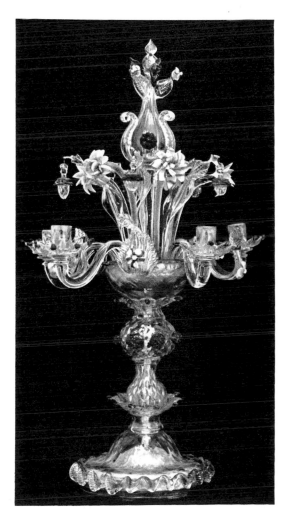

277. Venetian candelabrum. 17th cent. Glass. The Metropolitan Museum of Art, New York (gift of James Jackson Jarves, 1881). This candelabrum demonstrates the delicate, intricate elaboration to which glass so easily lends itself.

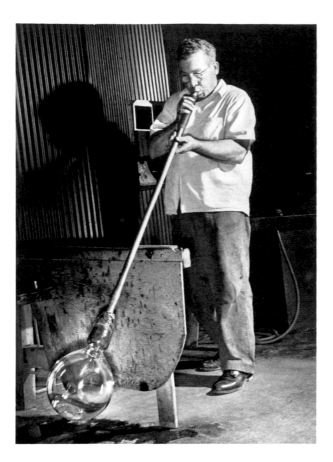

Shaping Glass

A material as plastic and ductile as hot glass can be shaped in many ways, but there are two basic processes.

Blowing Glass   When glass is blown by hand, the blowpipe (a hollow metal rod) is dipped in molten glass and then withdrawn with the desired amount clinging to the end. It is rolled on a polished slab, then blown into a bubble (Fig. 278). Working with the simple tools used for centuries—workman's bench, flow iron, shears, calipers, and wooden paddles—the craftsman in "offhand blowing" expertly develops the final form by rolling, twisting, and shaping with tools while the glass is hot and plastic. Because glass can be worked only at high temperatures, the object is frequently reheated in small ovens. Stems, feet, handles, or blown ornaments are formed separately and laid on. Molten glass can be blown into a single mold for efficient reproduction of one shape, or it can be shaped in a series of molds for more complex, sculptural results. Most blown glass nowadays is produced by machine (Fig. 279) with, of course, greatly increased efficiency.

Pressing, or Molding, Glass   Although the Egyptians pressed glass more than 3000 years ago, the process was not fully developed until rather recently. A mold is made, the right amount of molten glass is dropped into it, and a plunger forces the glass into the desired shape. Done either by hand or by machine (Figs. 280, 281), pressed glass can emerge in a great many shapes, and sometimes with a textured surface (Fig. 282).

Glass can be blown by hand or by machine.
opposite above :
left : 278. "Offhand" blowing requires great skill but can produce shapes impossible by any other process.
right : 279. In machine-blown glass, a puff of air makes a bubble of molten glass that is then shaped in a mold.

Pressed glass shapes often have textural patterns, although this is not inherent in the process.
opposite below :
left : 280. In pressing glass by hand, a white-hot glob is dropped in the mold and pressed into shape by a plunger.
right : 281. Mechanized pressing of glass has greatly speeded up the production of such items as casseroles, dishes, and glass blocks.

282. These pieces are typical of contemporary machine-pressed glass.

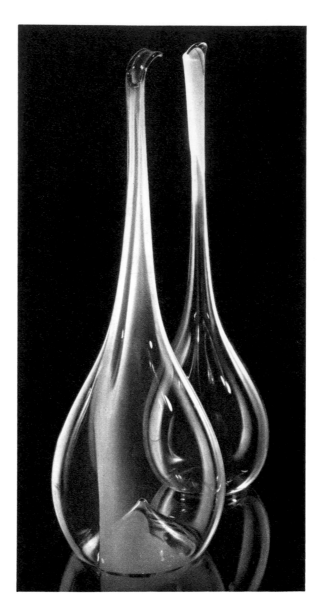

283. Two contemporary Dutch vases of thin, clear glass retain the bubble shape that develops naturally in blown glass. F. Maydam, designer.

What shapes are most appropriate for this completely amorphous, supercooled liquid with its chameleonlike qualities ? When molten glass is taken out of the furnace on the end of a blowpipe, it tends to assume globular shapes somewhat like those of the two Dutch vases in Figure 283 or the ornament around the chalice bowl in Plate 23. If air is blown through the pipe, a bubble is formed inside the mass that can be refined into contours such as those of the body of the chalice. Molds will entice glass into almost any shape desired. In handmade glass, diverse shapes can be joined together (Figs. 277, 285). Cutting can produce the hard, faceted, angular shapes characteristic of much old "cut glass," or it can lead to the softly rounded shape of the Pavel Hlava vase (Fig. 287). One can validly question any shape that seems appropriate to another material but foreign to glass or any form that is too fragile to hold up under the specific use for which it was planned. But most people today are not sympathetic toward rules that were formulated in terms of the past and that are unnecessarily restrictive. Man shapes glass to meet his needs, and the forms immediately suggested by the material are important, but they are only one set of determinants.

Plate 23. Chalice with Adoration of the Magi and Flight into Egypt. Venice, c. 1495. Enameled glass, height 7 ¹/₂″. Museo Civico, Bologna. A deep blue, slightly translucent glass chalice from Italy has a flaring base that rises into a sturdy stem punctuated with a knob and then swells out to hold the bowl in elongated globular strips. The Biblical scenes are of enamel.

left : Plate 24a. In *Aerial* (1967), a hand-blown vase by Dominick Labino, the free-form air sculpture floating between layers of glass is achieved entirely while the object is being free-blown. The body is reminiscent of the globular shape of glass as it comes from the furnace.

below : Plate 24b. Dominick Labino's vase (1968) with an iridescent surface effect shading from gold through green to purple is also free-blown. The decoration (called *prunted*) on the amethyst glass is a variation of the oldest form of decorating glass, that of adding glass upon glass as a kind of laid-on ornament.

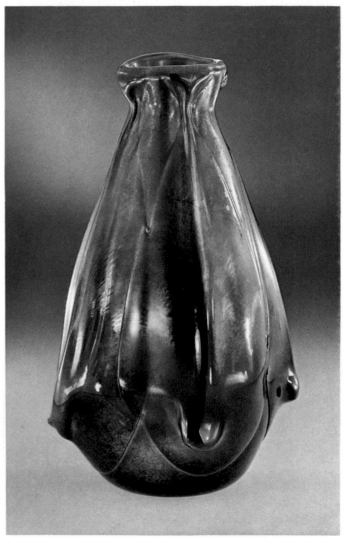

In terms of visual delight, the almost unique manner in which glass and light interact is consequential. When glass is transparent but thick, patterns of light develop *inside* as well as on the surface of the material. These patterns can be as serenely simple as in the Finnish vases (Fig. 284) or as complex as the forms floating in the walls of Dominick Labino's vase in Plate 24a. The patterns in glass imply motion, perhaps because we know that if the light changes or if we move our position the lights and darks will actually change dramatically. Colored transparent glass not only creates colored shadows but seems to radiate its luminous color to the space surrounding it. Moving away from completely plain, colorless transparency, to varying degrees of translucency and opacity and to the use of texture either on the surface or in the glass, one enters a field of far-ranging possibilities. Then there are the techniques of cutting and engraving that can set glass ablaze with a chromatic brilliance rivaling that of diamonds. Glass can glitter, sparkle, and scintillate, or it can glow with an opalescent luminosity. The vase in Plate 24b has an iridescence that responds to changing light with lustrous modulations of hues. It seems logical, therefore, to say that the appropriate uses for glass as a material, rather than as an object for use, are those in which full consideration is given to the effect that light can have on the material.

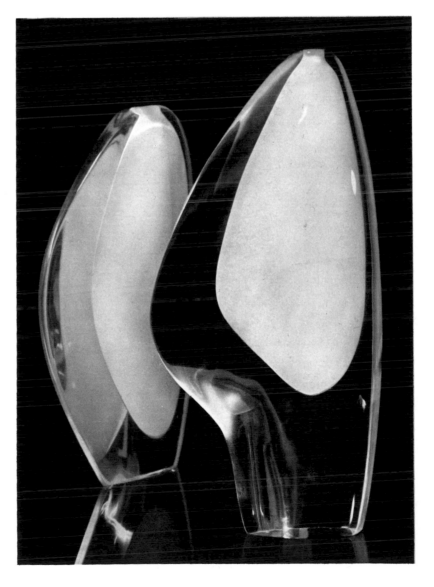

284. Two modern Finnish vases (c. 1960) preserve the globular character of hot, molten glass. The asymmetrical, free-form shapes are sensuously sculptural. Timo Sarpenva, designer.

right : 285. Venetian beaker with cover. c. 1500. Glass, height 5 $\frac{7}{8}$". The Metropolitan Museum of Art, New York (Munsey Bequest, 1931). The beaker is enriched by colored glass "laid on" clear glass.

below : 286. Blown and enriched by hand, these examples show some of the design possibilities of the process. The bases of the wine glasses were shaped while the pieces were hot and workable. The owl on the plate was engraved. The globs on the bottom of the vase and the ridges around the neck of the decanter were laid on.

Enrichment of Glassware

As with ceramics, much glassware does not need ornamentation. The material can be beautiful in itself and the basic shapes handsome. Certainly, no added decoration is needed on such pieces as the Dutch and Finnish vases or the glass sculpture in Figure 291. But there are numerous ways of enriching glass that, when sensitively carried out, may enhance the material and cause the shape to give intensified pleasure.

Laid-on Ornamentation Additional pieces of glass can be added to, or *laid on*, the basic shape for further enrichment of varied kinds. The Corning glass pieces in Figure 286 show that they can be precisely regular, as are the rings around the decanter's neck, or they may have a globular, less formal quality, as on the base of the vase next to the decanter. They can also be as ingeniously fanciful and delicate as the Venetian candelabrum in Figure 277 or preserve the plasticity of molten glass (Fig. 289).

Cut Glass Like precious jewels, glass can be cut to increase its sparkle, to provide decoration, and to create new shapes. The cutting is done on revolving stone or steel wheels fed with coarse abrasives; then the piece is successively polished on stone and felt wheels. When the design, material, and workmanship are good, cut glass produces a brilliance difficult to equal with any other material and process. With the development of flaw-free glass and the trend away from elaborate decoration, the saw-toothed, heavily patterned cut glass that graced our grandmothers' sideboards fell from favor for a while, but it is now regaining its popularity. That the cutting technique also holds new possibilities is demonstrated in the vase designed by Pavel Hlava (Fig. 287).

Engraved Glass Because glass is as smooth and as uniform as metal, it lends itself to delicate or vigorous engraving. The engraving of glass is an old technique that has enjoyed considerable popularity in the past few decades. Good hand-engraving takes time and great skill; therefore, it is expensive and done only on the finest crystal. Engraving is done with copper wheels of many sizes and shapes turned rapidly by motors. The glass is pressed upward against the revolving wheel, which is fed with a fine abrasive of emery dust mixed with oil. The result is a shallow intaglio that, by optical illusion, may seem to be in low relief (see the engraved owl on the plate in Fig. 286). Although the engraving is seldom deep, the effects can range from delicate lines to strongly realized forms. It is easy to distinguish from etched glass (described below) and from ornamentation produced by sandblasting through a stencil, for neither of these methods gives quite the clarity of line or full modeling of form that comes from engraving.

Enameled and Gilded Glass Glass, like ceramics, can be painted with enamels of many colors or with gold and silver, and these can be fired onto the surface. In recent years, glass enriched by this technique has been of disappointingly low quality, but the potentialities of the technique have been proved by many pieces of historic glass treasured in museums.

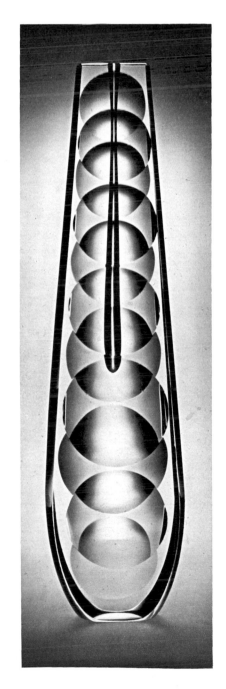

right : 287. A contemporary vase (c. 1958, height 14 ¼") of clear, colorless glass, designed and cut by Pavel Hlava, is enhanced by a succession of overlapping circular motifs that underscore the gently swelling, vertical form and add their own lively rhythmic pattern.

288. A bottle and a low bowl (1966; height, *left,* 10½", *right,* 6¼"), both of clear, blue glass, enriched with intricate, asymmetric motifs produced by sandblasting and acid etching are through one layer of glass to a heavier layer, either on the inside or outside. Bertil Vallien, designer.

Etched Glass　Etching is a common method of decorating glass. The areas not to be etched are coated with a waxy substance. Then the glass is exposed to hydrofluoric acid that eats the unprotected areas to a frosted texture. That the technique has possibilities for fresh and free approaches is shown in the two pieces (Fig. 288) designed by Bertil Vallien, a young Swedish artist.

Other Techniques　There are innumerable other ways of enriching glass that prove its versatility as a material. Romans, Venetians, and modern artists have made vessels out of multicolored glass mosaics fused together (Fig. 211). Objects with two or more layers of different colors have been carved in cameo fashion; and ornamentation has been sandwiched between two layers of glass. Varying the thickness of glass and introducing controlled bubbles or textures produce results such as those in Dominick Labino's bubble vase (Pl. 24a) and in Bengt Edenfalk's bottle (Fig. 289). Colors can be fused on the surface, and mineral flakes can be suspended like snow. The Venetians were masters of decorative spun threads and drawn bands. *Pâte de verre* (or paste glass), made by fusing finely powdered glass in molds, has produced velvety surfaces and a depth and subtlety of color unobtainable by other techniques. The surface of glass can be made iridescent and illusive, as in Plate 24b. And in the vase designed by Maydam (Fig. 290) unconfined colors appear to drift through the body.

　Glass is indeed a versatile material, one subject to many uses and to a considerable range of treatment for both form and expression.

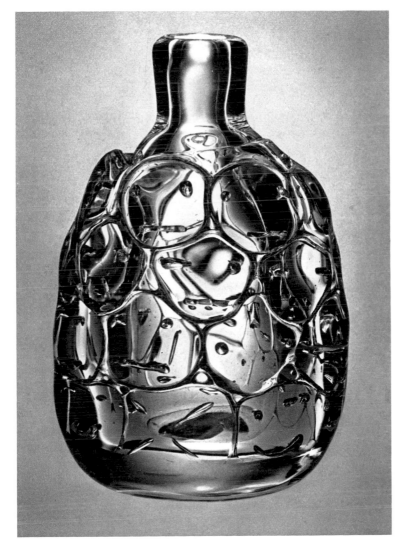

right : 289. A small glass bottle (1959, height 6 ¾″) exemplifies the ingenuity and skill that Sweden has brought to glassmaking. Bubbles in the glass and a fluid network of laid-on glass combine to produce an intricate pattern. Bengt Edenfalk, designer.

below : 290. A thick, solid contemporary vase (c. 1960, 5 × 8″) from Holland has a subtle design in gray and black that appears to float within the glass. F. Maydam, designer.

291. Robert C. Fritz's free-blown sculptural form (c. 1966, height 11″) of turquoise and smoky glass was made by joining two forms. The piece preserves, to an unusual degree, the fluidity and viscosity of molten glass and creates a vivacious contrast of lights and darks.

The ancient art of making durable vessels out of soft clay is still practiced throughout the world with processes that are similar to those of early potters although greatly improved and expanded. Glass production progressed more slowly but has in comparatively recent times enjoyed a tremendous development as a material of unique importance in art, architecture, and science. Glass and ceramics are used in hundreds of ways that directly affect our daily living, yet man has only begun to explore their full range of potentialities.

292. Susan Weitzman's *Phase* (1967, 54″ square) is a boldly patterned wall hanging of black and white wool.

8 Fabrics

Almost every minute, day or night, we are in visual and physical contact with fabrics. Not only do we use them to upholster furniture, to cover floors and beds, and to hang at windows, but we wear them for protection and adornment. Pliant and responsive, infinitely variable in color and texture, they soften, humanize, and enhance our environment.

Some fabrics are primarily utilitarian, and a few are created solely for esthetic pleasure, but the majority combine usefulness and beauty. Contemporary weavers and textile designers have at their command many materials and processes with which to produce a profusion of fabrics to meet our varied needs. We, the consumers, can select intelligently only when we have some knowledge of the basic materials and the ways in which they are fabricated and some understanding of the specific considerations of fabric design.

The Materials

Most fabrics are made from fibers, which are slender threadlike filaments. Plants and animals provide an abundance of natural fibers, and scientists have recently given us a host of new man-made materials.

Natural Fibers

Of the hundreds of fibrous materials found in nature, four are preeminent. Two of these, cotton and wool, deserve to be called "wonder" fibers because no man-made filaments yet developed are so versatile. Although somewhat more limited in range, linen and silk are valued for their unique qualities.

Cotton, used in more than two-thirds of today's textiles, comes from the fibers covering the seeds of cotton plants. The short fibers are separated from the seeds, carded and drawn to clean them and to make them parallel, spun into threads and yarns, and then woven into textiles. Cotton is inexpensive, wears fairly well, and is versatile—it is found as cool summer clothes, easily laundered "linens," thin curtains and heavy draperies, thick rugs, and tents. Special treatments can increase its softness and luster, make it water-repellent, wrinkle-resistant, and quick drying.

Linen comes from the fibers around the woody pith of flax plants, which have been cultivated for some 7000 years. One stem may yield as many as 25,000 fibers, each averaging 1/1000 inch in diameter and measuring up to 3½ feet long. Linen is the strongest, most pliable *vegetable* fiber. Because of its strength, linen can be spun into extremely fine threads and woven into thin and durable textiles, such as those used for handkerchiefs. Linen tablecloths and napkins look and feel smooth and fresh even after years of use. Heavier yarns are used for draperies, upholstery, and rugs. Today it can be processed so that it resists soil and wrinkles.

Silk is the luxury fiber without equal because of its unique luster and crunchy softness. It has the greatest tensile strength of any *natural* fiber, is somewhat elastic, and resists abrasion. Because silk fibers are long and strong, they can be spun into very thin yarns and woven or knitted into gauzy textiles, such as translucent chiffon. And silk yarns give shimmering satins, rich velvets, and lustrous rugs. Coarser silk fibers, from worms fed on oak leaves, are woven into the pleasantly rough textures of shantung and pongee. The way in which silkworms transform mulberry and oak leaves into this remarkable fiber is quite as wondrous as the processes by which man makes his artificial fibers, and basically it is similar to those used in making rayon.

Wool is not hair, but a fine undercoat that may later develop into hair. Sheep, and not all sheep at that, are among the few animals that bear a fleece of wool but not hair. Wool fibers vary in thickness: some are thin as a spider web, while others are as coarse as hair. They also vary in length, growing from about 1 inch to over 18 inches a year. Like cotton, wool fibers are combed out, twisted into yarns, and woven into textiles of remarkably varied qualities. There are thin challis; smooth, firm gabardines; or rough, loose tweeds and homespuns. Its durability, resiliency, and soft luster have made wool a standard fiber for rugs. Dyes penetrate deeply to give unequaled richness and subtlety of color. Much less widely used are the fibers obtained from such animals as alpacas, camels, goats, rabbits, and vicuñas.

Man-made Fibers

Until late in the nineteenth century man got along with nature's fibers. Then two independent developments—rayon and glass fibers—laid the foundations for an enormous program of making fibers tailored to our specific requirements. As with plastics, however, not much progress was made until the 1930s. Now over 40 percent of the textile fibers used in the United States are manufactured rather than grown.

Rayon, or artificial silk as it was first called, was predicted by a British scientist in 1664, but commercial production began in 1886. The process, although complex, can be described simply. Wood pulp or cotton linters are chemically treated to

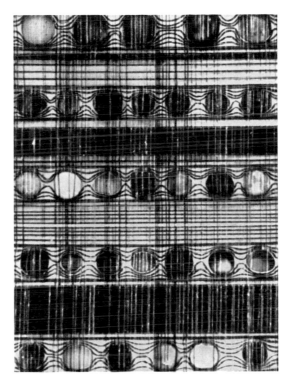

left : 293. The warmth and durability of wool and the strength of linen make them excellent fibers for an eighteenth-century coverlet (detail) handwoven by Mehitabel Harriman in New Hampshire. National Gallery of Art, Washington, D.C., Index of American Design.

right : 294. Ted Hallman's wall hanging (c. 1962, 6 × 9″) exploits the luminosity of brightly colored circles and strips of Plexiglas held together by plastic bands and fiber warp.

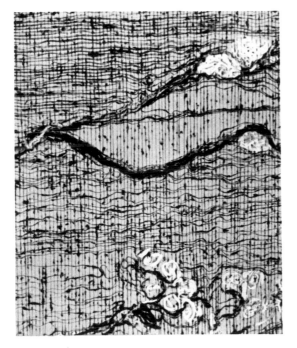

left : 295. Lenore Tawney's transparent wall hanging (c. 1962) combines cotton, silk, wool, and goathair in a way that accentuates the qualities of each fiber. Meandering lines float freely through the weaving.

right : 296. Mildred Fischer uses varied techniques in weaving abstract wool tapestries (c.1962) that express her reactions to the colors and patterns seen in the sky and in water.

produce a honeylike solution. This is forced through tiny nozzles (much like the spinnerets of silkworms and spiders) into a chemical bath, where it hardens into hairlike threads. These are then twisted into yarns and woven into textiles. All rayons are strong, absorbent, and mothproof, but vary greatly in other respects. They range from sheer to heavy, glossy to dull, and can be processed to resemble cotton, linen, silk, or wool. Often they are combined with other fibers. Rayons are widely used for sheer curtains and heavier draperies, rugs and upholstery, and clothes.

Glass fibers were first woven into textiles in the 1890s but were not seriously studied or widely used until the 1930s. While most glass is brittle, glass fibers are pliable because they are extremely fine—from 100 to 400 filaments are combined to make a fine yarn. Fiber glass, as the material is usually called, is noninflammable, nonabsorbent, and strong. It can be sleekly smooth or show many textures. It is used for thin curtains or heavier draperies, as reinforcing in plastic lamp shades or laminated sheets, and for many industrial purposes.

Nylon was developed in 1928 by combining in a very special way coal, wood, natural gas, air, and water. It is the strongest textile fiber commonly used; therefore, it can be woven into very sheer stockings or into very durable rugs. Highly elastic and resilient, nylon textiles will return to their original shape after stretching or twisting. They are slow to soil, easy to clean, and resist moths and mildew. Although as yet nylon does not have the deeply satisfying richness of silk, it is less expensive and more durable.

These are three of the earliest man-made fibers, the still-vigorous progenitors of a constantly enlarging family. All of the synthetic fibers share some desirable qualities: unlimited length of fiber in contrast to the comparative shortness of wool or cotton and the ability to dry quickly. Some of them are more soil-resistant, or retain pleats and creases better, or do not wrinkle and require little ironing. Most are unappealing to insects, some are fireproof, others have great elasticity. Some synthetics are better suited to specific uses than are any natural substances, but few have the range of qualities that make the natural fibers suitable to a broad spectrum of uses.

Each textile fiber has its assets and its liabilities. None of them is equally suitable for every purpose, but for each set of conditions there is a fiber, or a combination of fibers, that will do the job. Much, though, depends on the manner in which they are fabricated.

Making Fabrics

Animal skins and the bark of trees were the forerunners of fabrics, but at some early time men discovered that they could make their own fabrics, which were more responsive to their needs. Felts probably came first, then knitted fish nets and textiles as well as baskets or mats woven of grass and rushes. The controlled spinning of fibers into yarns led to more pliable and diversified cloths. As with ceramics and glass, there have been few basic changes in the making of fabrics from natural fibers, but there have been stupendous technological developments. Today the fabric industry is one of the three largest in the world. Designers and engineers have invented new processes and refined old ones to produce a seemingly inexhaustible variety of fabrics at great speed. Relieved of the necessity to produce quantities of cloth, designer-craftsmen are free to experiment in new directions.

The term *fabric* refers to anything manufactured, but it is often applied specifically to cloth. *Textile* refers only to fabrics that are woven.

297. A four-harness hand loom permits many complex weaves. Notice the four foot treadles that separate the warp threads in four ways and the shuttles on which the filling is carried back and forth. Robert Peterson, designer.

298. Plain weave.

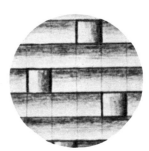

299. Satin weave.

300. Twill weave.

Weaving

Weaving is the process of interlacing, usually at right angles, two systems of pliable materials. It can be done on a piece of cardboard cut into a crude loom, on hand looms (Fig. 297), or on the complex power looms of a great mill. The lengthwise threads are called *warp*, the crosswise are known as *filling* (also *weft* or *woof*). There are four fundamental steps:

- Stringing the loom with the warp threads
- Separating the warp threads into two or more series to form an opening for the passage of the filling
- "Picking" the filling through this opening, usually with a shuttle
- Beating back the filling just run through to make the interlacing of the desired tightness

When one looks at the variety of textiles in a large store or mail-order catalog, it is hard to believe that there are only three basic types of weaves.

Plain weave, the simplest and strongest, accounts for about 80 percent of all woven goods (Figs. 298, 301). In this kind of weave, one filling yarn passes over one warp thread and under the next, as in broadcloth, burlap, or muslin. The many variations include *basket weaves*, in which two or more warps are crossed by two or more filling yarns, as in monk's cloth, and *rib weaves*, in which a rib is formed by having a warp thicker than the filling (or the reverse), as in rep or poplin.

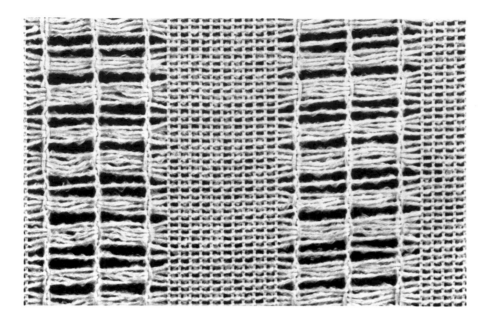

Machine-woven textiles have a fabulous range of expressive qualities.

above : 301. Texturized Fiberglas is soft and bulky. Marie Nichols' design (c. 1962), in which vertical stripes of plain weave alternate with open weave, celebrates the textile's structural character.

left : 302. Made of rayon in a satin weave, *Mobara* (1967) has a semiformal series of slightly irregular rosettes anchored in an interlaced grid.

Floating yarn, or *satin*, *weave* differs from plain weave in that the filling yarns float over or under several or even many warp yarns (Figs. 299, 302). This produces the smoothness of satin, in which long floats minimize the over-and-under texture of most woven products.

Twill weave interlaces warp and filling yarns so that diagonal lines show on the surface (Fig. 300). Many flannels, gabardines, and serges are examples.

Two frequently seen elaborations of the basic type weaves are the *pile* weave (Figs. 304, 312) and the *figure* weave (Figs. 293, 296). The pile weave utilizes, in addition to the flat-lying warp and filling, another set of yarns that stands up in loops. These loops can be cut, as in velvet, or uncut, as in bath towels. Figure weaves have simple to complex patterns, as in coverlets, brocades, and carpets. They can be produced on hand or power looms. Machine weaving of this type is usually done on

When closely inspected, fabrics reveal patterns and textures that cannot be fully appreciated from a distance.

left: 303. *Plume* (c. 1962), handwoven from silken rickrack, bronze metallic, and heavy cotton fibers, is an intricate interplay of coarse and fine, light and dark elements.

right: 304. José Cleón's *End of Summer* (c. 1962) is a deeply textured pile-weave rug of vibrantly colored wool yarns.

a Jacquard loom, a complex mechanism in which the weaving is controlled by perforated strips of cardboard in intricate designs. (They look much like the old player-piano rolls, and the principles are much the same.)

Although most fabrics are woven, four other techniques are regaining importance because of their design and production potentials.

Felting is the matting together of a web of fibers, usually with heat, water, and pressure, to form a continuous dense cloth. Felts are much used industrially, and new techniques give promise of distinctive, ornamental design (Fig. 314). In *bonding* (or *fusing*), the latest method of making nonwoven fabrics, the web is saturated with a binder and then dried or cured.

Knitting is the interlocking of loops of yarn by needles. In knitting, a single yarn (or set of yarns), moving in one direction only, is looped through itself to make a chain of stitches. With power machines, it can be five times as fast as weaving (Fig. 310).

 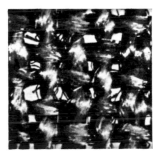 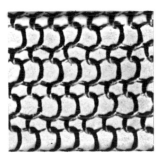

305–307. Enlarged photographs show how the structure of felt (*left*: 305) differs from that of a woven fabric (*center*: 306) and a knitted fabric (*right*: 307).

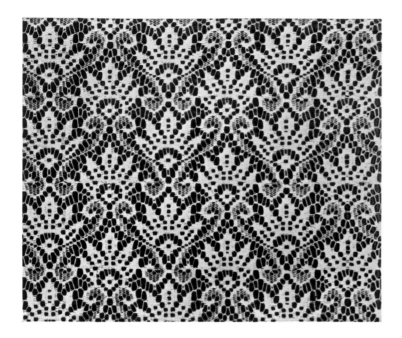

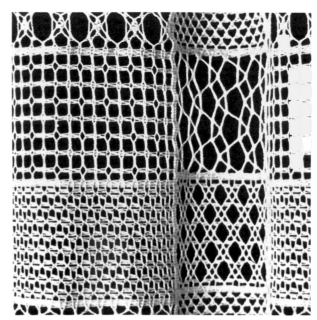

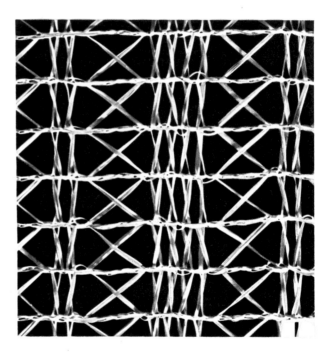

Lacemaking and knitting, historic ways of making fabrics, still hold unique possibilities for the present and future.

above : 308. A cotton Nottingham lace net (c. 1966) is a crisp transcription of a familiar motif.

above right : 309. *Bobbin Cloth* (c. 1962) is a thoroughly contemporary exploration of the open-and-closed nature of lace. Made of permanently white cotton, it is slip-proof, wilt-resistant, and drip-dry.

right : 310. Strong, dimensionally stable synthetic yarns can be knitted into flameproof open casement cloths (c. 1962) that hold their shape.

Lacemaking, the interlocking of yarns in openwork patterns, has been given vitality with fresh designs (Figs. 308, 309). Machines with as many as 4000 bobbins can with great speed make lace from cotton, linen, nylon, rayon, or wool.

Forming is the method by which plastic film or sheeting is made. It is the newest fabric technique and the only one in which fibers are not used. Synthetic resins are spread on wheels, extruded through wide dies, or pressed through rollers into thin, transparent or translucent, or heavier, opaque membranes. Coated fabrics, used for upholstery and wall coverings, are textiles with a durable surface coating of vinyl. Both plastic sheeting and coated fabrics can be embossed or printed with any pattern desired or molded into three-dimensional designs (Fig. 313).

Each of these processes leads to fabrics with distinctly different physical and esthetic characteristics.

Fabric Design

All fabrics have a *purpose* that is fulfilled through *materials* organized into a *structure*. The major factors in fabric design are therefore:

- The *purposes*, or *functions*, of the fabric
- The *materials* of which it is composed
- The *processes* by which it is fabricated
- The *applied ornamentation* (if any) that is added

Designers find inspiration in the purpose or function of a fabric.

above : 311. New stretch fabrics are designed to fit tightly over complex forms. Olivier Mourgue, designer.

left : 312. Matt Kahn's *Menorah* (1967), a wall hanging for a synagogue, depicts the seven-branched candelabrum used in Jewish religious services. The pile weave is varied in height and richly vibrant in color.

Designers and craftsmen may start with any one of these determinants—the desire for a warmth-giving coverlet (Fig. 293) or a compelling tapestry (Fig. 296), or the exploitation of synthetic fibers. His interest may be in a process, such as the molding of plastic (Fig. 313), or primarily in the applied ornamentation of printed designs. But all the factors must be considered at some time in the process.

Functions

A few handmade textiles are created for the sheer joy of making something, and some fabrics are developed in the hope that a use will be found for them. But almost all of our textiles are produced with some purpose in mind. It can be as mundane as merely confining the water from a shower bath with noncommittal plastic sheeting, as venturesome as developing stretch fabrics that because of their suppleness conform to complex furniture shapes, as in the Larsen apartment (Pl. 25) and in Figure 311, as inspiring as the wall hanging for a temple in Figure 312. Thus, the ways in which a fabric will be used and enjoyed are first factors in design.

Materials

New materials and processes invite exploration.

left : 313. *Curvilinear* (1962), a molded plastic wall covering gives a vigorous play of light and shade. Estelle and Irwine Laverne, designers.

right : 314. An enlarged detail of a Japanese papermaking technique shows a handsome, open, structural pattern. Soft, flexible felt cloth could also be made rapidly by this process.

In looking for satisfactory fibers, a designer considers the qualities of many kinds in relation to the specific problem. Also, he thinks about how the material can best speak for itself. For luxurious upholstery he might regard soft, gleaming silk as the ideal fiber. But if moderate cost and durability are important factors, he might well give consideration to rayon, nylon, or wool. Vinyl-coated fabrics would be even less expensive and more durable. The manner in which the fibers or resins are handled is as important as the material itself. We think of silk as soft and fine, of wool as rougher and thicker—but coarse silk roughly spun into thick yarns makes sturdy rugs, while some wools can be sheer and lustrous. Synthetic fibers can be smooth, continuous filaments or bulky, textured staple fibers. In the Op Art wall hanging (Fig. 292), Susan Weitzman chose fine wool because it can produce an evenly textured surface

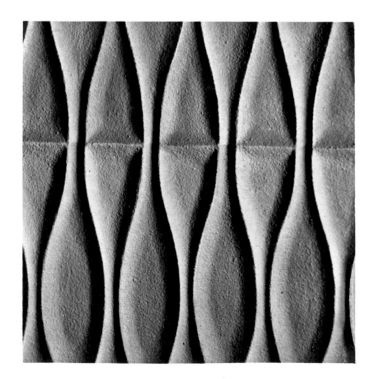

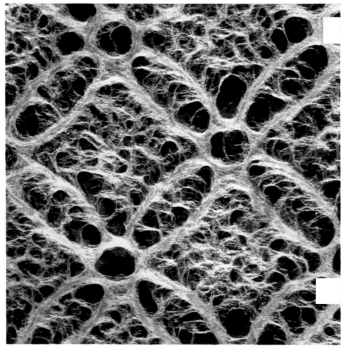

Plate 25. The flowing contours of some contemporary furniture have been made possible by the development of stretch fabrics that fit like stockings. In fabric designer Jack Lenor Larsen's New York apartment, his own *Firebird* fabric, backed with foam, stretches to cover completely the sofa recently designed by Olivier Mourgue. Plain stretch-wool *Contura* sheathes the unusual shapes of the Pierre Paulin chairs. The shell panels that arch over the ceiling are of a white translucent stretch material. As counterpoint to these soft fabrics and curvilinear forms, Larsen has used a firm, slightly textured sisal rug and transparent Plexiglas tables whose simple, rectangular, almost graphic outlines are echoed in the silver painting. (See also Fig. 311.)

Plate 26. The printed design on *Rifugio*, a heavy linen and cotton fabric, moves across the surface in jagged rhythms. Green, blue, white, and red stripes, angled and intermittent, are interspersed with curved forms that soften the predominant angularity and strengthen the flow of the pattern.

that allows the opposition of black and white to stand out clearly. On the other hand, in *Plume* the materials were chosen precisely for the lively pattern they would develop even in a simple weave (Fig. 303).

Fabricating Processes

Each of the fabricating processes described earlier leads to different physical and visual qualities. Each has its own *structural* pattern, as can be seen by comparing the illustrations in this chapter. The patterns can be as simple as the plain weave in the texturized Fiberglas (Fig. 301) or as intricate as the three-dimensional designs at the end of the chapter. There is almost no limit to the kinds of structural enrichment that can originate in the process of fabrication.

Applied Enrichment

Once again, we repeat that applied ornamentation is not necessary. Many fabrics need nothing beyond appropriate materials sympathetically fabricated for visual appeal. But we appreciate variety and stimulation, a holding and releasing of attention, and an intensity of expression not always achieved without some additional ornamentation such as printing, appliqué, and embroidery.

Printed Fabrics   Fabrics ornamented with print are so abundant that they deserve special attention (Pl. 26 and Figs. 315–321). Little is known about when and where they were begun, but evidence indicates that the Egyptians stamped designs on cloth as early as 2100 B.C. Apparently, though, it was many centuries before this process was widely known and used.

The three basic ways of printing designs on fabrics are block printing, roller printing, and screen printing, processes that are almost identical with those for printing on paper, discussed in Chapter 9.

Block printing, the oldest of the three, is done from blocks, usually of wood, into which a design has been cut (Fig. 315). A coloring agent is applied to the block, which is then pressed onto the fabric, and the raised portion of the block prints the design. Typically, each color requires a separate block. And since block printing

Two American textiles (Figs. 315, 316) are enhanced with curvilinear designs based on natural forms. In both, the dominant verticality is balanced by horizontal movements.

315. An eighteenth-century handblocked cotton shows conventionalized birds and foliage organized as intertwining motifs. Small leaves and flowers in the background strengthen the feeling of continuity. Museum of Fine Arts, Boston.

316. *Papilio* (1967), inspired by the intricate patterns of color on butterflies, is printed on sheer Dacron or on a textured linen. Overlays of translucent printing inks and the over-all crackle pattern produce a luminous iridescence.

is usually a laborious hand process, it is suited to relatively simple designs in which the repeated motifs are not large and the colors are few. It can, however, go beyond these circumscriptions.

Roller printing is a machine process that uses engraved copper cylinders on a rotary press. Each cylinder prints only one color, but many colors can be printed in one run through the press. It imposes few limitations on the designer. The pattern can be simple or complex with repeated motifs as large as the circumference of the cylinder. Because of its flexibility, speed, and precision, roller printing is widely used.

Screen printing is a stencil process, sometimes referred to as silk-screen (Fig. 317). The basic procedure is forcing a thick, pasty dye through the uncovered mesh of a stencil screen. Nowadays an electronically controlled mechanism prints up to seven times as fast as the older hand process. Although slower and more expensive per yard than roller printing, screen printing readily permits larger repeats and heavier pigments that give the fabric a handcraft look.

In looking at the diversified printed fabrics on these pages one might wonder whether there are any valid principles for ornamentation applied to fabrics. It

would be better to assume that there were none than to devise constricting rules. But thinking about the distinctive qualities of fabrics does provide some clues. Fabrics are essentially two-dimensional structures that are typically continuous and pliable.

■ *Flatness* suggests patterns that acknowledge the two-dimensionality of fabrics by staying on the surface (Fig. 317). This does not preclude some suggestion of depth, but it may make questionable designs that seem to bulge out from the fabric or that plunge into deep space, unless the designer wishes particularly to exploit one of these characteristics for its ambiguous effect.

■ *Continuousness* of textiles indicates ornamentation that is uninterrupted and is without definite beginning or conclusion. This can be achieved in many ways: stripes that call attention to the length or breadth of the material, plaids that move in two directions, or patterns that are multidirectional, as in *Rifugio* (Pl. 26), or have flowing continuity (Fig. 318). This does *not* rule out motifs that appear in isolation because, if knowingly handled, they can, in their surprise and impact, provide a welcome departure from customary approaches. The fabric design *A Crown for the Empress* (Fig. 319), almost overwhelming in the size of its single motif, would be effective as a foil either for busy patterns elsewhere in a room or for broadly simple architecture and furnishings. Its stark simplicity is similar to much of the Minimal Art (see pp. 444–448) now established as a major artistic expression.

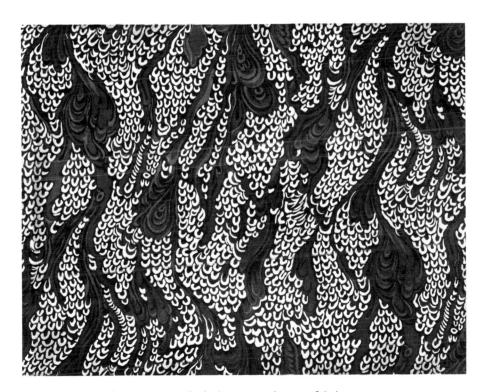

Flat, over-all designs seem particularly appropriate on fabrics.

opposite : 317. Alexander Girard's inventive graphic array of the word *love* in nineteen languages is as two-dimensional as the cloth on which it is printed (1967).

above : 318. In *Euterpe* (1967) a succession of curvilinear forms flow supply over the surface of the linen and cotton textile on which it is printed. Falconetto, designer.

right : 319. Maija Isolde's *A Crown for the Empress* (1967) relies on simplified abstract motifs 4 ½ feet in length for visual impact.

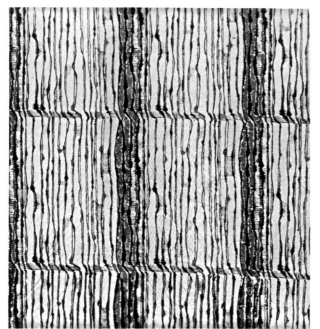

Some designs emphasize the pliant or structural qualities of textiles.

above : 320. The swirling lines of *Hellespont* (1965), a reversible cotton Jacquard, suggest the flexibility characteristic of an upholstery fabric and are also reminiscent of tides rushing through narrow straits.

left : 321. Fagya Ostrower, a Brazilian etcher, brings the imagination nurtured by print-making to textile design. Beginning with the basic rhythm of lines recalling the warp of the textile, she has lightly connected them with horizontal strokes that echo without duplicating the construction of the fabric.

■ *Pliability* makes fabrics particularly receptive to supple, flexuous designs but does not outlaw those that are geometric. The flowing lines of *Hellespont* (Fig. 320) and the softened geometry of *Rifugio* (Pl. 26) are both at ease with this quality.
■ *Structure,* especially the crisscross of weaving, can be highlighted by figures that reflect the construction of which they are part (Fig. 321). But, like any other factor, if this is interpreted too rigidly, the range of designs would be critically limited.

These major factors deserve consideration, but the intended purposes of fabrics are sometimes more consequential.

 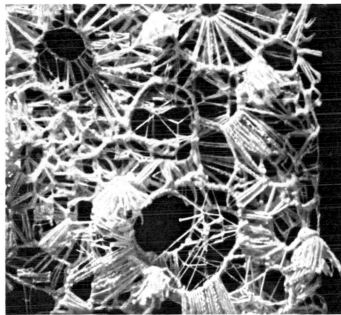

Although knitted and woven fabrics are usually two-dimensional, some contemporary craftsmen have experimented successfully with sculptural effects.

left : 322. Ron Goodman's *Composition* (1968, diameter 29″, depth 7″) is inventively knitted from violet and blue wools. The asymmetric curved forms interlock with one another in depth as well as in length and breadth. Collection Dr. and Mrs. H. T. Linn, Michigan.

right : 323. Haan Conrad and Dian Budko Thomas, both of whom are sculptors and painters, have created intricate forms woven on both sides of a double warp (1968), to be used as curtains or wall hangings. A detail shows the intricate, unexpected quality of their work.

Handcrafted Fabrics and Enrichment   Varied types of stitchery, appliqué, and embroidery are once again receiving the attention of serious craftsmen. And hand weaving, knitting, and lacemaking are being explored in new directions, most notably that of fabric sculpture or three-dimensional wall hangings. Ron Goodman, employing the old technique of knitting, has created a round wall plaque with ridges and hollows accentuating the several layers of the piece (Fig. 322). The intricacies of the dimensional weaving in Figure 323 are far removed from conventional weaving; they become a new kind of abstract, open tapestry that is especially effective when hung at a window.

As with other types of art, in appreciating textiles we think about the way in which they will be used and concern ourselves with their functional qualities. And, equally important, we look for textiles that have spirit, imagination, creativity.

9 Printing and the Graphic Processes

The book you are reading is an example of the art and science of printing. The type-face for the text is called *Times Roman*, and the type has been set on a *composing machine*, by a process termed *monotype*. The black-and-white photographs are *halftones*, and they have been reproduced by *gravure*, a process that depends upon an *intaglio cylinder* plate. The color chart in Plate 38 (p. 324) and the color reproductions throughout the book are printed in *four colors* (yellow, red, blue, and black) by a process identified as *lithographic offset*. Good results could also have been had from *letterpress* printing, whose plate has a *raised surface*.

So accustomed have we become to the printed page—newspapers, magazines, books—that we easily forget that machine printing on paper had been known in Europe for only fifty years when Columbus discovered the Western Hemisphere.

But the principles and processes on which printing is based had long been known. In Egypt and in India, designs from wood blocks had been impressed on textiles for centuries, and early in their history the Chinese were familiar with block printing on paper. There is evidence that the Chinese used movable type of clay and tin in the eleventh century, and that a Korean book was printed from cast type in 1409. However, it was not until the middle of the fifteenth century in Europe that Johannes Gutenberg began making movable type of individual letters.

At first this type was set by hand and printed on simple platen or job presses in which two flat surfaces are forced together to make the printing. The capacity of such early presses was about 300 pages a day. By 1814, power-driven cylinder presses were producing 1000 pages an hour, and modern giant rotary presses have many times that capacity. The *cylinder* press differs from the platen press in that the paper is fed on a cylinder, but the type is carried on a flat surface. In the *rotary* press, both type and paper are on cylinders, making possible much greater speed and efficiency.

As the speed of printing increased, attention was turned to the process of setting the type, and in 1885 the *linotype* was patented. The improved form of the linotype in use today is a very complex machine. A skilled operator works at a keyboard similar to a typewriter. As he presses each key, a matrix, or mold, of the letter is released and carried to an assembler. When molds for a full line of words have been assembled, a cast, or slug, is made. Then the molds are returned automatically to their proper places, and the printing is done from the cast.

Monotype—a process often used for composing technical copy and other types of text in which corrections are likely to be heavy and accuracy is important—sets type in lines of individual metal characters, instead of a solid slug for an entire line. Recently, *photocomposition* has been developed, a process by which characters are projected onto film. Even "computerized" composition is now possible.

As you look at the different kinds of typefaces used in magazines, you will probably think that there are hundreds of different ones. There are—but almost all of them relate to one of four basic families.

𝔅𝔩𝔞𝔠𝔨 𝔏𝔢𝔱𝔱𝔢𝔯   ROMAN   SANS SERIF   *ITALIC*

- *Black letter* type, introduced by Gutenberg in imitation of hand lettering, is the earliest. It is seldom used today.
- *Roman*, based on the inscriptions carved on Roman monuments, was developed in the fifteenth century. Some lines are thick, others thin; and most of the letters have *serifs* (small ornamental projections at the tops and bottoms).
- In *Sans serif* (or *Gothic*), all lines are of equal thickness, and there are no serifs, or at least only vestiges of them.
- *Italic*, of recent origin, has slanted letters, like those in the first word of this sentence.

Three other distinctions are worth mention. The *weight* (lightness or heaviness) of type is described in four standard classifications:

lightface   **standard**   **boldface**   **extrabold**

Letters also vary in *width*, and, again, there are four categories:

extended   standard   **condensed**   extra-condensed

In addition to different weights and widths, typefaces can express innumerable ideas and feelings through their *character,* as illustrated below:

DIGNITY or *Playfulness*
SIMPLICITY or *COMPLEXITY*

325. The visual appearance of the letters in a word is a potent means of expression. Robert Carola, designer.

Type can also be imaginatively manipulated or combined with pictorial images to emphasize the meaning of a word (Fig. 325).

Any printing job demands many decisions: page size, typeface, quality of paper, kind and quantity of illustrations, and size of margins around the printing. When sensitively and creatively handled, printing can be an art in its own right. Look at the printing you see every day and ask questions such as these:

■ Is it legible? Printing is one way of communicating ideas, and if it is not easy to read, it has little to recommend it—except as a device to capture attention.
■ Is the style of printing appropriate to the publication's purpose? Much printed material is intended to be read quickly and discarded, but some printing can give lifetime enjoyment.
■ Are the printed words and illustrations well organized? Design is as important in printing as in any other art.

The printing of words is only one branch of this field, and we now turn to the creation and reproduction of pictures by hand and machine.

The Graphic Processes

Today, visual images can be transmitted around the world with the speed of electricity. Satellites can produce and transmit with incredible immediacy photographs of weather conditions around the world or of the surfaces of objects in outer space. These can be reproduced by the thousands in a few minutes. Strikingly different is the work of the printmaker, who may labor long and patiently to produce a comparatively small number of drypoints or lithographs that he prints by hand (although the tedious parts of the process are sometimes relegated to assistants or mass-production techniques). Yet all are examples of the graphic arts and sciences.

The *graphic processes* can be defined as the making of plates or screens and from them the printing of pictures, designs, or letters. Some, such as drypoint and etching, are hand processes by which art is *created*. Others, such as the gravure processes, are mechanical methods of *reproducing* art. A few, notably lithography and silk screen, can be either.

A basic problem in all printing is treating a surface so that parts of it will print and parts of it will not. Four ways of achieving this goal have been developed:

326-328. Three major techniques of printing are shown in magnified details of mechanized rotary presses: relief printing (*left* : 326), intaglio printing (*center* : 327), and planographic printing (*right* : 328). The processes are the same when the printing surfaces and paper are flat. The upper cylinders carry the paper; the lower ones are the printing plates. The inked designs on the plates are at the left; the impressions made on the paper are on the right.

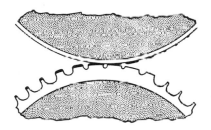
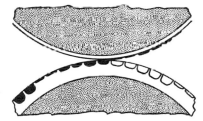
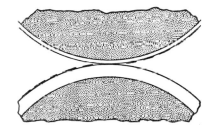

■ *Relief* printing is that in which the design stands above the general level of the plate's surface (Fig. 326). Rubber stamps and fingerprints, woodcuts and halftones are examples. The letterpress used for books is relief printing.

■ *Intaglio* printing is the opposite—the design is scratched, engraved, or etched into the plate (Fig. 327). These depressions are filled with ink, the plate's surface is wiped, and with great pressure paper is forced into the depressions to absorb the ink. Etchings and drypoints are examples. Gravure printing is the industrial equivalent, the process used for the black-and-white pages of this book.

■ *Planographic* (or surface) printing is done from an almost smooth surface treated chemically or mechanically so that some areas will print and others will not (Fig. 328). Lithography is the only common example. Offset book printing is a type of lithography.

■ *Stencil* printing is accomplished by cutting designs out of special paper or by making some portions of thin cloth impervious to liquids. Ink goes through the open portions but not through those that are impervious. Silk-screen prints are the best-known type.

Prints with more than one color can be made by any of these methods. Usually each color requires a separate plate and a separate printing, but different colors can be applied to one plate and printed together.

Hand Processes: Relief

In creating handmade prints of any kind a typical early step is musing about what the print is intended to do. In the past almost all prints represented a scene, interpreted an event or story, or depicted specific emotions with recognizable objects. But contemporary printmakers have extended the scope by exploring less tangible experiences and expressing them in abstract forms, much as musical composers

329. Leonard Baskin. *Man of Peace*. 1952. Woodcut, 59 ½ × 30 ⁵/₈″. The Museum of Modern Art, New York. Baskin vigorously explores some of the potentialities of the woodcut technique.

left : 330. Katsushika Hokusai. *The Great Wave of Kanagawa.* c. 1823–1829. Woodcut. The Metropolitan Museum of Art, New York (Howard Mansfield Collection, Rogers Fund, 1936). Large areas of flat and shaded color are accentuated by lines and dots in the waves and boats.

opposite : 331. Arthur Deshaies. *The Insects Go Up*. 1957. Relief engraving on Lucite, 13 ⁷/₈ × 23 ³/₈″. Print Council of America, New York. The opulent textures of this fanciful, semiabstract comment on the habits of insects are framed by velvety black areas and demonstrate the versatility of plastic as a printmaker's material.

have always done. Graphic artists usually make preliminary sketches on paper, and these range from rough sketches to detailed drawings. Some transfer their drawings to the printing surface, while others hang them on the wall as guides. Some make no preliminary studies but work directly from nature or from their own imaginations, responding only to their feelings and the potentialities of the graphic process.

Woodcuts and Related Techniques   One of the most ancient graphic processes, *woodcuts* (Figs. 329, 330) still retain their great popularity. In addition to wood, linoleum and many other materials are often used. Here are the basic steps in the standard approach.

- The design or picture is drawn or mentally projected on the *side grain* of such even-grained woods as beech, apple, or sycamore. (Sometimes the grain of the wood is visible in the print, as in Fig. 324.) Thick linoleum mounted on a block of wood is another favorite material, and this results in *linocuts*.
- Knives or gouges cut out those parts that are not to be printed.
- The block is inked and the design printed on suitable paper with the pressure of a printing press, a foot, or hand rubbing. Usually a few "proofs" are "pulled" and studied to see if changes are needed.

Wood engravings were originally done on the *end grain* of hard, fine-grained wood, but nowadays *Lucite* (Fig. 331) and other dense, hard substances are employed. The engraving is done with *burins*, which are small, sharp, steel tools. The prints typically have greater and more refined detail than do woodcuts, but there is no longer a hard-and-fast distinction between the two processes.

Contemporary printmakers, with an insatiable desire for discovery, have explored many new approaches and produced genuinely creative prints. Two or more processes are often combined, as in Figure 324. Cardboard, chipboard, composition board, and plastics have supplemented wood as basic materials. Innumerable textures can be created by imprinting the surface with such things as wire screen and nails or by roughening it with carpenters' files or power tools. The block can

be coated with glue or shellac, which before it dries can be impressed with paper-clips, the bark of a tree, or whatever the artist may deem desirable.

Instead of cutting into the block, a composition can be built up with pieces of cardboard or many other materials that are cut out, glued to the block, coated with shellac, and printed in the customary way. Paper reliefs involve both building up and cutting away. Variously shaped cardboard forms are glued to a rigid base, and then other patterns can, if desired, be cut into them. This technique allows great freedom, for the artist can add or subtract until he gets what he wants.

Multicolored prints, available from any of these processes, call to mind Japanese colored woodcuts. Keen observation and rich inventiveness in penetrating surface appearances to reveal essentials, combined with sureness of design, have carried these prints to remarkable heights. *The Great Wave of Kanagawa* (Fig. 330) depicts with powerful intensity one of the enormous waves that periodically strike Japan's coast. In the distance, Fujiyama is serene and aloof in contrast to the menacing turbulence of the ocean. Notice the dynamic asymmetrical balance, the rhythmic movement of water and spray, and the adroit placing of the mountain. Japanese prints are among the many sources that have inspired printmakers to evolve new, exhilarating modes of expression.

Hand Processes: Intaglio

Line engraving, drypoint, and etching are the major hand intaglio processes. Fine detail and intricate textures are typical characteristics. The printed lines or areas are slightly raised, and a depressed *plate mark* shows that the plate was pressed into the paper.

Line Engravings Also referred to as *engravings in metal, steel engravings,* or *copper engravings,* line engravings are sometimes called the "severest form of print-making." They give clean, assured, sweeping lines. Engraving in metal is done as follows:

- Plates of copper, steel, or zinc are engraved with burins (or gravers) that are pushed into the plate to gouge out V-shaped channels. The deeper a line is engraved, the wider it becomes, and the heavier it prints. Typically, the lines are crisp and definite, become thicker toward the middle, and taper toward the end.
- The plate is cleaned and heated; then the engraved lines are filled with ink and the surface is wiped clean. The plate is centered, face up, on the bed of a heavy press. Dampened paper is laid on top of it, and blankets of felt are placed over the paper.
- When a heavy roller is pulled over the plate, paper, and felt, the pressure forces the damp paper into the incised lines and the ink is transferred to the paper as slightly raised lines.

Calling cards and wedding invitations, postage stamps and paper money are the most common examples of line engravings seen today. If you examine a dollar bill with a magnifying glass, you will see some of the many fine textures—parallel lines of varied widths, dots, dashes, and crosshatching—that are possible in this graphic process. In the past, engravings made by hand were a major way of reproducing paintings and illustrating books: the lines can be so fine that 1000 can be put on an inch of plate.

Recently, line engraving has been revitalized as a creative, expressive process. Freed from binding stereotypes, contemporary engravers move from the austere

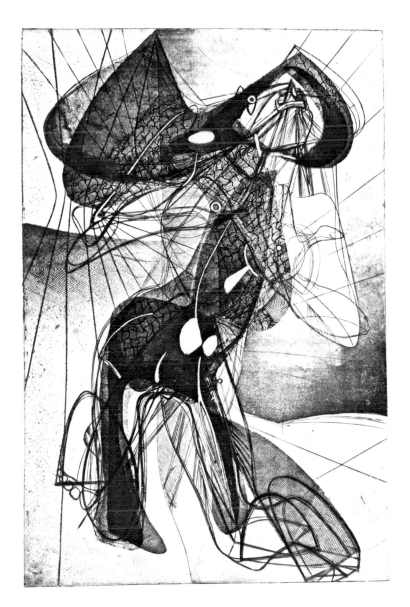

332. William Stanley Hayter. *Amazon*. 1945. Engraving and soft-ground etching, 24 $^1/_2$ × 15 $^7/_8''$. The Museum of Modern Art, New York (gift of Philip Johnson). This swirling composition combines decisive engraved lines with atmospheric areas of soft-ground etching.

and controlled to the energetic and impulsive. Often, as in Figure 332, engraving is combined with other incised techniques, and the prints are referred to as *intaglio*.

Drypoints   Superficially only slightly different from line engravings, drypoints are sometimes called *drypoint engravings*. With study, the differences assume significance. In making a drypoint:

■ Lines are cut into copper (also zinc, aluminium, Lucite) plates with needle-like points of sharpened steel or with points made from diamonds or rubies. These, in general, make a finer indentation than the engraver's burin and suggest a freer, sketchier line. A second important distinction is that the drypoint needle throws up tiny, irregular edges of metal, called a *burr*, that are left on the plate. In contrast, the engraver's burin, if sharp, leaves no burr, and any left by a dull tool is scraped off.

■ Printing drypoints is much like printing line engravings. Ink is rubbed onto the warmed plate—but in wiping it off, some ink is left in the burr to give the drypoint's characteristically soft, velvety line, and a light film of ink is usually left over the whole surface to give the background a pale tone.

Thus drypoints are generally distinguished from line engravings by such characteristics as these: the line quality is less formal and precise; the printed line is softly fuzzy; and the print generally has a toned background. *La Caresse* (Fig. 333) shows subject matter ideally suited to drypoint, for it seems unpremeditated and tender, sensitive and yielding. The composition has the informality often associated with the subject and the medium. Had this subject been carried out in line engraving, it would have been much clearer, harder, sharper.

Editions of drypoints are limited in number (unless the plate is coated with steel) because the burr wears off in the printing. The first twenty-five to thirty prints have the greatest richness, and from then on the quality declines.

Etchings   Although etchings are not easily distinguished from drypoints, their special qualities will become clear as we consider the way in which they are made. For etchings:

- A plate of copper or zinc is coated with a thin layer of *ground*—a dark, waxy material that resists acid but is easily penetrated by a metal needle.
- With a needle blunter than that used in drypoints, the lines to be printed are drawn through the ground. This exposes parts of the plate but does not scratch the metal.
- The plate is then immersed in an acid bath that eats away the exposed metal. The depth of the lines on the plate—and the consequent darkness of the lines

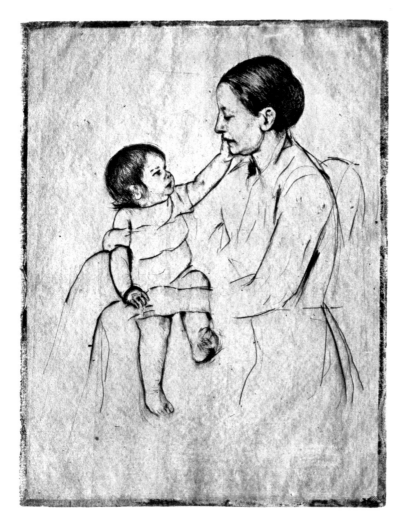

333. Mary Cassatt. *La Caresse.* 1891. Drypoint. The Metropolitan Museum of Art, New York (gift of Arthur Sachs, 1916). Many of the lines in this serene, tender drypoint show the soft, blurred quality produced by the "burr" on the plate.

334. Rembrandt. *Christ Healing the Sick (The Hundred Guilder Print)*. c. 1649. Etching, 10 $^7/_8$ × 15 $^3/_8$". The Metropolitan Museum of Art, New York (bequest of Mrs. H. O. Havemeyer, 1929, H. O. Havemeyer Collection).

on the print—is determined by the length of time the plate remains in the bath. A single immersion gives lines of equal depth. Variety is achieved by removing the plate from time to time, covering with a *stop-out* varnish those lines that are deep enough, and returning the plate for further biting.

■ Printing is identical with that of drypoint.

The etching *Christ Healing the Sick* (Fig. 334) by Rembrandt stands today, as it did three centuries ago, as one of the truly great works of art in any medium. The intense, sympathetic treatment of this moving subject matter makes it a noble expression of religious ideals. The dramatic diagonal organization of darks and lights gives great force to the group of figures with Christ in the center. Notice the virtuosity with which lines have been used. At the extreme left the lines stand clear and distinct, defining form and space by merely enclosing areas. As we move into the center of the picture, the lines are woven into a pattern of textures and values so that we are less conscious of the individual lines. Finally, at the extreme right, the lines are hardly noticeable in the rich grays and blacks. But line is the element on which the composition is built and is a major factor in giving it a flexible, lucid, almost transparent quality.

Other intaglio processes, used alone or more often with other techniques, as Peterdi has done in *Eclipse IV* (Pl. 27), include the following:

Aquatints   The aquatint process consists of covering a metal plate with resin dust and then heating it. Each particle of resin adheres to the plate as a hardened crystal, and the spaces between are etched with acid. Some areas are stopped-out with varnish while others are exposed to the acid. Repeated many times, this leads to textured areas that range from almost pure white to pure black (Fig. 335).

Soft-Ground Etchings   These are made by coating metal plates with a greasy ground that does not harden. A sheet of paper is laid on the ground, and the artist draws with a pencil or impresses the ground with anything he wishes. When the paper is removed, some of the ground comes with it. Then the plate is immersed in acid that eats into the metal in direct proportion to the amount of ground that has been removed.

Gabor Peterdi's *Eclipse IV* (Pl. 27) illustrates some of the possibilities of combining two or more techniques in one print. In this case segmented plates were used, and by employing etching, soft-ground etching, and relief etching processes, the artist achieved a variety of surface textures in a single work, some of which are slightly raised and others depressed. Peterdi was one of several artists who helped to spark the current revival of interest in printmaking. His interest and success in using innovative techniques influenced students and the printmaking community in general, resulting in the establishment of a number of graphic workshops where professional artists—painters, sculptors, and graphic artists—could work and experiment in what is essentially a mass-production medium. This in turn has led to the concept of the *multiple,* the duplication of a work of art by the hundreds, which is then available to the public at reasonable cost, rather than to the wealthy alone.

335. Karl Schrag. *Self-portrait.* 1963. Aquatint. Kraushaar Galleries, New York. Freely drawn strokes build up a convincing likeness.

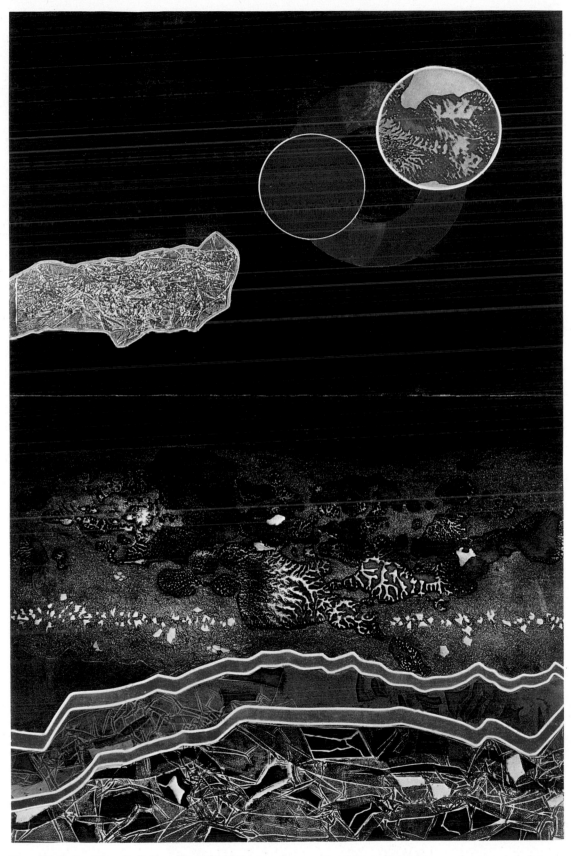

Plate 27. Gabor Peterdi. *Eclipse IV*. 1966. Etching, soft-ground etching, relief etching, and segmented plates. Courtesy Kovler Gallery, Chicago. A combination of techniques can result in a remarkably varied composition. Peterdi's etching interpolates crisply defined lines and broader courses and patches; irregular, blurred, and textured areas; and smoother conformations of color, a diversity of effects that could only be achieved through the different etching processes employed.

Plate 28. James Rosenquist. *Expo 67 Mural—Firepole, 33 × 17′*. 1967. Lithograph. Courtesy Leo Castelli Gallery, New York. The gradations of color and texture possible in lithography are demonstrated in this work. The colors shade into one another in some areas, but in others they sharply delineate forms. The graininess of the lithographic stone has been allowed to show through many of the hues, imparting richness and textural character to the simple composition.

242

336. Honoré Daumier. *The Hot Bath*. 1839. Lithograph, 10 $^7/_8$ × 8 $^1/_2$″. Minneapolis Institute of Arts (gift of Mrs. C. C. Bovey, 1924). This humorous print shows the textured grays and luminous blacks that can be achieved with lithographic crayons and pencils.

Hand Processes: Planographic

Lithography   The only important type of planographic printing, lithography, is based on the mutual antipathy of grease and water rather than on raised or lowered surfaces of printing plates. The major steps in the process are these:

■ The drawing is done on a slab of special Bavarian stone or on a zinc or aluminum plate. Such ingredients as wax, shellac, tallow, and lampblack are combined to form crayons, pencils, paints that can be applied with brushes, or inks that will flow from a pen. The image can be created with one or more of these compounds applied with conventional techniques of drawing and painting, or they can be rubbed on the plate with fingers or cloth, even spattered or dripped. White lines can be produced by scratching the plate with razor blades or steel needles, and dark areas can be lightened by scraping with knives or blades.

■ The stone or plate is then flooded with a solution of gum arabic, which makes the drawn portions insoluble in water, and with nitric acid, which makes the undrawn areas repellent to ink. Thus, the surface is chemically changed so that part of it repels water, the rest repels grease.

■ When ready for printing, the stone (or metal plate) is moistened with water, which soaks into those parts not drawn on. Printing ink, rolled over the surface, adheres only to those portions that are not wet. Paper is applied, pressure exerted, and a print is produced. Lithographs can also be printed in one or many colors. Plate 28 shows the many subtle variations of hue, value, and intensity that can be achieved by this process. Although the surface is neither raised nor lowered noticeably, a print with white, black, and all values of gray is possible.

337. Grace Hartigan. *Inside-Outside.* 1962. Lithograph, 24 $^7/_8$ × 19 $^{15}/_{16}''$. The Museum of Modern Art, New York (gift of the Celeste and Armand Bartos Foundation). Energetic and impulsive, the large forms and decisive brush strokes of this print preserve the fluidity of lithographic ink and the artist's gestures in creating them.

The expressive and technical scope of lithography is vast. Lithographic pencils and crayons give soft and grainy lines, crosshatched or solid areas (Fig. 336). Brush and ink give freedom akin to that in painting (Pl. 28), while pen and ink can be sketchily freehand or mechanically precise.

Hand Processes: Stencil (or Serigraphy)

Serigraphs   Also called *silk-screen prints*, serigraphs (literally "writing on silk") have been extensively produced and developed only since the 1930s. But they represent a branch of stencil printing, which has a long history. These are the steps:

- A special silk or synthetic open-mesh textile is tightly stretched to a wooden frame with sides several inches high, and the cloth (or screen) is treated so that the mesh is left open in some areas to allow paint to pass through but is made impervious in others.
- In printing, the surface on which the printing is to be done is placed below the screen, and a thick but light paint is poured along the edges of the printing frame. The paint is drawn across the screen with a squeegee and forced through the porous sections. A separate screen is required for each color.

Silk-screen prints can be made with simple, plain, or patterned areas as illustrated in Figure 339. Or they can be as richly textured as *The Beginning of Miracles* (Fig. 338), which was printed from twenty-three separate screens. This process is also used for posters and other commercial art when relatively small quantities of the print are needed, since the initial cost of preparing the stencils is much less than that of the plates for most other printing methods. Serigraphy is also used in the

left : 338. Sister Mary Corita. *The Beginning of Miracles,* detail. 1955. Serigraph. International Graphic Arts Society of New York. Complex, vibrating textures, the result of numerous screens, communicate a message of wonder and reverence.

below : 339. Roy Lichtenstein. *Moonscape.* 1965. Serigraph on metallic plastic, 20 × 24″. The print shimmers and changes, as does moonlight on clouds. A band of regularly placed dots at the top and strong black forms at the bottom steady the composition.

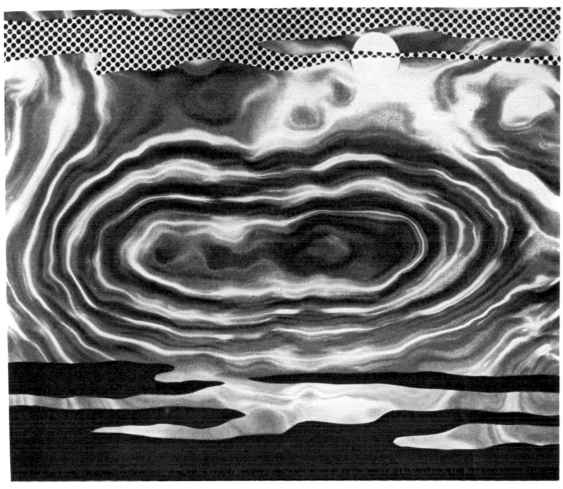

printing of "limited editions" of textiles, either by hand or by semimechanical means. It is widely used for machine printing on glass—labels on milk bottles, decorations on tumblers—because it is difficult to print from metal plates on this material.

In addition to the processes described above, there are newer ones that do not fit into the established categories.

Collographs   Printed from collages of all kinds of materials, such as fabrics, pieces of metal, or "found objects," that are glued to sheets of cardboard, collographs may also include intaglio plates. *Ljubljana Night* (Fig. 340) was built up from cardboard, paper, fabrics, metal washers and wires, and easily modeled acrylic gesso. Photoengraved, halftone plates were incorporated into the plate, as can be seen in the three rectangular, pictorial inserts. The freedom of this procedure can lead to an infinite diversity and produce results unlike anything done in the past.

Embossed Prints   Unlike most graphic prints, the surfaces of embossed prints are three-dimensional (Figs. 324, 341). Embossment takes advantage of the fact that paper is a fibrous membrane and that the better grades, surprisingly strong in tension, can be shaped as the printmaker wishes. The printing plates can be built up with a wide array of materials and processes: thin or thick pastes can be dripped, applied with a brush, or modeled; or actual objects can be glued to a base of card-

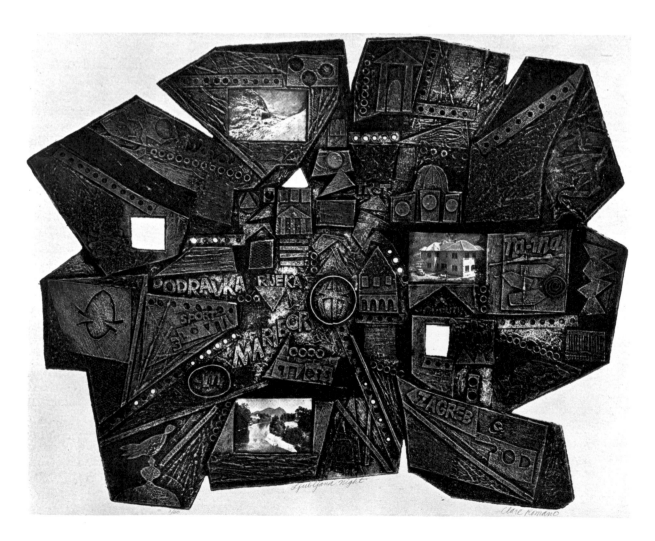

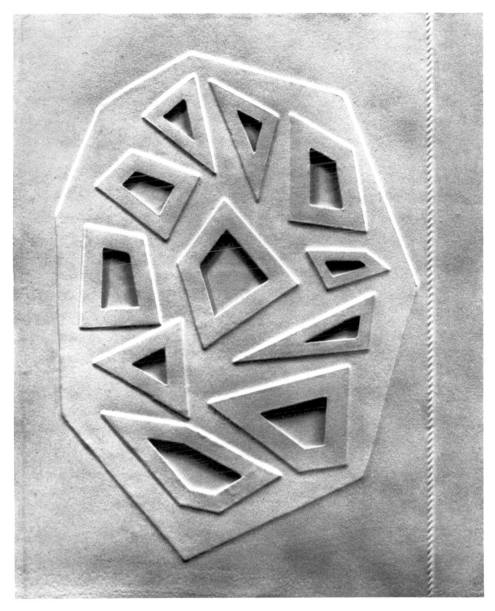

opposite : 340. Clare Romano. *Ljubljana Night.* 1965. Collograph, 27 × 21". Collection the artist. This record of the artist's responses to the city of Ljubljana, Yugoslavia, is printed in black and white and also in a color version.

above : 341. Angel Savelli. *Plato.* 1965. Embossment. Brooklyn Museum, New York. The clear-cut geometric forms of Savelli's relief print suggest Plato's philosophic concepts.

board or any other suitable material. Other possibilities include deeply carved woodcuts or blocks of plaster of Paris. Cast bronze plaques have also been used. The embossment can be delicate and linear or so vigorously sculptural that the paper becomes heavily wrinkled or even torn. To maximize the patterns of light and shadow, the plates are often printed without ink.

Object-Prints   Artists have also experimented with printing, especially silk-screen, on three-dimensional, vacuum-formed plastic (Fig. 342), as well as with covering the surface of sculpture with printed areas. They have also made "paintings" by printing on canvas or by incorporating such techniques as lithography into sculptural

left: 342. Claes Oldenburg. *Teabag*. 1967. Serigraph on Plexiglas, 39 × 28″. Multiples, Inc., New York. This serigraph, printed on vacuum-formed Plexiglas, is an example of an object-print in which graphic and forming techniques were combined.

below: 343. Gerald Gooch. *American Game 1*. 1967. Lithograph on Plexiglas, 2 ½′ square. Hansen Gallery, San Francisco. Images of the same man are lithographed in naturalistic colors. Two rows of balls that flash on and off in sequence give the effect of a ball being bounced back and forth. A dark floor and transparent walls produce many reflections.

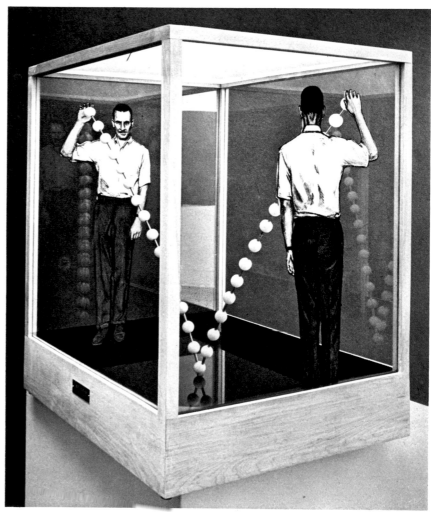

compositions, as in *American Game 1* (Fig. 343). Thus, as in many other areas, distinctions based on traditional concepts have given way to broader, more imaginative ideas and inventions.

Mechanical Processes: Relief

Almost all pictures seen in books, magazines, and newspapers are reproduced by one of the *photomechanical* printing processes. These processes permit reproductions to be printed in almost unlimited quantities. As the name implies, light plays an important part in these highly mechanized methods. In all of them, the design or picture, known as the *copy*, is photographed onto a photosensitive plate that is acted on by chemicals to prepare it for printing. Of the more commonly used mechanical processes for printing illustrations, letterpress is relief, lithography is planographic, and gravure belongs to the intaglio group. The types of image normally reproduced by these printing processes are two: illustrations made from *line* copy, and those made from *continuous-tone* copy. In letterpress, these two types of copy are prepared for presswork in the following way:

Linecut   A linecut is printed in one value only, usually but not necessarily black (Fig. 344), because it derives from copy consisting solely of lines or of solid black and unshaded white, such as pen-and-ink drawings, woodcuts, and the architectural plans and sections reproduced in this book. In line illustrations the appearance of intermediate values can be obtained by the use of *halftone screens* and *benday tints* (Figs. 344, 599). The technique of preparing line copy for printing is complex in detail, but in its essentials the process is relatively simple. It resembles the method by which an etching plate is prepared and is often called "zinc etching."

■ The copy is photographed onto a photosensitive glass plate to produce a negative.
■ This negative is printed on a zinc plate that has been coated to give it a photosensitive surface, just as an ordinary photographic negative is printed on paper to produce a positive. Those parts exposed to light become hard and insoluble in water; careful washing removes the unexposed coating.
■ The plate is inked and dusted with a fine ground much like that used on etching plates. The ground adheres to the inked portions and is brushed off the remainder.
■ The plate is immersed in an acid bath to etch out those portions not coated with ground.

The plate is printed like a woodcut: it is inked and then impressed directly on paper. Thus, it too is relief.

344. Linecopy can be enriched with ready-made repetitive benday textures that are available in hundreds of patterns.

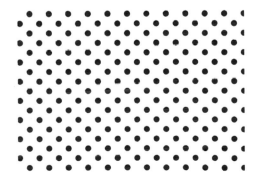

Halftone   Continuous-tone copy is usually a photograph, a wash drawing, a painting, or any sort of image that contains a range of intermediate values as well as the absolutes of black and white. Because of their intermediate values, the illustrations produced from continuous-tone copy are often referred to as *halftones*. Such material is prepared for printing in the following way:

■ Two sheets of plate glass, each engraved with parallel diagonal lines that are filled with black pigment, are placed face to face with the lines at right angles to each other. This produces a grid of opaque black lines with spaces between, similar to that in window screens.

■ The copy is photographed onto a photosensitive metal plate through the grid, which breaks the picture up into a series of dots (Fig. 345). The variation in size of dots depends on the amount of light striking the plate. Light causes the corners of the squares to appear round so that the squares come to look like round dots. The effect conveyed by these myriad microscopic dots is to create an illusion of the full range of values evident in the original copy. The finer the grid, or screen, the more convincing the illusion.

■ From here on, the process is exactly like that for linecuts—applying a ground, etching, and printing.

Four Color   This is the reproduction by printing of full-color subjects such as paintings and color photographs. Usually, color reproduction derives from copy

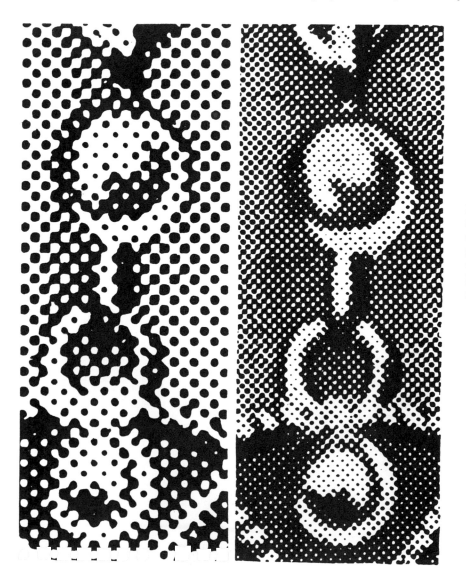

345. Halftones, greatly magnified, show the *varisized* dots that are hardly visible at ordinary size. A coarse screen was used for the example on the left, a fine screen for that on the right.

that is transparent color positive film, such as Ektachrome and Kodachrome. The preparation of color material for printing is an extension of the halftone process into the field of color. To recreate with ink on paper a full-color image, it is necessary to separate the color in the basic copy into independent negative films for the three primary hues—yellow, red, and blue—and black, which four colors, once on the press, recombine through superimposition to create the effect of full color. Additional colors can be separated from the original transparency and run on the press so as to obtain refinements in color fidelity not possible with just the basic four colors.

The colors are separated by photographing the copy first through a blue filter, which permits only the yellow rays to pass and thus gives a record of all the yellow in the original; second through a green filter to obtain reds; and third through a red-orange filter to obtain blues. The fourth separation negative is made with practically all the hues eliminated, recording only the major values. The separation negative films, which are continuous tone (unscreened), are then exposed against a sensitized film to make positive films, and these are exposed against another film with a halftone screen in the middle. The result is a set of screened halftone negatives that are used to make plates, in the manner appropriate for the printing process involved. The halftone screens are placed at different angles for each color, so that the colored dots will print alongside, rather than on top of, each other.

Since full-color reproduction is achieved with at least four plates, superimposed on each other to create a single image, it is imperative that the impressions made by the four plates be in perfect register —that is, accurately aligned along their outer perimeters. When plates are out of register, the image they produce is blurred, sometimes even creating the effect of a double image.

Mechanical Processes: Planographic

Lithography   Originally a process that printed from inked stones (as described on pp. 243, 244), commercial lithographic printing is now done from metal sheets treated to duplicate the stone grain. A modern offset lithography plate is a thin sheet of lightweight metal wrapped around a rapidly turning cylinder. Like the Bavarian stones, offset plates have areas that print by accepting ink and have others that repel it. The steps in the platemaking process are similar to those for letterpress, except that instead of terminating in a relief plate, they create a flat plate whose surface has varying degrees of hardness and softness. The hard areas are ink-receptive, or printing parts; the soft areas are water-receptive and are nonprinting.

As the cylindrical plate revolves on the press it comes in contact first with a set of water rollers, then with a set of ink rollers, and then with a cylinder wrapped in a rubber blanket. An impression cylinder carries the paper and presses it against the rubber blanket, from which the inked image, picked up from the metal plate, is offset (printed).

Offset printing offers a number of advantages over letterpress. Whereas the photoengraver for letterpress produces individual cuts or pages, the lithographer strips in all the pages, both text and illustrations, of a form (often as many as thirty-two pages to a form) on a single plate. Not only does this technological facility make an economic advantage, but it increases the range of the designer for creating imaginative layout of type and illustrations. By printing offset from a rubber blanket instead of directly on paper, lithography offers these advantages: plates last longer; the resilient rubber cylinder permits printing finer copy on rougher paper; and speed is increased. Although an eminently workable process and the type of printing now most often used for illustrated books, offset still does not produce an image quite as sharp and lifelike as can the best quality work in letterpress.

Mechanical Processes: Intaglio

Gravure   Printing from an engraved plate is a process even older than that of letterpress. Again, the illustrations are prepared for plating much as they are in letterpress, but the gravure plate is intaglio rather than relief or flat. To engrave, the entire area of the gravure plate is covered by a grid similar to a halftone screen. The square spaces between the lines of the grid are etched to depths varying in relation to the degree of light and dark in the image being engraved. The darker the tone in the original copy, the deeper the square is etched. The deeper the etched square or cup, the greater the amount of ink it can hold, and the darker will be the printed impression. Because the squares are all the same size (unlike the dots in letterpress and offset) and vary only in the amount of ink they contain and deposit on paper, gravure is a true halftone process, whereas letterpress and offset only simulate tones by optical illusion.

The gravure plate is cylindrical like that of offset, but the printing is done directly by the plate onto the paper, as in letterpress, except that once the plate is inked, a flat bar, or *doctor blade*, wipes the ink off the surface, leaving it in the recessed cups, or wells, only.

Printed words and pictures are one of the most potent means of communication among men. Newspapers, magazines, and books quickly carry facts and ideas, verbally and pictorially, to millions of people in all parts of the world. Scientists and artists, working together, have developed the reproduction of photographs, drawings, and paintings to a point permitting their use in almost all publications. Through them our understanding of the visual aspects of our environment has been greatly extended.

At one time it was thought that the inexpensive ease with which illustrative matter can be multiplied would end the need for prints made by hand in limited editions. Happily, the exact opposite has come true. Perhaps because we see so much that is mechanized we find new delight in hand prints. They are original works of art, which gives them an immediacy and individuality that are treasured because these qualities are rare. Contemporary printmakers have engendered and maintained a remarkable level of creativity. Original paintings of quality are relatively expensive to acquire, but beautiful, enduring, and imaginative art from printmakers is within the economic range of almost everyone.

346. Karel Appel. *Wild Heads Everywhere.* 1966. Lithograph, 18 × 26". International Graphic Arts Society of New York. Appel's composition, printed in black, yellow, red, green and two blues, is vigorously spontaneous.

347. Earl Reiback. *Lumia Aurora*. Light composition photographed by Elliot Moss Landy. Worcester Art Museum, Mass., and Howard Wise Gallery, New York. Using light as his medium, Reibach has created an intricate, abstract spatial composition.

10 Photography

Man's understanding of and delight in the world in which he lives has been enormously extended by photography. Photography is used in such varied ways and for such diverse purposes that basic questions about its nature arise. Is photography an art or a science, creative or mechanical? Are photographs literal reports or expressive interpretations? Is it easy or difficult to take a good photograph? The answer to each of these questions depends on the intent and skills of the photographer.

Photography is a science in which the physics of light and of lenses and the chemistry of making light images permanent are basic. It is also an increasingly useful adjunct of science in probing and revealing the physical universe from the depths of the oceans to outer space, in tracing the path of a proton or of a hurricane.

Photography can be an art when the photographer perceives and reveals the significance of his subject matter. Like painting, it is creative if the man behind the camera discloses the qualities of the image he records. Mechanics are important, but they need not be routine. Because cameras record images seemingly with little human interference (or help), we are inclined to believe that photography tells the literal truth. It does tell *a* truth, because cameras record the external appearance of the objects on which they are focused. But if we saw photographs of the same subject taken by twenty photographers, it would be evident that the individual who presses

left : 348. Paul Nadar. *Sarah Bernhardt.* 1859. George Eastman House, Rochester. Nadar's photograph dramatizes the beauty of a famous actress.

opposite above : 349. Dorothea Lange. *Migrant Mother.* 1936. Oakland Museum, Calif. This photo is an eloquent and stark revelation of poverty and depression.

the button determines which phase of the truth is of consequence to him. Photographers, like printmakers, select the aspects of their subjects they wish to emphasize, for no single photograph can tell everything about anything. To the creative photographer the inner, essential truth is of most consequence. As early in the history of photography as the 1850s, a group of Parisian photographers sought to make portraits something more than small, dim, standardized records. Paul Nadar, one of this group, knew well the many actors, painters, and writers who came to his studio, and through careful attention to lighting and posing, he succeeded in transmuting this personal vision into penetrating portraits of his sitters (Fig. 348).

Dorothea Lange, too, searched for the essentials that lie beneath the surface. Reminiscing about her assignment to photograph the conditions of migratory workers during the depression of the 1930s, she wrote of her *Migrant Mother* (Fig. 349):

> I saw and approached the hungry and desperate mother, as if drawn by a magnet. . . . I made five exposures, working closer and closer from the same direction. . . . There she sat in that lean-to tent with her children huddled around her, and seemed to know that my pictures might help her, and so she helped me. . . . The pea crop at Nipomo had frozen and there was no work for anybody. But I did not approach the tents and shelters of other stranded pea-pickers. It was not necessary; I knew I had recorded the essence of my assignment.*

* *Popular Photography*, Vol. 46, No. 2 (February, 1960), pp. 42–43, 126.

Sometimes called the easy art, photography at its lower levels of achievement offers beginners some degree of success more quickly than do the other arts. "You press the button, we do the rest" describes how easy it is—to do only a small part of the work! Professional photographers know that technical mastery takes time but is far less difficult than cultivating an individualized mode of seeing and thinking in terms of the whole photographic act.

Photography became a practical reality in the early decades of the nineteenth century (see Fig. 362). This is surprising because for centuries scientists knew the underlying principles—that light produces visual images and that it alters the chemical nature of some materials. Leonardo da Vinci explained the process, and Renaissance artists traced pictures made by the *camera obscura* ("dark room"), which admitted

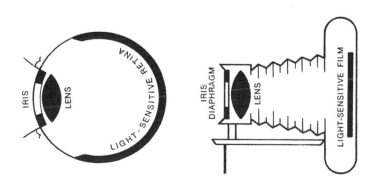

350. Human eyes and cameras have marked similarities.

light through a pinhole into a lightproof room and produced an inverted picture on the opposite wall. But not until recently could such pictures be made permanent.

The technique of *photography*, which means drawing or writing with light (see Fig. 347), is basically simple. The light from the object to be recorded is focused on a light-sensitive surface in a darkened box, and this image is fixed so that additional exposure to light will not produce further change. Years of research have increased technical control and extended the scope of photographic possibilities, while the leadership of great photographers has shown how far creativity can rise above mechanics.

The Materials and Processes

Although complex, expensive apparatus enables photographers to have more control over their work, some of the greatest photographs have been made with simple equipment. The basic equipment consists of a camera, usually with a lens, shutter, and diaphragm; films or plates; filters; paper on which the image is printed; and the paraphernalia needed to develop the negative and make the print. It is possible, however, to dispense with the camera and the film altogether. Figure 351 is a photo-

left : 351. Photograms offer opportunities for the creation of realistic or abstract patterns.

opposite : 352. Lenses concentrate the light reflected from objects to produce a small inverted image on film.

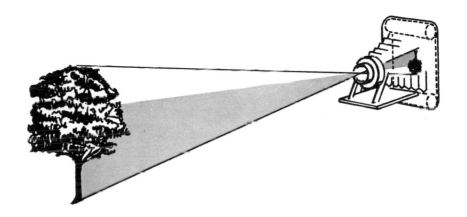

gram—a print made by putting objects directly on light-sensitive paper and exposing it to light, and then making the result permanent.

Cameras

The simplest *camera* is nothing more than a lightproof box with a simple lens and shutter at the front and film at the back, and is appropriately called a nonadjustable camera. Designed for amateur use under average conditions, it records well-lighted, stationary objects with minimum effort. But if a photographer wishes to take pictures with sharp detail, with near and far objects in focus, with a full range of values from black through all the different grays to white or with the complete spectrum of color; or if he wishes to work under poor light or with atmospheric effects or to record rapidly moving objects, more precise and complex equipment is necessary. There is an ever increasing, ever more sophisticated array of cameras and accessories from which to choose, from cameras with an electric eye that automatically sets the various mechanisms in response to prevailing conditions, through those that both take and print the photograph, to the enormously complicated scientific instruments that probe the secrets of life.

Lenses

The most important part of a camera is the lens or a combination of lenses, even though photographs can be produced without them. A pinhole will produce an image in moderately sharp focus, but the image will be so faint that an extremely long exposure or very bright illumination is required. A larger hole will admit more light, but the image will be fuzzy. A good lens, in contrast, gathers and concentrates much light to produce a sharply focused image quickly (Fig. 352). As lenses get larger, less light on the subject or less time for the exposure is needed, which permits good photographs of dimly lighted subjects or of those moving rapidly. Good lenses must be precisely ground and free from defects so that they approach those most remarkable of lenses, the ones in human eyes and in the eyes of some animals.

Various types of lenses have been developed for specialized photography:

■ Telephoto lenses magnify distant objects and allow the camera to get a detailed image of anything that is far away from it.
■ Wide-angle lenses are used when a photographer cannot back away from his subject far enough to include all that he wishes. They are much used by architectural photographers who wish to record a large section of a small room.

below : 353. A fish-eye lens was an apt choice of photographer J. R. Eyerman to accentuate the role of the freeway in the Los Angeles cityscape.

opposite above : 354. The diaphragm of a camera, like the iris of an eye, changes the size of the opening to admit little or much light.

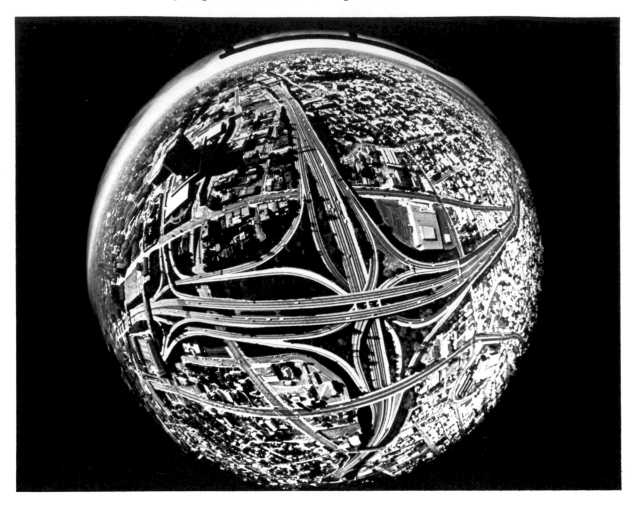

■ Fish-eye lenses are extremely wide angled. The resulting image is circular, with the elements in the center of the composition greatly magnified. This produces an unusual perspective with an emphatic center of interest, such as appears in the photograph of Los Angeles in Figure 353.

Shutters

The camera opening, or *aperture*, must have a mechanism to keep it closed until the moment of exposure—the crucial moment when, for a short time, light is allowed to enter the camera. This mechanism is called a *shutter*, and the time it takes to open and close is its *speed*. Nonadjustable cameras have one speed, which varies from $1/30$ to $1/60$ of a second. More complex cameras have shutters that provide a wide choice of speeds, from one second to $1/1000$ of a second, or time exposures of any length. Thus there are two means of controlling the amount of light that hits the film. First, the shutter controls the duration of the exposure. Second, the diaphragm, discussed next, increases or decreases the size of the aperture.

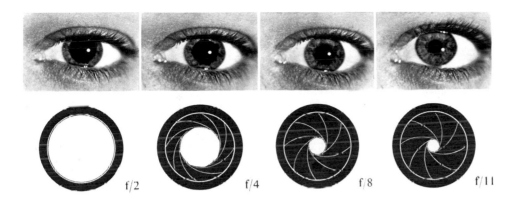

f/2   f/4   f/8   f/11

Diaphragms

The usefulness of a lens is greatly increased if the amount of light that it gathers while the shutter is open can be controlled. A window shade allows one to increase or decrease the light entering a room by covering more or less of the window. The iris of the eye acts in much the same way, contracting over the pupil in bright light, expanding in dim light (Fig. 354). Whereas cheaper cameras have one fixed opening, better cameras have diaphragms that can make the aperture very small or as large as the diameter of the lens to control the amount of light that enters.

The relation between size of aperture and time of exposure is important, and for most subjects there are varied combinations from which to choose (Fig. 355). The choice affects the photograph. These are the major factors:

- Large openings take shorter exposures; small openings take longer ones. This tends to equalize the quantity of light striking the film, but large and small openings produce different effects.
- Short exposures (with large openings) are required for reasonably sharp pictures of moving objects. When pictures of athletic events are taken at slow shutter speeds the figures become blurred. Sometimes this is intentional for special effects, but in order to "stop" the action of a fast runner or of a racing car, shutter speeds of $1/500$ of a second or less are necessary. (The exact speed is also determined by how brightly the subject is illumined and how fast the film is.) But at such speeds only that part of the picture on which the photographer has carefully focused his camera will be sharp. In some scientific work, speeds are needed that far exceed those possible with mechanical shutters, and it is then necessary to provide a sudden burst of intense light for as little as $1/100,000$ of a second (Fig. 372).

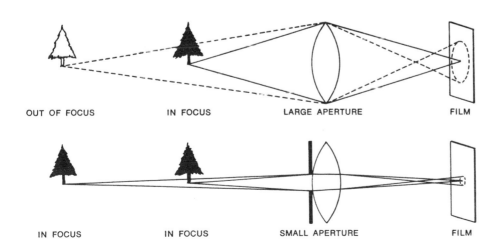

OUT OF FOCUS   IN FOCUS   LARGE APERTURE   FILM

IN FOCUS   IN FOCUS   SMALL APERTURE   FILM

355. Nearby and distant objects can be in focus if the diaphragm is adjusted to make the aperture small.

■ Long exposures (with smaller openings) produce greater depth of field (the distance between those near and far objects that are in sharp focus).

Films

Black-and-White Film   Film for black-and-white pictures is a thin, multiple-layered sandwich. The layer that does the work is the *emulsion*, a thin coating of gelatin in which millions of tiny crystals record the subject in terms of the amount of light reaching them. When developed, those particles struck by light darken to produce the negative. Under the emulsion is the *support*, which provides a strong yet flexible transparent base for the emulsion. The bottom layer, or *antihalation backing*, absorbs any excessively bright light that might scatter and produce halos around bright points.

Black-and-white films differ from one another in four basic qualities:

■ *Color sensitivity* describes how well the film responds to different colors. Early film, called *orthochromatic*, was not sensitive to red light but was oversensitive to blue light and produced strong contrasts. It is still used commercially for copying black-and-white illustrations or printed material. *Panchromatic* film, which is sensitive to most of the colors, gives natural-looking pictures with many steps of gray as well as black-and-white and is the most common type of roll film.

■ *Film speed* refers to the amount of light needed to get a satisfactory image, and this in turn determines the size of the aperture and the length of the exposure. For specialized photography of subjects that have an enormous range of brightness, from very intense to almost invisible, as in atomic explosions, extended-range films have been developed that are a sandwich of varied-speed layers—a slow-speed layer that records only extremely bright light, a medium-speed layer that captures intermediate degrees, and a high-speed layer for very faint phenomena.

■ *Graininess* comes chiefly from the large grains of silver bromide used in high-speed films. It is usually noticed only in enlargements.

■ *Contrast* describes a film's sensitivity to subtle differences of light in the subject. Some films produce harsh contrasts of lights and darks; others differentiate between many shades of gray.

Color Film   The story of color film is long and complex, but these are the basic facts. Color films typically have three layers of emulsion, each one of which is affected by one primary color of light. When developed, color films give either "positives" or "negatives." The most common type gives a positive transparency that, when looked at through a viewer, projected on a screen, or engraved in four colors for printing (Pl. 29, p. 275), reproduces the colors approximately as the photographer saw them. The other type gives a negative transparent film in which the colors are represented by their opposites. When printed on special paper, the colors are again reversed so that the subject is seen in its natural colors.

Filters

When it seems desirable to modify the dark-and-light pattern of the colors of a subject, *filters* can be used. These are pieces of transparent, colored gelatin or glass placed between the subject and the film. Filters lessen the amount of light reflected from objects of all colors except that of the filter. Of the many filters available for special effects, the commonest are the red, orange, and yellow ones used to intensify

Films and filters alter photographs of the same subject, taken by photographer Charles Swedlund.

left : 356. Photographed with orthochromatic film, which is not sensitive to red but is oversensitive to blue. The result is a barn that is almost black in value and a sky whose clouds are virtually indistinguishable.

357. In these two renditions filters were used. A K2 (yellow) filter was added to panchromatic film *(left)* to obtain a result relatively sensitive to all colors. A red filter supplementing panchromatic film *(right)* has created a dramatic contrast between the white clouds and blue sky.

the contrast between blue skies and white clouds (Figs. 356, 357) or to penetrate through a thick and hazy atmosphere.

Developing Negatives

Although chemical changes occur when film is exposed to light, the *latent image* is not visible until the film is developed. In a darkroom, exposed films are first immersed in a *developer*, an aqueous solution of several chemicals that transforms the exposed grains of silver bromide to bromide, which is washed away, and to metallic silver, which turns black, clusters together, and adheres to the film support. Some kinds of developers yield negatives with strong contrasts of dark and light, while others give a long scale of grays from almost black to almost white. The film is then rinsed either with cool *water* or a *short-stop solution* to halt the action of the developer, and then bathed in a *fixing agent*, commonly called *hypo*, that prevents light from making any further changes. After being rinsed again in water, the film is dried, and the image, in reversed values of the original subject, is ready for printing.

358. The same negative can produce markedly different results depending on the length of exposure during printing. An exposure of twenty seconds makes the most brilliant print.

Printing

The paper on which the printing is done is of consequence in the final result. Papers vary in tone, which may be warm or cool; in surface, textured or mat; in the speed with which they respond to light; in thickness; and in their ability to record contrasts in the film.

The process of printing is similar to exposing and developing a negative. In a darkened room, light is passed through the negative onto paper coated with a light-sensitive emulsion. The quantity of light that passes through is determined by the lightness or darkness of each portion. Thus, the values are again reversed so that the print has a light-and-dark pattern similar to that of the subject. The length of exposure depends on such factors as the brightness of the light, the density of the negative image, and the sensitivity of the paper. Figure 358 shows the different effects obtained from the same negative by varying the time of exposure. The exposed paper is then developed, fixed, and dried.

Contact prints are the same size as the negative. They are made by placing a piece of photographic paper in firm contact with a negative and exposing it to light. *Enlargements* are made by passing light first through the negative and then through a lens to produce a large focused image at some distance from the negative. They offer many possibilities. Using the whole image, the size of the print can be changed. By using only part of the negative, the shape can be changed and undesirable parts eliminated. Parts of the picture can be darkened or lightened. Portions of two or more negatives can be combined—clouds from one negative added to the negative of a landscape in which the sky is uninteresting, or images can be superimposed or combined to create and express a photographer's personal vision (Fig. 359). Such darkroom manipulation is abhorrent to the purists who believe that the record on the exposed negative should be altered little if at all. It is, however, a common practice among many photographers, who do it simply to upgrade the finished picture. But it is also an exciting field for exploration.

In the preceding sections the mechanical techniques of photography have been stressed because they are fundamental in enabling the photographer to get the result he wants. But the photographer makes many personal decisions to record in communicable form his inner concept. These include:

- Finding his subject and deciding which aspects of it he wishes to emphasize—what to include and what to omit, the angle from which to shoot, and what light is most appropriate, problems similar to those solved in the two photographs of trees illustrated in Figures 360 and 361
- Choosing his camera and accessories
- Selecting the most suitable film and filter (if any)
- Determining the size of the aperture and the length of the exposure
- Deciding which developer to use and how long the film should stay in it
- Selecting the photographic paper best suited to his intent
- Controlling the printing in many ways

Although all but the first of these seems mechanical, each demands judgment, a creative assembling and evaluation of many factors. The first step, however, is the crucial one that separates the journeyman photographer from the creative artists who will now be discussed.

below : 359. Carl Fischer's *Boy with Bubble-Gum Cards* (1966) was achieved by printing two negatives on one piece of paper. Collection the artist.

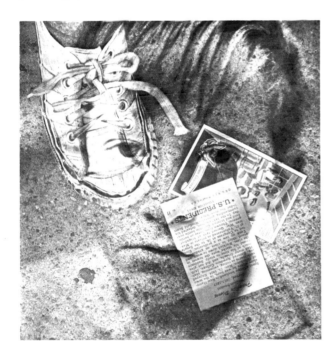

The creativity of the artist determines the impact of a photograph.

above right : 360. Ansel Adams. *Aspens near Santa Fe, New Mexico.* 1958. Light striking the leaves of the small trees and shrubs in the foreground makes them sparkle against the gradations of gray and black in the background.

right : 361. Harry Callahan. *Chicago c. 1950.* Bare trees become stark black shadows against the light of white snow and a misty gray background.

Looking at Photographs

Today's newspapers, magazines, and books carry so many photographs that one tends to look at them only long enough to see what they are pictures of; in short, one begins and ends with the subject matter. That is natural, since the great majority of photographs are nothing more than literal visual reports. But from time to time a photograph arrests one's attention not only for its subject matter but because the photographer has stripped the commonplace from what he saw and penetrated deeper than surface appearances. Then one is likely to experience an esthetic emotion akin to that offered by any other field of art.

In the early decades of the eighteenth century three men working independently established the basis from which modern photography has developed. In 1816 Joseph Nicéphore Niepce wrote that he had recorded an image on paper, but the only example of his work that we know was probably made in 1826. At the same time, Louis Jacques Mandé Daguerre was conducting his own experiments and improving Niepce's technique. During the same years, William Henry Talbot Fox discovered a way of making negatives from which positive prints could be made. Although each of these men made significant contributions, Daguerre's are the best known.

Four Nineteenth-Century Photographs

The Artist's Studio (Fig. 362), taken by Louis Jacques Mandé Daguerre in 1837, is one of the first successful photographs. Daguerre had established his reputation as a painter who could depict with astonishing accuracy natural scenes, but he wished to go farther and to make light paint the picture. After much experimentation, he succeeded in recording on a silver-plated piece of copper what he saw. The still life is remarkable for its composure, its sculptural three-dimensionality, and its varied textures. The photographic process Daguerre used was slow and complex, but a remarkably beautiful image was captured. Following his example of high standards of excellence, other men produced outstanding *daguerreotypes*. Later, to satisfy the public craving for pictures, chiefly portraits, the process was modified and cheapened to produce thousands of commonplace *tintypes*.

362. Louis Jacques Mandé Daguerre. *The Artist's Studio.* 1837. George Eastman House, Rochester. Daguerre succeeded in making a permanent record of one corner of an artist's studio.

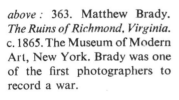

above : 363. Matthew Brady. *The Ruins of Richmond, Virginia.* c. 1865. The Museum of Modern Art, New York. Brady was one of the first photographers to record a war.

right : 364. William Henry Jackson. *Camp in Baker's Park.* 1875. The Museum of Modern Art, New York. The rugged expansiveness of the West was effectively revealed by the new medium.

By the time of the American Civil War, photography had progressed a long way. Although the equipment was cumbersome, a photographic negative could be made on a glass plate from which any number of prints could be created. Matthew Brady headed a large group of photographers who saw the potentiality of faithfully recording important events. Traveling in a horse-drawn buggy loaded with all of the paraphernalia needed for taking and developing pictures, the group made some seven thousand glass-plate negatives of aspects of the Civil War. *The Ruins of Richmond, Virginia* (Fig. 363) is a stark comment on destruction. Silhouetted against a white sky, the scarred buildings speak grimly of the empty wantonness of war in a way that is hard to forget.

Exploration of the West in the 1870s gave photographers a chance to try their skill in recording the undreamed-of vastness of the Rocky Mountains. William Henry Jackson's *Camp in Baker's Park* (Fig. 364) proves that they and their improved equipment were equal to the task. With a sure sense of expressive composition, Jackson contrasts the smallness of men and animals and the flimsiness of tents with the monumental solidity of great trees and mountains. Detail, near and far, is faithfully recorded, and the fact that there is no blur caused by the movement of men or animals shows that it had become possible to use comparatively short

above : 365. Alfred Stieglitz. *The Terminal.* 1893. San Francisco Museum of Art (Alfred Stieglitz Collection). Photography can capture revealing moments in an inimitable way.

opposite : 366. Berenice Abbott. *Night View of New York City.* 1933. An intricate pattern of lights and darks produces a striking vision of the city.

exposures. But to accomplish this, Jackson used a camera that would accommodate glass plates two feet square, because enlarging was still not practical. Developing the plates was done in a portable tent. To those who use miniature cameras and develop negatives and prints at leisure in a well-equipped darkroom, the difficulties of making photographs under such conditions will be quite apparent and the results commendable.

In 1893 Alfred Stieglitz photographed *The Terminal* (Fig. 365) after having waited hours in a snowstorm for his subject to compose itself as he wished it. Using the newly developed hand camera for outdoor work, he championed the "straight" or "pure" approach, establishing a tradition of realism in American photography that lifted the representation of the ordinary and factual to a high plane of significance and excellence and paralleled similar approaches in other branches of the arts. Not imitative of painting or burdened with tricks, his photographs seem to let the observer see the subject through the camera lens but in a new, more vivid way. *The Terminal* transforms a commonplace scene into a profound revelation of an ordinary occurrence. The large, powerful curve of men, horses, and tram boldly unifies an intricate composition of many interdependent parts. Atmospheric conditions and movement are captured in instantaneous vision.

Four Twentieth-Century Photographs

In order to demonstrate the potential of modern photography for creative individuality, attention is now focused on four examples of subjects found in cities.

Berenice Abbott's *Night View of New York City* (Fig. 366), taken forty years later than *The Terminal*, presents a totally different aspect of a city that had changed drastically in the intervening period. Photographed from a high vantage point, it portrays the metropolis as a series of luminous, cellular edifices separated by traffic arteries. Rigid geometric line is softened, differences are de-emphasized by concentration on the myriad pinpoints of light. The viewer's eyes are left free to wander and explore as they wish, for there is no single center of interest. By contrast, the unlighted roofs, the scarce areas of land without buildings, and the low, unlighted structure (slightly left of and below the center) tempt one to pause while looking more closely to see what is there. It is a compact, dense composition without beginning or end that stands for the seeming endlessness of urban centers.

Ernst Haas's *New York Reflection* (Fig. 367) is a bold, arresting arrangement in which flat, shadowy planes seem to plunge in and out of the space that contains them. The buildings only hint at their massive, three-dimensional substantiality. Some of the forms are clearly identifiable because of their rows of windows and their outlines; others appear as abstractions symbolizing the power and thrust of a megalopolis. Obliqueness pervades the entire composition, for almost no line or form parallels the edges of the photograph. Although each force is adroitly counterbalanced by others, no conformist stability can be found. The great heterogeneity of unanticipated shapes, sizes, textures, and directions is firmly bound together by the dark, angular frame that encloses them. Through means quite different from Berenice Abbott's, Haas communicates the overwhelming size and presence of the city and its stark dehumanization.

opposite above : 367. Ernst Haas. *New York Reflection.* 1962. Haas reduces the reality of the city to an overlapping pattern of flat planes.

opposite below : 368. René Burri. *Railway Station, Frankfurt.* 1962. Burri has captured the transient convergence of strangers in a city by combining two photos.

right : 369. Henri Cartier-Bresson. *Abruzzi.* 1953. The photographer snapped his shutter at the decisive moment when his subject was in equilibrium.

An entirely different aspect of city living is portrayed with great immediacy in *Railway Station, Frankfurt* (Fig. 368). Momentarily, a fragment of the urgent bustle and tension of rush-hour traffic has been arrested in a way that implies imminent change. Although the photograph shows only four persons and isolated details of the station, the impression is so vivid that one almost inevitably envisions the multitudes around the world who are in similar situations. Deliberately disparate in organization, the photograph has no central focal point. Attention tends to jump back and forth from the woman at the left to the man at the right. Of secondary interest are the man, woman, and electric sign in the background. The almost-blank area near the center has minimal interest, except to arouse curiosity about what cannot be seen. The direct confrontation is so strong that the viewer feels he is on the spot, a participant in the action rather than a detached observer.

Many miles and almost as many years separate Frankfurt from the small towns of the mountainous Abruzzi region of Italy. Henri Cartier-Bresson, impressed with the space and quiet movement of the old urban spaces in Abruzzi, recorded them on film (Fig. 369). He has written that his camera is an extension of my eye. I prowled the streets all day, feeling very strung-up and ready to pounce, determined to "trap" life—to preserve life in the act of living. Above all, I craved to seize the whole essence, in the confines of one single photograph, of some situation that was in the process of unrolling itself before my eyes. . . . In photography there is a new kind of plasticity, product of the instantaneous lines made by movements of the subject. . . . But inside movement there is one moment at which the elements in motion are in balance. Photography must seize upon this moment and hold immobile the equilibrium in it.*

Abruzzi invites our eyes to roam around in many directions and to pause at strategic points. We can follow the plunging diagonal of the railing and notice the events along the way: The woman at right center establishes a relationship with the church door, while the woman carrying a tray leads us down into the picture. The angle of the woman's tray makes us wonder whether she will continue down the steps or turn toward the church. Looking from one woman to the other, we see a boy aligned with the lamp support and then notice a girl half hidden by the railing. To the left of the church a woman walking away calls attention to the background, where there are three separate groups of people who make a handsome geometric pattern with the woman. No matter where we look there are suggested paths of movement to enjoy, exemplifying Cartier-Bresson's statement that ". . . the world is movement, and you cannot be stationary in your attitude toward something that is moving."

The sense of vitality in *Abruzzi* is heightened by bringing many opposites into unison. Most conspicuous is the interplay throughout the photograph of slender dark metal strips against solid masonry. Textured paving, rough stone walls, and tile roofs enhance the plain surfaces. Straight or angular lines accentuate those that are curved. And the people, dark and silhouetted, give meaning to the motionless stone-work that is their town.

Diverse as the masterworks seen thus far are, they have some general qualities in common. Each is technically excellent, and this is a basic consideration. Without technical competence a photographer can succeed in communicating his vision to others only by rare chance. Proficiency, however, is even more a matter of judgment than of manual skills and knowledge of rules. It entails choosing the materials, the processes, the aspect, and the moment most appropriate to the photographer's intent. In *The Terminal* (Fig. 365), for example, many objects are indistinct because that quality was inherent in the subject, whereas in *Aspens near Santa Fe, New Mexico* (Fig. 360) the photographer explores the effect of light illuminating the small leaves against shadowy tree trunks.

In each of these photographs the subject has been brought into some kind of order for two reasons. First, most people have an inherent urge to organize their environment, and they enjoy the success of others in this respect. Second, an appropriate coordination of forms, lines, and textures can be instrumental in expressing and communicating the essence of a subject. Ideally, the composition seems inevitable, it seems to have been created for that photograph alone. In the portrait of Sarah Bernhardt (Fig. 348), the actress, supported by a classical pedestal and cloaked with a luxuriantly draped robe, adopted a graceful, relaxed pose. All is soft and smooth, fluent and harmonious. Not so with the worried, overworked migrant mother (Fig. 349). Harsh, angular lines and rough, ill-assorted textures bind the mother and her children in their weary, bitter endurance.

Finding a subject and unveiling its special qualities is the crucial test of a photographer. Thousands can produce pictures that are technically perfect and attractively composed. We acknowledge their competence and walk on. But once in a while we

---

* Henri Cartier-Bresson, *The Decisive Moment*. New York: Simon and Schuster, 1952.

see a photograph that affects us deeply, that gives a heightened awareness of something not previously experienced or that had been viewed with eyes and mind half closed. There is no point in pretending that this can be explained by words. At present, it cannot. We simply know at such moments that someone has allowed us to see and feel more deeply than we customarily do (Pl. 29, p. 275).

Specialized Photography

Fantastic technological advances in photography have enormously extended scientists' knowledge of the inner structure of materials and of the exact nature of many physical processes and of the universe. In many instances, these advances have also disclosed new sources of inspiration to artists.

Movement is a natural concern of man, but until a century ago it was imperfectly understood because human eyes cannot "stop" it long enough to perceive precisely what happens. By the 1870s, however, the "instantaneousness" of photography had made it possible to establish permanent visual records of the successive motions of a horse galloping, a bird flying, or a man walking (Fig. 370). In more recent developments, the extremely brief, repeated flashes of intensely bright stroboscopic light have produced a succession of multiple exposures on one negative of such activities as a ballerina dancing (Fig. 371). Stroboscopic light and appropriate

right : 370. Thomas Eakins. Man walking. 1884–1885. Multiple exposures. The American painter Eakins took these multiple exposures in order to study the action involved in walking.

below : 371. Gjon Mili. Ballet dancer. Consecutive images recorded in the repeated flashes of stroboscopic light become the flow of motion of a ballet dancer.

above left : 372. The splash of a drop of milk taken (c. 1930) at $\frac{1}{100,000}$ of a second reveals a new aspect of reality.

above right : 373. To measure and evaluate the performance of an airplane propeller revolving at 4080 revolutions per minute, this photograph was taken in a smoke tunnel.

right : 374. Bruce Lauritzen. City at night. California College of Arts and Crafts, Oakland. By opening his camera shutter and driving around city streets at night, the photographer created a pattern of unusual rhythmic interest.

films and cameras have also been used to freeze an instant of movement (Figs. 372, 373). Another way of studying moving patterns is illustrated in the time exposure of the lights of automobiles in Figure 374.

As man has moved out into space to study the earth from a different viewpoint (Fig. 375) and to explore the regions beyond, the camera has become an even more invaluable tool. No longer need the scientist actually see what he wishes to examine. Photographs taken by cameras on space vehicles and then beamed to earth can be studied at leisure and in depth. For example, photographs taken in this way reveal the craters and elevations of the surface of the moon (Fig. 376) and help to predict a suitable landing spot for the first moon explorers. Combined with telescopes, cameras can concentrate enough light over a period of time so that objects in outer space invisible to human eyes are revealed, and successive photographs yield permanent records of their patterns of movement.

Through microphotography, scientists can study, in greatly magnified detail, the structure of the intricate patterns of inert materials (Fig. 377), the inside of blood vessels, or a tiny cross section of the tube foot of a marine animal called the feather star (Fig. 378).

top : 375. A photograph of the earth taken from space reveals the cloud formations that govern weather around the world.

right : 376. Photographs taken at an oblique angle by Lunar Orbiter II record the surface of the moon in the crater Copernicus.

below left : 377. The intricate structural pattern of the crystalline compound asparagine is exposed when photographed with transmitted polarized light at 200 times natural size.

below right : 378. A photograph produced by Delbert E. Philpott and Gladys Harrison with the aid of an electron microscope and later magnified 45,000 times allows scientists to study the anatomy of a cross section of a marine animal known as the feather star.

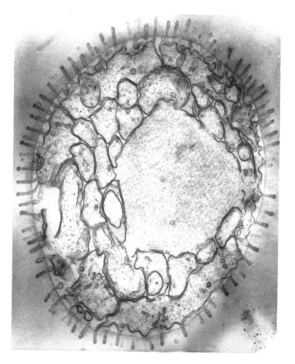

Holograms, produced by the intense beams of light called laser, create truly three-dimensional images that appear to be suspended in space and that can be inspected from almost any angle. Different parts of the plate record a scene differently, so that, in projecting it, a laser beam through one part of the hologram will reveal a different image from one sent through another section. The potentials of the process are revolutionary, ranging from the study of dust particles suspended in air to the use of holograms for data storage, because a single plate can contain thousands of separate images. Eventually, it is predicted, the process may be used to create truly three-dimensional movies and television.

Motion Pictures

Motion pictures, the cinema, the movies, are today quite often termed simply "the film." Whatever the nomenclature, moving pictures, in theaters or on the home television screen, are the most pervasive of all visual influences on modern life, and serious observers have long conceded that the film is a powerful medium of artistic expression. Film with sequential images creating the effect of motion is a medium of almost magical quality that makes possible a seemingly limitless range of visual experience. It can record the growth of a chicken in an egg, observe masses of objects and minute images in motion, and produce totally abstract compositions of light, color, and movement. Because of its fluidity, the film can treat both space and time in a dynamic, heterogeneous way that corresponds closely, more so than in painting, sculpture, architecture, and the other visual arts, to the open, organic, unpredictive character of life. Once sound is synthesized with space and time, the film offers the kind of total experience that has long been a concern of artists (see Fig. 379).

379. *Trajan's Campaign against the Dacians,* detail of Trajan's Column. A. D. 106–113. Marble, height of frieze band c. 4′ 2″. The scenes reproduced in the bands spiralling around Trajan's Column are a narrative sequence recapitulating the Emperor's exploits in the Danube Valley. The serial scenes have a cinematic quality that anticipates the modern motion picture.

Plate 29. Charles Steinhacker. *Sequoia Tree, Sequoia National Park, California.* 1964. Nikon F, 135 mm lens, Kodachrome II film. "Straight" photography can produce works of great beauty and subtlety. Through the use of side lighting, Steinhacker has created an abstract composition from the natural forms in a grove of Sequoias. By basing the exposure on the brightest areas he produced rich velvet-black in the shadows and chromatic color in the objects that reflect light. The interplay of colors transcends actuality to become an almost nonobjective interpretation of a deep forest scene.

Plate 30. A deliberately paced but onrushing flow of luminous energy streams across the panoramic screen and saturates the consciousness of the spectator in the psychedelic sequences of the movie *2001 : A Space Odyssey*. The aurora of colors, instantly perishable, infinitely varied, and underscored with soaring, rhapsodical music, creates a space-time continuum that carries its message in abstract, resplendent images. Stanley Kubrick, director; Metro-Goldwyn-Mayer, producer.

Historically, the film is man's latest achievement in his age-old attempt to make permanent records of action. Many murals in prehistoric caves and Egyptian temples, Greek and Roman carved friezes (Fig. 379), and Oriental scrolls portray sequential events by a series of successive, static forms. Having no control over the way in which observers would look at his work, the artist could only hope that due time would be given to each part and that the intended order would be followed. In motion pictures, the action unfolds before the observers' eyes, and each part is seen in the order and for the exact amount of time that the director deems best. The feeling of immediacy is also augmented by the addition of sound, the human voice explaining the action, music underscoring the mood, offstage noises extending the scene. Thus, time, the fourth dimension of our existence, and our sense of hearing, bolstering that of sight, draw us into the picture and surround us with it, often to the degree that we seem no longer viewers but participants emotionally involved in what is taking place. In this age of relativity, the space-time characteristics of the film, much like "Happenings" and "Environments" (see pp. 468, 469), offer the means for making an imaginative statement of the multidimensionality of modern experience (Pl. 30).

The Nature of Motion Pictures: Space and Time

The motion picture can be considered a temporal extension of the still photograph. It consists of a series of still pictures supported by a continuous film of cellulose acetate or cellulose nitrate. The illusion of motion that the moving picture produces from a sequence of related images in frames on a continuous strip of film is dependent on the phenomenon of persistence of vision. Persisting or lingering visual awareness is the retension by the retina of an image after the stimulus has disappeared. Most of us have experienced "after images"—the shapes and outlines of objects that we "see" immediately after we close our eyes or transfer them to other objects—and this in effect is the persistence of vision. It enables us to make a visual "liaison" between the images framed in a film sequence so that we perceive not a series of discrete and jerkily joined pictures but continuous action. The ability to fuse the images filmed on a strip into a visual continuum is essential to the motion picture medium, for in actual fact the film spectator sits almost half the time in darkness peering at a blank screen, at the interstices separating the filmed images.

When motion picture films, as we know them, were first exhibited in 1895, the basic theoretical and practical requirements for making pictures move had been understood in a general way for some time. The Alexandrian astronomer and mathematician Ptolemy (A.D. c. 150) recognized that vision could persist in after images, and the persistence of vision had been under systematic investigation since the eighteenth century. By the 1830s, it was recognized that the camera, to produce "moving" pictures, would require a means of effecting *intermittent* movement—of alternately blacking out and illuminating "still" pictures so that the spectator can distinguish clear, stable images in a series rather than the blur of photographs that themselves move. The film moves during the blackouts; the illusion of movement is produced by still "frames" illuminated serially. The genuinely modern development that made possible the unification of all the ideas into working motion pictures was the production of a strong, flexible support for the image sequences—the photographic *film*—and this came in 1887–1889.

The desire to record life in action (not at all alien to the motivations of painters and sculptors), to observe scientifically the process of locomotion (Figs. 370, 371), and to achieve a new medium of education and entertainment (still the primary uses of the film) was so strong in the nineteenth century that the invention and early

technical development of moving pictures evolved quite rapidly. Historically we associate "sound" movies with the late 1920s, color with the 1930s, wide-screen and the three-dimensional images with the 1950s, and 360-degree projection with the 1960s, but all these techniques had been researched and tried experimentally by 1903. Subsequent history of the film is one of refinement and elaboration of the ideas and processes produced during the first few years of the modern cinema.

The development of the film as an art form of consequence was, however, much more gradual. Initially, motion pictures were used to record other performing arts, such as plays and vaudeville acts. They then became narratives and in this mode imitated the short story, longer fiction, and full-length drama. The impact of the earliest movies came from their subject matter, heightened by appropriate photographic techniques and composition (Fig. 380).

At the same time, however, other trends have been in evidence, and now the "cinematic movie" exists in a very advanced, mature form. Camera techniques and the dimensions of time and space have been greatly emphasized. The viewers' eyes are induced to dart here and there, pausing for close inspection, scanning a panoramic view, catching a transitory glimpse, racing at breakneck speed, slowing down to snail's pace, or seeing an event backwards. Zoom shots instantly give blowups of objects in the distance and then bring back the total, larger scene (Fig. 381). Cameras may be pointed in any direction, tilted at odd angles, and distorting lenses used to heighten the emotional impact. Stroboscopic lights, photomontages of superimposed or contiguous images, and kaleidoscopic effects are other possibilities. Often, much as in James Joyce's writings, there is no strict time line, but rather snatches of time and place parallel the disjointed sequences of the mind.

As an esthetic medium, the film is unique in its synthesis of space and time. We perceive space in large part by observing movement in it, and this takes time. We comprehend time by the action that takes place in space, such as the expansion and contraction of lungs. Thus, in speaking of the film, we probably should use the composite term *space-time*. The filmmaker creates space and time by modifying his materials and by building them into space-time structures. His materials are light and color, space, time, and sound. The latter, however, is, like actors, not essential to the realization of a film. The units of structure are the shot (a continuous, uninterrupted view, or a kind of space-time "cell" within a more complex film sequence) and the sequence (a series of related shots, or cells). The traditional devices for structuring the materials of film are the cut (abrupt change of image), the dissolve (simultaneous fading out of one image and fading in of another), the fade in and the fade out (gradual appearance or disappearance of images), the iris in and the iris out (expansion of an image from a point to the full screen, or contraction from the full screen to a point), the wipe (pushing one shot off the screen by another of any shape in any direction or directions). Each of these is concerned with a time period. The cut is immediate, the dissolve somewhat longer, and the fade, the iris, and the wipe still more leisurely.

The units of structure and the transitional devices can be controlled and modulated by a variety of means. In any shot *space* can be controlled—that is, created—by the selection of configuration and light and color, by the distance and angle of vision, by the use of various lenses (including distorting lenses), and by the development process, as in solarization. Two or more separate spaces can be shown simultaneously by superimposition of images (double exposure) and many may appear by juxtaposition (split screen). The *time* can be modulated by passing the film through

opposite : 380. The interior scenes of Edwin S. Porter's *The Great Train Robbery* (1908) were shot in conventional stage fashion, even having the actors move right to left and left to right.

right : 381. The next-to-last shot in Sergei Eisenstein's *Ivan the Terrible,* Part I (1944), in which the Czar looks through an arch at the assembled populace, is a striking example of the "cinematic" approach to filmmaking.

above and opposite : 382. Frames selected from the "Odessa Steps Sequence" in Sergei Eisenstein's *Potemkin* (1925).

the camera at various speeds so as to create normal, slow, and fast motion as well as lapsed-time photography. The latter technique was used in a famous sequence that reproduced the demolition of an old theater. The camera was set up and left to photograph the wrecking site once every half hour. When the sequence was completed the film was run at normal speed. It created the illusion of the structure collapsing in exactly thirty seconds!

In sequences the idea of space can be modified by the character of the shots selected to appear in the series. A foot leaving the ground in New York and coming down in Paris would have the effect of eliminating both space and time and of creating a new space-time relationship. A different space-time relationship could be created by showing in sequence a number of shots taken from different distances and angles of a man raising a cup of coffee. In this instance, both space and time would be stretched well beyond the limits of reality.

Editing is the process by which much of a film's structure is established. Here, the editor and director can decide whether to have a contrasting or a harmonious relationship between one shot and another. The editor also determines the rhythm of the sequences in his decisions on the length of the time individual shots will remain on the screen. The succession of images can be accelerated and retarded in a rhythmic pattern, much as a composer treats note values in music.

A sequence much admired for the genius with which the full technical range of the film medium was exploited to high dramatic purpose is the famous "Odessa Steps Sequence" in Sergei Eisenstein's *Potemkin* (Fig. 382). Here, through the selection and composition of shots into a sequence of no more than a few minutes the horror of both group and individual tragedy is produced with appalling impact.

The film concerns a 1905 mutiny in the Russian navy. On a series of very high and broad steps at the port city of Odessa a great crowd of citizens is massed to cheer the victory of the mutineers aboard the ship *Potemkin*. Above them, at the top of the steps, appear ranked Cossacks, who march relentlessly down the steps in a total, sweeping slaughter of the defenseless people. The disaster is recreated on film from an immense array of well-conceived shots brilliantly edited into what has been called "one of the most influential few minutes in cinema history."

While the frames reproduced from the sequence in Figure 382 give effective expression to dreadful violence, the sequence is not an exercise in how to commit violence. These shots show the confrontation on the steps between a Cossack and an old woman. Eisenstein edited the sequence to omit the frame that would have had the saber actually strike the woman's face and concentrated on the expressions of the assailant and his victim just before and just after the blow fell. Surrounding this locus and moment of specific, personal catastrophe are the shots in the sequence

of the crowd, the Cossacks in formation with guns cocked, and the steps littered with butchered bodies.

The "Odessa Steps Sequence" is an example of how separate images placed in temporal juxtaposition can create a sense of relationship in space when none, or a different sort, may actually have existed. By shifting from one head to another and from the crowd to the individual, and by creating a rhythm among static and action shots of long and short duration, Eisenstein has, even in the few frames selected for reproduction here, demonstrated the breadth and the extreme concentration of space and time that are possible in the film medium.

The use of multiple screens can also strengthen the spectator's sense of involvement. In Cinerama, the projection of three films on adjoining curved screens partially encloses the viewer and puts him physically almost in the middle of the action. The effect can be intensified by projecting different images on many screens that may be angled in tiers on a wall, set at right angles horizontally and vertically, or that may completely surround the viewer. Films may also be projected onto moving sculptural objects, which distorts the image and compounds the feeling of action.

Since 1950 the esthetic and expressive range of the film has been extended with great imagination, even brilliance, by such directors as Antonioni, Bergman, Brakhage, Cassavetes, Shirley Clarke, Fellini, Goddard, Kubrick, and Resnais. The vision of these people, like that of most artists, is individual, distinctive, and egocentric in an extreme way. For this reason, the audience for the "new" film is relatively more limited than that which continues to support such traditional mass-culture movies as *The Sound of Music*. Using materials more sensitively and equipment with greater economy, creative filmmakers can produce films without the compromises that large-scale commercial sponsorship would impose upon form and content. Often, beautiful, original films are made by individuals, many of them—such as Andy Warhol and Norman Mailer—trained in the other arts. Academic institutions also offer training and research in film history and production, and it is now possible to earn the doctorate for study in the film.

Typically, the works of the avant-garde depart from traditional narrative methods and become more intensely concerned with powerful, direct expression of personal attitudes, psychic states, difficult, even prohibited subject matter, and abstract composition. Weary of what can be an overemphasis on techniques, some filmmakers merely set the camera going and let it record whatever images reach the lens. Others believe that the hand-held camera, exploring the happenings in the environment or the private and select images of the filmmaker, can result in incisive confrontations. Still another field of exploration has been that of mixed media, in which music, dance, and strobe lights are combined, not *in* the film itself, but *with*

top : 383. Stanley Kubrick. *2001 : A Space Odyssey.* 1968. Metro-Goldwyn-Mayer.

above : 384. *2001 : A Space Odyssey.*

film to create a new and totally involving environmental experience in which the viewer becomes a part of the action.

2001 : A Space Odyssey

Stanley Kubrick's *2001 : A Space Odyssey* is one of the most "filmic," or "cinematic," movies in both content and form ever produced as a major commercial enterprise. Its story derives from science fiction and Buck Rogers, and as an adventure narrative, it is an advanced expression of the grand tradition established by such classic films as *Birth of a Nation* and *Gone with the Wind.* At the same time, the work is considerably more than a fantasy of real and imagined science and the explorations of people in the early twenty-first century on an experimental mission in outer space. It becomes more under the impress of its ingenious creator, whose attitudes toward art and life are not only intense but informed by a sophisticated compound ranging from humor and irony through pessimism toward a kind of transcendental poetry. This fluidity and comprehensiveness of idea and purpose is supported by enormous expertise in the means and materials of filmmaking and by a relentless pursuit of perfection in the film medium.

It is significant for the filmic character of *2001* that the movie appeared before the novel form of its scenario was published. In this instance, the literary version is altogether secondary to the film. Indeed, the movie opens and proceeds for a good twenty minutes of fascinating visual exposition before a single word of dialogue is uttered. From beginning to end the camera scans in constant movement that is close to a *perpetuum mobile* not only the face of the earth but the infinite reaches of outer space (Fig. 383) and the inner lights of the human eye. And the movement is itself a stylistic element in the movie. Filmed for Cinerama projection, the wide screen seems as vast as space itself, and the movement has the slow, leisurely, perpetual character of weightlessness. When there is no movement, the stability has the manufactured quality of weight produced by centrifugal force rather than gravity.

2001 is about man's eternal search—from his initial, prehistoric, anthropoid discovery of weapons and power, through total rebirth in outer space—for a higher order, a more complete intelligence, for some sort of absolute, which in *2001* takes the abstract physical form of a smooth-surfaced, perfectly squared slab of pure sentience. As an ape creature, man revered the slab (a form associated with Mosaic tablets and Druidical monoliths), and in a universe populated by scientists with multiple Ph.D.s, Kubrick's man discovers anew and excavates on the moon a slab of total intelligence. In the orthodox manner of science, man then sets out on a mission to Jupiter (the planet of planets, the god without peers?) to gather still more daring evidence of the "most significant discovery in the history of science." En route, he at last experiences infinity, out of which is cast forth a wide-eyed, human-looking embryo, swimming inside a container much as the space man peers from the interior of his helmet, a new life whose destination appears to be birth, or rebirth, on earth.

In such a cosmic scheme as this, verbal language, or the language of *2001*, seems hopelessly inadequate, even irrelevant. The scant and exhausted dialogue in the context of brilliantly realized technology suggests man's intellectual advancement and his spiritual retardation. The most engaging character in the movie is the space ship's computer, called Hal, so perfectly programmed it becomes emotional and must be replaced. Like the dialogue, the plot of *2001* is not as tight and central an element as it would have been in a more conventional movie. The real action is in our discovery of the marvelous complexity of the space ships and stations (Fig. 384), the infinite openness of space, the textures of primordial earth, and, in the "breakthrough" scene, the gorgeous radiances of psychedelic colors and compositions (Pl. 30, p. 276). In a single cut, *2001* follows the course of a desiccated bone tossed by an ape as it arcs through the sky and becomes a space ship gliding elegantly at the same angle through an empyrean atmosphere. It is, however, in the pure color sequences (Pl. 30) that the film reaches its height, providing a rich, sensual experience. A still shot can only hint at the impact of the lyrical receding and advancing color sensations that rush across the screen and envelop the viewer in a drama of chromatic brilliance. Time, space, movement, and a vision of reality— these are what *2001* and the art of the film are about. *2001* offers a new kind of artistic logic, one that is difficult to verbalize, but it can be experienced in a very powerful way.

Films: the Art of the Real

The film, like all art mediums, is most fully realized when it exploits in an imaginatively relevant way those qualities that inhere in its medium. The qualities unique

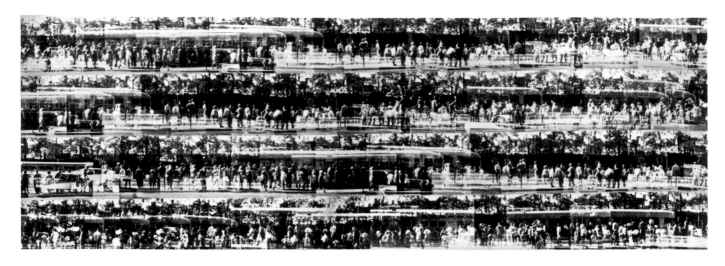

385. Ray K. Metzker. *Trolley Stop,* detail. 1966. The Museum of Modern Art, New York. The multiple imagery in Metzker's photograph is a personal visualization achieved through imaginative manipulation of the photographic medium.

to the film are those that fuse time, space, movement, and sound into a new, enhanced treatment of the reality that has perceptual significance for the audience the film is made for. The art of the film involves imitation, selection and arrangement, creation, expression, and even composition of wholly abstract beauty. At the same time, it must be allowed that of all mediums the film is meant to communicate, and since its language is primarily pictorial, rather than verbal, the film can communicate, after the manner of a true visual art, in a concrete, nonrational way directly to the human sensibilities. And since the film is the only medium that can work simultaneously in as many as five dimensions—vertical, horizontal, space, time, and sound—it is the medium with the greatest potential for penetrating, surrounding, and reproducing life. It is very much part of reality, and reality, therefore, may well be the subject matter most suited to communication by films. But the "reality" that is central to the film, or to any visual art, is not the literal transcription of visible objects but the creation of filmic experiences informed by a reality that emotionally, psychologically, and esthetically is meaningful for a representative number of viewers. Even the economics of filmmaking reinforces the pertinence of the real for motion pictures, because generally the most modest film could not be financed by a single person, and its existence is dependent upon a certain amount of group support, which the group will provide only if it feels realistically involved.

For the film, however, it is ultimately the imagination that arbitrates the real. In the words of the late Erwin Panofsky: "The problem is to manipulate and shoot unstylized reality in such a way that the result has style."

The extension of man through the use of the camera has enabled him to conquer space and time in ways previously impossible. Man stops time in a single photograph or speeds it up in a motion picture. Through the magic of the filmed image, he can see beyond his range of vision: he sees again things that happened in the past; he views events that are taking place simultaneously around the world and in inner and outer space; he can envision happenings in the mind, the emotions, and the future. The camera is the tool that makes this possible, but it is also a tool that can be used to create art (Fig. 385).

part III The Visual
Elements and
Their Organization

overleaf: 386. Richard Frazier. Sculptural environment. 1966.
Wood. California Design 10, Pasadena Art Museum.
The visual elements are organized into a sculptural environment
that draws the observer into the action.

left : 387. *Panathenaic Footrace.* 6th cent. B.C. Attic black-figured amphora. The Metropolitan Museum of Art, New York (Rogers Fund, 1912). This vase displays in its composition the order and freedom characteristic of certain aspects of early Greek life.

below : 388. Venetian glass plate. 16th–17th cents. The Metropolitan Museum of Art, New York (Jarves Collection). Enrichment takes the form here of irregular radiating bands of intricate linear patterns.

Introduction

A contemporary sculptural environment (Fig. 386), a Greek vase from the sixth century B.C. (Fig. 387), and an Italian glass plate from the sixteenth or seventeenth century (Fig. 388) are dissimilar in specific purposes and materials and in time and place of origin, but they are related to one another in that they all make use of form, line, texture, space, light, and color. These visual elements have been purposely organized to fulfill the utilitarian functions, if any, of the objects and to provide an esthetic experience to those who see or touch them.

The human needs and concerns from which art emerges were investigated in Part I, and in Part II the roles of materials and processes were discussed. Attention will now be focused on a third major aspect of art, the visual elements and their organization. The way in which these design elements are ordered can best be considered in terms of the principles of balance, rhythm, emphasis, variety in unity, and form follows function. A work of art may exemplify all the positive aspects of the principles of design, or it may seem to be incoherent and chaotic and imply a negative approach. Studying the work in the light of these principles is one way that the viewer may arrive at the message the artist is trying to communicate.

All art has *organization*, the arrangement of interdependent parts to form a coordinated whole. Organization can be referred to as *design, composition,* or *order*, but *organization* seems a more fundamental and inclusive term. It suggests that this aspect of art is inherent in the process and product, not superficially applied or arbitrarily imposed. It implies a purposeful integration of all factors.

Garo Z. Antreasian's *Shield* (Fig. 389), for example, is a balanced organization of rectangular forms surrounding five blurred discs and almost encompassed within a circular line. The artist seems to have concentrated on the sureness and certainty of precise, compact forms and on solid colors. These are varied by the dim discs, the shadowy outer square, and the freely drawn outer circle, which serve to intensify the orderliness of the other forms. David Hockney's *A Rake's Progress* (Fig. 390), on the other hand, seems unordered, undisciplined, composed of a variety of styles and techniques dropped on the paper. But by forcing the viewer to gain his equilibrium in the process of seeking out the reasons for the apparent imbalance, for the de-emphasis on the man's figure, for the broken rhythms, the ephemeral, disorganized quality of the rake's life is exposed. Hockney has used some of the negative aspects of the principles of design to give his work meaning.

Why is the organization of these two works, done within two years of each other, so different? Why does the history of any one field of art, such as architecture or painting, show so much variety? One answer is that works of art are created by individuals to satisfy specific and general needs in various parts of the world at different periods of time. Each work arises from its own complex of conditions that includes the spiritual, social, economic, and geographic. Art, however, does not merely reflect the environment in which it was created; it is, rather, an active component of the culture to which it belongs.

The contribution of the artist himself is of the highest importance. He may work as a member of a team or alone. Some artists are content to follow along in the footsteps of their predecessors and peers; others find new ways to express truths, their own truths and those of their epoch. Of inner necessity, the innovative artist remakes design in accordance with his individual ideas, and thus works of art created in the same period and country show numerous organizational approaches. Two artists may respond to different aspects of the same culture, but each by ordering his impressions can get his personal vision across to the public. Significant organization in art involves an intense search for forms and colors that eloquently communicate what the artist has found most authentic in his world.

An understanding of the basic principles of design can help to relate varied experiences that might otherwise remain disconnected. To be comprehensive and flexible, the principles should develop out of the widest possible variety of perceptions: human responses to diverse relationships of form, line, texture, space, light, and color; the characteristics of materials, new and old; design in nature, in a tree or a rock or in the movements of waves or clouds; and contemporary and historic art from all the world's cultures. New developments in chemistry and physics, anthropology, philosophy, and psychology, to mention but a few fields, open exciting new vistas for those who create or appreciate art.

above : 389. Garo Z. Antreasian. *Shield.* 1965. Lithograph, 27 × 19″. International Graphic Arts Society of New York. The strong, assertive, symmetrical organization promises stability and security.

right : 390. David Hockney. *A Rake's Progress.* 1963. Etching and aquatint, 12 × 16″. The Museum of Modern Art, New York (Ralph F. Colin, Leon A. Munchin, and Mrs. Alfred R. Stern Funds). Fast but uncertain drive is suggested in this print.

288

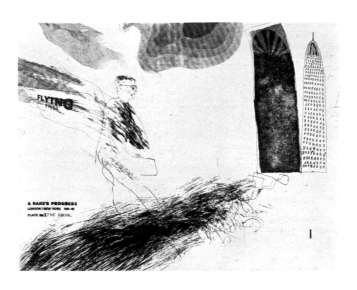

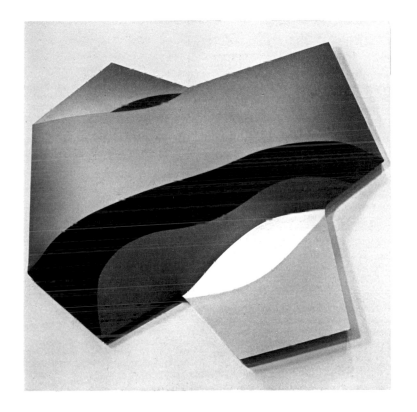

391. Charles Hinman. *Red/Black*. 1964. Acrylic on shaped canvas, 5'7" × 5' × 9". Richard Feigen Gallery, New York and Chicago. The artist has concentrated on the interaction of form and space. The smooth texture and the hard, sharp edges that become lines reinforce this.

11 Form, Line, Texture, and Space

Poets and novelists use words to make known their verbal ideas. Musicians use varied sounds to convey their musical ideas. And artists, whether painters, sculptors, architects, designers, or craftsmen, use form, line, space, texture, light, and color to express their visual and tactile ideas. A human arm, for example, is generally cylindrical in *form*, its edges can be interpreted as *lines*, and it exists in *space*. It is more or less smooth in *texture*, can be seen only in *light*, and its *color* is variable. The visual elements are the vocabulary of art, and artists give special attention to them, not as separate entities, but as interrelated components of what they see, touch, and know. When illiteracy was common, painting, prints, and sculpture were major means of communication. And they still are, but their significance has changed. The spread of literacy and the development of photography decreased the need for pictures and statues that are merely descriptive or that tell a story, and this increased sophistication has encouraged artists to explore the unique potentialities of their mediums. Like music, the visual arts can induce experiences that cannot be completely translated into words.

The visual elements are seen in relation to their surroundings, and these relationships determine the total effect. If the Great Pyramid (Fig. 106) were transported from the expansive sands of the Egyptian desert to a Rocky Mountain valley, it

Optical illusions demonstrate the significance of relationships.

above : 392. The two central circles are exactly the same size.

below : 393. The vertical lines are parallel.

right : 394. Giambattista Piranesi. *The Drawbridge* (*Gli Carceri* series, Pl. 7). 1745. Etching, 21 5/8 × 16 1/8″. New York Public Library (Astor, Lenox, and Tilden Foundation). The soaring complexity of a prison interior is characterized by ambiguous relationships of form, line, and space.

would still be large and pyramidal. But in comparison with the surrounding peaks, the Great Pyramid would seem smaller and less impressive. Or try to think of the town of Williamsburg (Figs. 49–51) set down on a New Mexican desert. The soft light of Virginia welcomes these buildings, but the brilliant New Mexican sunlight would make the colors seem weak and the ornament too delicate.

The relationship of the visual elements to one another, even of a part of one element to another part, is equally important. Figures 392 and 393 demonstrate that identical shapes may not always appear the same size in different contexts and that parallel lines do not always look parallel. In the twentieth century these phenomena underlie the movement called Op (for optical illusion) Art, but artists in many eras have been fascinated by the possibilities. In Piranesi's etching of the interior of a prison (Fig. 394), stairs and bridges crisscross the space and lead the eye in so many contradictory directions that the space becomes a pulsating enigma. Another concept is evident in Escher's *Three Spheres* (Fig. 395), in which lines depict very concrete but disturbingly different form and space relationships. By subtly changing

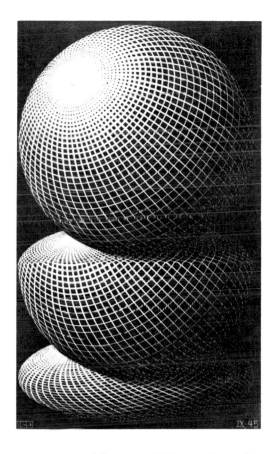

right : 395. M. C. Escher. *Three Spheres.* 1953. Lithograph. Three different earth planes create impossible relationships of elements.

far right : 396. The inner structure of leaves, which determines their external shape, is revealed when the covering membrane has been eaten away.

below right : 397. Wei tomb figure. Chinese, A.D. 386–557. Unglazed pottery with polychrome, $9\,^3/_4 \times 9\,^1/_2''$. The Metropolitan Museum of Art, New York (Rogers Fund, 1928). Mastery of significant forms is seen in this small ceramic figure from the Wei Dynasty.

the direction of the lines, the top form appears as a globe, the middle one has a flat top, and the bottom one has been so squashed that the roundness of the form is almost but not quite lost. The resulting ambiguity is both fascinating and disconcerting; the viewer endlessly searches for certainty in a world in which reality is often contradictory.

Form

To understand what form is and what it can do, it is easier to look at it isolated from other visual elements, even though in actuality it is always bound up with them. *Shape, mass,* and *structure* are alternative words, each with a slightly different connotation, but *form* is the most inclusive. We use the word *form* to describe the inner structure as well as the visible shape of objects, the mass that determines the outline and external configurations. It refers to the unseen but basic skeleton and muscles of a body as much as or more than to the covering skin, to the weblike structure of a leaf more than to the protective surface (Fig. 396). In Chapter 13 the meaning of form is further expanded to refer to the total organization of all the elements, but its basic meaning remains that of interaction between the interior and exterior portions of an object.

Form in Sculpture

The Chinese camel in Figure 397 was shaped by the sculptor's creativity from clay that at first was an unformed mass with as little plastic meaning as bread dough. The subject matter is a camel, but the result is not a literal copy. The sculptor studied

camels not only with his eyes but with his mind and feelings. External appearances were less consequential to him than the forces and structure underneath. He did not attempt to imitate surface textures, yet his sculpture conveys a vivid sense of the hidden muscles and framework. He emphasized those qualities that differentiate camels from other animals—the small head and large neck, the peculiar differences between the front and hind legs, and the humped back (even though a saddle pack covers it, one knows full well that it is there). Yet he also strengthened the head, neck, body, and legs by stressing their similarity to such basic forms as cylinders, cones, and spheres. This is an example of one of the many paradoxes in art. The sculptor particularized his forms to emphasize the essence, or "camelness," of his subject, and at the same time he generalized his forms to relate them to many other natural shapes. By such means he imbued the sculpture with individuality and a timeless, universal quality.

A quite different approach to form is seen in Richard Frazier's sculptural environment (Fig. 386). Crude wood shapes, some only slightly refined from the original tree trunks, are placed so as to emphasize their forms and to create the illusion of form out of the spaces between them. By walking through the environment, the spectator becomes a participant, a form that also delineates other forms.

Form in Painting

Painters, too, deal with form, and much of what was said about sculpture pertains to painting. Let us take the example of an artist painting a picture of a young man. The subject wears a coat and his arms are bent. Folds appear in the sleeves, and each time he moves, the folds take a different pattern. Even if the sitter is motionless, the folds look different under different lighting. With natural illumination the sleeves do not look the same at noon as in late afternoon. On a cloudy morning the details are less sharp than when it is sunny. We *know* that the structure of the arms remains the same, but what we *see* changes and this may lead to varied *emotional responses*. If the painter wants to emphasize essential forms, he concentrates on their basic shape established by bones and muscles. To some artists this is most important. But the essence of physical structure is not necessarily the most significant aspect of our world; certainly, it is not the whole truth. We see our world only through the changing light and color that objects reflect or transmit; this, too, is a reality.

Wayne Thiebaud's *Two Sitting Figures* (Pl. 31) seem real, almost disturbingly so. They sit in their chairs, caught in a moment of suspended time, matter-of-fact, flesh, muscle, and bone, wearing commonplace clothes. Nevertheless, they also transcend prosaic actuality. Thiebaud has said that staring at an object does something to the visual field, especially if it stares back. It makes the moment seem "expanded and clarified by focus and engagement." He is conscious that the two views that the human eyes see are composed into a composite view by the brain, and he has used this phenomenon in his work. Because to him the two views do not always merge perfectly, he surrounds his figures with halos and high-edge lighting in the color lines that both delineate his forms and make a transition from the solid shapes to the light-filled background.

If a painter wishes to draw attention to form and space, he may go as far as to actually build out the canvas over an inner structure and then to paint the surface in a way that further emphasizes the resulting shapes. Charles Hinman in his shaped canvas called *Red/Black* (Fig. 391) has eliminated all nonessentials to reduce his expression to pure form and the colors and space that define it.

Whether we are conscious of it or not, everything is in motion. Some painters, like Willem de Kooning, regard light, movement, and change of all kinds as deeply

Plate 31. Wayne Thiebaud. *Two Sitting Figures*. 1965. Oil on canvas, 5 × 6'. Collection the artist. Thiebaud makes as many as eight to twelve superimposed drawings on the primed canvas in as many colors, starting with diluted lemon yellow, and proceeding to golden yellow, cadmium red, alizarin crimson, cerulean blue, lime green, and so on. He then begins to paint, allowing many of the lines of pure color to show through, to outline and enliven the composition. The paint itself may vary from thin to a quite thick impasto that causes shadows and increases the illusion of space. This painting exhibits a sympathetic regard for the individuality of the sitters, a recognition of life as it is, and great tenderness despite the over-all clarity of the work.

Plate 32. Willem de Kooning. *Easter Monday.* 1956. Oil and newspaper transfer on canvas, 8′ × 6′ 2″. The Metropolitan Museum of Art, New York (Rogers Fund, 1956). De Kooning, one of the most influential of the Abstract Expressionist painters, reveals in his work the courageous attempts of man to assert himself in a precarious world. The forms in this painting are powerful but unstable. In the act of becoming, they disintegrate into near-chaos but still struggle to retain their identity. Broad swaths of color intimate shapes but are instantly overlaid by slashing lines and strokes that set loose opposing forces. The vitality of the painting lies in de Kooning's ability to unify these complex, aggressive forces into a reciprocal interplay of form.

revealing aspects of existence. In Plate 32 his disquieting brush strokes lay bare a tense struggle to discover order and form in a world marked by conflict and restlessness. Beyond objective fact is the universe of the spirit, of nonspecific, subjective feelings and insights. They may or may not be most vividly transmitted through recognizable objects permanently stationed in static space. In the dynamic act of creation the identity of individual shapes emerges and is lost as background forms advance and recede in the picture plane of de Kooning's paintings.

Form in Architecture and Industrial Design

The handling of form in architecture and industrial design evokes a wide range of responses. Unlike form in painting and sculpture, it usually satisfies a specific utilitarian need, and the interior is at least as important as the exterior. People get inside buildings and automobiles, they sit in chairs, and put their hands in refrigerators and chests of drawers. Each of the chairs discussed in Chapter 4 would cause a sitter to respond physically to the disposition of forms, and the response would have its psychological echo.

A comparison of the living room of the Huygen's house (Fig. 398) with the exterior illustrates the close relationship between interior structure and exterior form that is possible in architecture. Not only does the soaring ceiling determine the peaked roofline, but the repeated theme of voids and solids has made form, mass, and volume all-important in the design both inside and out. The large mas of the fireplace wall rises up through the roof, and on the interior it secludes one end of the house from the living room. The fireplace itself is a deep, wide recess with a suspended shelf on one side and a small opening into the dining room beyond. The volume of the sitting area is defined by dropping the floor two steps below the general floor level and by placing a built-in sofa wall along one side. The solid mass of the concrete piers that support the roof provide a protected area for the doors that pivot outward. The handling of form is consistently expressive. Massiveness and solidity contrast with openness and transparency to create a feeling of well-protected spaciousness.

398. The living room of the Remmert W. Huygens residence (1967) in Wayland, Massachusetts, reveals the interplay of substantial forms and spatial volumes that characterizes the design of the house. Huygens and Tappé, Inc., architects. (See also Figs. 33, 34.)

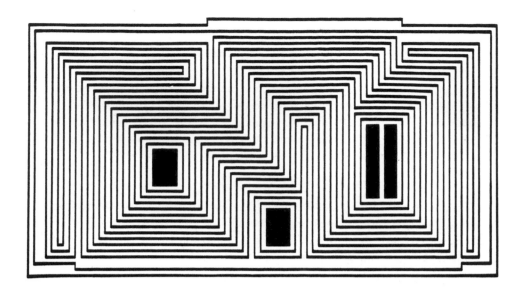

Angular forms have an extensive repertory of expressive meanings (Figs. 399, 400).

399. Josef Albers. *Sanctuary.* 1942. Lithograph. The Contemporaries, New York. Although the print seems at first to be rigidly static, the rectangles soon begin to recede and approach.

Families of Forms

In art and in nature forms tend to fall within "families" of similar shapes. In Figures 399 through 402 four examples, each with its own generic character, are shown. Other illustrations in this book demonstrate that each type can be infinitely varied.

Rectangular forms usually seem clear and definite, assured and certain, perhaps rigid and unyielding, because a right angle is always 90 degrees. Sometimes, however, the organization of rectangular forms can lead to an illusion of moving in and out (Fig. 399), and if, as in much architecture, there are abrupt contrasts of forms going up and down, crosswise and lengthwise, the effect is one of considerable activity (Fig. 412), because diagonal elements are introduced.

Triangular and other diagonal forms are generally more dynamic than rectangular forms, and their expressive range is extensive. When low and broad, as in the Egyptian pyramids, their gentle movement suggests stability and permanence. But tall, slender pyramids lead eyes and the spirit rapidly upward in an aspiring way, as in the Washington Monument or the steeple of the Bruton Parish Church (Fig. 95). If a pyramid stands on its apex, it becomes unstable, suggesting top-heaviness, uncertainty, or imminent change. These variations of position only introduce the possibilities inherent in one basic form. Triangular and diagonal forms can be large or small. If large and ordered, they develop tremendous thrust; if small and disordered, they may fritter away their potential energy by opposing each other. No matter how they are treated, they retain the distinctive characteristic of progressing toward one or more points. By organizing many small, flat, triangular shapes so that their apexes flow in opposing directions across the picture plane, Francis Celentano, for example, created a feeling of flickering movement (Fig. 400).

Geometric, curved forms have a different effect from those that are angular. Spheres, bounded by one continuing surface on which all points are equidistant from the center, have no top, sides, or bottom. They seem self-contained, with all forces in sustained equilibrium. Yet they are also unstable, for they can roll easily in any direction. In durability and permanence, however, spheres exceed even the pyramid: there are no corners or angles to break off or wear away. The other members of this group—cylinders, cones, hyperbolas, and ellipses—seem at once more active, because they have one dominant directional force, and more stationary, because they have either one straight or one slightly flattened side that could conceivably act as a base (Fig. 401). As with triangles and pyramids, however, placement of these forms on their more-convex ends increases the effect of instability.

400. Francis Celentano. *Flowing Phalanx*. 1965. Synthetic polymer paint on canvas, 34 ¹/₈ × 46 ¹/₈″. The Museum of Modern Art, New York (Larry Aldrich Foundation Fund). Light triangles push the dark background into a rhythmic progression of angular planes.

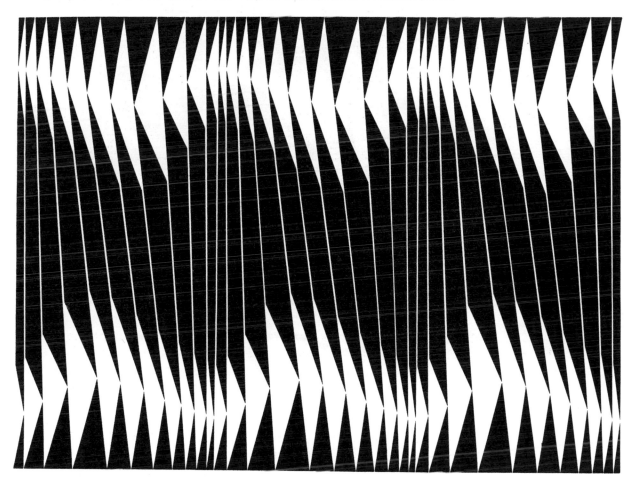

Curvilinear forms come in almost infinite variety (Figs. 401, 402).

401. Josef Albers. *Aquarium*. 1934. Woodcut. Philadelphia Museum of Art. The rhythms of a swimming fish are suggested in semigeometric curves.

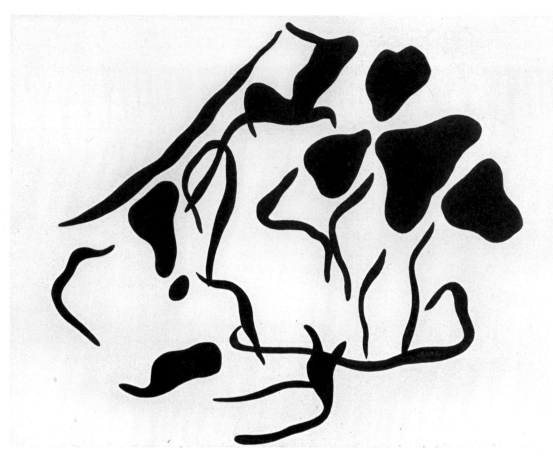

402. Jean (Hans) Arp. *Automatic Drawing*. 1916. Brush and ink on brownish paper, 16 ¾ × 21 ¼″. The Museum of Modern Art, New York. The free-form, or biomorphic, curves are fleetingly reminiscent of natural forms.

Free-form and biomorphic, organic curves abound in nature. Pears and squash, eggs and amoebas, the shell of a snail or the inner structure of a leaf, and most parts of the human body are but a few examples. These forms seem directly related to life and growth. They have been copied or modified in many kinds of art; and they have been completely abstracted (Fig. 402). But even without specific relation to any particular growing object, they recall the essence of nature.

Frank Lloyd Wright used organic forms to vitalize the design of the Guggenheim Museum (Fig. 416), and Isamu Noguchi used them in his sculptural table (Fig. 417). Modern freeway interchanges are composed of flowing curves because they allow a natural, fluid motion (Figs. 418, 419).

Texture

Every substance has an *internal, structural texture*. This may be the organically ordered, cellular grain of wood (Fig. 419) or the sharp, angular crystals found in some rocks and metals. Each material also has an *external, tactile quality* that is determined by the internal structure or the way in which the material is processed. Glass naturally tends to have a smooth surface, but it can be pressed, cast, or engraved to give varied degrees of roughness. Metals and woods can be given any texture the artist deems suitable. Oil and acrylic paints can be applied so that they

403. Robert Seyle. *Nail Relief VI.* 1966. Nails in wood, 3 × 4'. Ankrum Gallery, Los Angeles. Robert Seyle uses varied sizes and colors of nails in his construction to create the textures that constitute his forms.

have a satiny or shiny smoothness, but they can also have a vast array of textures. Finally, *visual or simulated textures* can be applied, as on printed fabrics.

Tactile Textures   Tactile texture, the actual, three-dimensional manifestation of structure or finish, is directly related to the sense of touch. It is the way satin and sandpaper feel when one runs a hand over them, but it can also be appreciated visually. Robert Seyle's *Nail Relief VI* (Fig. 403) shows variations of textures from large to small, and many degrees of regularity and irregularity, with resulting variations of tactile responses that can be both felt and perceived.

Visual Textures   Two-dimensional, visual textures can be seen but not felt. Long familiarity with tactile sensations, however, has so conditioned us that we respond to the look or appearance of these textures almost as we do to the real things. Painters depend on this when they create implied textures through color differentiation in order to evoke the sensory responses that actual textures would bring. Other examples include printed textiles (see Chap. 8) and many graphic prints, such as William Majors' *Burning Bush* (Fig. 410).

In any work of art tactile and visual textures may correspond to or differ from each other. Of the two Natzler vases (Fig. 404), the one on the right looks and feels rough and corroded, but the one on the left has its bland surface enlivened with a visual texture that comes from various colors in the glaze. This produces a flowing,

404. Two vases (c. 1960) by Gertrud and Otto Natzler show how visual and tactile textures alter the expressiveness of similar forms. One invites handling, the other discourages it.

light-and-shadow pattern reminiscent of structural undulations. Great textural interest can also be provided by disclosing inner structure, and this may result in a curious mixture of tactile and visual sensations. Polishing wood reveals its organic pattern, which may look rugged, but the surface is smooth to the touch.

The Effects of Texture   When one thinks of texture, one invariably uses a touch-sensation adjective to describe it. Textures differ from one another in many ways, two of which are the range from smooth to rough and from soft to hard. The adjectives one uses tell much about what texture does for an object and how it makes us feel.

Smooth textures are usually unobtrusive and undemanding. They underscore form, color, and spatial relationships, often to the degree that the observer is un-aware of texture as an element. They seem cool, tranquil, and precise; although, if hard, they sometimes seem unfriendly. Rough textures attract attention. They activate surfaces and may overshadow form and color. They tend to look warm and informal and may be pleasantly irregular or painfully harsh. Soft surfaces tempt us to touch them, for they seem friendly and appealing—that is, until they become so soft that they are flabby. Hard surfaces are less inviting, especially if they are rough, but fieldstone walls and the bark of trees are reassuringly strong and vigorous. As hard surfaces approach the brilliance of crystal or polished marble, their smooth-ness is visually and tactually satisfying.

Between these two sets of extremes there are, of course, many variations to fill in the range of sensory experiences. And there can be incongruities of texture that are unsettling. The soft, appealing texture of fur is almost repellent on the fur-lined cup, saucer, and spoon in Figure 405, because dinnerware needs an impervious surface and because a napped finish seems unpleasant for oral use. Oppenheim used this dipslacement of expected tactile sensations as a surrealistic manifestation of texture.

Use of Texture

Sculptors, working in the most tactile branch of art, have great concern for textures that make a significant contribution to the expressiveness of their work. In

opposite : 405. Meret Oppenheim. *Fur-covered Cup, Saucer. and Spoon.* 1936. Cup, diameter 4 ³/₈″; saucer, diameter 9 ³/₈″; spoon , length 9 ³/₈″. The Museum of Modern Art, New York. Textures can drastically alter the visual, tactile, and emotional reactions to common objects.

above : 406. Duayne Hatchett. *Largo.* 1966. Painted steel, 6′ 10″ × 7′ 2″ × 2′ 5 ¹/₂″. Royal Marks Gallery, New York. The relatively even painted surface of Hatchett's intriguing, large steel sculpture stresses the size and shape of the geometric forms.

order to focus attention on abstract forms in tenuous equilibrium, Duayne Hatchett, in *Largo* (Fig. 406), reduced all surface variations to a uniform visual and tactile smoothness. The primary shapes are immediately accepted by the observer, who is then left free to concentrate on the precarious stability of the forms. In *Nail Relief VI* (Fig. 403) the sculptor approached his work with the desire to create a scintillating textural composition out of such commonplace materials as a board and nails. Although one can let his imagination range freely in evaluating the forms, the relief makes no reference to anything specific, other than the materials from which it was constructed.

Painters, too, are aware of the power of textures. In Edouard Vuillard's painting *The Interior at l'Etang-la-Ville* (Fig. 407), a profusion of patterned areas imparts a soft, intimate character to a domestic interior. Figures seem to emerge from and then almost dissolve into the background. To Vuillard, who is said to have been in love with wallpaper, merging textures were more important than sharply delineated form or line. Hinman, in *Red/Black* (Fig. 391), went to the opposite extreme and avoided any indication of surface variation or pattern so that the basic form-space relationship is all-important.

Textures endow surfaces with significance, but, as always in art, relationships largely determine the final effect. In the living room of the Tugendhat house (Fig. 411), one of the early examples of the International Style, Miës van der Rohe set off sleek, shiny, plain surfaces of glass, metal, and concrete against the equally hard but visually exciting textural pattern of a marble wall and the softer, yielding intricacy of trees and plants beyond the windows. In this way the coldness of many of the materials was mitigated, their severity both heightened and compensated. Paul Rudolph's buildings for the Southeastern Massachusetts Technological Institute (Fig. 412) are composed of massive, strongly modeled and articulated forms. The corrugated surface of the concrete blocks and the projecting and recessed elements provide textural interest at both small and large scale, which humanizes the almost overwhelming size of the structure. In each of these buildings textures were purposefully and coherently organized to express the architect's concepts.

407. Edouard Vuillard. *The Interior at l'Etang-la-Ville*. 1893. Oil on Millboard panel, 12 1/2 × 14 5/16″. Smith College Museum of Art, Northampton, Mass. Elusive textures suggest without clearly defining the compressed form and space of a small room.

Line

In the drawing of three youths by Pablo Picasso (Fig. 408) there is no shading or modeling; yet without these devices the artist has convincingly defined human figures and a low bench in the corner of a room. The three-dimensional quality of the figures and of the space in which they exist as well as the differences between flesh, hair, textiles, furniture, and architecture are represented by line alone. More remarkable is the feeling of tender sensitivity communicated with comparatively few curved and straight lines.

When Picasso's drawing is compared with one by Diego Rivera (Fig. 409), marked differences are apparent. One is delicate, relaxed, and in repose; the other is strong, plodding, somber, and determined. Even if the subject matter is minimized or the drawings are turned upside down, the differences are still apparent, because they are rooted in the quality of the lines and the manner in which they are composed.

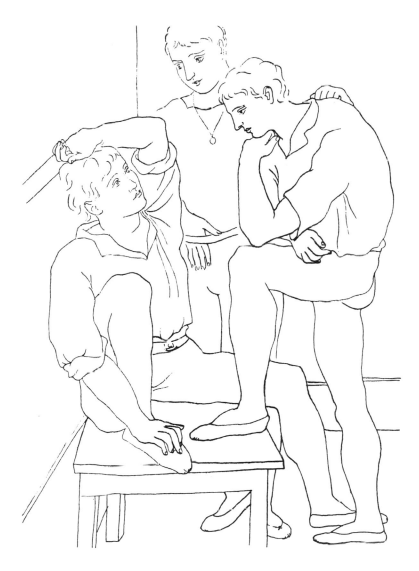

left : 408. In a drawing by Pablo Picasso solid forms and empty space are convincingly represented through line alone.

below : 409. Diego Rivera. *Mother and Child.* 1936. Ink drawing, $12 \times 9\,{}^1/_4{}''$. San Francisco Museum of Art (Albert N. Bender Collection). Rivera used heavy lines to depict a Mexican peasant and child. As in Fig. 408, line quality expresses and represents the subject.

The examples just discussed are comparatively uncomplicated, but lines can also be the basic element in complex statements. *Burning Bush* (Fig. 410) is an intricate organization of many kinds of lines that are strongly directional in their movement outward from the center. Small areas of white contrast brilliantly with areas of black and with innumerable grays. In some places, especially at the top and lower left corner, individual lines can be distinguished, but in general they are interwoven or crosshatched into textural planes that have a marked three-dimensional, spatial quality. Lines and forms have expressive power, because a line, no matter how thin, has form and because lines delineate form. This expressive power may derive from certain essentials of human experience. When a person is tired and lies down to sleep, he assumes a horizontal position, compliant to the pull of gravity. The things that suggest repose to us are likely to be horizontal objects, such as large calm bodies of water or low, gently rolling hills and meadows. When a person is up and about, he moves in a vertical position, and when vertical lines are seen they look alert, upward striving, and stable in their resistance to the force of gravity. When running or otherwise very active, the body assumes a diagonal position, head thrust forward, balance somewhat precarious, elbows and knees forming angles. So, too, diagonal lines form angles and they suggest continuous and energetic movement to maintain equilibrium and to resist gravitational forces. Artists use these expressive qualities to make a building, a statue, a painting, or a piece of furniture look restful or imposing or perhaps excited and moving, as in *Burning Bush.*

Line, however, is not always used to express human experience in this manner. Often it is used merely to represent objects: the line drawing of a building prepared by an architect or the drawings of a bridge made by an engineer; the lines drawn

left : 410. William Major. *Burning Bush.* 1967. Etching, 19 ½ × 15 ½″. International Graphic Arts Society of New York. Line has been used in this abstract composition to create expressive forms that attest to the artist's faith in religious hopes, aspirations, and beliefs.

opposite : 411. The living room in the Tugendhat house (1930) in Brno, Czechoslovakia, exemplifies architect Miës van der Rohe's philosophy of "less is more," in that nothing unnecessary distracts from the serene flow of space from indoors to outdoors.

on maps to represent rivers, roads, or contours; or the lines drawn on paper to represent words. Such use of line is primarily utilitarian, a convenient way of communicating ideas to other people. Whichever the emphasis—expression of human emotion or representation of factual materials—line is an important plastic element at the disposal of the artist. As architect Henry Van de Velde wrote, "A line is a force; it derives its force from the man who drew it."

Space

Space is the three-dimensional expanse in which living objects and inanimate objects exist. It is also the distance, void, or interval between things, akin to moments of silence in music or to a pause in a speech that can be more effective than sound. Space envelops us completely, but its reality is in the forms that give it definition. By day, the sky gains significance from the horizon that seems to separate it from the earth and, by night, from the solar bodies that act as points of reference. An area is shaped into a room by its enclosing planes. Space and form are inseparable elements, because all forms are contained in space, and at the same time they shape space. Space is also allied with time, because an empty area suggests and allows the possibility of change, of movement to fill the emptiness. These two concepts—space-form and space-time—have particular importance in architecture. People live and move in space, and their actions are affected by the forms they encounter.

Space, the Vital Element in Architecture

In the living room designed by Ludwig Miës van der Rohe (Fig. 411), the architect of the Bauhaus (Fig. 152), and in the college buildings designed by Paul Rudolph

(Fig. 412), the spatial compositions each have a definite character. Both are basically rectangular, but the similarity stops there. In the Miës van der Rohe living room,
space is subtly defined rather than enclosed by a minimum number of smooth-
textured planes and slender structural supports. Window walls make the outdoor
areas a vital unit in the spatial composition, and a freestanding marble screen allows
the interior space to flow into the adjoining areas. It is precise, serene, and unconfining. In the college buildings, space is vigorously articulated and positively defined.
From the broad, open terrace in the foreground, space is channeled into and up a
staggered stairway between rectangular boxes intended for eventual planting. At the
top of the stairs, the space divides and flows into and around the structure, a movement expressed by the concrete grid of the building and by the overhanging units.
This adds up to a progression from outdoor expansiveness to smaller indoor
volumes. In contrast to the calmness of the Miës van der Rohe dwelling, Rudolph's
architecture is a bold, assertive, interplay of exterior and interior space, bounded
but developing, and full of surprises.

Since prehistoric times man has sought space that is sufficiently enclosed to protect him and yet open and flexible enough for his body and soul. Natural caves were
a ready-made solution for early man, but he soon began to construct simple huts.
In the massive Egyptian burial structures, thick walls and columns provided security
but minimized openness. Later the Greek, Roman, and Gothic builders erected
edifices with greater and more flexible space. Recently these trends have been
accelerated by new materials, new ways of construction, and, in a world that is
growing ever more crowded, by an urgent desire for both usable space and a sense of
spaciousness.

opposite : 412. Paul Rudolph's buildings for the campus of Southeastern Massachusetts Technological Institute in North Dartmouth (1966) form a unified composition of flowing space and strongly modeled forms.

The Expression of Space

In architecture, space is tangible, but in the graphic arts three-dimensional form and space are expressed on a two-dimensional surface. In Figure 408, Picasso handled this problem with simple devices: overlapping planes, position on the vertical plane, and converging lines. We know that the middle figure is behind the others because their bodies *overlap* him and he is thereby partially obscured. The placement of his head and body *higher on the vertical plane* also pushes him back. The *converging* lines of the stool and lightly indicated walls and floor make room for the figures. Picasso intentionally misplaced the feet of the central figure too low in the picture to make them visible, to reaffirm that the figure is standing on the floor and leaning to the left. But it is Picasso's uncanny skill that makes the forms really seem rounded and the space so tangible that we feel we could reach into it. Rivera's drawing (Fig. 409) is considerably flatter, not because Rivera lacked skill, but because his subject suggested a more compact spatial organization. Even so, some parts stand in front of others. The shawl overlaps the woman's left shoulder, envelops the boy, and seems to carry around to the woman's right hand.

The illusion of space in a two-dimensional painting can be compelling even when the forms are almost completely nonobjective. In Roy Lichtenstein's *Little Big Painting* (Fig. 413), the visual reversal of the broad stroke in the bottom half of the composition establishes a strong back-to-front movement. The four other strokes take their places as overlapping planes one behind the other. The diagonal thrust

413. Roy Lichtenstein. *Little Big Painting*. 1965. Oil on canvas, 68 × 80″. Whitney Museum of American Art, New York. This is one of a series in which the artist isolated brush strokes and presented them as a kind of abstract subject matter or a greatly magnified detail in which the visual elements such as space are present but any literary meaning is hidden.

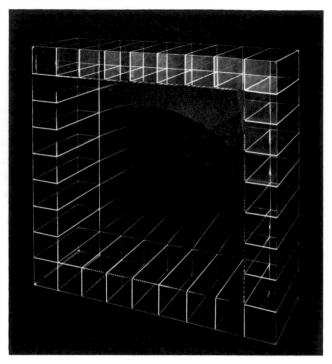

left : 414. Max Finkelstein. *Black Plus* 200. 1966. Brushed aluminium, 34 ½ × 36 × 2″. University of Illinois (Krannert Art Museum Purchase Award). Both two- and three-dimensional handling of space is displayed in this construction.

right : 415. Robert Stevenson. *La Mentira Verde.* 1967. Acrylic plastic, 36 × 36 × 12″. Hansen Gallery, San Francisco. Stevenson used transparent sheets of Plexiglas (acrylic plastic) to create a sculpture that looks like a three-dimensional drawing of spatial volumes.

of the stroke that drips paint furthers the back-to-front movement, while the gray-and-black band clearly seems behind the horizontal form with its strong dark-and-light contrast that is so much more demanding. The uniform background of regularly spaced gray dots recedes into the distance behind the boldness of the other forms. Lichtenstein, like Picasso, used many of the traditional techniques of indicating space, but in a fresh, direct way.

In three-dimensional forms of art, actual space can, of course, be an integral element. In Duayne Hatchett's *Largo* (Fig. 406), the observer is acutely conscious of the narrow space between the two balanced forms, and the sharp outlines of the sculpture carve positive shapes of space between the segments. Max Finkelstein's approach, however, is quite different in *Black Plus 200* (Fig. 414), a construction of aluminum rectangles. Although some of the forms are handled three-dimensionally, the illusion of depth is strongest in the diagonal streaks of light caused by the way in which the artist worked the surfaces of the metal segments. The resulting textures refract light, reflect colors, and set up a dynamic interplay of recessions that are abruptly terminated.

With the use of a transparent medium, space relationships can be completely exposed, as in Robert Stevenson's *La Mentira Verde* (Fig. 415). In this construc- tion of colorless Plexiglas subdivided by yellow Plexiglas planes, space is the domi- nant element. The piped light along the edges of the subdividers continues as reflec- tions on the clear plastic of the back of the frame and appears to extend into the void behind the actual construction. It also sets up a rhythm of variously spaced parallel dashes of light along some of the edges of the construction that changes when viewed from different angles. Unlike most sculpture, this work makes the observer more aware of the space contained within the structure than of the material from which it is made or of the surrounding openness.

Contemporary Concepts of Space

In the second half of the twentieth century artists and architects have become increasingly concerned with the *sense of space*. This is a recurring theme in the history of man's discoveries of new ways of manipulating space and perhaps of new needs to do so. The Gothic builders were entranced by the possibilities of the pointed arch and of vaulting devices and thus created new kinds of spatial experiences. Painters in the fifteenth century explored with delight the results of linear perspective. In the last one hundred years, the invention of steel-cage construction techniques has led to new ways of utilizing vertical volumes in skyscrapers, and the availability of glass in large sheets has allowed the visual expansion of the interior into the surrounding environment. In a time marked by two contradictory prospects—the steady decrease of useful open land and the dizzying possibilities of outer space—the concept of space has taken on new meanings.

Artists make the viewer aware of *being in space* by constructing compositions such as Richard Frazier's sculptural wood environment (Fig. 386), into which one walks and becomes another component.

Space is regarded as being *integral with* the other visual elements of art—form, line, color, light, and texture—and just as important. In fact, it often transcends the forms and materials that define it. The wood supports of Noguchi's table (Fig. 417) vigorously carve space into forms that are only lightly bounded by the glass top. In Stevenson's *La Mentira Verde*, spatial volumes are indicated by transparent plastic.

Greatly increased emphasis is placed on the *continuing character of space*. In Paul Rudolph's buildings (Fig. 412), interior and exterior spaces interpenetrate and expand. Cantilevered elements jut out over outdoor terraces; concrete stairs and paths continue man-made spatial boundaries into the environment; and roof-top terraces are half enclosed, half open.

The *multidimensionality of space* is recognized and exploited. Not only horizontal and vertical space but an infinite variety of diagonal and curvilinear relationships

left : 416. In Frank Lloyd Wright's Guggenheim Museum (1959) in New York City, the multidimensional expansion of space that swells upward in an inverted spiral is a major compositional factor.

309

are expressed in such examples as the spiraling Guggenheim Museum (Fig. 416), which shapes the interior volume into new dimensions.

The concept of *simultaneity*, in which many aspects are presented and perceived at the same moment, led to Cubist works, such as Juan Gris's *Landscape at Ceret* (Fig. 421), and to such architectural works as Paul Rudolph's (Fig. 412), in which there is no single dominant focus of attention but rather a moving point of reference that opens the way to multiple, successive images.

The *ambiguity* inherent in depicting space is pointed out by many artists. In Feininger's *Town Gate-Tower II* (Pl. 34) a figure apparently walking across an open city square is stopped short by a high wall; or perhaps he is disappearing around the corner of a building? The buildings exist on different spatial planes, and the resulting ambiguity reflects the dilemmas inherent in our contemporary urban experience.

Mobility and *fluidity*, two potentials of space, have been the subject of experimentation. Charles Mattox has incorporated actual movement into a sculpture (Pl. 33) through the use of oscillating shapes. The large, green-painted fiber-glass shape rolls gently back and forth on its base in response to the mechanical impulse of the small red square. Together they describe patterns in the air. Highway engineers have designed complex traffic intersections for fast-moving traffic (Fig. 418). De Kooning and Celentano (Pl. 32 and Fig. 400) express the dynamic experiences of life with lines and forms that weave and progress through space.

417. Isamu Noguchi brought his sculptural talents to the design of a coffee table in which space flows through and around the transparent and opaque forms. Designed in 1947, it was still in production in 1968.

below left : 418. The modern freeway, a twentieth-century innovation, is designed to speed a mobile society in continuous, fluid movement.

below right : 419. The rhythmic flow of vital forces in a microphotograph of wood from an Australian tree (*Banksia serrata)* is reminiscent of automobiles traveling on highways.

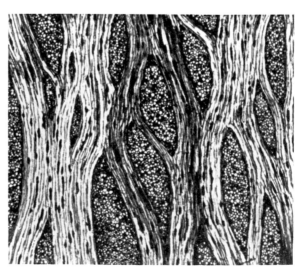

Plate 33. Charles Mattox. *Green Triangle with Red Cube*. 1966. Painted fiber glass and metal, 4′ × 4′ × 10″. Joseph H. Hirshhorn Collection, New York. Mattox calls attention to the space in which his sculpture stands and that flows through the hollow center by incorporating motion in the work itself. The configurations assumed by the triangular and square shapes as they move through space have been caught by repeated exposures of the camera, and the effect of their multiple images is to make the viewer aware of the void through which the forms travel.

Plate 34. Lyonel Feininger. *Town Gate-Tower II*. 1925. Oil on canvas, 39 ³/₈ × 31 ¹/₂″. Staatliche Kunsthalle, Karlsruhe. The shapes of the city inspired Feininger to explore both the interrelationships of form and space and the simultaneous vision of buildings and open areas from different points of view. By such contrapuntal devices as rhythmically repeated, inverted, overlapping, and interpenetrating forms, he makes evident the correlation of light-filled space and sunlit buildings with dark forms and mysteriously shadowed voids.

The particular concepts just discussed were not invented in this century. Great artists have always been concerned with the sense of space, and many historic works use linear perspective to produce the illusion of space (Fig. 420). In *Town Gate-Tower II* (Pl. 34), executed in 1925, Lyonel Feininger painted the reciprocity between light and air and the somber, overpoweringly geometric forms of the city. In 1930 the Tugendhat house (Fig. 411) ushered in a new era of space consciousness; and today Paul Rudolph (Fig. 412) shows yet another way of organizing space.

This discussion is brief because the useful and expressive organization of space has already been dealt with extensively in Part I and will be considered again in Part IV. Space, far from being merely "what is left," stands with form as one of the two major visual elements. Understanding of its complexity, diversity, and significance has greatly expanded with scientific advances. With telescopes and other space-probing devices scientists explore the interstellar vastness, and with electronic instruments they delve into the forms and voids of tiny bits of matter. In this age, artists, too, avidly explore and experiment with many new spatial concepts.

Three Landscape Paintings

In *Wheatfields* (Fig. 420), painted around 1670, Jakob van Ruisdael showed his mastery of expressive form and space. At first glance the painting may look almost photographically realistic. The easily recognized fields, trees, and clouds give the illusion of being three-dimensional forms existing at definite points in an expansive atmospheric space, following as they do the system of perspective developed in the fifteenth century. But then the viewer may begin to notice that each form has its own inner vitality. It is not an isolated chunk of inert matter but a lively part of great natural forces. In this painting, line is of little consequence, but space is tremendously important. The landscape is seen from one fixed viewpoint and progresses from the foreground along the road and on through the grove of trees. In this movement into space, sweeping, horizontal curves flow into, across, and beyond the fields, up into the limitless sky. Textures are used to evoke the surface qualities of nature, in the filmy, sensuous clouds, the feathery trees, and the roughness of the road against the smooth sweep of the wheatfields. Not content merely to reproduce a pleasant scene, Ruisdael reasserts the power and grandeur that lies beneath surfaces.

420. Jakob van Ruisdael. *Wheatfields.* c. 1670. Oil on canvas, 2′ 6³/₈″ × 4′ 3¹/₄″. The Metropolitan Museum of Art, New York (bequest of Benjamin Altman, 1913). This Dutch landscape is of seemingly infinite spaciousness.

421. Juan Gris. *Landscape at Ceret*. 1913. Oil on canvas. Present whereabouts unknown. This landscape shows the Cubists' interest in simultaneity, interpenetrating planes, and angular forms.

Juan Gris painted *Landscape at Ceret* (Fig. 421) one year before the beginning of World War I, while in the Pyrenees Mountains. His outlook, and that of many other persons in 1913, had little in common with the unbounded assurance that Ruisdael enjoyed. Bearing slight relation to a natural scene, the form, line, and space present a new way of seeing, thinking, and feeling. In searching for forms that reveal the dynamism of the modern world, Gris analyzed what he saw into many flat, angular planes, accentuated by a few curved and shaded forms. Instead of portraying objects as self-contained entities, each in its own allotted space, he shows facets of many things or multiple views of the same thing presented simultaneously. Vigorous diagonals, interpenetrating planes, and sudden contrasts of light against dark lead the viewer's eyes abruptly from one place to another. A single static viewpoint has given way to multiple, changing viewpoints, for the canvas can be visually entered at any point. With study, the first impression of a flat, crowded, cut-up canvas changes. Clear, consistent juxtapositions of dark and light make it seem as though there are lines where there actually are none. Decisive color contrasts produce a kaleidoscopic vibrancy of textures that are simplified and generalized rather than naturalistic. Some forms are clearly in front of others, and the diagonal areas diminishing toward the top suggest considerable penetration into space. Gris did not want to imply that this was an actual scene, and yet it corresponds with surprising truth to the way the surroundings appear when the viewer moves rapidly or looks quickly from one thing to another.

In the more than fifty years since Gris painted *Landscape at Ceret*, profound changes have taken place in the way many artists view the world. Douglas Snow, in his painting *Storm and Sunset* (Fig. 422), does not describe a pictorial image but one of sensations emerging from a heightened consciousness of the creative act.

From its title the painting can be interpreted as a landscape, although it does not suggest external forms but rather the forces of nature. A road of sorts enters the painting at the bottom leading to an indeterminate horizon. However, the shifting structural organization, in what can be imagined as the deep space of the sky, captures attention. Powerful forms in the center of the canvas express the turmoil contained in a storm and in the colorful explosion of a sunset. This mass of action is silhouetted against a lighter background plane that recedes into the distance, while the surprising energy of some of the horizontal lines evokes the vastness of a desert or a great plain. Textures are generalized and given new interpretations by the handling of the paint. The relationship of form to space is ambiguous. The line of the horizon can be placed at the edge of any one of the horizontal bands, but it will not stay there when viewed in relation to another part of the dominant vertical element. This ambiguity, coupled with the lack of recognizable shapes, makes the painting not a representation of an actual scene but a sensational image of storms and sunsets.

Each of these three paintings presents a landscape in terms of the time and culture within which the artist worked and expresses the way in which he saw nature. The visual elements that were used—form, line, texture, and space—are constant in their universality but varied in expression because of the complexity of their interrelationships and because of their interaction with human experience. A new interpretation of one of the elements can cause reappraisals of the others. In the 1960s, man has become aware of space as environment and of the need to control nearby space as well as the air above and around his cities. Buckminster Fuller, who designed the United States Pavilion at Expo 67 (Pl. 61 and Figs. 238, 634, 637) as a freestanding spherical cover, has envisioned a similar space shelter that would protect the central section of the borough of Manhattan and make possible complete air conditioning. Such a concept of environmental space would inevitably result in new forms for buildings, which would no longer be required to keep out winter winds and spring rains but might need even more sound- and air-conditioning.

The ultimate fantasies to date are spacecrafts and free-floating environmental balloons in the sky, livable habitations in the ocean's depths, and climatically comfortable communities near the Arctic Circle and in deserts. These would result in even more drastic changes in the forms and space with which people live. It is anyone's guess as to what kinds of painting and sculpture these developments would inspire.

422. Douglas Snow. *Storm and Sunset.* 1963. Oil on canvas, 40 × 48″. Feingarten Galleries, Los Angeles. The artist has identified with the forces of nature and revealed them subjectively in vivid and expressive forms.

12 Light and Color

Light and color, the most ephemeral, least tangible of the visual elements, can be perceived only through vision, whereas form, texture, and space can be experienced through sight or touch. Our response to light and color is instantaneous and powerful. Light wakes us up. Typically, man sees color more quickly than he sees form, and his emotional response may be more vivid. Greater understanding of the environment is derived from sight than from all the other senses combined. This is due in part to the fact that the human eye, unlike other sensory receptors, is a direct extension of the brain. Light and color are as inseparable as space and form; without light there is no color, and all light has color.

Light

Light is a form of radiant energy, a force to which all but a few organisms react immediately, either consciously, subconsciously, or both. In man, at least, the reactions are a complex of physical and psychological responses as yet only partially explained. For that matter, the exact nature of light is not precisely understood, but it is known that light varies enormously in brightness. The light from strong sunlight is approximately four hundred thousand times that from the full moon and one

316

million times that from some of the stars. White light is composed of all the hues of the spectrum, while absolute blackness has none.

For all practical purposes light can be regarded as traveling in straight lines. Light is affected by the nature and the surface qualities of any material it strikes. Transparent or translucent substances allow the penetration of light to varying degrees, but the color of the light is altered if the material is pigmented. Opaque objects, depending on their pigmentation, absorb some of the brightness and hues in light and reflect the remaining hues as the color of the object. A few materials, such as opals, faceted diamonds, and cut glass refract, or break up, light into its components, much as the prism does. Smooth polished surfaces, notably metals, produce bright, sharp reflections, but rough surfaces soften and diffuse light.

Conversely, the appearance of objects is affected by light, because forms and textures can be emphasized or subordinated by the direction from which the light comes and by the size of the light source. The degree of brightness, the levels of contrast, and the color of light are also influential. Uniform light is seldom noticed as such, but its effect varies with the quantity of light. Bright light tends to be stimulating, while low levels are quieting. Warm-colored light is generally cheerful, but light that is cool in color may be either quieting or depressing. Strong contrasts of brightness and darkness are emphatic and dramatic, and they attract attention.

Two photographs of Lincoln Center demonstrate these points. In Figure 424 broad, general daylight exposes the exterior of the buildings, shows the textures and patterns created by the materials used in the walls and in the plaza, and casts shadows wherever the direct rays of the sun do not penetrate, making the interiors look like dark caverns. Thus the outward appearance is emphasized, and the buildings appear heavy, massive, almost stolid, despite the tall colonnaded fronts. In Figure 425, taken at night, man-made and man-controlled illumination articulates the brightly lighted interior volumes, which are curtained with glass and protected by roofs that float on slender columns and almost disappear in the general blackness of the night.

Lincoln Center for the Performing Arts (1962–1966), New York.

left : 424. By day, Lincoln Center is revealed as a complex of several large buildings arranged around two interconnecting plazas.

right : 425. By night, the center comes alive with floodlights, and attention is drawn to the brightly illumined interiors.

The fountain is a shifting cone of light in the center of a mysteriously shadowed plaza. The massive solidity of the buildings has become much less evident, replaced by a sense of space and life.

Sculptors have long been concerned with the element of light and the patterns of brightness and shadow that it creates. One factor in their choice of material is the way it will absorb or reflect light, and they carve or model shapes to achieve whatever effects they seek. Until recently, sculptors worked chiefly with opaque or slightly translucent substances, and the light came from outside sources. Today, the materials at their disposal range in quality from completely opaque through all degrees of translucency to absolute transparency. In #3807-11 (Fig. 426) Norman Zammitt used clear and opaque, colorless and pigmented plastic to prevent, impede, and facilitate the passage of light. In a solid box of clear, colorless acrylic plastic that allows light to pass through without hindrance, triangular planes of shaded orange are suspended one behind the other. As the viewer walks around the sculpture, these triangles allow more or less light to penetrate, according to the number of the planes through which the light must travel. Hanging in the center of the box are curved pieces of plastic—some of dark, translucent hues, others finished with baked enamel in brilliant colors—that transmit, absorb, and reflect light as the materials permit.

426. Norman Zammitt # 3807-11. 1965. Acrylic, baked enamel, and phenolic plastic, 16 × 15 × 11″. Hansen Gallery, San Francisco. Light reveals and activates transparent orange triangles and the colors of translucent and opaque curves that are suspended in a clear plastic box.

Painters and graphic artists also regard light as a vital element, but because until lately almost all of their work was done on two-dimensional surfaces, they relied on the gradations and contrasts of pigments and inks to give the illusion of light. There are, of course, exceptions. Some painters, such as Vincent van Gogh (Fig. 436), have used bold, thick strokes of paint that are noticeably raised above the canvas and that reflect light and cast shadows. Printmakers are experimenting with processes in which raised, inkless areas produce three-dimensional prints (Figs. 340, 341). In most historic painting and prints, the effects of light were based on the artist's perceptive study of nature and were creatively adapted to his medium. In some modern work, however, this problem is faced more directly, and a strong sense of actual light is created. In his untitled painting in Figure 427 Arnold Schmidt produced an optical illusion of pulsing light by gradually altering the direction of bright streaks until they almost completely cover the dark background and merge into an illusionary source of radiant energy.

Nature puts on a continuous "light show," although much of it passes unnoticed. From dawn until night the light of the sun gradually changes in brightness, color, and direction. The modeling of objects and the shadows they cast are altered as the earth rotates. On clear days the natural illumination is sharp and bright. Haze and fog reduce and soften it, and scattered clouds cast patterns of moving shadows. The

427. Arnold Schmidt. Untitled 1965. Synthetic polymer paint on canvas 4′1⅛″ × 8′1⅛″. The Museum of Modern Art, New York (gift of Mr. and Mrs. Herbert Bernard). In this composition light, space, and form are vividly conveyed by paint alone.

sky on a cloudless night is an intricate pattern of sparkling dots against a dark background. Much more conspicuous and dramatic are rainbows, flashes of lighting, and the aurora borealis.

Prior to this century, the only consequential man-made visual arts in which light was the primary element were spectacles of fireworks and the processes of photography and motion pictures, discussed in Chapter 10. Today, many artists are exploring the vast possibilities of using controlled illumination as a basic ingredient in their work (Pl. 57, p. 471). In some cases, such as Chryssa's *Fragment for the Gates to Times Square II* (Fig. 428), the light source is emphatically visible and static, and only the spectator moves. In others, typified by LeParc's *Continuous Instability—Light* (Fig. 423), the electric bulb cannot be seen, but it illumines dangling aluminum blades that, together with four interchangeable pierced screens, create an endless succession of visual images. Kepes's *Mobile Light Mural* (Fig. 429), a very large, complex organization of light in action, is constructed of a gray aluminum screen with some sixty thousand random perforations and larger cutouts, in back of which are a vast number of incandescent and fluorescent bulbs and tubes and many thousands of filters of varied colors. These are controlled by timing and switching mechanisms that produce continuously changing, nonrepetitive patterns.

An even more direct and dynamic use of light and motion is found in the light shows in which the spectator is enveloped in pulsating, flashing lights and colors, sometimes fleetingly representational, but more often abstract or nonobjective. In these shows, the sense of sight is as completely engaged as is the sense of hearing with music, with the result that the object or environment is not just something to be looked at but to be experienced, an immediate, sensual involvement (Pl. 35).

Color*

Every stimulus of color that our eyes perceive produces emotional as well as physical responses. Knowingly or not, we react to the colors in our man-made environment and to those of the natural surroundings. There is some evidence, for example, that the vascular system, the pulse, blood pressure, and nervous and

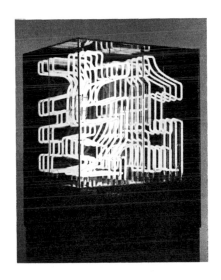

above : 428. Chryssa. *Fragment for the Gates to Times Square II*. 1966. Neon tubing and Plexiglas, 43 × 34 1/16 × 27 1/16″. Pace Gallery, New York. Appropriately, this light sculpture is of neon tubing whose hot and cool colors are reflected on the gray, boxlike enclosure.

top : 429. Gyorgy Kepes. *Mobile Light Mural*. 1959. Light mosaic, 51 × 18′. KLM, New York. Kepes' mosaic of moving lights evokes the impression of flying at night over the cities of the world.

---

* This discussion will be concerned only with color obtained with pigments. Colors produced by light behave differently. The system followed here was developed by Sir David Brewster and is the simplest of the several theories and the one typically used by painters. The color systems evolved by Albert Munsell and Wilhelm Ostwald, used in commerce and industry because they have a precisely standardized color notation, are based on different primary hues. In practice the results produced by the several theories differ slightly, if at all.

muscular tension are affected by color; certainly many persons feel much better when surrounded by light or bright hues. There is no consistency in the effects of different colors except that those liked by the individual are more inspiriting. In part, this is brought about by the emotional states, the associations, and the memories that color arouses, but there may be more immediate physiological reactions. Not many persons have strong likes or dislikes regarding forms and textures, but nearly everyone has decided color preferences.

The history of color is a fascinating study of human diversity, because attitudes toward color have varied enormously with each age, community, and group. In contemporary American culture, for example, there have been great changes in the past few decades. Not long ago many homes were almost without noticeable color: clear, positive colors were thought to be in poor taste. In the commercial and industrial arts, color was used timidly. Advertisements were mostly in black and white, kitchen and bathroom fixtures were always white, and automobiles were usually black or in sober, formal colors. This, of course, is not the case today.

In recent years much has been learned about the power of color, and this knowledge has increased courage, inventiveness, and skill in using color for practical purposes. For instance, the evaporation loss in gasoline storage tanks was reduced by almost one-third when the tanks were painted white instead of red. By painting a shipping lane in the frozen Yukon River black it was opened to navigation three weeks earlier than usual, because dark, warm colors absorb heat. Factory employees who had said that they felt cold when the temperature was 72° ceased their protests when the blue-green walls were painted coral. Men lifting black metal boxes complained of strained backs, but when the same boxes were painted pale green they reported that the "new, lightweight" boxes made a real difference. Other findings have been equally useful: flies tend to avoid blue; night insects do not like orange light; and barnacles spurn the hulls of ships painted white or light green. Clearly, color is a forceful element, and artists, too, have used it since early days as a potent means of expressing and communicating their emotions and ideas. As has been mentioned earlier, the elements of light and color are currently being integrated with movement into total experiences that seek to involve the spectators as deeply as possible (Pl. 35).

The Nature of Color

Color is the response of vision to the different wave lengths of visible light that form a narrow band on the known spectrum of radiant energy. White (or apparently colorless) light, such as that from the sun at noon, contains all the colors of the spectrum: violet, blue, green, yellow, orange, and red with their intermediate gradations. These are so balanced and blended that the effect is colorless, but the fact that they are there can be demonstrated by passing white light through a prism, which refracts it into a spectrum. When white light strikes an object, some of the colors are absorbed and others are reflected. A lemon, for instance, absorbs almost all color rays except the yellows, which, reflected to our eyes, give the lemon its color. Leaves reflect primarily green rays, and therefore we say that leaves are green. Thus the color of an object is determined by the rays that are reflected to our eyes. In transparent objects the light passes through instead of being reflected from the surface; in passing through, all but the dominant rays are filtered out.

This, however, only begins to describe color. To say that an object is red is not a very accurate color description, for it may be scarlet or maroon. To describe the color with any reasonable preciseness at least three terms are needed, which correspond to the *three dimensions* or attributes of color:

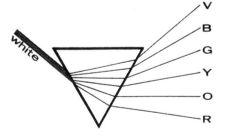

430. Light refracted through a prism.

Plate 35. Nicolas Schöffer. *Lux 2*. 1967. Kinetic metal sculpture in a "prism" of mirrors at fixed angles. The dynamics of light, space, and movement are captured in a photograph of *Lux 2* as it appeared in an exhibit entitled "Light and Movement" at the Musée d'Art Moderne in Paris. The kaleidoscopic play of light through the revolving sculpture onto the surrounding mirror-prism involved the photographer-spectator, Pierre Comte, in an almost psychedelic experience of swirling, ever-changing color and perpetual movement that surrounded him and receded into seemingly infinite space. The reproduction is made from a composite photograph in which the upper half is the original image and the lower half a mirror image of it. This device accentuates the sense of involvement, but only actual participation would lead to the totality of the encounter.

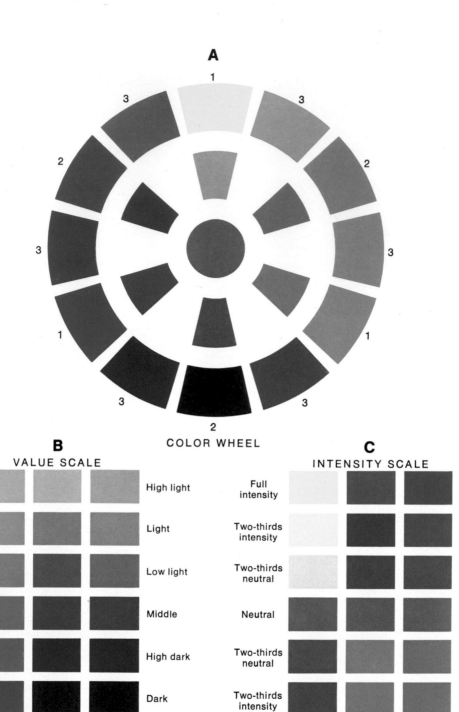

A

1

3 3

2 2

3 3

1 1

3 3

2

COLOR WHEEL

B

VALUE SCALE

High light

Light

Low light

Middle

High dark

Dark

Low Dark

C

INTENSITY SCALE

Full intensity

Two-thirds intensity

Two-thirds neutral

Neutral

Two-thirds neutral

Two-thirds intensity

Full intensity

Plate 38a. The color wheel shows a sequence of hues in the following order, beginning with yellow at the top and proceeding clockwise: yellow, yellow-green, green, blue-green, blue, blue-violet, violet, red-violet, red, red-orange, orange, yellow-orange. The numeral *1* indicates primary hues; *2*, secondary hues; and *3*, tertiary hues.
Plate 38b. The value scale shows seven values each for three hues: green, orange, and violet.
Plate 38c. The intensity scale shows two different degrees between full intensity and neutral for six hues. Adapted from *The Art of Enjoying Art* by A. Philip MacMahon, as adapted from *Commercial Art* by C. E. Wallace; by permission of McGraw-Hill Book Co., Inc.

■ *Hue* is the name of a color, such as red, blue, or green. Hue indicates the color's position in the spectrum and on the color wheel in Plate 38. It also indicates the warmth or coolness of a color: for instance, red is warm, blue is cold, and green is intermediate.

■ *Value* refers only to the lightness or darkness of a color, the amount of light reflected or transmitted by the object. Any hue can vary in value: red can become light pink or dark maroon.

■ *Intensity* indicates a color's degree of purity, strength, or saturation. This is determined by the quantity of the dominant hue. Scarlet, which is red of high intensity, is almost pure red. Rose beige is neutralized red.

Hue: The Position of a Color in the Spectrum

The color wheel in Plate 38 has the same progression of hues as the spectrum but bent into a circle and with the two end colors blended into red-violet, a color not in the spectrum. The twelve hues on the wheel can be divided into three categories:

■ *Primary hues*, labeled (1), are red, blue, and yellow. They cannot be obtained by mixing other hues, but, if combined in the proper amounts, will produce nearly every other known hue.

■ *Secondary hues*, labeled (2), are green, orange, and violet. Each stands midway between the two primaries that produce it when mixed in the right amounts. Green comes from blue and yellow, orange from red and yellow, and violet from red and blue.

■ *Tertiary hues*, labeled (3), stand between a primary and a secondary hue and result from a mixture of the two. Their names—yellow-green, blue-violet, and red-orange—indicate their components.

Hues are changed or new ones produced by combining neighboring hues, as is indicated above. Blue, for example, becomes blue-violet when it is combined with violet. If even more violet is added, the hue is changed again. The twelve hues on the color wheel are only a convenient beginning, for there can be an almost infinite number of hues.

When placed next to each other, hues produce effects ranging from harmony to contrast. Some combinations, such as blue, blue-green, and green, produce a harmonious and restful sequence. But if blue is placed next to orange, there is excitement and contrast.

Two adjectives are used to describe these relationships between colors:

■ *Analogous hues* are adjacent to each other on the color wheel, as are blue, blue-green, and green.

■ *Complementary hues* lie directly opposite each other. Blue and orange, red and green, or yellow-orange and blue-violet are examples.

Any two complementary colors can either cancel or intensify each other. If they are mixed in proper amounts, they will produce a grayish neutral tone. But if they are placed next to each other, each hue will seem brighter, as though its power had been released. Red appears redder next to green than when alone, and the green appears greener than when seen in isolation. Blue and orange, yellow-green and red-violet—in fact, any pair of complements—affect each other similarly. This phenomenon, known as *simultaneous contrast*, is of great importance in combining colors and is much used in Op Art.

This discussion of the mutual intensification of hues leads to a basic generalization that applies to almost every phase of art: *Distinctly visible contrasts accentuate*

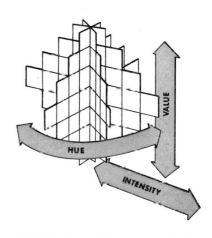

431. The three dimensions of color are often shown by a "color solid." Pure hues are located on the outer edges. Value is represented on the vertical axis, going from the lightest value at the top to the darkest at the bottom. Maximum intensities occur on the periphery and become increasingly neutralized as they approach the central axis.

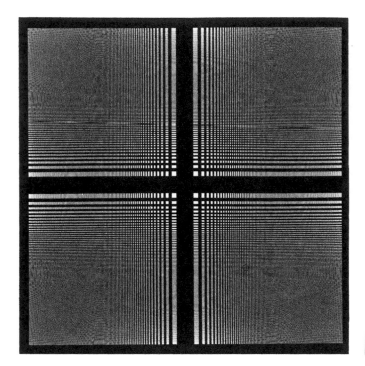

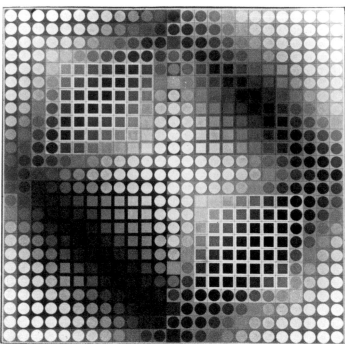

left : 432. A grid-Fresnel zone plate, which perfects alignment of electronic beams, demonstrates how perceivable contrasts accentuate differences. As the color areas diminish in size, they tend to merge and produce an optical mixture of the two colors. At the outer corners, the sensation is not of black and white but of gray.

right : 433. Victor Vasarely. *Sende.* 1967. Tempera on board, 20 × 20″. Sidney Janis Gallery, New York. Circles and squares form illusive patterns of brightness and darkness.

differences. Black looks blacker next to white (Fig. 432), and angular forms seem more pointed when seen with rounded shapes; the list is almost endless. If, however, the units are so closely related in color or so small or indistinct that they blend visually, the opposite effect—cancelling out or neutralizing—occurs. Vasarely, in his painting *Sende* (Fig. 433), made use of both analogous and complementary hues to produce a lively interaction between just two types of form. By means of the degree of harmony or contrast between the colors of the circles and squares and between them and the background grid, he has made some of these forms clearly stand out or recede, and in some areas he has deliberately created evanescent configurations that are spatially ambivalent, because the viewer cannot always keep them in sharp focus.

The relative warmth and coolness of hues affect us and our environment. Red, orange, and yellow are warm hues, associated with sun, fire, and heat. Conspicuous, cheerful, and stimulating, these hues stand out so prominently that they seem to come forward. In contrast, blue-green, blue, and blue-violet are comparatively cool, inconspicuous, and restful. They suggest distance, in part because faraway trees or mountains are often bluish. Additionally, warm hues tend to make objects seem larger and to soften their outlines, while cool hues do the opposite.

Since 1949, Joseph Albers has been intensively studying, in his words, "the interaction of color." Through an endless series of paintings of squares mathematically nested within other squares, he has explored the relativity of colors and has demonstrated conclusively that color is never absolute but that its effects and its values vary in intensity in accordance with the surroundings. In his *Study for an Early Diary* (Pl. 36), the orange-yellow and deep pink, which we ordinarily think of as advancing colors, here recede behind the clear, cool, blue square. The viewer can, however, cause the blue to recede by altering his focus so that the innermost square becomes a hole cut in the canvas, revealing the blue sky in the background.

Artists make good use of these characteristics. If a painter wishes a landscape to impart gaiety, he may emphasize warm hues. For the opposite effect, cool hues might predominate. But in neither case will the painting be uniformly warm or cold because contrast is vital. Important objects in the foreground would be in warm, advancing hues; background forms would be in cooler, receding hues. This is one means of implying distance. In *L'Appel* (Pl. 37), Paul Gauguin combined these two effects to create a work at once paradisiacal in the warm, bright colors in the foreground and brooding and mysterious in the deep, cool hues in the landscape across the stream. If, however, a painter wants to keep a feeling of the actual two-dimensionality of his canvas, he may deliberately reverse this illusionistic relationship in some parts, as Gauguin did. The green and lavender clothes on the figures recede slightly, and the orange-red tree trunk, which contrasts with the background blues and greens, comes forward to enter into the composition of the three figures and three trees in the foreground. Although the painting can be analyzed in terms of spacial effects, Gauguin's chief interest was undoubtedly in the creative autonomy of color to produce the emotions and sensations he felt so strongly. The colors are for the most part intense and luminous, perhaps more so than even an idyllic south sea island could produce. In these ways, Gauguin conveyed not only the feeling of space, but also his reaction to the exotic nature of this faraway land.

Value: The Lightness or Darkness of a Color

The lightness or darkness of a color depends on the amount of light reflected or transmitted. The value scale in Plate 38 shows seven steps of the colors green, orange, and violet, their degrees of lightness or darkness. There can, of course, be an almost limitless number of degrees of lightness and darkness, but (excluding black and white) seven is a convenient number and corresponds to the value steps of the hues in the color wheel. Yellow is very light, violet is dark, and the other hues range between these extremes. The values in which the hues are shown in the color wheel are known as *normal values*; that is, they are the values at which each hue reaches its greatest purity. Thus, starting at the top of the wheel and then going down either side we get:

Hue	Value Step	Hue
Yellow	High light	Yellow
Yellow-orange	Light	Yellow-green
Orange	Low light	Green
Red-orange	Middle	Blue-green
Red	High dark	Blue
Red-violet	Dark	Blue-violet
Violet	Low dark	Violet

A moment's reflection will show that we ordinarily think of hues in somewhat this way. Yellow, for instance, usually comes to mind as a light, bright yellow—the color of a lemon or a dandelion. Violet usually is thought of as dark—the color of violets, grapes, or plums. To be sure, there are dark yellows, such as olive drab, and light violets, such as orchid, but these are not the most characteristic values. *Tints* are values above the normal; *shades* are values below the normal. Thus pink is a tint of red, and maroon is a shade of the same hue; sky blue is a tint, and navy-blue is a shade.

The value of a color is raised by making it reflect more light. To lower the value, the amount of light it reflects is reduced. With pigments this is most readily done by adding white or black, which also usually changes the hue and intensity as well as the value. The lightness or darkness of values seems to change with different backgrounds. In Figure 434 the gray circles are identical in value, but they look darker against white, lighter against black.

above : 434. A value scale shows how greatly the appearance of anything is affected by its background. The gray circles are identical.

Intensity: The Degree of Purity or Saturation

Any color can vary as to the quantity of the dominant hue it contains. Red, for example, can be brilliantly saturated or subdued and neutralized. Mixing it with anything else—such as black, white, gray, or its complementary, green—reduces the amount of red and thereby reduces its intensity. Intensity can also be lessened by thinning out the color with water, oil, turpentine, and so forth. Usually this is accompanied by a change of value, unless whatever is added has the same ratio of light reflectance as the original hue. Although the intensity of any hue value can be varied, the fullest intensity occurs when each hue is at its normal value, as illustrated in the outer circle of the color wheel. Both the value scale and the intensity scale in Plate 38 illustrate this fact.

The apparent intensity of a color can be changed by the surroundings in which it is seen. Colors usually appear more saturated when seen against white, gray, or black backgrounds, or when they are placed near an area of their complementary hue. Somewhat the same phenomenon occurs if they are used with unsaturated colors of their own hue. Thus, green looks purer when seen against an achromatic background, a red background, or one that is gray-green.

Effects of Hue, Value, and Intensity

Color is an inexhaustibly rich and powerful means of expression and communication. It has direct bearing on our emotions and our attention. Color also affects the apparent size of forms, their spatial position, and the sharpness of their outlines. Hue, value, and intensity each makes its special contribution, but the three properties of color are usually regarded as integrated components dependent on each other for their total impact. Their effects are the following:

Arousing Emotions   Paul Gauguin, whose *L'Appel* is reproduced in Plate 37, was a master of the emotional possibilities in color and was able to transform his feelings and insights into powerful color-form relationships. Disillusioned by materialism, he sought escape in the exoticism of the south seas. *L'Appel* dramatizes the ambiguity Gauguin found in primitive life—the intense brilliance of the vegetation set against an enigmatic background, the simple beauty of the people placed in the rich landscape. In the foreground, the heat of reds, red-violets, pinks, yellows, and oranges is heightened by neutralized greens and blues. The warm, brown flesh of the women reflects this brilliance and forms a bridge over the cool blue and lavender of the stream to the mysterious lushness of the green grassland and the foreboding purples

left : 435. Fernand Léger. *The City.* 1919. Oil on canvas, 7'7" × 9'9 1/2". Philadelphia Museum of Art (A.E. Gallatin Collection). Léger employed maximum value differences, and the result is strong and stimulating.

right : 436. Vincent van Gogh. *Rain.* 1889. Oil on canvas, 29 7/8 × 36 3/8". Collection Francis P. McIlhenny, Philadelphia. The individual units in the landscape lose their separate identities in a web of neutralized colors with little value differentiation.

in the distance. This is not a painting that can be viewed dispassionately. The richness, the variety of values in the analogous hues, and the juxtaposition of the complementary warm and cool colors command response.

Catching Attention   Attention can be guided by choice and organization of hue, value, and intensity. Gauguin's *L'Appel* demands attention, but Albers' *Study* (Pl. 36) quietly invites observation. Warm hues attract more notice than cool ones, but a vigorous contrast of hot and cold is more strongly noticed than either one used alone. Red, black, green, and orange are conspicuous against white, but black on yellow is the most legible combination at a distance, which explains its use on road signs. The more intense the color, the greater its power of catching our attention. Painters and advertisers typically reserve their brightest colors for important parts of their pictures.

Influencing Apparent Size and Distance   The ways in which color seems to alter the size of objects are often dramatic. Painting the walls of a room in light, neutral, cool colors makes the room seem more spacious than would bright red or dark brown. A marked difference between an object and its background usually calls the object to one's attention and thereby makes it seem larger. Thus, a dark blue sofa against a white wall may look larger than it would if upholstered in light tan. In general, warm hues, high values, and strong intensities increase apparent size.

Apparent distance is drastically affected by color. In a view that includes distant as well as nearby trees, the far trees look bluer, lighter, more neutral, and show less light-and-dark contrast. Interior designers and landscape architects, as well as painters, can increase or decrease apparent distance with color. A ceiling that is too high, for instance, can be made to look lower. Background plants in a garden can be chosen to seem farther away.

Affecting Outlines   A glance at Albers' *Study* (Pl. 36) shows that the intersecting edges of the yellow-orange and pink squares, which are related warm colors of comparable middle values and intensities, tend to blur and merge, while the outline of the cool, contrasting, high-value, moderately intense blue stands out sharp and clear. Léger's and Van Gogh's paintings, even when reproduced only in black and white, show that conspicuous value differences emphasize outlines and that closely related values minimize them. In *The City* (Fig. 435) the individual parts are clearly delineated by decided lights and darks. In full color, hue and intensity can contribute almost as much as does value: bright reds and yellows stand out from dulled blues and greens in *The City*. Quite different is *Rain* (Fig. 436), in which close values of grayed, harmonious hues subordinate outlines to create a quieter, over-all effect. In Rubens' *Descent from the Cross* (Pl. 40, p. 334) a complete range of values, from subtle nuances to bold distinctions, produces an orchestral effect. Observe how differently the nine heads relate to their background—no two are the same. Artists normally strengthen the outlines of important parts of their composition by contrasts and minimize the subordinate parts with subtly connected colors.

Color Preferences   Color preferences have been extensively studied. Under laboratory conditions, red and blue are the most favored hues, orange and yellow-green the least favored. Fairly intense colors are preferred to neutrals, and women prefer colors lighter than those liked best by men. However, there is little agreement on combinations of colors. Outside the laboratory, these findings are not necessarily valid. For example, most people find pleasure in orange sunsets and in the yellow-greens of spring foliage.

Summary of Effects of Color

	Hue	*Value*	*Intensity*
SIZE	Warm hues increase apparent size of objects.	High values increase apparent size, but strong contrast with backgrounds also has a similar effect.	Full intensities increase apparent size.
DISTANCE	Warm hues bring objects forward; cool hues make them recede.	Low values advance; high values recede. Marked value contrasts within an object bring it forward.	Full intensities decrease apparent distance.
OUTLINE OR CONTOUR	Warm hues soften outlines slightly more than do cool hues, and contrasting hues make outlines clearer than do related hues.	Value contrasts emphasize outlines.	Intensity contrasts emphasize outlines.
ATTENTION	Warm hues attract more attention than do cool hues. Contrast of warm and cool is also attention-getting.	Extremely high or low values attract attention, but contrasts or surprises are even more effective.	Full intensities attract our attention, especially when contrasted with neutrals or complementaries.
FEELINGS	Warm hues are stimulating, cool hues quieting. Warm and cool together give a balanced effect.	High values are cheering, low values restful or depressing. Contrasts are stimulating.	Full intensities are heartening, strong, exciting. Low intensities are peaceful and relaxing.

AGAM (Jaacov Gipstein). *Double Metamorphosis II.* 1964. Oil on aluminum, in 11 sections, 8′10″ × 12′ 2¹/₂″. The Museum of Modern Art, New York (gift of Mr. and Mrs. George M. Jaffin).

left : 437. In a front view, the clean outlines of the figures are lost in the over-all activity of a reticulated surface.

right : 438. A side view reveals strongly defined color forms on shallow slats.

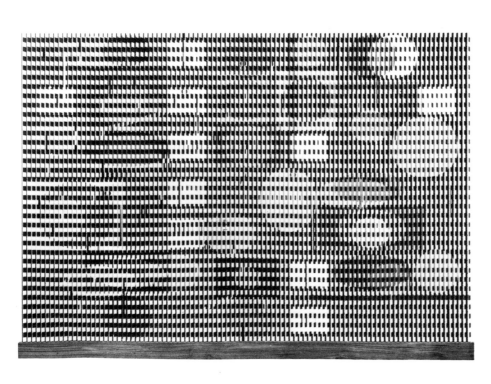

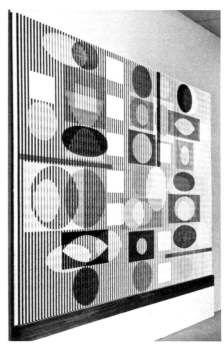

Using Color

There are no laws governing the use of color, as is abundantly proved by widespread differences of opinion and by the sterile results of constricting systems. One might ask whether color, like form or texture, is most vital when it grows out of and contributes to function or when it is meaningfully related to material, form, and space, or whether it is a completely independent element. Obviously, it can follow any of these directions, and it also can have varying kinds of interdependence. Much depends on the degree of integration wanted and on the specific situation.

Painters have complete freedom in their choice and manner of using color. AGAM (Figs. 437, 438), for example, alters the color relationships in his paintings by attaching thin triangular strips vertically on the face of the work and painting two or more motifs on the three-dimensional surface thus created. This adds still another dimension to his paintings, that of time, for as the spectator walks past the composition, it seems to move, and changing color experiences are revealed. Viewed from an angle, precise geometrical figures stand out in decisive color contrasts; when viewed straight on, they disintegrate and merge, and the forms are largely lost in a play of related colors.

Principles of color harmony, however, have been studied intensively by philosophers, scientists, and artists. Harmony is often thought of as a consistent, orderly, or pleasing arrangement of parts. Most people agree that consistency and order are basically desirable, but, especially in art, they can be deadening if not sparked by the unexpected or even the discordant. There are, nevertheless, several somewhat formalized types of color schemes that can be put into major categories. Stressing easily recognizable, ordered relationships, these types are widely used by designers, especially those concerned with interiors, chiefly as points of departure; painters, printmakers, and sculptors seldom pay any attention to these "color schemes."

Related Color Schemes   Schemes of related colors tend toward quiet, restful effects—*if strong value contrasts and high intensities are avoided.*

Monochromatic color schemes, the simplest of all, use only one hue. Blue, for example, could range in *value* from almost black to near white and in *intensity* from saturated cobalt to an ashen gray (Fig. 439). Such schemes are often vitalized with white, gray, and black, and with varied textures. The Retti Candleshop (Pl. 39) juxtaposes orange fabrics with the luminosity of gray aluminum and silvery mirrors.

Analogous schemes are based on any degree of value and intensity of from three to five hues that are adjacent to or near each other on the color wheel and all of which contain a common hue. Examples are blue-green, blue, and blue-violet, as shown in Figure 440. Analogous schemes obviously have more variety than do monochromatic schemes.

Contrasting Color Schemes   Based on opposing hues, contrasting color schemes are likely to seem stimulating and balanced because they include warm and cool hues.

Complementary schemes are built from any pair of hues directly opposite each other on the color wheel, such as orange and blue, yellow and violet (Fig 441).

Double-complementary schemes use two adjacent hues with their respective complements, as red-orange and orange with blue and blue-green for example (Fig. 442).

Split-complementary schemes use any hue plus the two hues located on each side of its complement. If the color is yellow, the other hues will be red-violet and blue-violet—because violet, yellow's complement, was split into red-violet and blue-violet (Fig. 443).

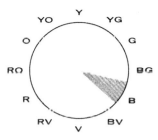

439. Monochromatic scheme.

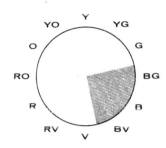

440. Analogous scheme.

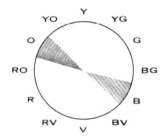

441. Complementary scheme.

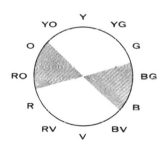

442. Double-complementary scheme.

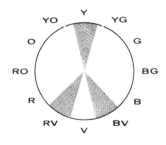

443. Split-complementary scheme.

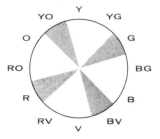

444. Triad scheme.

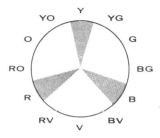

445. Tetrad scheme.

The Retti Candleshop (1965) in Vienna expresses the quality of its products by the setting in which they are displayed. Hans Hollein, architect. (See also Pl. 39.)

left : 446. The extreme restraint of the exterior is underscored by precise detailing and by the glimpsed radiance of the interior.

right : 447. The interior is characterized by clear functionalism and maximum economy of space.

Triad schemes are made from any three hues that are located equidistant from each other—red, yellow, and blue; or yellow-orange, blue-green, and red-violet (Fig. 444).

Tetrad schemes include any four hues equidistant on the color wheel, as exemplified by red, yellow-orange, green, and blue-violet (Fig. 445).

These color schemes are all based on an orderly relationship of hues that is sufficiently obvious to be recognizable. By no means do they cover all of the possibilities. They do, however, allow for considerable individuality. Remember, every *hue* can vary tremendously in *value* and *intensity*. A triad scheme can bring together scarlet, chrome yellow, and cobalt blue, or it can include these same hues as rose gray, chartreuse, and slate blue. Identical hues are found in the combinations of ultramarine violet and lemon yellow, charcoal gray and beige. Furthermore, the proportional amount and disposition of the hues are unlimited. However, many artists—painters in particular—want to explore beyond the familiar, and while most of the works of art illustrated in this book may be analyzed and assigned to one of these classifications, they will not have originally been based on such seemingly constricting concepts.

The Visual Elements Viewed Together

Although we have looked at the visual elements of art separately in order to concentrate on each one, they are almost never experienced in isolation.

A Candleshop in Vienna

The Retti Candleshop (Pl. 39 and Figs. 446–448), on a handsome fashionable street in Vienna, is an elegant advertisement and a showroom of great technical perfection. In sharp contrast to the eclectic style of the older building in which it is set, the exterior plane is a continuous surface of brushed aluminum, devoid of any ornament, even a name. The perfect symmetry of the façade is emphasized by the light reflected in shimmering luminosity on the linings of the deeply recessed openings. The name of the firm, in plastic lettering, appears only on the sides of the deep, narrow doorway. Two smaller openings curve inward on either side of the entrance, with show

Plate 39. The showroom of the Retti Candleshop in Vienna is reserved but elegant, luminous, glowing, and perfectly detailed. Subdued general lighting and brighter spotlighting visually enlarge the small space by focusing attention on the perimeter of the room, while the quiet display of candles becomes part of the total design. Hans Hollein, architect. (See also Figs. 446–448.)

Plate 40. Peter Paul Rubens. *Descent from the Cross.* c. 1611–1614. Oil on panel, 13′ 10″ × 10′ 1″. Cathedral, Antwerp. By his masterly integration of the visual elements, Rubens created a profoundly impressive painting. Form, line, texture, and space provide the basic structural framework, but it is the handling of light and color that deepens the intensity of the composition. The lighted shroud and the body of Christ illuminate the surrounding figures, uniting the group in an emotive relationship. The colors used, the full scale of values from white to black, and the gradations of intensity from neutrality to full saturation vividly express the turbulent passions and deep sorrow of the Deposition.

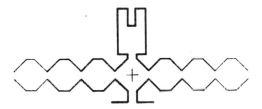

windows placed at a 45-degree angle to catch the attention of the passerby. Instead of blatantly shouting its name and its wares, the shop relies on the highly individual architectural treatment to symbolize the firm and to invite inspection.

The interior, originally an uninspiring space only 13 feet wide, with a floor area of 160 square feet, was made into an expanding and contracting visual experience. The rectangular rigidity of the space was not denied but brought to life by imaginative variation of the forms and by opposing them with circular elements. The main showroom is diamond-shaped, with the angles cut off and placed diagonally on the long axis. A door at the rear opens into storage and sales rooms. Air-conditioning grilles are used as further rectangular design elements; the glass entrance door is divided into two units by a safety bar, which is lightened by two smaller rectangular openings that echo the grilles. In a similar way, half-cylinders on two mirrors are a safety factor, alerting visitors to the fact that these are not open doorways, but they are worked in as design features by repeating the circular forms as quarter-cylinders in the exhibition cases and as globes in the overhead lighting fixture. Triangular niches along each side of the showroom display the candles.

Although unobtrusive, line is important in the total effect. The edges of all the forms are sharply delineated and repeat the elongated shapes of the candles. Most of the lines are straight; a few are geometric curves; and the angles of some of the forms are softly rounded. Textures also are undemanding, but they reinforce one another and impart a rare quality of serenity: the aluminum is brushed to a soft luminosity, the exhibition cases are backed by smooth, light-reflecting silk, and the carpeting is an unpatterned, supple plush. Without becoming obvious, the textures soften the rigidity of the forms and materials. The two mirrors facing each other across the horizontal axis of the showroom reflect the opposite diagonal walls and create endlessly receding vistas that greatly enlarge the sense of space.

General lighting comes from the suspended fixture of four frosted globes, and spotlights illumine the larger showcases but throw into shade the smaller intervening niches. A monochromatic color scheme of orange silk walls and a deeper orange carpet is partially reflected on the aluminum walls and imparts a glowing ambience to the space. Glimpsing this jewel-box interior through the narrow openings on the closed, mysterious front, the passerby is enticed inside to inspect the candles and is encouraged to buy them by the soothing yet stimulating design and color.

Peter Paul Rubens' *Descent from the Cross*

In Rubens' religious painting (Pl. 40) the visual elements are fused into a momentous expression of human values. The painting was one of many works through which the Counter-Reformation Catholic Church reasserted its doctrines in compelling, emotional terms. Three and a half centuries have not diminished its power.

The body of the dead Christ sinking into a white shroud commands first attention and implores compassionate participation in the tragedy. Although every inch of the painting holds interest, we repeatedly return to the central figure. Basically, the design is simple—a strong diagonal supported by an almost vertical ladder—

448. A diagram illustrates the way in which the illusion of indefinite space is created by the twin mirrors that face each other across the horizontal axis of the Retti Candleshop.

but its ingenious development is another matter. Eight figures are grouped around Christ's body in a dynamic organization of downward curves expressive of tragedy. Fluent and painterly, the forms are plastically modeled—sharply defined at some points, merging into the enveloping space at others. Flesh is softly rounded, and the robes fall in folds. Although the figures are stretched and twisted, an uncommon feeling for balance and rhythm brings repose. Line is subsumed in the plenitude of form.

Set in fathomless space, the figures advance. Those at the top, pushed forward by the sky, seem almost as near as those at the bottom. Within the group, however, there is complex interplay of advancing and receding forms. The top-left figure stretches back into space while coming forward to touch Christ's shoulder, in contrast to the tensely hunched figure at his right. The vehement stances of the men at the right cleave space sharply, the three Marys supplely modulate it. Only when one looks from the base of the ladder to the horizon at the left does one sense the great space that extends beyond the figures.

Although brush marks are visible, the surface of the painting is tactually quite smooth. Visually, the oil paint ranges from thick impasto to transparent glazes. The textures of fabrics, wood and metal, ground and sky, flesh and hair strengthen the representation of form and add visual enrichment.

In order to communicate deep-felt grief, the artist used colors that are mostly neutral and dark. The lightest values are concentrated in Christ's body and shroud but spread outward into the surrounding faces and arms. Nearly all else is below middle value. The one large, intensely colored area is John's red robe, which makes Christ's body seem more pallid and seems to imbue John with strength to support the Master. At John's left, Mary Magdalene's dark green robe complements the nearby red. Paintings such as this show how subject matter can be made emotionally vivid through the evocative use of the elements that constitute all visual art.

A shop built to promote the sale of candles is admittedly far removed from a deeply inspired religious painting, because the reasons for their creation are so different. The concept behind the shop is the stimulation of the buying urge; the motive behind the *Descent from the Cross* is to release psychic energy. But within the limits of their objectives, both can be analyzed and assessed, for the visual elements of form, texture, line, space, light, and color are part of their organization and contribute to their success or failure in their own terms. This is true in every area of the arts, and while the degree of lasting consequence may be vastly different, all of the visual aspects of life can benefit from perceptive and skillful design.

449. A pink conch shell from the Bahamas exemplifies the remarkable beauty that can result from order in nature.

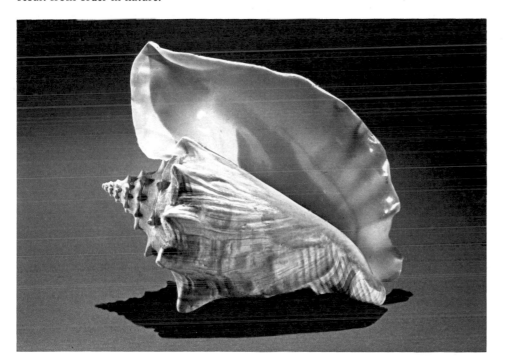

13 Design: Formal Organization in Art

Man has an innate need to find or to make meaningful order in his world. Without the presence of order in the important aspects of his life, man cannot live. He therefore tends to create around him the kind of order he finds most congenial. Although man is also capable of creating disorder—often of the most disastrous sort—he is, in general, an order-producing creature. The large number of words in constant use that relate to the ordering of experience testifies to the large part the urge to organize plays in our everyday lives: we *form* a committee; we *compose* a letter; we *organize* a dance; we *plan* a course of action; we *design* a garden. Order, of course, can be pushed to extremes. A life that is too ordered is dull and featureless, but a chaotic, undirected life is ruinous. Order, then, must play a moderating part in productive and pleasurable living.

All order may well have an esthetic base. Certainly we are affected by relationships we consider beautiful but that are not directly related to art. The manipulation of figures and symbols in mathematical formulas often discloses the majesty of numerical relationships. The sight of a complicated machine in operation stirs a viewer to reactions that go beyond the appreciation of efficiency. And objects such as suspension bridges or telescope reflectors, designed and built only to serve utilitarian functions, can evoke an esthetic response. In the arts, the esthetic aspects of order are intensified and given special meaning. The arts, of course, have no corner on esthetic qualities, but it is their esthetic aspects that give them their distinctive character.

In this chapter we will discuss the bases and aims of order in art and in the following chapter the principles of design. In both discussions the emphasis will be on formal relationships—that is, on the relationships among the plastic elements: line, form, space, texture, color, and light—for they are the vehicles the artist uses to give reality to his ideas. In these analyses the terms *organization* and *design* will be used almost interchangeably but with preference given to *design,* because it is more suggestive of an esthetic dimension and because *organization* is a much broader term.

The Importance of Design

The significance of design is well illustrated in Figures 450 and 451. Figure 450 is a diagram of the Kandinsky painting *White on Black,* in which a number of white, generally rectangular forms appear on a black background. In Figure 451 these same forms have been randomly scattered over an identical background. The difference is striking. It is readily observable that although the second diagram is not without effect, its casual and unplanned distribution of forms is monotonous, whereas the first diagram has an exciting strength and coherence. There is a sense of rightness in the diagram of the original—in the grouping of the forms, in their relation to the edges of the composition and to each other, and in the interest generated by variety. In short, the diagram of the Kandinsky is organized: it is designed.

Design is important in a number of ways. First, it is a kind of universal syntax through which artists communicate their ideas. A comparison of the designs of the *Great Buddha* at Kamakura, Japan, and Mark di Suvero's *New York Dawn* (Figs. 452, 453) shows how design can be the vehicle of expression. In the *Great Buddha* a relaxed equilibrium is achieved through quiet symmetry. The rhythms are gentle, and the serene face and joined hands are emphasized. The effect produced is conducive to contemplation, peace, and self-containment, in keeping with the religious beliefs the sculpture portrays. *New York Dawn,* in contrast, is composed of a group of rough, aggressive, and tense forms. Although the composition as a whole is balanced, it has no repose. For di Suvero, dawn in New York is not a relaxed or sentimental period, as the strong cantilevered forms extending into space, the harsh upturned points, and the straight, threatening metal shaft all state. Both sculptures come from different periods and countries, but the emotional content of each is equally apparent, because the language of design knows no national or temporal boundaries. All artists, intuitively or consciously, employ the kinds of formal relationships that will convey their concepts in a vital and persuasive manner.

To communicate his ideas an artist must engage the viewer's attention and then hold it until his message is comprehended. Designs that are forceful but easily understood attract attention. This is a basic guideline in commercial art, because an unnoticed advertisement is a failure. Furthermore, commercial art must be designed

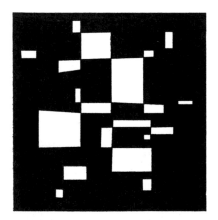

Organization makes the difference between interest and monotony.

above : 450. In the diagram of Kandinsky's painting *White on Black* the forms are arranged in a coherent order.

below : 451. The same forms randomly distributed produce a dull and disjointed effect.

above left : 452. *Great Buddha.* 1252. Bronze. Kamakura, Japan. The symmetry, rounded forms, and slowly descending rhythms of the Buddha convey a calm repose.

above right : 453. Mark di Suvero. *New York Dawn (for Lorca).* 1965. Wood, steel, and iron, 6′6″ × 6′2″ × 4′2″. Whitney Museum of American Art, New York (gift of the Howard and Jean Lipman Foundation, Inc.). The asymmetry and the sharp, projecting forms convey tension and uneasiness.

below : 454. Herbert Leupin's poster (1949) for a Swiss newspaper is a compelling composition. Silhouetted against a dark background, the newspaper and the "world" stand out sharply, but one's attention always returns to the name of the paper.

to get the basic idea across quickly, and for that reason it is often superficial. But in painting, sculpture, and architecture—arts that embody profound and complex ideas—more time is required for understanding. Works of fine art are designed to hold our interest longer and to make familiarity with them a rewarding experience. Compare the design of the Swiss advertisement in Figure 454 with that of Duccio's *Maestà* (Fig. 494). Both have a strong, arresting composition, but Duccio's painting is infinitely richer in its development.

The second way in which design is important is in making our environment more comprehensible. Design provides a structure to which a multiplicity of parts can be meaningfully related. A well-organized lecture can present a wide array of ideas and facts with clarity. In a poorly organized lecture these same facts may seem meaningless and disparate. Every work of art of any consequence has a basic organization upon which a large measure of its excellence depends. Even in more commonplace objects design has a central role. Industrial designers make the switches on kitchen ranges and the dials and buttons on automobile dashboards easy to see and to use. Architects and city planners design buildings and urban areas for convenience of movement. In the complex twentieth century, a welter of demands are made of everyone in pursuing his daily routines. Were it not for design, which orders

455. *Form follows function* is epitomized in the body of a sea gull.

the demands made on us and simplifies our responses, life would be untenable. A third significance of design, therefore, resides in the formal relationships of any work of art, which can and should be stimulating and satisfying in themselves. A vase, for example, can arouse us esthetically through its form and color alone, without any concern for its use or materials. A statue or a building can provide a vitalizing experience through its rhythm. Magnificent organization of color, whether in a sunset, an Oriental rug, or an abstract painting, can lift the viewer out of the routine pattern of commonplace activities. The natural and man-made visual world abounds in organizations and relationships that are rewarding to the emotions and the senses.

Nature and Art

To watch a sea gull soar effortlessly through the air, dive suddenly for a fish, or float buoyantly on the water makes it clear that the "design" of the gull's body is wondrously adapted to its way of living (Fig. 455). This is one of the chief reasons that sea gulls continue to exist, for in nature anything that is not well adapted to or capable of changing in response to new environmental conditions is in danger of extinction. If we observe a gull more closely it becomes apparent that although its parts exhibit a remarkable unity, they are quite unlike one another. There is, in fact, great diversification among them. Wings, legs, beak, and tail are considerably differentiated in shape, because each has a particular function, yet they are integrated into a coherent whole.

The example of the sea gull relates to art, because nature, of which man is a part, provides the artist with the bases for his art. The artist has always turned to nature for inspiration and guidance, and it has offered him subject matter of enormous variety. But it is its diverse systems of organization that have been nature's great gift to the artist. Art can be viewed as an extension of man, because man utilizes the relational principles and seeks in his art the essential unity that he observes in natural forms, including himself. This does not mean that any one kind of unity is superior to all others, for nature is richly varied (Figs. 456–458), and man is endlessly ingenious. As man discovers more about himself and his world, he extends the range of his views of life and of the possible relationships within those views. What is more, through the aid of such devices as electron microscopes and giant reflectors in telescopes, new micro- and macro-worlds are being revealed and other marvels of organization are becoming known. Artists, being eminently vital and contemporary beings, respond to the rich diversity in nature and are guided by the principles on which natural phenomena are organized.

Form and Function

Man develops forms to fulfill functions of many kinds. At one extreme are tools, in which utility is the basic determinant of form: hammers for driving nails and skillets for cooking food. In such objects, few people will put up with any element of design that lessens efficiency, yet man has seldom been completely satisfied with tools that are merely practical. Primitive peoples and modern efficiency experts find that beauty increases productivity and work satisfaction for the simple reason that the use of an attractive object is in itself pleasurable. Thus the form of a useful object is often refined or ornamented in ways that serve no directly useful purpose. Primitive

456–458. Even lower forms of life, such as these corals, have wonderously varied and organized forms.

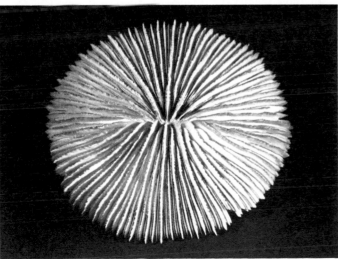

peoples often ornament tools to invest them with a kind of magic. For technological man, increased efficiency through the pleasure that comes from using beautiful things is no less magical. At the other extreme are the "fine arts," which include paintings and sculpture, much architecture, and many smaller articles that transcend utility, where esthetic and spiritual expression and satisfaction are paramount concerns. In other words, there are two orders of function: one in the sphere of utility, the other in the sphere of emotional and psychological response. The artist must be attentive to both of these types of function, giving each its appropriate emphasis and fusing them into an integrated whole.

Because art ranges from those products that are almost entirely (but seldom exclusively) practical to those created out of spiritual necessity but that may or may not have useful aspects, the artist must deal with a broad spectrum of functions. Occasionally, he works at one extreme or the other, but for the most part he must weld both the utilitarian and the emotional into one work.

The short history of American automobile design in Figure 459 illustrates the complexities of developing appropriate forms for anything that has several purposes. Early designs resembled carriages minus the horse. They were economical and straightforward but visually uncoordinated, because at this time designers saw the automobile only as a means of locomotion. As greater speed became possible, engineer-designers developed more coherent bodies that implied motion. Then manufacturers began to realize that the relationship of many Americans to their automobiles went far beyond usefulness. The automobile owner regards his vehicle as a symbol of independence and prosperity and as something to be admired. This introduces problems that have little to do with utility. Automotive advertisements now put about as much emphasis on social and esthetic factors as on mechanical performance. Thus the designer's task is complicated, for he must find forms to satisfy diverse, often contradictory needs and whims. The models introduced each year show changes just great enough to arouse the buying urge in new-car customers. Many innovations are superficial, faddish, and esthetically questionable. Trivial or secondary functions are too often given disproportionate attention. Faced with this change-for-the-sake-of-change philosophy, it is reassuring to find that some cars are altered only when they can be improved (Fig. 460).

It is interesting to note that as cars have become more complex, the outer forms have become simpler. Much of the mechanical complexity is hidden by the outer form of the car body, which has been subjected to extreme refinement. An analogy might be drawn with the sea gull, for the basically simple yet subtle form of both the car and the bird encloses the most remarkable complexities.

Sullivan and Form Follows Function

An unparalleled creative opportunity was presented to the architects of the United States with the innovation of the skyscraper in the latter part of the nineteenth century. The rapid growth of cities and the development of steel construction and elevators made the use of high-density land essential and the building of high-rise structures feasible. The age of the skyscraper had begun. However, architects failed to realize

opposite above : 459. The stylistic evolution of the Ford motor car. American automobile design has undergone many changes, most of them in response to popular taste for concealing mechanical parts and for commercial elegance.

opposite below : 460. The design of some cars, such as this two-seat coupé Jaguar, is modified only when superior performance or greater beauty can be attained.

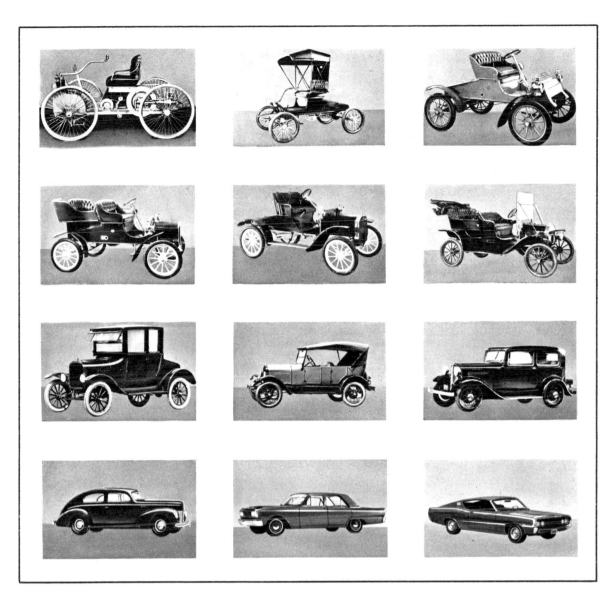

Greek columns and Romanesque arches make an esthetic event out of structural necessity.

top : 461. View through the "Basilica" (c. 550 B.C.) to the "Temple of Poseidon" (c. 460 B.C.), Paestum, Italy.

above : 462. Main arcade, gallery, and clerestory of the nave, Ely Cathedral, Cambridgeshire, England. c. 1100–1135.

opposite : 463. The inventive ornament in Louis Sullivan's Wainwright Building (1890), St. Louis, is an integral part of the structure. (See also Fig. 586.)

that a new structural system demanded a new architecture and that, as history has proved countless times, esthetic events could be made out of structural necessity (Figs. 461, 462). Most builders ignored the implications of a new structural system and clothed magnificently engineered steel frames with irrelevant ornament created for and copied from Greek temples, Roman baths, and Gothic cathedrals. Louis Sullivan, a young architect working in Chicago, saw the absurdity of frosting these new kinds of structures with classical columns and cornices or with Gothic pinnacles. He began to search for forms that would eloquently express the use, structure, and materials of new edifices, that would be consonant with the time and place in which they were built, and that would nourish the spirit of contemporary man (Figs. 463, 586). It was he who reminded his contemporaries of the timeless concept, exemplified by nature, that *form follows function.* Early man not only fitted his pottery to its intended task but shaped and decorated it to delight the eye. The same principle underlies such achievements as Greek columns and modern typewriters. When the Industrial Revolution disrupted the civilized world, however, this precept was forgotten by all but a few creators, and it was Sullivan who revitalized this concept for the twentieth century.

In basic shape, Sullivan's buildings nobly express their use, structure, materials, time, and place. They avoid doing this in a deadening, solely practical way by their exquisite proportions and subtle details, and by their rich ornamentation in appropriate places. Sullivan put such care into his designs because they were built for people with souls and hearts as well as minds and bodies. In his writing, he emphasized the quest for an organic, vital, living architecture for that "large abundant moment which we call *today.*" He writes of man, who with "five senses all awake" pursues "realities—a word I love because I love the sense of life it stands for, the ten-fingered grasp of things it implies, the animation and spirituality of it. . . ." This glimpse into Sullivan's thinking reveals that he was not talking about utility alone.

Other Formal Considerations

Although a revolutionary and essential concept when Sullivan first formulated it, *form follows function* has proved too simplistic an approach for the plurality of modern design needs. As a concept it is limited primarily by its implication that design is a purely rational undertaking, that function can be precisely determined, and that for each function there is *a* form. It ignores the mixed and mutable character of function and cannot explain why in many instances a multiplicity of forms is equally satisfactory for a particular object, or how a form that satisfies a function in one material may be radically unsuitable if another material is used.

This dependence of form upon function would seem to ignore the fundamental fact that even a simple object is often put to conflicting purposes and no one design can serve them all. The designer, therefore, must make choices among the demands he is to meet. In a complex design problem, such as a multipurpose public building, a simple solution could be achieved only at the expense of some of the needs the building is supposed to satisfy. Much modern architecture has achieved notable simplicity by fulfilling only some of its functions and ignoring the others. In the hands of a good designer or architect, the solution to a limited set of functions can be pure and intense. In the hands of less gifted designers the search for simplified design usually has results that are merely flat and banal.

In works of art, whether visual, literary, or lyric, there is a place for the tensions of ambiguity, for the clash of opposites when conflicting demands make compromise impossible or untenable. Factors such as these have been accepted in poetry, painting,

above : 464. The diverse shapes of efficient light bulbs demonstrate that there is seldom, if ever, one "best" design.

left : 465. Ansei Uchima. *Between Silences.* 1966. Woodcut, 10 $^1/_2$ × 14 $^1/_2$″. International Graphic Arts Society of New York. The artist has conveyed his idea through his choice of the forms and colors and their disposition and relationships.

and sculpture, but much less so in architecture and industrial design. As a result, much modern design has been superficial and has offered a machinelike simplicity that is debased and dehumanized. Designers, and their patrons, have addressed themselves to certain of their problems and have ignored the others. Only by meeting the need for beauty as well as use is an article truly functional, and this requires imagination and inspiration, discrimination and judgment on the part of the designer. Even when use and economy are primary concerns, one design is almost never unquestionably superior to all others. We have only to look at the many models of available chairs to realize the range of solutions that are both satisfactory and beautiful (Pls. 12, 14 and Figs. 123, 124, 133–140). Of course, some chairs are comfortable yet unattractive, and the reverse is also true. Typically, however, there are at least a handful of designs for almost any object that are equal in merit, as the silhouettes of the electric light bulbs in Figure 464 demonstrate.

In the highly expressive arts, however, the functions are as plural as the range of solutions designed to serve them. Religious architecture, for example, must do more than afford a place for contemplation and prayer; it must instill a feeling of reverence in the viewer. A church dare not resemble a bank or a gymnasium for it has a sharply different function, and the likeness would evoke responses hardly appropriate for a church. As the examples in Chapter 3 make clear, forms developed for religious purposes differ widely yet serve their purposes well.

Form and Expressions

In his five-color woodcut *Between Silences* (Fig. 465) the Japanese artist Uchima is commenting on the discontinuity of experiences in modern life. The picture contains an idea, and its communication is the function for which the artist has developed a form. Discontinuity is the antipode of continuity, and because the latter is one of the attributes of most art, Uchima has taken an idea not usually treated artistically. He has, furthermore, used nonobjective forms, which, although they evoke certain associations, are in no way portrayals of things we are familiar with. The composition is sharply broken near the middle into two unequal parts. Where there is often a major dominating element, there is almost empty paper—silence. The two parts of the composition are in conflict. Furthermore, the area occupied by the forms is in the upper part of the print, thus leaving the lower part empty (more silence)—an unusual compositional treatment. Note, in particular, that each of the forms has an integrity and independence of its own. They are not continuous and are largely unrelated, yet their freshness and spontaneity give the print a compelling quality. Uchima has taken a basically nonvisual idea and has served it well by giving his picture an attractive form.

This analysis is, at best, partial and ignores other esthetic dimensions of the print, such as the use of color and the techniques employed, to mention only two. Also, it is not meant to suggest that an artist searches for the solution to creative problems and ideas in a completely rational, analytic manner. Much of the creative process is intuitive; the questions are felt rather than precisely articulated. The presence of ambiguity in so many works of the twentieth century demonstrates that there is a plurality of functions in many expressive products. Yet behind every valid creative work there is a compelling idea to which the artist has given meaningful form.

Bernini in his *Ecstasy of St. Theresa* (Fig. 466) used recognizable forms to portray a state of mind and of spirit. He depicts a moment in the saint's life in which

466. Gian Lorenzo Bernini. *Ecstasy of St. Theresa.* 1645–1652. Marble, life-size. Cornaro Chapel, Sta. Maria della Vittoria, Rome. The nervous, fluttering folds of the saint's garment spirit of this masterpiece of Baroque sculpture with as much eloquence as does her facial expression.

347

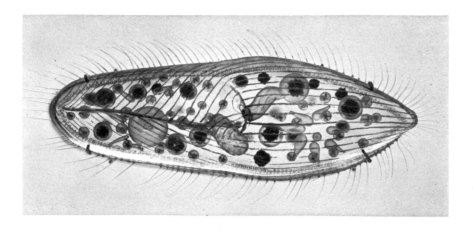

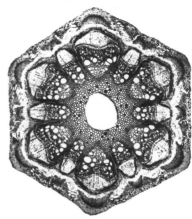

an angel appeared to her in a dream and transfixed her body with an arrow, causing her to experience a combination of extraordinary pleasure and intense agony. The saint is shown at the moment of her swooning, when she sinks back in a state of exquisite transport. Bernini has conveyed much of the spirit of the moment in the facial expression of St. Theresa, but the organization he has given to the sculptural forms is equally eloquent. No semblance of stability or balance is suggested. The edges of the saint's figure form a triangle that rests on a point, her foot. Within the figure itself the folds of St. Theresa's garment billow and writhe in patterns of great nervous intensity. They define a moment of spiritual agitation rather than a human body and speak more eloquently of her ecstacy than does her face. Above the saint, as a heightening contrast, is the angel, sweet and serene in its composure. The theatricality of this sculptural production has never been surpassed, and for many people it is overly dramatic. Yet Bernini's masterful organization of forms to convey his intent cannot be disputed.

The emergence of form from expression and function is basic in art, and by observing the relationships among form, expression, and function the viewer has the means to penetrate the dynamics of works of art. What are the purposes of a painting, a sculpture, a building? Do its forms fulfill them? These are general questions, and their intelligent consideration can often lead the way to an understanding of a work. In many other instances—mainly those in which the purpose of the work, or the artist's idea, is not clear or is not understood—such broad questions may be only partially helpful. However, the study of form as it grows out of function and expression can provide the excitement of engaging the spectator in a meaningful dialogue with the statements put to him by artists and designers.

Variety in Unity

When form and function are integrated, *variety in unity* is almost inevitable. Because every object has more than one function, and because some functions are very complex, the parts of each object are differentiated to perform their specific roles. And because inefficiency is the result when the parts do not work well together, some degree of unification is essential.

There are few natural objects that do not show both unity and variety. Even a microscopic unit such as paramecium (Fig. 467) displays a nucleus differentiated from an enveloping protoplasm that varies in density and has discernible contractile and food vacuoles. The cross section of a twig (Fig. 468) shows, in a more ordered and unified fashion, a high degree of differentiation due to the increasing specialization of parts. As we look higher in the scale of life to birds and mammals, we find a multitude of diversified parts functioning together as a whole. In art, also, variety in unity is a fundamental necessity and a source of lasting satisfaction.

Unity, the Quality of Oneness

Unity, or the quality of oneness, is almost unavoidable when something develops out of a strong, clear purpose or idea. Contemporary aircraft are good examples of this quality, and so are the paintings by children, where lack of subtlety is usually compensated for by directness. Mature artists also penetrate superficialities in their search for unifying essentials but in a more complex and skillful way. A twentieth-century painter whose works are unsurpassed in the unity they convey is Piet Mondrian, whose *Composition* of 1929 is reproduced in Plate 41. Using only rectangular forms, white, primary colors, and careful proportioning, Mondrian achieved works of the most refined sort. To a casual observer, his paintings may seem dull; to an attentive one, the exquisite relationships have a compelling purity.

Unity in art is important in several ways. First, it helps to attract and hold our attention, which is an initial step toward understanding. Second, a unified work of art is easier to "grasp" than is one marked by uncoordinated diversity. Third, oneness aids memory by providing the viewer with a central theme to cling to.

Advertisers seek unity in their work because it helps promote products (see Chap. 5). Merchandisers want their displays unified so that customers will not be perplexed. Painters, sculptors, and architects aim for "an inner consistency that is always the mark of a genuine spiritual event," but they may prefer a subtle unification of discrepancies, the excitement of tamed opposites, to a barren unison or commonplace harmony. Great art often brings together paradoxes and tensions, the juxtaposition of mystery and clarity.

There are many ways to arrive at unity. However, the following four methods are among the easiest to understand and to use.

Surrounding Objects with a Strong Enclosure   Frames around paintings and fences that enclose gardens are examples of elementary unifying devices. A frame separates

469. Masaccio. *The Trinity with the Virgin, St. John, and Donors.* 1425. Fresco. Sta. Maria Novella, Florence. The strong arch form enclosing the major figures of the composition provides a unifying device that is both simple and satisfying.

349

a painting from its surroundings and visually holds it together. Garden walls and hedges shut out distracting views and keep one's attention within bounds. In Masaccio's painting *The Trinity with the Virgin, St. John, and Donors* (Fig. 469) the strong arch form unifies the most important figures in the composition.

Limiting the Number of Elements   Enforced concentration on one or a few things ensures some degree of oneness, for there is nothing to distract the viewer from the basic idea. But unless skillfully done, such enforced concentration may not hold one's interest for long. The Lieberman painting in Figure 470 could hardly be more simple or more unified. The viewer's attention is held by the purity of the circle and its enclosing square. By way of contrast, Louise Nevelson gives unity to her complex sculptures by painting them black or in another monochrome (see Fig. 570).

Repetition of Elements   Similarity in shape, size, or color ties parts together, especially if they have a strong compositional and substantive relationship with one another. Although repetition is basic in such fields as architecture (see Figs. 604, 618) and textile design, it can quickly lead to dullness unless the elements are interesting in themselves and the pattern they establish is distinctive. In the Byzantine screen in Figure 471 there are fifteen units of identical size and five different designs.

Similarity or Harmony of Parts   The viewer's interest is likely to be aroused and held if the components share some common qualities but are not identical. The paving pattern in Figure 472 makes use of only circular shapes, but they have been ingeniously varied. The Bernini sculpture (Fig. 466) also exemplifies this treatment.

The four preceding devices are among the ABC's of unity. They have been used effectively by amateurs and professionals, both contemporary and historic. However, they are devices and rules-of-thumb that when used alone almost never produce more than a pleasant but tasteless porridge. Complete artistic unity is not gained by merely limiting the number of objects or ideas in a painting, any more than a garden can be genuinely integrated by fencing it in. Fruitful unity is the result of a powerful, significant oneness that develops out of differences that have an inevitable consequence. The unity of two identical buttons is weak when compared to the vital unity of a button and buttonhole. To put it simply, vital interaction is fundamental to the most profitable use of the principle of unity.

Variety, the Quality of Diversity

Variety, the partner of unity, arises from contrast or opposition: diversity of materials and differences in forms, colors, or textures. It ranges from just noticeable

above : 470. Alexander Lieberman. *Minimum.* 1950. Enamel on composition board, 4 × 4′. Collection the artist. Unity has been assured in this painting by the use of a single form.

below left : 471. Byzantine screen, Chiesa Metropolitana, Ravenna. c. 547. Marble. The repetition of identically sized squares is enlivened by differences in the treatment of the squares.

below right : 472. Marquetry of colored stones, San Miniato al Monte, Florence. After 1013. The design is unified by the use of only circular forms.

Plate 41. Piet Mondrian. *Large Composition with Red, Blue, and Yellow.* 1928.
Oil on canvas, 4′ ³/₄″ × 2′ 7¹/₂″. Courtesy Sidney Janis Gallery, New York.

Plate 42. Stuart Davis. *Hot Still-Scape for Six Colors*. 1940. Oil on canvas, 35 $^3/_4$ × 44 $^3/_4$".
Collection Mrs. Edith Halpert, Downtown Gallery, New York.

473. Stuart Davis. Study for *Hot Still-Scape for Six Colors*. 1940. Oil on canvas, 9 × 12″. The Museum of Modern Art, New York. This sketch for Davis' painting in Plate 42 shows the comparatively simple pattern on which the painting was developed.

differences to open conflict. Although variety is the antipode of unity, the two come together in dynamic interrelationships in art and nature. Diversity intensifies unity. It keeps us alert by inviting us to participate actively in the search for unity among variants.

An example of variety developing out of unity can be found in the following, quite common experience: A boy decides to learn how to ski. First, he gets a pair of skis, the most important element in the situation aside from himself and the snow. Then he purchases ski poles and a pair of ski pants, and then a ski jacket, cap, mittens, and scarf. Next, he improves his skills. He studies types of snow; he buys different kinds of wax; he practices a variety of turns: stem turns, Christiana turns, jump turns. Thus a complex pattern of behavior develops out of a simple interest in skiing. In the act of skiing, all these diverse elements are brought together. Art, too, can be as organically unified and varied as nature or our behavior patterns when it grows from a central idea.

Variety can be developed in a number of ways.

One way is *to unfold and expand a basic idea*. This method can be seen when a small, apparently simple seed grows into a large plant with many contrasting and specialized parts. In music there is the device of "theme-and-variations," in which the parts, different as they may be in tempo, rhythm, or key, evolve from a central theme. Often some of the variations depart so radically from the theme that they take on a completely different character. Artists, too, may take this evolutionary course of creating variety out of unity, as *Hot Still-Scape for Six Colors* (Pl. 42 and Fig. 473) by Stuart Davis shows. Seymour Lipton's *Sanctuary* (Fig. 569) and Eero Saarinen's TWA Flight Center (Figs. 615, 616) also illustrate this same unity in variety.

In other works, *two or more themes*, usually contrasting, are pitted against each other, interwoven, and eventually brought into some kind of agreement, as in the di Suvero sculpture (Fig. 453). At times *strong contrasts* stand alone with no attempt at a harmonious resolution, with only the tension of their opposition providing a unifying link. In just this manner does Philip Johnson's glass house (Pl. 2a and Figs. 9, 10) affirm its crystalline geometric line against nature's organic complexity.

Stuart Davis' sketch and painting humorously titled *Hot Still-Scape for Six Colors* (Fig. 473 and Pl. 42) offer a striking example of the method an artist employed to solve the problem of creating variety. The sketch states in simple terms the basic theme—the dynamic interplay of forces that characterizes many aspects of contemporary living. This is expressed in a diagonal organization of intensely colored, overlapping, and interpenetrating planes. The strongest movement is a diagonal thrust from the upper left of the work to the lower right. A number of lesser movements oppose it. The area of major interest is clearly in the center. With only minor exceptions, the forms are angular and straight-edged, and on each side of the sketch is a receding plane that moves into a large dark area that suggests a surface parallel to the picture plane. It is as if the forms of the composition were set into the interior of a box. Looked at another way, these enclosing planes constitute a kind of frame holding together the energetic composition.

In the completed painting, Davis has kept the basic forms established in the sketch almost intact, but he has changed the proportions of the picture and of some of the units and has added several forms. Most noticeably, he has enriched the canvas with a dazzling array of details. The spirals and intertwining lines, the crosses and circles are not only unlike one another, but they are not repetitious of the angular planes they enliven.

At first glance, the "still-scape" seems almost chaotic, for the underlying framework is not immediately obvious. But close scrutiny reveals this as a remarkable display of unity forged from almost fantastic variety. The improvisations and the abrupt changes of pace make the painting as exciting as jazz, of which it is strongly reminiscent. Davis obviously prefers extracting order from dissonances and conflicts to accepting soft harmonies. In a similar vein, architect Marcel Breuer (see Figs. 100, 101) has written, "The real impact of any work is the extent to which it unifies contrasting notions—opposite points of view. *I mean unifies and not compromises.*"

474. The number of shapes used in the design of a courthouse in Brooklyn, New York, is few, but the building lacks unity and coherence. The openings seem uncoordinated within the total form of the building.

Great Architecture Fuses Variety into Unity

Let us compare an early twentieth-century courthouse (Fig. 474) in Brooklyn, New York, the recently completed library of the University of California at Irvine (Fig. 475), designed by William L. Pereira, and the Farnese Palace in Rome (Fig. 476), designed by Sangallo and Michelangelo and built over 400 years ago. Which of these three architectural works looks as if it were *one* building developed from *one* idea? Which looks like a series of separate units piled together? Which is richest in variety?

The Farnese Palace is noticeably longer than it is high. The horizontality of the three rows of windows is accentuated by continuous moldings, and the structure is capped by a magnificent cornice. The university library has about the same

top : 475. Narrow, vertical openings comprise the major mass of the library of the University of California at Irvine and bestow on it a compelling unity. William L. Pereira, architect.

above : 476. The Farnese Palace in Rome (1534–1546), designed by Antonio da Sangallo, embodies subtle differences in window treatments to enrich the unity of the façade. The top story was added by Michelangelo (1546).

proportions as the palace. It also is marked by strong horizontals. The courthouse, a little higher than it is long, shows no such definite proportions. There is no consistent force integrating its major units, no real sense of its basic form, and consequently the viewer receives no dominant single impression of the whole.

Another important factor relating to the three structures concerns consonance with time and materials. The Farnese Palace is a masonry structure created in the spirit of its time. The library, a steel-structured building that seems to float above the small supports on which it rests, is also of its time. But the courthouse is a large, twentieth-century steel-and-concrete structure disguised by a pseudo-Renaissance veneer of stone. This is the approach to architecture that Louis Sullivan fought.

As to the matter of variety, the diverse window shapes and sizes as well as the different surfacing materials give the courthouse this quality, but the variety seems dull and unmotivated. Both the rounded and rectangular windows are bland holes in the stone façade, linked neither by an inclusive rhythm nor by an energizing juxtaposition of forms. Both the library and the palace have less variety. But neither building is, in any sense, dull. The tall, thin, vertical windows in the campus library break up the major rectangular form and reflect the book stacks behind them. These are echoed in smaller windows both directly below and in the setback central section, which thrusts through at the top. The detail around the windows on each of the three stories of the Farnese Palace is fundamentally similar, yet each story shows enlivening differences. The rectangular windows on the ground floor are topped by projecting, horizontal moldings; the windows on the second floor are rectangular, but have alternating pointed and arched pediments; while the rounded windows of the top floor fit nicely into triangular pediments. Thus straight, rounded, and pointed shapes are progressively integrated into a rhythmic pattern. Any building requires the bringing of disparate elements into some order. The three examples just dealt with illustrate solutions of a similar nature yet of widely contrasting success.

Unity and variety are fundamental in art. A pair of opposites, they complement and supplement each other. Unity leads to order, variety brings vitality through contrasts. They interact with and balance each other so that an active oneness precludes monotony or chaos. If variety gets out of control, unity is endangered, and the whole is lost in the parts: a building becomes a collection of doors, windows, and walls; and a painting looks like an assemblage of forms and ideas. But too much consistency is deadening. It has been said that the greatest art is that which intensely unites the most variables. In a well-organized object the differing parts, much as citizens in a democracy, interact without losing their individuality. Unity does not imply conformity or regimentation, because the units have to be differentiated for maximum effectiveness. The conflicts and contrasts mature into an unfettered totality.

477. Organization in such natural forms as this elm leaf provides the basis for the principles of design.

14 The Principles of Design

Even a lowly elm leaf (Fig. 477) is, on close scrutiny, a thing of impressive beauty. In its handsome organization, it reveals both unity and variety. The pattern of veins denotes particular functions, and even without botanical knowledge one can be sure that its form fulfills its functions well. The leaf also can be looked at in terms of the *ways* it is organized: the emphasis of the center vein, the rhythmic patterns of the lateral veins and the edges, the balance of the whole. It is such relationships in nature that are used as the bases for organization in art.

In this chapter, we will explore in works of visual arts the coherent, expressive relationships of the parts to one another and to the whole. These relationships offer esthetic stimulation and satisfaction and are closely related to the aspects of art that have already been discussed: physical, emotional, and spiritual needs, and the characteristics of materials that are used.

The principles of design can be considered means of relating the elements of the visual arts, and no painter, sculptor, architect, designer, homemaker, or student can avoid using them. Everything we touch has form, texture, and color, and involves light and space. It is the way these elements are handled that makes the difference between clumsy ineptitude and consummate artistry.

Two Houses

The purpose of the following analysis of the exterior of two houses is to identify basic relationships existing in works of visual arts—that is, the principles of design—and to demonstrate some of the varied ways in which the principles can occur. The houses in Figures 478 and 479 both have considerable elegance, but they are separated in time by over 150 years. The Gardner-White-Pingree house was built in 1810 by Samuel McIntyre in Salem, Massachusetts. The house in Purchase, New York, designed by Charles Gwathmey and Richard Henderson, was built in 1968. In discussing the latter house, only the front on the left will be considered.

The two houses have a number of things in common. Their proportions are similar, both being wider than high. Their major subdivisions—rectangular units—are also similar. Both have a strong semicircular form that contrasts with the general rectangularity and strong horizontals that mark each floor. And, when built, both made use of contemporary forms and were thus considered "modern."

In looking at any work of art from the standpoint of design, the first question to ask is: What is the major impression that one gets from observing it? And second: What is its major feature?

The major impression one gets of the Gardner-White-Pingree house is of a consistently horizontal building. It is given this character by the rows of windows on each floor, by the cornice, by the balustrade that hides the sloping roof, which, if seen, would detract from the rectangularity, and by the white stone divisions between the floors. A large number of lesser verticals opposes this horizontality: the windows and the shutters, the pedestals in the balustrade, the chimneys, and, most noticeably, the entrance door and the stoop. The last two elements present the additional contrast of curved forms, which appear in the fanlight above the door and in a semicircular stoop that projects from the house. These vertical and curved elements are not as emphatically stated as the horizontal ones; however, the contrasts they offer intensify the generally horizontal character of the house.

There is no doubt that the major feature of the house is the entrance door, for it is centrally placed and is the largest element in the façade. In addition, the contrasts in direction and form (vertical and curved) make it stand out from the main mass of the building. The entry is a fitting point of emphasis for a house facing a street.

The house in Purchase, New York, is also predominantly horizontal. The rectangular forms that compose the front, however, are larger in size and fewer in number. Unlike the Salem house, there are few repeated units, and none occurs more than twice. Although each of the rectangular areas fits into the total design of the house, each seems to possess a singular independence. Opposing the major horizontal forms is the white chimney and, more emphatically, the projecting semicircular form. This house does not have a direct center like the Gardner-White-Pingree house, but the clear points of emphasis are the window areas, especially the one on the ground floor. These areas, contrasting with the white walls, dominate the house by their location and their dark values. The glass section on the ground floor is especially emphasized by the form of the walls that flank it, a splayed wall on one side, a curved wall on the other. The point of dominance is again the entrance to the house, except that here it is on the garden side. From this comparison we can conclude that *emphasis* is a significant factor in design.

A second design question to ask is: Are the various parts and subparts of the design related in an attractive manner?

In the Gardner-White-Pingree house the openings are regularly spaced across the façade. The series of repetitions of windows, shutters, and intervening brick areas on each floor is attractive and satisfying. In the balustrade above the cornice, the pedestals occur at the midpoint between the windows and at the ends in a kind of counterpoint to the windows themselves. The repetitive order of the windows is contained by the chimneys, which appear at each side of the house. The structure is also divided into three unequal horizontal areas, each one smaller than the one below it. The cornice and balustrade crown the house and serve as a fourth unit. Both horizontally and vertically, there is a continuity in the design.

opposite : 478. Centrality, repetition, and symmetry mark the design of the Gardner-White-Pingree house in Salem, Massachusetts, designed by Samuel McIntyre in 1810.

right : 479. Subtle relationships among the asymmetrical and variously sized and proportioned elements characterize this home (1968) in Purchase, New York. Charles Gwathmey and Richard Henderson, architects.

In the Purchase house there is also a strong relationship among the parts. Whereas in the Salem house there was a rhythm of repetitive units, here there is a rhythm of proportions, much as in a Mondrian painting (Pl. 41, p. 351). Each form and surface—flat, rounded, and sloped—has a justness of relation to the adjoining form and surface. The viewer's eye moves easily from one unit and part to the other. From this observation we can infer that *continuity* is another factor with significance for design.

The third design question to ask is: Is the design a balanced one? The Gardner-White-Pingree house is symmetrically balanced, one half being the mirror image of the other, and this produces an assured and quickly understood stability. The center of the building is immediately identified as a vertical axis bisecting the front door, the two center windows, and indeed the entire house. In the Purchase house, on the other hand, no similarly exact center can be located. However, both optically and physically there is a center, and it falls in the window areas. The varying wall treatments, projected and splayed on one side, rounded on the other, complement each other. Although the house is asymmetrical, it has a design equilibrium and is thus balanced. *Balance,* therefore, is also a design characteristic to consider.

These two houses have been used to introduce a discussion on principles of design, because both are basically simple in organization, although developed with elegance and refinement, and are similar to other buildings we all have seen. Although noticeably dissimilar in appearance, both houses reflect the design characteristics of emphasis, continuity, and balance, and a consideration of them brings to light qualities common to both houses. This, indeed, is one of the major functions of design principles—to reveal the fundamental structure of works of art.

Formal Relationships

New art works are often rejected by both critics and the public. Such rejection, however, tends to be generated more by the new subject matter or new materials of these works than by their design. The design of works by the Ash Can group of American painters now seems tame and conservative to us, although when first exhibited early in the century, the group startled many people by their portrayal of scenes and objects of everyday urban life, which were judged as unworthy subject matter for good painting. The same reaction greeted Pop Art in the 1950s (see Chap. 15). Now it too, when seen in perspective, takes its place as a movement in which important works have stature not only because of their content but also because of their design, or structure. Being attentive to design, therefore, enables one to get beyond subject matter and to view the formal relationships among the various elements within art works that give the visual arts their esthetic value.

Furthermore, works of art similar in organization can convey markedly different effects, as can be shown in a comparison of El Greco's *St. Francis in Ecstacy* and Lee Bonticou's *Untitled, 1961* (Figs. 480, 481). The former, a sixteenth-century work, portrays the well-known saint in an intense religious experience. Dominating the canvas is St. Francis, his oval-shaped head at upper center. The painting has two major types of movement: one begins in the shape of the head and gradually enlarges as it approaches the edges of the canvas; the other radiates outward, like spokes in a wheel, from a center located near the area of the figure's heart. A restless, ecstatic energy pervades the work, and there are in it many nervous, attenuated forms.

The Bonticou work is of the machine age. Large and small saw blades are used as well as grilles, vents, intakes, and exhausts—all set in a patchwork of heavy

Two works of differing material and content can have similar organizational bases. The paintings in Figs. 480 and 481 both have strong circular and radial movements.

left : 480. El Greco. *St. Francis in Ecstacy.* 1585–1590. Oil on canvas, 42 1/4 × 32″. Detroit Institute of Arts. A nervous pulsation permeates all the forms in this evocation of an intensely religious experience.

below : 481. Lee Bonticou. *Untitled, 1961.* Welded metal and canvas, 6′ × 5′6 1/4″ × 2′2″. Whitney Museum of American Art, New York. The use of canvas and metal objects gives this work a strikingly different appearance. It is a dynamic and energized work of our machine culture.

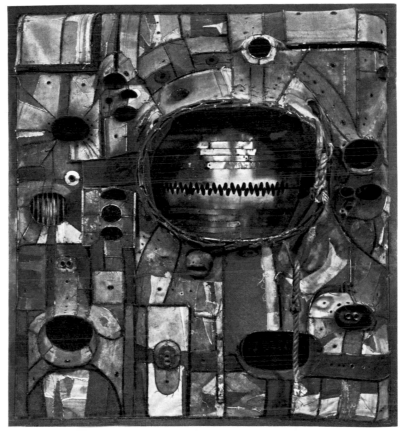

canvas on a metal frame. Here, too, the composition is both circular and radial and has a remarkable similarity to the El Greco, even to the use of a knotted rope. Study of the two works leads one to conclude that although very different in subject matter, they are closely allied in composition. Both have a nervous vibrancy springing from the organizational devices used. However, the flamelike forms in the El Greco, which give it an ethereal and spiritual quality, are rightly not present in the Bonticou, where rectangular forms produce a more stolid character. Nevertheless, the basic structural similarities between the two works make clear the other qualities which they have in common.

The design of a work, of course, is always related to its expressive purpose and to the materials the work is made of. Its appreciation must also consider these factors, for design practiced or appreciated apart from other bases of art is arid and useless.

Three Principles of Design

With few exceptions, art works have characteristics that identify them almost immediately with specific cultures and periods. Even a novice can tell a Gothic cathedral from a Classical temple, but it takes a little more awareness and discernment to distinguish between Greek temples of the sixth century B.C. and those of the following century. We also know that artists develop personal styles and that individual works can be accurately dated from stylistic evidence. It is the manner in which the plastic elements have been used and organized—determined by cultural interests and ideals, materials and technology, and individual artistic personalities— that makes particular works different from all others and stylistically, historically distinctive. The plastic elements and their organization can, in a real sense, be said to *be* any particular art object.

Although it is the differences that distinguish individual works of art from one another, there are factors relating them. Of these, perhaps the most important are the principles of design—those relationships among the plastic elements that enable one to observe affinities between a Chinese painting and medieval embroidery, between Etruscan tomb painting and Pop Art. This suggests that the principles of design are flexible instruments. Nothing, in fact, demonstrates their versatility more than the multiplicity of styles, both cultural and personal, in which they can be seen to operate.

The use of design principles in furthering appreciation and creation is both considerable and limited. As already pointed out, they enable an observer to cut through cultural and stylistic idiosyncrasies and discover basic relationships, for principles of design are, in reality, broad and sound generalizations. Their chief limitation is that of any generalization: however sound it may be, it can offer only a partial solution and explanation. Within their limitations, however, principles of design can nonetheless convey a great deal. For both the creative artist and his audience principles of design serve as working guides to the analysis of works in progress and works that have been completed. The study of design is an important part of the training of persons in all fields of art. It is no less useful a discipline to the spectator generally interested in art.

There have been numerous formulations of principles of design, each with its own validity. To avoid confusion and to establish a firm basis for the present discussion—as well as for subsequent, perhaps more refined understanding of principles in art—we will here concentrate on three major considerations already introduced : *emphasis, continuity,* and *balance.*

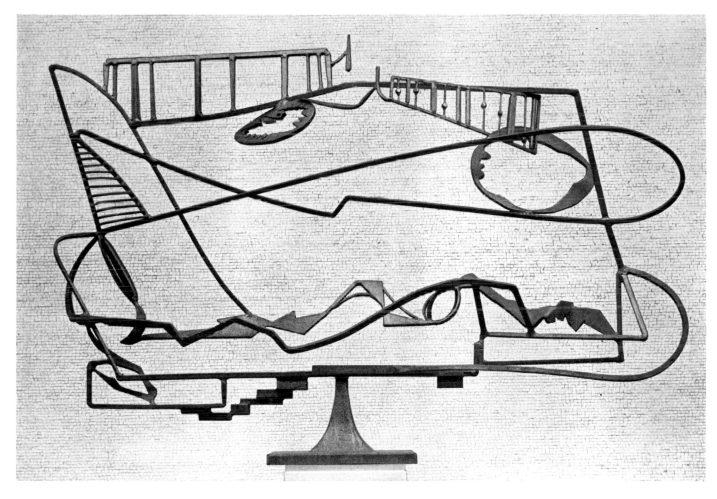

482. David Smith. *Hudson River Landscape*. 1951. Steel, length 6'3". Whitney Museum of American Art, New York. The most striking forms in this work occur at the edges rather than in or near the center, where compositional interest is usually placed.

In speaking of principles in art, we have to acknowledge that to be relevant and useful in the analysis of art works, or in their creation, the principles of design must be applied with flexibility and intelligence. For example, the principle of emphasis is basic: something in the work must dominate. However, emphasis is usually interpreted as referring to centrality—to a kind of high point or climax occurring in the work. In recent years, there have been many works that avoid compositional centrality. David Smith's *Hudson River Landscape* (Fig. 482) is such a work. The most interesting aspects of the composition do not appear in or near the center but around the periphery in a fascinating variety of forms and edges. There is emphasis, however, and it is in the flowing, almost meandering line that suggests a river and that ties together all the incidents along the way. The Jackson Pollock painting in a later chapter (Fig. 546) is a work in which every part of the canvas is as important as every other part and one in which centrality does not exist. Yet the painting is dominated by an intricate interlacing of lines, which vitalize the canvas with patterns of great power. Emphasis is present in the Pollock but of a sort that demands a different interpretation of emphasis than is usually given it.

Balance is another principle that is occasionally violated. In most works of art the composition as a whole, regardless of the vigor of the various parts, involves some resolution of the forces in it and thus achieves a general equilibrium. However,

483. John Chamberlain. *Essex*. 1960. Automobile body parts and other metal relief, 9′ × 6′8″ × 3′7″. The Museum of Modern Art, New York (gift of Mr. and Mrs. Robert C. Scull and Purchase). The state of imbalance in *Essex* is basic to the impact of the work.

from time to time powerful works are produced that are deliberately out of balance, such as John Chamberlain's *Essex* (Fig. 483). The composition leans toward the left, thus suggesting motion. The parts within the large form, bright in color but bent and mashed, connote dreadful impact. Is not this clearly a statement of the commonplace tragedy of our times, the automobile accident? Here are forms made of strong material but altered almost beyond recognition by a powerful force or by a meeting of two forces. This work could not convey its message if it were in balance. Artists such as Chamberlain would probably justify their license with design principles by stating that many of the events in today's world are irrational—our appalling automobile death rate, two world wars of colossal destruction within the first half of the century, and the constant threat of ultimate, imminent annihilation. Such a world cannot always be seen as in balance. Rules are made to be broken, but when this is done the idea in the work must be sufficiently strong to justify the rejection of a principle.

Emphasis: Dominance and Subordination

In Jan van Eyck's *Van der Paele Madonna* (Pl. 43, p. 369, and Fig. 484) there is no doubt about what dominates. In the center and elevated on a double-tiered platform are the Madonna and Child. They dominate the work, first, by virtue of their elevated and central position within the composition and, second, by color—the intense red of the Madonna's robe and the strong red, blue, and green in the patterned carpet spread before the throne. The oval of the Virgin's face radiates outward to the larger oval of her over-all silhouette, and this places a pronounced emphasis on the center

of the painting. Several rectangular forms frame the central heads and figures, and there are a number of radial forms, especially in the rug and floor patterns, in the canopy, and in many of the lines of the surrounding figures. The three men at the sides are clearly subordinate by their position and by the darker, cooler hues of their clothing. Other subordinate elements, however—columns, arches, windows, pedestals—are related to the basic system of oval and curved, rectangular and diagonal forms and directions, which are the bases of the composition. This masterful, complex organization was created by one of the greatest of the Northern Renaissance painters. He achieved a stunning composition from a wide variety of forms, materials, and colors. The relation of the subordinate to the dominant elements is always clear.

In Nathan Oliveira's *Standing Man with a Stick* (Fig. 485) the major object of emphasis is also obvious. In the center of the canvas is a solitary figure, roughly and

above : 484. Jan van Eyck. *The Madonna of Canon George van der Paele with Sts. Donation and George.* 1434–1436. Panel, $4'1/_8'' \times 5'2^1/_8''$. Groeningemuseum, Bruges. This magnificent composition is clearly dominated by the enthroned Mother and Child. (See also Pl. 43, p. 369.)

right : 485. Nathan Oliveira. *Standing Man with a Stick.* 1959. Oil on canvas, $5'8^7/_8'' \times 5'1/_8''$. The Museum of Modern Art, New York (gift of Joseph Hirschhorn). With only one major feature in it, this painting abounds in compositional subtleties.

heavily painted, erect but not quite balanced. Standing against an almost feature-less background, he is the image of alienation and emptiness. Yet for all its apparent simplicity, the figure has been emphasized in a number of ways. On both sides of it are parallel dark areas that are subordinate but that strengthen the figure; around its upper part there is a soft horizontal, repeated more strongly at the base, which opposes the decisive vertical. Within the predominantly gray form are touches of warm color, contrasting with the generally gray background. Other subordinate directions are in the texture of the pigment, and these, too, are echoed in the back-ground. *Standing Man with a Stick* is a picture of eloquent and haunting beauty.

Although very different in effect, the emphasis in both these paintings is similarly achieved: by the position of the figure and by the repetition, echo, and opposition of it or some of its parts. Dominance presupposes subordination, or the existence of lesser elements. Contrast also emphasizes dominance, although if dominance is to be maintained, the contrast must be subordinate. Both subordination and contrast are effective devices for emphasizing dominance in the *Van der Paele Madonna* and in *Standing Man with a Stick*.

Dominance, or emphasis, can be asserted in many ways—in form, color, direc-tion, texture, and position, among others. Limiting the number of elements is also effective. Many objects of the same size and character tend to compete with one another. Size is also important. A sofa usually demands more attention than a chair, a skyscraper more than a residence. Making important figures larger than others in paintings is both an obvious and a satisfactory device. Decisive character is quickly noted, and bold shapes are more important than timid or neutral ones. Unexpected or unusual elements rivet our gaze. When first exhibited, Marcel Duchamp's *Nude Descending a Staircase* (Pl. 44, p. 370) startled, intrigued, or irritated almost every-one who saw it. After fifty years, it still does not seem ordinary. Likewise, the unique interplay of straight and curved lines, of spontaneous and reasoned forms in *Hudson River Landscape* (Fig. 482) set it apart from the commonplace. Finally, the grouping of elements gives them significance. A fireplace allied with bookshelves and a sofa can dominate a room more readily than any one of them alone. In paintings, the major forms—figures, buildings, or trees—are often organized in one dominant group. Emphasis is thus a principle productive of unity and variety. It can serve either or both.

Continuity: Organized Movement, or Rhythm

It is satisfying to watch the organized movements of a good dancer, but it is dis-turbing to watch one whose motions are without pattern. The varied kinds of dances, from the stately minuet to today's vigorous gyrations, have earned their popularity because they are rhythmic patterns of bodily movements that express the feelings of the participants. Continuing, recurring, and developing patterns, although most obvious in the dance, pervade all phases of art.

Repetition, *alternation*, and *progression* are as fundamental in nature as in art (Fig. 486). Repetition occurs in the beat of the heart; alternation occurs in the ebb and flow of tides, in the cycle of day and night, and in the changing of the seasons. Progression is seen in any tree or river system: small twigs lead to the sturdy trunk, small streams to the broad river. The human body, too, is an incredibly complex design with continuity in its various parts.

Many of the illustrations in this chapter show that continuity can be a decisive unifying factor and also convey highly diversified feelings. The clear-cut rhythms of the Gardner-White-Pingree house (Fig. 478) are measured and stabilized; the studied placement of forms in the house (Fig. 479) at Purchase, New York, convey a different

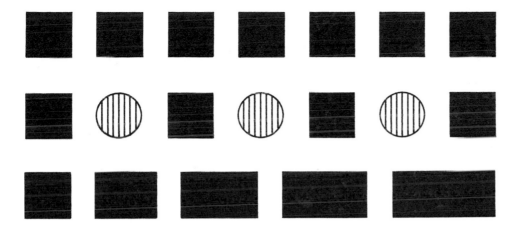

486. The three elementary rhythmic devices are repetition (*top*), in which the same form is duplicated; alternation (*center*), in which two forms follow one another; and progression (*bottom*), in which a form undergoes sequential change.

but equally valid continuity. Gentle, harmonious curves reinforce the peaceful nobility and assurance of the *Buddha* in Figure 452. The basic rhythm pattern of Duccio's *Maestà* (Fig. 494) is firmly established in the steady and strong rectangular throne, but a succession of curved, gently swaying forms dispels rigidity.

Mark di Suvero's sculpture (Fig. 453) reveals repetition in its three major horizontals: the base, the form at the right, and the one directly over it. There is also a directional sequence in the work's three major upright forms. Much of this sculpture's impact is due to the sharp contrasts that it embraces.

In general, repetition is very successful in advertising. A slogan or trade name used again and again establishes a pattern that is remembered. In architecture, textiles, and many other art forms, repeating the same motif, usually at equal intervals, brings regularity. Repetition, though, must be well handled or else the constant reiteration will become irritating or go unnoticed. The ticking of a clock, after a time, sinks unheard into the background. On the other hand, television commercials too frequently heard and seen can annoy and thus repel rather than attract. Alternation, the interspersed repetition of two or more units, is more active and complex than a repeated single unit. The effectiveness of either device depends on the appropriateness of what is repeated and how sensitively the recurrence is handled. In a culture of mass production, however, everyone has constant confrontations with repetition, from the row of identical soup cans on the supermarket shelf to the rows of windows in any large structure. A significant phenomenon, however, occurs in spatial repetition or in alternation or in both. The head-on view of a building with a colonnade is a good example of repetition of identical units, the columns (Fig. 461). It is also an example of alternation, since the columns alternate with the spaces between them. This will be seen clearly in the model of the Parthenon in Chapter 17 (Fig. 593). When, however, the same repetitive units are viewed in perspective (Fig. 592), the repetition becomes progression of the most perfect sort. That visual repetition can also be, and usually is, perceived as progression is probably one reason why it is so attractive. It seldom is boring in the way temporal repetition can be.

Progression is, of course, more dynamic than repetition or alternation, involving as it does sequential change of one or more qualities. Sizes may range from small to large, shapes may change by degrees from angular to rounded, and colors may move from gray through a sequence of dull greens up to pure green. Notice in El Greco's *St. Francis in Ecstasy* (Fig. 480) the gradations in size, shape, and direction of the v-shaped forms in the left sleeve that pull attention down toward the hand and over toward the skull. Throughout the painting, elongated, pointed forms are dominant, but no two are identical. There are also many repetitions, contrasts, and sequences in the Bonticou work (Fig. 481).

The American Embassy, Dublin   An unusual and attractive example of architecture that embodies continuity in a number of ways is the American Embassy in Dublin (Fig. 487), designed by architect John M. Johansen. A circular building, it is constructed of precast concrete units that, in their flowing and interlaced forms, are reminiscent of designs in early Celtic crosses and in the *Book of Kells* (Fig. 488). The window embrasures, when seen as single units, alternate on each floor level. The openings can also be looked at as two- or three-story units, introducing other kinds of repetition and alternation. Furthermore, as the building curves away from the viewer the rhythm of the repetition and alternation of the architectural forms intensifies, and the forms even change in character as the depth of the window openings becomes visible.

Benedictine Basilica, Ottenbeuren   Another remarkable example of continuity is shown in the Benedictine basilica (Fig. 489) at Ottenbeuren in southern Germany. This church, finished and dedicated to the Holy Trinity in 1767, is an example of

above : 487. Forms that exhibit unusual continuity mark the design of the United States Embassy Office (1964) in Dublin. John M. Johansen, architect.

above right : 488. Chi rho monogram (XPI), *Book of Kells.* 7th–8th cents. Illuminated manuscript. Trinity College Library, Dublin.

right : 489. The Benedictine basilica at Ottobeuren (1767) in Germany is an example of German Baroque, a style marked by dramatically turbulent yet rhythmic forms.

Plate 43. Jan van Eyck. *Madonna of Canon George van der Paele with Sts. Donation and George.* 1434–1436. Panel, 4' 1 1/8" × 5' 2 1/8". Groeningemuseum, Bruges.

Plate 44. Marcel Duchamp. *Nude Descending a Staircase, No. 2.* 1912. Oil on canvas, 4′ 10″ × 2′ 11″. Philadelphia Museum of Art (Louise and Walter Arensberg Collection.)

German Baroque, a style unequalled in its curvilinear, writhing, even turbulent forms. Very sensibly, the architect left the main structural elements—columns, entablatures, and arches—largely untouched. Between these structural members, however, are convoluted, exuberant, immensely energetic decorative shapes. The excitement is further heightened by the introduction of painted and gilded elements. Although the Baroque style, often given to decorative excesses, was out of favor for a long time, it has been rediscovered recently, perhaps as a reaction to the austerity of much modern architecture and our preoccupation with simple forms. As a style, it may well seem overly complex and theatrical, but it has strong emotional appeal. German Baroque exceeded all other styles in its complications, but as architecture with strong, powerful, and, at times, almost unbelievably rhythmic elements, it is also without peer.

A Modern Painting and a Greek Sculpture   A twentieth-century painting, Marcel Duchamp's *Nude Descending a Staircase* (Pl. 44), and a Greek sculpture of the fifth century B.C., *Victory Adjusting Her Sandal* (Fig. 490), are of interest because of their similar rhythmic patterns. Women are the subject matter of both works, and in both they are engaged in quite ordinary actions. The major forms are similar and taper toward the base. In the Duchamp work the sense of movement is greater, a reasonable impression since it is a series of sequential images of a single figure. The Greek sculptural relief, however, is considerably more graceful. Transcending these contrasts is the fact that, separated by some 2400 years, two artists, one entranced with the grace of a single female form, the other intent on portraying movement, have produced works of remarkable similarity. It is the intent of the artists that separates them more than the finished compositions.

Continuity therefore would seem in several ways to be a significant factor in art. It can help attract and hold attention by giving compositions vitality and intensity. It can make compositions seem more orderly and, therefore, more readily comprehensible. Transition is a kind of continuity that relates two otherwise unconnected

490. *Victory Adjusting Her Sandal*, relief from the balustrade of the Temple of Athena Nike, Athens. 410–407 B.C. Marble, 42 × 20″. Acropolis Museum, Athens. There is a remarkable similarity here in rhythmic structure to Duchamp's *Nude Descending a Staircase* (Pl. 44).

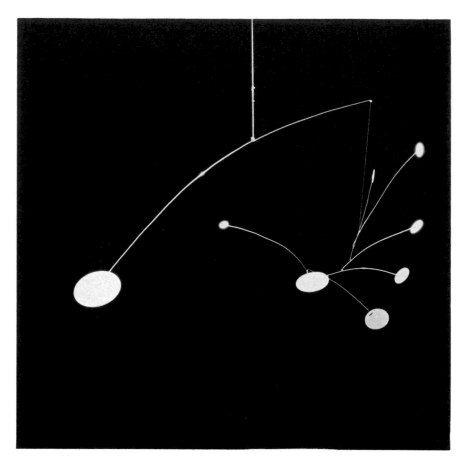

Alexander Calder. *Hanging Mobile*.
1936. Aluminum discs and steel wire,
width c. 28″. Collection Mrs. Meric
Callery, Paris. Whether at rest or
in motion, Calder's mobile is an
invigorating interpretation of balance in ever changing relationships
among the parts.

above : 491. When at rest, the sculpture resembles an unusually subtle
diagram of asymmetric balance. The
discs progress rhythmically from
large to small, their supports from
long to short.

right : 492. When in motion, each
disc describes a curved path through
space.

or opposed factors in a composition. Repeating certain forms, colors, or textures establishes unity, while modifying any of those elements provides the variety that vitalizes unity. It is, then, unity and variety that continuity produces.

Balance: Equilibrium

A sense of balance is fundamental to a person's ability to function well. If it is seriously disturbed, one is unable to walk and feels disoriented. It is only natural, therefore, that some kind of equilibrium be sought in art. If an object is clearly balanced, a sense of security is engendered. If, however, the stability is too obvious, the work is boring. Often a work of art is more stimulating if it challenges us to discover, as in solving a problem, just how the equipoise was attained. The illustrations in this chapter show a number of ways to obtain balance, each of which is vital to the expressive content of the work of art.

The classical illustration of balance is a pair of scales with identical weights equidistant from the center. These weights, responding only to the downward pull of gravity, seem motionless. But balance is more energetically shown in such sports as skiing. The skier must balance himself in ever changing ways or suffer a spill. As he speeds down a slope, he continually shifts his weight to maintain equilibrium. When his weight is equally distributed on both feet, the skier proceeds in a straight line. If he wants to change direction, he shifts his weight. In life, equipoise is almost never stationary because change is constant. Art can in fact be moving forces and tensions, as in Alexander Calder's mobile (Figs. 491, 492).

Balance is a strongly unifying principle, for its purpose is always to bring the parts of a composition into a well-ordered relationship. It has no qualitative aspect: nothing is suggested about the attractiveness or unattractiveness of what is in balance. This does not lessen its significance, however, for balance is such an important principle in life that human experience cannot tolerate its absence for long.

There are three basic types of balance: *symmetrical*, *asymmetrical*, and *radial*, each of which has its own distinctive characteristics and effects (Fig. 493). Much variety is possible within each type and much overlapping of effects among them.

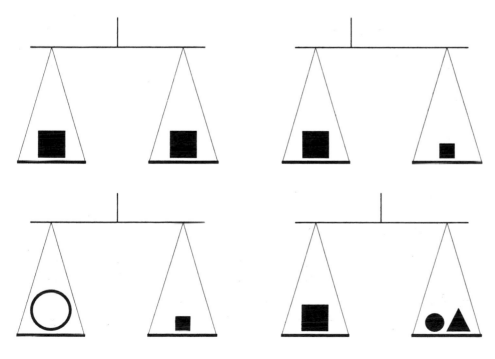

493. Symmetrical balance (*upper left*) is strictly defined as bilateral symmetry in which identical forms equidistant from the center equalize each other. In asymmetrical balance (*upper right*) forms that are not of the same visual weight are counterbalanced by being placed at unequal distances from the center. There are, however, intermediate steps (*lower left and right*) in which forms that are dissimilar except in visual weight are the same distance from the center.

Symmetrical Balance   Sometimes called *formal* or *passive* balance, symmetrical balance is the type in which one-half of the object is the mirror image of the other. It occurs in many aspects of nature, in many plants and animals, and in the human body when standing at attention and viewed from either front or back. Because of man's bilateral symmetry, many of the objects he uses—clothing, chairs, tables, and desks—are symmetrically balanced. Formal balance is a determining factor in classical architecture, of which the Governor's Palace in Williamsburg (Fig. 50), the Farnese Palace (Fig. 476), and the Parthenon (Fig. 592) are examples. It is not often found in painting or sculpture, although the *Buddha* (Fig. 452) and Duccio's *Maestà* (Fig. 494) show a high degree of symmetry.

As these examples reveal, formal balance *usually* gives a sense of stateliness, dignity, and formality. Generally, the effect is poised rather than dynamic, passive rather than active. But what about the Presbyterian Church in Stamford (Pl. 9, p. 79) or the Cathedral at Rheims (Figs. 603–608)? These too are symmetrical, but they are active rather than passive. The rising, pointed forms in both structures and the lively ornament on the cathedral activate these buildings. Symmetrical balance helps stabilize them. This demonstrates that every characteristic of an art object is affected by all of the others, and that there are exceptions to every generalization. Another factor clearly operates in architecture, however. A building may be absolutely symmetrical when viewed frontally, but asymmetrical when viewed laterally, as most large buildings generally are. The same is true of sculpture. Thus three-dimensional symmetrical art forms must meet the demands of both formal and informal balance.

When, therefore, can formal balance be effectively used? Essentially, it is when we wish to produce a reposeful, formal effect or when we wish to stabilize a design that might otherwise be hyperactive. Often, however, symmetrical balance is used merely because it is easy. Hanging a picture or placing a window or fireplace in the center of a wall automatically produces equilibrium, even though it may be uninteresting and unmotivated equilibrium. The absolutely centered picture, window, door, or fireplace is frequently neither attractive nor workable. Thus formal balance, useful as it may be, should be employed only when it is genuinely purposeful.

Eduardo MacEntyre's *Generative Painting* (Fig. 495) is composed of what are essentially two rows of thinly drawn circles placed in such a way that a new form is fortuitously generated. The spacial displacement of the composition is ambiguous, and various parts can be seen as either projecting or receding. The rounded shapes on the undifferentiated background seem to be suspended. The center and most conspicuous form tapers to a point. Here is a work using symmetry in which the effect is totally alien to the massive, classical balance of the Parthenon. Instead of dignified repose, there is lightness and buoyancy.

Asymmetrical Balance   An object in which the weights or attractions on each side are equated but not identical illustrates asymmetrical balance, also called *informal* or *active* balance. The side view of the human figure displays this type of equilibrium. In fact, when the figure is engaged in any kind of action the relationships are asymmetric. The principle of the lever, as used in physics, further illustrates the idea of informal balance: a man can lift a freight car if the proper leverage is supplied him. In symmetrical balance, however, a man must be equalized by another his own size.

Asymmetrical balance differs in its effect from symmetrical stability. It stirs us more quickly and more vigorously and arouses a curiosity to explore the object and find out what keeps it in equilibrium. It suggests movement, spontaneity, and sometimes casualness. Emphatic points are not so much dead stops in the design as pauses strategically located in a dynamic whole.

The majority of works illustrated in this chapter are asymmetric in their design, for clearly asymmetry offers the artist more opportunities for freedom. Superb design is apparent in Esteban Vicente's paper collage *Blue, Red, Black, and White*

opposite : 494. Duccio di Buoninsegna. *Maestà.* 1308–1311. Tempera on wood, 6′11″ × 13′10″. Cathedral Museum, Siena. The assured nobility of the Madonna and Child is signified in an almost exactly symmetrical composition. Repeated spherical forms and circular halos build up to the central figure.

right : 495. Eduardo A. MacEntyre. *Generative Painting : Black, Red, and Orange.* 1965. Oil on canvas, 5′5″ × 4′11¹/₄″. The Museum of Modern Art, New York (Inter-American Fund). Two rows of overlapping circles produce a strong central form.

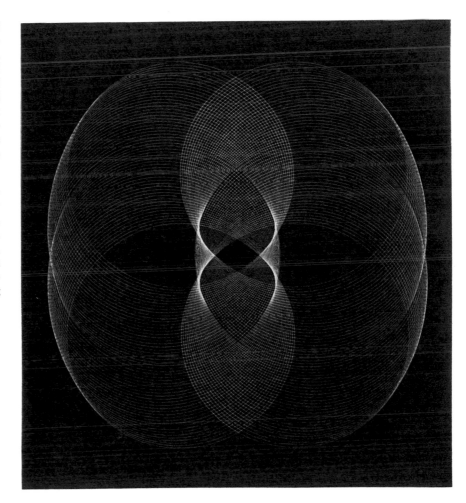

right : 496. Esteban Vicente. *Blue, Red, Black, and White*. 1961. Mixed media, 29 $^7/_8$ × 40 $^1/_4$″. The Museum of Modern Art, New York (given anonymously). The asymmetric balance, the rough-torn edges, and the singularity of each form of this collage of paper on cardboard give the appearance of spontaneity.

below : 497. The interior of the Fred I. Smith house (1968), with its carefully proportioned rectangular areas, gives the appearance of being a three-dimensional Mondrian painting (see Pl. 41). The exterior is shown in Pl. 4. Richard Meier, architect. (See also Figs. 38, 39.)

(Fig. 496). The large, irregular, dark form clearly dominates and establishes a major diagonal axis and a minor vertical one. The other forms support and oppose the dark major element in size, disposition, edge, and hue. The large form is exceptionally vigorous, with an edge that, although varied, remains consistently strong. There is no repetition here: each incident seems to be one of a kind. Clearly, however, there is emphasis, subordination, continuity, and balance, and the similarity of material effects a unity among the variety of shapes and directions. The work is suffused with a kind of unfettered freedom and spontaneity, as if it had "just happened"; yet the relationships are studied and basic.

Many art problems suggest informal balance. Note the advertisements in any magazine or those in Chapter 5. Very few are symmetrical, because advertisers know that an active design attracts and holds attention. Observe, too, that painting and sculpture depicting action, such as Duchamp's *Nude Descending a Staircase* (Pl. 44), or works expressing passion, such as the *Ecstasy of St. Theresa* (Fig. 466), are usually asymmetric. However, not all informally balanced art is highly activated; sometimes it is peacefully quiet, as in many domestic interiors. In modern homes that are planned for practical convenience, rooms, windows, and doors are seldom symmetrically located. In furniture arrangements designed for use and visual comfort rather than solely for beauty this is also true.

Figure 497 shows an interior of the Smith house in Darien, Connecticut, the exterior of which was illustrated in Chapter 1 (Pl. 4, p. 26). This beautifully designed room looks like a constructed painting by Piet Mondrian (Pl. 41, p. 351) with its precise, rectangular relationships. Just as informal balance can be used to depict action, attract attention, or convey strong emotion, it can also be used for efficiency and comfort.

Radial Balance   In radial balance the major parts radiate from a center like spokes in a wheel or the petals of a daisy or even the ridges on certain types of corals (Fig. 458). The center is thus a potential focal point, but it may or may not be emphasized. Usually there is a sense of circular movement. When symmetrical, the effect tends toward the formal, as it does in radial city plans (Fig. 67) or the rose windows in Gothic cathedrals (Figs. 603, 604). The designs on dinner plates are often radial (Fig. 388). Asymmetrical examples include expanding spirals and offcenter mobiles (Figs. 491, 492).

Conclusion

Through the principles of design works of art are organized to fulfill their intent and to communicate to the viewer. Emphasis, continuity, and balance deal only with the formal relationships in works of art, with the way in which the various elements are combined and arranged. Their purpose is to provide the coherence a work of art needs in order to convey its intent.

Principles of design are useful chiefly as critical tools, either by an observer in testing the formal qualities of a work, be it a building, a painting, or a piece of jewelry, or by an artist in judging the validity of a work in progress. An artist does not *apply* a design principle as he works. Rather, the organization emerges as the work develops. The artist may, in the process of creation, wish to review his work critically from time to time, to withdraw somewhat from it and examine what he has done with an objective eye. It is at such moments of removal and evaluation that the artist consciously or unconsciously uses the principles of organization as checks.

Principles of design are, of course, only vehicles for the intent of the artist. If his idea or message is trivial, no amount of good organization can make it significant. But without organization, consonant with purpose, a valid and profound idea will remain inconclusive and unconvincing.

Principles of design are enormously flexible generalizations that derive from the entire field of art and from nature. Their wide applicability is proof of their validity. They are not arbitrary in their derivation. Their use in art should be as organic and vital—and flexible—as in life and nature. When this occurs, the art that emerges and embodies them takes life and becomes meaningful.

The final example in this chapter demonstrate what may be maximum flexibility in the application of design principles. Robert Rauschenberg's *Revolver* (Fig. 498) is composed of a base in which rest five clear plastic discs, that can be revolved, hence the name of the work. On each of the discs various figurative and lettered patterns drawn from many sources have been printed. These include a photograph of a Classical temple, a large portion of Ingres' painting *The Turkish Bath,* and photographs of rockets and athletes. A number of words also appear, each with its own burden of meanings. This is a do-it-yourself composition; the discs can be rotated so that the images fall into an enormous range of combinations. There is freedom in time and space; images from the Classical period impinge on those from the space age, and the upside-down tennis player seems as weightless as an astronaut. Tastes in art vary, and what appeals to one person may well disappoint the next. So as to please everyone Rauschenberg here provides the means for each "user" to bring together a series of images and to create compositions that respond to his own individual sense of design. Another important factor behind this work, is its use of chance relationships, of randomness and spontaneity. In this age of conformity, compositions that are too tightly organized are suspect; freedom and openness seem more relevant. The Rauschenberg work embodies these values in an ingenious manner.

498. Robert Rauschenberg. *Revolver.* 1967. Mixed media, 6'6" × 6'5" × 2'1/2". Courtesy Leo Castelli Gallery, New York. The Plexiglas discs in this construction can be rotated independently to create a wide variety of compositions from the images on the discs.

499

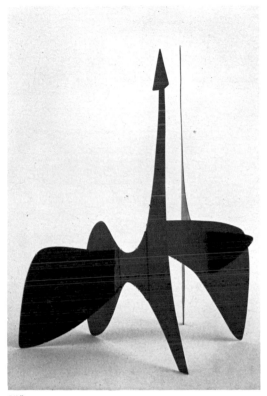

500

501

part **IV** Painting, Sculpture, and Architecture

overleaf :

top left : 499. Mark Rothko. *Number 10*. Oil on canvas, 7′6 ³/₈″ × 4′9 ¹/₈″.
The Museum of Modern Art, New York (gift of Philip C. Johnson).

top right : 500. Alexander Calder. Model for "*Teodelapio,*" *Spoleto*. 1962.
Painted sheet aluminum, 23 ³/₄ × 15 ¹/₄ × 15 ³/₄″.
The Museum of Modern Art, New York (gift of the artist).

below : 501. Lower Manhattan skyline, 1963.

502. Bridget Riley. *Movement in Squares*. 1962. Tempera. Arts
Council of Great Britain, London.

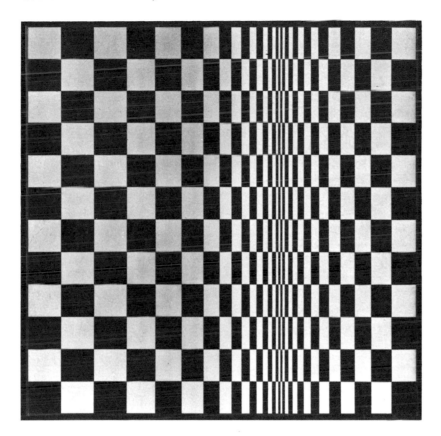

Introduction

The first three parts of this book reproduce many examples of painting, sculpture,
and architecture, for without frequent reference to these three major arts there
could be no valid discussion of human needs, materials, processes, and organization
insofar as they relate to art. Throughout history, painting, sculpture, and architecture have been vehicles for varied and profound expressions of man's thoughts and
feelings, for the development and use of his highest technical skills, and for the
exercise of his capacity for organization. In all justice, these forms have traditionally
been called the *fine arts*.

All of the arts embody and communicate feelings and ideas, but because they are
less affected by utilitarian considerations than are other forms, painting and sculpture
offer artists the greatest freedom for making in a direct way their most intense
statements and expressions. Thus, painting and sculpture are the artistic mediums for
conveying the inner needs and concerns of man, his ideals and aspirations, his fears
and frustrations. Throughout most of the history of art, however, painting and
sculpture have also been assigned utilitarian roles; they have been supported by and
been placed at the service of religion and the state. Painters and sculptors have from
time immemorial created murals and carvings for cathedrals and temples, for public
buildings and communal squares. Through their art they have instructed people in

the tenets and history of their religious beliefs and impressed on them the glories of the state and the wisdom and power of its rulers. They were seen as highly gifted craftsmen who had a clearly defined social role. The artist as an individual—painting, carving, and constructing alone and uncommissioned in his studio on work designed for no particular patron or location—is a phenomenon of modern times.

Today, most artists produce their works without reference to place or person. They hope for patrons or purchasers and for exhibitions in galleries and museums. However, for artists in general, certainly for the young ones, if and when acclaim and support occur, it is after their works have been created. The benefit of this is that in pursuit of their "own thing" artists enjoy the freedom of being responsible to no one but themselves; they work on what they please when they please. They can be as obscure, experimental, or revolutionary as they may wish. The interests of patron or sponsor are not their concern.

This freedom for artists occurs at a time when our culture has become extraordinarily complex and diversified. As a result of these factors, and others, the works of painters and sculptors have never in history been as mixed and varied in form, content, and materials as now, nor have they dealt with as broad a range of human, esthetic, and technical problems. It may be noted that when artists had patrons—the church, the state, or powerful personages—their work was generally executed as visual supplement to and illustration of the ideas and purposes of those patrons. Now, independent of patronage, artists are frequently strong social critics.

As long as the artist was in the service of a patron, whether public or private, his work was primarily public in character. For example, religious sculptures in a medieval cathedral were designed to instruct the faithful of the community in Christian virtues and the dogma of orthodox Christianity. They narrated in visual form the texts of the Old and New Testaments for a populace that was illiterate. In New Guinea, the ancestor poles and figures that sculptors create are for particular public ceremonies, and it is intended that their magical powers benefit all members of the community.

By contrast, we in recent times *expect* that the work of an important artist will at first be criticized and even rejected, and indeed this has been a reality of the artist's experience during the last two hundred years. A striking example is Vincent van Gogh, now regarded as one of the great masters of modern painting, who sold only two paintings in his lifetime. One may ask whether artists have alienated themselves from the public by being gratuitously obscure and by dealing with forms and ideas that have no relevance for present-day life. One might answer that quite the opposite is true. The creative artist is always contemporary, and it is his very involvement and direct confrontation with the issues of his time that make him appear ahead of and out of phase with his contemporaries in the general public. Later, often much later, when the common experience catches up with the artist's advanced vision, his work is accepted and praised, and its value acknowledged. But delayed acceptance means that for a period of time we are deprived of the illumination and intensification of life that artists through their works make possible for us. In another context, this is called the generation gap, here the cultural gap. In the age of science, we are still a long way from accepting the creative contemporary artist as an essential member of and primary contributor to our culture, despite the

opposite above : 503. George Sugarman. *Two-in-One.* 1966. Polychromed wood, 7′ × 11′6″. Courtesy Fischbach Gallery, New York.

opposite below : 504. Installation of paintings by Kenneth Noland. 1967. André Emmerich Gallery, New York.

505. Joern Utzon, architect; Ove Arup and Partners, consulting engineers. Opera House, Sydney, Australia. Scheduled completion date, 1969. Possibly the most complex design ever engineered into architecture, the Sydney Opera House exists by virtue of sophisticated and advanced developments in materials, processes, and computer science.

international acclaim and commercial success realized in recent years by a limited number of American artists.

In their great ingenuity and devotion to experimentation, painters and sculptors continue to create an astonishing array of expressions that delight, baffle, annoy, and stimulate us. They are breaking down the barriers between painting and sculpture as they produce works that in their forms and materials are impossible to classify as either. Artists are exploring new techniques and new substances. Painters are using cloth, papers, and actual objects as well as pigment; sculptors work more with a welding torch than with a chisel and, more often than not, with steel rather than stone.

In architecture also, diversity is characteristic of the contemporary scene, as our demands on structure become more varied and as the range of building materials and our knowledge of them increase. Architecture is basically utilitarian, for buildings are constructed only when they are sufficiently needed to pay the cost of their construction. Because large and complex structures such as churches, office buildings, law courts, schools, theaters, transportation terminals, and state houses are public in purpose and serve the needs of many people, much of our most ambitious architecture has a broad social basis that permits little of the distinctively personal quality of painting and sculpture. Furthermore, since in both construction and use such architecture involves many people, it is inevitable that the interests and ideals of the group are expressed in the buildings it sponsors. Gothic cathedrals, growing out of the Christian religion of the Middle Ages, dominated the lives of medieval men. In our century, towering skyscrapers in large American cities are evidence of the importance we attach to commerce, and each individual building has its own expressive qualities that are the architect's response to the plurality, often the puerility, of modern commercial taste.

Still, once the function and purpose of public architecture have been acknowledged, we must also cite the purely formal qualities of architecture. Even the most casual examination of Eero Saarinen's TWA Flight Center at Kennedy International Airport in New York (Fig. 616) will reveal that this structure is as much an enormous environmental sculpture as it is a functional gateway for airline passengers. Now, in the age of Pop culture, even the Empire State Building seems more like a giant piece of Pop sculpture than it does an office building, especially since its thirty-year-old engineering would render it somewhat obsolete in relation to current needs and expectations. Thus, architecture, like painting and sculpture, participates in the ambivalence distinctive of modern esthetic perception.

In this concluding part of *Art Today*, we look at painting, sculpture, and architecture from the points of view presented in the three preceding parts: expression of human needs and interests; materials and processes; and organization. Both contemporary and historic examples will be examined, but the emphasis will fall on recent productions. Historic arts reveal much about the character and times of the people who created them. In the same way, modern paintings, sculptures, and buildings tell us much about ourselves and the time in which we live.

15 Painting

Frank Stella's *Tuftonboro 1* (Pl. 45, p. 395; Fig. 506) is a recent work. Large in size and painted in strong, flat, uncompromising, tension-creating colors, it has no suggestion of atmosphere. There is no subject matter—only severe geometric shapes that carry few or no associations for the viewers. Stella is a leader in the development of what is called *Minimal Art,* a style that goes counter to most of the time-honored values we have come to associate with painting.

Most Western painting, particularly from the period of the Renaissance to the middle of the nineteenth century, is what can be considered *illusionistic*; that is, it creates an illusion of real people and objects in a rational space. All the abstract paintings of this century are *allusive*: although they distort and alter the appearance of the real world, they still allude to people or to things. Minimal Art is neither illusionistic nor allusive. It demands that it be accepted for itself.

In most paintings we feel the artist has chosen a subject and has made some comment about it that he submits to the viewer for his acceptance and enjoyment. By contrast, the Minimal artist wishes to create objects that are as real, and that speak to us as directly, as the objects with which we live. He does not comment or interpret; he confronts us with a shape or a form without handing us any ideas about it. He gives us no clues and makes no value judgments. Rather, he asks us to respond directly to the perceptual experience his work provides. In Minimal Art, to quote E. C. Goossen, "the new attitude has been turning art inside out: instead of perceptual experience being accepted as a means to an end, it has become an end in itself."

Because the artist does not "intervene" in these new works, they make particular demands on the viewer. Lacking clues from the artist to the proper responses he should have, he is thrown entirely on his own resources. The viewer thus confronts himself.

Two important aspects of *Tuftonboro I* that are not conveyed by the illustration and need comment are its colors and size. The colors, in the order of their values from dark to light, are a lustrous black, brilliant cardinal red, tan, and bright yellow, each separated from the other by a fine line of unpainted canvas (see Pl. 45). The colors, like the forms, are nonallusive. The physical size (over 8 feet high by 9 feet wide) is impressive, and the viewer feels a *presence*, a *confrontation*, which, if he is at all responsive, he cannot avoid. Giant scale is a characteristic of much painting and sculpture produced during recent decades, a quality bound up with the *role* of new art forms (Figs. 503, 504).

Here, then, is a movement that seems to fly in the face of accepted purposes and functions of art. It is typical of most developments in art in that they seem to react against commonly and currently held values. In spite of its revolutionary appearances, however, Minimal Art has developed quite reasonably out of the movements that preceded it. This indeed seems to be a characteristic of most new styles.

An anecdote about the American painter James McNeill Whistler might serve as an introduction to the thick press of the sublime and the ridiculous that generates the art we will review: Whistler was invited to a friend's home for dinner. He was then executing his now-famous paintings of London fogs (Fig. 507). Shortly after the painter arrived at his host's house another guest rushed up to him and exclaimed excitedly, "Mr. Whistler, I just crossed the Thames River, and it looked exactly

opposite: 506. Frank Stella. *Tuftonboro I.* Synthetic polymer paint on canvas, 8'3" × 9'1". 1966. Collection Mr. and Mrs. Victor W. Ganz, New York. (See also Pl. 45, p. 395, and p. ii.)

right: 507. James A. McNeill Whistler. *Old Battersea Bridge : Nocturne—Blue and Gold.* c. 1872. Oil on canvas, 26 1/4 × 19 3/4". Tate Gallery, London (by courtesy of the Trustees).

like one of your paintings!" Whistler smiled and replied, "Thank you, Madam. Nature is improving."

This is an amusing story about a painter who was also a remarkable wit, but it raises a basic point about painting. Whereas the usual assumption (however unthinking) is that in the forms, structure, and colors of his work the artist follows nature, Whistler is saying the reverse. We see in life that which the artist has chosen to portray. The artist, then, does not "hold a mirror up to nature" and attempt to make his pictures a reflection of the visible world; rather, he interprets his subjects and in this manner provides the spectator with new knowledge of the world about him.

Whistler makes clear in his response to his admirer that he is an artist whose paintings bear a close resemblance to nature and are thus, to a degree, illusionistic. Because painting has for most of its history been dominated by the use of subject matter to create illusions, let us continue our examination of painting by looking at two examples done in styles that can be considered illusionistic. This review can also provide a comparison with *Tuftonboro 1* and insights for understanding Stella's approach to that work.

A Cityscape and a Landscape

Edward Hopper, an American, painted *Early Sunday Morning* (Pl. 46, p. 396; Fig. 508) in 1930, and Vincent van Gogh, a Dutchman working in France, painted *Starry Night* (Pl. 47, p. 397; Fig. 509) in 1889. The paintings provide strong contrasts in subject and in treatment. Both depict commonly perceived subjects. The cityscape is an unpretentious stretch of small shops with living quarters above, a row of structures still typical of the inner core of many American cities; the landscape is dominated by a brilliant star-filled and moonlit sky. Hopper's subject is so commonplace that in daily life it is something we would scarcely notice; Van Gogh's subject is compelling for its own intrinsic beauty and grandeur. *Early Sunday Morning* is illumined by the clear, steady light of day; *Starry Night* evokes the mystery and awesomeness of the night. Both artists were faced with the necessity of transformation: Hopper, to take an ordinary and unattractive subject and make it a work of art; Van Gogh, to capture within the confines of a small canvas the great energies and vastness of a brilliant summer night.

Hopper's *Early Sunday Morning*

At first glance one might say that in *Early Sunday Morning* Hopper has done nothing to his subject but record it. Such a reaction, however, ignores the fact that even the simplest painting requires the artist to make many decisions. Hopper, first of all, had to determine what he wanted to paint. Among the questions he could have posed for himself are these: Should the subject, once chosen, be given a vertical or horizontal format? Will the painting be low key or high key in its emotional and color values? If it is a group of buildings, will people be included? How much space will be given to sky, to foreground? These questions, and many others, must be answered in some way before work is begun. Sometimes, small sketches are made to assist in arriving at decisions. It is essential, of course, that the artist have some kind of feeling about his subject if he is to produce a painting of vitality; the attraction cannot be half-hearted or desultory. One might then ask why Hopper chose such an ordinary subject. Rather than answer that question directly, let us look closely at the picture he produced and some of its features.

508. Edward Hopper. *Early Sunday Morning*. 1930. Oil on canvas, 2'11" × 5'. Whitney Museum of American Art, New York. (See also Pl. 46, p. 396.)

The first thing we note about *Early Sunday Morning* is its horizontality. The shape of the entire picture reinforces the shape of its major feature, the building. Horizontal lines, of course, suggest repose. This effect is entirely in keeping with the title, for Sunday morning, in contrast to other mornings of the week, is a time when the practical affairs of life are temporarily in abeyance, when one can enjoy the luxury of sleeping past the usual rising time, when a general air of peace and quietude is most likely to prevail. The last point is especially pertinent here, for this is an area of shops and stores, where on weekdays most people would be up and about their business.

The composition of the picture is essentially a series of horizontal bands running lengthwise across the painting. The narrow top band, the sky, extends the width of the picture, unbroken except by a small dark rectangle at the right that suggests a taller (and newer?) building nearby. The bottom, and more narrow, rectangle is bisected by the line of the curb, and the area depicting the sidewalk is broken by the water plug, the barber pole, and long early-morning shadows. The major rectangular form, the building, is also bisected by an unbroken line dividing the first floor from the second. Most apparent, however, is the division of the building itself into a host of predominantly vertical rectangular shapes that serve as foils for the major horizontal areas. The second-story windows, in a two-two, three three grouping, alternate with the cornice brackets, the latter occurring in pairs at two points. On the ground floor, in somewhat larger scale, the openings are more varied, being both doors and windows. There is a beguiling variance in their treatment, differences in structural materials, in size and disposition of lettering, and in the kinds of awnings, window shades, and curtains that are used. But particularly basic to the unity of this picture is the fact that for all the variation confronting us, the major forms and subforms are all either long narrow or nearly square rectangles. Observe the second and third windows from the right edge of the painting. They are tall and slender in shape, but each is broken into three rectangles that vary from narrow to almost square, and at the bottom and top of each, the sill and the lintel form two more narrow rectangles. These rectangular forms run like leitmotifs throughout the picture, and their variety and pervasiveness contribute to the structural richness of the composition.

Hopper has introduced two gentle yet important contrasts into the picture. Opposing the basic rectangular forms are a number of circular and curved ones—

the water plug, the barber pole, the three little metal forms on the ledge in front of the second-story windows, the scallops on the awnings. The other contrast is in direction. There are two systems of diagonals, one created by the shadows cast by the three projecting signs, the other by the shadows projected into the openings on the street floor and the shadows from the brackets. The placement of the water plug and barber pole also establishes an important diagonal movement. The painting abounds in other subtleties, enough to reward the viewer for careful and systematic study.

With the identification of the subject never in doubt, *Early Sunday Morning* is readily classifiable as realistic. But, quite apart from the literalness of the subject matter, the painting simply exudes overtones that radiate from Hopper's treatment of it. The artist has saturated the building with a sense of being lived and worked in. He comments on the idiosyncracies of people that give life its quality, its pace, texture, and color. Along with the general air of quiet and lassitude in the painting, there is a feeling of the strain and fatigue of life, perhaps even a touch of the melancholy. There is also a strong suggestion of mystery and uncertainty, which are most evident in the long shadow in the middle of the sidewalk extending from one side of the painting to the other. We have no hint of what might be casting the shadow, but we do note that it does not parallel the direction of the other shadows. This leaves us ignorant of both the light source and the shadow-casting object that give form to one of the purest and most striking lines in the entire composition.

Hopper, unlike Stella, has come between the observers and the painting to point out things that he feels are important and to offer his observation for their review and understanding. Without portraying people, Hopper has produced a human document.

Van Gogh's *Starry Night*

By contrast, *Starry Night* (Pl. 47, p. 397; Fig. 509) impresses us by its tremendous vitality and sense of movement; a restless energy pervades the canvas. The universe is portrayed as a system of mighty and tremendous forces, which make the works of man, typified by the church and the houses, appear static and inconsequential. It is to the might of nature, to the natural laws that order the stars and determine the forms of hills and the growth patterns of trees that Van Gogh's art is responding.

We have all experienced starry nights in which we feel the gigantic forces of nature and realize ourselves as only tiny parts of a universe that is awesome in its magnitude and magnificence. It is these feelings that Van Gogh has stated, and he accepted the fact that the magic of a starlit night can no more be portrayed by literal painting than by literal photography. To convey his ideas he distorted sizes and shapes. Movements of light pattern the sky with all the energy and much of the form of nebulas; individual stars in their brilliance take on tremendous size (compare them with the buildings); the moon, usually the dominant feature of the night sky, is given a lesser place in this firmament. The giant cypress tree on the picture's frontal plane—also a part of nature—is filled with the same restless energy as the sky. The small village in the foreground seems secure and protected, and both the repose of the forms of the buildings and the stability of their treatment are in sharp contrast to the almost explosive vigor in the rest of the picture. *Starry Night* is a romantic subject, romantically portrayed, highly emotional both in content and in the means used to convey its ideas. It is the work of an individual who felt deeply and intensely the wonder and the awesomeness of nature.

In looking at *Starry Night*, one is immediately conscious of Van Gogh's technique, because it is in large part responsible for the dynamic quality of the canvas.

Every stroke is visible, each is part of the larger forms that make up the composition. The areas occupied by sky and ground are generally horizontal, as are the lesser forms within them. Opposing these, both in direction and value, is the form of the cypress tree (with a faint echo in the church spire). Its startling darkness adds brilliance and luminosity to the sky; its verticality makes the earth forms appear more stable and placid. We have already commented on the tree's restless quality, which serves as a link between it and the sky, giving the two a basis of unity even though in direction, hue, and value they are drastically opposed.

It is within the sky, and properly so, that the most compelling and unusual forms are found. Almost directly in the center are two large, interlocking spiral shapes (with a lesser one slightly below and to the right) that are part of a great movement entering the picture at the left and climaxing in the spirals. The spiral, with its constantly changing direction and speed, is an admirable form for producing a sense of movement and energy. Filling the rest of the sky are the stars and the moon, all burning with a terrible intensity. These are all circular, and they appear restless and mobile. The erratic forms hanging in the sky are in stunning contrast to the stable, rectangular solids of the buildings. The hills, with their gently rounded forms, serve as transition between ground and sky. In color, the hot, piercing yellow of the moon and stars is in strong opposition to the cool greens and blues in the tree, land, and sky.

There is another compositional arrangement that should be observed, one based on a system of diagonals. A strong line is established along the lower right edges of the cypress tree extending generally to the upper left-hand corner. Note in how many places this direction is repeated in the forms of the building, the ground, and the sky. These diagonals are opposed by other diagonals set at right angles to them, structural lines that appear most sharply in the contours defining the tops of the hills and that are confirmed in other parts of the composition. The picture involves horizontals, verticals, opposing diagonals, circles, spirals, rectangles, and triangles, all skillfully interwoven and further unified by the bold technique.

Starry Night is an example of Expressionism, a kind of art that springs from the emotional involvement of the artist with some aspect of the subject. Expressionist works are charged with the energy of particularized passions. They are never detached

509. Vincent van Gogh. *Starry Night*. 1889. Oil on canvas, 29 × 36 ¹/₄″. The Museum of Modern Art, New York (Lillie P. Bliss Bequest). (See also Pl. 47, p. 397.)

or objective but rather are filled with emphases and distortions of a highly subjective character. In the hands of a person with little taste or discipline, expressionistic art can be tawdry and banal. Van Gogh, however, with his skill in both composition and technique, was able to control his explosive visions and give coherence to forms of fantastic energy.

Early Sunday Morning and *Starry Night* are examples of differing facets of modern painting. One is a calm and reasoned yet compassionate portrayal of an ordinary feature of the American urban environment. The other is intensely emotional, a passionate outpouring in response to a spectacular display of natural phenomena. Although Hopper has remained rather close to the appearance of his subject, he was consciously discriminating in his selection of what he would portray and of the conditions under which he would present it to us. Van Gogh, by contrast, went far beyond the appearance of his subject, and his painting has become a more personal and subjective statement. Both men, by quite different means, have produced works of compelling artistry and power.

The Field of Painting

The paintings by Hopper and Van Gogh make it clear that, as was discussed in Part I (and as we shall consider further in this section), the *form* of a work of art grows out of expression. Painters vary widely in what they want to *say*; therefore, they make use of widely divergent means and forms in their expressions. Let us look now at some general considerations.

Historically, painting has been a representational art, although the range of expression within representational statements is great indeed. Verisimilitude, of course, is never a criterion of excellence: we must look instead for factors in which esthetic criteria can reside, such as formal organization and color. With the development of photography, a medium now in use for well over a hundred years, the painter has been liberated from the necessity of recording and reporting, which were among his chief responsibilities prior to the perfection of the camera. The artist is now free for other kinds of exploration, and he has used his new freedom and responsibility well. Some artists, as we shall see, employ photographs as images in their pictures. Thus, technology has released artists to explore new areas of expression and at the same time provided a new tool for their experimentations.

Today, as always, painters deal with the problems or aspects of life that they see as important. They explore the physical and spiritual world in which we live and devise ways to state their discoveries. Sometimes they direct us to aspects of nature

510. Ben Shahn. *Reconstruction.* 1945. Tempera on pressboard, 26 × 39″. Whitney Museum of American Art, New York.

that we, unnoticing, have passed by. Painters may experiment with mechanized forms and thus provide a machine esthetic; they may investigate space and movement and thereby be as much a part of the space age as any scientist. They may also be involved with feelings and sensations and discard all subject matter. And painters may express the fears, anxieties, and frustrations of the world, comment on social injustice, or reaffirm basic human dignity (Fig. 510). In many varied and wondrous ways, painters offer vital insights into the condition of man and his relation to the world.

In the quickening tempos of the twentieth century, in the atmosphere of accelerating change and expanded pluralism, painters, very much like scientists, have become the vanguard of the experimentalist and innovatory experience of modern life. Indeed, it is their very eagerness to change and innovate that makes the work of contemporary painters relevant for its time. As a result, we the spectators are the beneficiaries of a range of artistic expression, produced for our pleasure and enlightenment, that is unparalleled by the art of any period. Very often the manifestations of heightened, advanced artistic vision baffle and annoy us—perfectly reasonable responses to new and intensely imagined art, but not justification for thoughtless dismissal.

One striking aspect of change in twentieth-century culture is the weakening of traditional barriers, among social classes, between the sexes, within fields of learning, and in institutions and ideas. The dissolution of established structures is symptomatic of a cultural transition that leads inevitably to new outlooks and systems of organization in all areas of human behavior. The disappearance of barriers is nowhere more apparent than in the fields under discussion here.

One has only to look at the history of art to realize that man's ideas and feelings, his beliefs and concerns are molded by the kind of world in which he lives. The artist in any culture searches for answers to the questions of his age. The artists of Greece directed themselves to a quest for the ideal. The craftsmen and the builders of the Middle Ages were searching for salvation through the mystical experience of religion. The cultural ambience of any period provides a matrix for the expressive content of its art. Contemporary painters, no less than those of other periods, are confronting and in their own ways dealing with the multiplicity of problems in modern life. In a diverse age, diversity of expression is a notable feature of today's paintings.

The range of materials available to the artist has been enormously increased. Not only can he select from among many new kinds of pigments and surfaces for his painting, but, in addition, he has incorporated into his work a plethora of materials not traditionally used in painting—sand, stones, torn paper, wood, found objects of all sorts, and the devices of industry and technology. Modern paintings often include none of the materials we usually associate with panels and canvases. And as the range of materials expands, so do the possibilities for esthetic statement.

Finally, the painter concerns himself with expressing his idea in and with the materials he is using. In applying materials of any sort, the artist immediately becomes involved with the visual elements and with the principles of organization. His method of working may be deliberate and controlled, spontaneous and impulsive, or automatic and free of conscious manipulation. But whatever his means of working, the result can be evaluated in terms of organization.

Expression: Subject Matter and Content

Many people are afraid to respond to a painting or to express an opinion about it. "Am I having the 'proper' reaction?" "Is this the way I am 'supposed' to feel when I look at this painting?" "This picture does not affect me—perhaps I have no esthetic sensibilities." These are all-too-typical reactions.

In many respects, paintings are like people: They are richly varied, and each has a distinct personality. They can be serious, profound, trivial, humorous, tragic, upsetting, or have any one of a wide range of characteristics that could also be applied to people. In meeting someone, you react to his behavior traits, to his speech, his clothes, his ideas, and to his responses to situations. On such bases you form your opinion: You like him; you dislike him; you are neutral; you wish to withhold judgment until you have seen him again. Sometimes on further acquaintance you reverse your opinion: A person toward whom you were neutral may become a valued friend as various aspects of his personality are slowly revealed; another who at first seemed to possess charm and graciousness may before long seem superficial and inept.

Carrying further the analogy of pictures and people, we may state a few generalizations. First, the cultivation of paintings and persons repays one in abundant measure, because in the process new and richer aspects of both are revealed. A profound picture can in a short space of time no more reveal all that it has to offer than can a profound individual. In fact, the real depths of either are never fully plumbed; hence their continued appeal. Second, we have something in common with all people and with all pictures; the bases exist for an effective and growing relationship between us and both people and paintings. The matter of *liking* the individual picture or the specific person is not necessarily relevant. And last, each spectator has his own reactions. Do not fear your own! Do not be afraid either of suspending judgment until you have broader bases for intelligent response than are possible in an initial encounter. Do not be afraid to modify your reactions either, for only through a revision of attitudes and understandings can growth take place. The American artist Robert Rauschenberg has stated these points most emphatically: "If you do not change your mind about something when you confront a picture you have not seen before, you are either a stubborn fool or the painting is not very good."

We now turn to two more paintings which we will scrutinize closely. The subject matter is the same in both—people—but they differ widely in content. As with the Hopper and the Van Gogh, we can compare divergent treatments. In discussing them we will focus on such questions as: What is the general effect of the picture? What is the artist trying to "say"? What means has he used to communicate his idea?

Two Paintings of People

In his picture *American Gothic* (Fig. 511), Grant Wood left no doubt about what he was painting. It is a portrait of an American farmer and his wife against their Gothic Revival farmhouse and one of their barns. It is a picture of two people who, to the artist, typified the Midwest American farm folk of their time. The couple appear severe but not unkind, hardworking and thrifty, clean and unpretentious. There is much evidence of pride in their well-tended farm. The farmer grasps his pitchfork as a king would hold a scepter, the expression of his wife implies a humorless concern for her neatly kept home, an image of pride reinforced by the thriving house plants, the living room shades drawn to keep the rug from fading, and the lace curtains in the bedroom.

Yet for all its unpretentiousness, the composition is artfully organized and unified. It is generally triangular and stable; the two figures are held together, pictorially, by the gable and the porch roof. The area between the two heads is given importance by the dark windows, and they too take on a triangular form. The pitchfork serves as a symbol in the picture, and its characteristic form is presented in a number of ingenious

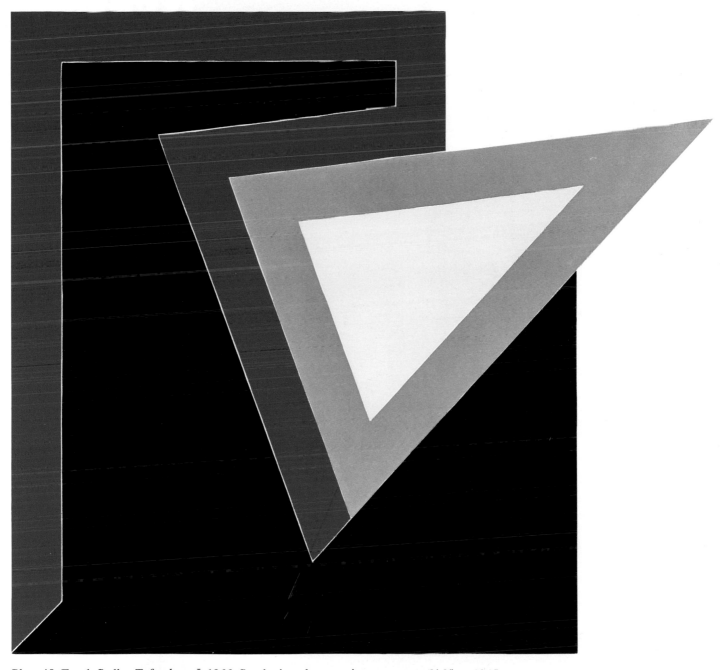

Plate 45, Frank Stella. *Tuftonboro I*. 1966. Synthetic polymer paint on canvas, 8′ 3″ × 9′ 1″.
Collection Mr. and Mrs. Victor W. Ganz, New York. (See also Fig. 506.)

Plate 48. Pablo Picasso. *Girl before a Mirror*. March, 1932. Oil on canvas, 5′ 3 ³/₄″ × 4′ 3 ¹/₄″.
The Museum of Modern Art, New York (gift of Mrs. Simon Guggenheim).

511. Grant Wood. *American Gothic.* 1930. Oil on canvas, 29 ⁷/₈ × 25″. Art Institute of Chicago (Friends of American Art Collection).

variations: in the stitching on the front of the man's overalls; in the hand grasping the pitchfork handle; in the vertical stalks of the plant on the porch to the left; and, somewhat more modified, in the tracery of the windows, the joint lines of the sheet-metal roofs, and the pleating on the man's shirt. The pitchfork, in addition, strikes a note of thin verticality, echoed in the variations just cited and the vertical siding of the house and barn. These linear, angular, vertical forms are associated with the man. Opposed to these are the rounded forms found mainly on the left, or woman's side, of the picture. Note the softly curved lines and forms that appear in her dress and apron and in the cameo she wears. In the background behind the woman, next to the plant with the forked canes, are begonia plants whose leaves repeat the shape of her cameo. The man stands in front of the barn, the woman in front of the kitchen, and the living and bedroom areas are between them. The man standing slightly ahead of the woman tells us something of their personal relationship.

Here is a skillful painting of two persons that is rendered with realism and composed with subtlety. It presents a specific situation, at a particular time, and in a definite place.

Girl before a Mirror (Pl. 48) does not attempt to depict a particular person with fidelity. The subject is not someone we could recognize, because no one has ever looked like that. What, then, has the painter, Pablo Picasso, done?

This is clearly a picture of great complexity. It is easy to identify the major elements in the composition—the girl, the mirror, and her reflection. But we note that the girl reflected in the mirror is quite different from the one looking into it. We can see at once that Picasso is not painting surface appearances; in fact, in this picture they interest him little. Other ideas are attracting him here.

The total picture is bold and vigorous in treatment, rich and sumptuous in color. The composition is cut into two almost equal parts by the edge of the mirror, but the arm of the girl, as it reaches across, connects the two halves. The figure, its reflection, and the mirror are composed primarily of curved and circular forms that in considerable variety are displayed handsomely throughout the composition. (The use of

curved forms to convey feminine qualities is thus a device used by both Wood and Picasso, a basic similarity that lies beneath the surface differences.) The girl and her reflection are painted generally in cool hues of low intensity with a few touches of warm color. The color is thus in keeping with the soft and nonaggressive character of the forms. By contrast, the background is made up of vigorous diagonals painted mostly in brilliant reds and yellows, colors that are both hot and advancing. This presents us with a visual paradox: The soft and recessive major forms appear against a harsh and aggressive background. But there are aspects that the figure, the reflection and the background have in common: Some straight lines and warm colors appear in the figure and its reflection; a small circular form is the central element in the background pattern; and green in small amounts is used throughout the picture. The variations in which these relations occur are many. Note, for example, the variations and dispositions of the circular forms in the two figures (head, eye, breast, abdomen, buttocks) and the subtle changes worked on the green in the background.

The figure and its reflection are the dominating elements of the composition, and they are "simultaneously clothed, nude, and X-rayed." On the left the head is shown as a full circle, and within it we see both a profile and full-face view. This head, with its full, bold forms, is serene and outgoing in its effect. In the mirrored head the profile is more dominant, and the effect is one of introspection and withdrawal—an impression suggested chiefly by the sunken and heavily shaded eye as well as by the color. It is as if the young girl were looking into rather than at herself. The mirror is, therefore, given another connotation.

In *Girl before a Mirror* Picasso's intent was very different from Wood's. He has shown us that aspects of people other than their surface appearances may provide the content of a painting. By combining different views, which suggest not only what he sees but also what he knows, by invoking many reactions about mental states as well as physical appearances, Picasso has added new dimensions to pictorial presentation. The painting is a powerful work of art with strong forms and rich colors, oppositions and harmonies, coherence along with contrast and variety.

American Gothic and *Girl before a Mirror* were painted within two years of each other, in 1930 and 1932 respectively, and they illustrate two among the many trends

in twentieth-century painting. People are the subject matter in both, but the content is markedly dissimilar. Wood's painting is a literal, factual document of two Iowans in front of their house and barn. Picasso's painting is an imaginative and inventive portrayal of many physical and psychic attributes of a young girl. Whereas *American Gothic* is specific, *Girl before a Mirror* is generalized. Another way of saying this is to refer to the one as *realistic* and to the other as *abstract*, the latter term meaning that essentials of the subject are portrayed rather than surface appearances.

The Man behind the Easel

Look at the photograph and three portraits of Maria Lani (Figs. 512–515) and the four portrayals of Marilyn Monroe (Figs. 516–519). In each group of works, the subject was identical, yet the interpretations differ markedly.

At the time Maria Lani's portraits were painted (in the late 1920s), the subject was an actress of great talent and beauty. She lived in Paris, where a number of artists either painted or modeled her remarkable head. It has several distinguishing characteristics: the lovely triangular shape of the face, the large lustrous eyes and heavy eyelids, the strongly arched eyebrows, the wide, full mouth, the general amplitude of form. All these combine to make a head that is handsome and distinguished. Hers is a beauty of structure and form; it is not superficial or cosmetic.

The three portraits of Maria Lani are sharply different, and they are at the same time very much alike in that they resemble the subject. All three artists chose a three-quarter view; all have taken note of the characteristic shape of her face, of the wide forehead tapering to the full chin, and of the heavy-lidded eyes. Yet the differences are even more striking than the similarities. These three portraits were done by Henri Matisse, Georges Rouault, and Chaim Soutine, all of whom are important figures in twentieth-century art. In the Matisse, done with the simplest of means, we see a person who is alert, gay, and charming. As portrayed by Rouault, she is tragic, her face a mask, the eyes large and unseeing, but with forms that are full and rounded. The Soutine is generally somber, and the expressionistic elongation and distortion of her head give us a characterization that is tense, ascetic, and neurotic.

It so happens that the particular character of each of these paintings is like that of the major works of the three artists. We can only conclude that Matisse brought to the subjects he painted a gay and cheerful view, that Rouault's was grave and tragic, Soutine's moody and introverted. Artists, we may say, interpret their subjects in terms of their general outlook and personalities. The subject—whatever or whoever it may be—contributes something of itself to the appearance of the finished work, but in the end it is the artist's own vision that predominates over the subject matter.

Marilyn Monroe was one of the most popular motion picture stars of all time. Voluptuously beautiful, she was a fabulous figure who became still more legendary— virtually mythic—after her suicide in 1962. In an age of world-wide film distribution and electronic media, she was a sex goddess to millions of people throughout the world. The epitome of the glamorized movie queen—sought after, adored, idolized, and pampered—she was also a tragic figure, quite possibly driven to her death by the relentless pressure of fame and publicity. It is only natural that artists should be attracted to Marilyn Monroe as a subject, symbolizing as she did so many aspects and conflicts of our culture. While still alive, she was portrayed by a number of artists, and after her death a great many more painters took her image as their subject. The four portraits reproduced here are by Mimmo Rotella, Willem de Kooning, Andy Warhol, and James Rosenquist (Figs. 516–519). The differences among these portrayals are even more striking than those exhibited by the characterizations of Maria Lani.

The Rotella is a *décollage*, a composition made by the removal of material. Parts of a large poster advertising a Marilyn Monroe movie have been torn away to reveal fragments of other advertisements. We are presented with an alluring photographic image of the star along with lacerated and torn-edge forms. What is exposed is texturally interesting but formless and chaotic. The attractiveness of the image is heightened and made poignant by the ragged paper ends and the rough

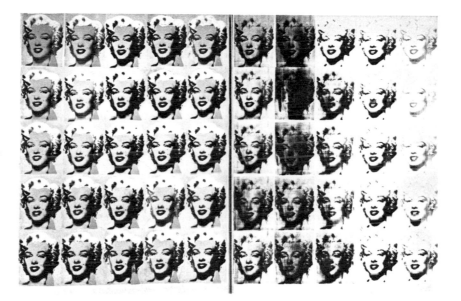

opposite left : 516. Mimmo Rotella. *Marilyn.* 1963–1964. Décollage, 4′5″ × 3′1 ¹/₂″, Courtesy Sidney Janis Gallery, New York.

opposite right : 517. Willem de Kooning. *Marilyn Monroe.* 1954. Oil on canvas, 4′2″ × 2′6″. Collection Mr. and Mrs. Roy Newberger, New York.

above : 518. Andy Warhol. *Marilyn Monroe.* 1962. Serigraph diptych, 4′4″ × 4′9″ each panel. Collection Mr. and Mrs. Burton Tremaine, Meridan, Conn.

left : 519. James Rosenquist. *Marilyn Monroe.* 1962. Oil on canvas, 7′9″ × 6′. Collection Mr. and Mrs. Sidney Janis, New York.

textures that surround it. Rotella seems to suggest here that a film star's success is indeed a fragile thing, a thin covering over many griefs and pressures.

De Kooning, a leading figure in the Abstract Expressionist movement, has executed a famous series of paintings featuring women, of which this portrait of Miss Monroe is one. Identification of the subject is made possible primarily through the title, and creating more than the slightest resemblance to her was clearly not his intention. This painting, and others in the series, is characterized by an almost savage application of paint. As in the Van Gogh landscape, all the brush strokes are visible, but whereas Van Gogh caused brushwork to clarify form and organization, de Kooning seems to have used his brush to attack and break up the form. The figure is lacerated, and there is no sharp differentiation between it and the background. One senses a feeling of struggle against dissolution, of identity being lost in its dynamic, volatile surroundings. The picture is overpowering in its brutal energy.

Warhol, employing a recently developed technique, duplicated a photograph of Miss Monroe by means of the silk-screen process. We have not one picture of her but fifty, twenty-five on each half of the diptych. The frequent repetition of the image is clearly derived from mass media, and we get the suggestion not only of their power but the inevitable vulgarization of what they deal with. This, as well as the Rotella portrait, is an example of Pop Art, a style that has embraced the forms of popular culture, such as comics, Coke bottles, beer cans, Green Stamps, old clothes, and hamburgers, and has viewed them with combined fascination and disgust.

Rosenquist is also a Pop artist. In a style reminiscent of billboards he makes use of a number of juxtaposed images. The various parts of the painting have the tantalizing character of motion picture closeups. Several of them are inverted, and the bits of lettering create a tension with the fragments of the human image as we search out each fragment separately. The details are inviting to the viewer, yet they are scrappy and disjointed.

The portraits of Marilyn Monroe even more than those of Maria Lani make clear the extent to which artists impose their attitudes on the subjects they choose. They have a view of life to which they apply their esthetic sensibilities. They give us, the observers of their work, a way of examining our world and of reacting to it. What the artist does adds new dimensions to our experiences or deepens the vision we already possess. It is the man behind the easel, the artist, who guides and directs the course of art. He is formed, in part, by the world he lives in, but he both forms and and transforms the world by his work.

The contrast in the two sets of portraits also underscores a major change that occurred in painting during the forty-year interval separating them. These seven works cannot, of course, typify all that has transpired during that time, but they are sufficiently representative to allow some generalization. The chief difference between the two groups is the attitude toward the subject matter. In the earlier portraits, it was clear that despite wide variations in style the sitter was central to the picture. In the more recent group, the subject becomes a peg on which the artist hangs his point of view. The approach is less specifically humanistic in that the concern is more for broad social issues than for individual people. The artists are even more diversified in their methods of statement. The differences may be in degree rather than kind, but they are real and striking. Our new art is indeed new.

Materials and Processes in Painting: Traditional Mediums

What the painter wishes to say in his work determines not only his choice of subject, but also his choice of medium and the way he uses it. Each medium exerts a pronounced effect on the finished product, yet each responds to varied and individual treatment. The painter must have an intimate knowledge of the qualities and characteristics of the medium he chooses, for it is only by learning to control and exploit them that he can cause materials to serve his purpose.

Despite the great variety of results that artists obtain in their paintings, the mediums they use are few in number. Until recently, all paintings could be classified under three main headings: oil, watercolor, and fresco.

Painting in Oil

Ever since oil paints were developed around the beginning of the fifteenth century, painters have used them more frequently than any other medium. They have many advantages. Oils offer an enormous range of hues, values, and intensities; they lend themselves to extraordinarily varied handling; they can be worked and reworked many times; and they are durable.

In *View of Toledo* (Fig. 520), El Greco utilized the potentialities of oils to achieve in a vivid and dramatic manner his monumental conception of landscape. Within the forms of the painting we can see how the artist has used the medium to achieve a wide range of effects. The ominous sky has been rendered in great, sweeping passages of color that are in sharp contrast to the fine detail of the buildings. In the lower left, the medium has been applied in small areas of varying color and value to describe the leafy details of trees. These again form a contrast with the feathery, flamelike foliage to the right, where the colors have been subtly blended with the brush. The artist's blending of pigment is also strikingly apparent in the swelling ground forms toward the upper right, where gradation of color and tone gives the effect of massive solidity. Through a masterly use of the medium, El Greco created a stunning array of effects in color and value, form and texture, all assimilated by artistic genius into a unified whole.

521. Claude Monet. *Sunflowers.* 1881. Oil on canvas, 39 3/4 × 32″. The Metropolitan Museum of Art, New York (H. O. Havemeyer Collection, bequest of Mrs. H. O. Havemeyer, 1929).

In looking at *View of Toledo*, we are barely conscious of the paint *as paint*. It has been applied to make a relatively smooth surface and used to simulate the colors and textures of the forms depicted. However, as we examine *Sunflowers* by Claude Monet (Fig. 521) we are immediately conscious of the paint itself and the way it has been applied to the canvas. The individual brush strokes are clearly visible, and the texture they create becomes, in itself, a major ingredient of the work. This is an Impressionist painting, one in which the *impression* of a scene was sought rather than detailed description. The ultimate aim of the Impressionists was to achieve a greater reality in their art, the kind of reality the eye itself would perceive, not a record of what the mind would know to exist. Even in a black-and-white reproduction it is clear that the artist has used "broken" color. Each surface is painted with independent strokes of varying hues that "mix" in the eye of the observer. The petals of the flowers have, for example, received their very form from the thick, buttery strokes of yellow, orange, and red pigment. The background is made shimmering and luminous by the juxtaposed patches of cool and warm hues. Impressionist paintings are undisguised celebrations of the splendor of nature. Curiously, when they first exhibited their works, the Impressionists were accused being inept technicians!

In de Kooning's painting of Marilyn Monroe, there is even greater concern with how the pigment is applied. In the Monet we "discover" that a leaf has been painted with strokes of pigment; in the de Kooning we do the reverse. We see the handling first. We note such things as the vigor of the brushwork, the texture left by the strokes, the splash of pigment made by heavily loaded brushes struck against the canvas. These compel our attention. Obviously the medium has been exploited as a source of pleasure. We are almost a witness to the act of painting, for every step of the painting process is there to be seen. *Action painting*, of which this is an example, is one aspect of a long sequence of developments in which artistic interest increasingly has been directed toward the qualities of medium and its potential for expression, painterly or otherwise.

The Process There is no limit to the ways in which oil pigments can be handled, and in no other paint medium is it possible to get a wider range of effects. The pigment can be applied in separate strokes, in thick and heavy opaque masses, or in washes of almost watercolor transparency. Variations and nuances of color and subtle modeling of form are restricted only by the painter's ingenuity and skill. Another characteristic is also of considerable importance. In watercolor painting the artist begins with white paper to which he applies color, and each touch of pigment darkens the paper. Thus, unless opaque white pigment is added to watercolor, the painter necessarily works from light to dark. The same is true of fresco. In oil painting, however, it is possible to work either from light to dark or from dark to light because, as typically used, oil paint is opaque enough to cover what is beneath it.

In working with oils the artist needs a suitable surface on which to paint—one that will receive the paint freely and yet not absorb it, that can withstand temperature changes and not crack the pigment on it. Canvas is the most widely used support, although wood, paper, and metal have been used. Many of the great paintings up to the time of the Renaissance were painted on wood, but the lightness, cheapness, and flexibility of good hemp for linen canvas have made painting on wood a rare practice. Recently, there has been an increased use of hard-pressed wall boards, as well as other materials, for oil paintings.

Pigments Colors come from many sources: minerals, vegetable matters, coal tars, and other chemical combinations. These are ground until the grains are extremely fine; then they are mixed with oil (linseed usually) and sometimes with wax to bring them to a suitable consistency. For oil painting the pigments are mixed on the palette with oil and turpentine to whatever degree of thinness the painter may wish. Colors vary in their permanence. Some, particularly earth pigments, never fade; others, including several very desirable ones, are quite impermanent. Oil pigments dry quite slowly and over a long period of years tend to darken in color as the oil yellows.

Some painters do not use brushes but apply their pigments with a palette knife or with other tools, or directly from the tube or can. In this way the artist can apply his paint thickly and produce a bold, textural effect. *One* (Fig. 546) displays the "action" style that Jackson Pollock developed by placing his canvas on the floor and pouring liquid pigment on it. The effect he achieved derived from the fluid quality of the paint as it fell on the canvas. But even with the apparent freedom of this technique the artist exerted many controls, over color, direction, and thickness of paint, to cite only a few. In fact, Pollock's technique was so fully seasoned that, like Van Gogh, he has had no successful imitators.

Modern oil painters are actively experimental and have greatly extended the range of possibilities of their medium. The ways in which they use it are as complex and diverse as the ideas they express. After more than five hundred years of use, oil paint as a medium can still astonish and delight us with its versatility.

Painting in Watercolor

In its broadest sense, the term watercolor refers to any paint medium that is soluble in water and uses water as a thinner. More often, however, it refers specifically to a kind of transparent paint that is applied to paper. *Lower Manhattan* (Fig. 522), by John Marin, is a watercolor of this type. It is a view of the financial center of New York City as it appeared several decades ago, with lower Manhattan's distinctive skyline in the background and the elevated railroad (now gone) in the foreground. In its headlong diagonals, its sharp contrasts, and its impetuosity, the sketch captures the dynamic quality characteristic of a throbbing business and commercial center. It would be difficult to get the effects Marin achieved in any other medium than a watered pigment applied freely on paper. Good watercolor paintings are not easy to make, despite their impromptu appearance. Watercolor painting, as much as any other medium, requires a high degree of technical dexterity.

The Process   The most notable characteristics of the watercolor medium are fluidity and transparency. The pigments come in tubes or in cakes that are soluble in water; hence their fluidity. They are available in a wide range of colors, but sumptuous and varied effects can be achieved from a few basic ones.

The transparency of watercolor gives a special importance to the surface on which it is painted, and most painters use a paper that is rich in texture. In oil painting the surface is selected primarily for the way it responds to the strokes of the brush and holds the paint, but in most oil paintings the surface itself is almost completely obscured by the opaque pigments. With watercolor, however, the surface of the paper is visible through the transparent pigment, and in many watercolors, parts of the paper are left unpainted. The paper thus becomes integral to the painting, for the surface texture comes from the paper the medium is applied to.

The manner in which the paint is applied can further enhance the textural quality of the paper. The brush can be passed lightly over the surface so that only the tops of the "bumps" on the rough paper catch the pigment, or a wet brush can be applied to make the pigment settle into the hollows between the bumps. In either technique, the textural quality of the surface is accentuated. Smooth paper is sometimes used by watercolorists, with a marked difference in effect. In particular, it produces paint surfaces without texture. The colors dry more evenly, and if textures are desired, they can be obtained by applying strokes to a dry surface.

The watercolorist's brushes are also carefully selected. Generally, "soft" brushes are used, made from the hair of such animals as camels, oxen, and red sable. Brushes made from sable are expensive but much the best, for they are very pliant yet spring back to their original shape as soon as pressure is released and they are lifted from the paper. Hard, bristle brushes are also used, and these are best suited to paintings in which dry textural effects are wanted.

The fluid and transparent qualities of watercolors exert a pronounced influence on the methods of working with them. They must, for example, be mixed on a white palette, since any color in the palette would distort the color of the transparent pigments. When colors are mixed on the palette and applied in a "wash," they produce an even, ungraded tone. Colors can be blended on the paper by allowing them to flow into each other, or the artist can load his brush with two or more colors by pressing it directly into the undiluted pigments and then applying it to the paper to produce a stroke that is richly varied in color. He can achieve gradations in value by putting a stroke of full color on the paper and then brushing clear water into the edge of the stroke, thereby carrying the diluted color over a larger surface.

As noted earlier, the transparency of the medium also imposes upon the artist the necessity of working from light to dark, for once a dark color has been applied it cannot be lightened with further applications of paint. It is largely for this reason that watercolors cannot be worked and reworked as can the opaque pigments of oil paint. Although some artists work with a meticulous technique, carefully building one color over another, the medium is especially well suited to the kind of spontaneous, vigorous treatment exemplified by *Lower Manhattan*.

Paul Cézanne's Watercolors   There are, however, many ways of painting with water-soluble pigments, and each has its merits. A great contrast to the Marin is provided by Paul Cézanne's *Mont Sainte-Victoire* (Fig. 523). Here the medium is used with restraint. Actually, only small areas are painted, and the blank paper carries most of the responsibility of the painting. But the effect of great scale has been achieved, and the mountain towers massively over the trees and buildings in the foreground even though it is mostly flat white paper. Note how both the forms of

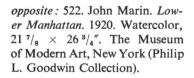

opposite : 522. John Marin. *Lower Manhattan.* 1920. Watercolor, 21 $^7/_8$ × 26 $^3/_4$″. The Museum of Modern Art, New York (Philip L. Goodwin Collection).

right : 523. Paul Cézanne. *Mont Sainte-Victoire.* c. 1900–1906. Watercolor, 16 $^3/_4$ × 21 $^3/_8$″. The Museum of Modern Art, New York (gift of David Rockefeller).

the pigmented areas as well as the brush strokes within them suggest the basic structure and nature of the various elements. Look at the photograph in Figure 535 of the mountain that was Cézanne's subject. The interesting thing is that the painting looks more like a mountain than the photograph.

A Chinese Watercolor   The Chinese have a tradition of watercolor that goes back many hundreds of years. Chang's *The Evening Tolling of a Distant Temple Bell* (Fig. 524), like many works of this sort, is painted on a silk whose original whiteness or light color must have produced a stunning effect. Age has darkened the fabric and robbed the painting of much of its former brilliance. Chinese artists have traditionally been interested in atmospheric effects, and they use subtle washes to suggest the softness of mist, the forms of mountains, the flow of streams. Foliage forms, both large and small in scale, are painted in with brushwork of dazzling dexterity. Colors are muted, and much use is made of dull greens and browns. In *Lower Manhattan*, Marin celebrated the energy and accomplishments of man. Chang contemplated the grandeur and inscrutable vastness of nature.

Other Types of Watercolors   So far we have discussed only transparent watercolors, but many contemporary painters prefer to use one of the several types of opaque water-soluble paints. Far from being new, opaque watercolors are among the most ancient of painting mediums. *Tempera*, a mixture of ground pigments with an albuminous or colloidal vehicle (egg, gum, or glue), was employed by Egyptian, medieval, and Renaissance painters, and it is still used today, as in Andrew Wyeth's *Ground Hog Day* (Fig. 525).

Sharp and precise detail is possible with tempera, and Wyeth has exploited this quality to the full. He has applied the paint in small strokes, which makes possible the remarkable gradation and modeling in the work. Like Hopper, Wyeth has taken a simple and homely subject and invested it with a kind of magic. As observers we relate to the subject—the clear air, the immaculate house, the appetizing meal ready to be eaten, the evidence of honest labor—but at the same time we view it with a detachment that makes us feel we have never really looked at a table or freshly cut logs before. Wyeth occupies a unique position in American art. He is independent of the rapid succession of movements that have changed the character of American art and has continued to paint Pennsylvania and New England subjects with a sharp and loving eye. A mature and fortunate artist, Wyeth commands the admiration and respect of critics and public alike.

Gouache, another type of watercolor, is made by grinding opaque colors with water and mixing the product with a preparation of gum, or by adding Chinese white, which is opaque and water-soluble, to transparent watercolors (see Pl. 52, p. 434; Fig. 526). *Poster paints* are the most familiar, least expensive, and least satisfactory (as far as permanence and flexibility are concerned) of the opaque watercolors. *Casein* paints, which have an alkaline solution of casein as their vehicle, are comparatively new and hold many possibilities, for they can be used as transparent washes or as thick, opaque areas, either smooth or textured.

opposite : 524. Chang Lung Chang. *The Evening Tolling of a Distant Temple Bell.* Ming Dynasty, 1594. Painting on silk. Philadelphia Museum of Art.

right : 525. Andrew Wyeth. *Ground Hog Day.* 1959. Egg tempera on board, 31 × 31″. Philadelphia Museum of Art.

below : 526. Morris Graves. *Bird Singing in the Moonlight.* 1938–1939. Gouache, 26 ³/₄ × 30 ¹/₈″. The Museum of Modern Art, New York.

Any medium is used well when it serves the artist as a suitable means of expressing his ideas, and almost any exhibition of contemporary watercolors will show the great ingenuity with which today's painters approach their work. Often they combine different kinds of watercolors or use them with such materials as charcoal, crayon, and chalk. Although watercolors are still likely to be smaller than oil paintings, many of them are far larger than they were forty years ago. Not only has their scale been increased, but modern watercolors are bolder, richer, and infinitely more variegated in expression. Beginners and experienced painters alike can learn much by experimenting with watercolors, for they are a fascinating and challenging medium that can reveal many insights into the techniques and materials of painting and the problems that are central to art.

Painting in Fresco

Sixty-three feet above the floor of the Sistine Chapel in Rome, Michelangelo in the early sixteenth century painted a monumental series of scenes illustrating the ideas and events of the Hebrew-Christian and Neo-Platonic traditions. To cover the ceiling's 700 square yards of surface, the great artist worked almost entirely alone and completed the cycle after four years of appallingly hard labor. Today, more than four centuries later, the Sistine Ceiling remains one of the truly staggering achievements in world art. The medium Michelangelo used for painting the Sistine vault is fresco, whose characteristics can be seen in the *Creation of Man*, a detail from the scenes of the Old Testament (Fig. 527).

Fresco, an Italian word meaning fresh, is a technique of painting on fresh, wet plaster with pigments that have been mixed with water. A finished fresco has something of the transparent, fluid quality of watercolor, but there the similarity ends, because fresco is a medium for painting in monumental scale. It is an ancient process, one that can be found in wall paintings unearthed on the island of Crete and dated about three and a half millenniums ago. From a later period in antiquity, A.D. c. 70, we have frescoes preserved in the remains of Pompeii and Prima Porta. Their remarkable freshness attests to the extraordinary durability of fresco. The most brilliant use of fresco was during the Gothic and Renaissance periods, especially in Italy, where the walls and ceilings of countless cathedrals, churches, chapels, and palaces were covered with frescoes of exceptional beauty and power. Giotto's *Lamentation* (Fig. 111) is one of the great fresco paintings of the late Middle Ages and one of the first sure steps leading toward the Italian Renaissance. During the seventeenth and eighteenth centuries, interest in the use of fresco as a medium generally declined, but from the middle of the nineteenth century until our own time there has been a renewed interest in paintings done in this medium. Throughout the centuries of its use the technique of fresco painting has changed little, although contemporary artists do have a wider range of colors available to them than did earlier practitioners.

The Process   For the fresco painter, faced with the problem of covering a large area of wall or ceiling while working on a high scaffold, it is advisable that a project be well planned before beginning to paint. Usually, the artist makes preliminary sketches that, once perfected into a design, are enlarged to full size. Such full-scale sketches are called cartoons, and for a large fresco they are cut up into pieces, each of which represents a day's work. Fresh plaster is applied over the area to be painted, the cartoon is fastened to it, and the necessary outlines and details are transferred to the wet plaster. (Michelangelo used an iron stylus.) Plaster beyond that which has been painted in a single session is cut away. The requirements of painting in wet

527. Michelangelo. *Creation of Man*, detail of the Sistine Ceiling. 1511. Fresco. Vatican, Rome.

plaster are such that the artist should be careful to make the limits of each day's work coincide with the edge of a figure or of some prominent feature—to search for lines and formal needs of the composition so that the characteristics of the medium can be placed at the service of the artist's esthetic purpose.

Pigments are mixed with water and applied to the damp plaster. As the water evaporates, the lime in the plaster absorbs carbonic acid gas from the air, and a thin transparent layer of crystalline carbonate of lime forms on the surface. This protects the fresco to the degree that it will not deteriorate as long as the plaster is not damaged. Frescoes cannot be reworked in the way oils or watercolors can. If a major change is to be made, the artist can only remove the plaster he has painted on and redo the unsatisfactory portion on a fresh base. A certain amount of touching-up with tempera paint is frequently done, but colors applied to dry plaster lack the permanence of those bonded into it. Leonardo da Vinci painted his *Last Supper* on dry plaster, and the deterioration of that masterwork, already a ruin in the artist's own lifetime, is evidence of the inadequacy of painting in *secco*, or on dry plaster.

Two Frescoes The composition in the *Creation of Man* consists of two masses, each of which stands out clearly against the background. On the left is Adam rising from a sloping land form in response to the shock of life God has given him. The event is conveyed by Michelangelo's rendering of the figure. While one side remains

above : 528. José Clemente Orozco. *Gods of the Modern World.* 1932–1934. Fresco, 10′6″ × 14′8″. Dartmouth College, Hanover, N. H.

opposite : 529. Al Held. *The Dowager Empress.* 1965. Synthetic polymer paint on canvas, 8 × 5′. Whitney Museum of American Art, New York.

inert in a smooth, simple curve, the other is a taut complex of contours quickening to the suggestion of life and movement. On the right and against the sky is God, both borne and surrounded by heavenly creatures, his arm embracing the yet-uncreated Eve. It is at the tips of the index fingers of God and Adam that the two masses in the composition are brought together, and each of the extended hands reflects its possessor. The hand of Adam is limp with the first stirrings of life; the hand of God powerful with creative energy.

José Clemente Orozco's *Gods of the Modern World* (Fig. 528) is also part of a larger fresco, one that this Mexican artist painted for the library of Dartmouth College. The deities here are educators, and the setting for them is an academic one, a library. The major figure is a skeleton lying on rows of substantial tomes, in the act of giving birth to a baby skeleton already adorned with a mortar board. In attendance, like a team of surgeons, are the gods, all wearing the formal academic robes representative of their professional erudition. But they too are skeletons. Orozco is protesting arid and lifeless scholarship that, despite its educated appearance, is able only to produce equally arid and lifeless learning.

These two frescoes have in common the depiction of the transmission of life. One painting is concerned with Genesis, the birth of humanity, the other with the still-birth of acquired nonfunctional knowledge. In the former we have a glimpse of man, who, created in the image of God, gives promise of the wonder and greatness of human life. In the latter we are reminded that learning is valid only if it has life, that much erudition is dead and thus a mockery of itself.

Materials and Processes in Painting: New Mediums

All of the traditional painting materials are composed of natural substances that have been processed in one way or another to produce a medium suited to the artist's needs. In recent years, technological advances in the production of synthetic compounds have led to the development of totally new painting mediums. As early as the 1930s some few artists were working with synthetic materials, notably a group of Mexican painters that included José Clemente Orozco and David Alfaro Siqueiros. In the years since, both scientists and artists have given increased attention to the development of synthetic mediums, and today there are a number of them that rival, and in some ways surpass, the traditional mediums of painting.

Polymer Tempera

The most widely used synthetic mediums today are polymer temperas (Fig. 529). They are of two distinct types—one a polyvinyl acetate and the other an acrylic resin—but there are only minor differences in the way they behave. In both types a synthetic emulsion, or base medium, acts as the binder to which dry pigments are

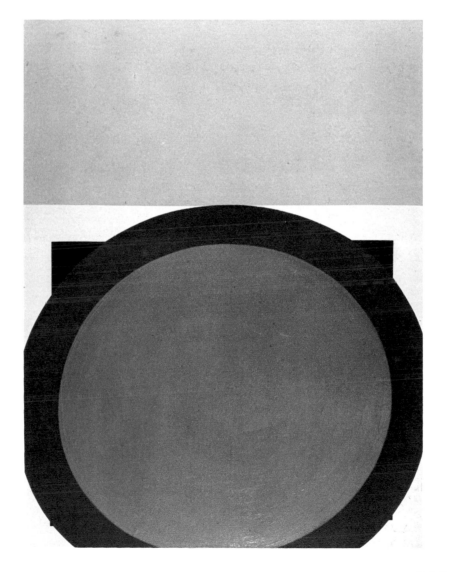

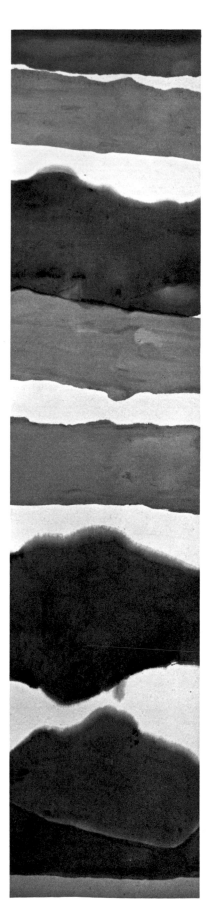

added. Applied to a surface without the addition of pigment, the emulsion dries to a tough, transparent film. The paints are water compatible; that is, water is used for thinning them and for cleaning brushes and palettes. However, once they have dried they are completely resistant to water; thus, overpainting may be done without any possibility that color will bleed through from the underpainting. Although the working texture of the polymer tempera paints is very different from oils, they can, like oil paint, be thinned to the consistency of transparent watercolor or be applied in a thick impasto. They have the great advantage over oil paint in drying rapidly. Oil painters may have to wait days, and sometimes weeks, before overpainting, but new layers of polymer tempera may be applied in from twenty minutes to two hours, depending upon the thickness of the underpainting. Another and distinct advantage of these paints is their ability to adhere to a variety of surfaces, including paper, canvas, and wood, as well as various wallboards, plaster, masonry, stucco, and stone. In fact, they may be applied to any surface except those that are oily or are excessively nonporous and slick.

The necessity of painting oils "fat over lean" need not concern the artist in working with polymer tempera. An oil painting dries layer by layer, and each succeeding application must be more "fat" (that is, contain more oil) and therefore more flexible than the last to prevent eventual cracking and flaking. Polymer tempera, however, dries as a homogeneous mass, for as each new layer is applied it forms a chemical bond with those beneath it. This remarkable characteristic also makes possible the use in a polymer tempera painting of materials that otherwise would be incompatible. Textures may be achieved by mixing with the paint such diverse materials as sand, ground cork, and shredded asbestos. Color and pattern may be introduced by using materials such as colored papers or textiles and fixing them to the painting with the clear medium that, as it dries, bonds them permanently to the surface.

One of the problems of working with any of the traditional water-soluble mediums is that as they dry they change in value, in most cases becoming noticeably lighter. With the polymer temperas, no color change is brought about by drying. Thus the artist has more control over his color, and he finds it much easier to mix fresh pigments to an exact match with colors that have dried.

Numerous tests have indicated that the polymer tempera mediums are quite resistant to light, heat, and exposure. They do not yellow and darken as do oil paints, and because of the uniformity and flexibility of the paint film, are less easily damaged.

Other Synthetic Paints

There are a number of other synthetic paints that artists use today. The following two mediums appear to have gained the widest acceptance.

Oil-Compatible Acrylic Resin Paints Acrylic resin paints differ from polymer tempera mediums in that they are oil-compatible; that is, the artist, in working with them, uses linseed oil and turpentine as thinning agents. The working texture of these paints closely approximates that of oil paints (see Fig. 530). They can, in fact, be used in combination with oils, though when the artist does this he forfeits the advantage of quick drying, which characterizes the medium when it is used alone.

Another important characteristic of these paints is that they are soluble in turpentine long after they have dried. Thus paints that have dried on the palette can be softened and used, and sections of a painting can be washed out and reworked well after they have dried. With respect to permanence and durability, these paints are comparable to the polymer temperas.

Pyroxylin Pyroxylin paint is not an especially new material, although it is only in recent years that it has gained any degree of acceptance as an artist's medium. It is more commonly known as "lacquer" and is sold commercially under a number of trade names, the best known of which is Duco. It was again the Mexicans who pioneered in the use of this medium, and it was used by Siqueiros for several of his major works (Fig. 531). Jackson Pollock also recognized the possibilities of the medium and used it in many of his large paintings, the medium's high liquidity being responsive to Pollock's "action" technique (Fig. 546).

One of the most outstanding characteristics of pyroxylin is its extremely short drying time. Within a few minutes the surface is dry to the touch, and the artist is free to work without interruption. Because it becomes brittle as it dries, the medium must be applied to a rigid support such as wood, Celotex, or Masonite. The surface of the support can be varied, however, by sprinkling a textural material such as sand or sawdust onto the wet paint.

Pyroxylin lends itself to a sizable array of technical treatments. It can be applied in flat glazes or built up to form a modeled surface. On the other hand, it can be

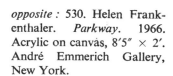

opposite : 530. Helen Frankenthaler. *Parkway.* 1966. Acrylic on canvas, 8′5″ × 2′. André Emmerich Gallery, New York.

right : 531. David Alfaro Siqueiros. *The Sob.* 1939. Duco on composition board, 4′1/2″ × 2′1/4″. The Museum of Modern Art, New York.

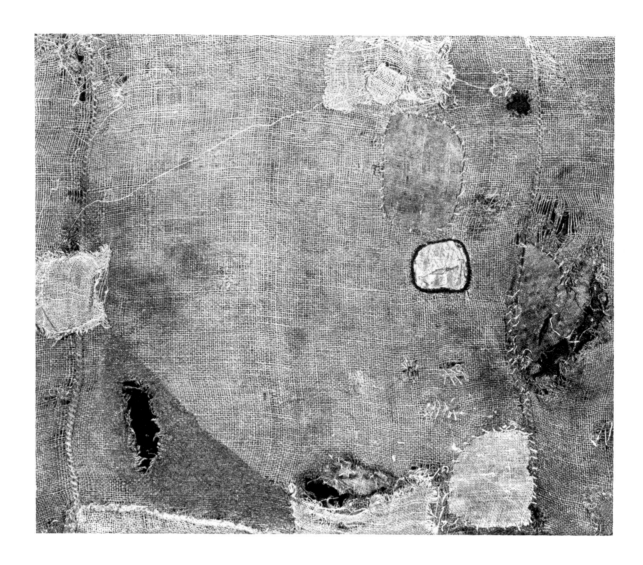

thinned to the transparency of watercolor and, in this form, applied to paper. By following certain technical procedures, it can be used to imitate exactly the effect of fresco. But the composition of the medium is such that, in combination with the lacquer solvent, it can be manipulated to produce unique effects of dripping, blending, and textures. The one disadvantage of the medium is its high inflammability and the penetrating fumes it gives off. These necessitate working always in a well-ventilated area and with extreme care.

The development of new painting mediums is generally greeted enthusiastically by the artist for it offers the challenge of new relationships with his work and the possibility of widening and extending his expressive range. At their least, the new mediums supplement the technical and expressive capabilities of the traditional mediums. It is the view of a growing number of artists that, freed by the new materials from many of the technical limitations of the traditional mediums, they are inspired to find and develop new creative directions.

Other New Mediums

Artists have been particularly ingenious in extending the range of materials they find useful. In looking at many recent works one is tempted to say that there are few materials which in the last several decades artists have not used and even made

central to the esthetic significance of their work. They have drawn not only upon the great store of natural materials generally found in the world about us—twigs, leaves, stones, sand, soil, seeds—but upon the products of modern life—photographs, newsprint, charts, metals, maps, wood, fabrics, plastics. The use of such common and untraditional materials has done much to give modern art its unique quality. It has also raised problems in the classification of works incorporating such elements. Now, even the basically two-dimensional creations can no longer be properly identified by the simple term "painting."

The Italian artist Alberto Burri made *Composition 8* (Fig. 532) of burlap, a material that is inherently textured. In "forming" his medium, the artist has sewn, patched, and glued it to a canvas. We respond not to a painted surface but to the woven texture of an actual material that has been manipulated to give effect to the artist's esthetic purpose. *Composition 8* achieves considerable intensity, much of it from the direct presentation of torn and mended surfaces and edges. A handsome abstract pattern is also created by the disposition of forms and textures.

Progressions by Mary Bauermeister (Fig. 533) is made entirely of stones and sand mounted on board. It is, actually, four distinct but related compositions combined into one work. What strikes us initially is the extent to which the raw materials have been transformed, and it is only on a second or third look that we realize the nature and presence of the raw materials this work is made of. On two of the square areas the stones, meticulously graded in size, have been arranged to suggest deep perspective, and the differing horizon lines create a tension from one to the other. The other two squares are less clearly ordered. There is no regular progression here but a feeling of eroded and restless forms, which, although made of identical materials, provide a contrasting effect. In each of the four panels the artist has left uncovered a small square of the board on which the stones are mounted. The flatness of the exposed board causes us, as we discover it in each of the panels, to perceive another kind of tension between the raw board and the patterns and illusions of the covered areas. The stones have their individual colors and values, but these remain within the warm and gray part of the spectrum.

Joseph Cornell's *Space Object Box* (Fig. 534) is a wooden construction that includes a variety of objects. Although small in size, it produces a sense of scale that derives chiefly from the cork ball (a planet?) set against the dark space of night. The spherical shape is repeated in the marble at the bottom of the cordial glass, and this takes us suddenly to a microworld. In between we see a chart with a moonlike form on it (which is smaller than the marble) and a metal ring that hangs in the foreground and sets up a plane opposed to the one suggested in the cork ball. The high-value area below is a lighted space, and at the bottom is a small starfish. The ambiguity of the various spherical and circular forms gives the work a strong poetic quality. The objects are things that are familiar to all of us. Presented in new and engaging contexts, they enchant us as we lose ourselves in their magic.

The Cornell work is identified as a *construction*, a general term that can distinguish a work in which a mixed multiplicity of materials are brought together. *Assemblage* is another term identifying the same kind of creation. Generally, however, it refers to constructions that are clearly three-dimensional; thus, assemblage is more commonly associated with sculpture. A work assembled and composed from

534. Joseph Cornell. *Space Object Box*. 1959. Wooden construction with painted wood, metal rods and ring, cork ball, cordial glass containing marble, starfish, pasted paper, $9\,^1/_2 \times 15 \times 3\,^3/_4''$. Present whereabouts unknown.

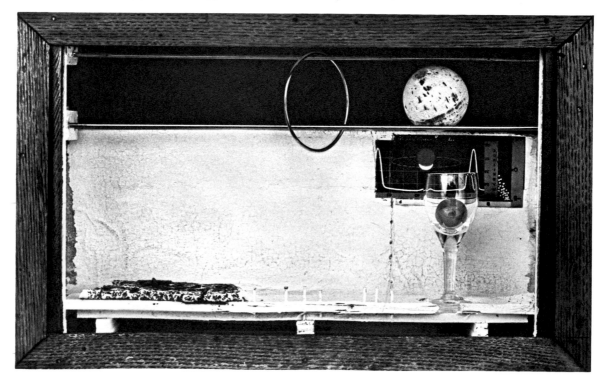

a variety of flat materials—paper, fabric, canvas—is called a *collage*. Artists, of course, are not particularly concerned with how a piece will be labeled after it is finished, and terminology usually is invented to fit the completed facts, not the reverse. Still, the etymology of the language of modern art does suggest the exhilarating scope and multiformity of the inventions wrought by contemporary artists.

Organizing a Painting

One has only to walk through a museum gallery to know that there are many different kinds of organization in painting. This general principle, set forth in Part III of this book, has also been demonstrated in the several comparative analyses of paintings already made in this chapter. Organizational methods range from meticulous and extensive preplanning to acceptance of the results produced by chance and accident.

For his *Guernica* (Fig. 536) Picasso made dozens, even hundreds of sketches (of which four are shown in Figs. 537–540) investigating many possible organizations both of the entire composition and of small and large portions of it. This is a method that has been used by most artists, for it enables them to develop, refine, and intensify their ideas before beginning the serious and final work of painting itself. For projects of great scale, such as ceiling and wall murals, extensive preplanning is imperative. It is also essential in paintings such as those of Mondrian (Pl. 41, p. 351), in which relations and proportions of the greatest refinement are sought.

A common method of working on small canvases or sketches is to draw in the major outlines of the compositions and, with these as guides, to develop the smaller areas in the process of painting. In his watercolors, the pencil lines Marin sketched in to guide his painting are often still visible.

Many contemporary artists have rejected the approach to painting that requires the establishment of the major areas of a picture before beginning to paint. Robert Rauschenberg, in commenting on his own method of working, has said:

> I'm opposed to the whole idea of conception-execution—of getting an idea for a specific picture and carrying it out. I've always felt as though, whatever I've used and whatever I've done, the method was always closer to a collaboration with materials than to any kind of conscious manipulation.

What Rauschenberg suggests is a method that is improvisational and spontaneous, and these traits are clearly evident in his work. His reference to "collaboration" suggests an interaction and a working with his mediums, but he would not view this as an essentially conscious process.

The Dadaists and Surrealists at times made use of automatism and chance in their paintings. In automatism the hand, using a pencil or brush, moved with no conscious control over the picture surface. The purpose of this was to help in "overcoming" the forms of art as the artist had learned them. It also enabled him to draw on the subconscious as a source of forms. The lines generated in this way served as a fresh foundation for the composition. Accidentality, the chance disposition of forms, also served as a basis for their composition. Interest in both automatism and chance in art strongly persists today.

There really is no end to the methods by which the artist can organize his paintings. In general, the more precise his forms, the more careful will have been his planning prior to painting. Hopper obviously detailed *Early Sunday Morning* with considerable care before applying pigment because the finished work exhibits a host of calculated proportional relationships. Van Gogh, by contrast, painted much more spontaneously, relying more on the textured strokes and vigorous forms to unify his composition than on carefully planned forms and areas. For all the thrilling, brisk deftness of Van Gogh's work, however, we today have come to believe that this artist may have prestructured his compositions more than was formerly assumed.

Three Examples of Organization

Three paintings will now be examined closely, with particular attention paid to the organization imposed upon them. Of the three works, one is distinctly realistic in its treatment of subject matter; a second is somewhat abstracted through its use of known forms that have been reordered and modified; and a third is entirely abstract.

William Harnett's "Realism"   In his engaging work *After the Hunt* (Pl. 49) the American artist William Harnett attempted to create a painting of almost photographic realism. Seeing the picture reproduced on page 423, the reader might in fact mistake the painting for a photograph. This type of painting is called *trompe l'œil* (fool-the-eye), and its objective is to produce an illusion of actual objects. This is no longer an important function of painting, despite the pleasure such works can give us, if they are handsomely composed and painted with affection. In the Harnett picture the hunt is over, and on a beautifully hinged door the hunter has hung his hat, horn, jug, shotgun, and other paraphernalia, along with a rabbit and three fowl that he netted. Harnett clearly painted from the actual objects; thus, he was responsible not only for the selection of the subject matter reproduced but for the arrangement of its individual parts as well. We note with pleasure the compositional forms and directions in the picture—the circle and the variations of it, the horizontals, the verticals, and the opposing diagonals. We are presented with contrasts among materials—grained wood, shiny metal, soft fur, and feathers. Harnett had much greater control over the objects in the picture than a landscape painter, for instance, would have had, for they are relatively small and portable, and subject to whatever organization the artist may have wanted physically to impose upon them.

But Harnett's task in painting this picture involved considerable modification of what he saw. It is an obvious fact that while most objects exist in three dimensions, the artist painting them on a flat surface has only two dimensions to work with. To arrive at three-dimensionality with two dimensions only, Harnett used color and value and created an illusion of forms in space. The framing of the composition within the limits of a rectangular shape also involved conscious selection and a modification of what the painter actually saw. The boundaries of our vision are circular, and what we see at the periphery of the visual field is soft and indistinct. Thus, when the artist puts a frame around a selected segment of the visual field and excludes what is beyond it, he is making a choice and modifying what he has seen. Furthermore, because the range of values in nature is many times that which can be achieved with pigments, the artist must make changes to suggest with the limited value range at his disposal the value contrasts in the objects he is painting. Every painting is to a degree an abstraction by virtue of the changes the artist must make in the economy of his materials and means. This is true of a work such as *After the Hunt* even though it was Harnett's purpose to imitate as closely as possible the actual appearance of the objects he painted.

Cézanne's Abstracted Landscape   In *Mont Sainte-Victoire* (Pl. 50) Cézanne, by contrast, set out to make major modifications in his subject matter. The extent of his changes can be appreciated by looking at a photograph of the same subject

Plate 49. William Harnett. *After the Hunt*. 1885. Oil on canvas, 5′ 10 ¹/₂″ × 3′ 11 ¹/₂″.
Palace of the Legion of Honor, San Francisco (Mildred Anna Williams Collection).

Plate 50. Paul Cézanne. *Mont Sainte-Victoire.* 1904–1906. Oil on canvas, 27 ⁷/₈ × 36 ¹/₈″.
Philadelphia Museum of Art (George W. Elkins Collection).

535. Photograph of Mont Sainte Victoire, near Aix-en-Provence, France.

(Fig. 535), that, while pleasant, is certainly not distinguished. It has the cluttered effect of many views of the countryside, with trees and shrubs, particularly in the foreground, obscuring the view or concealing the major ground forms they are growing on.

In relation to the haphazard character of the photograph, the painting has a striking clarity. The foliage and ground shapes have been presented in an orderly arrangement; the sky, instead of being merely a light area, has become an integral part of the picture, with variations of both value and form. Set off and dramatized by the ordered foreground, Mont Sainte-Victoire becomes the dominant feature of the painting and thus achieves a noble grandeur. In particular, the viewer experiences the sense of organized space, for the voids are as carefully structured as the forms. Whereas the photograph appears to be a jumbled mixture of many kinds of trees, the foliage in the painting has a pleasing visual rhythm, an effect produced by the shapes of the foliage masses and the consistent brush strokes. Throughout the painting, movements and forces have been organized in relation and in opposition to one another.

Identified as a Post-Impressionist, Cézanne is generally regarded as the father of modern art. Among his many contributions are his treatment of all forms in terms of their simple geometric shapes, his modeling of form with color, and his distortion of forms in response to compositional needs. The influence of these innovations has been apparent in all subsequent developments of Western art.

Picasso's Abstraction   Let us look closely at another work, different in content and treatment from the preceding two. Picasso's *Guernica* (Fig. 536) is acknowledged to be one of the great paintings of the twentieth century. Virtually everyone agrees that it is an anguished protest against the horrors and senselessness of war; it has been described as a "piercing, gripping, strident, and everlasting shriek." At the same time, there has been endless discussion and controversy over the meaning of and relationships among the various symbols in the painting.

Picasso painted *Guernica* in 1937 as a commission for the Pavilion of the Spanish Republic at the Paris International Exhibition. The Spanish Civil War was in progress, and on April 28, 1937, the Germans, who were assisting in the rebellion against the Loyalist government, carried out an aerial attack on the town of Guernica, the ancient Basque capital in northern Spain. There was no military reason for the attack; it was an early experiment in saturation bombing to see if a town could be

536. Pablo Picasso. *Guernica*. 1937. Oil on canvas, 11′6 × 25′8″. The Museum of Modern Art, New York (on extended loan from the artist).

entirely destroyed from the air. The defenseless community was devastated, and the world reacted in horror to the event. Picasso, a Spaniard, was deeply moved and in a little over a month executed both the preliminary sketches of the whole composition and the individual parts of it, and the mural itself.

Guernica is a remarkable fusion of formalism and expressionism. There is a general economy of line and color, and many of the painting's elements are clearly derived from Cubism, an essentially formal style that enabled Picasso to show multiple views of heads, bodies, and buildings. Along with this, however, the painting displays an emotionalism of the most extraordinary sort that creates an inescapable feeling of terror, hysteria, and doom. No chromatic color is used, only blacks, grays, and whites. The sole contrasts are in value changes. It is as if the scene had first been fractured and then drained of all color.

There is one large dominating form in the composition, a triangle that extends across the bottom from the hand on the left to the foot on the right and that has its apex in the hand holding aloft the small lamp. This is basically a stable form, but Picasso has shattered it with a concentration of angular, contrasting, and convulsive forms. The two sides of the triangle also set up diagonal movements that are carried with strong effect throughout the composition. Note also that the major triangle, and therefore the entire composition, is bisected and that to the middle right a large white triangular area appears resting on one of its points. *Guernica* is composed of such stable and unstable forms, of serene yet exploded areas.

The actual objects in the composition are few. In the major triangular form there is to the left a fallen and dismembered warrior; above him a dying horse that has been gored from above; at the apex, the small lamp; and to the right, the figure of a woman struggling into the area of light cast by the small lamp. Immediately above her head is the head of another woman, also moving toward the light. To the left an anguished mother holds a dead child, and over her, looking away from the light, is a bull. To the right we see another woman trapped in a burning house.

It is on the meaning of the specific elements in the composition—especially the bull, the horse, the lamp, and the radiant eyelike form slightly to the left of center at the top—that differences of interpretation have centered. Picasso has made use

537. Pablo Picasso. *Head*, study for *Guernica*. May 24, 1937. The Museum of Modern Art, New York (on extended loan from the artist).

of personal symbols in *Guernica,* and his observations on them have been contradictory. However, we know that Picasso, a Spaniard, has had a continuing preoccupation with the bullfight, a spectacle in which the horse and the bull both figure prominently, and in his work he has frequently used the bull as the symbol of brutality and the horse as a symbol of innocence. About the people there is little doubt. Seldom have the horrors of war been depicted with such agonizing intensity as in the fallen fighter, in the women on the right, and in the woman on the left and the dead child. Even though the distortion in the figures is violent, we are never distracted by it, but through the treatment of figures, faces, hands, and feet, we are made aware of human suffering of the most appalling sort. A key factor in the picture is the small lamp in the center. It is placed at the apex of the major form in the picture, and it is the source of light for the area of greatest brilliance. Although the triangular form it dominates also includes the dead warrior and a part of the body of the expiring horse, the lamp suggests the light of the human spirit toward which the two women, the least anguished figures in the mural, are drawn. Beyond this central form, in the areas of darkness at the sides, we see the triumphant bull surveying the scene of grief and desolation.

In Figures 537–540 are reproduced four sketches representative of the many studies Picasso made for *Guernica.* Early in his planning, he seems to have decided upon the basic compositional arrangement, the large central triangle, but he experimented extensively with problems of the placement of major figures, their relationships, and the treatment of details. Some possibilities had to be discarded; only those were used that seemed to contribute most forcefully to the total statement. But in the series of sketches we have a remarkable record of what an artist may do in organizing a picture—the tentative planning, the exploration of alternatives, the decisions about basic relationships, the testing of ideas and specific forms, and finally the welding of all these into a final comprehensive composition. They reveal an overriding concern for the effectiveness of the contribution of each part and its relation to the end result.

Harnett, Cézanne, and Picasso used quite different forms, colors, and relationships in their pictures, and they achieved works that are indeed distinct from each other. In examining all three, the spectator will probably conclude that each artist organized his painting in terms of the problems he was dealing with, and each had a deep understanding of and commitment to his subject. Detachment from subject or work would, until recently, have been inconceivable for an artist, yet many of the young contemporary avant-garde artists, especially those working in such styles as Op and Minimal, believe that engagement is not important, that feelings of passion and involvement are not essential. Much recent art is "cool" in that it appears detached, yet the new art is vital and impressive. It is too soon to judge whether this is a new characteristic of the artist or merely a stance he is taking as part of his rejection of previous ideas and models. Time, as always, will tell.

below : 538. Pablo Picasso. *Head,* study for *Guernica.* June 8, 1937. The Museum of Modern Art, New York (on extended loan from the artist).

bottom left: 539. Pablo Picasso. Study for *Guernica.* May 9, 1937. Pencil on white paper, $9\,^1/_2 \times 17\,^7/_8$". The Museum of Modern Art, New York (on extended loan from the artist).

bottom right : 540. Pablo Picasso. *Horse and Woman with Dead Child,* study for *Guernica.* May 8, 1937. Pencil on white paper, $9\,^1/_2 \times 17\,^7/_8$". The Museum of Modern Art, New York (on extended loan from the artist).

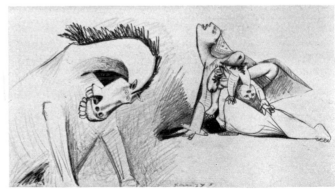

Organization of Space

From the time man as a painter first started to compose his pictures he has been concerned with the organization of space. Some suggestion of space occurs in any painting or design in which there are changes in values or hues, lines that converge or cross, or forms that vary in size or overlap. Each of these is a device for suggesting that certain parts of a composition are in front of or behind other parts. It is, of course, implied rather than actual space that a painter works with, and this can range from the flat space of Rothko's *November 10* (Fig. 499) to the illusion of very deep space in Magritte's *Le Château des Pyrénées* (Fig. 544). For the past century, painters (with a few notable exceptions) have not been interested in creating illusions of deep space. Artists have given their paintings a flatter treatment as they have become involved with relating the organization of their works to the flat plane of the painting surface. Picasso's *Guernica* is, basically, nonillusionistic. The abstraction of the entire composition is so considerable that we do not view it with illusions of deep space, however clearly depth may be suggested by the placement of various elements in front of or behind each other.

Space can also be suggested by less obvious devices. In Gottlieb's *Blast I* (Fig. 547) the two contrasting forms seem suspended in space. In Rothko's *Number 10*, the soft edges of the rectangular forms convey the impression of atmosphere. Recently, especially in Minimal Art, references to any sort of space or atmosphere are eliminated, as in Stella's *Tuftonboro 1* (Pl. 45 and Fig. 506).

Because, however, implied space is a manifestation of practically all painting, we should examine some of the devices artists have developed for making this implication. Space as a primary factor in art was analyzed in Chapter 12; here, the review will supplement and extend the earlier discussion by looking briefly at some of the elemental relationships that our perceptual experience causes us to understand as space when we see them in a painting. The fact that they are obvious does not diminish their significance or the variety and ingenuity with which they can be used.

Size When a number of objects are portrayed, the larger ones generally appear to be closer to the spectator. This is an optical effect that we all know well. A person standing nearby *looks* larger than one who is a block away. In actuality, a larger image of the person who is closer appears on the retina of the eye. In Van Gogh's *Starry Night* (Pl. 47) the trees are made larger than the rounded hills, which visually sets them off in the distance and brings the tree up into proximity with the spectator. Size, of course, is related to scale, and it tends to give relative importance to an object. The sheer size of the rock in Magritte's *Le Château des Pyrénées* gives it a physical significance that commands our attention.

Vertical Location *View of Toledo* (Fig. 520) is a good illustration of the effect the vertical placement of elements can have. With objects that are clearly below eye level—towers, trees, road, and river—the farther down they are in the picture the nearer they appear to be. Conversely, with objects that are above eye level—the clouds for instance—the higher they are the closer they appear to be.

Overlapping Forms When one form overlaps and partially obscures a second, the first form seems nearer. In Grant Wood's *American Gothic* (Fig. 511) the farmer and his wife overlap their farm buildings, and the farmer's right arm overlaps the figure of his wife. Spatial relationships are thereby established. Even in an abstract picture such as Picasso's *Girl before a Mirror* (Pl. 48) space is suggested by the overlapping of forms.

Linear Perspective   For centuries artists were concerned with ways of suggesting space realistically on the flat surface of a painting. The devices just discussed are only partial means of achieving this. It was the discovery of the principles of perspective in the fifteenth century that provided a technique whose precision suggested science. Linear perspective is the depiction of space by means of diminution of size in relation to lines that converge as they approach the horizon line. Railroad tracks or the edges of roads on flat terrain demonstrate the operation of the principles of perspective in their convergence as they recede from the spectator. More complex examples appear in views of streets lined with buildings and of open landscapes with trees, streams, and mountains. An image of a scene as it falls on the retina of the eye is composed in terms of linear perspective. In the twentieth century we are accustomed to this way of perceiving and construing spatial recession because in photographic prints, especially of urban subjects, sets of parallel lines converging toward vanishing points can readily be identified. Western artists have made considerable use of linear perspective during the last five centuries and through its use have achieved an effect of great "naturalness." Tooker's *The Subway* (Fig. 545) as well as El Greco's *View of Toledo* are clearly based on it. Although effective, linear perspective is limited in that it freezes the position of the spectator in relation to the picture and may produce a static, lifeless effect.

Even though perspective is a visually accurate method of depicting space, there is considerable psychological evidence to prove that we do not always *see* according to the laws of perspective. A round table as seen by the spectator from the image that falls on the retina is an ellipse, but the spectator may still see it as round. In other words, we see many things in terms of what we know. Linear perspective is not an essential for the production of great art. There have been many periods— the Middle Ages, for example—in which art of the highest excellence was produced without recourse to it. A great deal of Oriental painting makes use of parallel delineation of the planes of architectural forms in which lines do not converge, and of inverse perspective in which lines, instead of converging, diverge. Whereas linear perspective closes spaces in relation to the observer, inverse perspective opens it, and a sense of spatial freedom is achieved. Many contemporary painters, although they understand perfectly the principles of linear perspective, choose not to use them. Perspective techniques are of little use to artists concerned with such problems as simultaneity, dissolution of forms into surrounding space, and nonillusionism in general.

Aerial Perspective   Aerial perspective is a means of depicting space by the weakening of values and intensities and the alteration of hues as they recede from the spectator. For example, a tree in sun seen nearby presents strong contrasts of hue, value, and intensity. The parts in sunlight are bright greens and yellows; those in shade or shadow are dark in value and mostly blue-green in hue. If this same tree is seen at a distance, the contrasts of hue and value tend to disappear, the edges become softer, and the whole object turns bluer in hue. Aerial perspective can also be seen quite clearly in the treatment of mountain ranges. *The Evening Tolling of a Distant Temple Bell* (Fig. 524) is a painting in which aerial perspective is used to suggest depth.

Interpenetration and Transparency   The relationships among objects in a painting, whether animate or inanimate, have always been a concern of painters, but it is the intensity and extent of these relationships that have led to modern experiment and innovation. So conscious are many artists of the effect of one object on another that, in their representation of objects, they cause the objects literally to penetrate one another. To make these penetrations apparent, artists frequently treat objects as

541. Georges Braque. *The Table*. 1928. Oil on canvas, 5′10 ³/₄″ × 2′4 ³/₄″. The Museum of Modern Art, New York (Lillie P. Bliss Bequest).

if they were transparent. This can be observed in *The Table* by Georges Braque (Fig. 541) and Joan Miró's *Painting* (Pl. 53, p. 435). Note that these devices achieve both a sense of flatness in a painting and a lively sense of movement. The clear articulation of space, as when one opaque object appears in front of another, has been destroyed, and spatial ambiguity is substituted. Pictures like these have been influenced by such developments as the X ray and the fluoroscope as well as by a culture-wide concern with interaction observable not only in art but in physics, psychology, the social sciences, and practically all areas of modern inquiry.

Although present-day painters feel free to employ the older systems of construing space, they have felt compelled to explore fresh ways that are dynamically related to the exciting and vital age in which they live. It is the expressive intent of each painter that determines whether he depicts space realistically or whether he flattens, distorts, and abstracts it.

Diversity in Modern Painting

This chapter will conclude with a look at some additional examples of modern painting and will explore its diversity. This will be done by discussing specific works in relation to a few of the extraordinary number of major movements. The arts have been as subject to rapid change as have all other aspects of our culture, and the multiplicity of artistic expression is simply a reflection of the complex age we live in. The rich and variegated character of modern art is a direct and sensitive response to the impulses generated by a many-faceted world.

Each artist of stature is an individualist whose paintings have unique qualities. Usually, however, the works of a number of artists contemporary with one another have a great deal in common, because artists tend to work on the general problems current in their time. The concurrence of interest and treatment can be seen as the development of a *style*, and so as to verbalize about phenomena that are visual we devise such terms as Cubist, Pop, and Minimal as labels convenient for identifying in some rudimentary way the factors distinctive of the work of a group of artists. Style labels can characterize the production of both the group and the individual artist, but they should be accepted as labels only, not definitive for either the group or the specific exponent. Many works actually defy classification—and are all the more significant for it. Artists often dislike being placed in a style category, feeling that identification with a style group compromises the special value of their uniqueness and originality. There are, however, several broad generic categories that can serve for the purpose of summarization and clarification.

Objective painting is that in which the artist portrays his subject matter with little alteration of the colors and forms as the eye sees them. The attitude toward the subject may be realistic or idealistic, but the subject of the painting remains clearly recognizable. Wood's *American Gothic* (Fig. 511) and Harnett's *After the Hunt* (Pl. 49) are both objective. Before the twentieth century most Western painting was objective, even the highly stylized painting of the Byzantines, but recent painting styles have been abstract or nonobjective.

All paintings are *abstract* to a degree, but the term typically is applied to those works in which essentials or fundamentals of the subject are portrayed rather than its surface appearance. Objects in abstract painting are often identifiable, but they may be radically modified in appearance. Abstract paintings tend to be disciplined in structure. Picasso's *Girl before a Mirror* (Pl. 48) and Braque's *The Table* (Fig. 541) are both abstract paintings.

As the term is used in modern art, *expressionism* denotes a kind of art in which the primary source of the values expressed in the art derive from the artist's instinctive response to the basic materials and techniques of his artistic activity. It is the expression in art of the artist's value-laden reaction to contemporary spiritual and intellectual conditions. Van Gogh, an expressionist, said: ". . . instead of trying to record what I see, I use color arbitrarily to express my feelings forcibly." Expressionistic painting usually has an emotional content that is emphasized by the artist's treatment of his work. It almost always exhibits a measure of distortion, often in both color and form. Van Gogh's *Starry Night* (Pl. 47) and Soutine's portrait of Maria Lani (Fig. 515) are both expressionistic paintings.

Nonobjective is a term used for those paintings that have no subject matter and rely only on form, color, and relationships for effects. Nonobjective paintings are often referred to as abstractions, and as with much art terminology, this assignment is not precisely accurate. Mary Bauermeister's *Progressions* (Fig. 533), Bridget Riley's *Movement in Squares* (Fig. 502), and Jackson Pollock's *One* (Fig. 546) are all monobjective paintings.

There is clearly no sharp division between these categories, and some paintings simply resist all attempts at classification. But, in general, they can be helpful as points of departure in our efforts to organize our understanding of art—which is about all that can be said of any classification.

Some Major Styles in Modern Painting

The isms and schisms in the art of the twentieth century have been as prodigious in number as modern artists have been prodigal in the rich abundance of their imagination and production and in the ideas and inventions that have taxed human language to manufacture terms equal to the visual flux and multiformity of our time. To reflect even partially the strain placed on language by the burgeoning, volatile movements in modern art, we can cite here only a few of the terms devised to identify certain of the style groups that have in their moment of influence commanded a measurable degree of interest. Out of the Tower of Babel in the throbbing center of artistic activity we have had such esthetic systems as Constructivism, Dadaism, Dynamism, Fauvism, Intimism, Orphism, Parallelism, Purism, Supremism, Synthetism, and Vorticism. All of these have passed into the accelerating recession of more or less recent history, each of the isms producing certain works and ideas of abiding interest. Transcending the diversity and continuity of so many artistic expressions have been several movements of such power and influence they simply must be acknowledged as among the truly great styles of the age. They are genuinely styles in that they not only have been acknowledged through the sheer distinctiveness and force of the works originally defining the styles, but they have radiated influence and inspired greater artistic activity and achievement where weak and neutral quality might well have lingered. Of those movements in the great mode we will here examine eight of the most significant, styles that informed and have been informed by contemporary life, styles that relate as much to sculpture as to painting. They are Fauvism, Cubism, Dada, Surrealism, Abstract Expressionism, Pop Art, Op Art, and Minimal Art.

Fauvism The French word *fauve* means wild beast, a term that the Parisian critic Louis Vauxcelles used to describe certain works exhibited in the Salon d'Automne in 1905 and 1906. Thus was characterized the first genuinely modern art movement of the twentieth century. Unwitting as the remark was, it accurately registered the response many spectators felt to the fantastically colored and distorted compositions of Henri Matisse, André Derain, and Maurice Vlaminck. Each of these artists could have said, "I use color arbitrarily to express my feelings forcibly." Their colors were brighter than any ever used in painting before, and these colors were antinaturalistic—that is, expressionistic. It is the Fauves who first abandoned themselves to one of the great obsessions of modern art—color!

Among the paintings in the 1905 exhibit that caused the scandal justifying the label *Fauve* was Henri Matisse's *Woman with the Hat* (Pl. 51). Even today the extraordinarily vivid colors, arranged and painted in what would suggest a chaos of disfunctional technique and perception, still generate a terrific shock on the first encounter. They are "deliberate disharmonies" of red, green, orange, purple, and blue. What seemed merely willful in 1905 is in fact an intentionally planned experience in visual violence. Each of the major hues has its carefully plotted secondary expressions. It is the insistence on the integrity of feeling and the systematic exploitation of instinct and intuition.

Such art as this took inspiration from the general interest of the late nineteenth century and the early twentieth century in "primitive" art and culture, an interest that had enormous consequence for Picasso and the Cubists. For Matisse, the reference to primitivism would have been in search of his instinctual sources: "What I am after, above all, is expression. . . . I am unable to distinguish between the feeling I have for life and my way of expressing it. . . . Composition is the art of arranging in a decorative manner the various elements at the painter's disposal for the expression of his feelings."

Add to the hot colors of an intense personal sensibility the coolness of an orderly French mind, and we have the *Woman with the Hat* and the greatness of Henri Matisse. What we see as feeling, color, and control, Matisse, quoting Baudelaire, termed *luxe, calme, et volupté.*

Cubism   Such was the magnetism of the new style called Cubism in the early part of the twentieth century that around 1910 it temporarily polarized the careers of most of the artists active at the time. It was Braque and Picasso who, working in close collaboration, perfected the system and viewpoint we have long termed Cubism. The style wrought one of the major transformations in Western art. In place of the traditional artistic concern for form and space, Cubism introduced a wholly new fusion of mass and void. It substituted unstable structure, disconnected planes, and uncertain spatial relationships for the centuries-old system of perspective and the precise placement of identifiable objects in simulated depth. Instead of placing art in the service of illusory reality, Cubism offered art itself as reality, the reality of the process by which natural phenomena are translated into art. For an age committed to the principle of relativism, Cubism formulated a visual language of conscious ambiguity. In Cubist art, and in most art of the twentieth century, it is impossible to interpret precisely the shifting elements and images the artist's swelling imagination has fashioned. This imprecision and ambiguity expresses the paradoxical nature of reality, and Cubism, by describing it in mixed, multiple, and contradictory ways, created a visual syntax that articulates something primary and fundamental in modern experience.

Picasso described Cubism as "an art dealing primarily with forms," an idea and purpose in art that derived from Cézanne, who concerned himself with fundamental forms rather than surface appearances. Cubist paintings are usually characterized by many straight lines and angular planes, arrived at either through drastic simplification of forms or through fragmenting and then rearranging them in such a way that multiple views of the forms are presented. Because of the preoccupation with structure, color in Cubist pictures is generally muted. There is also a concern for the

Plate 51. Henri Matisse. *Woman with the Hat*. 1905. Oil on canvas, 32 × 23 $^1/_2$″.
Collection Mr. and Mrs. Walter A. Haas, San Francisco.

433

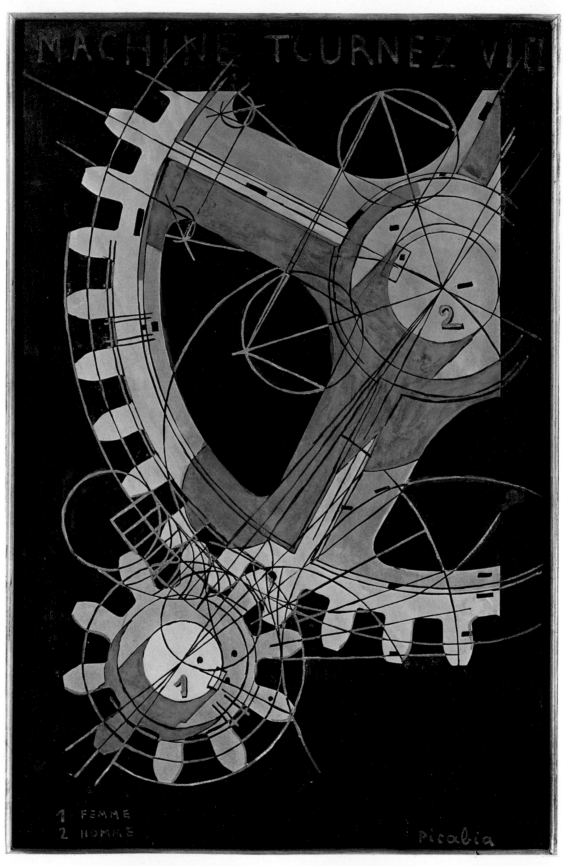

Plate 52. Francis Picabia. *Machine Tournez Vite.* c. 1916–1917.
Gouache, 19 $\frac{1}{4}$ × 12 $\frac{5}{8}$″. Galleria Schwarz, Milan.

Plate 53. Joan Miró. *Painting*. 1933. Oil on canvas, 5'8 ¹/₂″ × 6'2 ¹/₄″. The Museum of Modern Art, New York (gift of the Advisory Committee).

Plate 54. Pablo Picasso. *Portrait of Ambroise Vollard.* 1909–1910.
Oil on canvas, 36 $^1/_4$ × 25 $^9/_{16}$″. Pushkin Museum, Moscow.

relation of the subject and its background to the surface of the canvas—the picture plane. Cubists were also the first artists to introduce such materials as fabric, newspaper, wallpaper, and other printed matter into their paintings. In this way they discarded the notion of art as something crafted entirely by the artist and thereby blurred the distinction between art and nonart.

Many of the characteristics peculiar to Cubism are manifest in Picasso's portrait of Ambroise Vollard (Pl. 54). In the abstract language of Cubism, behind the network of lines and planes—like irregular, flinty pieces from a cracked slate—emerges, miraculously, a human presence even more convincing than that Picasso produced of the same subject in a line and value portrait (Fig. 542) so classic in its literal description the drawing could have been done by an academic traditionalist rather than by one of the most experimental artists of the twentieth century. In Cubism, it is important to realize that however abstract the individual work, there remains in it an ultimate reference to reality. It is in this way that Cubism establishes its fundamental tension between the demands of nature and those of art.

Braque's *The Table* (Fig. 541) is a late example of Cubism, as are Picasso's *Girl before a Mirror* (Pl. 48) and *Guernica* (Fig. 536). Explicated by Cubist principles, *Girl before a Mirror* becomes an uncanny evocation of the dualities of human experience, the polar extremes of life and death, the outer and the inner self, or, in the Freudian terminology of its time, the ego and the id. Even as late as 1937, the esthetic of Cubism served well the artist's expressed ends in *Guernica's* grim documentation of the wanton destruction of human lives and moral values. Marcel Duchamp's *Nude Descending a Staircase* (Pl. 44, p. 370) made Cubism notorious among the general American public when it was exhibited in the famous Armory Show of 1913.

Dada and Surrealism   The movements we call Dada and Surrealism were as much concerned with ideas—with philosophy, psychology, poetry, and politics—as with the plastic arts. They proposed life attitudes that, once assimilated, constituted working, cogent philosophies. So dependent were Dada and Surrealism on conscious conceptualization that the very terms preexisted the art they identify.

Dada—a nonsense vocable suggesting infantile gibberish—arose out of the disgust Europeans felt at the failure of their society in the disaster of World War I. Its purpose was to undermine the hoax of the bourgeois ethic and make way for a better order that would, in the manner of Freudian psychology, take account of the irrational in human behavior. Dada looked for the "gratuitous act," the random, spontaneous gesture that by its very lack of premeditation could explain the unreason and inanity in the conventions of moribund Western society. While improvisation was at the heart of Dada, the movement did program certain of its activities, and these "manifestations" or *gestes* of gratuitous and irrational pranks and performances were the precursors of the "Happenings" of the 1960s (see pp. 468, 469). The significance of the "act" in Dada also anticipated such post-World War II painting as Abstract Expressionism. In reacting against their antecedents, the Dadaists rebelled also against the "art-art," or pure painting, of pre-World War I and promoted such "anti-art" and "engineered" pieces as Marcel Duchamp's "ready-made" *Bicycle Wheel* (Fig. 543) and the machine imagery of Francis Picabia's *Machine Tournez Vite* (Pl. 52), an exercise in the symbolism of union of man with woman, with the two principal players identified in the picture by numbers keyed to a legend. Throughout Dada there seems always to have been an element of black humor, a kind of poetic sarcasm.

Surrealism evolved from the Dada experiments and became a major movement in the years following World War I. Like Dada, it sought social revolution through

542. Pablo Picasso. *Ambroise Vollard.* 1915. Pencil, 18 3/8 × 12 1/2". The Metropolitan Museum of Art, New York (Whittelsey Fund).

543. Marcel Duchamp. *Bicycle Wheel.* Original, 1913, lost; replica 1951. Bicycle wheel on wooden stool, 4'2 1/2" × 2'1 1/2" × 1'4 5/8". The Museum of Modern Art, New York (Sidney and Harriet Janis Collection).

free association, biomorphism, accident, automatism, and "found" objects; but in place of the relative anarchy of Dada, Surrealism was an attempt by artists, poets, writers, and thinkers to construct a system, or dialectic, from the ideas of Sigmund Freud. In the words of the movement's principal spokesman, André Breton, Surrealism was meant "to designate a certain psychic automatism that corresponds rather closely to the state of dreaming, a state that is today extremely difficult to delimit." Its ultimate purpose was to bring about a kind of super or absolute reality—*surréalité*. The three paintings reproduced here represent contrasting demonstrations of this fascinating movement.

Joan Miró's *Painting* (Pl. 53) is serene and elegant. None of the forms is anchored; they float and move on a soft, slightly differentiated background of red, green, and blue planes. The forms are biomorphic in that they overlap and interpenetrate, are transparent and opaque. Some of the forms change shape as we look at them, and others seem to appear. The forms suggest, they are not explicit. The dreamlike quality, the use of forms that seem to have sprung from the unconscious, and the free associations, all characterize this work as Surrealist.

René Magritte's *Le Château des Pyrénées* (Fig. 544) embodies another aspect of Surrealism. Here the forms are explicit to the point of being photographic, and the colors have the reality of empirical observation. No distortion is suggested. But the viewer is fascinated by the very unreality of the reality before him. Hovering against a blue-and-white clouded sky and over a large body of water is a boulder of mountainous size on top of which sits a medieval castle. The rock is not falling; rather, it is suspended, and the irrationality of what we see is compelling. This picture too is dreamlike, and the remarkable incongruity of its images gives the picture both a magic and an illusory, phantasmal quality.

There is another kind of dream in the scene George Tooker painted in *The Subway* (Fig. 545). At first glance we notice a number of people in the passages and stairways of a subway system, all well and attractively dressed. But a closer look suggests that the title has other meanings. Thrust into the frontal plane of the picture, at the convergence of three axes, is a woman who seems gripped by unknown fears. She dominates the composition by her size and placement. All the other figures are disposed around her, although at first glance they have no relation to her. As we look at them, however, we make some unnerving discoveries. The two men behind her are identical in appearance, and they seem as distraught as she. To the right and left of these three figures are four other men, also identical except for differences in the color of their topcoats. They look furtive and seem to share the common fear. A number of women appear in the painting, and although they are of different ages, they all wear the same style of coat and shoes and through their similarity seem to achieve a kind of relationship.

All of these discoveries strengthen the hallucinatory atmosphere of the picture, and the appearance of identical figures and those with selected features in common suggests a psychotic fixation or a stereotype. Psychiatrists instruct us that the dreamer is always the central figure in his dreams, and within this context we can accept the woman at the center of Tooker's painting as the dreamer. We are witnesses to her visions.

Still other disturbing aspects of the picture present themselves. Everyone is alone. There is no communication from one person to the other; each seems preoccupied with his own anxieties. In several places we get partial views of people—fragments of faces, edges of coats. These people seem incomplete and "cut off." They are suggested but not revealed. Some figures, although visible, are separated from the central grouping by iron grilles. While all the corridors and stairways are well lit, none seems inviting or even possible as an exit.

This too is a picture of a dream, a nightmare taking place in the subways of the mind. The fears in this painting are not those of dark, unlighted recesses. They are the terrors of the unconscious, the illuminated corridors of emptiness, peopled by the imaginings of the dreamer.

Abstract Expressionism   Since the mid-1950s the United States, specifically New York, has been the center of the art world, taking over the position held by Paris since the seventeenth century. The development that gave international preeminence to art produced in America was Abstract Expressionism, a style with strong indigenous qualities and a rich variety of manifestations. For more than a decade it was a powerful movement whose worldwide influence is not yet totally diminished. Its principal exponents—painters like Jackson Pollock, Willem de Kooning, Adolph Gottlieb,

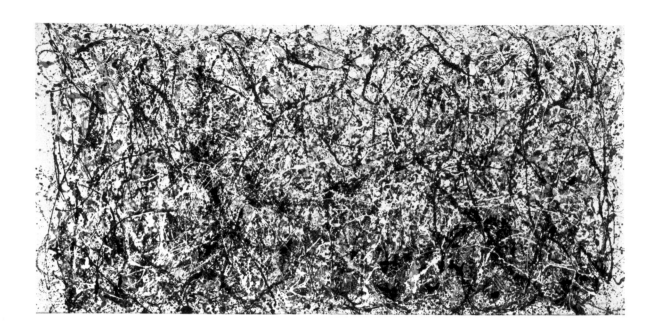

546. Jackson Pollock. *One*. 1950. Oil, Duco, Dev-o-lac, and aluminum paint on canvas, 8'10" × 17'5 ³/₈". The Museum of Modern Art, New York (gift of Sidney Janis).

Arshile Gorky, Hans Hoffmann, Mark Rothko, Franz Kline, William Baziotes, Robert Motherwell, Philip Guston, Conrad Marca-Relli, Bradley Walker Tomlin, and Barnett Newman—have become the old masters of post-World War II painting, whose works are owned by museums and collectors everywhere.

Abstract Expressionism is rooted both in the geometric forms of Cubism and in the automatism and free-associational aspects of Surrealism, and it is these two opposing sources that gave the style much of its vigor. The movement's esthetic of the random dribble and chance splash is also not far from Dada's search for meaning in the gratuitous act. It reflects the turmoil and despair of World War II and the period immediately following it. The Abstract Expressionists placed emphasis on personal, even emotional involvement with art and its creation and on the affirmation of individuality and its expression in art. All the artists had in common an interest in the process of painting itself, and this took precedence over the more usual practice of conceptualizing prior to executing a picture. The result, often, is rawness, tremendous vitality, and the evidence of extremely rapid execution, as if the work had been painted with the quickness and fury of a tornado. There is therefore a sense of immediacy in Abstract Expressionist paintings, a feeling that one is not only a witness to the finished work but to the act of painting that led to the completed canvas. Sheer size of canvas is another characteristic of this style. Such works have the power of enveloping the spectator and of drawing him into the picture through his mere contemplation of it. The observer seems automatically to become a participant with the artist in the work, for the ambiguous forms typical of Abstract Expressionist painting invite personal interpretation.

Willem de Kooning's portrait of Marilyn Monroe (Fig. 517) was an introduction earlier in this chapter to the work of one of the leaders of the Abstract Expressionist movement. No one has surpassed de Kooning in the vigor of his brushwork and in the painterly quality of his canvases (see Pl. 32, p. 294). More than most of the Abstract Expressionists, he has sustained a relatively consistent interest in figuration, an interest that makes possible such pictures as the portrait of Marilyn Monroe.

Of the group of painters who became famous as Abstract Expressionists none is better known than Jackson Pollock, whose *One* (Fig. 546) is a characteristic example of the fluid style his painting technique could produce. Pollock painted by placing his canvas on the floor and pouring extremely liquid pigments on it from above. The initial response to this use of medium was one of outrage. Pollock's "action" painting seemed a thing of arrogance and irresponsibility. Yet it soon became clear that here was an artist of exceptional power who had brought a new freedom to art. As a painting, *One* has neither edges nor "centers of interest" nor subject matter. It is composed of a complex of lines differing in weight, color, size, and the visual dynamics related to the controlled variations in the speed with which the lines were created. The painting fairly bursts with restless energy and rage, and the curved lines turning back on themselves suggest a painful anxiety. As the streams and streaks interweave and overlay one another they create a labyrinth of marvelous intricacy. We are at once and in a detached way keenly aware of the process by which the painting was achieved. The next moment we are drawn into the painting itself by following with fascination the mazes of seemingly infinite variety created by the interlace of dribbled paint lines. Pollock has exploited his technique in an ingenious way, for poured pigment creates lines that possess their own dynamics. This produces in the picture a strong sense of the random and accidental, and the controls the artist exerted in handling the pigment have not diminished the fantastic energy and spontaneity the composition communicates.

Blast I (Fig. 547) by Adolph Gottlieb is a painting in a series the artist has done in which two objects are disposed one above the other. In this picture the upper object with its brilliant color and rounded, even form may be the sun; below in muted earth tones is a rough-edged form that seems to be both energized and dissolved, or exploded, by the great and concentrated force above it. The burning disc may, at least partially, represent an atomic blast, an interpretation the title invites. Whatever the meaning chosen, the violent opposition of the two forms—hot against dull, serene against anguished, upper above lower—creates a visual tension that is totally compelling. Although as reproduced on the printed page the work's extreme abstraction offers no clues to actual size, the painting somehow manages to imply great scale.

Number 10 (Fig. 499), by Mark Rothko, is a very large canvas—approximately 7½ feet high by 5 feet wide. The viewer becomes enveloped by the size of the painting as well as by the luminous rectangles of color (white, yellow, and blue) that float before him. The edges are soft and irregular, enlivened at times by the introduction of touches of contrasting colors. Basically, the painting could hardly be simpler. There are no figurative elements, and the space is flat. Rothko has rejected most of the means used by artists to create paintings. Yet, the large color areas with their variances and irregularities have a mysterious, captivating quality. Color and scale are the basic ingredients of Rothko's art, and so crucial are they that color and scale in *Number 10* have an almost mathematical interdependence.

Rothko, like all gifted artists, is a sincere, committed painter, and as there is an integrity on the part of the artist, so should it exist in the attitude of the viewer. The ethic in this requires that the spectator view such art with all the sincerity that went into making it. As Rothko put it: "A picture lives by companionship, expanding and quickening in the eyes of the sensitive observer. It dies by the same token."

Pop Art   One of the marked characteristics of Abstract Expressionist paintings is the extreme individualism with which they have been treated. So intent were the artists on producing strong statements, they often achieved something uncogent and failed to communicate with the inadept among their observers. Pop Art was in large part a reaction against the obscurity of image and composition in Abstract Expressionism. On the more positive side, it originated as a move by a group of artists—at first working separately and independently—to incorporate well-known and common forms and cultural artifacts into their art. As a result, objects of a

547. Adolph Gottlieb. *Blast. I.* 1957. Oil on canvas, 7'6 ¹/₈" × 3'9 ¹/₈". The Museum of Modern Art, New York (Philip C. Johnson Fund).

radical familiarity became subject matter: soup cans, neckties, cream pies, comic strips, hamburgers, Coke bottles, pneumatic tires, and, significantly, people. For the first time in several decades the human figure reappeared in a major movement as the subject of serious art. The response to Pop Art has been generally enthusiastic, for the public enjoys the element of recognition in Pop and is beguiled by the ambivalent humor and irony with which Pop artists have employed and juxtaposed commonplace things.

But for all its charm Pop Art is mordant in its commentary on the ugliness and futility in much of mass culture, on the sideshow vulgarity, materialism, and spiritual fatuousness evident in affluent American society, and on the absurd and dehumanized sexuality that has permeated the puritan realm.

The sources of Pop esthetic can be found in Malraux's "museum without walls," for Pop finds its themes, images, and materials everywhere. Pop is also an art for the McLuhan age. In its destruction of the barriers between art and life, Pop is an illustration of the thesis of "everything influencing everything." By its reference to the full range of everyday life, Pop takes on an environmental character, and in certain forms it becomes a "Happening," a theatrical event in which people are incorporated as active art objects, much as bits of junk are included in Pop paintings.

Pop can, in addition, be dignified by its references to a number of distinguished antecedents. In Dada, Pop has an ancestor for its black humor. Also like Dada, it is the art of the double take—the discredited, ordinary object lifted from the place common to its kind and exhibited with all the singularity of an icon. The "Happenings" staged by Allan Kaprow hark back to the *gestes* of the Dadaists. Unlike Dada, an anti-art, Pop is art-art. Indeed, much of the irony in Pop emerges from the virtuoso treatment of common, commercial things according to the grand manner of Western pictorial traditions. In Cubism, Pop has found its collage technique. Pop is also not altogether alien to the work of Edward Hopper (Pl. 46) and Andrew Wyeth (Fig. 525) in its depiction of the sterility of unrealized expectations in American life. Like Hopper and Wyeth, Pop artists have a taste for nostalgia, which, in Pop, seeks satisfaction in the clothes, the movies, the cars, the radios, plumbing, and refrigerators of the 1930s and 1940s.

Among the portraits of Marilyn Monroe reproduced earlier in this chapter, three are by Pop artists—Mimmo Rotella, Andy Warhol, and James Rosenquist (Figs. 516, 518, 519). Robert Rauschenberg's *Canyon* (Fig. 548) shows us quite another aspect of Pop Art. Here we have a remarkable combination of familiar forms and images. Printed matter of mixed sorts is composed in patterns of almost classic beauty. At the bottom of the picture a stuffed eagle flies directly off the surface of the canvas, and below, hanging on a piece of cord, is a pillow. Unifying these disparate parts are a number of painted surfaces, the oil paint applied with all the vigor and sensitivity of an Abstract Expressionist. The subject matter is clearly popular, and the real, three-dimensional character of the objects assembled into the picture is a challenge to the vague spatial quality of Abstract Expressionism. As the "found" materials invade the spectator's own space, they demolish the barrier between art and life. The painting becomes a time capsule of human experience.

Rauschenberg's use of three-dimensional objects also exemplifies the dissolution of the distinctions between painting and sculpture. *Canyon* has some of the characteristics of both. It is painted, yet it is, in considerable part, three-dimensional. The artist's employment of such things as stuffed birds, pillows, and sticks of wood demands that we reexamine what art is, for here are objects used in a serious, accomplished work that in themselves are not esthetically significant. Yet through the vision and skill of his artistry Rauschenberg compels us to look at them and experience a whole new range of sensibilities.

left : 548. Robert Rauschenberg. *Canyon.* 1959. Combine painting, oil on canvas, wood, printed matter, stuffed eagle, pillow tied with cord, etc., 7'1" × 5'10 ¹/₂" × 1'11". Collection Mr. and Mrs. Michael Sonnabend, New York.
below : 549. Noel Mahaffey. *My Brother with Janis.* 1966. Oil on canvas with photography, 5'6" square. Oklahoma Art Center, Oklahoma City.

The images in *Canyon* are not programmatic, and the artist has not intended that together they should add up to a pat summary explanation of life and art. The fact that the images together cannot be resolved into a single, closed meaning sustains tension within the art and between it and the viewer. It is this tension that the artist sought. Rauschenberg has posed questions, not answers.

Noel Mahaffey's *My Brother with Janis* (Fig. 549), an oil painting that incorporates photographs, gives us a series of painted and photographed views of two attractive young people. In a kind of montage we see various relationships and reactions. The images, differing in size, in placement, and in presentation, intrigue us, for in a work suffused with warmth and affection they suggest many moods and dimensions.

As Pop Art developed it explored still more and newer forms and values, and as it became increasingly complex the style lost much of its original vigor. Nonetheless, Pop has surveyed and declared valid whole vast areas of our lives as subject matter for art. It has also attracted to art a new audience to which uncompromisingly abstract, nonobjective work communicated little or nothing. This fresh, lively, and intelligent audience is not likely to be lost to art as its practitioners continue their innovations with ideas, images, techniques, and materials.

Op Art　Optical art, generally known as Op, can be defined as the art that, free of allusive or atmospheric qualities, appeals directly to the eye for its responses. It usually is completely nonobjective and "hard-edge." The surfaces of these paintings, whether in black and white or in vivid color, delight us with their suggestion of movement and life. At the head of the Introduction to Part IV, on page 381, is

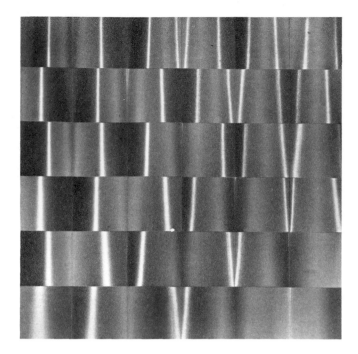

Bridget Riley's *Movement in Squares*, a two-dimensional painting that for all its simplicity projects an image of continuous motion and restlessness. Here the artist is playing on our optical responses. The progressive diminution of the width of the squares suggests that they are on a plane receding from the eye, and try as one might, this painting *cannot* be viewed as a flat plane. In addition, when the squares become extremely foreshortened, a sense of movement is set up that is impossible to control. Furthermore, if one looks fixedly at the top of the picture, where the squares seem to have receded to their greatest depth, the lower part of the picture, which will be seen in peripheral vision, takes on a very different aspect than when one looks at it directly. And the reverse is also true.

LL 36 Q 14 × 14 inv. (Fig. 550), by Getulio Alviani, demonstrates another facet of Op Art. This work is composed of thirty-six squares of burnished aluminum mounted on composition board. Each square is flat, but the way in which it is burnished causes light to be reflected in a way that suggests the metal, instead of flat squares, is a series of undulating strips. Here again, the effect is totally convincing. If the viewer steps up to the picture and assures himself that it is flat, this knowledge is of no avail to him as he looks at the work while stepping back from it. His eye sees what he knows is an illusion—the undulating bands of aluminum.

Optical artists have investigated many aspects of our visual apparatus and have created works that demand a direct retinal response. It is the directness of the demands of Op Art and the apparent mystery of our responses that account for much of the popularity of the style. It may baffle the eye, but it also provides excitement and delight. It carries no message, it does not touch our spirit, but once again, the artist has impressed us with his inventiveness.

Minimal Art   Like Op Art, Minimal is a reaction against the tactile, extempore, impassioned, structureless, egocentric characteristics of Abstract Expressionism that, along with Op, has been identified by the general rubric "post-painterly abstraction." Paintings of this kind are not only abstract but totally nonallusive works, whose effect derives from conscious conceptualization about pure color and from execution of extreme, almost immaculate care (see Pls. 55, 56). Instead of the

Plate 55. Morris Louis. *Aleph Series II.* 1960. Acrylic on canvas, 6′ 6″ × 8′ 10″. Courtesy André Emmerich Gallery, New York.

Plate 56. Ellsworth Kelly. *Blue-White Angle*. 1966. Painted aluminium, 6 × 3 × 6′.
Courtesy Sidney Janis Gallery, New York.

446

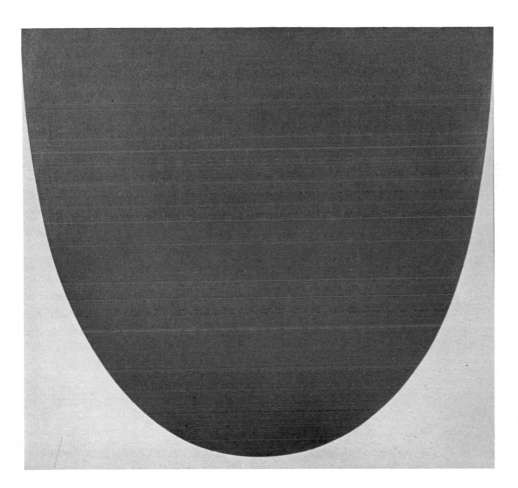

552. Ellsworth Kelly. *Red White.* 1963. Oil on canvas, 6'11" × 7'6 ³/₄". Courtesy Sidney Janis Gallery, New York.

impasto surfaces of Abstract Expressionist canvases, the pictures of the post-painterly movement typically have no overpainting and suggest a free, breathing quality. In theory, they are paintings in search of their own thing—those qualities that make a painting a painting and not anything else, for instance sculpture. The post-painterly artists strive to exploit the properties that inhere in their medium—two-dimensionality and specificity of shape—and achieve a result that is purely pictorial. Such refined and quintessential visual experience seems distant from Pop's total assimilation of art and life. The esthetic of color and of concreteness in art is one more reference to the sources of twentieth-century painting—to Fauvism and Cubism. The antecedents of post-painterly abstraction can also be found in Matisse's late compositions made of large cut-out gouaches (Fig. 551) and of Joseph Albers' experimental series of coloristic paintings of squares-on-squares (Pl. 36). Thus, "hard-edge" is characteristic of a good many of the post-painterly works, although such painters as Morris Louis (Pl. 55) arrived at direct, naked color by saturating unprimed canvas with veils of pure pigment. Certain of the qualities associated with post-painterly abstraction can be found even among the Abstract Expressionists, in Gottlieb's *Blast I* (Fig. 547), in Rothko's *Number 10* (Fig. 499), and in the open, free, "breathing" quality in Pollock's *One* (Fig. 546).

Minimal, the most reductive of the post-painterly movements, can be seen in Frank Stella's *Tuftonboro 1* (Pl. 45). *Red White* by Ellsworth Kelly (Fig. 552) is another example illustrating the Minimal principle. It too is impressive by its very scale. The style is hard-edge, and the painting offers no suggestion of atmosphere. The large red shape is remarkably simple and is reminiscent of a motion-picture closeup. Except for the white across the bottom, it fills the canvas.

Yet the shape, despite its sharp edges and simplicity, is ambiguous. The concave form of the background area is alive with tension. The red shape can appear light, heavy, flat, rounded, threatening, or recessive. Because of the curved form at the bottom, one thing it cannot be is static or stable. But in large part *Red White* is what we bring to it, and the painting is rewarding in proportion to the extent that we confront ourselves with it. In *Blue-White Angle* (Pl. 56), also by Kelly, we have a Minimal painting developed in two planes. The conception is audacious, for the painting is no longer confined to the wall but meets the spectator on, so to speak, his own ground. The hinge elaborates a radically reduced form, and this, along with the flat, strongly contrasted colors, results in a work of truly singular visual power.

Minimal is a style that demands intensive discipline from the artist. Rejecting space, texture, and atmosphere, and relying as he does almost entirely on form and color, the artist has only limited means for achieving his effect. Therefore, statements are minimal and in their understatement are filled with potential for many dimensions of experience.

Diversity has often been acknowledged in this chapter, and it is one of the few obvious consistencies of modern painting. Never have artists attempted to express in pigment such an array of ideas or so many and such mixed manifestations of life. Still, modern painters are regularly accused of turning their backs on life, of ignoring the public and its sensibilities, of willfully cultivating obscurity in their work. On the contrary, the very diversity of their production gives witness to the profound involvement artists have with today's concerns, and since they are artists and committed to visual expression, they articulate their awareness with the most powerful and relevant language available to them—that of vision, of space, of motion.

A humanistic function, the practice of art has as its chief concern the human condition. If many paintings seem relentlessly subjective and individualistic, it is because, in an age of regimentation and conformity, the artist believes it necessary to emphasize the central importance of the individual. Increasingly, during this century, the viewer has been considered by the artist less as a passive spectator and more as an active participant. In Minimal Art, more than ever before in painting, the response depends largely on what the observer brings to a painting. Clearly, this assigns to the artist a different role—and to the observer a critical one.

After a long period of apprenticeship, mainly in following the lead of European artists, American painting is now in a position of leadership. It has accepted the responsibilities of its new role by providing ideas whose vitality and significance command the attention and respect of the world. As we have already observed several times, painting has changed rapidly and radically within a very few generations. It is likely that the rate of change will accelerate rather than diminish. In any event, American painting—and American art generally—faces a future of great promise from a position of solid, even spectacular achievement.

553. Robert Mallary. *In Flight*. 1957. Relief of wood, dust, sand, synthetic polymer resin on painted plywood, 3′7 1/2″ × 6′7 5/8″ × 4 3/8″. The Museum of Modern Art, New York (Larry Aldrich Foundation Fund).

16 Sculpture

At first glance, Robert Mallary's *In Flight* (Fig. 553) seems a confirmation of its own title. Our initial impression is of a large, dark form airborne against a ground of stark white. On closer inspection, we find, as something of a surprise, that the major unit is the battered section of a 12-inch wooden beam, apparently salvaged from a demolished building. Below it are large splinters of wood, as well as dust and sand. We observe that *In Flight* is an arrangement of discarded materials. What is more important, we discover that it is a superb composition of forms, colors, and textures. All the elements of this relief are ambiguous: we see them in two roles. Careful consideration, however, can reveal the special truth of what Mallary has done. He has taken materials of the most ordinary sort—literally wreckage and dirt—and has transformed them into a work of art.

The use of common, even rejected materials as the substance for works of art has been an accepted practice of a good many artists for several decades and has created whole new realms for artistic exploration. Certainly, the introduction of junk, refuse, and "debased" objects into the context of art has expanded the range of modern esthetics, and sculpture, no less than painting, has evolved with all the speed and daring typical of our time.

Because modern sculpture and painting are related in an immense number of ways, much of the reasoning presented in the preceding chapter on painting can apply to a consideration of sculpture. The most obvious difference between painting and sculpture, however, is that painting traditionally has had two dimensions only, relies heavily on color, and suggests form and space through a clever use of hue and value, while sculpture is three-dimensional and gains its effects primarily from actual form and genuine relief or space. Thus, even though both painters and sculptors may work with the same ideas, the objects they create, and their effect on us, will not be the same. *Relief sculpture*, of which *In Flight* is an example, is a form that finds its place somewhere between painting and freestanding sculpture and has some of the characteristics of both. It often claims about the same range of subject matter as painting, and, like painting, it is almost invariably designed to be viewed from a single position, usually frontal.

Sculpture, again like painting, has for most of its history dealt with recognizable forms, and the human figure has been, by all odds, the favorite subject of sculptors. Nonetheless, abstraction, such as that in the Mallary relief, has proved just as relevant for sculpture as it has for painting, and a number of nonobjective sculptural works have been reproduced throughout this chapter. In dealing with identifiable subject matter, however, the sculptor is more limited than the painter in the kinds of subjects that he can treat effectively. The reason is simple. Because sculpture (with the exception of reliefs) *can* be seen from all sides, those subjects that involve perspective from a fixed viewpoint, such as landscapes and interiors, are seldom suitable to treatment in a sculptural medium. Although sculptors have often designed their freestanding works to be seen from a single, or fixed, viewpoint, there inhere in sculpture, as well as in architecture, the problems that relate to three-dimensionality, especially the problem of composing works so that they can be viewed with satisfaction from all sides.

The following works have been selected as an introduction to the expressive problems of sculpture.

Six Sculptures of Women

Of the six sculptures illustrated on pages 451–454 one has survived from Classical antiquity. The so-called *Hera of Samos* (Fig. 556) is by an unknown Greek sculptor who worked in the sixth century before Christ. The other works are modern, all having been done during the middle third of the twentieth century. All six sculptures have as their subject the female figure, which has indeed been one of the great themes for sculptors and spectators alike. In treatment, however, these works reveal that their creators had distinctly different and quite independent expressive purposes.

Standing Beach Figure (Fig. 554) by Frank Gallo, an American, is the most recent of the six and is made of a newly developed material—*epoxy resin*. It is by any measure the most realistic of the group, its realism due not only to the pose of the figure but to the medium, which has much the same texture and luminosity as human skin. The statue clearly represents a contemporary woman, who, clad only in the tight slightness of a bikini, stands in a pose of unselfconscious awkwardness. No attempt seems to have been made to idealize or abstract the subject. It is as if we were viewing a sculptural snapshot. But at the same time, for all the apparent verisimilitude, Gallo has, at many points, deviated from reality. Note, for example, the figure's left side, where the area from the head to the arm is treated with a full, simple form on which is drawn a line suggesting quite another form. This kind of generalized treatment also appears on the figure's right leg just below the hip. These

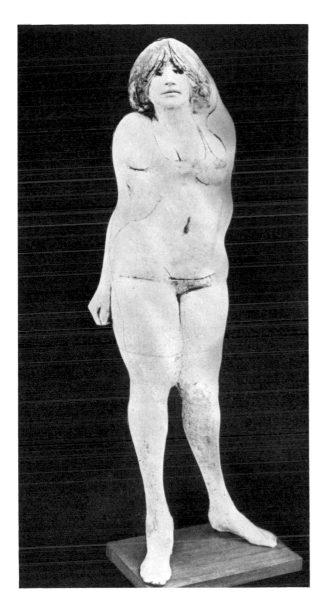

left : 554. Frank Gallo. *Standing Beach Figure*. 1965. Epoxy resin, 5′5″ × 1′7″ × 1′3″.
Courtesy Graham Gallery, New York.

right : 555. Alexander Archipenko. *Walking*. 1936. Red terra-cotta polychrome. Collection
Mme. Alexander Archipenko.

variants of observable form give the figure a life and a vitality that are almost
preternatural. Gallo has said that he finds the postures of human figures
"potentially expressive" and that for him "the celebration of the ordinary, a passion
for the commonplace, or subtleties of the incidental are grave concerns." We feel
that in the image Gallo has given us we have the figure as she truly is, that her
reality has been heightened for us by the liberties the artist has taken in modeling
the commonplace and incidental qualities of his subject.

Walking (Fig. 555), by the Russian-born American Alexander Archipenko, has
much in common with *Standing Beach Figure,* for in both these sculptures there is a
predominance of full, rounded curves distinctive of the female form. In certain
details the resemblance between the two sculptures is remarkable, especially in the
form of the legs and in the shape of the silhouette created by the line connecting
their heads and shoulders. But whereas *Standing Beach Figure* is realistic and

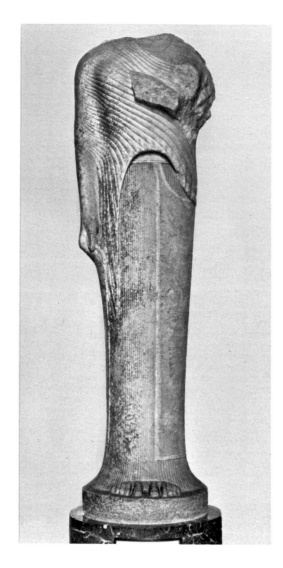 

explicit, *Walking* is generalized and abstract. In addition, the latter is presented, not at one instant in the process of walking, but at several instants somewhat after the Cubist manner of Marcel Duchamp in *Nude Descending a Staircase* (Pl. 44, p. 370). There is also the complexity of two kinds of form: the forms toward the edges of the sculpture are convex and positive, while those in the center are concave and negative. Part of the figure, therefore, is seen in a reverse impression, yet it is both attractive and convincing. Several such oppositions present themselves—concave and convex, the smooth and the rough, advancing and receding. Compared to the Gallo work, *Walking* seems reserved, withdrawn, and impersonal, but it is nonetheless ripe with a feminine essence.

Walking is a terra-cotta sculpture, that is, made of clay that has been fired. The nature of the material and the process the artist used on it are evident in the finished work, especially in the coarse texture of the outermost areas, where pieces of the plastic clay have been pressed onto the basic surface. The disposition and sequence of the several textures are also revealing of the artist's intentions toward his work. In all, the elements and their treatment in *Walking* constitute an esthetic purpose quite distinct from that in Gallo's *Standing Beach Figure*.

Hera (Fig. 556) is a religious statue carved over 2500 years ago for a Greek temple on the island of Samos. It is the most formalized work in the group of six figures assembled here. The sculpture is of a type called *kore*, or maiden, that was designed for a temple enclosure and represented a female figure bearing a votive offering. It is not known precisely that this kore was to portray Hera, the wife of Zeus and queen of the skies, but the commanding and austere character of the sculpture suggests no ordinary woman, perhaps even Hera. The figure is carved from marble, a fine-grained material that can be worked in infinite detail. There are many details in the *Hera*, but they are all subordinated to the columnar form. The arms are held close to the body. The folds of the garment, highly stylized, repeat the vertical line of the figure. The lower edge of the dress curves outward and, by repeating the line of the feet, provides a transition from the mass of the figure to the circular base. The general symmetry of the form, the patterning of the folds of the garment, the consistent tapering of the figure from the shoulders to the base all make it a sober, patrician presence. The facts of *Hera*'s anatomy and dress have been generalized according to the archaic style of sixth-century B.C. Greece. The effect of the stylization is one of power, control, nobility. It is interesting to compare *Hera* with *Hermes* (Fig. 109), a statue, possibly by Praxiteles, from a later period when the Greeks had invested their gods with greater humanity and given them a somewhat different role to play in religion.

Julio Gonzalez's *Woman Combing Her Hair* (Fig. 557) is also a highly abstracted form, but while *Hera* is reserved, monumental, and archetypal, this figure is active and spontaneous in the performance of a specific and intimate act. The material is wrought iron, which is singularly intractable, yet the figure possesses exceptional freedom and vigor. The major movements convey a sense of posture, and the small forms catch the essence of gesture. Because iron is tough and strong, many of the small parts are fine, open, and attenuated. *Hera* and *Woman Combing Her Hair* provide stunning contrasts in the effects possible in sculpture and, more narrowly, the effect possible in particular materials.

Most of the forms in *Torso* by César (Fig. 558) are ample and rounded, qualities that are feminine, but here the effect is less than pleasant and seductive. Full as the forms may be, they have a grossness that defeats any element of refinement. The surfaces particularly demand our attention, and they are rough and corroded.

opposite left : 556. *Hera*, from Samos. c. 550 B.C. Marble, height c. 5′3″. State Museums, Berlin.

opposite right : 557. Julio Gonzalez. *Woman Combing Her Hair*. 1936. Wrought iron, height 52″. The Museum of Modern Art, New York (Mrs. Simon Guggenheim Fund).

right : 558. César (Baldacchini). *Torso*. 1954. Welded iron, height 30 ³/₈″. The Museum of Modern Art, New York (Blanchette Rockefeller Fund).

559. Wilhelm Lehmbruck. *Standing Woman.* Cast in New York 1916–1917 from original plaster. Bronze, height 6'4". The Museum of Modern Art, New York.

This is a figure of despair; its once-healthy forms are now aging, the members and limbs lost and useless. Yet, curiously, the figure strikes a note of affirmation. It connotes the indomitable qualities of the human spirit surviving in the face of formidable odds, and it inspires a response mixed with admiration and disgust. *Torso*, too, is of iron, but here the figure is built up of small, generally rectangular plates that have been welded together. They are clearly visible in the reproduction on page 453. In the arms and the abdomen several of the metal rods forming the structure of the figure have been allowed to penetrate the surface. It is as if tendons and ligaments of the body had become exposed in the general process of the form's gradual disintegration.

Wilhelm Lehmbruck, a German, created the graceful bronze we call *Standing Woman* (Fig. 559). Like the Gallo work, this figure is a fully recognizable female form, but Lehmbruck has idealized it through systematic generalization. There is nothing of the casual stance or random gesture. Instead, we see a woman of timeless and mature physical beauty, an elegiac figure that gazes at the world with melancholy and sadness. The sculpture, in its great quietude and pathos, has a remote, antique quality, but the subdued glow of life in the delicately modulated surfaces saves it from neoclassic emptiness.

The nature of the various materials the artists have used in their works accounts in part for the differences we can identify among the six sculptures of female figures. More fundamental, however, are the distinctions among the moods, attitudes, ideas, and purposes that the artists have required their materials to serve as vehicles for. Such a limited number of examples as these six works makes it clear that sculpture has no less potential as an expressive form than painting.

With this general introduction to sculpture, let us now turn to more particular considerations of the art.

A Sculptor on Sculpture

Henry Moore, in the quotation that follows, gives us an original and well-articulated statement about sculpture and some of the problems that he—a sculptor—has found relevant for expression in this form. Moore, one of the towering artists of our time, responds with great intelligence and sensibility to the complexities of his field, and he speaks not only about sculpture but about his methods of working. Two figures by Moore are reproduced in Figures 560 and 561, and the artist's comments can do much to help us understand these works.

> It is a mistake for a sculptor or a painter to speak or write very often about his job. It releases tension needed for his work. By trying to express his aims with rounded-off logical exactness, he can easily become a theorist whose actual work is only a caged-in exposition of conceptions evolved in terms of logic and words.
> But though the nonlogical, instinctive, subconscious part of the mind must play its part in his work, he also has a conscious mind which is not inactive. The artist works with a concentration of his whole personality, and the conscious part of it resolves conflicts, organizes memories, and prevents him from trying to walk in two directions at the same time. . . .
> This is what the sculptor must do. He must strive continually to think of, and use, form in its full spatial completeness. He gets the solid shape, as it were inside his head—he thinks of it, whatever its size, as if he were holding it completely enclosed in the hollow

of his hand. He mentally visualizes a complex form *from all round itself*; he knows while he looks at one side what the other side is like; he identifies himself with its center of gravity, its mass, its weight; he realizes its volume, as the space that the shape displaces in the air.

And the sensitive observer of sculpture must also learn to feel shape simply as shape, not as description or reminiscence. He must, for example, perceive an egg as a simple single solid shape, quite apart from its significance as food, or from the literary idea that it will become a bird. And so with solids such as a shell, a nut, a plum, a pear, a tadpole, a mushroom, a mountain peak, a kidney, a carrot, a tree trunk, a bird, a bud, a lark, a lady-bird, a bulrush, a bone. From these he can go on to appreciate more complex forms or combinations of several forms. . . .

As far as my own experience is concerned, I sometimes begin a drawing with no preconceived problem to solve, with only the desire to use pencil on paper and make lines, tones and shapes with no conscious aim; but as my mind takes in what is so produced, a point arrives where some idea becomes conscious and crystallizes, and then a control and ordering begin to take place.

Or sometimes I start with a set subject; or to solve, in a block of stone of known dimensions, a sculptural problem I've given myself, and then consciously attempt to build an ordered relationship of forms, which shall express my idea. But if the work is to be more than just a sculptural exercise, unexplainable jumps in the process of thought occur; and the imagination plays its part.

It might seem from what I have said of shape and form that I regard them as ends in themselves. Far from it. I am very much aware that associational, psychological factors play a large part in sculpture. The meaning and significance of form itself probably depends on the countless associations of man's history. For example, rounded forms convey an idea of fruitfulness, maturity, probably because the earth, women's breasts, and most fruits are rounded, and these shapes are important because they have this background in our habits of perception. I think the humanist organic element will always be for me of fundamental importance in sculpture, giving sculpture its vitality. Each particular carving I make takes on in my mind a human, or occasionally animal, character and personality, and this personality controls its design and formal qualities, and makes me satisfied or dissatisfied with the work as it develops.

My own aim and direction seems to be consistent with these beliefs, though it does not depend on them. My sculpture is becoming less representational, less an outward visual copy, and so what some people would call more abstract; but only because I believe that in this way I can present the human psychological content of my work with the greatest directness and intensity. *

An artist can explain only in part his work and the processes he uses to shape it—the experience of translating abstract feelings and ideas into concrete, visual forms—but Moore has made several penetrating observations about art and its creation. He speaks only of his own views on sculpture and from his own experience, but his remarks nonetheless have a measure of universal relevance. Of particular interest is his observation that an artist should not speak often about his job, for such verbalization can cause essential tensions to go slack. Artists—who, after all, are committed to visual rather than verbal expression– generally tend to be reluctant to discuss what they have done, and Moore may well have identified the source of their natural apprehensiveness. Moore also points out that the artist works not only with the "nonlogical instinctive, subconscious part of the mind" but with the "conscious mind" as well. Although the artist may, through preliminary sketches, arrive at an idea that is "conscious and crystallizes" or may start with a "set subject," there are "inexplainable jumps in the thought process" that occur as he works. This interplay between conscious and unconscious, between logical thought processes and imaginative and intuitive leaps is no doubt very near the generative center of all creative endeavor.

---

* Reprinted with the permission of Penguin Books. Inc.

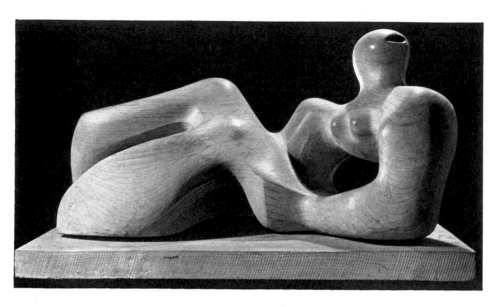

Reclining Figures by Henry Moore

The two reclining figures by Moore are of the same subject—the female figure—but twenty-five years separate the dates of their completion. The earlier one is carved in wood; the later sculpture has been cast in bronze. We can thus make a fascinating comparison of two sculptures using the same subject carried out in different materials at rather widely separated moments in the artist's life. The similarities are clear: both figures recline and in much the same posture; both have an elemental quality as if they derived their vitality and strength from the earth; and both have a primordial and timeless character.

In the wooden figure the forms are full, sensuous, and powerful. With only generalized anatomical references, they move, swell, and contract. Just below the breasts there is an opening in the figure, which is a penetration of form that Moore developed to relate the front of a figure with its back. Because of his deep respect

opposite above : 560. Henry Moore. *Reclining Figure*. 1935. Elm wood, 19 × 35 × 17 ¹/₄″. Albright-Knox Art Gallery, Buffalo.

opposite below : 561. Henry Moore. *Reclining Figure II*. 1960. Bronze, 4′3″ × 8′6″. The Museum of Modern Art, New York (given in memory of G. David Thompson, Jr., by his father).

for the materials he works with, Moore has not only revealed the grain of the elm wood but used it to accentuate the form and its surface contours. This heightens the elemental quality of the work, for wood is a material that by its grain reveals its growth and life. He has given the sculpture an organic rhythm that resonates both the wood and the great forces of nature.

The later figure is more abstracted, having been composed of two masses that, although related, are separate and distinct. The penetration below the breast of the first figure has been enlarged and now severs the figure into two segments. Large in scale, powerful rather than energetic in its rhythm, the work seems more substantial, a more thoroughly seasoned version of the original image. This work also has a visible relationship with the human figure, but, at the same time, it is a vast earth form articulated by the crags, cliffs, and caves of unconquered nature. It is as if the sculptor, even more than in the earlier work, had mastered the relationship between the enduring nature of man and the physical world—the relationship through which we are shaped by the forms of nature and, in turn, see nature in our own image. Both of these sculptures are large, convincing visual statements of the spiritual and psychological complexity of human experience.

Processes in Sculpture

There are three major processes by which sculpture traditionally has been executed—by subtraction, by addition, or by replacement. The carving of stone is an example of the first, a process in which unwanted material is cut away. The construction of a sculpture by putting together bits of clay or by welding together pieces of metal typifies the second. Sculpture cast into molds where a more permanent material replaces that with which the sculptor worked is the third major process.

Sculpture by Cutting Away: The Subtractive Process

In the subtractive process the sculptor begins with an unformed mass and by the removal of material brings into being the finished sculptural form.

The Materials   Stone and wood are the two major mediums used to make sculpture by the subtractive process. In many respects they are notably dissimilar. Stone is hard and durable, inorganic, and almost without limitation in size. Indeed, many hundreds of years ago entire temples were carved out of cliffs both in Egypt and in India. More recently, at Mount Rushmore in South Dakota and at Stone Mountain in Georgia, whole mountainsides have been carved into gigantic portrait heads of famous American presidents. Wood, on the other hand, is relatively soft and subject to decay. It is an organic material, showing through its grain the fact that it came into being by a process of growth. Furthermore, wood is limited in the size of the pieces it can offer. But both materials exist generally throughout the world, and both occur in diverse types. In Chapter 6 the qualities of color, texture, and hardness of wood were examined.

Stone is extremely varied in all respects—in color, in hardness, and in texture. Colors tend to reds, browns, and grays, although there are white, blue, and green stones. In hardness it ranges from soapstone, so soft it can be scratched with the fingernail, to granites, which are harder than many metals. In texture it can have the fine, even grain of marble or the coarseness of sandstone. Many stones are streaked, mottled, or otherwise variegated. In all, stone offers the possibility for a considerable array of effects in sculpture.

During the nineteenth century, white marble was especially favored because its fine grain could support the detailed carving current taste demanded. In this century sculptors have generally found marble too cold, even lacking in character, and they have preferred stones with pronounced color and texture. Moreover, contemporary interest in such new materials and processes as plastics and welding has drawn many sculptors away from the tradition of stone carving. Still, a modern, radically abstract sculptor like Constantin Brancusi (Fig. 562) has found marble an eminently successful material for his work, and even Henry Moore, whose sculptures seem so completely realized in wood and bronze, has worked right at Carrara, the age-old site where Michelangelo quarried blocks of white marble for his monumental sculptures. Wood is still favored by certain modern artists, often as "found" pieces of drift, tooled, or industrial wood for such assemblages as Louise Nevelson's *Sky Cathedral* (Fig. 570). Whatever the future may hold for them in art, stone and wood have over the centuries been the two major materials of sculpture.

The Tools and Processes   Chisels and hammers are the sculptor's basic tools in the subtractive process, although those for wood are different from the implements used for stone. The task of chipping and carving even a modest piece of sculpture demands not only artistic judgment but great stamina. Power tools have materially lightened the physical effort required of the sculptor, but the very resistance of the material has an effect on the result. The artist is, in a real sense, pitted against the stone or wood he is working on, and the toughness of the material makes its own special demands. It is time, space, and energy that make carved sculpture possible, and unless the artist has a strong commitment to carving, work is not even begun. This, in part, accounts for the historic prevalence of painting over sculpture, although the very toughness of the materials of sculpture has caused statues and reliefs to survive from antiquity, while virtually all of Greek painting, except that on pottery, and most of Roman painting perished long ago. It is also one explanation for a difference in the kinds of ideas that are developed in sculpture and painting. Since stone and wood sculpture is produced only by sustained physical effort and cannot be "dashed off" like a pencil or watercolor sketch, the subjects treated by carving sculptors tend to be monumental and deliberate. Nevertheless, we have seen in the Gonzalez work (Fig. 557) that spontaneous, movemented effects have been captured even with hard and resistant materials.

When stone sculpture assumes monumental proportions it becomes necessary to do a preliminary study of the ideas for the sculpture in a small model made of some easily worked material, such as wax. For sculpture this is the equivalent of a sketch in which the sculptor plans in small scale the basic organization of the large work. An often-used term from Italian for the preliminary model of a sculpture is *bozzetto*. Because wood sculptures are generally smaller in size and the material is more readily worked, they are rarely prestudied with wax or clay models. Often the artist makes his initial sketch directly on the block of wood and begins carving.

In both materials the sculpture is first "roughed out" in general masses, and at first attention is given only to the major proportions, the general movement, the over-all relation of parts. As the cutting continues, the work becomes more careful and precise. Details begin to emerge—the swell of a muscle, the folds of a drapery, the curl of a lock of hair. In the ultimate finishing the sculptor treats the surface to bring out the qualities he wants in texture, light, and reflection. Many stones and woods are capable of a high polish that emphasizes subtleties of form and modeling. It is then that some of the special characteristics of the material become most apparent—the fineness of marble, the crystalline sparkle of granite, the grain of wood.

Carving in Stone and Wood In Figure 563 we see the portrait head of the Egyptian Queen Nefertiti who, along with her husband King Akhenaten, reigned during the fourteenth century B.C. The head is from limestone that once carved was coated with a sealing ground and then painted. The right eye is inlaid with crystal set in black paste. The socket of the left eye is empty. The left eye may not have been finished, for the bust was discovered in 1912 during excavations of what had been the studio of a sculptor. That the head was buried for so many centuries accounts for its excellent condition.

Limestone, a fine-grained material, is, as the bust shows, subject to subtle modeling. Much of the detail, such as that in the necklace, is painted on the surface rather than carved in relief. The head is of an extraordinary beauty; the forms are all strong yet plastically refined, the expression both regal and serene. The long, graceful neck with its slightly swollen form responds to the thrust of the crown. In fact, seen in profile, the two major forms—the crowned head and the neck flowing into the shoulders—are closely related in their trapezoidal outline.

left : 562. Constantin Brancusi. *Mlle Pogany.* 1912. Marble on limestone base, height 17 ¹/₂″. Philadelphia Museum of Art (Louise and Walter Arensberg Collection).

right : 563. *Queen Nefertiti.* c. 1360 B.C. Carved and painted limestone, height c. 20″. State Museums, Berlin.

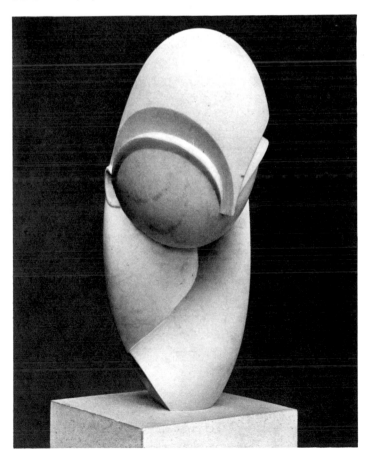 

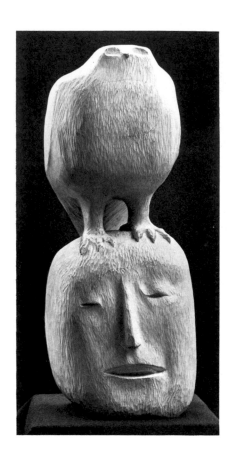

left : 564. Leonard Baskin. *Oppressed Man.* 1960. Pine painted white, 31 × 13 × 11 ¹/₂″. Whitney Museum of American Art, New York.

opposite left : 565. John B. Flannagan. *Jonah and the Whale.* 1937. Bluestone, height 30 ¹/₂″. Collection the sculptor.

opposite right : 566. *Kuan-yin.* Chinese, 12th century. Polychromed wood, height 42 ¹/₂″. Rijksmuseum, Amsterdam.

Leonard Baskin's *Oppressed Man* (Fig. 564) is carved from pine and, like Nefertiti, is composed of two similar forms. The head, however, shows none of the repose expressed by the Egyptian sculpture. Rather, the man's features are pulled out of position and distorted into the shape of anguish. The head rests directly on the base and is severed altogether from its body. There is perhaps a riddle in the bird, which, ordinarily a symbol of freedom, is here the only visible source of the oppression wrought upon the head. Like the bust of Queen Nefertiti, this too is painted, but the coating of white does not obliterate or supplant the handsome, textured surface left by the chisel marks. These, in turn, relate through their consistency the two major forms. Baskin, by leaving the gouges of the chisel clearly revealed, makes the process by which he created the work part of the esthetic of the finished sculpture.

Stone and wood are the materials used respectively in John Flannagan's *Jonah and the Whale* (Fig. 565) and the Sung Dynasty *Kuan-yin* (Fig. 566). The former is heavy, compact, and "stony"; the latter is light, open, and comparatively delicate. In *Jonah and the Whale* one has the feeling that Flannagan was as interested in the form and surface of the stone as a piece of stone as he was in suggesting a whale. He has used the density and weight of the material to convey the feeling of massiveness. The figure of Jonah is finely modeled, but it too is compact. There is a handsome contrast between the huge simplicity of the whale and the subtle treatment of the figure of Jonah trapped in the whale's belly, and Flannagan has humorously conveyed the discomfort of both participants in the sculptural drama.

The *Kuan-yin* is Chinese. It is a Buddhist religious figure, a seated female bodhisattva, a person who has attained enlightenment but who postpones Nirvana so that she may help others to attain it. Two traits, therefore, are clearly to be expected in the figure—repose and kindness. Part of the weight of the seated figure rests on one arm. The other is extended across a raised knee. The relaxation of the hand, the downcast eyes, the hanging garments, the sense of undisturbed weight all convey a feeling of utter peace and quietude. Kindness is also conveyed in the soft curves that give the work a gentle energy. This general sensibility is reinforced by the warm tones with which the sculpture has been painted. The openness and detail of the figure are the gifts of the material the figure is carved of. Because wood is not brittle, it will permit the sculptor to work thin and extended forms, such as the hands of *Kuan-yin*. Since it is fine-grained, much detail is also possible.

The dissimilarities between wood and stone sculpture derive largely from differences in their physical substances. Artists are generally great respectors of materials and use them with a sense of their natural integrity. In the instance of carved sculpture, wood and stone are related in that for both mediums the finished product is brought into being by a process of removing material, that is, the sculpture emerges as the sculptor cuts away unwanted stone or wood from the original block.

Sculpture by Joining or Combining Materials: The Additive Process

In sculpture that is built up the sculptor achieves the expression of his idea by joining or combining separate pieces of material, usually small ones. These can be

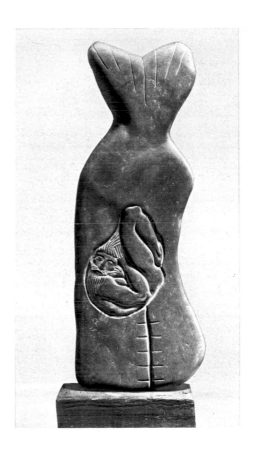

very plastic, such as moist clay, but rigid or semirigid materials—metal wire, rods, and plates, as well as wood—are combined in additive sculpture by such processes as riveting, soldering, welding, nailing, and glueing.

Sculpture in Terra-cotta   Few materials are as immediately reponsive to a sculptor's hands and tools as clay. A very plastic substance when moist, clay yields readily to the slightest pressure. Sculptors model in this medium by adding and pressing small bits of clay together until the desired form has been built. Once it has dried, clay becomes brittle and is a very impermanent material in this form. If remoistened, unfired clay can, however, be worked and reworked many times.

There are several ways by which a sculptor can make durable a work constructed from wet clay. He can fire the original in a kiln by a process discussed in Chapter 7. To be suitable for kiln firing, however, the piece must have been built so that the clay in its various parts is of a relatively uniform degree of thickness. Large clay figures are generally made ready for firing by building them around a hollow core. Should the sculptor want to obtain a number of replicas of a sculpture, he may make a plaster of Paris mold similar to those discussed in Chapter 7, cast the replicas in it, and then fire them. (This, then, becomes cast sculpture, which is discussed more fully in the following section, on pages 465–468.) In either case the result is usually referred to as *terra-cotta,* an Italian term meaning "cooked earth" that describes a coarse earthenware clay product fired at comparatively low temperatures. Although much more durable than unfired clay, terra-cotta is not strong. It breaks and chips quite easily and cannot survive any great strain or weight. It is a risky medium for very large works (although even in antiquity the Etruscans could fire lifesize statues from clay), and it is not suited to the sharp and thin shapes in which metal behaves so well. Terra-cotta, nonetheless, is a handsome, relatively inexpensive medium for sculpture.

Archipenko's *Walking* (Fig. 555) and Andrea del Verrocchio's *Virgin and Child* (Fig. 567) demonstrate what results can be had from working in clay and finishing in terra-cotta. In *Walking* Archipenko has exploited the soft, plastic quality of clay. He created the coarse, pebbly texture on the outside of the figure by pressing on and flattening small lumps of clay. The finer texture next to the rough surface comes from the artist's use of a modeling tool. In both *Walking* and Verrocchio's *Virgin and Child* there is a predominance of bold relief and rounded forms, characteristics that appear as naturally in clay sculpture as they do in pottery. The Verrocchio relief is also notable for its conspicuous variety. The softly rounded forms of the Madonna's face and hands and the Child's body are accentuated by the crisp, somewhat angular treatment of the clothing. Fine detail contrasts with broadly handled, simple masses. Like the Egyptian head (Fig. 563) and the Chinese figure (Fig. 566), the Renaissance work is painted and gilded, the polychrome enlivening the underlying forms of the relief. Verrocchio's terra-cotta sculpture resembles the Mallary piece (Fig. 553) in that both are relief sculptures. *Virgin and Child* is not a freestanding sculpture; its forms are attached to a background, and it is meant to be seen only from the front. In fact, a frame, complete with moldings, has even been made a part of the composition. The Verrocchio work is what is known as *high relief*; that is, its forms project boldly from the background, but in relation to sculpture in the round they have less body and depth. Relief in this kind of sculpture can range from very low to very high, and given the interest and the skill, a sculptor can achieve in relief a sense of form and space that is uncanny.

The present-day visitor to Mexico is invariably intrigued by the variety of hand-crafted figurines offered for sale in the markets. The subjects are numerous, but many are of people engaged in everyday activities and caught in all their familiar postures and attitudes. These little figures have a long history, for Indian craftsmen throughout the Western Hemisphere, especially in Central and South America, have

for centuries produced clay figures of strong character and excellent workmanship. Within recent decades pre-Columbian art has become the object of refined connoisseurship and avid collecting. *Laughing Man* (Fig. 568) is a Mexican work that is difficult to date with certainty. It may have been done anywhere from 600 to 1200 years before Columbus first came to America. But the figure's gesture and exuberance are timeless. The pudgy, nattily outfitted man is presented without pretense, and its very forthrightness infects us with the good humor it exudes.

Sculpture Built Up from Rigid Materials   A second kind of built-up sculpture is that in which material of a rigid or resistant nature is formed and joined to produce the finished work. We have already discussed the wrought-iron figure by Gonzalez (Fig. 557) and the fact that the techniques he explored set in motion methods of working that have been attracting the interest of an increasing number of artists. Succeeding sculptors have diversified not only the materials but the methods of handling them and the effects produced from the expanded range of materials. An important reason for the popularity of metal sculpture is that it utilizes both materials and processes of the machine age—iron, steel, copper, and brass worked by cutting and welding and by brazing with oxyacetyline torches. The results thus secured could have emerged only in the twentieth century.

We have also looked at *Torso* by César (Fig. 558), a sculpture that is built up of small plates of iron welded together. Seymour Lipton's *Sanctuary* (Fig. 569) is made of a combination of metals. Nickel, silver, and steel are all cold in color and highly reflective, but they also vary slightly in their color. Also, the surfaces created by melting silver and nickel over steel are richly variegated. The title suggests protection or refuge from threat. In the center of the sculpture we find a group of small geometric forms enclosed and shielded by large organic shapes. The work suggests a plant—seeds perhaps within a pod. The harsh, metallic form and strong, rhythmic

opposite left : 567. Andrea del Verrocchio. *Virgin and Child.* 15th century. Terra-cotta, polychromed and gilded, $30^1/_2 \times 23''$. The Metropolitan Museum of Art (Rogers Fund, 1909).

opposite right : 568. *Laughing Man*, from Mexico. Pre-Columbian A.D. 300–1200. Clay, height 14″. Memorial Art Gallery of the University of Rochester (R. T. Miller Fund).

right : 569. Seymour Lipton. *Sanctuary.* 1953. Nickel-silver over steel, height. $29 \, ^1/_4''$. The Museum of Modern Art, New York. (Blanchette Rockefeller Fund).

composition make a powerful image of the generative source. Lipton, like the Surrealists, is interested in the universal cycle of birth and death, and *Sanctuary* suggests the dark, enveloped inner core of life's primary force in a state of hibernal repose. It is enlightening to compare Lipton's *Sanctuary* with that of Albers (Fig. 399). In these works two gifted artists have used the same theme but pursued it in different mediums to make vastly different interpretations.

Teodelapio by Alexander Calder (Fig. 500) makes a striking contrast with the Lipton sculpture. Whereas the latter is coiled up into concentric introversion, the former is vigorously open and extroverted. Calder uses the term *stabile* for such works in order to distinguish them from *mobiles*, a form of sculpture Calder devised in the early 1930s to create moving three-dimensionality (Figs. 491, 492). But nothing is stable about the visual effect of this work. Touching the floor chiefly on points of curving edges, it seems literally to spring into the air. With their lively edges, the forms never repeat themselves and change constantly in appearance as one moves about the work. Made of sheet aluminum, the various parts of the work seem from certain views to be flat, organically shaped planes (reminiscent of the shapes in Miró's *Painting*, Pl. 53, p. 435), and from others to be thin lines like those to the right of the high, arrow-topped vertical. The illustration is the model of a large finished work that Calder made for the Festival of Two Worlds at Spoleto, Italy. On a public plaza in this little Italian hill town, the quiet of the medieval world confronts, in *Teodelapio*, the dynamism of the twentieth century.

570. Louise Nevelson. *Sky Cathedral*. 1958. Painted wood construction, 11'3 $\frac{1}{2}$" × 10' $\frac{1}{4}$" × 1'6". The Museum of Modern Art, New York (gift of Mr. and Mrs. Ben Mildwoff).

Louise Nevelson's *Sky Cathedral* (Fig. 570) is a construction of wood over 11 feet high made of a large number of variously sized and proportioned rectangular boxes and crates fitted together and filled with a miscellany of forms, many of them the "found" wood products of ordinary industry. Some of the boxes are open and reveal interiors with meticulously arranged contents. A few are largely closed and exclude our view. In the assemblage we recognize bits and pieces of familar forms—chair and table legs, balusters, arms and splats of chairs, newel posts, discs and cylinders, as well as planks and shafts of raw and finished wood. The boxes at the base are somewhat larger than those farther up, and the arrangement of objects within them is somewhat simpler. A coat of black paint assimilates the hundreds of disparate parts into a somber unity.

Sky Cathedral is an endlessly fascinating work. Each of the boxes with its mixed contents provides a complete and self-contained rectangular relief composition. More important, however, is the interplay throughout the construction among forms rounded and flat, thick and thin, open and congested, revealed and masked, horizontal, diagonal, and vertical. It is a man-made world that we view, with each part expressing its own history and purpose and all of it brought together by uniform black paint and a cold, raking light into a stunning concentration of artistic relevance. Even without the title, the construction would probably call to mind the richness and intricacy of Gothic carving. But this is a cathedral of modern times, an assemblage of the uprooted and discarded ends and scraps of our environment treated with remarkable poetry and magic.

For built-up sculptures made of other materials see Naum Gabo's *Linear Construction in Space Number 4* (Fig. 575) and Sol LeWitt's *Untitled* (Fig. 581).

All kinds of materials lend themselves to built-up sculpture. Paper sculpture, although very fragile, is capable of surprising and crisp effects, for paper—creased, folded, twisted, torn—is a highly plastic medium. *Papier-mâché* is both light and tough, and is used for such things as masks and stage properties. Sculptors are also using such mediums as mosaics, plastics, wire, and glass with ingenious and varied effect.

Today sculptors build up their works, using various kinds of materials, more than they carve and cast. Probably, it is not that the method intrigues them; rather, it is the necessity of using it in order to work with such materials as sheet metal, plastic, plywood, and found objects. Certainly, sculptors have worked with great genius to meet the challenge of the modern world image for image, employing built-up construction as their technique.

Sculpture by Replacement: Casting

In the process of casting, a mold is formed around the original model and into it is cast the material of which the final version of the sculpture is made.

Sculpture in Cast Metal   Building a model in clay is usually the first step toward producing sculpture cast in metal. In most cases, the finished product is in bronze. Henry Moore's *Reclining Figure II* (Fig. 561), the Benin head (Fig. 571), Jacob Epstein's *Social Consciousness* (Fig. 572), and Barbara Hepworth's *Sphere with Inner Form* (Pl. 20, p. 170) are all cast-bronze sculptures. Bronze is hard, strong, and durable with none of the softness of clay. Nonetheless, the cast piece may reflect the plastic quality of the clay from which the original was made.

If a sculptor intends a piece to be cast in bronze, he usually designs it with metal in mind. Long, or extended, forms are suited neither to clay nor to stone. In the Epstein work, however, the arms and legs are slender and attenuated, for the great strength of bronze makes them possible. Bronze, too, can support intricate detail, and it is often given complex surfaces.

Bronze castings are generally made by the *lost-wax*, or *cire-perdue*, process, which dates back many hundreds of years. In this method, the artist prepares a model of the piece to be cast exactly as he wishes it to appear when finished—in form, size, and detail. Over this a gelatin piece mold is prepared. Because of its softness and flexibility, gelatin reflects all details and can be removed from the undercut areas without losing shape. The inside of this mold is coated with wax to the thickness that is wanted for the bronze—about 1/8 inch. A core of investment material (mostly plaster of Paris and silica) is poured into the mold, and the gelatin mold is removed leaving the wax shell and the core. Wax rods are attached to the shell. These form a system of canals for the bronze to enter and the air to escape. The core is held in place with iron nails. A plaster-silica mix, reinforced with wire, is used to build up the outer mold. The core, wax covering, and outer mold, together, are called the *flask*, and when it is heated to 600° F, the wax melts and runs out through the canals. It is then heated to 1500° F to burn out any remaining wax. What remains is the core separated by a narrow space from the surrounding mold. Into this free space the molten bronze is poured. The outlets enable the air to escape as the bronze fills the mold. When cool, the outer mold and core are removed, and the final finish is given to the sculpture. Whereas in stone sculpture there is only one "original," in bronze a number of replicas can be made.

The casting of sculpture is an old process that has been used by such diverse groups as the ancient Greeks and Romans, the Chinese, and certain African tribes. From about 1500 to 1900 at Benin in Nigeria, bronze casting was developed to a high level, and the head in Figure 571 is a superb example from the sixteenth century. Bronzes such as this exemplify a court style and were dedicated to the ruler's glorification. As in most African sculpture, the features of this head have been distorted for expressive purposes. The abstraction is especially apparent in the forward thrust of the lower part of the face. The forms that connect the head covering with the ornament around the neck give the piece a simple, basic shape. But our attention is directed chiefly to the features, which are full and bold in form, making a strong, regal, and imperious image.

Social Consciousness (Fig. 572) is an important bronze by the controversial American-born English sculptor Sir Jacob Epstein. Planned for the Philadelphia park where it now stands, the sculpture is large in size and monumental in effect. In keeping with its theme, the work is filled with compassion, yet it is not in the least sentimental. It is a magnificent piece of design. There are majestic rhythms in the repetitions of the diagonals and verticals, in the relation of straight to curved and of taut to relaxed forms. But the humanity pervading the work is more than equal to the strength of the design. Here is a great human theme—that man is his brother's keeper—and it is given an expression consonant with its nobility. Significantly, too, Epstein was one of the few modern sculptors who could give an idea of this nature compelling form and avoid trite and hackneyed treatment. During the last hundred years we have had a surfeit of sculptures with noble titles and empty forms. In the twentieth century, sculptors, like painters, have largely turned to ideas that are subjective and that deal with private inner worlds rather than public problems. It is to Epstein's credit that he could deal meaningfully with a great human theme of the world common to everyone.

Other metals also are used for casting sculptures, such as lead, aluminum, and copper. Through electroplating, a sculpture in one metal can be covered with another. In some instances gold leaf is applied. Sculpture cast in metal is attractive to the artist because the result is very durable, yet it enables him to prepare the model

571. Altar head, from Algeria. Benin, 16th century. Bronze, height 8 3/8″. Museum of Primitive Art, New York.

in a material that is easily worked and that does not demand the great physical effort required to carve sculpture in stone or wood. In spite of their durability, however, comparatively few cast-metal statues survive to great age. This is not, however, because of a limitation of the materials, but because metals, especially bronze, are in themselves substances of such worth that many sculptures have been destroyed and the metal melted down for use in other products—often in cannons. But because of its many advantages, metal will continue to be an important sculptural medium.

Sculpture Cast in Other Materials *Polychrome No. 1* (Pl. 58, p. 472; Fig. 573) was made by David Weinrib of a material entirely new in sculptural history—plastic—and in using the mass-made medium for sculpture the artist has given it a distinguished treatment. The several forms in this sculpture (all cast by the artist) range from geometric to organic; some are compact, others attenuated. They are mostly warm in color—in the red and red-orange range—and with their highly polished surfaces they glow like jewels. Independent forms, they can be variously arranged and interlocked. Sculptors see in plastic a new, challenging, increasingly acceptable medium

above : 572. Jacob Epstein. *Social Consciousness.* 1954. Bronze, over lifesize. Philadelphia Museum of Art (Ellen P. Samuel Memorial, Fairmont Park Association).

left : 573. David Weinrib. *Polychrome No. 1.* 1966. Plastic, $1\frac{1}{2} \times 3 \times 3'$. Courtesy Royal Marks Gallery, New York. (See also Pl. 58, p. 472.)

for sculpture. Devoid of historical associations with art, plastics do not predispose the artist to any particular esthetic form, and with them he can feel freer to express his ideas in fresh and innovatory ways than he would with such traditional mediums as stone and wood.

Still other materials have been used successfully in creating cast sculpture. Jacques Lipchitz' *Man with a Guitar* (Fig. 574) is of cast stone, a material that can be worked with considerable variety in both color and texture. Compounded of stone and dust and a binder, it has the same general characteristics as stone— weight, hardness, and durability. Plaster is also used for casting sculpture. While it lends itself to an easy production of copies and can be given a number of different finishes, plaster is so soft that any sharp edges on the cast form become blunted, and its mat, lusterless quality prohibits replicas with sparkle and vitality. Being a fragile substance, it chips and breaks easily.

As in sculpture by subtraction, sculpture by replacement is a method with less interest for artists than it had formerly. But it possesses a great history and is a process that artists have used to ennoble world culture with some of its most illustrious monuments.

Happenings: A New Kind of Experimentation

A Happening is an event that takes place in an "environment." It may be an ordinary occurrence as when "spaghetti is eaten and cooked by at least two people," or it may be so unusual as an occasion when "at least ten people are packaged up in plastic film and are dumped or delivered by truck." These events, and others like them, are caused to occur in environments such as a supermarket on a Thursday or a Friday at 9 A.M., on a street at 5 P.M., or at a city dump at noon. And further directions may be given: "Each action may be performed once or twice and at one or two prescribed environments at their respective times, as desired." Allan Kaprow, in writing the score from which these quotations have been taken, listed five actions and three environments along with times. No action was tied to any environment, and all five might occur at the same place. Thus, in a Happening a large measure of chance is involved. Ordinarily, no Happening is to be performed more than once. If it is, it then takes on some of the aspects of formal theater prepared for spectators who come and pay to see a performance. If, however, two people cook and eat spaghetti at a city dump, and a number of other people happen to see it and stop and watch, that is another matter: however theatrical the situation, the participants in it have created a Happening.

Happenings are not sculpture, and some explanation is needed for their appearance in the middle of a chapter devoted to sculpture. Because they involve participants and settings, they seem logically to relate more closely to theater than to any of the other major art forms. On certain occasions they have been treated as theatrical events, but this actually eliminates one of the most significant features of Happenings—their essential randomness. Happenings seem relevant here, in the midst of our review of modern sculpture, because they demonstrate the extent of esthetic experimentation artists are given to today and can serve as an introduction to some consideration of the diversity of form and expression that modern sculptors have developed in their work.

In the preceding chapter a number of the concerns of contemporary artists were cited. These included the demand for the spectator's active participation in art, the importance of chance in determining certain aspects of art, and the blurring of traditional distinctions among the various arts. The creators of Happenings have as their major goals the realization of these very concepts, and their purpose is to develop new awarenesses that are not touched by traditional art forms. Many painters and sculptors have been actively engaged in the scoring and staging of Happenings and view them as important manifestations of the creative impulse. Whatever the ultimate contribution of Happenings to the accumulating heritage of Western culture, they have already had a salutary effect on the arts. In the theater they have succeeded in diminishing the distinction between performers and audience. At their most ordinary, such as the preparation and consumption of spaghetti by two people, they can heighten human consciousness of the multidimensional experience called life, and in their more outrageous and anarchic antics they can alter our whole awareness of reality. By fostering a fluid relationship between art and life Happenings extend still further the frontiers of the artist's acknowledged domain of interest.

Diversity of Form and Expression in Modern Sculpture

Sculpture recently produced and exhibited reveals an astounding range of subject, idea, and form, for contemporary sculptors, like their fellow artists in painting, have with the full scope of modern perception been exploring the subjective realms of feeling, the products and materials from technology, space and relativity, and all the forms generated by our century. Throughout the book, and especially in the first part of this chapter, we have examined a number of recent works, and in the remainder of the chapter we will consider still more specifically the problems and triumphs of modern sculptural art, especially its diversity.

Influence of Science and Technology

It would be difficult indeed to find a recent work of art that is not in some way or ways influenced by science and technology. Our attitudes, our beliefs, and our actions—and those of artists—are all part of the age of science, and are affected by it. The four sculptors cited in the following discussion have been selected to illustrate the influence science has had on modern sculpture.

Some observers are either apprehensive or pessimistic about the effect of science on art. Despite the anxiety, science need not be an unfortunate influence. In fact, the reverse may be the case. Artists have always created their works in terms of the major preoccupations of the period they live in. For them to ignore science would in all likelihood serve only to diminish their contribution to modern life. Artists should be depended upon to provide the humanistic values that can make life bearable in a mechanized world. They will at one moment use science and at the next warn us against its effects. But they will not ignore it.

The Cubist sculpture *Man with a Guitar* (Fig. 574) was done around 1915 by Jacques Lipchitz, an American citizen born in Lithuania. Cubism developed early in the twentieth century and was a semiscientific study of nature. The angular and mechanized forms that we see in the sculpture are the hallmark of Cubism. The figure has been geometrically structured and organized to express the interdependence of form, space, and time. Even with the considerable abstraction in the sculpture, the man and his guitar are discernible, but we are more strongly conscious of the work's structural organization, the forms vigorously complementing one another in shape, size, and movement. In *Man with a Guitar* form has been given precedence over subject.

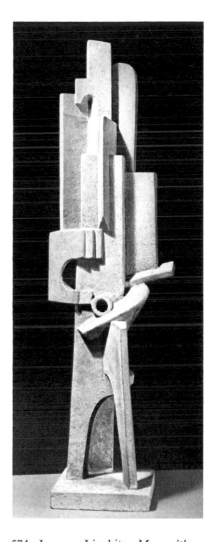

574. Jacques Lipchitz. *Man with a Guitar*. 1915. Cast stone, height 38 $1/4$". The Museum of Modern Art, New York (gift of Mrs. Simon Guggenheim Fund).

Linear Construction in Space Number 4 by Naum Gabo (Fig. 575) represents a search for rational, logical form. It is a descendant of the movement known as Constructivism, which developed shortly after World War I. Basing their esthetic on "an optimistic acceptance of scientific and technological progress," Constructivists regarded space and time as the essential elements of real life and, therefore, of art. They also believed that if they are to be creative and to produce work that is spiritually satisfying, artists must cease trying to represent the surface appearance of objects. One would expect to find in works based on such concepts a cordiality toward new materials. In *Linear Construction* the major shapes are made of plastic, and the artist has interrelated them with webs of nylon cord, which, although strung with mathematical regularity, produce patterns that cross, converge, and diverge in visually exciting ways. There is a consistent purity in *Linear Construction*. The forms are sharp, clear, and open. Tension is achieved only in ways that are clearly visible, and no psychological overtones are suggested. It has the beauty of a mathematical equation, with majestic and clearly perceivable relationships. And it is with little emotional involvement that we enjoy this poetry of form and tension.

All sculptures involve light. As with any object, we can see them only if light rays are reflected from their surfaces. So, in a very real way, sculptors have always dealt with light, for it reveals the subtleties of modeling, the changes of plane, the reflective or absorptive qualities of texture. But the sculptor was always dependent upon the light that fell *on* his work. Now, of course, because of electricity, we have devices for generating light in a controlled, efficient, and basically safe manner so that it is only reasonable for contemporary artists to develop works that *give out* light. Experiments in this direction go back some years, but recently the idea has gained momentum, and a number of artists have been developing sculptures that include incandescent bulbs and neon tubing. It seems somewhat strange that artists should take so long to exploit these materials. Perhaps it is the ordinariness of electricity in modern life that makes electrical material seem unfit for sculptures. Indeed, the reaction of many people to such works as Stephen Antonakos' *Marie's First Neon* (Pl. 57) is that neon light is not a medium with esthetic potential. In responding to the Antonakos sculpture, we must remember that because of our conditioning to the use of neon lights for the commercial advancement of such products as pizzas and beer, it is we who may be unfit to perceive neon as an esthetic material, although the material itself could be perfectly suited to any role we may want it to play.

Neon, of course, is a gaseous element that, when voltage is applied to it, emits a brilliant orange-red glow. We are familiar with neon encased in the coiled and tortured tubes of commercial signs. Now, other related gases are available that can produce different colors, and any commercial area at night is an active witness to the range of colors tubed light can create. Neon is used to refer to all these varicolored lights; thus, while a common term, it is no longer a precisely accurate one. All neon lights come in glass tubing of uniform diameter, and before the gas is introduced, this can be bent into any desired shape. They also require rather bulky transformers to lower the voltage of the electricity before it is passed over the electrodes.

In *Marie's First Neon* the sculptor had the tubing blown to the dimensions and shapes that he wanted. He also encased the transformers in the enameled aluminum base on which he placed the lights. At the base of the sculpture are four rows of blue lights parallel to each of the work's four sides. Rising from them are an arch form and a spirelike vertical shaft—both in colors that are primarily hot—and two angular projections that move, in the picture, off to the left. The entire sculpture is programmed so that individual parts light at different times and in combinations and patterns that are visual rhythm itself. Although not a large work, it possesses

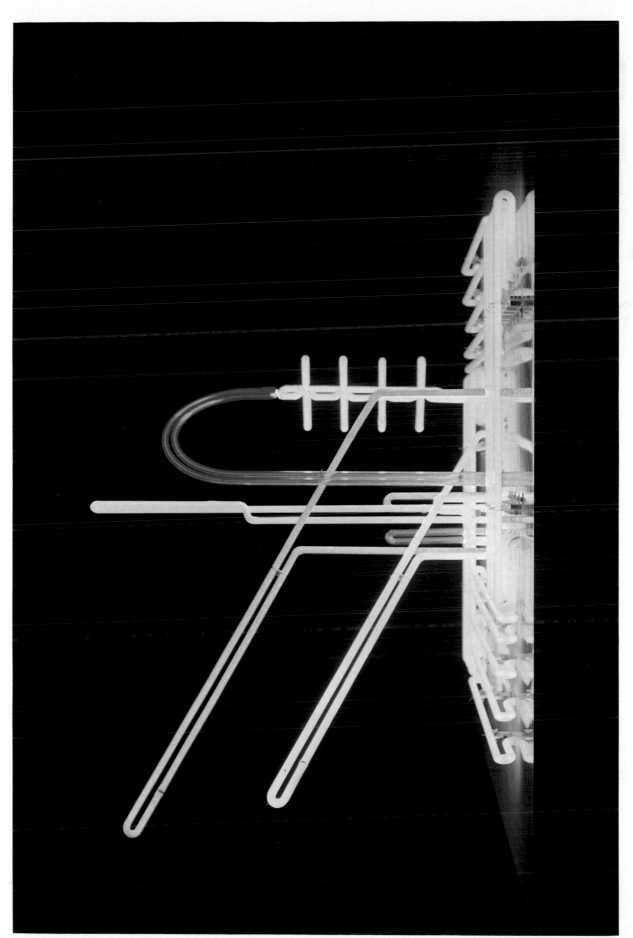

Plate 57. Stephen Antonakos. *Marie's First Neon*. 1965. Neon tubing and enamel-coated aluminum, 3′ 8″ × 4′ × 4′. Whitney Museum of American Art, New York.

Plate 58. David Weinrib. *Polychrome No. 1.* 1966. Plastic, 1′ 6″ × 3′ × 3′. Courtesy Royal Marks Gallery, New York. (See also Fig. 573.)

Plate 59. Marisol. *Women and Dog*. 1964. Wood, synthetic polymer paint, plaster, miscellaneous items, 6′ × 6′10″ × 1′ 4″ over all. Whitney Museum of American Art, New York (gift of the Friends of Whitney Museum of American Art). (See also Fig. 578.)

Plate 60. Isamu Noguchi. *Cube*. 1969. Painted welded steel and aluminum, total height 28′. 140 Broadway, New York. (See also Fig. 582.)

considerable scale. It is best seen, of course, in a darkened area, and in such an environment the work takes on a fascinating power.

Ernest Trova takes a different view of science and technology: its effect on man. For a number of years he has been working on the *Falling Man Series*, of which Figure 576 is a study. An image common to all the studies in the series is a figure without facial features, arms, or sex, a smoothed-down or unemerged demicreature who appears always in many duplicates and who seems inert and immobilized as if he were waiting for instructions from a computer to tell him what to do. The "falling man" is an exquisitely tooled standard part ready to perform whatever function may be required in the giant engine of life. In Figure 576 there is some slight variation in the posture of the figures and in the direction they face, but the differences seem external rather than intrinsic. Several have wheels or other devices attached to them, appendages that are mechanical rather than organic. In others, the bodies are covered with lines like those on graph paper, as if to prepare them for some sort of physical or psychological measurement. All the figures are isolated in separate boxes; all except the first and the last appear against dark backgrounds. It is an intriguing and disturbing work. We see man pressured into a state of conformity and stripped of individuality, isolated and robotized. These too are fruits of science, and Trova has named them for us in an appropriate and convincing visual language.

Pop Sculpture

Pop Art, the movement introduced in the last chapter as art that takes its ideas and forms from mass, commercial culture, has had as many sculptors as painters among its practitioners. The use of found objects, the technique of assemblage, and the conscious aggression upon the barriers between art and life all suggest three-dimensionality, the true realm of the sculptor.

576. Ernest Trova. Study, from *Falling Man Series.* 1964. 18 plaster figures in a compartmentalized wooden box, 4′ × 2′8 $^3/_4$″ × 6 $^3/_4$″; each figure, height 12 $^1/_2$″. The Museum of Modern Art, New York (John G. Powers Fund).

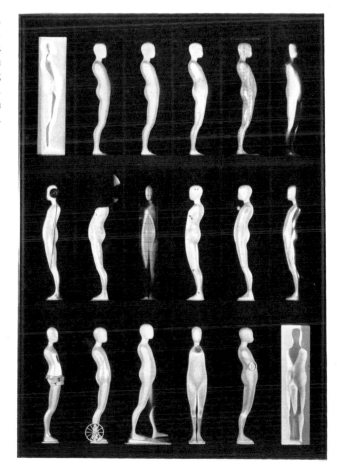

The Swedish-American artist Claes Oldenburg has done a series of sculptures simulating the common and ubiquitous foods available not only in millions of kitchens and supermarkets but in drive-ins, quick-lunch counters, and automats. He has produced such edibles as *Hamburger with Pickle and Tomato Attached*, *Double Hamburger*, *Ice Cream Cone*, *Cake-Pie*, and *Baked Potato* (Fig. 577). All the sculptures in the popular foods series are large in size. Monumental is the term that comes to mind, but the mind somehow balks at the notion of a monumental hamburger or baked potato. All of the food sculptures are painted in bright colors by a technique reminiscent of Abstract Expressionism, yet the effect is vastly different. Enlarged to macroscopic size, food seems, and is, vulgar, and Oldenburg makes no attempt to soften the impact. He is both attracted and repelled by his subjects. They recall the giant signs and food replicas that promote restaurants and roadside cafés, making a hash of the American street scene and countryside.

Oldenburg has sometimes been dismissed as a gag man, but entertaining though he may be, he also mocks and mourns the debasement of life and its good things, such as food, by crass commercial drives. Like most Pop Art, there is humor in Oldenburg's work, and part of it is in the discrepancy between the appetizing, almost luscious appearance of his foods and the hard dryness of their plaster substance. There is also humanity in it, for Oldenburg's subjects invariably have an intimate, close relationship with human tastes, needs, and desires. The artist has stated: "I am for art that takes its forms from the lines of life, that twists and extends impossibly and accumulates and spits and drips, and is sweet and stupid as life itself." It is interesting also to know that Oldenburg is one of the masters in the organization of Happenings.

Marisol, a Venezuelan, is author of a series of sculptures combining three-dimensional forms with drawn and painted surfaces. *Women and Dog* (Pl. 59, p. 473; Fig. 578) is representative of her work. Typically, Marisol has people (often herself) as the subject of her sculpture. In the Pop tradition she introduces identifiable artifacts into her compositions and uses materials as materials. The stuffed dog's head, the leash, the purse, and the hair ribbon in *Women and Dog* blur the distinction between the real and the depicted. The strong patterns and modish styles also characterize the sculpture as Pop. In *Women and Dog* we see not one woman but three, and a little girl as well as a dog. The three women, however, all have identical features (those of Marisol) and may be considered a trinity of images for a single person. The child and dog too might well be images from Marisol's own childhood. The absorption with self has the psychological associations of Surrealism, while the multiple images are a pictorial device from Cubism.

Although the figures—excluding the heads and legs—are rectangular blocks of wood, each is painted, decorated, and worked in ways that dramatize the flatness of surface and the nature of the base material while, at the same time, denying the surface and its material to suggest, almost as in *trompe-l'œil*, depth and dimension. In some areas, especially in the legs, the grain of the wood is clearly visible. The heads of the center and right figures are featureless ovoid forms that have naturalistic images adhered to or sketched upon them. Throughout the sculptural complex there is a continuous alternation between reality and illusion, the tension of the ambiguity held taut by the virtuosity of the sculpture's execution.

Minimal Sculpture

Die (Fig. 579), the 6-foot, black-painted, steel cube by the American Tony Smith, embodies many of the characteristics of work by recent avant-garde sculptors. It is remarkably simple; no details mar the absolute flatness of the cube's planes.

It is large, and like the recent work of many painters, it impresses and achieves *presence* by its very scale. It has no base or pedestal; rather, it rests directly on the ground, thereby proclaiming that sculpture is a reasonable and legitimate part of any environment and does not need to be set aside as something rare and special. It is made of a modern material, steel. Having been used little for works of art, steel has no sculptural history to predispose and distract the artist. The sculpture suggests nothing but itself. There are no allusive overtones to the work, and the observer brings to it whatever his own sensibilities may permit.

Die is an example of Minimal sculpture, a movement in which Smith has been one of the leaders. We feel at once *Die*'s relation to Minimal painting (see pp. 444–448), and the objectives of painters and sculptors working in the Minimal mode are much the same. In most of the movements of modern art it is the painters who have been the leaders and who generally have pointed the way for sculptors. In Minimal Art the edge is with the sculptors, and they are pointing out directions to painters.

The size of *Die* is worth further consideration. Its 6 feet rise slightly above the eye level of all but a few observers, and the work is thus somewhat over human scale. This gives it something of the character of architecture, and, indeed, much Minimal sculpture is architectural in its forms. At times, it appears that what has happened to painting and sculpture is also happening to sculpture and architecture, which is that the distinction between them becomes increasingly diffuse. To a degree, this is true, but the extremely large-scale effects of architecture cannot be incorporated into sculpture, nor can any of its distinctly functional aspects. Perhaps it could be stated that sculpture is taking on a number of architectural qualities, and these, as we shall see shortly, have renewed a relationship between the two fields that had all but disappeared.

It is interesting to note that Smith did not fabricate *Die*. In his own words, he "picked up the phone and ordered it," and workmen in a metal shop made it to his specifications. The cube, therefore, lacks the personal imprint of the artist that we

579. Tony Smith. *Die*. 1962. Steel, 6′ cube. Courtesy Fishbach Gallery, New York.

usually associate with works of art. We have already seen that Stephen Antonakos had the neon tubes made for his sculpture in Plate 57. Once artists use materials that demand machine fabrication, this practice is inevitable. It also coincides with the general feeling of detachment that artists have recently exhibited toward their work.

Larry Bell's *Untitled* (Fig. 580) is, compared to *Die*, relatively small, being only 20 inches on its cubic side. Mounted on supports above the floor, it appears to have a base, but the sheets of glass on which it rests are so transparent that one is not conscious of them. The desired effect—and this is achieved—is of the cube virtually suspended in the air. The glass on the interior of the cube is coated to produce iridescent colors—yellows, greens, reds, blues. These are spatially ambiguous and atmospheric in suggestion. The sense of space is real but not precise. The fascination of this work resides in the fact that one is presented with a cubed void. One looks into nothing and sees a great deal.

Sol LeWitt's *Untitled* (Fig. 581) is a 5-foot cube. But unlike the preceding two, this cube is divided into many subforms. Each edge of the cube is divided into six equal intervals with connections between them. There are 216 small cubes within the large one, all visible to the viewer. The material of this work is aluminum that has been coated with flat enamel. One set of dividers (those going directly into the sculpture in the view shown) is painted a dark value. The other two are light. This gives the work a striking optical variation.

Although this is basically a simple sculpture, it presents itself as appealingly complex. It is the vistas provided by the thirty-six "corridors" on each face of the cube that are intriguing. Each view is slightly different, each changes as one moves, each has its own set of diminishing rhythms that recede from the viewer.

A cube (actually a rhombohedron) of very substantial scale—28 feet high—is the sole adornment of the area in front of 140 Broadway in the financial district of New York (Pl. 60, p. 474; Fig. 582). It was designed by the Japanese-American sculptor Isamu Noguchi, whose long career has been one of the most productive and enriching in all modern art.

We can perhaps best appreciate the Noguchi sculpture by first considering its site and environment. The bank building occupies a rectangular plot edged by four streets. The building and zone codes of New York City permit a higher building where less of the total surface ground plot is used. In this instance, the architects and sponsors chose to take advantage of the law for esthetic reasons. Consequently,

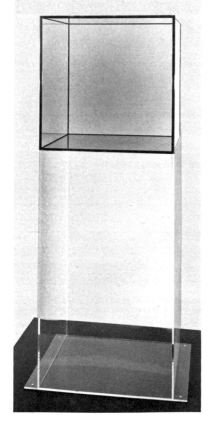

above : 580. Larry Bell. *Untitled.* 1966. Vacuum-plated glass, metal, 20″ cube. Courtesy Pace Gallery, New York.

right : 581. Sol LeWitt. *Untitled.* 1966. Aluminum and flat enamel, 60″ cube. Courtesy Dwan Gallery, New York.

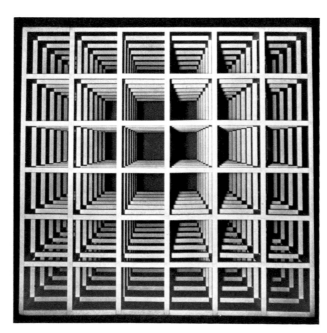

there is a broad, open plaza in front of the building and wide sidewalks on the other three sides, all paved in travertine, a handsome, coarse-textured stone, which extends in a flat, unbroken plane from the base of the building to the curbstones.

From the expanse of inert pavement, the building—its exterior consisting of four flat planes of metal and glass—rises abruptly and without interruption, tapering, or setback for 52 stories. It presents itself as a tremendous grid, a soaring shaft of severe, modern design. Its large glass windows, almost flush with the dark metal cage, mirror without distortion the Beaux-Arts elaborations of the older skyscrapers in the adjoining areas. The entire building is elegance restrained, and few equal it in refined understatement.

Noguchi's cube is a confident foil to the dark, gleaming, radically reduced architecture. Bright, almost tomato red in color, it acquires additional brilliance by being set off axis against the deep, bronze tones of the metal building. The tall structures surrounding the plaza keep it in shadow much of the time, and the sculpture's radiant color makes the area glow with warmth even on cloudy days. Poised on one corner, the cube sets up directional contrasts with the structure immediately behind it. Against the rectangular reserve of the building, the diagonals appear free, even exuberant. Although small in relation to the bank, the cube is yet more "minimal" in its statement than the architecture. The planar directions it establishes become, therefore, enormously powerful. Through the center of the cube and connecting two sides is a cylindrical opening lined with light, reflective aluminum (Fig. 582). The circular shaft penetrating the cube is echoed on the site of 140 Broadway only in the shape of the bench planters that punctuate the plaza on one side of the building. Against the severe rectangularity of this environment the rounded forms appear special, pure, and elegant. A well of light, a gene of color, Noguchi's dancing cube is the life factor in an environment that cried out for humanization.

We have referred earlier to the architectural nature of Minimal sculpture. There is a long tradition of architecture and sculpture complementing one another, and while currently there is close cooperation between architects and sculptors—in an age when sculpture is architectural and architecture is sculptural—there was a period in modern design during which neither form seemed to be able to enhance the other. Minimal sculpture can hold its own in the tremendous scale of modern commercial and institutional architecture, and the future seems promising for still more intimate collaboration between architects and sculptors.

Much Minimal sculpture is more complex than the examples illustrated and discussed here. The four cubes, however, demonstrate the eagerness and ability of sculptors to break with the past and to create freshly. They are thus turning to forms of great simplicity. Even within the limitation of a severe geometric form, sculptors can arrive at both effect and a remarkable variety of image.

Sculpture, one of the major forms of art, has been important in almost every culture. Twentieth-century work is marked by great diversity—in mediums, in methods of working, and in content. The human image, historically the sculptor's principal subject, is now less frequently used. Minimal sculpture, a current movement with strong impetus, has rejected all subject matter and aims toward a new direction unlike any that has preceded it. But Minimalists are not the only artists working in sculpture, and there are other significant expressions in modern sculptural art. Given their curiosity and sense of adventure, the sculptors of this technological age can assure us of constant change in their artistic production. Relying on their creative, often intensely personal vision, contemporary sculptors have given clear evidence of their genius to invent brilliantly. The ways of artists are such that the future of sculpture may seem unimaginable, but a future it will definitely have.

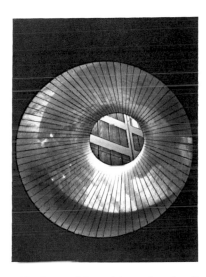

582. Isamu Noguchi. *Cube*, detail. 1969. Painted welded steel and aluminum, total height 28'. 140 Broadway, New York. (See also Pl. 60, p. 474.)

583. Andreas Feininger. *Windows*. 1967.
Photograph. New York City.

17 Architecture

The rulers of ancient Egypt built for eternity. Thus, the early Pharaohs drove their builders to design and construct massive, largely solid stone pyramids and funerary temples in which their dead bodies would be stored and preserved against decay, until the time when, according to the Egyptian religion, their souls would once more return to their bodies. The great temple complexes of Egypt were in fact necropolises, whole cities for the dead, complete with food, tools, and furniture. The Great Pyramid of Khufu has already been illustrated and discussed in Chapter 3 (Fig. 106).

In striking contrast, the eighteen buildings of Rockefeller Center in New York City (Fig. 584) are thin shells of steel, concrete, and stone providing offices, stores, restaurants, and broadcasting studios for thousands of people who work, visit, and have business in midtown Manhattan. The section diagram in Figure 585 compares the Great Pyramid with the three blocks of Rockefeller Center buildings that front on Fifth Avenue. (The tall center silhouette is of the seventy-story RCA Building.) The structures in the New York complex were built to be used, not by mummies waiting for eternity, but by radio (and now television) stars, executives, janitors, office boys, and the visiting public, all of whom are very much in the here and now. Rockefeller Center is literally aswarm with human activity of the most intense sort, and the human needs satisfied by these skyscrapers are vastly different from those the Egyptians had in mind as they made their incredible exertions to construct the Great Pyramid. However, our concern in this chapter is not only with human needs but with organization of space and with problems of materials and methods of construction and how they relate to and are integral parts of the design and appearance of buildings.

Man's problem in architecture has generally been one of enclosing space so as to make it usable for the practical and symbolic purposes deemed significant at any one historical moment. Progress in most fields of art is difficult, if not impossible, to identify and measure. Change we are certain of, but increase in esthetic quality is never easy to determine. With regard to the technology of architectural construction, however, one can state without equivocation that there has been enormous progress in the use of materials, and that today man is able to enclose more space with greater ease and less material than ever before. The American engineer R. Buckminster Fuller has said that "if you want to determine the degree of development of a building, just weigh it." By such a criterion, the Egyptians lose! The evolution of construction from the massive temples and tombs of Egypt to the light, open, steel

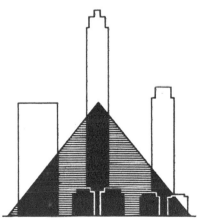

left : 584. Henry Hofmeister, H. W. Corbett, Raymond Hood, and others. Rockefeller Center, New York. 1931.

above : 585. Diagram showing the scale of the Great Pyramid of Khufu in relation to some of the buildings in Rockefeller Center. The RCA Building is in the center.

and concrete of modern, functionally designed architecture is as exciting as that of any natural phenomenon observed by Darwin.

But once man has enclosed space he can use it to serve as many purposes as there are human needs. Architecture can nourish the spirit by expressing human ideals and aspirations. And we find that such structures as homes, churches, temples, and governmental buildings in different cultures throughout the world tell us as much about the people who built them as the activities they shelter. Architecture functions in ways that are both symbolic and directly utilitarian, expressive and esthetic as well as practical.

In the preceding chapters there have been a good many comments on and illustrations of architecture, domestic and institutional. Here, the concern for architecture will be somewhat more particular; it will concentrate on the problems of design, construction, and expression in architecture. The discussion will begin by reviewing an architectural form that has evolved in recent decades.

The Skyscraper

Skyscrapers are an American art form, representing new conquests of space and materials. These "poems in steel" have added a new dimension to the urban scene. At the same time, they are, in their domination over the rest of the community, expressive of the place that commerce and industry occupy in contemporary life. In the Middle Ages the cathedral was the cultural and visual center of the community; in twentieth-century America, the "cathedrals of commerce" tower above all else.

What should a skyscraper look like? Does the architect, like the painter and sculptor, have problems of expression? What is the relation between structural systems and the appearance of a skyscraper? What are the effects of technological developments? Such questions have been the preoccupation of architects since steel construction and elevators first made tall buildings possible.

The Wainwright Building

One of the early skyscrapers was the Wainwright Building (Fig. 586) in St. Louis. Although built in 1891, it retains a remarkably "modern" look. It was designed by Louis Sullivan, a member of the "Chicago School" and one of the great architects of modern times. Sullivan was the first to realize that the skeletal frame of a skyscraper should be reflected in the design—that a tall office building should look like what it is and not like a Greek temple or a Gothic cathedral.

Sullivan's imaginatively sensible and revolutionary ideas flourished initially but were submerged by the revival styles of the Beaux-Arts School (so called for the conservative École des Beaux-Arts in Paris, where many American architects were trained in the late nineteenth century). This defeat of the first manifestations of modernism in architecture was wrought, curiously, by the success of the Chicago Fair of 1893, for whose design Eastern "palace" architects prevailed over the local designers. Chicago architects invented the modern skyscraper, and their legendary progressivism has earned them the title "Chicago School." In the 1890s and the early decades of the twentieth century, however, the new rich of the United States wanted architecture that could suggest "enduring" values, and they most frequently chose classicism. But eclecticism—which drew its forms and details from virtually all the historical styles (and was in vogue even before the 1893 Fair)—enabled architects to dress the new architecture in what appeared to be familiar clothing.

Sullivan recognized that skyscrapers are *lofty steel structures* typically used as *office space*. In the Wainwright Building height is stressed by emphatic vertical piers. The nature of the interior space, which is a series of small rooms similar in size and shape, is expressed by an organization of windows that is strictly regular but subtly proportioned. Sullivan's great contribution, ignored for decades but now fully appreciated, has eventually become a major influence in contemporary architecture.

There are several other features in the building that should be observed and kept in mind when comparing it with later skyscrapers. It has three major horizontal divisions: a base (the two bottom floors), a shaft (the seven identical floors making up its main mass), and a cap, or cornice. This is a design concept that developed originally in antiquity, and it is exemplified in the classical column (Fig. 592). Furthermore, the corners are conspicuously heavier than the vertical elements between them. Sullivan was designing in terms of a masonry tradition in which corners were for structural reasons heavier. And last, even though the Wainwright Building is multistoried, it remains human in scale. In recent tall structures, these three concepts have been rejected, but demonstrating Sullivan's links to the past does not in any way lessen the magnitude of his contribution. One has only to observe other buildings constructed at the same time—and later (see Fig. 587)—to realize the extent to which he was radically innovative in his designs.

The Chicago Tribune Building

The tower of the Chicago Tribune Building (Fig. 587) was built in the mid-1920s, and as we look at it today we wonder why a twentieth-century structure should be ornamented with fifteenth-century Gothic detail. The prototype of this building

588. "Butter Tower," Rouen Cathedral. 15th cent.

is the "Butter Tower" of Rouen Cathedral (Fig. 588), an excellent example of late French Gothic architecture. Built of stone, by virtue of the Gothic structural system of piers, arches, and buttresses, the tower and its forms derived from a method of construction that was integrally related to medieval life. Essentially a vertical style, the Gothic imparts a feeling of aspiration entirely in keeping with the religious fervor of the period.

Perhaps it was the common factor of verticality in a medieval tower and a modern skyscraper that led architect Raymond Hood to use the Butter Tower as a model. But this kind of choice could only have been made at a time when people generally were not bothered by depositing their money in classical temples, housing their governmental agencies in Romanesque palaces, or printing their newspapers in Gothic towers. Although they could accept the engineering that made tall buildings possible, architects and their clients could not embrace an esthetic based on technology. "Good taste" was an imperative that made them mask their structures in forms adapted or "lifted" from historic periods. Eclecticism was dominant throughout the first third of this century, and American cities became veritable encyclopedias of architectural styles. The leading architects of the time were men of taste and judgment. They believed their proper mission to be the responsible transmission of the great historical styles into the twentieth century. But our views of architecture—as recent buildings show—have changed substantially in the intervening decades.

In designing the Tribune Building on a Gothic model, the architect, of necessity, made many concessions and changes from the original source. For example, the Tribune Building is very much taller than the Butter Tower, and to achieve this height and meet the demands of space and economy, it had to be constructed with a steel frame. Still, Hood thought it important that the Tribune Building have an authentic Gothic appearance, and he therefore designed the external stonework to suggest that the entire structure had been done in masonry. Yet the slender piers of stone could not possibly stand if they were built apart from the steel frame. Near the top of the tower, where the first setback occurs, the designer (following the model) has introduced a series of flying buttresses that in Gothic construction resisted the thrust outward of the arches in the center and thereby held the structure together. In the Tribune Building the forms are false; they support nothing, perform no structural function, and are pure decoration.

Withal, the building is handsome, and one could apply to it, with favorable results, all the principles of design. It is subtly detailed and proportioned and was clearly conceived by a designer of taste and discrimination. Yet, while making use of modern technology, the Tribune Building attempts to conceal it; while housing the complex of activities involved in the production of a newspaper for a large American city, it arbitrarily takes on the appearance of an architectural style that now seems totally unrelated to its time, place, and function.

The New York Daily News Building

Hood also designed the New York Daily News Building (Fig. 589), built six years after the Chicago Tribune Building. It is definitely in the Sullivan tradition, but in starker terms. There is an irony in the triumph of Chicago ideas in a newspaper building in New York, whose own designers were responsible for the eclipse of the Chicago School and for the Gothic revivalism in the Chicago Tribune Building. The bold and simple forms of Hood's Daily News Building proclaim the verticality of the skyscraper. The bands of masonry are clearly nonsupporting, and the space between is given over to the windows and the medium-brown panels that separate them between floors. On the shafts themselves, there is no detail; their great effectiveness comes from the design inherent in the structure. The facing is light in value, almost white, and presents a dazzling contrast with the sky, especially on sunny days. The window shades in the entire building are a soft rust color, and these provide a note of warmth in the generally severe design.

The extent to which the design of the Daily News Building was revolutionary can be seen by contrasting it with the Wainwright and Chicago Tribune buildings. In this wholly modern, twentieth-century structure, an esthetic based upon the precision and duplication of machined forms has been realized. An attendant feature is the loss of human scale. Even the windows as individual elements tend to disappear in the general design. The Daily News Building served to direct the attention of architects to franker statement and to the utilization of structure as the basis for design. As we look at some of the skyscrapers designed after it we see how the innovation introduced by Hood became the design imperative of much modern architecture. Our sensibilities have adjusted to these skyscrapers, and we have come to accept the absence of human scale and the use of machined forms as the established environment of modern life.

Lever House

In the Lever House (Fig. 590), designed by Gordon Bunshaft of Skidmore, Owings, and Merrill, and situated on New York's Park Avenue, the stainless steel and glass surfacing of the building mark it as a product entirely of the machine age. It has nothing of the masonry tradition that for thousands of years characterized most Western architecture. Here is an uncompromisingly frank and lucid architectural

left : 589. Raymond Hood. Daily News Building, New York. 1929–1930.

right : 590. Gordon Bunshaft of Skidmore, Owings, and Merrill. Lever House, New York. 1952.

statement. It is a steel and concrete *cage* that has been sheathed in a glass and stainless steel *envelope*. The walls, or *skin*, constituting the envelope have been separated from the structure.

There is a brilliant clarity about the Lever House design. At the base of the building a horizontal unit is supported one story above the ground on gleaming metal piers to create an unbroken pedestrian space extending over the entire plot, except for that occupied by the glass-enclosed lobby directly beneath the main mass of the building. Above the horizontal form, but separated from it by an indentation or "notch," rises a handsomely proportioned rectangular solid that is encased in green-tinted glass and stainless steel. The two major forms are opposed and sharply articulated. The free walkway at grade level, the concentration of the tower in no more than 25 percent of the available air space, and the disposition of the slab structure along one edge of the site all invest the Lever House with an extraordinary lightness and clean, immaculate grace. It seems simply to float on its platform, well above the ground. On the sunlit side of the slab the horizontal bands dividing the floors are visible. On the shaded side the sheathing serves as a gigantic, reflecting surface for adjacent buildings and passing clouds. The depth of the reflected images makes the Lever House seem almost ephemeral. This, too, heightens the impression of lightness.

The Lever House set a new style in skyscraper design, but many of the "slab" buildings imitating it use glass and metal sheathing to encase structures of indifferent, often inferior design. Nonetheless, the Lever House and buildings like it represent a brilliant exploitation of twentieth-century technology in skyscraper design.

The John Hancock Building

The hundred-story John Hancock Building (Fig. 591) in Chicago, also by Skidmore, Owings, and Merrill, presents several quite original features. First, its tall shaft is *tapered*, or, more precisely, its form is that of a stretched and truncated pyramid. The designers have thus rejected the glass-curtained rectangular solid that has dominated tall-building design since the early 1950s.

A structure of this altitude would stand out whatever its architectural environment. However, the tapered form of the John Hancock Building sets it even more sharply apart from its neighbors and visually gives it still greater height than it actually has. It virtually dwarfs the surrounding structures, for the giant cross-girders (a structural system used also in San Francisco's Alcoa Building, Pl. 6, p. 44), although basically simple forms, are so vast in size that they diminish the scale of all other forms to the level of mere fussiness. The John Hancock Building is also a departure from much high-rise design in that its skeleton is exposed, not masked by a sheath. Although clearly a product of advanced technology, it has none of the sleek elegance and reserve of Lever House. Rather, it is an aggressive, powerful building in a city noted for the strength and originality of its architecture.

In addition, the building is unusual in combining offices and apartments. The upper floors, at the tapered end of the shaft, offer close integration of interior space with window exposure and are thus more suitable to domestic occupation. The lower, more expansive floors are, because of their larger interior spaces, designed to be used as offices.

The John Hancock Building is as radical in its break with current practice as were the Wainwright, Daily News, and Lever buildings at the time of their completion. It suggests that our architecture may be going into yet another phase, one of superscale—architecture that would be in keeping with the supercities now emerging. Our urban communities have grown to such grotesque and uncoordinated size

591. Skidmore, Owings, and Merrill. John Hancock Building, Chicago. 1968–1969.

that in their sprawling inefficiency they have become prodigally wasteful of time and energy. The development of superconcentrations in the form of buildings even taller than the ones we are accustomed to, offering contiguous living and working areas, may well be one manifestation of the architecture of the future.

The Lever House, Philip Johnson's home (Pl. 2, p. 8; Figs. 9, 10), and the United Nations Headquarters (Figs. 84,85) exemplify the International Style in architecture. In these buildings form is clearly stated, the surfaces are clean, even stark, and the picturesque has been rejected altogether. They represent a style that was formulated primarily at the Bauhaus (see pp. 119, 120), a style that during the 1920s had a parallel expression in the American architecture of Rudolf Schindler and Richard Neutra. Its presence in the United States was reinforced by Bauhaus designers and teachers who arrived in North America just prior to and during World War II. Rather than look back, the International Style readily accepts the present and finds within it the rationale and sensibility for an esthetic that expresses its own time. The John Hancock Building, however, is not readily classifiable. It has the same frank statement, the same starkness, but in its several departures from the primary expressions of the Bauhaus formula, it may have taken the first step toward a new and independent style yet unnamed.

Skyscrapers have, obviously, changed in design since they first became possible in the closing years of the nineteenth century, but as technology advances they seem to become a still more vitally relevant form of construction. As long as they offer a meaningful reality for human needs, skyscrapers will be designed and built, and in the organic play between needs and solutions, designers will certainly innovate and develop well beyond the most visionary and monumental achievements of the present. Shaping as they do much of our environment, architects and builders can, within the limitations imposed by general consent, be a significant factor in the success or failure of modern culture.

Architectural Construction

In general, architecture has three components directly comparable to the human body: the *skeleton*, or frame, that supports the building; the *skin* that encloses it; and the *equipment*, or "vital organs," through which air, light, sound, and sanitation are controlled. In early architecture little distinction was made between skeleton and skin, and little provision was needed for equipment; today each of these components has been the subject of careful study, although in some recent work the distinction between skeleton and skin is again disappearing as new materials and techniques make possible new methods of construction.

Systems of Construction

Historic systems of architectural construction are generally classified in four categories:

- *Post-and-lintel*, in which horizontal beams are laid across the spaces between upright supports (Fig. 595). If the upright support is a continuous wall instead of separate posts, the system is more aptly called *wall-and-lintel*.
- *Cantilever*, in which load-carrying beams, or members, project beyond their supports (Fig. 628).
- *Arch*, in which small wedge-shaped pieces of material are placed with joints at right angles to the curve (Fig. 597). This defines the *true*, or *radial*, arch, but the term has come to describe any structure with curved elements.

- *Truss*, in which members such as beams and bars are assembled into a rigid triangular framework (Fig. 625).

A great many architectural styles have throughout the world been developed from these basic systems. But useful as the four categories may be in studying historic work, they are completely inadequate for understanding contemporary practice. Today architects and engineers usually divide buildings into two major categories:

- *Bearing-wall construction*, in which the wall supports not only itself but the floors and roof as well: skeleton and skin are one and the same thing. For example, in a log cabin or a solid masonry building the walls *are* the structure. Two specialized variants of this system deserve mention: (1) *monolithic construction*, in which the material is continuous—that is, not jointed or pieced together—as in concrete structures (Figs. 609, 610, 615, 616), and (2) *structural skin construction*, in which sheet materials (such as plywood or sheets of metal) are placed and held under stress to assume a structural form. In this second variant skin and skeleton are fused, but they are more or less continuous, thin sheet materials rather than "chunks," and their shape exploits their potential strength. Typical examples in nature are the shell of an egg or of a turtle. It is seen also in inflated balloons, silos, grain elevators, and oil storage tanks of wood, concrete, or metal, such as the Hortonspheres (Fig. 636). This is also called *stressed skin*, *shape engineering*, and, in the airplane industry, where it is used for wings and fuselages, *monocoque*.

- *Skeleton frame construction*, in which a framework supports the building, and the walls (or skin) are merely fastened to it (Figs. 617, 623). This is called *balloon framing* in wooden-house construction, *steel-cage* in skyscraper construction. Two specialized types of skeleton frame construction merit attention: (1) *cantilever construction*, as explained above, and (2) *suspension construction*, in which the structure is suspended from a tower mast, as in suspension bridges (Fig. 228) and the roof of the Kagawa Gymnasium (Figs. 631–633).

The following, major portion of this chapter will examine architecture in relation to the four principal materials that have shaped it—stone, concrete, wood, and steel—for it is out of the properties of these materials and their uses that the basic structural systems have been developed. A general understanding of the primary building materials and systems can help explain all the building forms, whether contemporary, historic, or derivative.

Building in Stone

Because of the actual and suggested permanence of stone, most of the world's great architecture, public and private, has been constructed from this material. Thus, the stone tradition has permeated even contemporary architectural thinking and has determined much of today's taste and judgment.

In the United States, however, there has never been a genuine stone tradition. At first, the need for quick shelter led the colonists to use wood. By the time brick became common, Colonial architecture was a reflection of English work, and stone was not used extensively until the revivals of Greek, Roman, Gothic, Romanesque, and other styles set in. There are, therefore, many American buildings in which stone and brick are important but not live components of a contemporary tradition. For the most part, the masonry in American buildings has been used as surfacing over metal skeletons, and while often attractive, the bricks and stones are skins, or curtains, without structural significance.

Post-and-Lintel: The Parthenon

Post-and-lintel construction was superlatively employed in one of the seminal and most illustrious buildings in the Western world—the Parthenon on the Acropolis in Athens, Greece (Figs. 592–594). Built about 2500 years ago (448–432 B.C.) as a temple in honor of Athena Parthenos, the patron goddess of Athens, the Parthenon remains the crowning glory of the Athenian Acropolis. The illustrations are of the building in its present state and of a model that conjectures its original appearance. With the advent of Christianity the cult of Athena was replaced by dedication to the Virgin Mary. After the Turkish conquest, the Parthenon became a mosque. During a conflict with the Republic of Venice the Turks stored gunpowder in the building, and in 1687 a random bomb set off the ammunition that blew out the central section. From 1801 to 1803 much of the sculpture was removed by the British diplomat Lord Elgin to England, where it now is displayed in the British Museum. Thus, the Parthenon comes to us as a legendary, damaged magnificence, a noble ruin.

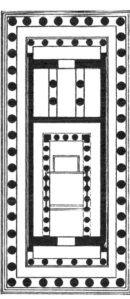

above : 592. Ictinus and Callicrates. The Parthenon, Athens. 448–432 B.C.

right : 593. Reconstruction of the Parthenon. The Metropolitan Museum of Art, New York (Purchase, 1890, Levi Hale Willard Bequest).

above right : 594. Plan of the Parthenon.

The plan (Fig. 594) shows the rectangular simplicity of the building. It was surrounded by a colonnade, with a second row of columns at each end. Of the two rooms composing the interior, the larger housed an ivory-and-gold statue of Athena, the smaller was a treasury. The temple, as the plan makes clear, was not designed to hold large groups of worshipers, for the religious festivities of the Athenians took place mainly outside the building.

The Parthenon is built on the basic post-and-lintel system (Fig. 595). The structural logic of the upright posts supporting horizontal beams (or lintels) can be readily demonstrated by standing two books on end and bridging the gap with a third. Through this system builders and architects have given us some of the world's most distinguished buildings. The Parthenon, however, reveals one of the major limitations of post-and-lintel construction when stone is used. Notice that the columns (posts) are set relatively close together, not necessarily because the designers, Ictinus and Callicrates, wanted them that way, but because stone lintels of great length are not feasible. As a building material, stone is strong in compression but weak in tension (that is, when stretched or strained). Stone posts can be high because the weight above merely compresses them. Lintels, however, are another matter. The upper half is in compression; the lower half is in tension. Therefore the tensile strength of the material used is a determinant of the design—lintels of wood or steel can be much longer than those of stone.

One of the most convincing theories about the genesis and development of the Parthenon's form, now considered the acme of classical perfection, is that the parts of the building and their interrelationship derive from earlier constructions in wood. Columns are natural forms in wood, for a straight tree trunk provides one ready made. The translation of wooden columns into stone is less natural, because to make a tall column, marble must be built up in separate pieces called *drums*. The vertical fluting, or channeling, on the columns could have originated in the woodsman's adz marks. In marble the flutes serve to integrate visually the several drums into a single shaft. The triglyphs—the rectangular forms that appear directly above the columns in the frieze—are modified beam, or lintel, ends. The Greeks would have employed stone because it was a more durable material, especially since Greece itself is blessed with some of the finest marbles in the world.

A brief description of the parts of a classical building such as the Parthenon is pertinent because the forms themselves have been in use ever since they were developed, and there are few towns in the Western world that do not have one or several buildings that are classical in design. The temple rests on a sturdy base of three high steps, called the *stylobate*. Above this rise the *columns*, vertical *shafts* surmounted by simple but delicately curved *capitals*; the columns are *channeled* to make them seem more slender, and the capitals form an admirable transition between the vertical columns and the horizontal *entablature*. The *architrave*, adorned with bronze shields, acts as a good foil for the sculptured panels in the *frieze*, above which is the *cornice*. Architrave, frieze, and cornice make up the entablature, just as the shaft and capital make up the column. Surmounting all is the *pediment*, filled with sculpture subtly adapted to the triangular space. The Parthenon is built in the Doric Order—a style in classical architecture that is identifiable by its column and the entablature it supports. The other classical orders are Ionic, Corinthian, Tuscan, and Composite.

To attempt to describe the beauty of the Parthenon is difficult, for beauty seems always to remain in some measure ineffable. To be sure, the proportions are exquisite; the glistening Pentelic marble is one of the finest building stones the earth produces; the resplendent sculpture both inside and outside the building, originally painted in vibrant polychrome (as was the entire structure), enriched it

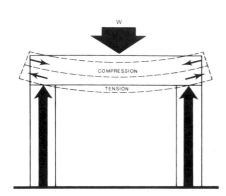

595. Post and lintel.

immeasurably. Yet none of these alone can explain why the Parthenon is a symbol of the beautiful. It is a basic fact, however, that every part is inextricably related to the whole design. Beauty is often considered a matter of harmonious, functional relationships, of adjusting each part to its neighbors through careful refinements. The Parthenon is remarkably refined both in its parts and in their interrelationships.

Of the many ingenious devices employed by the architects, only those concerned with correcting optical illusions will be mentioned here. Although we are not generally aware of it, forms and lines do not always appear to the human eye as we know them to be. For example, long horizontal lines seem slightly concave; identical spaces do not always appear equal. Through several centuries, Greek builders observed these phenomena in their temples and developed means of overcoming them. The architects of the Parthenon used a number of refinements to help give the building a vibrant, living, perfectly integrated quality that accounts, in part, for its enduring reputation. Some of the major modifications are listed below.

Optical Illusion	*How It Was Corrected*
Long horizontal lines in a building appear to sag.	All the long horizontals, such as the steps and the cornice, are bowed up in the center. The amount of this correction across the front is about $2^1/_2$ inches.
Columns with straight sides appear concave.	The columns are given a slight bulge, or swell, called *entasis*.
A building rising straight up from the ground often appears to be leaning forward.	The whole front of the Parthenon is tilted backward slightly (about $2^1/_2$ inches).
Equal spaces between columns in a colonnaded front do not appear equal.	Distances between columns are different to make them all appear equal. The space at the center is the largest, and the spaces get progressively smaller toward the corners.
Columns silhouetted against the sky appear slenderer than when seen against a darker background.	The corner columns, often seen against the sky, are heavier than the other columns in the colonnade.

596. Roman aqueduct, Segovia. A.D. 10.

It is a testament to the sensitivity of the Greeks that they built with such discernment. The Parthenon expresses great repose, due probably to the horizontality of its major mass. The contrast of the vertical columns, the enrichment of the capitals, moldings, and sculpture, all give it an air of restrained vitality. It remains an ultimate achievement in post-and-lintel stone construction.

The Round Arch: The Roman Aqueduct at Segovia

The aqueduct built by the Romans at Segovia, Spain, shows clearly the characteristics of arch construction (Fig. 596). Unlike the Parthenon, in which each opening was spanned by a single beam or piece of material, each opening in arch construction is spanned by a number of pieces of material. The advantages of the arch are immediately apparent. An opening is not limited by the length of a beam, and, through the use of relatively small pieces of material, areas of great dimension can be spanned. The Greeks knew the principle of the arch, but they made little use of it.

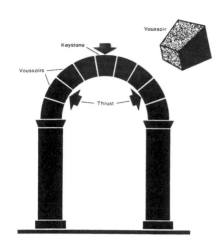

597. Round arch.

Perhaps the arch form was incompatible with their ideals of beauty, concerned as they were with harmony and repose. It was the Romans, their immediate followers in the evolution of architecture, who exploited the possibilities of arch construction. Indeed, the arch and its perfection in varied forms were a central preoccupation of builders for about two thousand years.

The type of arch the Romans used was the round or semicircular one, and it became so integral a part of their building that arches of this form are still referred to as Roman. Its development was intimately related to the development of the Romans as a people. We know that they were more aggressive and materialistic than the Greeks. Their commercial activities, big public assemblies, fabulous banquets, and renowned trials demanded buildings with larger, more flexible interiors. The arch provided a structural basis for such buildings, but the Romans found other uses for it as well. Monumental arches commemorated the conquests of triumphant leaders. Vast amphitheaters permitted multitudes to enjoy circuses and pageants. Arched bridges over rivers, together with good roads, enabled armies to march swiftly. And arched aqueducts, built so well that some are still standing, brought water great distances to key cities. The arch was a dominant motif in Roman architecture.

As can be seen in the Segovia aqueduct, an arch is made up of wedge-shaped pieces of materials (*voussoirs*) with joints at right angles to the curve. Stone is a material uniquely suited to arch construction because all material in an arch is in compression. Stone can stand great pressure and is, of course, extremely durable.

The arch, by its nature, is subject to lateral thrust, or *spreading* (see Figs. 597, 605). This may be easily demonstrated by arching a piece of paper and then slowly bringing weight to bear on top of it. The arch, when depressed in the center, spreads at the sides. These movements, indicated by the arrows in Figures 597 and 605, are characteristic of all arches. Furthermore, the flatter the arch, the greater its tendency to spread. Tall, pointed, or parabolic arches have less tendency to spread and therefore need less support. To counteract this lateral thrust, arches need to be supported or braced at the point of weakness. This is done in various ways—with a solid wall, with another arch, or with a buttress.

The difference in effect between post-and-lintel and arch construction can be made apparent by comparing the Parthenon with the interiors of St. Peter's in Rome and Rheims Cathedral (Figs. 601, 604). Whereas the Parthenon, composed of balanced horizontals and verticals, seems almost inert or static in its settled equilibrium, the Christian buildings, whose structural continuity derives from interdependent arched forms, suggest energy and movement. The highly dynamic effect of the arch stems not only from its shape but from the fact that it is a basically unstable architectural form. For this reason, structures supported mainly by arches are likely to present a vigorous, activated image.

The Vault and the Dome: St. Peter's in Rome

The principle of the arch gave rise to *vaults*, which are arched coverings in masonry. The most basic form of vaulting, the projection of a simple arch, is a *barrel vault* (Fig. 598), and the name is an apt one, since in appearance it looks like a barrel cut lengthwise. The barrel vault has the characteristics of the simple round arch. It is, in fact, an arch repeating itself along a passage. There is the same tendency to spread, the same need for support at the place where the lateral thrust makes for weakness. In the interior of St. Peter's, the voluminous spatial quality of a large barrel vault is evident. Here the surface is enriched with coffers, depressed rectangular forms that lighten the weight of the vault and articulate it in both color and shape.

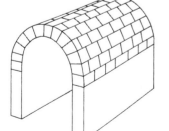

598. Barrel vault.

There are many variations of vaulting. When vaults intersect each other, *cross vaulting* results (Fig. 599), and the support can be localized rather than continuous, as it is in a barrel vault. The development of vaulting is discussed briefly in the succeeding section on the pointed arch.

The *dome* is also an extension of the principle of the arch (Fig. 600). In the instances where semicircular arch forms are used, the dome is a hemisphere—like a tennis ball cut in half. A dome is a round arch which has been rotated using the midpoint of the arch as the center. It becomes, in a sense, a multitude of arches so arranged that all the bases rest on a circle and the tops all cross at a common point. In the dome all the characteristic weak points of the arch remain, and consequently, it requires support at the points of lateral thrust. Usually, but not always, this is taken care of by properly designed buttresses, which may become a decorative feature of the exterior.

The magnificent dome of St. Peter's (Figs. 601, 602) crowns this largest of all churches. Here, the intent was to design a dome that would be impressive both

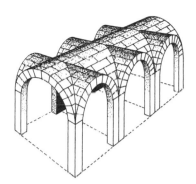

599. Cross vaulting.

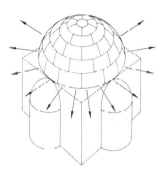

600. Dome.

above : 601. St. Peter's Basilica, the Vatican, Rome. Apse and dome by Michelangelo, 1547–1564; dome completed by Giacomo della Porta, 1588–1592; nave and façade by Carlo Maderno, 1606–1626; colonnades by Gian Lorenzo Bernini, 1656–1663.

right : 602. Michelangelo and Carlo Maderno. Interior, St. Peter's Basilica, the Vatican, Rome.

as a culminating exterior form and as an interior space. Designed by Michelangelo and completed after his death in 1564, it is the ultimate realization of the type developed in Italy during the fifteenth and sixteenth centuries. It is also the prototype of most of the monumental domes subsequently constructed, including the dome on the United States Capitol in Washington, D.C. (which is formed of cast iron).

In order to be a spectacularly dominant form, the dome of St. Peter's is raised on a drum, the lower part of which can be seen in the interior view. On the exterior the drum is surrounded by paired columns that, with their bases and entablatures, are 50 feet high. These serve as buttresses to counteract the spread of the great structure and act as transitional elements to the main mass of the building. Even the force of the ranked columns has not been sufficient to counteract the thrust of the masonry, for at various times as many as ten encircling chains have been placed in the dome to keep it from spreading. The dome itself, including the lantern (the windowed superstructure at the top), is 450 feet high and is constructed of an outer and an inner shell, the latter 137 feet 6 inches across on the inside. The base of the dome is nearly 250 feet above the floor; the distance from the floor to the top of the internal cupola, 335 feet, a height greater than a thirty-story building. This vast space creates a strong vertical axis, and the high altar is logically centered under the dome. It is readily understandable that the dome of St. Peter's is an architectural achievement of astounding monumentality.

Domes, especially those raised high above the main mass of the structures supporting them, are imposing forms, and they have been much favored as crowns for important public buildings. Powerful forms, they are symbols of power. Their interior spaces, altitudinous and free of supports, create a sense of soaring infinity, an infinity that nonetheless seems rational and palpable, for the dome is a central form with a definite point of focus.

Today few domes are constructed on the true arch principle. But the basically simple, geometrically satisfying form of domes has merited their continuance in modern architecture. In place of stone, however, they can be constructed of a newer material, such as steel in the Pittsburgh Civic Arena (Fig. 630), or of an old material, such as concrete (used even by the Romans) in Eero Saarinen's TWA Flight Center (Figs. 615, 616), where the poured concrete has been reinforced with structural steel.

The Pointed Arch: Rheims Cathedral

Scarcely any record of man's accomplishments is more dramatic than the development of the Gothic cathedrals, of which Rheims Cathedral (Figs. 603, 604, 606–608) is a representative example. Like the Parthenon, it is the result of many factors— of climate and geography, of thoughts, actions, and aspirations, of knowledge of architectural construction. As we look at Rheims Cathedral, we are impressed chiefly with its ascending, aspiring, uplifting character, the product of people concerned with God who were eager, literally, to reach heavenward with their lofty houses of worship.

The Gothic period was a deeply religious one; men were intensely interested in all matters related to the soul's salvation. Most of the people were illiterate, and in order that they might know more of the life of Christ and of other holy persons, and might visualize and feel more of the glory of their God, biblical incidents and stories from the lives of the saints were depicted in richly carved stone and in colorful stained glass. The glass windows and stone images integral to the Gothic style were developed not as technical flourishes but as direct answers to deeply rooted human interests and needs.

Climate was still another factor affecting the construction and the appearance of Gothic cathedrals. The Greeks did not have to build against the rigors of bitter winter weather, and they took advantage of the mild climate by erecting buildings with open porticoes and colonnades. But farther north architects had to reckon with severe weather. Northern France has long periods of driving rain and cold, dark, sullen days. Chill, wet, and gloom had to be kept out of the buildings, not only physically but psychologically, and architects made windows richly colored so that the dull light from the outside was transformed into warm, glowing tones. The windows also expressed medieval notions about heavenly light, its appearance and transmission.

In Rheims the pointed arch was used (Fig. 605)—a form found in all cathedrals that can be considered Gothic. It possesses structural advantages in having less lateral thrust than a round arch and greater flexibility. Whereas the height of a round arch is determined by its width, the height of a pointed arch can be readily altered by changing the curve of the sides. Thus, the Gothic style, far from being characterized merely by details, is primarily a system of construction. Most of the characteristics of arch construction in the seasoned Gothic system can be seen in Rheims Cathedral.

Note in the picture of the interior (Fig. 604) that the *nave*, or central aisle, of the cathedral is defined by two corresponding series of *piers* that support the *vaulting* over the nave and the side aisles. By following two of the adjoining piers up into the vaulting, one can see that these, with the two corresponding ones across the nave, define a rectangular area, or *bay*, and that the outer edges of the bay in the vaulting are defined by pointed arches that connect the piers. In addition, arches are sprung across the bay, dividing it into four areas that are filled in with masonry.

left : 603. West front, Rheims Cathedral. 1211–1290.

right : 604 Interior (view toward the west), Rheims Cathedral.

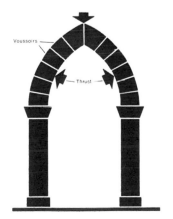

605. Pointed arch.

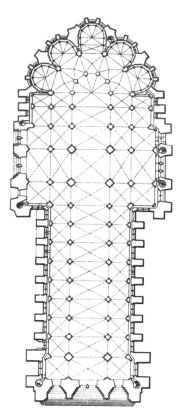

above left : 606. Lateral view, Rheims Cathedral.

above right : 607. Plan, Rheims Cathedral.

left : 608. Rheims Cathedral. *left :* Longitudinal section of the interior along the nave. *center :* Transverse section across the nave. The function of the flying buttresses in supporting the interior vaulting can be clearly seen. *right :* Elevation of a portion of the exterior along the nave.

The *groin lines* (which mark the intersection of the *cross vaults*) are marked with protruding masonry called *ribs*. All of these features can also be observed in the plan.

The piers at each corner of the bay bear the weight of the masonry above them. As we know from the earlier discussion, arched vaulting exerts an outward thrust that must be countered if the building is to stand. The pointed arch has less lateral thrust than the round one, but its thrust outward is still considerable. Italian builders often "tied" arches together with iron rods to keep them from spreading. This solution was unacceptable to the French, who, instead, developed a more organic solution to this difficult problem. Look at the lateral view of the cathedral in Figure 606 and the diagrams showing sections through the structure and a partial elevation of the exterior (Fig. 608). These reveal how the thrusts from the vaulting in the interior are met by the construction of arches outside the building whose thrusts counterbalance those from within. These exterior arches are great soaring constructions that span the side aisles and become in their bases part of the outer wall of the cathedral. These are *flying buttresses*, for they "fly" over the side aisles to perform their structural function of providing support from the ground up to the top vaults. They create for Gothic structures a feeling of freedom, daring, and movement.

Gothic buildings are not inert. Rather, they are structures in which the forces and counterforces that reside within the structure are given exciting and esthetic form. The thrust-counterthrust that exists in nearly every part of a Gothic cathedral means that it is in a delicate and amazingly complicated state of equilibrium. Theoretically, at least, the removal of one of the arches would mean the collapse of the whole building, because every part depends on every other part for support. Thus, the term *organic* is often used to describe the Gothic style.

In stone construction, therefore, Roman and Renaissance architects used the round arch and Gothic builders the pointed arch. Arch forms have also been developed in concrete, wood, and steel. At this point an elementary principle of forces should be stated, namely that forces, like water, tend to flow more easily around smooth bends than around sharp angles. Thus, the arch, minimizing the break between vertical and horizontal elements, represents a great structural development. This principle is further developed in structural skin construction.

Building in Concrete

Concrete, often regarded as a new material, was used regularly and well by the Romans more than two thousand years ago for large, imposing buildings.

The Romans were the first to perfect the dome as well as the arch, and in the Pantheon (Figs. 609–611) they have left us one of the most remarkable structures of all time. In form it is extremely simple, the interior being almost exactly as high as it is wide (140 by 142 feet). The interior of the dome is a perfect half-sphere resting upon a circular wall. There is only one entrance, and the remainder of the circular wall is enlivened and adorned with seven large niches. The light comes from a single source, a great "eye," or *oculus* opening, 29 feet across in the center of the dome. Built during the years A.D. 120–124, it was originally a temple to all the gods, but in 609 it was dedicated as a Christian church in memory of all the martyrs. The altars now in the Pantheon date from the Renaissance.

The base of the Pantheon's dome is a 20-foot-thick concrete wall. The dome itself, the thickness of which continually diminishes as it rises to the "eye," is of brick work with heavy mortar joints. Embedded in it are arches that relieve and transmit the

below left : 609. Interior, the Pantheon, Rome. A.D. 120–124.

above : 610. The Pantheon, Rome.

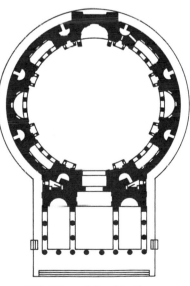

611. Plan of the Pantheon.

Architecture   497

thrust of the giant structure. The exterior is sheathed in brick, the lower part of the interior in richly colored and variegated stones. The interior of the dome is decorated with coffers.

Its basically simple forms are monumental. The geometric character of the interior seems fundamental, the scale is impressive, and the progression of the coffers in the dome, with their diminution in size as they extend up into the dome, gives the interior a sense of vitality. The thickness and height of the supporting walls, however, almost conceal the dome on the exterior, where, quite unlike St. Peter's, it appears as a low saucerlike form. The Pantheon, however, was a source for the domes that architects fashioned during the Renaissance, including that over St. Peter's.

The Nature of Concrete

Structures built from concrete differ significantly from the stone buildings discussed in the previous section in that they are *monolithic* (the material is homogeneous and continuous), whereas masonry constructions are built up of relatively small pieces of stone that, even in the finished structure, retain separate identities. The concrete structures of the Romans depended for structural strength on bulk and mass rather than on precise knowledge of material. Concrete is a conglomerate made by uniting cement and water with sand, broken stone, slag, cinders, and the like. It withstands great compression and very little tension. Also, like stone, it does not rot or corrode and is fire-resistant. Beginning in a liquid state, concrete assumes the contours and textures of any "form" into which it is poured. It can be given the massiveness of the Pantheon or the slender rectangularity of cage construction, the continuous ribbons of our highways and sidewalks, or the small building blocks in common use. It has been well named "the original plastic." The following two buildings represent recent constructions in concrete whose architects used the material in ways that are new and quite fundamentally different.

Notre-Dame-du-Haut, Ronchamp   The Chapel of Notre-Dame-du-Haut at Ronchamp, France, designed by the Swiss architect Le Corbusier, exploits both the heavy and the fluid nature of concrete (Figs. 612–614). The massive exterior wall (composed partially of brick) is perforated with windows of varied sizes, asymmetrically but precisely organized. The tall towerlike form houses a small chapel above the roof. The structure is covered with a great roof form that swells plastically and lifts as it leaves the supporting wall. Actually, the roof is built much like an airplane wing, which it strongly resembles. It has two thicknesses of poured concrete, and the

below left : 612. Le Corbusier. Notre-Dame-du-Haut, Ronchamp, France. 1950–1955.

below right : 613. Le Corbusier. Interior, Notre-Dame-du-Haut, Ronchamp.

above : 614. Perspective diagram of Notre-Dame-du-Haut, Ronchamp.

above : 615. Eero Saarinen. TWA
Flight Center, Kennedy International
Airport, New York. 1962.

left : 616. Eero Saarinen. Interior,
TWA Flight Center.

space between is braced with struts. A uniformly rough surface has been given to all
the walls by spraying them with a coarse stucco. In the interior the window openings
are broadly splayed, and the deep geometric forms thus created provide varying
views of the stained glass set in the windows. It has been said that the Ronchamp
chapel is more a piece of sculpture than architecture. Clearly, the nature and disposition of the forms produce a building that is structurally dynamic and spiritually
moving.

TWA Flight Center   The TWA Flight Center (Figs. 615, 616) at Kennedy International Airport in New York City was designed by Eero Saarinen. The architect
stated that he wanted to produce a building "in which the architecture itself would
express the excitement of air travel." To realize this purpose, he chose concrete as
the building material.

617. Alcoa Building (under construction), Pittsburgh.

The initial fluid nature of concrete is apparent in this building, for here is a structure of shapes that flow. To secure them, it was necessary to build forms for the entire building, both inside and out, into which the concrete was poured. And since the building is monolithic, the pouring of the concrete, once started, was not stopped until it was completed. Then the concrete was allowed to dry and cure, and the forms were removed.

There is a similarity between the shell of concrete in a structure such as the TWA Flight Center and the shell of an egg. Both are extremely strong in relation to the amount and thickness of the material involved. But sheer size makes its special demands. The TWA building has a 2-acre roof made of 6000 tons of concrete and 700 tons of steel. In some places, where the roof has little weight to carry, it is only 7 inches thick; at the buttresses, where the weight of the roof is transferred to the supporting piers, it is 3 feet thick. By allowing the potentialities of the materials to suggest the form and then refining that form creatively, Saarinen showed that today's architects need not always follow "the cult of the cube" into a boxlike conformity.

Basically, the TWA terminal is composed of four concrete intersecting shell vaults that seem to float above the ground. The free, spreading forms are reminiscent of birds and of airplanes. Not only the vaults but the Y-shaped buttresses suggest flight. Light is another vital factor that gives the structure buoyancy. In the interior, narrow bands of windows between the vaults add natural illumination from above to the light that floods in from the large windows at the ends of the vaults. The colors are predominantly high in value, and the gray and tan surfaces reflect the light coming from many directions. The integration of exterior and interior, from the major forms to the smallest details, creates a compelling unity. A strong sense of movement pervades the entire development. Inside or out, the curvilinear forms and space seem to be in perpetual change as one moves in or around them. Unlike most rectangular structures, which often seem absolutely fixed once they become familiar, Saarinen's TWA building discloses new and unexpected relationships.

Precast Concrete

In most buildings in which concrete is used the material is cast *in place*, as in the framework of the Alcoa Building in Pittsburgh (Fig. 617). Here, wooden frames were placed around the steel framework and then filled with concrete. After the concrete had hardened, the forms were removed. This is satisfactory for rough structural work designed to be covered with a sheathing material or where a finished surface is not desired. However, the difficulties in pouring refined or complex forms on the edge of a building 300 feet above ground are obvious. With the development of new forming materials this difficulty has been partially overcome. Precasting, however, makes possible the prefabrication of precise, refined, and reinforced concrete units under controlled conditions, usually at a plant or factory. The precast units must be transportable. When finished they are taken to the building site for incorporation into the structure. Precast concrete thus resembles stone in the way it is used in design and in the way it is handled. Like stone, the units are discrete. Precasting has made concrete a much more usable material in modern architecture than natural stone.

Ferroconcrete

Ferroconcrete (or reinforced concrete) has metal reinforcing embedded in the concrete so that the tensile strength of metal is united with the compressive strength of concrete. It is most often seen in buildings in which a steel *skeleton frame* is first erected and then enclosed in concrete (Fig. 617). Later, the outside wall, or skin, is hung on the frame. Steel encased in concrete is also more resistant to fire, for an exposed steel frame can be distorted by high heat.

Ferroconcrete technology, which was developed and first used in the nineteenth century, has moved toward increased lightness and flexibility. Thus, some bridges use thin slabs of ferroconcrete shaped to become strong structural elements. Thin, curved shells are very efficient for large, unobstructed, open spans.

Prestressing and post-tensioning, which are discussed in the following section, are both technically sophisticated ways of strengthening concrete with metal reinforcement.

Prestressed and Post-Tensioned Concrete

Because concrete is weak in tension, the distance that can be spanned by concrete beams is limited. To give concrete the needed tensile strength it has become a common practice to reinforce the material with metal beams and rods. *Prestressing* is one of the techniques used for reinforcing concrete. In this method metal rods, cables, wires, bars, and so on, which are under *tension*, are embedded in concrete and arranged in ways to cause the structural forces to flow in predetermined directions. If weight is placed on a beam between the uprights that support it, the lower part of the beam will be in tension. When the concrete is cured (set), the forces holding the bars in tension are removed and the tension is distributed along one edge of the beam, causing it to deflect (bend) slightly. When each end of such a beam is placed on supports so that the edge containing the bars is on the top, with the deflection upward, it is capable of carrying greatly increased weights. Prestressing can be used in beams, cantilevers, flooring slabs, vaults, domes—in fact, in almost all structural forms. In particular, it makes possible beams of great length that are strong but relatively light.

Post-tensioning involves the introduction of the same kind of stressing as in prestressed concrete, except that in post-tensioning the stressing is done *after* the concrete has been poured and has hardened. Like prestressing, this technique has made concrete an extremely versatile building material.

The 27-story Gulf Life Tower (Figs. 618, 619) in Jacksonville, Florida, is a strikingly bold, square building, designed by Welton Becket in association with the firm of Kemp, Bunch, and Jackson. On each of its sides two tapered columns support a series of sturdy horizontal beams. The length and size of the beams immediately indicate that either prestressing or post-tensioning has been used. In this instance, it is the latter. The significant point is that the long horizontal members,

above : 618. Welton Becket with Kemp, Bunch, and Jackson. Gulf Life Tower, Jacksonville, Florida. 1968.

left : 619. Welton Becket with Kemp, Bunch, and Jackson. Gulf Life Tower.

which post-tensioning makes possible, introduce a new kind of scale into high-rise building and a greater flexibility in design. It should be noted also that the window wall is *behind* the structural frame. The structure-skin relationship is thus the reverse of that in buildings like the Lever House (Fig. 590).

The structural framework of the building was erected one floor at a time. The exterior columns were formed by first putting into place the necessary steel reinforcement and a precast outer shell and then pouring the inner core of the columns. The beams are each over 40 feet long and weigh about 15,000 pounds, and each one is composed of 14 precast units. The units were lifted separately into place by a crane and then shored into precise position on a cantilevered "strongback," or heavy truss, which was lifted from floor to floor as work progressed. Once the units in a beam were in place, 12-strand metal tendons were inserted through a continuous opening in all the units—a process that is much like stringing a line of beads on a wire. The opening undulates both horizontally and vertically, and this movemented disposition places the tendons for proper stress control along the full length of the beam. After the beams were positioned and "threaded," the tendon was placed under the necessary tension. The beams, therefore, have become *post-tensioned*.

As Figure 619 shows, the beams are distinctly sculptured. They taper both upward and inward from the supporting columns, their basic form determined by structural requirements. They are thinnest at the ends of the cantilevers and at the midpoints of the center beams, that is, at those points where the load carried is lightest. They are heaviest where they adjoin the columns, for it is there that the load of each beam is transferred to the vertical supports. Prestressing was used to provide interior support for the floors between the exterior and a central core of elevators, stairwells, and utility spaces. Another audacious design feature is the second floor (housing a bank), which is *hung* from the post-tensioned floor above.

What sets the Gulf Life Tower apart from other recent tall buildings is the difference in its scale, established by both the size and the length of the beams. With this kind of success to prove its validity for modern design, concrete—prestressed and post-tensioned—is likely to be used still more frequently and with yet greater versatility.

Increasingly, prestressed concrete is utilized to solve the complex engineering problems of elevated roadways designed to carry live loads of heavy traffic. Since the supports for elevated roadways can obstruct other traffic areas below, the fewer the supports the better. The elevated highway in Berlin (Fig. 620) is particularly spectacular. The structure's graceful sweep is carried on single, widely spaced piers over railway tracks. Directly under the roadways are box beams. Here, the prestressed concrete allows for spans of 225 feet, which is unusually long for any kind of construction.

In 1967, *Architectural Forum*, a professional journal, called the concept of building with boxes "an idea whose time has come." The idea of prefabrication is not new. Its use in domestic housing was examined in Chapter 1, where the Techbuilt house was shown to employ modular units that have been prefabricated for rapid assembly on the building site. To a considerable degree, prefabrication is involved in all current building. In "building with boxes," however, the new unit—the box—is a room or two or more rooms. The unit, or module, therefore has become considerably larger and more complex. Technically, box building is not dependent on any particular material, but thus far concrete has been most frequently used.

Architects are always devising ways of lowering construction costs, but the building industry has been only to the slightest degree affected by mass-production techniques. Current construction costs remain so high that much shelter must yet be built for millions of people who now live in inadequate housing. At the present

620. Elevated highway, West Berlin, Germany. 1963. Hollow box beam 225', total length 767'.

left: 621. Moshe Safdie. "Habitat 67," Montreal. 1962. (See also Fig. 26.)

right: 622. Moshe Safdie. "Habitat 67."

rate of population growth millions upon millions of new dwelling units will be needed within the next few years. Enormous social problems can be solved only if satisfactory housing at realistic costs can be provided.

The first large-scale demonstration of building with boxes was "Habitat 67" (Figs. 621, 622), an experimental high-density community complex designed by the Israeli architect Moshe Safdie and built for Expo 67 at Montreal. A major objective for Habitat was to provide "the essentials of a complete environment, privacy, garden, identity and choice, commercial spaces, fresh air, and sunlight." These goals, usually associated with suburban living, were to be achieved in an urban setting.

Habitat consists of 354 modular construction units comprising 158 houses. The units contain from 1 to 4 bedrooms. Some units have all their rooms on a story; others are arranged in 2 stories. Each unit boasts a garden terrace. The modular boxes measure 17 feet 6 inches by 38 feet 6 inches by 10 feet. They were precast with metal reinforcement and once cast were fitted by an assembly-line technique with such essentials as floors, windows, walls, and wiring. Preassembled kitchens and bathrooms were lowered into place through the tops of the modular box units. The number of ways in which the boxes could be divided was ingenious. A single box could become a living-dining room and a kitchen, or two bedrooms and a bath, or a living room with kitchen, bathroom, and bedroom. Where needed, partitions were added. The approximate weight of each modular box was 90 tons.

After the interior was finished to the degree prefabrication would permit, the box was lifted into place. Here again, remarkable ingenuity made possible a variety of combinations (Fig. 621). The units were post-tensioned into proper place with rods, cables, and welding, and the result is a continuous, albeit visually complicated structure.

Access to the houses is provided by "streets" that at various levels, sheltered from the weather, connect the houses with playgrounds and elevators. Beneath each of the walkways is an enclosed mechanical space sufficient to contain the utilities.

The views of Habitat suggest a new kind of architecture. Despite its commitment to high-density occupation, it is intimate and human in scale. The pattern of shadows created by the diverse interrelationships among the modular boxes is lively, even picturesque. Thus far, the large multiple-dwelling, moderate-rental apartments erected in the United States have, for the most part, been dismal, dehumanized structures devoid of esthetic interest and hopelessly monotonous and overscaled. Habitat suggests that high-density housing at low cost need not be deadly and overpowering, that identity and interest are indeed possible.

It is inevitable that still larger populations will concentrate in major urban areas. The United States has become a nation of city dwellers, and urban sprawl has already devoured most of the open country surrounding its cities. Long-distance commuting, now a commonplace of modern life, is chronically wasteful of time and energy. Making cities habitable again is a virtual necessity—and this involves the architect. The ideas developed in Habitat suggest one way of making high-density living both attractive and feasible. Already, a number of architects, including Safdie, have designed urban communities of much greater size than Habitat using many of the ideas initiated in it. It is only a matter of time until some will be built (see Fig. 26).

The possibilities of concrete are now being explored more creatively than any other of the major building materials. Architects ignored concrete for many years; now they find it responsive to a wide range of building problems. The Romans used this material to produce great and monumental architecture. Modern architects are proving themselves no less ingenious in their application of concrete to design goals, and they have the advantage of knowing more precisely than the Romans its structural capabilities. Working with engineers, contemporary designers have discovered new ways of handling concrete, of increasing its efficiency and extending the range of its versatility. After centuries of oblivion, concrete has become one of the great building materials of modern times.

Building in Wood

The plentiful supply of wood in the United States has made it our most common building material; it accounts for over 80 percent of our structures. Most of us are familiar with the wood-frame house in which a frame of studs and joists (a skeleton) is erected; the exterior (the skin) of wood, brick, or plaster is added; and the interior wall finish is applied. Called *balloon framing* or *light frame structure*, this is a type of *skeleton frame construction* developed in Chicago in the 1830s (Fig. 623). Its invention was a major factor in the rapid development of the land beyond the Alleghenies, for it permitted much more rapid construction than did the older heavy frame structure. Even before Sullivan's time, Chicago was a center of architectural innovation. In contrast to masonry structure, in which the wall is both load bearer and surface, balloon framing is closely related to steel construction in its separation of structure and surface. Wood is also suited to *cantilever construction*, as in the eaves projecting beyond the walls of buildings; to *trusses*, as found in wooden barns and contemporary structures; and to *structural skin construction*, similar to that in the molded plywood chairs by Charles Eames (Fig. 227). One of the major uses of wood in large contemporary construction is as a material for forms into which concrete is poured.

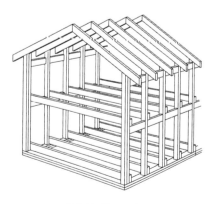

623. Balloon frame.

Lamination of Wood

The characteristics of wood, discussed in Chapter 6, reveal its potentialities and limitations as a building material. Technological developments have greatly extended its uses. Increasingly, laminated wood, especially plywood, is being used in construction, for it possesses remarkable and highly predictable strength. When bonded with synthetic resins it is made weatherproof. In contrast to metals, which require high heat for shaping, plywood can be shaped permanently at low temperatures. Fabrication is thereby greatly simplified. In relation to its weight, it is probably stronger than any known material. It can be a moldable "skin" material of considerable structural strength. Architecturally, molded plywood has not as yet found wide application—but it has the potential and holds promise for use in *structural skin construction*.

Plywood sheets are not the only new development in wood. Related to these are larger laminated structural members in wood, such as beams and trusses, of great size and strength. A *beam* is typically a large single piece of wood (or metal) much longer than wide or thick and is used horizontally to bridge the gap between upright supports; thus, it is the same as a *lintel*. Beams of single pieces of wood are limited in length and known strength, but lamination makes possible beams and other structural members of increased size and efficiency. Like plywood, these structural members become precise building materials.

A striking example of the use of laminated wood structural members occurs in St. Paul's Lutheran Church of Sarasota, Florida, a structure designed by the architect Victor Lundy (Fig. 624). Most of the interior is of wood, a material whose surface is warm and rich. It is the form of the ceiling that gives this interior its distinctiveness. The laminated beams suggest lower branches of great trees that diminish in size as they ascend. The interior conveys the impression of buoyancy, lightness, and aspiration. The supports meet at regular intervals in the ceiling, like groin lines in Gothic vaulting, except that here the curve is reversed. As they approach the top of the ceiling, and as the load they support becomes less, they diminish in size. Forms of this shape and lightness are possible in wood only through lamination.

624. Victor A. Lundy. St. Paul's Lutheran Church, Sarasota, Florida. 1959.

626. Frank Lloyd Wright. Taliesin West, Phoenix, Arizona. 1938.

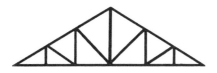

625. Trusses. *above :* Howe truss. *below :* bowstring truss.

The Truss in Wood

A *truss*, as defined earlier, is a rigid framework of beams, bars, rods, and the like. It is in the form of a triangle, or a series of triangles, because the triangle is the only geometric figure that cannot change shape without altering the length of one or more of its sides (Fig. 625). Originally made of a number of single pieces of timber (later of metal), trusses are now also made of laminated wood. Although the principle of the truss is remarkably simple, it has been developed precisely only within recent times.

The view of Taliesin West (Fig. 626) is a striking example of wood used to give a monumental effect. The forms at the left are the ends of large trusses that extend over a workroom. The organic texture of the wood is in handsome contrast to the brightly colored stone in the base below, and the strong forms of both the wood and the masonry are suited admirably to the landscape. Like all of the work of Frank Lloyd Wright, this building is characterized by its relation to site and by the forthrightness of the forms.

Through such processes as lamination, wood has become still more variously usable than before. Its limitations, however, exclude it from use in major structural projects in all but a few instances. In domestic construction it remains the most practical and most often employed material.

Building with Steel

Steel has made possible our present industrial age. From tiny precision instruments to hundred-story buildings and mile-long bridges, one sees the extent to which it and other metals have entered into and affected our lives. With good reason, the steel industry is regarded as a barometer of American business, which is largely dependent on it. The importance of steel in present-day life is all the more remarkable when we realize that its manufacture began just a few years before the Civil War.

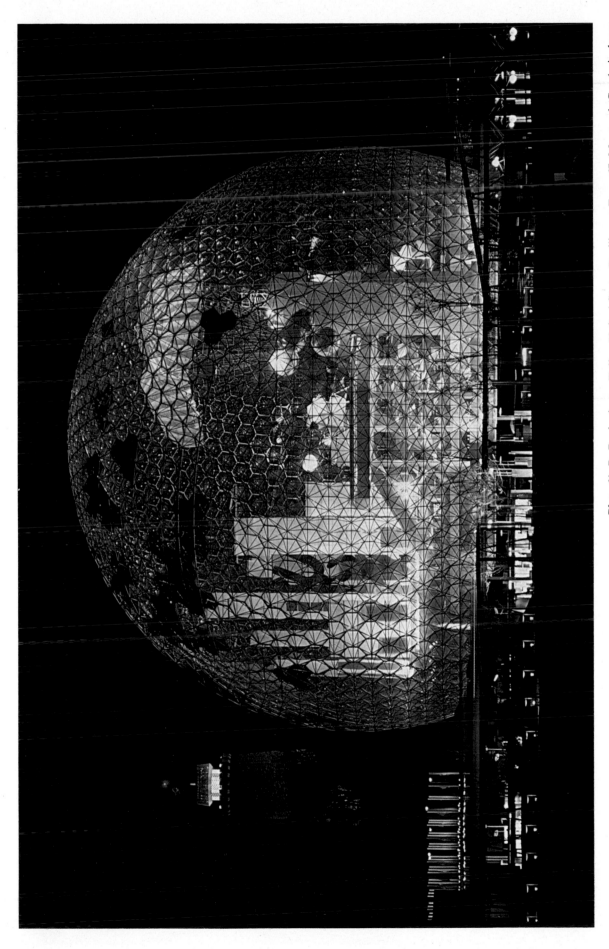

Plate 61. R. Buckminster Fuller. United States Pavilion at Expo 67, Montreal. Geodesic dome constructed of steel pipes and transparent acrylic, 250' in diameter. (See also Figs. 238, 634.)

above : Plate 62a. Kevin Roche, John Dinkeloo, and Associates. Ford Foundation Building, New York. 1967. (See also Figs. 638, 639.)

right : Plate 62b. Interior, Ford Foundation Building.

508

Plate 63. Schipporeit-Heinrich, Inc. Lake Point Tower, Chicago. 1968. (See also Fig. 641.)

Government buildings at Brasilia, the new capital of Brazil. Lucio de Costa, city planner. (See also Fig. 119.)

above : Plate 64a. Oscar Niemeyer. Congress and Administration buildings. 1959.

right : Plate 64b. Oscar Niemeyer. Presidential Palace. 1960.

510

In the first half of the nineteenth century iron was used, although not widely, as a building material; but steel—finer and denser in structure and stronger in compression and tension than iron—was seized upon for widespread use as soon as it became available. Since then, it has been under constant study and development.

Steel-Cage Construction

It is only logical that in use steel was first channeled into *steel-cage construction* (Fig. 627), which is found in most tall buildings. Like balloon framing, it also was developed in Chicago. The first multistory steel frame covered with a nonstructural skin was built there in 1883, approximately half a century after the invention of balloon framing. At first called "Chicago construction," it received most of its early attention in that city.

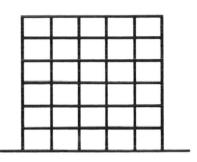

627. Steel-cage construction.

It is the great strength of steel that makes skyscrapers possible. When load-bearing walls of stone are built, the base must become thicker as the walls increase in height. One of the early Chicago skyscrapers, the 16-story Monadnock Building, completed in 1891, is of stone construction and has ground-floor walls 6 feet thick. If a stone structure thirty stories high were to be built, most of the space on the ground and lower floors would be taken up with walls and supports. With steel-cage construction, the supports take surprisingly little space, and even on the ground floor of very tall buildings they are not large. In addition, steel buildings resist the forces of wind and earthquakes with a resilience that stone structures do not have. Steel-cage construction, like the older post-and-lintel system, leads to architecture that is basically rectangular, although, as the John Hancock Building (Fig. 591) and others indicate, it can be treated in a more modulated form. Nevertheless, large contemporary structures are assembled from many prefabricated parts that must relate to the repetitive grid of the steel cage. To make this unified, but essentially monotonous, framework into a humanly satisfying work of art is the challenge presented to architects by modern technology.

Cantilever Construction in Steel

628. Cantilever construction.

The tensile strength of steel is exploited in *cantilever construction*. As can be seen in the diagram in Figure 628, a cantilever requires that the material resist tension without breaking or distorting.

The increasing size of aircraft, expecially passenger jets, creates the problem of constructing shelters large enough to provide maintenance for the aircraft. Figure 629 shows a United Airlines hangar under construction. It appears considerably different in its completed state, with the walls and doors obscuring the great, free

629. Skidmore, Owings, and Merrill. United Airlines hangar (under construction), San Francisco. 1961.

630. Mitchell and Riley.
Civic Arena, Pittsburgh.
1961.

stretch of the roof supports. This hangar is planned with berths for four DC-8s. In the center is a maintenance core supported by seven pairs of reinforced concrete columns whose shape follows the theoretical curve of stresses. These support the great cantilevered steel girders on which were later hung the sliding doors of the hangar. The girders are 14 feet deep at the piers and taper to 5 feet at the ends. They are cantilevered for a distance of 142 feet, which, interestingly, is the same dimension as the interior of the Pantheon.

The Civic Arena in Pittsburgh (Fig. 630) is another recent structure that is dependent on steel for its audacious form. With a seating capacity of over thirteen thousand, it is covered by a stainless steel dome over 400 feet in diameter and thus has one of the largest clear-span roofs in the world. Even more remarkable is the fact that the roof is retractable. It is divided radially into eight 45-degree segments, six being movable and two stationary. In opening the roof, three movable segments on each side ride on a series of motorized carriages under the fixed sections. Only two and one-half minutes are required to open or close the roof. The main support for the dome is provided by a cantilever space frame—a triangular truss visible on the right—which projects 205 feet over the auditorium. This, too, is spectacular construction, and it is easy to grasp how unprecedented flexibility is provided by such a structure for concerts under the stars on clear summer evenings or for hockey games on cold winter nights.

Suspension Construction in Steel

Even greater utilization of the tensile properties of steel is made in *suspension construction*, where *all* the material is in tension. The possibilities of suspension construction were demonstrated by John Roebling in the Brooklyn Bridge he designed and built during the years 1869 to 1883. Architects generally ignored this great achievement, and almost fifty years elapsed before tension construction was seriously developed. There are now a good many magnificent and exciting suspension bridges throughout the country, such as the new Verrazano-Narrows Bridge in New York (Fig. 228). The tremendous size of the suspension bridges is difficult to grasp, set as they are well above water. The span between the towers of the

Verrazano-Narrows Bridge is 4260 feet, a distance greater than four-fifths of a mile. Yet this giant structure is suspended from four cables, each only a little over a yard in diameter. The cables themselves are entirely under tension, thus exploiting the greatest asset of steel. The daring of suspension bridges is perhaps best appreciated by viewing them from the level of the water below. From there the enormous spans between the towers and the seeming fragility of the entire structure are truly awesome. In the 4200-foot central span of San Francisco's Golden Gate Bridge the dynamic state of tension is such that the distance from the roadway at the center of the span to the water below can fluctuate as much as 10 feet depending on conditions of weather and load.

The Kagawa Gymnasium (Figs. 631–633), at the seacoast city of Takamatsu in Japan, makes use of tension construction in another way—to support a roof. The major form of the building is of concrete, and it is shaped, appropriately, like a giant watercraft or an ark, an impression that is heightened by the porthole-like openings along the sides of the building. The jutting ends of the structure—the "bow" and the "stern"—are, in reality, functionally formed, for they enclose the grandstands that flank the gymnasium floor. The interior provides a better view of the roof. It is carried on a series of small cables about 4 feet apart, each cable in

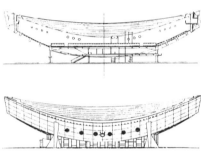

left : 631. Kenzo, Tange, and Associates. Kagawa Gymnasium, Takamatsu, Japan. 1966.

below : 632. Interior, Kagawa Gymnasium.

above : 633. Elevation and section of the Kagawa Gymnasium.

the form of a hyperbolic paraboloid. The curving shape of the roof is extremely handsome. For the spectators it forms a vast interior space unbroken by supports of any kind.

The Geodesic Dome

R. Buckminster Fuller possesses one of the most creative minds of the twentieth century. He is an American engineer, but his major concern is man, and his genius is committed to discovering how contemporary man can live a fruitful, satisfying life. For decades Fuller has been designing radical, far-out homes and automobiles, exploiting in the fullest way possible the methods, materials, and accumulated knowledge of modern science and technology.

Fuller's greatest achievement is the geodesic dome, a structure of remarkable lightness that can span large interior spaces. The most monumental of the Fuller domes (it has been called "Bucky's Biggest Bubble") was built for the United States Pavilion (Pl. 61, p. 507; Figs. 634, 637) at Expo 67 in Montreal. A three-quarter sphere, it is 250 feet in diameter and 200 feet high. It has 141,000 square feet of surface area and 6,700,000 cubic feet of interior space. The framework is of metal—some 720 tons of it. Even so, not counting the weight of the plastic skin, only about 4 ounces of material were required to enclose each cubic foot of space within the dome!

A detail of this dome is reproduced in Chapter 6 (Fig. 238) showing the form of the space frame. The triangle is the basic form, and it occurs most visibly on the exterior, where the triangles make three "great circles" upon the face of the dome. A hexagonal pyramid is bolted at each junction of these circles and is constructed of six triangles. In the discussion of trusses on page 506, the great strength of the triangle was pointed out. Geodesic domes, therefore, are not only light in weight but are great in strength, and they represent an enormous advance in technology suitable for architecture. In addition, the United States Pavilion possesses esthetic interest and technical sophistication. Each of the hexagonal pyramids has within it a small acrylic plastic dome. At night, or when the weather is cool and the natural light low, the pavilion is transparent (see Pl. 61). A number of the hexagonal domes have exhaust vents, and each domical unit has metalized sunshades that automatically operate to provide a controlled "interior climate." The sunshades, responding to the heat of the sun as it strikes the dome at different angles, change the structure's surface from complete transparency to polished "chrome."

Buckminster Fuller conceived the Montreal dome as a demonstration of an ultimate "controlled environment." From inside the dome he wanted there to be an "uninterrupted contact with the visual world." "The sun and the moon will shine in and the landscape and sky will be completely visible, but the unpleasant effects of climate, heat, dust, bugs, glare, etc., will be modulated by the skin to provide a 'Garden of Eden' interior." Geodesic domes have already been built for a number of purposes. Fuller sees their extended use as a means of altering our environment drastically to the greater comfort and satisfaction of everyone.

Arc Welding and Stressed-Skin Construction

Another development that has had a great effect on building is electric arc welding, the results of which are illustrated in the interior of the Lincoln Electric Company (Fig. 635). By this process, two steel members can be joined so that the joint is as strong as any portion of the members themselves. It can be seen that this is superior to riveting, where, in a sense, a joint is no stronger than the weakest rivet. The steel skeletons of recent skyscrapers are arc welded, but the potentialities of this process have, thus far, been explored primarily by the aeronautical engineer in airplane construction. Other common examples of welded structures of the "stressed skin" type are the Hortonspheres seen around oil refineries (Fig. 636). The

opposite : 634. R. Buckminster Fuller. United States Pavilion, Expo 67, Montreal. (See Pl. 61, p. 507.)

right : 635. Ammann and Whitney. Interior, Lincoln Electric Company, Cleveland.

below : 636. Hortonspheres of the Standard Oil Co. (N.J.), Baton Rouge, La.

geometric simplicity of these structures is stunning. The stairways ascending them assume curves of great beauty, and the scale of the welter of pipes in the surrounding area invests them with monumentality. The structural strength of the Hortonspheres in relation to their materials makes them perhaps the most efficient constructions ever built.

It is therefore steel, not the stone of the great historical monuments, that makes modern architecture possible, and steel is indeed the base material of twentieth-century building.

637. The Biosphere. The controlled environment established in the former U.S. Pavilion at Expo 67. (See Pl. 61, p. 507, and Figs. 238, 634.)

Environmental Control in Modern Building

Traditionally, the basic requirements of architecture are few: an efficient plan, solid construction, sound use of materials, and esthetic quality. But in almost any large structure built now, provision is made for a variety of special activities and facilities scarcely hinted at in historic work. Large buildings of today are used not by a few persons but by many thousands. Elevators and escalators as well as halls and stairs are needed; air-conditioning and artificial illumination as well as windows are necessities; precise information on construction materials and processes are the requisites of safety and economy. Thus, the expert knowledge of a host of specialists is needed in any extensive building enterprise. Each contributes his share, and each determines in his way the final form.

One factor—precise environmental control—merits mention, for it is central to many recent architectural developments (see Fig. 637). With heating and cooling systems our tasks need not be subject to the seasons. Because of artificial illumination we can carry on our activities by night as well as by day. Telecasting, radio broadcasting, and scientific research, for example, all require a high degree of environmental control. In fact, much twentieth-century work is possible only because we can regulate the temperature, humidity, light, and sound in our surroundings.

The extent to which it is possible for man to control his environment is best illustrated by recent space exploration. Using technically sophisticated capsules of incredible complexity, men can penetrate for periods of several days environments of such hostility that exposure for even a fraction of a second means instant death. Communities on the moon are being projected, as well as voyages, not only to other planets in the solar system but to other galaxies. These and similar ventures will not be feasible until even greater environmental control can be established, but there seems little doubt that such undertakings can, in time, be successfully accomplished. The point to consider, however, is that precise regulation of many aspects of our surroundings is a general preoccupation of our culture. This interest is particularly noticeable in architecture, because buildings constitute the immediate environment of most people.

Environmental control in architecture demands two things: precise analyses of human needs and advanced technology. Increasingly, man is being studied by physiologists and psychologists to determine optimal conditions for his productivity and welfare. For the first time in history, the use of materials in construction has become a matter of considerable exactness. So much is now known about the performance of the various materials that they can be used efficiently and economically. (It should be added that engineers and architects now design for a high margin of safety.) Computers, too, are used in organizing the vast amounts of data that must be considered. Understandably, the precise information available to architects and engineers on materials and structural systems can open the door for an unparalleled period of architectural experimentation.

Precise control of interior environment does not necessarily make good architecture. In fact, the multiplicity of specialists who must be involved in planning a structure—each seeing to it that some factor such as heat, light, sound control, and air conditioning is adequately provided for—vastly complicates the architect's job. He must coordinate the requirements of all the specialists without weakening his design. This is at best a difficult matter; at worst, impossible.

Significant architecture, however, not only meets the physical needs of its occupants but expresses their social and political outlook, their spiritual aspirations, and their esthetic values. With the complexity of modern life, the size and rigidity of large institutions, and the pressures for regulation and control, care must be taken not to reduce individuals to numbers or units on a graph. A home should be designed for a family unit of real people, as a setting for the joys and frustrations implicit in family life. It cannot be designed only for a group of persons at a particular income level. An office or a factory houses, for a number of hours each working day, groups of people with varying responsibilities. It also shelters individuals who bring with them to their tasks their particular personalities. They cannot be treated as inert materials to be shaped or as machines that perform precisely as directed. Fortunately, architecture is an art, and therefore it is humanistic in its orientation. The significant architects design first of all for people and for the human spirit. Environmental control, if pursued too narrowly, can make life mechanically and physically comfortable but spiritually arid.

Other Recent Innovative Buildings

Innovation in architecture is a somewhat different enterprise than in painting and sculpture. First of all, the structural and utilitarian requirements of architecture impose their special demands on the designer. Furthermore, any client, whether a homeowner or a corporation, wants a high measure of assurance that the building once designed will meet the needs for which it is being built. An experimental painting, if unsuccessful, can be put out of sight. An unsuccessful building cannot be hidden from view, and it is too expensive to be destroyed. It can be accepted or rejected, but it cannot be ignored. Architecture thus has built into it a number of deterrents to innovation, and the many new ideas now shaping modern architecture are not only a tribute to the resourcefulness of designers but a measure of the persuasiveness of architects in dealing with people who will pay for the buildings they propose. The purpose of this last brief section is to examine a few examples of the most exciting architecture recently developed from designers' abstract ideas into constructed buildings.

The Ford Foundation Building, New York City

The new home of the Ford Foundation (Pl. 62, p. 508; Figs. 638, 639) in New York City was designed by Kevin Roche, John Dinkeloo, and Associates on a site only several hundred feet from the United Nations Headquarters near the East River. The building's basic shape is that of an L. Remarkably, the two sides opposite the L are enclosed for the structure's full height with glass window walls to embrace what is in reality a small, beautifully planted and tended park filled with trees, shrubs, and ground cover. The enclosure makes an oasis of green, herbaceous growth that year round is available to both Foundation employees and the public in the midst of one of the busiest and most impacted areas of New York City. A second unusual feature is that not only do most of the offices face the enclosed park but they are

638. Kevin Roche, John Dinkeloo, and Associates. Plan of the Ford Foundation Building, New York. 1967. (See Pl. 62, p. 508).

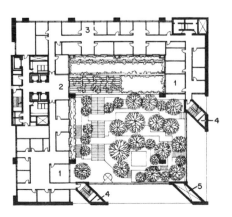

639. Kevin Roche, John Dinkeloo, and Associates. Section toward the west of the Ford Foundation Building. (See Pl. 62, p. 508; Fig. 638.)

themselves entirely visible from the park and from other parts of the building. The effect is one of great openness and spatial freedom within the larger confines of the building.

The piers and solids on the exterior of the building are unbroken shafts constructed of gray-red granite that is laid with such thin joints the effect is almost monolithic. These shafts are, as the plan shows (Fig. 638), slanted in an oblique angle to the axes of the building so that views from within the structure are directed diagonally toward the outside. Thus, another direction, a further opening of sight lines, is added to the strong rectilinear ones established by the main mass of the building. Between the granite piers is a rectangular grid of rust-surfaced steel. Inside, the banks of offices are supported by slender piers sheathed in the same granite used outside, and the glass walls are divided by thin verticals and heavier horizontals of darkened steel. The floors and furnishings of the offices partake of the general warmth of the building materials. The umber tones of steel, stone, and furnishings are nicely foiled by the green freshness of the planted heart of the building.

The building extends through a city block and has entrances on two streets whose difference in elevation is equal to the height of an entire floor. Consequently, the enclosed park serves as a transitional element and is designed on several levels to accommodate the variation in level. Three flights of stairs lead from one entrance to the other. The banks of offices project forward both at the base and at the top of the building (see Fig. 639), and the interior space is thereby shaped by the architecture almost like sculpture. At the top of the building the offices surround the entire court in the form of a crowning cornice. Thus, offices and park are independent of each other, yet visually they are closely integrated elements.

The Ford Foundation Building is both unusual and remarkable. It offers the contrast of precise, machined forms with natural plantings, of enclosed space with public view. The offices present the paradox of simultaneous protection and clear, unfettered spaciousness, of intense activity and repose, of organic growth as well as steel-and-granite stability. It is, in all, one of the most civilized institutional structures ever conceived and built.

The Mechanic Theater, Baltimore

The Mechanic Theater (Fig. 640), designed by John M. Johansen for Baltimore's Charles Center, is part of a central-city revitalization project. Baltimore needed a downtown theater, but to justify the high cost of a valuable commercial site, the planners had to find a number of uses, in addition to the theater, for the block cleared of old buildings. Below ground is a garage; at street level is a row of shops; and above them sits the theater itself. The shops provide a simple but ample base, and the roof is a terrace for theatergoers. The plain, open, glass fronts of the shops contrast with the closed, solid, and complex forms of the theater above, whose design proclaims that the action is indeed inside. Visual access into the mass of the theater's structure is provided only on the lobby side, through a large glass wall. Traditional playhouses have elaborate façades that are consonant with the heightened reality and make-believe of theater. The Mechanic Theater presents an exterior as spare as a fortress.

It is, however, a powerful and interestingly sculptured form that architect Johansen has wrought, in large part, by shrinking the exterior shell of the building and leaving exposed to the open elements what normally would have been contained in the envelope of a more distended outside wall. The vertical forms flanking the lobby are stairwells; the large horizontal forms beside them, lounges. The boxlike projections along the auditorium wall are banks of seats that literally project out

into space and from the inside have direct sight lines to the stage. The forms, though varied and strongly articulated, are never capricious. The theater resembles an enormous Cubist sculpture whose complex parts are unified by the warm color and texture of concrete.

The Lake Point Tower, Chicago

The 70-story, 645-foot Lake Point Tower (Pl. 63, p. 509) in Chicago was, when built, not only the world's tallest apartment building but also the world's tallest reinforced concrete structure. It was not erected on a steel-cage framework, but, like the Gulf Life Tower (Fig. 618), was built a floor at a time with metal rods used as reinforcement for the poured concrete. What is the most immediately striking feature in this building is its form, which has the most sensuously curved surfaces of any building designed since the Baroque period. The bronzed aluminum and glass of the undulating sheath glints and reflects light and images in distortions that are a remarkable departure from the flat planes of such buildings of the high International Style as the Lever House (Fig. 590). The Lake Point Tower depends wholly on its form for visual effectiveness. It is punctuated at top and at bottom only by form; there is neither base nor top elaboration to provide visual closure. The form and its edge do all. The number of floors could have been increased or diminished, like a garden hose, with no change in the design. Yet it is a stunning structure, mammoth and glittering against the Illinois sky.

top : 640. John M. Johansen. Mechanic Theater, Baltimore. 1968.

right : 641. Ludwig Miës van der Rohe. Project for a glass skyscraper. 1920–1921. (See Pl. 63, p. 509.)

642. I. M. Pei and Partners. Everson Museum of Art, Syracuse, N.Y. 1968.

This, too, is an example of technology triumphant, for it is indeed a precisioned product, one of giant scale. Schipporeit-Heinrich, Inc., prepared the building from a design projected in 1920–1921 by Miës van der Rohe (Fig. 641), the great German architect who taught at the Bauhaus and then settled in Chicago during the 1930s. The extent of Miës' influence on modern American architecture is incalculable. His dictum, "less is more," means that more is gained than lost by spareness, economy, and reserve. In works by him and his followers, the functionalism of the International Style "extracted architecture" from the simplest of means, and the austere high purpose of this approach has permitted a "purifying artistry to come to focus."

The Everson Museum of Art, Syracuse

"Museums must create a mood of excitement and anticipation, of mystery." I. M. Pei, the China-born American architect, obeyed his own injunction in the design of Syracuse's Everson Museum of Art (Fig. 642), one of the most individual museum structures ever built. It exemplifies much of the mood and view of recent architecture, its freedom from stereotype, its uncompromising esthetic, the forcefulness of its character. The building rises boldly above an extensive concrete plaza. Its design consists basically of four galleries cantilevered outward from a 50-foot-square central court according to a plan that resembles a squared pinwheel. The four galleries of the interior are connected by bridges, and as one passes from one gallery to the next a window offers views to the outside. Below ground are administrative offices, members' quarters, and a 320-seat auditorium.

Again, the material used for the Everson Museum is reinforced concrete. On most surfaces, it is faced with an aggregate of crushed rose granite that is bush-hammered and diagonally striated. The warmth of the facing contrasts with the neutral gray of the exposed natural concrete in the panel borders, interior stairs, balconies, and bridges.

Pei's design illustrates the limitations of the form-follows-function slogan. It is true that the Everson Museum functions well as an environment for exhibiting art, but the decisions that established the form of the museum were based more on esthetics than on function. Of course, the building "works" as does any good building, but the great merit of the Everson Museum lies in its superbly articulated esthetic statement, an asset so strong it becomes independent of the building's operational success. In the words of an architecture critic, the Everson Museum is "the architecture of today as art history will eventually record it."

The Salk Institute of Biological Studies

For Dr. Jonas Salk, the developer of the vaccine against poliomyelitis, architect Louis Kahn has designed an institute of biological research (Figs. 643–645) whose site is an irregular one facing the Pacific Ocean in La Jolla, California. The present two laboratory buildings face each other across a court (Fig. 643) and are "yoked together underground by a massive mechanical system." Each building has a large laboratory area on each of three floors, and above each laboratory is a floor with a 9-foot ceiling that is space designed to serve the many special requirements of biological research. With this facility, the laboratories can be serviced with no interruption of the work progressing in them. The laboratories are ringed with smaller-scale units: a stretch of study rooms on the court side, offices toward the ocean, a

below : 643. Louis I. Kahn. Salk Institute of Biological Studies, La Jolla, Calif. 1968.

right : 644. Louis I. Kahn. Salk Institute of Biological Studies.

below right : 645. Plan and section, Salk Institute of Biological Studies.

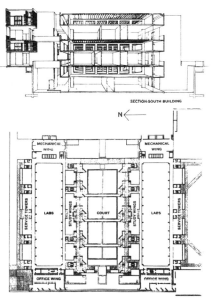

series of service towers away from the court, and a mechanical wing on the remaining side.

Like so many buildings of this generation, these are constructed of poured concrete, with plastic forms used to provide a smooth finish. The accented edges of the formwork have left a thin rectilinear pattern on the building surfaces (see Fig. 644). The tie-holes that remained after the forms were removed are plugged with lead. They are a residue of process that enriches the wall surfaces in an attractive way.

In the Salk Institute, Kahn has designed for what he calls a sense of "beyond the need." "The building must work . . . but anyone can do that: the building must also have the sense of man." He has provided an environment to "engage the full sentient capacities of the men who are its occupants."

The architecture of Louis Kahn is imbued with a quality that is particularly human. His buildings are so perfectly scaled they seem to be not only immediately made for man but openly cordial to him. The Salk Institute is suffused with the ineffable quality of a work of art. In the architect's words: "A great building must, in my opinion, begin with the unmeasurable and go through the measurable in the process of design but must again, in the end, be unmeasurable."

Brasilia

A view in Brasilia concludes this section (Pl. 64, p. 510; Fig. 646). Brazil's capital was long Rio de Janeiro, but its location there, at the extreme east of the nation's geographical center, was not satisfactory, and it was decided to move the federal government to the exact center of the country and closer to the vast natural resources that are Brazil's hope for future greatness. Here, the architect Oscar Niemeyer, working with Lucio Costa, the designer of the basic scheme for Brasilia, had the unique opportunity to create an entire metropolis from scratch. Brasilia was conceived as an automobile city, its streets and highways moving in long sweeping curves. There is little of the gridlike angularity of most traffic-choked American cities.

In commenting on the buildings of Brasilia, Edmund N. Bacon, the American architect, speaks of "architecture which interlocks." Shown in Plate 64a are the twin towers of the Administration Building and in front of it the dome of the Senate and the saucer form of the House of Representatives. These are splendidly powerful, plastic forms, and the play of one against the other is lyric and sustained.

Architects have long been bound to the single-building concept with little or no opportunity, or responsibility, to affect directly the areas surrounding the structures they design. Although the tradition of working on the single, set piece has produced many handsome buildings, even masterpieces, it has not invariably led to attractive or livable cities. The current and urgent need for urban renewal can be met effectively only when large areas are planned, where the talents of a group of specialists are involved, and where a complete environment can be created. Chief among these specialists should be the architect, and his task would be to relate the human, the technical, and the social factors to the production of visual surroundings suited to the air age and its aspirations. The experiments at Brasilia in large-scale planning for a multipurpose community may produce some of the solutions to the problems that press upon the cities whose traditional centers have, in mid-twentieth century, died of dilapidation and abandonment.

Conclusion

The chapter and book conclude with a picture of one of Frank Lloyd Wright's major works, the Kaufmann house at Bear Run, Pennsylvania (Fig. 647), because it

646. Bruno Giorgi. *The Warriors,* before the Supreme Court Building, Brasilia. (See Pl. 64, p. 510.)

647. Frank Lloyd Wright. Kaufmann house ("Falling Water"), Bear Run, Pa. 1936–1939.

epitomizes so much of the vigor and vision of modern architecture. The house is not new, having been built in 1937. Yet, it has an ageless quality, for the forms are as vital as when they were first built.

The site for the house, wooded and rocky, includes a brook and a waterfall. "Falling Water" is an expression of Wright's constant concern for relating architecture to its setting. The major mass of the houses is of stone, and it seems to grow directly from the rock ledges on which it rests. From these rock walls spring two dramatic and breathtaking terraces that, cantilevered from the house, project over the waterfall. Wright has written that "the good building is one that makes the landscape more beautiful than it was before." The rustic quality of the setting is not diminished in its attractiveness. In fact, it is heightened by the contrast of the man-made forms that have been placed in it. As for the house itself, we feel that man has come to terms with nature and is drawing from it the beauty, strength, and serenity it can provide. Although the forms in the house may seem new, the Kaufmann house is architecture in the grand tradition—the satisfaction of human needs, the sensitive use of materials, the incorporation in structure of technological advances. But most important, it is a statement of ideas and values that men cherish.

The close relationship that should exist between the technology of a period and vital architecture is both stated and implied in this chapter, whether the discussion deals with a Gothic cathedral or an American skyscraper. It is only reasonable that, in our recent period of rapid technological growth, architecture should have changed radically. In particular, the increasing ability of the machine to produce forms that are large in size and complex in composition has led to an architecture in which buildings are, in effect, vast, precisioned, and machined structures such as the Lever House and the Lake Point Tower. Our culture being what it is, the view of architecture that these structures exemplify will be with us for as long as we can foresee.

But at the same time, architecture of a quite different nature is also being built, as typified by the TWA Flight Center and the Kagawa Gymnasium. Although as structures they, too, make use of twentieth-century technology, their forms are fluid. This view of architecture, as well, gives promise of further and extensive development. Thus, we have approaches that, in a sense, supplement each other and provide a plurality that is the mark of cultural health.

As this book began with a discussion of architecture, so does it end; and in a sense, the presentation has run full circle. Each field of art has its own significance, each its own expression. Each too, in its visible aspects, speaks to us eloquently of the people who create, use, and enjoy it. The basis of all art is human experience, and its special function is to humanize and give meaning to a culture. It is through the arts that we become civilized, and all—the creators, the users, the appreciators— make their contributions in the kind of art they create and support. Each of us has a part and a responsibility.

Bibliography

General and Historical

Battcock, Gregory, ed. *The New Art*. New York: Dutton, 1966.

Encyclopedia Americana. 30 vols. New York: Encyclopedia Americana, 1969.

Encyclopedia Britannica. 24 vols. Chicago: Encyclopedia Britannica, 1969.

Encyclopedia of World Art. 12 vols. New York: McGraw-Hill, 1960–1969.

Fleming, William. *Arts and Ideas*. New York: Holt, Rinehart and Winston, Inc., 1968.

Gombrich, Ernest H. *Art and Illusion*. New York: Phaidon, 1962.

Gregory, Richard Longton. *Eye and Brain*. New York: McGraw-Hill, 1966.

Haefele, John W. *Creativity and Innovation*. New York: Reinhold, 1962.

Huxley, Aldous. *On Art and Artists*. New York: Harper & Row, 1960.

Janson, H. W. *History of Art*. New York: Abrams, 1962.

Larkin, Oliver W. *Art and Life in America*. New York: Holt, Rinehart and Winston, Inc., 1964.

Lucas, E. Louise. *Art Books: A Basic Bibliography on the Fine Arts*. New York: New York Graphic, 1968.

McCurdy, Charles, ed. *Modern Art: A Pictorial Anthology*. New York: Macmillan, 1958.

Mendelowitz, Daniel M. *A History of American Art*. New York: Holt, Rinehart and Winston, Inc. 1960.

Read, Herbert. *The Philosophy of Modern Art*. Cleveland: World Publishing, 1959.

Rodman, Selden. *Conversations with Artists*. New York: Putnam, 1961.

Rose, Barbara. *American Art since 1900*. New York: Praeger, 1967.

———, ed. *Readings in American Art since 1900: A Documentary Survey*. New York: Praeger, 1968.

Sewall, John Ives. *A History of Western Art*. New York: Holt, Rinehart and Winston, Inc., 1961.

Chapter 1

Alswang, Betty, and Ambur Hiken. *The Personal House.* New York: Whitney, 1961.

Aronson, Joseph. *The Encyclopedia of Furniture.* New York: Crown, 1965.

Berrall, Julia S. *The Garden : An Illustrated History.* New York: Viking, 1966.

Cantacuzino, Sherban. *Modern Houses of the World.* New York: Dutton, 1964.

Chermayeff, Serge, and Christopher Alexander. *Community and Privacy : Toward a New Architecture of Humanism.* Garden City, N.Y.: Doubleday, 1963.

Church, Thomas D. *Gardens Are for People.* New York: Reinhold, 1955.

Eckbo, Garrett. *The Art of Home Landscaping.* New York: McGraw-Hill, 1956.

Faulkner, Ray, and Sarah Faulkner. *Inside Today's Home.* New York: Holt, Rinehart and Winston, Inc., 1968.

Hayward, Helena, ed. *World Furniture : A Pictorial History.* New York: McGraw-Hill, 1965.

Heyer, Paul. *Architects on Architecture : New Directions in America.* New York: Walker and Company, 1966.

Hitchcock, Henry-Russell, and Philip Johnson. *The International Style.* New York: Norton, 1966.

Hoffman, Hubert. *Row Houses and Cluster Houses : An International Survey.* New York: Praeger, 1967.

Kaspar, Karl. *Vacation Houses: An International Survey.* New. York: Praeger, 1967.

Kassler, Elizabeth B. *Modern Gardens and the Landscape.* New York: Museum of Modern Art, 1964.

Moody, Ella, ed. *Decorative Art in Modern Interiors* (Annual), vol. 53. New York: Viking, 1966.

Pegler, Martin. *Dictionary of Interior Design.* New York: Crown, 1966.

Peluzzi, Giulio, ed. *The Modern Room.* New York: Universe Books, 1967.

Philip Johnson 1949–1965. Introduction by Henry-Russell Hitchcock. New York: Holt, Rinehart and Winston, Inc., 1966.

Rudofsky, Bernard. *Architecture without Architects.* New York: Museum of Modern Art, 1965.

Wanscher, Ole. *The Art of Furniture : Five Thousand Years of Furniture and Interiors.* New York: Reinhold, 1967.

Weisskamp, Herbert. *Beautiful Homes and Gardens in California.* New York: Abrams, 1964.

Whiting, Penelope. *New Houses.* London: The Architectural Press, 1965.

Whiton, Sherrill. *Elements of Interior Design and Decoration.* Philadelphia: Lippincott, 1963.

Wright, Frank Lloyd. *The Natural House.* New York: Horizon Press, 1954.

Yoshida, Tetsuro. *The Japanese House and Garden.* New York: Praeger, 1955.

Serial Publications
American Home
Architectural Record
Arts and Architecture
Better Homes and Gardens
California Home
Domus
Furniture Forum
House and Garden
House and Home
House Beautiful
Interiors
Interior Design
Progressive Architecture
Sunset

Chapter 2

ARCHITECTURAL RECORD editors. *Apartments and Dormitories.* New York: McGraw-Hill, 1958.

Bacon, Edmund N. *Design of Cities.* New York: Viking, 1967.

Blake, Peter. *God's Own Junkyard.* New York: Holt, Rinehart and Winston Inc., 1964.

Choay, Françoise. *Le Corbusier.* New York: Braziller, 1960.

Clapp, Gordon Rufus. *The TVA : An Approach to the Development of a Region.* Chicago: University of Chicago Press, 1955.

Crosby, Theo. *Architecture : City Sense.* New York: Reinhold, 1965.

Eichler, Edward P. and Marshall Kaplan. *The Community Builders.* Berkeley, Calif.: University of California Press, 1967.

Faltermayer, Edmund K. *Redoing America : A Nationwide Report on How to Make Our Cities and Suburds Livable.* New York: Harper & Row, 1968.

Gibberd, Frederick. *Town Design.* New York: Praeger, 1967.

Goody, Joan E. *New Architecture in Boston.* Cambridge, Mass.: MIT Press, 1968.

Gruen, Victor. *The Heart of Cities.* New York: Simon & Schuster, 1965.

Halprin, Lawrence. *Freeways.* New York: Reinhold, 1966.

Hilberseimer, Ludwig. *The Nature of Cities.* Chicago: Theobald, 1955.

Hoffmann, Hubert. *Row Houses and Cluster Houses : An International Survey.* New York: Praeger, 1967.

Howard, Ebenezer. *Garden Cities of Tomorrow.* Cambridge, Mass.: MIT Press, 1968

Jacobs, Jane. *The Death and Life of Great American Cities.* New York: Random House, Inc., 1961.

Johnson-Marshall, Percy. *Rebuilding Cities.* Chicago: Aldine, 1966.

Kyle, John H. *The Building of TVA : An Illustrated History.* Baton Rouge: Louisiana State University Press, 1958.

Le Corbusier (Charles Edouard Jeanneret-Gris). *The City of Tomorrow and Its Planning.* London: Architectural Press, 1947.

Lederman, Alfred and Alfred Trachael. *Creative Playgrounds and Recreation Centers.* New York: Praeger, 1959.

Lynch, Kevin. *The Image of the City.* Cambridge, Mass.: MIT Press, 1968.

Mayer, Albert. *The Urgent Future*. New York: McGraw-Hill, 1967.

Mumford, Lewis. *The City in History*. New York: Harcourt, 1961.

———. *The Urban Prospect*. New York: Harcourt, 1968.

Osborn, Frederic J. and Arnold Whittick. *The New Towns : The Answer to Megalopolis*. New York: McGraw-Hill, 1964.

Reps, John W. *The Making of Urban America*. Princeton: Princeton University Press, 1965.

Ritter, Paul. *Planning for Man and Motor*. New York: Pergamon Press, 1964.

Schmitt, Karl Wilhelm. *Multistory Housing*. New York: Praeger, 1966.

SCIENTIFIC AMERICAN. *Cities*. New York: Knopf, 1967.

Spreiregen, Paul D. *Urban Design : The Architecture of Towns and Cities*. New York: McGraw-Hill, 1965.

Weaver, Robert C. *The Urban Complex : Essays on Urban Life and Human Values*. Garden City, N.Y.: Doubleday, 1964.

Whiffen, Marcus. *The Public Buildings of Williamsburg*. Williamsburg, Va.: Colonial Williamsburg, 1958.

———. *The Eighteenth-Century Houses of Williamsburg*. New York: Holt, Rinehart and Winston, Inc., 1960.

White, Wilston H. *Cluster Development*. New York: American Conservation Association, 1964.

Chapter 3

Anson, Peter F. *Fashions in Church Furnishings : 1840 1940*. New York: Macmillan, 1960.

Bodrogi, Ribor. *Art in Africa*. New York: McGraw-Hill, 1968.

The Bronze Reliefs for the Door of Saint Peter's and Sculpture, Paintings, and Drawings (exhibition catalog). New York: Paul Rosenberg and Co., 1966.

Cuttler, Charles D. *Northern Painting : From Pucelle to Bruegel/Fourteenth, Fifteenth, and Sixteenth Centuries*. New York: Holt, Rinehart and Winston, Inc., 1968.

DeWald, Ernest T. *Italian Painting : 1200–1600*. New York: Holt, Rinehart and Winston, Inc., 1961.

Elisofon, Eliot. *The Sculpture of Africa*. New York: Praeger, 1958.

Gregor, Josef. *Masks of the World*. New York: Wittenborn, 1968.

Maguire, Robert and Keith Murray. *Modern Churches of the World*. New York: Dutton, 1965.

Mâle, Emile. *Religious Art from the Twelfth to the Eighteenth Century*. New York: Pantheon, 1949.

Meauze, Pierre. *African Art*. New York: World Publishing, 1968.

The National Museum of Anthropology, Mexico : Art, Architecture, Archaeology, Ethnography. Vazquez, ed. New York: Abrams, 1968.

Pepper, Curtis Bill. *An Artist and the Pope*. New York: Grosset & Dunlap, 1968.

Otto, Eberhard. *Ancient Egyptian Art : The Cults of Osiris and Amon*. New York: Abrams, 1968.

Richter, Gisela M. A. *A Handbook of Greek Art*. New York: Oxford, 1965.

Smith, G. E. Kidder. *The New Churches of Europe*. New York: Holt, Rinehart and Winston, Inc., 1964.

Wingert, P. *Primitive Art*. New York: Oxford, 1962.

Serial Publication
Liturgical Arts

Chapters 4 and 5

Bayer, Herbert and others. *Bauhaus : 1919–1928*. Boston, Mass.: Branford, 1952.

Christensen, Erwin O. *The Index of American Design*. New York: Macmillan, 1950.

Clauser, H. R. *Encyclopedia of Engineering Materials and Processes*. New York: Reinhold, 1963.

Constantine, Mildred, ed. *The Package*. New York: Museum of Modern Art, 1959.

——— and Alan M. Fern, eds. *Word and Image : Posters from the Collection of the Museum of Modern Art*. New York: Museum of Modern Art, 1968.

Drexler, Arthur and Greta Daniel. *Introduction to Twentieth-Century Design*. New York: Doubleday, 1959.

Dreyfuss, Henry. *The Measure of Man*. New York: Whitney Publications, 1967.

Giedion, Sigfried. *Mechanization Takes Command : A Contribution to Anonymous History*. New York: Oxford, 1948.

Gruen, Victor and Larry Smith. *Shopping Towns, USA*. New York: Reinhold, 1960.

Henn, Walter. *Buildings for Industry*, 2 vols. New York: Hayden, 1965.

Hulten, K. G. Pontus. *The Machine—As Viewed at the End of the Mechanical Age*. New York: Museum of Modern Art, 1968.

Hutchinson, Harold F. *The Poster : An Illustrated History from 1860*. New York: Viking, 1960.

Kaspar, Karl. *Shops and Showrooms : An International Survey*. New York: Praeger 1967.

Loewy, Raymond. *Never Leave Well Enough Alone*. New York: Simon and Schuster, 1951.

Mumford, Lewis. *Technics and Civilization*. New York: Harcourt, 1934.

Munce, James F. *Industrial Architecture*. New York: McGraw-Hill, 1960.

Panero, Julius. *Anatomy for Interior Designers*. New York: Whitney Library of Design, 1967.

Read, Herbert. *Art and Industry*. London: Faber & Faber, 1966.

Wallace, Don. *Shaping America's Products*. New York: Reinhold, 1956.

Serial and Annual Publications
Art Directors Club of New York. *Annual of Advertising and Editorial Art and Design*. New York: Reinhold (distributors).
Craft Horizons
Industrial Design
Graphis
Graphis Annual 1968–1969. W. Herdeg, ed. New York: Hastings.
Modern Packaging
Packaging
Pack I : An International Survey of Packaging Design. W. Crouwel, and K. Weidemann, eds. New York: Praeger.
The Penrose Annual. H. Spencer, ed. Hastings.

Chapters 6, 7, and 8

American Fabrics Magazine editors. *Encyclopedia of Textiles*. Englewood Cliffs, N.J.: Prentice-Hall, 1960.
American Federation of Arts. *Threads of History*. New York: Whitney Library of Design, 1965.
American Home Economics Association. *Textile Handbook*. Washington, D.C.: American Home Economics Association, 1966.
Billington, Dora M. *The Technique of Pottery*. New York: Hearthside Press, Inc., 1962.
Brady, George Stuart. *Materials Handbook*. New York: McGraw-Hill, 1963.
Burton, John. *Glass : Hand Blown, Sculptured, Colored : Philosophy and Method*. Philadelphia: Chilton, 1968.
Choate, Sharr. *Creative Casting*. New York: Crown, 1966.
Diamond, Freda. *The Story of Glass*. New York: Harcourt, 1953.
Dow, Francis. *The Arts and Crafts in New England 1704–1775*. New York: Da Capo Press, 1968.
Holden, Geoffrey. *The Craft of the Silversmith*. New York: Viking, 1954.
Hughes, Graham. *Modern Silver Throughout the World : 1880–1967*. New York: Viking, 1967.
Koch, Robert. *Louis C. Tiffany, Rebel in Glass*. New York: Crown, 1964.
Labino, Dominick. *Visual Art in Glass*. Dubuque, Iowa: Wm. C. Brown Company, Publishers, 1968.
Leach, Bernard. *A Potter's Book*. Levittown, N.Y.: Transatlantic Arts, 1965.
Meilach, Dona Z. *Contemporary Art with Wood*. New York: Crown, 1968.
Moseley, Spencer, Pauline Johnson, and Hazel Koenig. *Crafts Design*. Belmont, Calif.: Wadsworth Publishing Co., Inc., 1962.
Munsterberg, Hugo. *The Ceramic Art of Japan*. Rutland, Vt.: Tuttle, 1964.
Nelson, Glenn. *Ceramics*. New York: Holt, Rinehart and Winston, Inc., 1966.
Newman, Thelma R. *Plastics as an Art Form*. Philadelphia: Chilton, 1964.
Rhodes, Daniel. *Clays and Glazes for the Potter*. Philadelphia: Chilton, 1957.
———. *Stoneware and Porcelain*. Philadelphia: Chilton, 1959.
Savage, George. *Glass*. New York: Putnam, 1965.
Slivka, Rose, Aileen O. Webb, and Margaret Merwin Patch. *The Crafts of the Modern World*. New York: Horizon Press, Inc., 1968.
Tovey, John. *The Technique of Weaving*. New York: Reinhold, 1966.
Wildenhain, Marguerite. *Pottery : Form and Expression*. New York: American Craftsmen's Council, 1959.
Zielinski, Stanislaw W. *Encyclopedia of Hand-Weaving*. New York: Funk and Wagnalls, 1959.

Serial Publications
American Fabrics
Art in America
Craft Horizons
Design
Design Quarterly

Chapter 9

Biegeleisen, J. I. and E. J. Busenbark. *The Silk Screen Printing Process*. New York: McGraw-Hill, 1941.
Brunner, Felix. *A Handbook of Graphic Reproduction Processes*. New York: Hastings, 1962.
Chieffo, Clifford. *Silk Screen as a Fine Art*. New York: Reinhold, 1967.
Craven, Thomas. *A Treasury of American Prints*. New York: Simon & Schuster, 1937.
Croy, Peter. *Graphic Design and Reproduction Techniques*. New York: Hastings, 1968.
Escher, M. C. *The Graphic Work of M. C. Escher*. New York: Meredith Press, 1967.
Hayter, Stanley William. *New Ways of Gravure*. New York: Oxford, 1966.
Heller, Jules. *Printmaking Today*. New York: Holt, Rinehart and Winston, Inc., 1958.
Ivins, William M. *Notes on Prints*. New York: Da Capo Press Books, 1968.
Kosloff, Albert. *Elementary Silk Screen Printing*. Chicago: Nazdar Co., 1954.
Leach, Mortimer. *Letter Design in the Graphic Arts*. New York: Reinhold, 1960.
Peterdi, Gabor. *Printmaking : Methods Old and New*. New York: Macmillan, 1959.
Robertson, Ronald G. *Contemporary Printmaking in Japan*. New York: Crown, 1965.
Smith, C. *Experiments in Relief Print Making*. Charlottesville, Va.: University of Virginia Press, 1954.
Sternberg, Harry. *Modern Methods and Materials of Etching*. New York: McGraw-Hill, 1949.
Sutton, Jams and Alan Bartram. *An Atlas of Typeforms*. New York: Hastings, 1968.

Zigrosser, Carl. *The Book of Fine Prints.* New York: Crown, 1956.

Serial Publications

Eichenberg, Fritz and Andrew Stasik, eds. *Artist's Proof: Annual of Contemporary Printmaking* vols. 6–8. Barre, Mass.: Barre Publishers, 1968.

Chapter 10

Arnheim, Rudolph. *Film as Art.* Berkeley and Los Angeles: University of California Press, 1967.

Cartier-Bresson, Henri. *The Decisive Moment.* New York: Simon and Schuster, 1952.

————. *The World of Henri Cartier-Bresson.* New York: Viking, 1968.

Crist, Judith. *The Private Eye, the Cowboy, and the Very Naked Girl.* New York: Holt, Rinehart and Winston, Inc., 1968.

Elliott, George P. *Dorothea Lange.* New York: Museum of Modern Art, 1967.

Elisofon, Eliot. *Color Photography.* New York: Viking, 1961.

Feininger, Andreas. *The Anatomy of Nature.* New York: Crown, 1956.

————. *Successful Photography.* Englewood Cliffs, N.J.: Prentice-Hall, 1960.

————. *Successful Color Photography.* Englewood Cliffs, N.J.: Prentice-Hall, 1966.

Fulton, Albert Randthaler. *Motion Pictures.* Norman, Okla.: University of Oklahoma Press, 1960.

Gernsheim, Helmut and Alison Gernsheim. *Concise History of Photography.* New York: Grosset & Donlap, 1965.

Hauser, Arnold. *The Social History of Art,* vol. 4. New York: Vintage Books, n.d.

Herdeg, Walter, ed. *Film and T.V. Graphics.* New York: Hastings, n.d.

Laughton, Roy. *TV Graphics.* New York: Reinhold, 1966.

Lewis, Leon and William David Sherman. *Landscape of Contemporary Cinema.* Buffalo, N.Y.: Buffalo Spectrum Press, State University of New York at Buffalo, 1967.

Lyons, Nathan. *Photography in the Twentieth Century.* New York: Horizon Press, 1967.

MacGowan, Kenneth. *Behind the Screen.* New York: Dell, 1967.

Miller, Thomas H. and Wyatt Brummit. *This Is Photography: Its Means and Ends.* New York: Doubleday, 1959.

Newhall, Beaumont. *History of Photography from 1839 to the Present Day.* New York: Museum of Modern Art, 1964.

Newhall, Beaumont, and N. W. Newhall. *Masters of Photography.* New York: Braziller, 1958.

Panofsky, Erwin. "Style and Medium in the Moving Pictures," in David Talbot, ed., *Film: An Anthology.* Berkeley and Los Angeles, University of California Press, 1967.

Purves, Frederick, ed. *The Focal Encyclopedia of Photography.* London: Ford Press, 1965.

Renan, Sheldon. *An Introduction to the American Underground Film.* New York: Dutton, 1967.

Stephenson, Ralph and Jean R. Debrix. *The Cinema as Art.* Baltimore: Penguin, 1965.

Szarkowski, John. *The Photographer's Eye.* New York: Museum of Modern Art, 1966.

Zim, Herbert S. and R. Will Burnett. *Photography.* New York: Simon & Schuster, 1956.

Serial Publications

International Photography Yearbook. Ian James, ed. New York: A. S. Barnes, 1969

Photographis: International Annual Advertising Photography. Walter Herdeg, ed. New York: Hastings.

Chapters 11, 12, 13, and 14

Anderson, Donald. *Elements of Design.* New York: Holt, Rinehart and Winston, Inc., 1961.

Arnheim, Rudolf. *Art and Visual Perception: A Psychology of the Creative Eye.* Berkeley, Calif.: University of California 1954.

Birren, Faber. *Color, Form, and Space.* New York: Reinhold, 1961.

Brodatz, Phil. *Textures: A Photographic Album for Artists and Designers.* New York: Dover, 1966.

Collier, Graham. *Form, Space, and Vision: Discovering Design Through Drawing.* Englewood Cliffs, N.J.: Prentice-Hall, 1967.

de Sausmarez, Maurice. *Basic Design.* New York: Reinhold, 1964.

Ellinger, R. *Color, Structure and Design.* Scranton: International Textbook, 1963.

Fletcher, Alan, Colin Forbes, and Bob Gill. *Graphic Design: Visual Comparisons.* New York: Reinhold, 1964.

Garrett, Lillian. *Visual Design: A Problem-Solving Approach.* New York: Reinhold, 1967.

Gatz, Konrad, and Gerhard Achterberg. *Color and Architecture.* New York: Hastings, 1967.

Hornung, Clarence P. *Handbook of Designs and Devices.* New York: Dover, 1946.

Itten, Johannes. *The Art of Color.* New York: Reinhold, 1961.

Kandinsky, Wassily. *Point and Line to Plane.* New York: Solomon R. Guggenheim Museum, 1947.

Kepes, Gyorgy. *Language of Vision.* Chicago: Paul Theobald, 1949.

————. *The New Landscape.* Chicago: Paul Theobald, 1956.

————, ed. *Vision/Value.* Series of six volumes. New York: Braziller, 1966–67.

Maerz, A. and M. Rea Paul. *A Dictionary*

of Color. New York: McGraw-Hill, 1950.

Moholy-Nagy, Laszlo. *Vision in Motion.* Chicago: Theobald, 1947.

Nelson, George. *Problems of Design.* New York: Whitney Publications, 1965.

Pye, David. *The Nature of Design.* New York: Reinhold, 1964.

Renner, Paul. *Color, Order and Harmony.* New York: Reinhold, 1965.

Smith, Charles N. *Student Handbook of Color.* New York: Reinhold, 1965.

Strache, Wolfe. *Forms and Patterns in Nature.* New York: Pantheon, 1956.

Serial Publications
Design Quarterly

Chapters 15 and 16

Arnason, H. H. *History of Modern Art.* New York: Abrams, 1968.

Battcock, Gregory, ed. *Minimal Art : A Critical Anthology.* New York: Dutton, 1968.

———. *The New Art : A Critical Anthology.* New York: Dutton, 1968.

Canaday, John. *Mainstreams of Modern Art.* New York: Holt, Rinehart and Winston, Inc., 1959.

Elgar, Frank and Robert Maillard. *Picasso.* New York: Praeger, 1960.

Elsen, Albert E. *Purposes of Art,* New York: Holt, Rinehart and Winston, Inc., 1967.

Fleming, William, *Arts and Ideas.* New York: Holt, Rinehart and Winstons, Inc., 1968.

Fried, Michael. *Morris Louis, 1912–1962.* Boston: Museum of Fine Arts, 1967.

Goossen, Eugene C. *The Art of the Real : USA 1948–1968.* New York and Greenwich, Conn.: Museum of Modern Art and the New York Graphic Society, 1968.

Haftmann, Werner. *Painting in the Twentieth Century.* 2 vols. New York: Praeger, 1965.

Hamilton, George Heard. *Painting and Sculpture in Europe : 1880–1940.* Baltimore Md.: Penguin Books, 1967.

Janson, H. W. *History of Art.* New York: Abrams, 1965.

Jensen, Lawrence N. *Synthetic Painting Media.* Englewood Cliffs, N.J.: Prentice-Hall, 1964.

Johnson, Ellen H. "Claes Oldenburg," *Painting and Sculpture.* Toronto: Art Gallery of Ontario, 1963.

———. *Cézanne.* Milan: Fratelli Fabbri Editori, 1963.

Kaprow, Allan. *Assemblage, Environments and Happenings.* New York: Abrams, 1966.

Kultermann, Udo. *The New Sculpture : Environments and Assemblages.* New York: Praeger, 1968.

Lippard, Lucy. *Pop Art.* New York: Praeger, 1966.

Mayer, Ralph. *The Artist's Handbook of Materials and Techniques.* New York: Viking, 1957.

Mendelowitz, Daniel M. *A History of American Art.* New York: Holt, Rinehart and Winston, Inc., 1960.

O'Connor, Francis V. *Jackson Pollock.* New York: Museum of Modern Art, 1967.

Read, Herbert. *A Concise History of Modern Painting.* New York: Praeger, 1956.

———. *A Concise History of Modern Sculpture.* New York: Praeger, 1964.

Rewald, John. *The History of Impressionism.* New York: Museum of Modern Art, 1962.

———. *Post-Impressionism from Van Gogh to Gauguin.* New York: Museum of Modern Art, 1962.

Rose, Barbara. *American Art since 1900.* New York: Praeger, 1967.

Rosenblum, Robert. *Cubism and Twentieth-Century Art.* New York: Abrams, 1966.

Rubin, W. S. *Dada, Surrealism, and Their Heritage.* New York: Museum of Modern Art, 1968.

Seitz, William. *The Art of Assemblage.* New York: Museum of Modern Art, 1961.

———. *The Responsive Eye.* New York: Museum of Modern Art, 1965.

Solomon, Alan R. *Robert Rauschenberg.* New York: The Jewish Museum, 1963.

Tomkins, Calvin. *The Bride and the Bachelors.* New York: Viking, 1965.

Tuchman, Maurice. *American Sculpture of the Sixties.* Los Angeles: Los Angeles County Museum of Art, 1967.

Chapter 17

Burchard, John and Albert Bush-Brown. *Architecture of America : A Social and Cultural History.* Boston: Little, Brown, 1961.

Cichy, Bodo. *The Great Ages of Architecture.* New York: Putnam, 1964.

Collins, Peter. *Changing Ideals in Modern Architecture.* London: Faber, 1965.

Fitch, James Marston. *America Building–The Historical Forces that Shaped it.* Boston: Houghton Mifflin, 1967.

Fletcher, Bannister. *History of Architecture on the Comparative Method.* New York: Scribner, 1961.

Giedion, Siegfried. *Space, Time and Architecture : The Growth of a New Tradition.* Cambridge, Mass.: Harvard University Press, 1954.

Hamlin, Talbot, ed. *Forms and Functions of Twentieth-Century Architecture.* 4 vols. New York: Columbia University Press, 1952.

Heyer, Paul. *Architects on Architecture : New Direction in America.* New York: Walker & Co., 1966.

Hitchcock, Henry Russell and Philip Johnson. *The International Style.* New York: Norton, 1966.

Jacobus, John. *Twentieth-Century Architecture : The Middle Years, 1940–64.* New York: Praeger, 1966.

Joedicke, Jurgen. *A History of Modern Architecture*. New York: Praeger, 1959.

Mumford, Lewis. *The Roots of Contemporary American Architecture*. New York: Grove, 1959.

Nervi, Luigi. *Aesthetics and Technology in Building*. Cambridge Mass.: Harvard University Press, 1965.

Neutra, Richard. *Survival Through Design*. New York: Oxford, 1954.

Pehnt, Wolfgang, ed. *Encyclopedia of Modern Art*. New York: Abrams, 1964.

Rasmussen, Steen Eiler. *Experiencing Architecture*. New York: Wiley, 1959.

Rudofsky, Bernard. *Architecture without Architects*. New York: Museum of Modern Art, 1964.

Saylor, Henry H. *Dictionary of Architecture*. New York: Wiley, 1963.

Scully, Vincent, Jr. *Frank Lloyd Wright*. New York: Braziller, 1960.

———. *Modern Architecture*. New York: Braziller, 1961.

Sharp, Dennis. *Modern Architecture and Expressionism*. New York: Braziller, 1967.

Smith, G. E. Kidder. *The New Architecture of Europe*. New York: World Publishing, 1961.

Sullivan, Louis H. *Autobiography of an Idea*. New York: Dover, 1956.

Venturi, Robert. *Complexity and Contradiction in Architecture*. New York and Greenwich, Conn.: Museum of Modern Art, New York Graphic Society, 1967.

Wright, Frank Lloyd. *The Future of Architecture*. New York: Horizon, 1953.

———. *On Architecture*, ed. by Frederick Gutheim. New York: Grosset & Dunlap, 1959.

Zevi, Bruno. *Architecture as Space*. New York: Horizon, 1957.

Serial Publications
Architectural Forum
Architectural Record

Index

References are to page numbers, except for color plates and black-and-white illustrations, which are identified by figure and plate numbers. Titles of works of art are printed in italics; descriptive citations and titles of examples in architecture, in roman type.

Photographic Sources

References are to figure numbers unless indicated Pl. (plate).

ABC Television Ltd., Teddington Lock, England (185); Alinari–Art Reference Bureau, Ancram, N.Y. (111, 379, 466, 469, 476, 494, 527, 601–602, 610); Aluminum Company of America, New York (617); American Chair Company, Sheboygan, Wisc. (124); American Craftsmen's Council, New York (262, 292, 294–296, 314, 404); American Museum of Natural History, New York (396, 449, 456–458, 467); Ammann and Whitney, New York (635); Anderson–Alinari–Art Reference Bureau, Ancram, N.Y. (112, 609); Andrews, Wayne, Grosse Pointe, Mich. (478); Ansco, New York (358); *Architectural Record*, New York (34, 63, 81); *Architectural Record Houses of 1967* (13); *Architectural Record Houses of 1968* (36, 38); Archives Photographiques, Paris (603–604, 606); Auerbach, Alfred, Associates, New York (235); Australian Consulate General, News and Information Bureau, New York (505); Bacon, Edmund N., *Design of Cities*, The Viking Press, New York, 1967 (203–204, Pl. 18); Baily, I. W., photograph, courtesy of Professor E. S. Barghoorn, Cambridge, Mass. (468); Baker, Oliver, New York (499); Bank, Kurt (629); Beckhard, Robert L., for Jack Lenor Larsen, Inc., New York (320); Black Star Publishing Co., Inc., New York (353); Boesch, Ferdinand, New York (150, Pl. 21b); Boesch, Ferdinand, New York, and Museum of Contemporary Crafts, New York, "Fantasy Furniture" (140), "Plastic as Plastic"

(243); British Broadcasting Corporation, London (186); British Information Services, New York (42–43); Brose, Raymond E. (464); Brown, F. N. M. (373); Bryan and Shear Ltd., Glasgow, and Cumbernauld Development Corporation (75–76); Calif-Asia Company (137); California College of Arts and Crafts, Oakland (351); California Design/9, Pasadena Art Museum (147, 208); Canadian Consulate General, Press & Information Service, New York (637); Carr, George, New York (621); Carter, E. C. and Son, Port Chester, N.Y. (308); Castelli, Leo, Gallery, New York (548, Pl. 15); Chanel, Inc., New York (178); Chemstrand Company, New York (212); Ciba Corporation, New York (305–307); Clarence House, New York (318); Clements, Geoffrey, New York (335); Colonial Williamsburg, Inc., Williamsburg, Va. (44–45, 95, 187); Command Records Division of Grand Award Record Company, Inc., New York (172–173); Conn, Betty, Southfield, Mich. (322); *Contract Magazine*, Herman Miller, Inc., and Ruff, Kiek, and McAuliffe, Inc., New York (317); Copeland and Thompson, Inc., New York (264); Corning Glass Works, Corning, N.Y. (275, 279, 280–282, 286); Corning Museum of Glass, Corning, N.Y. (276, 287, 289); Cserna, George, New York (88, 624); Department of Construction and Housing, City of Berlin (620); Design Research, Inc., Cambridge, Mass. (319); Dickey and Harleen

Studios, Official Photographers, Golden Gateway Center, San Francisco (59–61); EB Foto, Hørve, and Georg Jensen, New York (138); Edgerton, Germeshausen, and Grier (372); Elenhank Designers, Inc. (316); *Engineering News-Record*, New York (26); Erwitt, Elliott, Magnum Photos, Inc., New York (73); Finnish National Travel Office, New York (92); Florian, Robert C., Berwyn, I., and American Craftsmen's Council, New York (459); Ford Motor Company, New York (459); Forest Products Laboratory, Toledo, O. (216–218); Frantz, Alison, Athens (592); French Government Tourist Office, New York (71); General Electric Company, Bridgeport, Conn. (125–126); Giraudon, Paris (110, 588); Gorham Company, New York (231, 233); Graber, Richard, Andover, Mass., and *Architectural Record*, New York (62); Graham, Bill, Posters, Inc., San Francisco (184); Graham, William A., Arlington, Va. (56); Gross, Richard, Los Angeles (269, Pl. 14); Gross, Richard, Los Angeles, and California Craftsmen Show, sponsored by the California Arts Commission (149); Gross, Richard, Los Angeles, and California Design/9, Pasadena Art Museum (222); Gross, Richard, Los Angeles, and California Design/10, Pasadena Art Museum (207, 209–210, 240); Grove, Miles R., Inc., New York, Boyle Midway Division, American Home Products Corp., and Gommi Associates (166); Guerrero, Pedro,

Fig. 174 reproduced by permission of Reinhold Book Corporation, book jacket of *Optical Illusions and the Visual Arts* by Ronald G. Carrher and Jacqueline B. Thurston, New York, 1966. Fig. 325, Robert Carola in *Playboy,* July 1961 (OPTOMETRIST); May 1960 (KISS); January 1964 (PSYCHOANALYSIS); May 1960 (NONCONFORMIST). Copyright © HMH Publishing Co., Inc. Figs. 350 and 355 reproduced by permission from *This Is Photography.* Works by Arp, Brancusi, Braque, Chagall, Duchamp, Gris, Miró, Picabia: © ADAGP, French Reproduction Rights, Inc. Works by Cassatt, Léger, Matisse, Monet, Picasso, Rouault, Soutine, Vuillard: © SPADEM, French Reproduction Rights, Inc.